THE AUTOBIOGRAPHY OF

LIEUTENANT-GENERAL

SIR HARRY SMITH

BARONET OF ALIWAL ON THE SUTLEJ
G.C.B.

EDITED

WITH THE ADDITION OF SOME SUPPLEMENTARY CHAPTERS

BY G. C. MOORE SMITH, M.A.

WITH PORTRAITS AND ILLUSTRATIONS

LONDON
JOHN MURRAY, ALBEMARLE STREET
1903

PREFACE.

THE Life of Sir Harry Smith here offered to the public consists of an Autobiography covering the period 1787 to 1846 (illustrated by notes and appendices), and some supplementary chapters contributed by myself on the last period of Sir Harry's life (1846–1860). Chapter XXXI. carries the reader to the year 1829. This, it is interesting to remark, is a true turning point in the life of the great soldier. Till then he had seen warfare only on two continents, Europe and America (the Peninsula, France, the Netherlands, Monte Video, Buenos Ayres, Washington, New Orleans); from that date onwards the scene of his active service was Africa and Asia. Till 1829 his responsibility was small; after 1829 he had a large or paramount share in directing the operations in which he was engaged. This difference naturally affects the tone of his narrative in the two periods.

The Autobiography (called by its author "Various Anecdotes and Events of my Life") was begun by Sir Harry Smith, then Lieutenant-Colonel Smith,

at Glasgow in 1824. At that time it was only continued as far as page 15 of the present volume. On
11th August, 1844, when he had won his K.C.B.,
and was Adjutant-General of Her Majesty's Forces
in India, he resumed his task at Simla. He then
wrote with such speed that on 15th October he was
able to tell his sister that he had carried his narrative to the end of the campaign of Gwalior, that
is, to 1844 (p. 490). Finally, on 7th September,
1846, when at Cawnpore in command of a Division,
he began to add to what he had previously written
an account of the campaign of the Sutlej, which
had brought him fresh honours. This narrative
was broken off abruptly in the middle of the Battle
of Sobraon (p. 550), and was never completed.
Accordingly, of Sir Harry Smith's life from
February, 1846, to his death on 12th October, 1860,
we have no record by his own hand.

The Autobiography had been carefully preserved
by Sir Harry's former aide-de-camp and friend,
General Sir Edward Alan Holdich, K.C.B., but,
as it happened, I was not myself aware of its
existence until, owing to the fresh interest awakened
in Sir Harry Smith and his wife by the siege of
Ladysmith early in 1900, I inquired from members
of my family what memorials of my great-uncle
were preserved. Sir Edward then put this manuscript and a number of letters and documents at
my disposal. It appeared to me and to friends

whom I consulted that the Autobiography was so full of romantic adventure and at the same time of such solid historical value that it ought no longer to remain unpublished, and Mr. John Murray, to whom I submitted a transcription of it, came at once to the same conclusion.

My task as Editor has not been a light one. In Sir Harry's letter to Mrs. Sargant of 15th October, 1844,* he says of his manuscript, " I have never read a page of it since my scrawling it over at full gallop ;" and in a letter of 14th January, 1845, " Harry Lorrequer would make a good story of it. You may ask him if you like, and let me know what he says of it." It is clear from these passages that Sir Harry did not contemplate the publication of his story in the rough form in which he had written it, but imagined that some literary man, such as Charles Lever, might take it in hand, rewrite it with fictitious names, and so fashion out of it a military romance. The chapters † on Afghanistan and Gwalior, already written, were, however, of a serious character which would make them unsuitable for such treatment ; and the same was the case with the chapters on the Sikh War, afterwards added. Whether Lever ever saw the manuscript I do not know ; at any rate, the author's idea was never carried out.

* See Appendix vi.
† Sir Harry's original narrative is not broken into chapters.

It is obvious that now that fifty years have passed, some of the reasons which made Sir Harry suggest such a transformation of his story are no longer in force. The actors in the events which he describes having almost all passed away, to suppress names would be meaningless and would deprive the book of the greater part of its interest. And for the sake of literary effect to rewrite Sir Harry's story would be to destroy its great charm, the intimate relation in which it sets us with his fiery and romantic character.

The book here given to the public is not indeed word for word as Sir Harry wrote it. It has often been necessary to break up a long sentence, to invert a construction—sometimes to transpose a paragraph in order to bring it into closer connexion with the events to which it refers. But such changes have only been made when they seemed necessary to bring out more clearly the writer's intention; the *words* are the author's own, even where a specially awkward construction has been smoothed; and it may be broadly said that *nothing* has been added to Sir Harry's narrative or omitted from it. Such slight additions to the text as seemed desirable, for example, names and dates of battles,* have been included in square brackets. In some cases, to avoid awkward parentheses, sentences of

* The Peninsular dates are generally borrowed from *A British Rifleman* (Major Simmons' diary).

Sir Harry's own have been relegated from the text to footnotes. Such notes are indicated by the addition of his initials ("H. G. S.").

Sir Harry's handwriting was not of the most legible order, as he admits, and I have had considerable difficulty in identifying some of the persons and places he mentions. Sometimes I have come to the conclusion that his own recollection was at fault, and in this case I have laid my difficulty before the reader.

I have not thought it my duty to normalize the spelling of proper names, such as those of towns in the Peninsula and in India, and the names of Kafir chiefs. Sir Harry himself spells such names in a variety of ways, and I have not thought absolute consistency a matter of importance, while to have re-written Indian names according to the modern official spelling would have been, as it seems to me, to perpetrate an anachronism.

I have, indeed, generally printed "Sutlej," though Sir Harry frequently or generally wrote "Sutledge;" but I have kept in his own narrative his spelling "Ferozeshuhur" (which is, I believe, more correct) for the battle generally called "Ferozeshah." Even Sir Harry's native place (and my own) has two spellings, "Whittlesey" and "Whittlesea." In his narrative I have preserved his usual spelling "Whittlesea," but I have myself used the other, as I have been taught to do from a boy.

Perhaps it is worth while to mention here that Sir Harry's name was strictly "Henry George Wakelyn Smith," and it appears in this form in official documents. But having been always known in the army as "Harry Smith," after attaining his knighthood he stoutly refused to become "Sir Henry," and insisted on retaining the more familiar name.* As the year of his birth is constantly given as 1788, it is worth while to state that the Baptismal Register of St. Mary's, Whittlesey, proves him to have been born on 28th June, 1787.

While the documents put into my hands by Sir Edward Holdich enabled me to throw a good deal of additional light on the events recorded in the Autobiography, I thought it a prime duty not to interrupt Sir Harry's own narrative by interpolations. Accordingly I have thrown this illustrative matter into Appendices. In some of these, especially in his letters to his wife of 1835 (Appendix iv.), one sees the writer, perhaps, in still more familiar guise than in the Autobiography.

But I had not merely to illustrate the period of Sir Harry's life covered by his Autobiography; I

---

* Sir Harry's ordinary signature was " H. G. Smith." His letters to his wife were commonly signed " Enrique "; to members of his family, " Harry Smith "; to his friend and interpreter for the Kafir language, Mr. Theophilus Shepstone, " Inkosi " (" Chief "). He addressed Mr. Shepstone as " My dear Sumtseu " (" Hunter ").

had a further task before me, viz. to construct a narrative of the rest of his life (1846–1860), including his Governorship of the Cape (1847–1852). For the manner in which I have done this, I must crave indulgence. At the best it would have been no easy matter to continue in the third person a story begun by the main actor in the first, and in this case the letters and personal memoranda, which were tolerably abundant for Sir Harry's earlier years, suddenly became very scanty when they were most required. Accordingly, for much of Sir Harry's life I had no more sources to draw on than are accessible to anybody—histories, blue-books, and newspapers. I can only say that in this situation I have done the best I could. My chief difficulty was, of course, in dealing with the time of Sir Harry's command at the Cape. It would have been inconsistent with the scope of the whole book to have attempted a systematic history of the colony or of the operations of the Kafir War. At the same time I could not enable my readers to form an estimate of Sir Harry's conduct at this time without giving them some indication of the circumstances which surrounded him. If I am found by some critics to have subordinated biography too much to history, I can only hope that other critics will console me by finding that I have subordinated history too much to biography.

Amid a certain dearth of materials of a private

kind, I do congratulate myself on having been able to use the packet of letters docketed by Sir Harry, "John Bell's and Charlie Beckwith's Letters." General Beckwith was an earlier General Gordon, and his letters are so interesting in matter and so brilliant in expression that one is tempted to wish to see them printed in full. Perhaps some readers of this book may be able to tell me of other letters by the same remarkable man which have been preserved.

The latter part of this book would have been balder than it is, if it had not been for the help I have received from various friends, known and unknown. I must express my thanks in particular to the Misses Payne of Chester, who lent me letters addressed to their father, Major C. W. Meadows Payne; to Mrs. Thorne of Chippenham, who lent me letters addressed to her father, Major George Simmons; to Mrs. Fasson, daughter of Mr. Justice Menzies of the Cape, and Mr. W. F. Collier of Horrabridge, who gave me their reminiscences; to Colonel L. G. Fawkes, R.A., Stephen A. Aveling, Esq., of Rochester, Major J. F. Anderson of Faringdon, R. Morton Middleton, Esq., of Ealing, Captain C. V. Ibbetson of Preston, Mrs. Henry Fawcett, my aunt Mrs. John A. Smith, Mrs. Farebrother of Oxford, Mr. B. Genn of Ely, Mr. Charles Sayle of Cambridge, Mr. G. J. Turner of Lincoln's Inn, Mr. A. E. Barnes of the Local Government Board, the Military Secretary of the War Office, and others, for kind assistance of various kinds. I am indebted to my cousins, Mrs. Lambert of 1, Sloane Gardens, S.W., and C. W. Ford, Esq., for permission to reproduce pictures in their possession, and to General Sir Edward Holdich for much aid and interest in my work in addition to the permission to use his diary of the Boomplaats expedition. Lastly, my thanks are due to my brothers and sisters who assisted in transcribing the Autobiography, and in particular to my sister, Miss M. A. Smith, who did most of the work of preparing the Index.

I shall feel that any labour which I have bestowed on the preparation of this book will be richly repaid if through it Harry and Juana Smith cease to be mere names and become living figures, held in honour and affection by the sons and daughters of the Empire which they served.

G. C. MOORE SMITH.

SHEFFIELD,
September, 1901.

For some of the corrections now introduced I am indebted to Lieut.-Col. Willoughby Verner, Rifle Brigade, and to the Rev. Canon C. Evans, late Fellow of Trinity College, Cambridge.

G. C. M. S.

UNIVERSITY COLLEGE, SHEFFIELD,
April, 1902.

DATES OF LIEUT.-GENERAL SIR HARRY SMITH'S COMMISSIONS AND APPOINTMENTS.

———•◦•———

REGIMENTAL RANK.

Second Lieutenant, 1st Battalion 95th Regiment ...	8 May, 1805
Lieutenant	15 Aug. 1805
Captain	28 Feb. 1812
Major, unattached	29 Dec. 1826
Lieut.-Colonel, unattached	22 July, 1830
Lieut.-Colonel, 3rd Foot	13 May, 1842
Lieut.-Colonel, unattached	25 Aug. 1843
Colonel, 47th Foot	18 Jan. 1847
Colonel, 2nd Battalion Rifle Brigade	16 April, 1847
Colonel, 1st Battalion Rifle Brigade	18 Jan. 1855

ARMY RANK.

Major	29 Sept. 1814
Lieut.-Colonel	18 June, 1815
Colonel	10 Jan. 1837
Local rank of Major-General in the East Indies ...	21 Aug. 1840
Major-General	9 Nov. 1846
Local rank of Lieut.-General in South Africa ...	1847–1852
Lieut.-General	20 June, 1854

STAFF APPOINTMENTS.

PENINSULAR WAR.

A.D.C. to Colonel T. S. Beckwith	Oct. 1810
Brigade Major, 2nd Brigade, Light Division under Major-General Drummond, Major-General Vandeleur, Major-General Skerrett, and Colonel Colborne successively	Mar. 1811 to the end of the war, Mar. 1814

WASHINGTON EXPEDITION.

D.A.G. to Major-General R. Ross	1814

b

New Orleans Expedition.

A.A.G. to Major-General Sir E. Pakenham   ...   1814
Military Secretary to Major-General Sir J. Lambert   1815

Waterloo Campaign.

Brigade-Major, afterwards A.Q.M.G. to 6th Division
    (Major-General Sir J. Lambert and Major-General
    Sir Lowry Cole successively)   1815
[Returns to his regiment.]

Occupation of France.

Major de Place of Cambray   1815–1818
[Returns to his regiment.]

Glasgow.

Major of Brigade to Major-General Sir T. Reynell
    (commanding Western District) and Lieut-
    General Sir T. Bradford (Commander-in-Chief in
    Scotland) successively   1819–1825
[Returns to his regiment.]

Nova Scotia.

A.D.C. to Lieut.-General Sir James Kempt, Governor   1826

Jamaica.

D.Q.M.G. under Lieut.-General Sir John Keane,
    Governor   1827

Cape of Good Hope.

D.Q.M.G. under Lieut.-General Sir Lowry Cole, Lieut.-
    General Sir B. D'Urban, Major-General Sir G.
    T. Napier, Governors, successively   1828–1840
Chief of the Staff under Sir Benjamin D'Urban in
    the Kafir War   1835

India.

A.G. to Her Majesty's Forces, under Lieut.-General
    Sir Jasper Nicolls and Lieut.-General Sir Hugh
    Gough, Commanders-in-Chief, successively   ...   1840–1845

Sikh War.

In Command of the 1st Division Infantry   1845–1846

CAPE OF GOOD HOPE.

Governor and Commander-in-Chief 1847–1852

HOME STAFF.

In Command of the Western Military District ... 1853–1854
In Command of the Northern and Midland Military
   Districts 1854–1859

STEPS IN THE ORDER OF THE BATH.

C.B. for Waterloo 1815
K.C.B. for Maharajpore 1844
G.C.B. for Aliwal and Sobraon 1846

BOOKS USEFUL FOR REFERENCE IN CONNEXION WITH SIR HARRY SMITH'S LIFE.

An Authentic Narrative of the Proceedings of the Expedition under . . Craufurd until its Arrival at Monte Video, with an Account of the Operations against Buenos Ayres. . . By an Officer of the Expedition (1808).

SIR WILLIAM F. P. NAPIER : *History of the War in the Peninsula.*

SIR H. E. MAXWELL : *Life of Wellington.*

SIR WILLIAM H. COPE : *History of the Rifle Brigade* (1877).

EDWARD COSTELLO : *Adventures of a Soldier* (1852).

A British Rifleman (Major George Simmons' Diary), edited by LT.-COLONEL WILLOUGHBY VERNER (1899).

SIR JOHN KINCAID : *Random Shots by a Rifleman.*

SIR JOHN KINCAID : *Adventures in the Rifle Brigade.*

Recollections of Rifleman Harris (1848).

SURTEES : *Twenty-five Years in the Rifle Brigade* (1833).

COLONEL JONATHAN LEACH : *Rough Sketches in the Life of an Old Soldier* (1831).

A Narrative of the Campaigns of the British Army at Washington and New Orleans. By an Officer (1821).

CHARLES DALTON : *The Waterloo Roll Call* (1890).

GEORGE McC. THEAL : *History of South Africa,* vol. iv. (1893).

R. GODLONTON : *A Narrative of the Irruption of the Kafir Hordes into the Eastern Province of the Cape of Good Hope,* 1834-5 (1836).

SIR J. E. ALEXANDER : *Narrative of a Voyage, etc.* (1837). This work contains in vol. ii. a history of the Kafir War of 1835, with illustrations.

H. CLOETE : *The Great Boer Trek.*

The War in India. Despatches of Viscount Hardinge, Lord Gough, Major-General Sir Harry Smith, Bart., etc. (1846).

J. D. CUNNINGHAM : *History of the Sikhs.*

McGREGOR : *History of the Sikhs.*

GENERAL SIR CHAS. GOUGH and A. D. INNES : *The Sikhs and the Sikh Wars* (1897).

J. W. CLARK and T. McK. HUGHES : *Life of Adam Sedgwick.*

HARRIET WARD : *Five Years in Kaffirland.*

J. NOBLE : *South Africa* (1877).

A. WILMOT and J. C. CHASE : *Annals of the Colony of the Cape of Good Hope* (1869).

ALFRED W. COLE : *The Cape and the Kaffirs* (1852).

W. R. KING : *Campaigning in Kaffirland* (with illustrations), (1853).

W. A. NEWMAN : *Memoir of John Montagu* (1855).

Correspondence of General Sir G. Cathcart (1856).

EARL GREY : *The Colonial Policy of Lord John Russell's Administration* (1853).

BLUE-BOOKS : *Cape of Good Hope* (1830-1852).

M. MEILLE : *Memoir of General Beckwith, C.B.* (1873).

CONTENTS.

LIST OF ILLUSTRATIONS.

On the Cover.

ARMS GRANTED TO SIR HARRY SMITH IN 1846.

They are thus described by Sir Bernard Burke :—

Arms—Argent, on a chevron between two martlets in chief gules, and upon
   a mount vert in base, an elephant proper, a fleur-de-lis between two
   lions rampant, of the first: from the centre-chief, pendant by a riband,
   gules, fimbriated azure, a representation of the Waterloo medal.

Crest—Upon an Eastern crown or, a lion rampant argent, supporting a
   lance proper ; therefrom flowing to the sinister, a pennon gules, charged
   with two palm-branches, in saltier, or.

The supporters are a soldier of the Rifle Brigade and a soldier of the 52nd
   Regiment.

THE AUTOBIOGRAPHY OF·

LT.-GEN. SIR HARRY SMITH,

BARONET OF ALIWAL, G.C.B.

———•◦•———

CHAPTER I.

MONTE VIDEO AND BUENOS AYRES.
1806-7.

Written in Glasgow in 1824.—H. G. SMITH.

I WAS born in the parish of Whittlesea and county of Cambridgeshire in the year [1787]. I am one of eleven children, six sons and five daughters. Every pains was taken with my education which my father could afford, and I was taught natural philosophy, classics, algebra, and music.*

* The birthplace of Sir Harry Smith in St. Mary's Street, Whittlesey, is now called " Aliwal House." In his MS. he left the year of his birth vacant, and it would appear that he was uncertain of his own age (cp. p. 73). This may account for the date of his birth having been often given wrongly as 1788. The east end of the south aisle of St. Mary's church was at this time partitioned off and used as a schoolroom, the vicar or curate teaching. It was here that Harry Smith received his education from the Rev. George Burgess, then curate, who survived to welcome him in Whittlesey in 1847 on his return after the battle of Aliwal. This part of the church, having been restored in 1862 as a memorial to him, is now known as " Sir Harry's Chapel."

Harry Smith's father, John Smith (son of Wakelyn Smith),

B

In 1804 the whole country was *en masse* collected in arms as volunteers from the expected invasion of the French; and being now sixteen years of age, I was received into the Whittlesea troop of

surgeon, born 1756, died 2 Sept. 1843, married in 1781 Eleanor (born 1760, died 12 Dec. 1813), daughter of the Rev. George Moore, M.A. (Queens' College, Cambridge), vicar of St. Mary and St. Andrew, Whittlesey, and minor canon of Peterborough Cathedral. They had in all fourteen children, but only eleven survived infancy, viz. 1, Mary Anne; 2, John Stona; 3, Eleanor Moore; 4, Elizabeth; 5, Henry George Wakelyn (b. 28 June, 1787); 6, Jane Alice (Mrs. Sargant), b. 1789; 7, William; 8, Thomas Lawrence (b. 25 Feb. 1792); 9, Anna Maria; 10, Charles (b. 10 Aug. 1795); 11, Samuel.

Mrs. Sargant, Harry Smith's favourite sister, resided for many years in Clapton Square, and died in 1869. She was the author of *Joan of Arc, a Play, Charlie Burton* (a tale, translated into French and German), and many other works.

Thomas Lawrence (frequently mentioned in this book) received his commission in the 95th (Rifle Brigade) on 3 March, 1808, and took part in the actions of Sir John Moore's expedition to the battle of Corunna. Like his brother Harry, he served with the Light Division throughout the Peninsular War to the battle of Toulouse, being dangerously wounded at the Coa. He was recommended for promotion for his conduct at Waterloo. He proceeded with his regiment to Paris, and riding as Adjutant at the head of the 2nd Battalion, was the first British officer who entered the city on 7 July, 1815. He went on half-pay in 1817. In 1824 he was appointed Barrack-master, in which capacity he served in Ireland till 1838, when he was transferred to Chatham. On the formation of Aldershot Camp in 1855, he was appointed Principal Barrack-master there, and held his appointment till 1868. On retirement he was made a C.B. and granted a special pension. He died in London on 6 April, 1877, and was buried in the cemetery, Aldershot.

Charles was present as a " Volunteer " with the 1st Battalion 95th at Quatrebras and Waterloo, after which he received a commission as Second Lieutenant. Two or three years later he retired from the army and settled at Whittlesey. He became J.P. and D.L. for Cambridgeshire, and Lieut.-Colonel of the Yeomanry Cavalry of the county, and died at Whittlesey on 24 Dec. 1854.

Further information about Sir Harry Smith's family was given to Mr. Arthur M. Smith, at his request, for his book *The Smiths of Exeter*, and will there be found, although, in the opinion of the present editor, no connexion between the two families can be established. See also p. 794 *inf.*

Yeomanry Cavalry, commanded by Captain Johnson. During this year the Yeomanry in the neighbourhood patrolled through Norman Cross Barracks, where 15,000 French prisoners were kept, when the Frenchmen laughed exceedingly at the young dragoon, saying, " I say, leetel fellow, go home with your mamma; you most eat more pudding." In the spring of 1805 the Whittlesea Yeomanry kept the ground at a review made by Brigadier-General Stewart (now Sir W. Stewart), when I was orderly to the General, who said, " Young gentleman, would you like to be an officer?" "Of all things," was my answer. " Well, I will make you a Rifleman, a green jacket," says the General, "and very smart." I assure you the General kept his word, and upon the 15th [8th ?] May, 1805, I was gazetted second lieutenant in the 95th Regiment Riflemen,* and joined at Brabourne Lees upon the 18th of August. A vacancy of lieutenant occurring for purchase, my father kindly advanced the money, and I was gazetted lieutenant the 15th September [August ?], 1805. This fortunate purchase occurred when the 2nd Battalion of the corps was raising and the

---

* In consequence of a representation made to the Government by Colonel Coote Manningham and Lieut.-Colonel the Hon. William Stewart, an "experimental Corps of Riflemen" was formed early in 1800, with Manningham as colonel and Stewart one of the lieut.-colonels. It was actually organized by Stewart. On the 25th of December, 1802, the corps was ordered to be numbered as the 95th Regiment. In 1803 they were brigaded with the 43rd and 52nd as part of Sir John Moore's Camp of Instruction at Shorncliffe. The 2nd Battalion was formed on the 6th of May, 1805, according to Cope, and joined the 1st Battalion at Brabourn Lees, near Ashford, in June (see Cope's *History of the Rifle Brigade*, p. 1, etc.).

officers had not been appointed, by which good luck twenty-seven steps were obtained by £100.

In the summer of 1806 a detachment of three Companies was directed to proceed from the 2nd Battalion of the corps from Faversham to Portsmouth, there to embark and form part of an army about to proceed to South America under the command of Sir Samuel Auchmuty. This detachment was under the command of Major Gardner, and I was appointed Adjutant, a great honour for so young an officer.* The army sailed for America, touching at Plymouth, Falmouth, Peak of Teneriffe, and Rio Janeiro, at which place it stayed one week to take in water, stores, etc., and, covered by the detachment of Riflemen, landed within a few miles of Monte Video upon the 16th of January, 1807. Some skirmishing took place the whole day with the light troops of the enemy. Upon the 17th and 18th the army halted for the artillery, stores, etc., to be landed. The outposts (Riflemen) were employed both of these days.

Upon the 19th the army moved forward, and a general action took place, the result of which was most favourable to the British, and a position was taken up in the suburbs of Monte Video. Upon the 20th the garrison made a most vigorous sortie in three columns, and drove in our outposts, and a heavy and general attack lasted for near two hours, when the enemy were driven to the very walls of the place. The

* For his diary of the voyage, etc., see Appendix I.

Riflemen were particularly distinguished on this occasion.

The siege of Monte Video was immediately commenced, and upon the morning of the 3rd of February, the breach being considered practicable, a general assault was ordered in two columns, the one upon the breach, the other an escalade. Both ultimately succeeded. Not a defence was destroyed nor a gun dismounted upon the works. The breach was only wide enough for three men to enter abreast, and when upon the top of the breach there was a descent into the city of twelve feet. Most of the men fell, and many were wounded by each other's bayonets. When the head of the column entered the breach, the main body lost its communications or was checked by the tremendous fire. Perceiving the delay, I went back and conducted the column to the breach, when the place was immediately taken. The slaughter in the breach was enormous owing to the defence being perfect, and its not being really practicable. The surrender of this fortress put the English in the possession of this part of the country.

I was now afflicted with a most severe fever and dysentery, and owe my life to the kind attentions of a Spanish family in whose house I was billeted. My own relations could not have treated me with greater kindness. My gratitude to them can never be expressed or sufficiently appreciated. *

---

* The following extracts from Hughes and Clark's *Life of Adam Sedgwick* (i. p. 76, etc.) refer to this time—

" Sedgwick went on December 17, 1804, to spend Christmas with

In the autumn * an outpost was established on
the same side of the river as Monte Video, but
nearly opposite to Buenos Ayres, at Colonia del
Sacramento. This had formerly belonged to the
Portuguese. It was situated on a neck of land,
and a mud wall was carried from water to water.
There were no guns up, and in one place a considerable breach. One particular night a column of
Spaniards which had crossed the river from Buenos
Ayres stormed this post, and were near carrying
it by surprise had it not been for the valour of
Scott and his guard of Riflemen, who most bravely
defended the breach until the troops got under
arms. The enemy were not pursued, as their
numbers were not known and the night was dark.
Why this breach was not repaired one cannot say,

Ainger at his father's house at Whittlesea. . . . He never forgot the
simple pleasures which he there enjoyed. . . . It was on this occasion
that he made the acquaintance of Henry Smith, son to the surgeon
of Whittlesea, then a boy of sixteen. Sedgwick watched his career
with affectionate interest.

"In 1807 he wrote to Ainger—

"'Pray has Henry Smith escaped the fate which many of our brave
countrymen have met in Egypt? I believe his Regiment was in the
expedition.'

"W. Ainger replies—

" 'Whittlesea, August 3, 1807.

"'Henry Smith, after whom you inquired, did not go into Egypt,
but to Buenos Ayres. His father had a letter from him after the
engagement. His Captain was killed by his side in the outset; the
command of the Company then of course devolved to Henry, who,
I believe, acquitted himself very creditably, and did not, to use his
own expression, get a single scratch. Last week brought his friends
another letter from Monte Video, which acquainted them that he was
then (in April) just recovering from the attack of a fever, which
appears, Sedgwick, to have been not less formidable than yours was.
He says he has lost all his flesh; but I find he retains all his spirit.'"

* *I.e.* the English spring.

except that in those days our commanders understood little of the art of war, and sat themselves
down anywhere in a state of blind security without
using every means to strengthen their posts.
Experience taught us better.

The enemy did not re-cross the river, but took
up a position about fourteen miles from Colonia,
in which Colonel Pack (afterwards Sir Denis
Pack), who commanded the British force, resolved
to attack them. The column consisted of three
companies of Riflemen, the 40th Regiment, two
6-pounders, and three light companies. It marched
upon the night of [6–7 June], and arrived in sight
of the enemy at daylight in the morning. They
were drawn up on an elevated piece of ground,
with a narrow but deep, muddy, and miry river in
their front. Their cavalry formed a right angle upon
the right of their infantry and they had seven guns
upon the left. The Rifle Brigade covered the
troops whilst crossing the rivulet, and in about
twenty minutes by a rapid advance the position was
carried, the enemy leaving behind him his guns,
tents, stores, etc., with a great quantity of ammunition. In the destroying of the latter poor Major
Gardner and fourteen soldiers suffered most dreadfully from an explosion. Some flints had been
scattered upon the field; the soldiers took the shot
to break the cartridges, and thus the whole blew
up. About two hundred shells also exploded.
The army at a short distance lay down, and not
an individual was touched. Colonel Pack, with his

army, the captured guns, etc., returned to Colonia in the evening.*

A considerable force having arrived under General Whitelock, who took the command, the army was remodelled and embarked in August [really on the 17th of June], 1807, to attack Buenos Ayres. The post of Colonia was abandoned, and the three companies of the 2nd Battalion Rifle Brigade were embodied with five of the 1st just arrived from England, and I was appointed adjutant of the whole under the command of Major McLeod. The army landed upon [28 June], and was divided into two columns, the one consisting of the light troops under General Craufurd, and of a heavy brigade, the whole under Major-General Leveson-Gower. [Some uncomplimentary epithets are here omitted.] His column was one day in advance of the main body commanded by General Whitelock in person. His orders were to march up to the enemy's outposts and take up a position. In place of obeying his orders, General Leveson-Gower immediately attacked the enemy in the suburbs of Buenos Ayres, and drove them in with great loss, leaving their cannon behind them. Having thus committed himself, in lieu of

* Cope says he could find no particulars of this affair of the 7th of June beyond the mention of it and the casualties. Pack's own report of the affair, however (with Whitelock's covering despatch), is given under his name in Philippart's *Royal Military Calendar* (1820). It is interesting to compare that account with the one in the text, as each has some details not in the other. It seems that the Spaniards, two thousand in number, were under Major-General Elio (see p. 79, below), and the name of their position was San Pedro.

following up the advantage he had gained and pushing forward into Buenos Ayres, which would have immediately surrendered, he halted his column and took up a position. The enemy recovered from his panic, and with the utmost vigour turned to and fortified the entrances of all the streets. (Buenos Ayres is perfectly open on the land side, but has a citadel of some strength within the town and upon the river. The houses are all flat-roofed, with a parapet of about three feet high.) The day after the affair alluded to, General Whitelock with his column arrived. The next day he reconnoitred the enemy, drove in their outposts, and partially invested the city. Some very heavy skirmishing took place in the enclosures, the fences consisting of aloe hedges, very difficult to get through, but making excellent breastworks. The Rifle Corps particularly distinguished themselves.

Upon the [5 July] the whole army attacked in four columns. The men were ordered to advance without flints in their musquets, and crowbars, axes, etc., were provided at the head of the column to break open the doors, which were most strongly barricaded. It must be stated that the streets of Buenos Ayres run at right angles from each other. Each street was cut off by a ditch and a battery behind it. Thus the troops were exposed to a cross fire. The tops of the houses were occupied by troops, and such a tremendous fire was produced of grape, canister, and musquetry, that in a short time two columns were nearly annihilated without effecting any impression. The column I belonged to, under Brigadier-General Craufurd, after severe loss, took refuge in a church, and about dusk in the evening surrendered to the enemy. Thus terminated one of the most sanguinary conflicts Britons were ever engaged in, and all owing to the stupidity of the General-in-chief and General Leveson-Gower. Liniers, a Frenchman by birth, who commanded, treated us prisoners tolerably well, but he had little to give us to eat, his citadel not being provisioned for a siege. We were three or four days in his hands, when, in consequence of the disgraceful convention entered into by General Whitelock, who agreed within two months to evacuate the territory altogether and to give up the fortress of Monte Video, we were released. The army re-embarked with all dispatch and sailed to Monte Video. Our wounded suffered dreadfully, many dying from slight wounds in the extremity of lockjaw.

The division of troops I belonged to sailed upon [12 July], under the command of Brigadier-General Lumley. I confess I parted from the kind Spanish family, who during my illness had treated me with such paternal kindness, with feelings of the deepest sorrow and most lively gratitude. The old lady offered me her daughter in marriage and $20,000, with as many thousand oxen as I wished, and she would build me a house in the country upon any plan I chose to devise.

Now that I am brought to leave the fertile

plains of the Plate, let me make some little
mention of its climate, soil, and productions. Its
summer is, of course, in January; during this time
it is very hot. Still you have a sea breeze and a
land breeze, which is very refreshing. During the
rainy seasons the weather is very tempestuous.
The climate altogether is, however, most mild and
salubrious. Corn of all descriptions grows with the
least possible care. The fertile grass plains are
immense. The country is not a dead flat, but un-
dulated like the great Atlantic a few days after a
gale of wind. Upon these plains thousands of oxen
and horses are grazing; they are so thick that were
an individual ever entangled amongst them he
would be lost as in a wood. These animals are,
however, all the property of individuals, and not wild
as supposed, and each horse and ox is branded.
You could buy a most excellent horse for two dollars
(I gave ten for one, he being very handsome, which
was a price unheard of before), a cow and calf one
dollar, a pair of draft oxen five (they are thus dear
in consequence of being trained). The country
abounds in all sorts of wild fowl and innumerable
wild dogs, which nature must have provided to eat
the carcases of the slaughtered cattle, many of which
are killed merely for their hides, a few of the prime
pieces alone being made use of for food. The
marrow is usually also taken and rendered into
bladders, with which they cook everything, using it,
in short, as we use butter, which makes their dishes
very palatable. The native inhabitants, called

"peons," or labourers, are a very superior race of men, almost Patagonians, are beautiful horsemen, and have a peculiar art of catching horses and oxen by what is termed the "lasso." This is a leathern thong of about thirty feet resembling the lash of a hunting-whip. An iron ring is at one end, through which the other end is passed, by which means a noose is formed; the end is then fastened to the girths of the horse. The lasso is collected in the man's hand, he swings it circularly round his head, and when the opportunity offers, he throws it over the head of the animal he wishes to catch. He is sure of his aim; the noose draws tight round the animal's throat, and he is of course choked, and down he drops.

In killing bullocks they are very dexterous. The moment the bullock finds himself caught he begins to gallop round; the end being fast to the saddle, the horse turns gradually round so that he is not entangled. A second peon with his lasso gallops after the bullock, and throws his lasso round the hind leg above the hough and rides in a contrary direction to the other horseman, consequently the bullock is stretched between the two horses. The riders jump off and plunge their knives into the bullock, and other persons are employed to dress it, etc.

The fleet separated in a gale of wind off the Azores. During this gale the transport I was in carried away its rudder. Our captain had kept so bad a reckoning we ran four hundred miles after he expected to make the Lizard. In the chops of the Channel we fell in with the *Swallow*, sloop of war, to whom we made a signal of distress, and she towed us into Falmouth Harbour [5 Nov.]. It blew the most tremendous gale of wind that night. A transport with the 9th Dragoons aboard was wrecked near the Lizard, and this would inevitably have been our fate had we not been towed in by the sloop of war. The rudder was repaired, we were driven into Plymouth, and in the middle of December anchored at Spithead, where we delighted to have arrived. However, to our great mortification, we were ordered to the Downs, there to disembark.

I obtained leave of absence, and was soon in the arms of a most affectionate family, who dearly loved me. My mother's delight I shall never forget. There are feelings we possess in our youth which cannot be described. I was then only nineteen. My brothers and sisters were all well, and every moment called to my recollection some incident of juvenile delight and affection.

CHAPTER II.

WITH SIR JOHN MOORE—BATTLE OF CORUÑA.
1808-9.

I STAYED in this happy land of my sires for two months, when I was ordered to join. The Regiment was then quartered at Colchester. Although there were many subalterns present who were senior to me, I had given to me, for my exertions abroad as Adjutant, the command of a Company. This was the act of my kind and valued friend Colonel Beckwith, whom I shall have occasion frequently to mention in these memoirs, but never without feelings of affection and gratitude. The Company was in very bad order when I received it, which Colonel Beckwith told me was the reason he gave it me. I now procured a commission for my brother Tom, who was gazetted over the heads of several other candidates.

In the summer [spring] of 1808 10,000 men were ordered to Sweden under the command of Sir J. Moore. Three Companies of the Rifle Brigade under Major Gilmour were to form part of the expedition. By dint of great exertion I was appointed Adjutant to this detachment. We marched to Harwich to embark. When the fleet was collected, we anchored

a few days in Yarmouth roads. The fleet arrived
at Gottenburgh [on 7 May], blowing a heavy gale
of wind. The harbour of this place is most beautiful.
The army never landed, but the men were drilled,
embarking and disembarking in flat-bottomed boats.
I jumped against three regiments, 95th, 43rd, and
52nd, and beat them by four inches, having leaped
19 feet and 4 inches.

Commenced at Simla, Himalayas, 11th Aug. 1844.—H.G.S.

At this period Napoleon announced his unjust
invasion of Spain, and Sir John Moore's army was
ordered to sail and unite with the forces collecting
on the coast of Portugal for the purpose of expelling
Junot's army from Lisbon. On approaching the
mouth of the Mondego, a frigate met us to say Sir
Arthur Wellesley's army had landed in Mondego
and pushed forward, and that Sir John Moore was
to sail for Peniche, and there land on arrival. The
battle of Vimiera had been fought [21 Aug. 1808],
and the Convention was in progress. Sir John
Moore's army landed one or two days after the battle
and took the outposts. The three Companies to
which I was Adjutant joined Colonel Beckwith and
the headquarters of the Regiment, and I was
appointed to Captain O'Hare's Company (subalterns Smith, W. Eeles, Eaton).

After the embarcation of the French army, an
army was formed under Sir John Moore for the aid
of the Spaniards, and it moved on the frontier of
Alemtejo.

The 95th were quartered in Villa Viciosa, in an
elegant palace. I occupied a beautiful little room
with a private staircase, called the Hall of Justice.
I was sent by Sir Edward Paget to examine the fort
Xuramenha and report upon it, the fords of the
Guadiana, etc., near the important fortress of
Badajos.

In the autumn of this year (1808), Sir John
Moore's army moved on Salamanca. As I could
speak Spanish, I was employed by Colonel Beckwith
to precede the Regiment daily to aid the Quarter-
master in procuring billets and rations in the different
towns, and various were the adventures I met with.
The army was assembled at Salamanca, and never
did England assemble such a body of organized and
elegant troops as that army of Sir John Moore,
destined to cover itself with glory, disgrace, victory,
and misfortune. The whole of this campaign is too
ably recorded by Napier for me to dwell on. I shall
only say that never did corps so distinguish itself
during the whole of this retreat as my dear old Rifles.
From the severe attack on our rear-guard at Calcavellos [3 Jan. 1809], where I was particularly distinguished, until the battle of Coruña, we were daily
engaged with a most vigorous and pushing enemy,
making most terrific long marches (one day 37 miles).
The fire of the Riflemen ever prevented the column
being molested by the enemy; but the scenes of
drunkenness, riot, and disorder we Reserve Division
witnessed on the part of the rest of the army are not
to be described; it was truly awful and heartrending

to see that army which had been so brilliant at Sala-manca so totally disorganized, with the exception of the reserve under the revered Paget and the Brigade of Guards. The cavalry were nearly all dismounted, the whole a mass of fugitives and insubordinates; yet these very fellows licked the French at Coruña like men [16 Jan.]. The army embarked the following day. I shall never forget the explosion of a fortress blown up by us—the report cannot be imagined. Oh, the filthy state we were all in! We lost our baggage at Calcavellos; for three weeks we had no clothes but those on our backs; we were literally covered and almost eaten up with vermin, most of us suffering from ague and dysentery, every man a living still active skeleton. On embarcation many fell asleep in their ships and never awoke for three days and nights, until in a gale we reached Portsmouth [21 Jan.]. I was so reduced that Colonel Beckwith, with a warmth of heart equalling the thunder of his voice, on meeting me in the George Inn, roared out, "Who the devil's ghost are you? Pack up your kit—which is soon done, the devil a thing have you got—take a place in the coach, and set off home to your father's. I shall soon want again such fellows as you, and I will arrange your leave of absence!" I soon took the hint, and naked and slothful and covered with vermin I reached my dear native home, where the kindest of fathers and most affectionate of mothers soon restored me to health.[*]

* See his reference to this time, p. 159.

c

CHAPTER III.

BACK TO THE PENINSULA UNDER SIR ARTHUR
WELLESLEY.

1809.

IN two months I rejoined the Regiment at Hythe.
From Hythe we marched for Dover, where we
embarked for Lisbon [25 May] to join the Duke's *
army. Having landed at Lisbon, we commenced
our march for Talavera. On this march—a very
long one—General Craufurd compiled his orders
for the march of his Brigade, consisting of the
43rd, 52nd, and 95th, each upwards of 1000 strong.
These orders he enforced with rigour (as it seemed
at the moment), but he was in this way the means
of establishing the organization and discipline of
that corps which acquired for it its after-celebrity
as the " Light Division."

We had some long, harassing, and excessively
hot marches. In the last twenty-eight hours we

---

* The author, writing many years after the events described, does
not discriminate the titles borne at different dates by his revered
commander, but speaks of him as " the Duke," even from the time he
was Sir Arthur Wellesley. At the risk of offending the historical sense
of some readers, I have made no attempt to remove such a harmless
anachronism.

marched from Oropesa to Talavera, a distance of
fourteen Spanish leagues (56 miles), our soldiers
carrying their heavy packs, the Riflemen eighty
rounds of ammunition.   But the battle of Talavera
was thundering in our ears, and created a spirit in
the Brigade which cast away all idea of fatigue.   We
reached the sanguinary field at daylight after the
battle [29 July], greeted as if we were demi-gods by
all the gallant heroes who had gained *such* a victory.
We took up the outposts immediately, and some
of us Riflemen sustained some heavy skirmishing.
The field was literally covered with dead and dying.
The bodies began to putrefy, and the stench was
horrible, so that an attempt was made to collect
the bodies and burn them.   Then, however, came a
stench which literally affected many to sickness.
The soldiers were not satisfied with this mode of
treating the bodies of their dead comrades, and the
prosecution of the attempt was relinquished.   After
our stay at Talavera [29 July—3 Aug.], during
which we were nearly starved, the army commenced
its retreat, passing the bridge of Arzobispo in the
most correct and soldier-like manner, our Brigade
forming the rear-guard.   The army retired on
Deleytosa, the Light Brigade remaining in a
position so as to watch the bridge of Almaraz.
Here for three weeks we were nearly starved
[6 Aug.—20 Aug.], and our position received the
name of Doby Hill.*   We marched every evening

* Cp. E. Costello, *Adventures of a Soldier*, p. 36: " For bread
we took the corn from the fields, and, having no proper means of

and bivouacked so as to occupy the passage of the Tagus, and at daylight returned to our hill. Honey was plentiful, but it gave dysentery. My mess—Leach's Company (Leach, Smith, Layton, and Bob Beckwith)—were not as badly off as our neighbours. We had a few dollars, and as I could speak Spanish, I rode into the lines of the Spanish troops, where I could always purchase some loaves of bread at a most exorbitant price. With this and some horrid starved goats we lived tolerably for soldiers in hard times. The army retired into quarters—the headquarters to Badajos, our Division (which had added to it Sir Rufane Donkin's Brigade, the 45th, 87th, and 88th Regiments) to Campo Mayor [11 Sept.], where sickness and mortality commenced to an awful extent. On our reaching the frontier of Portugal, Castello de Vidi, wine was plentiful, and every man that evening had his skin full.

During the period we were at Campo Mayor [11 Sept.—12 Dec.], the Hon. Captain James Stewart and I got some excellent greyhounds. We were always out coursing or shooting, and were never sick a day; our more sedentary comrades many of them distressingly so. The seven right-hand men of Leslie's Company died in the winter of this year.

winnowing and grinding it, were obliged, as a substitute, to rub out the ears between our hands and then pound them between stones to make it into dough, such as it was. From this latter wretched practice, we christened the place 'Dough Boy Hill,' a name by which it is well remembered by the men of our Division." Cp. p. 321, below.

While at Campo Mayor the convalescents of my Light Brigade were ordered to our old fortress, called Onguala, on the immediate frontier of Portugal, and opposite to Abuchucha, the frontier of Spain. They consisted of forty or fifty weakly men. I was first for Brigade duty, and I was sent in command, with a Lieut. Rentall of the 52nd Regiment and my brother Tom, who was sick. I knew this country well, for we had had some grand battues there, and shot red deer and wild boars. So soon, therefore, as I was installed in my command, lots of comrades used to come from Campo Mayor to breakfast with me and shoot all day. On one occasion Jack Molloy, Considine, and several fellows came, and while out we fell into the bivouac of a set of banditti and smugglers. We hallooed and bellowed as if an army were near us. The bandits jumped on their horses and left lots of corn-sacks, etc., in our hands ; but on discovering our numbers, and that we fired no balls (for we had only some Rifle buttons pulled off my jacket), being well armed, they soon made us retreat. This, after my friends returned to Campo Mayor, so disconcerted me that I made inquiry about these same rascals, and ascertained there were a body of about twenty under a Catalan, the terror of the country. I immediately sent for my sergeant (a soldier in every sense of the word) to see how many of our convalescents he could pick out who could *march at all.* He soon returned. He himself and ten men, myself, Rentall, and my sick brother Tom (who

would go) composed my army.   I got a guide, and
ascertained that there were several haunts of these
bandits; so off I started.   We moved on a small
chapel (many of which lone spots there are in all
Roman Catholic countries), at which there was a
large stable.   On approaching we heard a shot
fired, then a great and lawless shouting, which
intimated to us our friends of the morning were
near at hand.   So Pat Nann and I crept on to peep
about.   We discovered the fellows were all inside
a long stable, with a railed gate shut, and a regular
sentry with his arms in his hand.   They were all
about and had lights, and one very dandy-looking
fellow with a smart dagger was cutting tobacco to
make a cigar.   Pat and I returned to our party and
made a disposition of attack, previously ascertaining
if the stable had a back door, which it had not.   I
then fell in our men very silently, Mr. Rentall being
much opposed to our attack, at which my brother
Tom blew him up in no bad style of whispering
abuse, and our men went for the gate.   The sentry
soon discovered us and let fly, but hit no one.   The
gate was fast and resisted two attempts to force it, but
so amazed were the bandits, they [never] attempted
to get away their horses, although their arms were
regularly piled against the supports of the roof of
the stable, and we took twelve banditti with their
captain, a fine handsome fellow, horses, etc.   His
dagger I sent to my dear father.   I sent my prisoners
on the next day to Campo Mayor, galloping ahead
myself, in an awful funk lest General Craufurd

should blow me up.   However, I got great credit
for my achievement in thus ridding the neighbourhood of a nest of robbers; and the captain and five
of his men (being Spaniards) were sent to Badajos
and sentenced to the galleys for life, being recognized as old offenders.   The remainder received
a lesser punishment.   My men got forty Spanish
dollars each prize money, the amount I sold the
horses for.   I bought for forty dollars the captain's
capital horse.   The men wanted me to keep him as
my share, but I would not.   Dr. Robb, our surgeon,
gave sixty Spanish dollars for a black mare.   Thus
ended the Battle of the Bandits.

CHAPTER IV.

CAMPAIGN OF 1810—THE 1ST GERMAN HUSSARS.

IN the winter of this year [12 Dec. 1809] we marched towards the northern frontier of Portugal. We marched towards Almeida, and were cantoned in villages to its rear—Alameda, Villa de Lobos, Fequenas, not far from the Douro. Here too was good shooting and coursing; but I was not permitted to be idle. We moved into Spain [19 Mar. 1810], and at Barba del Puerco had a most brilliant night attack, in which Colonel Beckwith greatly distinguished himself.

At Villa de Ciervo a detachment of one sergeant and twelve Hussars (1st German) were given me by General Craufurd to go right in among the French army, which had moved on Ciudad Rodrigo and then retired. Many are the hairbreadth escapes my Hussars and I had, for we were very daring; we were never two nights in the same place. One night at Villa de Ciervo, where we were watching a ford over the Agueda, two of my vedettes (two Poles elegantly mounted) deserted to the enemy. The old sergeant, a noble soldier, came to me in great distress. "O mein Gott, upstand and jump up your horse ; *she* will surely be here *directly !*"   I was half asleep, with my horse's reins in my hand, and roared out, " Who the devil is *she ?* "   " The Franzosen, mein Herr.   Two d——d schelms have deserted." So we fell back to the rear of the village, sitting on our horses the remainder of the night, every moment expecting the weakness of our party would cause an attempt to cut us off.   At daylight we saw fifty French dragoons wending their way on the opposite bank to the ford.   I immediately got hold of the *padre* and *alcalde* (priest and magistrate), and made them collect a hundred villagers and make them shoulder the long sticks with which they drive their bullock-carts and ploughs, which of course at a distance would resemble bayonets. These villagers I stationed in two parties behind two hills, so that the " bayonets " alone could be seen by the enemy.   Then with my sergeant and ten Hussars (two having deserted) I proceeded to meet the enemy, first riding backwards and forwards behind a hill to deceive him as to my numbers. The French sent over the river about half their number.   I immediately galloped up to them in the boldest manner, and skirmished advancing. The enemy were deceived and rapidly retired, and I saved the village from an unmerciful ransacking, to the joy of all the poor people.

At this period General Craufurd had officers at two or three of the most advanced vedettes where there were beacons, who had orders to watch the enemy with their telescopes, and, in case of any movement, to report or fire the beacon. I was on this duty in rather a remote spot on the extreme left of our posts. The vedette was from the 1st Hussar picquet. These men would often observe a patrol or body of the enemy with the naked eye which was barely discernible through a telescope, so practised were they and watchful. Towards the evening my servant ought to have arrived with my dinner (for we officers of the look-out could take nothing with us but our horse and our telescope), but he must have missed his way, and as my appetite was sharpened by a day's look-out, I began to look back, contrary to the vedette's idea of due vigilance. He asks, "What for Mynheer so much look to de rear?" I, sad at the fast, "Hussar, you are relieved every two hours. I have been here since daylight. I am confounded hungry, and am looking out for my servant and my dinner." "Poor yonge mans! but 'tis notings." "Not to you," said I, "but much to me." "You shall see, sir. I shall come off my horse, you shall up clim, or de French shall come if he see not de vedette all right." Knowing the provident habits of these Germans, I suspected what he was about. Off he got; up get I *en vedette*. With the greatest celerity, he unbuckled his valise from behind his saddle, and took out a piece of bacon (I had kept up a little fire from the sticks and bushes around me), from a cloth some ground coffee and sugar, from his haversack some biscuit, and spread on the ground a clean towel with knife. fork, and a little tin cup. He had water in his canteen—his cooking-tin. He made me a cup of coffee, sliced some bacon, broiled it in the embers, and in ten minutes coffee, bacon, biscuit were ready and looked as clean as if in a London tavern. He then says, " Come off." Up he mounts, saying, " Can eat. All you sall vant is de schnaps." I fell to, and never relished any meal half so much ; appetite was perfect, and the ingenious, quick and provident care of the Hussar added another to the many instances I had witnessed of this regiment to make them be regarded, as indeed they were, as exemplary soldiers for our emulation.

My servant soon after arrived. The contents of his haversack I transferred to my kind friend the Hussar's, and half the bottle of wine, on which the Hussar remarked, " Ah, dat is good ; the schnaps make nice ; " and my servant put up his valise again for him. I was highly amused to observe the momentary glances the Hussar cast on me and my meal, for no rat-catcher's dog at a sink-hole kept a sharper look-out to his front than did this vedette. In the whole course of my service I never was more amused, and nothing could be more disinterested than the Hussar's conduct, which I never forgot.

CHAPTER V.

CAMPAIGN OF 1810—BATTLE OF THE COA.

Soon after this the French invested Ciudad Rodrigo, and regularly commenced the siege. The Light Division (into which fell the three regiments 43rd, 52nd, and two Battalions of Rifles, 1st and 3rd Portuguese Caçadores, the latter under Elder, a most brilliant Rifle officer), 1st Hussars, 14th Light Dragoons, 16th Light Dragoons occupied Gallegos, Exejo, etc., our advanced post being at Marialva, on the road to Ciudad Rodrigo. During the whole siege our alerts were innumerable, and at Marialva we had several very smart skirmishes, but so able were Craufurd's dispositions, we never lost even a vedette.

The French were in the habit of patrolling over the Agueda with cavalry and infantry, about 30 Dragoons and 200 foot. General Craufurd determined to intercept one of these patrols [10 July], and [moved out with] the cavalry, 1st Hussars, 14th and 16th Light Dragoons, and Light Division. It may now be asked, Was it necessary to take out such a force to intercept so small a party? Certainly. Because the enemy might have crossed the Agueda to support the patrols. We were all moved to where directed, the infantry were halted, some of the cavalry moved on. At grey daylight the patrols of the enemy appeared, their Dragoons some way in advance of the infantry. The patrol was very incautiously conducted (not like our 1st Hussars), and the Dragoons were taken in a moment. The infantry speedily retired to an eminence above the ford and formed square. Craufurd ordered them to be attacked by the cavalry, and several right good charges were made; but the French were steady, the dead horses in their front became a defence, and our cavalry never made the slightest impression. Craufurd never moved one of *us*. The charges of cavalry ceased for a few seconds— the fields around were high-standing corn. The gallant fellow in command gave the word, "Sauve qui peut." In a moment all dispersed, ran through the standing corn down to the banks of the river, and were saved without the loss of a man. The officer was promoted on his arrival in his camp.

Our loss was very considerable. Poor Colonel Talbot of the 14th (commanding) killed, and a lot of men. I and Stewart, Adjutant of the Rifle Brigade, asked leave to go ahead, and we saw it all. Indeed, it was in sight of the whole division. Had two Companies of ours only been moved to threaten the ford, the enemy would have laid down their arms. Such a piece of soldiering as that morning presented the annals of war cannot produce.[*]

[*] Cp. Cope, p. 55: "Why Craufurd did not use his guns or let loose the Riflemen at the French infantry, seems inexplicable."

While we were at a village called Valde
Mula, in the neighbourhood of Fort Concepcion,
that most perfect little work was blown up [21
July]. It was the neatest fortification I ever saw
(except the Moro in the Havana subsequently), and
the masonry was beautifully executed.

After the fall of Ciudad Rodrigo, which made a
brilliant defence, our advanced line fell back to the
Dos Casas, and in front of Alameda we had a
brilliant affair with the French, in which Krauch-
enberg 1st Hussars and McDonald Royal Artillery
greatly distinguished themselves. The 3rd Caçadores were this day first under fire, and behaved
nobly. After this our advanced posts were
retired behind the Dos Casas to cover Almeida.
While Massena prepared his army to invade
Portugal and besiege Almeida, we were daily on
the alert and had frequent skirmishes. General
Craufurd, too, by a variety of *ruses* frequently made
the whole French army turn out.

In the early morning of the 24th of July (I was
on picquet with Leach and my Company that night)
the enemy moved forward with 40,000 men. Our
force, one Brigade of Horse Artillery, three Regiments of cavalry, five of infantry, were ordered by
the Duke to remain as long as possible on the right
bank of the Coa, where there was a bridge over the
river on the road from Almeida into Portugal to
Celerico and Pinhel, posting ourselves between
the fortress and the bridge, so as to pass over so
soon as the enemy advanced in force. In place of

doing this, Craufurd took up a position to our right of Almeida, and but for Colonel Beckwith our whole force would have been sacrificed. Fortunately a heavy rain had fallen, which made the Coa impassable except by the bridge, which was in our possession, and the enemy concentrated his force in one rush for the bridge [24 July].

During the Peninsular War there never was a more severe contest. The 43rd lost 17 officers and 150 men, my Regiment 10 officers and 140 men. When we passed the bridge my section was the rear-guard of the whole, and in a rush to drive back the enemy (with whom we were frequently absolutely mixed), my brother Tom and I were both severely wounded, and a Major Macleod, a noble fellow, afterwards killed at Badajos, put me on his horse, or I should have been taken. The enemy made several attempts to cross, but old Alister Cameron, Captain in the Rifle Brigade, had posted his Company in a ruined house which commanded the bridge, and mainly contributed to prevent the passage of the enemy, who made some brilliant attempts. The bridge was literally piled with their dead and they made breastworks of the bodies. On this day, on going to the rear wounded, I first made the acquaintance of my dear friend Will Havelock,* afterwards my whipper-in, who was joining the 43rd fresh from England, with smart chako and jacket. I had a ball lodged in my ankle-joint, a most painful wound. We were sent to Pinhel,

* Elder brother of Sir Henry Havelock. See p. 297.

where the 3rd Division was seven leagues from
the action, the nearest *support* (?).   Sir Thomas
Picton treated us wounded *en princes*.

The wounded were ordered to the rear, so as
to embark on the Mondego at Pinhel.   In collecting transport for the wounded, a sedan chair
between two mules was brought, the property of
some gentleman in the neighbourhood, and, fortunately for me, I was the only person who could ride
in it, and by laying my leg on the one seat and
sitting on the other, I rode comparatively easy to
the poor fellows in the wretched bullock-cars, who
suffered excruciating agony, poor brother Tom
(who was very severely wounded above the
knee) among the rest.   This little story will
show what wild fellows we were in those days.
George Simmons' (1st Rifles) bullocks at one
stage had run away.   As I was the spokesman,
the surgeon in charge came to me in great distress.   I sent for the village magistrate, and actually
fixed a rope in my room to hang him if he did
not get a pair of bullocks (if the Duke of W. had
known he would have hung *me*).   However, the
bullocks were got, and off we started.   The bullocks
were not broken, and they ran away with poor
George and nearly jolted him to death, for he was
awfully wounded through the thick of the thigh.
However, we all got down to Pinhel [31 July], and
thence descended the Mondego by boats, landing
every night.   At one house a landlord was most
insolent to us, and Lieut. Pratt of the Rifles, shot

through the neck, got very angry. The carotid
artery must have been wounded, for it burst out in
a torrent of blood, and he was dead in a few
seconds, to our horror, for he was a most excellent
fellow. On the same bed with me was a Captain
Hull of the 43rd Regiment with a similar wound.
I never saw any man in such a funk.

On our reaching the mouth of the Mondego, we
were put on board a transport. In the ship with
me was a stout little officer, 14th Light Dragoons,
severely wounded, whose thigh afterwards dis-
gorged a French 6-lb. shot. On arrival in Lisbon
[7 Aug.] we were billeted in Buenos Ayres, poor Tom
and I in awful agony in our miserable empty house.
However, we got books, and I, although suffering,
got on well enough. But poor Tom's leg was in
such an awful state he was sent home. George
Simmons's wound healed.* My ball was lodged on
my ankle-joint, having partially divided the *tendo
Achillis*. However, we heard of the army having
retired into the celebrated lines of Torres Vedras,
and nothing would serve us but *join the Regiment.*
So our medical heroes very unwillingly sent us off to

---

* George Simmons writes in his diary for the 17th of September,
1810 : "I removed to Pedroso for the convenience of sea-bathing, my
thigh being much better, which enabled me, with crutches, to move
about. Lieutenant Harry Smith was also with me. I found great
benefit from the sea-bathing." Sir Harry Smith, writing to Major
George Simmons on the 16th of June, 1846 (soon after the battle of
Aliwal, when he had driven the Sikhs into the Sutlej), refers to
their bathing together at this time, though he says at Belem, not at
Pedroso (both places are close to Lisbon) : " Dear George,—We little
thought at Bellam [Belem], when hopping about there, I should become
a master of that art we were both 'girning' under, or a swimming
master for pupils in the Sutledge ! "

D

Belem, the convalescent department under Colonel Tucker, 29th Regiment, a sharp fellow enough. When I, George Simmons, and Charlie Eeles, 3rd Battalion, just arrived sick from Cadiz, waited on him to express our desire to join, he said, "Oh, certainly ; but you must be posted to do duty with convalescents going up the country." I was lame and could not walk. George Simmons cantered on crutches, and Charlie Eeles was very sick. However, *go* or *no go*, and so we were posted to 600 villains of every Regiment in the army under a long Major Ironmonger of the 88th (afterwards of Almeida celebrity, when the garrison escaped). We marched in a day [7 Oct.]. On the first day's march he pretended to faint. George Simmons, educated a surgeon, *literally* threw a bucket of water over him.*
He recovered the faint, but not the desire to return ; and the devil would have it, the command devolved on me, a subaltern, for whom the soldiers of other corps have no great respect, and such a task I never had as to keep these six hundred rascals together. However, I had a capital English horse, good at

* Simmons states in his diary that the Commandant was Major Murphy (not Ironmonger), and writes that at the end of the second day's march "another one hundred *heroes* had disappeared, which made our Commandant raving mad. Smith called upon me to assist him in a medical capacity. I had a bucket of spring water thrown upon him, which did him good ; he had several fits, but this put an end to them" (p. 111). According to the Army Lists, Major Barnaby Murphy, 88th Regiment, was killed at Salamanca, July, 1812. Lieut.-Colonel W. Iremonger, 2nd Foot, retired 2 May, 1811 (? 12 May). There is no Ironmonger in the Army List. The garrison of Almeida escaped on 11 May, 1811. In his despatch of 15 May, 1811, Wellington censures a Lieutenant-Colonel (name not given), but it is for "imprudence," not cowardice.

riding over an insubordinate fellow, and a voice like
thunder. The first bivouac I came to was the
Guards (these men were very orderly). The commanding officer had a cottage. I reported myself.
It was raining like the devil. He put his head out
of the window, and I said, " Sir, I have 150 men
of your Regiment convalescent from Belem." "Oh,
send for the Sergeant-major," he very quietly said;—
no "walk in out of the rain." So I roared out, "We
Light Division men don't do duty with Sergeant-
majors, nor are we told to wait. There are your
men, every one—the only well-conducted men in 600
under my charge—and these are their accounts!"
throwing down a bundle of papers, and off I galloped,
to the Household man's astonishment. That day
I delivered over, or sent by officers under me, all
the vagabonds I had left. Some of my own men
and I reached our corps that night at Arruda, when
old Sydney Beckwith, dear Colonel, said, " You are
a mad fool of a boy, coming here with a ball in
your leg. Can you dance?" " No," says I ; " I
can hardly walk but with my toe turned out." " Can
you be my A.D.C.?" " Yes ; I can ride and eat,"
I said, at which he laughed, and was kind as a
brother ; as was my dear friend Stewart, or Rutu,
as we called him, his Brigade Major, the actual
Adjutant of the Regiment.

That very night General Craufurd sent for me,
and said, " You have come from Sobral, have you
not, to-day, and know the road?" I said, " Yesterday." " Well, get your horse and take this letter

to the Duke for me when it is ready." I did not
like the job, but said nothing about balls or *pains*,
which were bad enough. He kept me waiting
about an hour, and then said, "You need wait no
longer; the letter won't be ready for some time, and
my orderly dragoon shall take it. Is the road
difficult to find?" I said, "No; if he keeps the
chaussée, he can't miss it." The poor dragoon
fell in with the French patrol, and was taken
prisoner. When the poor fellow's fate was known,
how Colonel Beckwith did laugh at my escape!

At Arruda we marched every day at daylight
into position in the hills behind us, and by the
ability of Craufurd they were made impregnable.
The whole Division was at work. As Colonel Beckwith and I were standing in the camp one day, it
came on to rain, and we saw a Rifleman rolling down
a wine-cask, apparently empty, from a house near.
He deliberately knocked in one of the heads; then—
for it was on the side of a rapidly shelving hill—
propped it up with stones, and crept in out of the
rain. Colonel Beckwith says, "Oh, look at the lazy
fellow; he has not half supported it. When he falls
asleep, if he turns round, down it will come." Our
curiosity was excited, and our time anything but
occupied, so we watched our friend, when in about
twenty minutes the cask with the man inside came
rolling down the hill. He must have rolled over
twenty times at least before the rapidity disengaged
him from his round-house, and even afterwards,
such was the impetus, he rolled over several times.

To refrain from laughing excessively was impossible,
though we really thought the noble fellow must be
hurt, when up he jumped, looked round, and said
" I never had any affection for an empty wine-cask,
and may the devil take me if ever I go near another
—to be whirled round like a water-mill in this
manner!" The fellow was in a violent John Bull
passion, while we were nearly killed with laughing.

When Massena retired, an order came to the
Light Division to move on De Litte, and to Lord
Hill to 'do the same on our right at [Vallada ?].
This dispatch I was doomed to carry. It was one
of the utmost importance, and required a gallop.
By Jove, I had ten miles to go just before dark,
and when I got to Colborne's position, who had a
Brigade under Lord Hill, a mouse could not get
through his works. (Colborne was afterwards my
Brigadier in the Light Division, and is now Lord
Seaton.) Such a job I never had. I could not go
in front of the works—the French had not retired;
so some works I leaped into, and led my noble
English horse into others. At last I got to Lord
Hill, and he marched immediately, night as it was.
How I got back to my Division through the night I
hardly know, but horse and rider were both done.
The spectacle of hundreds of miserable wretches of
French soldiers on the road in a state of *starvation*
is not to be described.

We moved *viâ* Caccas to Vallé on the [Rio
Mayor], where our Division were opposite Santarem.
The next day [20 Nov.] the Duke came up and

ordered our Division to attack Santarem, which was bristling on our right with abattis, three or four lines. We felt the difficulty of carrying such heights, but towards the afternoon we moved on. On the Duke's staff there was a difference of opinion as to the number of the enemy, whether one *corps d'armée* or two. The Duke, who knew perfectly well there were two, and our move was only a reconnaissance, turned to Colonel Beckwith. "Beckwith, my Staff are disputing whether at Santarem there is one *corps d'armée* or two?" "I'll be d——d if I know, my Lord, but you may depend on it, a great number were required to make those abattis *in one night*." Lord Wellington laughed, and said, "You are right, Beckwith; there are two *corps d'armée*." * The enemy soon showed themselves. The Duke, as was his wont, satisfied himself *by ocular demonstration*, and the Division returned to its bivouac. Whilst here, Colonel Beckwith was seized with a violent attack of ague.

Our outposts were perfectly quiet, although sentries, French and English, were at each end of the bridge over the Rio Mayor, and vedettes along each bank. There was most excellent coursing on the plains of Vallé, and James Stewart and I were frequently out. Here I gave him my celebrated Spanish greyhound, Moro, the best the world ever produced, with a pedigree like that of an Arab horse, bred at Zamora by the Conde de Monteron ; but the noble dog's story is too long to tell here.

* Cp. Kincaid, *Random Shots*, pp. 101, 102.

In one year Stewart gave me him back again to run a match against the Duke of Wellington's dog. But the siege of Ciudad Rodrigo prevented our sports of that description. Colonel Beckwith going to Lisbon, and I being his A.D.C., it was voted a capital opportunity for me to go to have the ball cut out from under the tendon Achillis, in the very joint. I was very lame, and the pain often excruciating, so off I cut.

Soon after we reached Lisbon, I was ordered to Buenos Ayres to be near the surgeons. A board was held consisting of the celebrated Staff Surgeon Morell, who had attended me before, Higgins, and Brownrigg. They examined my leg. I was all for the operation. Morell and Higgins recommended me to remain with a stiff leg of my own as better than a wooden one, for the wounds in Lisbon of late had sloughed so, they were dubious of the result. Brownrigg said, " If it were my leg, out should come the ball." On which I roared out, " Hurrah, Brownrigg, you are the doctor for me." So Morell says, " Very well, if you are desirous, we will do it *directly*." My pluck was somewhat cooled, but I cocked up my leg, and said, " There it is; slash away." It was five minutes, most painful indeed, before it was extracted. The ball was jagged, and the tendonous fibres had so grown into it, it was half dissected and half torn out, with most excruciating torture for a moment, the forceps breaking which had hold of the ball. George Simmons was present, whose wound had broken out and obliged him to go to Lisbon.* The surgeon wanted some linen during the operation, so I said, "George, tear a shirt," which my servant gave him. He turned it about, said, " No, it is a pity; it is a good shirt;" at which I did not ——— him a few, for my leg was aching and smoking from a wound four or five inches long. Thank God Almighty and a light heart, no sloughing occurred, and before the wound was healed I was with the regiment. Colonel Beckwith's ague was cured, and he had joined his Brigade before I could move, so when I returned to Vallé he was delighted to see his A.D.C.

* He was at Lisbon from 3 Dec. to 4 Feb., when he returned to his Regiment with Colonel Beckwith (*A British Rifleman,* pp. 124, 135).

CHAPTER VI.

CAMPAIGN OF 1811.

I FOUND the army in hourly expectation to move, and the Captain of my Company—Leach—was gone sick to the rear, so I said to my Colonel, "I must be no longer A.D.C., sir. However grateful I am, my Company wants me." "Ah, now you can walk a little, you leave me! Go and be d——d to you; but I love you for the desire." Off I started, and the very next day we marched [6 Mar. 1811], Massena retreating out of Portugal, and many is the skirmish we had. My leg was so painful, the wound open, and I was so lame. When others could lie down I was on horseback, on a dear little Spanish horse given me by James Stewart, afterwards an animal of still greater renown.

At Pombala I had with my Company a very heavy skirmish [11 Mar.]. At Redinha my Company was in the advance [12 Mar.], supported by Captain O'Hare's. A wood on our front and right was *full* of Frenchmen. The Light Companies of the 3rd Division came up. I asked, "Are you going to attack that wood?" A Captain of the 88th Light Company, whom I knew,

quite laughed at my question.   I said very quietly,
"You will be beat back, and when you are, I will
move on the edge of the wood and help you."   How
he laughed!   My prediction was very soon verified:
he was wounded, and picked up by my Company,
which I moved on the right flank of the French and
stopped them immediately.   I sent to my support,
O'Hare, to move up to me.   The obstinate old
Turk would not, and so I was obliged to come
back, and had most unnecessarily five or six men
wounded.

The Plain of Redinha is a fine field for
military display, and our lines formed to attack
Ney's rearguard were magnificent.   The enemy
had many guns in the field, with prolonged lines,
an excellent mode for retreat on such ground,
and no rearguard was ever drawn off in more
masterly style, while I thought our attack in lines
was heavy, slow, and not half so destructive as
a rush of many contiguous columns would have
been.   The enemy had to retire over a bridge
through the village of Redinha, and we Riflemen
sorely pressed them on their left.   A line of French
infantry, concealed behind an *atalaya* (or tower) on
a hill good for the purpose, were lying down as my
Company and the one commanded by that wonderful Rifleman, Willie Johnstone, got within twenty
yards of them.   To our astonishment, up jumped
the line, fired a volley (they did not hit a man), and
went about.   At them we all went like devils, a
regular foot race, except for me and my little horse

Tiny, from which I could not dismount. In the
pursuit he carried me down a rock twelve feet high,
and Johnstone and I got to the bridge and cut off
half a Battalion of French. So many Legions of
Honour I scarcely ever saw in a group, but the eagle
was off! We *never* told what we had done, though
we enjoyed the fun, but it is an anecdote worthy of
record in Napier's *History*.

We were engaged with the enemy every day.
The next turn up was at Condesia [Condeixa]; the
next at Casal Nova [14 Mar.], where we had as heavy
a skirmishing fight as ever occurred. We Light
Division gentlemen had our full complement of fighting, for the French were obliged to hold a village to
give their column time to retire, and if the Duke's
orders had been obeyed, our Division ought not to
have attacked until the 3rd and 4th Divisions were
well up on the Frenchmen's left. I lost several men
that day, as did all our Companies, and particularly
the 52nd. Poor Major Jack Stewart,* a dear little
fellow, a friend of mine, was shot through the
lungs and died in three days, (Beckwith's Brigade-
Major, Lieut. James Stewart, was in three days
[28 Mar., near Freixadas] killed off the very
same little English horse, called Tom); Strode, a
Lieutenant, received his death-wound while talking
to me, etc. That night I was on picquet. The
enemy were retiring all night, but their sentries and
ours were in sight. At daylight a thick fog came

---

* Cope says Major John Stewart was killed in this fight near Casal
Nova, and Lieut. Strode mortally wounded (14 March).

on. Beckwith's Brigade, with him at its head, moved up to where I was posted. He said, "Come, Harry, get your Company together, and fall in at the head of the column." At this moment two of the 16th Dragoons rode back, and Beckwith said, "Where do you come from?" "We have patrolled a league and a half in the front, and seen naught." "A league and a half, my friend," says old Sydney, "in a thick fog is a d——d long way. Why, Harry, you said the vedettes were close to you." "So they are," I said, "and you will be fired at the moment you advance." We had not gone fifty yards when "Pop! pop!" Oh, how old Sydney laughed! "A league and a half!" But the fog was so thick we could not move, and the enemy, hearing our column on their rear, being clear, moved off.

In a few days, as we had got well up to the French rear-guard and were about to attack, a General Order was received, to my astonishment, appointing me Brigade Major * to the 2nd Light Brigade, not dear old Sydney's. *He* expected it, since he and Colonel Pakenham (dear Sir Edward!) were trying to do something for me on account of my lame leg. Beckwith says, "Now give your Company over to Layton, and set off immediately

* The duties of a Major of Brigade are given in a letter of Sir W. Gomm, Sept. 19, 1808: "The pay and rank are the same as those of Aide-de-camp. The officer has the rank of Major during the time he holds the employment, and he is not considered as generally belonging to the General's family so much as the Aide-de-camp. The situation is more independent" (Carr-Gomm's *Life of Sir W. Gomm*, 1881, p. 106).

to Colonel Drummond," who commanded the
Brigade. Hardly had I reached it, when such a
cannonade commenced, knocking the 52nd about in
a way I never saw before and hardly since. We
were soon all engaged, and drove the French, with
very hard fighting, into and over the river, with a
severe loss in killed, prisoners, and drowned. A
very heavy fight it was, ending just before dark.
I said to my Brigadier, " Have you any orders for
the picquets, sir ? " He was an old Guardsman, the
kindest though oddest fellow possible. " Pray, Mr.
Smith, are you my Brigade Major ? " " I believe so,
sir." " Then let me tell you, it is your duty to post
the picquets, and mine to have a d—d good dinner
for you every day." We soon understood each
other. He cooked the dinner often himself, and I
commanded the Brigade.

Our next great fight was a bitter one, Sabugal
[3 April]. I shall never forget the German 1st
Hussars, my old friends, moving on that day ; their
singing was melodious. Sir W. Erskine commanded
the cavalry and Light Division, a near-sighted old
ass, and we got *melted* with Reynier's *corps d'armée*
strongly posted on heights above Sabugal, and
attacked when the Duke intended we should have
moved round their left to Quadraseyes, as the 5th,
4th, and 3rd Divisions were to attack their front in
the centre of their position. However, we began,
and never was more gallantry mutually displayed
by friend and foe than on this occasion, particularly
by dear old Beckwith and his 1st Brigade. Some

guns were taken and retaken several times. A
French officer on a grey horse was most gallant.
Old Beckwith, in a voice like thunder, roared out
to the Riflemen, " Shoot that fellow, will you ? "
In a moment he and his horse were knocked over,
and Sydney exclaimed, " Alas ! you were a *noble
fellow."*

My Brigadier, as I soon discovered, left the
command to me, so I led away, and we came in for
a pretty good share in preventing Reynier's turning
the left of Beckwith's Brigade. Fortunately, the
5th Division got into action just in time, for the
French at the moment were squeezing us awfully.
The Light Division, under the shout of old Beckwith, rushed on with an impetuosity nothing could
resist, for, so checked had we been, our bloods were
really up, and we paid off the enemy most awfully.
Such a scene of slaughter as there was on one hill
would appal a modern soldier. The night came on
most awfully wet, and the 5th and Light Division
were sent back to Sabugal for shelter. Most dilapidated the place was, but the roofs were on, and
Sir W. Gomm, A.Q.M.G. of the 5th, and I divided
the town between us, our poor wounded lying out
in the rain and cold all night. The next morning
was fine, and as the sun rose we marched over the
field of battle. Our soldiers' blood was then cool,
and it was beautiful to hear the remarks of sympathy
for the distress of the numerous dying and wounded
all around us. Oh, you kings and usurpers should
view these scenes and moderate ambition !

This evening [4 April] we had a long march into Quadraseyes, but did not see a vestige of the enemy all day, nor of our commissariat either. We were literally starving. That old rogue Picton had seized the supplies of the Light Division for his 3rd. If he be now in the Purgatory that we condemned him to, he is to be pitied.

We closely pursued the French over the frontier, but never had a real slap at them. Almeida, which was garrisoned by their troops, was invested by the 5th Division, while the Light Division moved into its old lines, Gallegos, Marialva, Carpio, and Espeja. From the French garrison of Ciudad Rodrigo the enemy frequently came out. The Duke had gone into the Alemtejo, and Sir Brent Spencer commanded—a regular old woman, who allowed the French to commit all sorts of extravagances under our noses, when a rapid move on their rear from Espeja would have punished them. Sir W. Erskine commanded the advance Cavalry and Light Division.

I was at breakfast one morning with Sir William Erskine, who, early in the morning, with his staff had taken out a small party to reconnoitre Ciudad Rodrigo. The enemy immediately sent over a detachment of cavalry to check the advance, and a great argument occurred between Sir William and his A.A.G., Macdonald, whether the enemy crossed one or two squadrons. During the discussion in came Sir William's orderly, a clever old dragoon of the 1st German Hussars. "Ah!" says Sir William, "here is my old orderly; he can tell us. Hussar, how many squadrons of the enemy crossed the Agueda this morning?" With a body as stiff and erect as a statue, and a salute with an arm braced as if in the act of cutting down his enemy, "Just forty-nine mans, no more; I count him." The laugh was against both disputants.

Now occurred the dreadful disaster of the escape of the French garrison of Almeida. I shall never forget the mortification of our soldiers or the admiration of our officers of the brilliancy of such an attempt, the odds being a hundred to one against success. My long friend Ironmonger, then of the Queen's, into whose face George Simmons threw the bucket of water when marching, as before described, from Belem,* was grievously to blame.

Massena's army were rapidly recovering. They had received reinforcements, and were preparing to throw into Ciudad Rodrigo a large convoy of provisions. For this, it was necessary for them to put us back, and the present moment seemed a favourable one, as it was the intention ultimately to withdraw the French army to Salamanca and the neighbouring large towns, so that no demand might be made on the ample supplies required for Ciudad Rodrigo. At this moment Soult was making a formidable demonstration in the Alemtejo and Estremadura, our attempt on Badajoz had failed, and a large portion of our army had moved towards the south; it was therefore a fair opening for Massena to drive us over the Coa.

* See p. 34.

However, the dear Duke of Wellington took a braver view of the situation, and concentrated his army behind Fuentes D'Oñoro, and there fought that celebrated battle which lasted a day and a half [5 May]. General Craufurd joined us here on the day of the general action. The soldiers received him with every demonstration of joy. The officers at that time execrated him. I did not; he had appointed me his A.D.C., though I would not go to him, and he was always most kind and hospitable to me.

On the morning of this day old Sydney again distinguished himself, for the enemy from Poza Velha turned our right flank and licked our cavalry (14th Light Dragoons and Royals) awfully, bringing 4000 fresh fellows against them. There never was a more heavy fight than for several hours in the village of Fuentes. Here I saw the 79th Regiment, in an attack on the head of a French column coming up the road, bayonet eight or nine French officers and upwards of 100 men, the only real bayonet conflict I ever witnessed. After the battle of Fuentes d'Oñoro, the French retired unmolested, for we were glad to get rid of them. As they had such a formidable body of cavalry, on that open country we literally could not molest them.

At this time almost all our army moved into the Alemtejo *via* Arronchas, where, on Sir John Moore's advance to Salamanca, I had a nice quarter which I occupied four different times during the war. The poor family were always delighted to see me. On our advance into the Alemtejo we heard of the bloody battle of Albuera [16 May], and many of us rode on to see the field, which was well demonstrated by the lines of dead bodies, a most sanguinary conflict, and beautifully and truly described by Napier.

I must here record a most ridiculous night alarm the Light Division had, although leagues from any enemy, on their march into the Alemtejo. A drove of bullocks galloped over our men asleep in the bivouac, and for some time the officers could hardly persuade our best soldiers they were not French cavalry. My Brigadier, Drummond, was sleeping under a tree on his little portable iron bedstead. The light of a fire showed him, to my amusement, in his shirt (not a very long one), endeavouring to climb into the tree. I fell in his guard, and manfully charged *nothing* up a road leading to our camp, while General Craufurd lay on his back laughing to hysterics, poor fellow. Drummond soon after died at Guinaldo, in my arms, of a putrid sore throat, and Craufurd was killed in the storm of Ciudad Rodrigo.

During all this summer our army was assembled watching Soult, who neither attacked us nor we him. Never did we spend a more inactive summer. The enemy from Ciudad Rodrigo moved on Castello Branco, and threatened thereby our left flank and line of communication over the Tagus. When Soult could no longer feed his assembled army, he retired, and our Light Division were rapidly moved on Castello Branco, the remainder of the army of the north following.

Our army this autumn was cantoned, as near as it could be fed, on the frontiers to watch Ciudad Rodrigo, which the Duke contemplated besieging. After the death of General Drummond, Major-General Vandeleur was appointed to my Brigade, a fine, gentleman-like old Irish hero. We were quartered at Martiago, and our Division, some at El Bodon, others at Zamora, Guinaldo, etc. It was a very hot autumn, but towards the end of the year, when the rains commenced, there was capital coursing.

General Craufurd this year, in one of his mad freaks, reported that the Light Division was in want of clothing, etc., and it must go to the rear. The Duke ordered us to march one cold night over the Agueda to Larade, not far from Guinaldo, for his inspection. A great scene occurred. Craufurd had not arrived before the Duke rode down the line, and the Duke laughed and said, " Craufurd, you are late." " No, my Lord ; you are before your time. *My watch* is to be depended on." (I was riding a brown mare which I gave £120 for to Charlie Rowan, who had been thrown by her, after buying her from General Craufurd because *he* could not ride her. The mare charged the Duke, I on her back. " Hallo, Smith," says the Duke, " your horse masters you.") The Duke, to *our* delight, says to General Craufurd, " I never saw the Light Division look better or more ready for service. March back to your quarters; I shall soon require you in the field." About this time Marmont moved up to Ciudad Rodrigo with an enormous convoy of provisions, and he compelled the Duke to assemble, and the brilliant affair of cavalry and squares of infantry behind El Bodon took place [24 Sept.].

About this time we had some heavy and laborious manœuvring, night marches, etc. During these movements we marched a dark night's march from Guinaldo, and, as the road was wet and far from good, we had several checks in the column, when I heard a conversation between a 16th Light Dragoon and one of the German 1st Hussars, neither of whom had abstained from the ingredient which formed the subject. 16th Dragoon: "I say, Hussar, I likes it strong and hot and sweet, and plenty of ——. How do you like it?" Hussar: "I likes him raw."

Marmont, having accomplished his object, fell back, and we returned to our old cantonments. The Duke of Wellington's dispatch dated "Quadrasies, Sept. 29," so fully details all these operations and shows the beauty of the manœuvres so distinctly, I may confine myself to what occurred the evening General Pakenham's brigade had such a formidable brush at Aldea de Ponte.

The 4th Division was to return at dusk, as was the Light. I was lying in bivouac, talking to General Craufurd and John Bell, when a dragoon rode up with a note from General Cole, requesting

Craufurd to send an officer as a guide to lead his division to the heights of Rendo at dusk. I said, "Oh, John Bell will go, of course." "No," says John; "Harry Smith knows the road best." So I was ordered to go. Before I reached Cole it was dark. I found his Division moving: they were all right. I reported myself to him—the first time I had ever spoken to him. Colonel Brooke, brother of the "Shannon" Brooke, his Q.M.G., was with him. "Oh," says Cole, "sent by Craufurd, are you? Do you know the road?" We Light Division gentlemen were proper saucy fellows. I said, "I suppose I should not have been sent if I had not." "Ugh," says Cole, as hot as pepper. Here I may remark upon the difficulty there is at night to know roads, even for one well acquainted with them. Fires lighting, fires going out, the covering of the country with troops—such things change the face of nature, and a little anxiety adds to the difficulty. Cole, a most anxious man, kept saying, "Are you sure you know the road, sir?" etc., etc., etc. At last I said, "General Cole, if you will let me alone, I will conduct your Division; if you thus attract my attention, I cannot." It was an anxious moment, I admit. I was just at a spot where I might miss the road, a great road which I knew was near. I galloped ahead to look for it, and oh, how General Cole did blow me up! I found my road, though, and so soon as the head of the column had fairly reached it, I said, "Good night, General," and in a moment was in full speed,

while he was hallooing to me to come back. I had
some difficulty in finding my own Division, which
was moving parallel with the force. When I told
Craufurd of my first acquaintance with that hot
Irishman Cole, how he laughed! Poor dear Sir
Lowry! I was afterwards A.Q.M.G. to him after
the battle of Waterloo, and served under him as
Commandant of Cape Castle and Senior Member
of Council when he was Governor, and many is the
laugh we have had at our first acquaintance.

On one of our marches from the Alemtejo to
the north, in a house where General Drummond
and I were quartered at Idanha a Nova, a very
facetious Portuguese gentleman showed us a sort
of a return of the British, so incorrect that General
Drummond laughed at it; but Charlie Rowan, our
A.A.G. (now the great policeman in London *), who
was dining with General Drummond, told this
anecdote at the Duke's table at Guinaldo, and I
was sent back about 150 miles to fetch my friend.
I could speak Portuguese as well as English. I
therefore persuaded our hero to accompany me to
the Duke without telling why, but a more un-
pleasant ride than this, in charge of my friend and
all alone, without groom, etc., I never had, and many
was the blessing I bestowed on Charlie Rowan's
tongue. I delivered my friend to the Adjutant-
General at Guinaldo, and had twenty-four miles to
join my General at Robledillo.

* Colonel Rowan (from 1848 Sir Charles Rowan, K.C.B.) was
Chief Commissioner of the Metropolitan Police Force from its institution in 1829 till 1850. He died in 1852.

CHAPTER VII.

CAMPAIGN OF 1812 : STORMING OF CIUDAD RODRIGO.

As the winter approached we had private theatricals. The Duke appointed so many days for horse races, greyhound matches, etc., and the very day they were to come off, which was well known to the French army, we invested Ciudad Rodrigo, namely, on the 8th of January, 1812, and that very night carried by storm the outworks called Fort San Francisco, up to which spot it took the French several days to approach. We broke ground, and thus the siege commenced.

When the detachments of the Light Division Brigades were parading, my Brigade was to furnish 400 men. I understood four Companies, and when Colonel Colborne (now Lord Seaton) was counting them, he said, " There are not the complement of men." I said, " I am sorry if I have mistaken." " Oh, never mind; run and bring another Company." I mention this to show what a cool, noble fellow he is. Many an officer would have stormed like fury. He only thought of storming Fort

San Francisco, which he carried in a glorious
manner.*

The siege was carried on by four Divisions—
1st, 3rd, 4th, and Light, cantoned as near Ciudad
Rodrigo as possible. One Division was on duty at
a time, and each had to ford the Agueda the day it
was for duty. The Light was at El Bodon. We
had a distance of nine miles to march every fourth
day, and back on the fifth, so that we had only three
days' halt. The frost was excessive, and there was
some little snow, but fortunately the weather was
fine above head.

The Light Division stormed the little breach
on the evening of the 19th of January (nine
o'clock). I was supping with my dear friend
Captain Uniacke, and brother Tom, his only subaltern not wounded. When I parted from Uniacke
—he was a noble, light-hearted fellow—he says,
"Harry, you will be a Captain before morning."
Little, poor fellow, did he think he was to make the
vacancy. I was senior subaltern of the 95th, and
I went to General Craufurd and volunteered the
forlorn hope that was given to Gurwood. Craufurd
said, "Why, you cannot go; you, a Major of

---

* Costello (p. 140) tells how, after the taking of Fort San Francisco,
many of the French wounded prisoners were stripped naked by the
Portuguese Caçadores. One of them, a sergeant, on being marched
in, and seeing his officer in the same plight with himself, "ran to
embrace him, and, leaning his head on his shoulder, burst into tears
over their mutual misery. Captain Smith, the General's aide-de-
camp, being present, generously pulled forth his pocket-handkerchief
and wrapped it round the sergeant's totally naked person, till further
covering could be obtained."

Brigade, a senior Lieutenant, you are sure to get a Company. No, I must give it to a younger officer." This was to me a laborious night. Just as my Brigade had to march, I discovered the Engineer officer had not brought up the ladders, fascines, and bundles of hay, and old George Simmons was sent for them.

In ascending the breach, I got on a ravelin at the head of the 43rd and 52nd, moving in column together. Colborne pulled me down again, and up the right breach we ascended. I saw the great breach, stormed by the 3rd Division, was ably defended, and a line behind a work which, as soon as we rushed along the ramparts, we could enfilade. I seized a Company of the 43rd and rushed on the flank, and opened a fire which destroyed every man behind the works. My conduct caused great annoyance to the Captain, Duffy, with whom I had some very high words; but the Company obeyed me, and then ran on with poor Uniacke's Company to meet the 3rd Division, or rather clear the ramparts to aid them, when the horrid explosion took place which killed General Mackinnon of the 3rd Division on the spot and many soldiers, awfully scorching others. I and Uniacke were much scorched, but some splinters of an ammunition chest lacerated him and caused his death three days after the storm. Tom, my brother, was not hurt.

I shall never forget the concussion when it struck me, throwing me back many feet into a lot of charged fuses of shells, which in the confusion

I took for shells. But a gallant fellow, a Sergeant MacCurrie, 52nd Regiment, soon put me right, and prevented me leaping into the ditch. My cocked hat was blown away, my clothes all singed; however the sergeant, a noble fellow, lent me a catskin forage-cap, and on we rushed to meet the 3rd Division, which we soon did. It was headed by a great, big thundering Grenadier of the 88th, a Lieutenant Stewart, and one of his men seized me by the throat as if I were a kitten, crying out, "You French ——." Luckily, he left me room in the windpipe to d—— his eyes, or the bayonet would have been through me in a moment.

Gurwood got great credit here unfairly. Willie Johnstone * and poor Uniacke were the two first on the ramparts, Gurwood having been knocked down in the breach and momentarily stunned, which enabled them to get before him. However, Gurwood's a sharp fellow, and he cut off in search of the Governor, and brought his sword to the Duke, and Lord Fitzroy Somerset buckled it on him in the breach. Gurwood made the *most* of it.

We had many officers of rank wounded. George Napier, of the 52nd, lost an arm; the General of Brigade, Vandeleur, was wounded severely in the shoulder; and Colonel Colborne, of the 52nd, received an awful wound, but he never quitted his Regiment until the city was perfectly

* There is an interesting account of this heroic soldier in the *United Service Journal* for 1837, Part I. p. 354, by J. K. (John Kincaid), written after Johnstone's death at the Cape.

ours, and his Regiment all collected. A musket-ball had struck him under the epaulette of his right shoulder, and broken the head of the bone right off in the socket. To this the attention of the surgeons was of course directed. Some months after Colborne complained of a pain four inches below where the ball entered, and suppuration took place, and by surgical treatment the bone was gradually exposed. The ball, after breaking the arm above, had descended and broken the arm four inches below, and was firmly embedded in the bone. The pain he suffered in the extraction of the ball was more even than his iron heart could bear. He used to lay his watch on the table and allow the surgeons five minutes' exertions at a time, and they were three or four days before they wrenched the ball from its ossified bed. In three weeks from that day Colborne was in the Pyrenees, and in command of his Regiment. Of course the shoulder joint was anchylosed, but he had free use of the arm below the elbow.

After this siege we had a few weeks' holiday, with the exception of shooting some rascals who had deserted to the enemy. Eleven knelt on one grave at Ituero. It is an awful ceremony, a military execution. I was Major of Brigade of the day. The Provost-Marshal had not told the firing off, so that a certain number of men should shoot one culprit, and so on, but at his signal the whole party fired a volley. Some prisoners were fortunate enough to be *killed*, others were only wounded, some untouched. I galloped up. An unfortunate Rifleman called to me by name—he was awfully wounded—" Oh, Mr. Smith, put me out of my misery," and I literally ordered the firing-party, when reloaded, to run up and shoot the poor wretches. It was an awful scene.

> " Blood he had viewed, but then it flowed in combat . . ."

CHAPTER VIII.

CAMPAIGN OF 1812: THE STORMING OF BADAJOS—
HARRY SMITH'S MARRIAGE.

AT this period of the year (February, March) the
coursing in this part of Spain is capital, and by
help of my celebrated dog Moro and two other
excellent ones, I supplied the officers' mess of every
Company with hares for soup. We had a short
repose, for the army moved into Estremadura for
the purpose of besieging Badajos. We Light, 3rd
and 4th Divisions, thought, as we had taken Ciudad
Rodrigo, others would have the pleasure of the
trenches of Badajos, but on our reaching Elvas
[17 Feb., 1812] we were very soon undeceived,
and we were destined for the duty,—to our mortification, for soldiers hate sieges and working-parties.
The Guards work better than any soldiers, from
their habits in London. Badajos was invested
by the 3rd, 4th, and Light Divisions on the
Spanish side, or left bank of the river, and by
the 5th Division * on the Portuguese side, or right
bank. On the night of the 17th March, St.
Patrick's Day, the Light Division broke ground

* Not till 24 March (Napier, iv. 105).

under a deluge of rain, which swelled the
Guadiana so as to threaten our bridge of boats.
Our duties in the trenches were most laborious
during the whole siege, and much hard fighting we
had, sorties, etc.   The night [26 Mar.] the outworks La Picurina was carried by my dear friend Sir
James Kempt, part of the 3rd Division (which was
his) were to compose the storming party. The Light
Division, the working party, consequently were sent
to the Engineer Park for the ladders. When they
arrived, General Kempt ordered them to be planted
(Sir H. Hardinge, D.Q.M.G. of the Portuguese
army, was here distinguished). The boys of the
3rd Division said to our fellows, " Come, stand out
of the way ; " to which our fellows replied, " D——
your eyes, do you think we Light Division fetch
ladders for such chaps as you to climb up ? Follow
us "—springing on the ladders, and many of them
were knocked over. A notorious fellow, a Sergeant
Brotherwood, a noble fellow on duty, told me this
anecdote. The siege was prosecuted with the same
vigour from without with which it was repelled from
within.

After some hours in the trenches, when we
returned I invariably ate and went out coursing,
and many is the gallant course I had, and many
the swift hare I and my dog Moro brought home
from the right bank of the Guadiana. One day
James Stewart, I, and Charlie Eeles set off, having
three hours off duty, to look for a hare or two
at a celebrated spot where the hares ran very

strong because there was a rabbit warren which saved them. Moro, of course, was of the party. We soon found an unusually strong hare, and, although the greyhounds fetched round a dozen times, she still worked her way for the warren. I was riding a great stupid Irish horse bought from General Vandeleur, called Paddy, and as it was important for the soup to kill this hare, however unsportsmanlike on quiet occasions it would be deemed, I rode to head her from the warren. My stupid beast of a horse put his foot into a hole and rolled over me. Stewart and Eeles picked me up, but I was insensible. Although I have generally managed on such occasions to get away from the horse, the animal had rolled over me, and when I came to myself I was sitting on Eeles' knee, my arms tied up with a whip-thong, and James Stewart, with a blunt-looking penknife, trying to bleed me, an operation I quickly prohibited by starting on to my legs. Moro killed his hare, though, without my help.

On the night of the 6th April the 3rd Division were to storm the citadel, the 4th and Light the great breach, the 5th the Olivença Gate, and to escalade, if possible. The command of the Light Division had devolved on Colonel Barnard. Vandeleur was wounded, and stayed at Portalegre, and poor Beckwith had gone to the rear with violent ague; he never joined us again, noble soldier that he was.

This escalade has been so frequently described,

I shall only say that when the head of the Light Division arrived at the ditch of the place it was a beautiful moonlight night.   Old Alister Cameron, who was in command of four Companies of the 95th Regiment, extended along the counterscape to attract the enemy's fire, while the column planted their ladders and descended, came up to Barnard and said, " Now my men are ready ; shall I begin ? " " No, certainly not," says Barnard.   The breach and the works were full of the enemy, looking quietly at us, but not fifty yards off and most prepared, although *not firing a shot.*   So soon as our ladders were all ready posted, and the column in the very act to move and rush down the ladders, Barnard called out, " *Now,* Cameron ! " and the first shot from us brought down such a hail of fire as I shall never forget, nor ever saw before or since.   It was most murderous.   We flew down the ladders and rushed at the breach, but we were broken, and carried no weight with us, although every soldier was a hero. The breach was covered by a breastwork from behind, and ably defended on the top by *chevaux-de-frises* of sword-blades, sharp as razors, chained to the ground ; while the ascent to the top of the breach was covered with planks with sharp nails in them.   However, devil a one did I feel at this moment.   One of the officers of the forlorn hope, Lieut. Taggart of the 43rd, was hanging on my arm—a mode we adopted to help each other up, for the ascent was most difficult and steep.   A Rifleman stood among the sword-blades on the

top of one of the *chevaux-de-frises*. We made
a glorious rush to follow, but, alas! in vain. He
was knocked over. My old captain, O'Hare, who
commanded the storming party, was killed. All
were awfully wounded except, I do believe, myself
and little Freer of the 43rd. I had been some
seconds at the *revêtement* of the bastion near the
breach, and my red-coat pockets were literally filled
with chips of stones splintered by musket-balls.
Those not knocked down were driven back by this
hail of mortality to the ladders. At the foot of
them I saw poor Colonel Macleod with his hands
on his breast—the man who lent me his horse when
wounded at the bridge on the Coa. He said,
"Oh, Smith, I am mortally wounded. Help me
up the ladder." I said, "Oh no, dear fellow!"
"I am," he said; "be quick!" I did so, and came
back again. Little Freer and I said, "Let us throw
down the ladders; the fellows shan't go out." Some
soldiers behind said, "D—— your eyes, if you do
we will bayonet you!" and we were literally forced
up with the crowd. My sash had got loose, and
one end of it was fast in the ladder, and the bayonet
was very nearly applied, but the sash by pulling
became loose. So soon as we got on the glacis,
up came a fresh Brigade of the Portuguese of the
4th Division. I never saw any soldiers behave with
more pluck. Down into the ditch we all went again,
but the more we tried to get up, the more we were
destroyed. The 4th Division followed us in marching up to the breach, and they made a most

F

uncommon noise. The French saw us, but took no notice. Sir Charles Colville, commanding the 4th Division (Cole having been wounded at Albuera), made a devil of a noise, too, on the glacis. Both Divisions were fairly beaten back; we never carried either breach (nominally there were two breaches).

After the attacks upon the breaches, some time before daylight Lord Fitzroy Somerset came to our Division. I think I was almost the first officer who spoke to him. He said, "Where is Barnard?" I didn't know, but I assured his Lordship he was neither killed nor wounded. A few minutes after his Lordship said that the Duke desired the Light and 4th Divisions to storm again. "The devil!" says I. "Why, we have had enough; we are all knocked to pieces." Lord Fitzroy says, "I dare say, but you must try again." I smiled and said, "If we could not succeed with two whole fresh and unscathed Divisions, we are likely to make a poor show of it now. But we will try again with all our might." Scarcely had this conversation occurred when a bugle sounded within the breach, indicating what had occurred at the citadel and Puerto de Olivença; and here ended all the fighting. Our fellows would have gone at it again when collected and put into shape, but we were just as well pleased that our attempt had so attracted the attention of the enemy as greatly to facilitate that success which assured the prize contended for.

There is no battle, day or night, I would not willingly react except this. The murder of

our gallant officers and soldiers is not to be
believed.   Next day I and Charlie Beckwith, a
brother Brigade-Major, went over the scene.   It
was *appalling.*   Heaps on heaps of slain,—in
one spot lay nine officers.   Whilst we were
there, Colonel Allen of the Guards came up, and
beckoned me to him.   I saw that, in place of con-
gratulating me, he looked very dull.   " What's the
matter ?" I said.   " Do you not know my brother in
the Rifles was killed last night ?"   " God help him
and you ! no, for I and we all loved him."   In a flood
of tears, he looked round and pointed to a body.
" There he lies."   He had a pair of scissors with
him.   " Go and cut off a lock of his hair for my
mother.   I came for the purpose, but I am not equal
to doing it."

The returns of killed and wounded and the
evident thin appearance of our camp at once too
plainly told the loss we had sustained.   O memorable
night of glory and woe ! for, although the 4th
and Light were so beaten, our brilliant and numerous
attacks induced the governor to concentrate all his
force in the breaches; thus the 3rd escaladed the
citadel, and the 5th got in by the Olivença gate.
Although we lost so many stout hearts, so many
dear friends and comrades, yet not one staff officer
of our Division was killed or wounded.   We had
all been struck.   My clothes were cut by musket-
balls, and I had several contusions, particularly one
on my left thigh.

Now comes a scene of horror I would willingly

bury in oblivion. The atrocities committed by our soldiers on the poor innocent and defenceless inhabitants of the city, no words suffice to depict. Civilized man, when let loose and the bonds of morality relaxed, is a far greater beast than the savage, more refined in his cruelty, more fiend-like in every act; and oh, too truly did our heretofore noble soldiers disgrace themselves, though the officers exerted themselves to the utmost to repress it, many who had escaped the enemy being wounded in their merciful attempts! Yet this scene of debauchery, however cruel to many, to me has been the solace and the whole happiness of my life for thirty-three years. A poor defenceless maiden of thirteen years was thrown upon my generous nature through her sister, as described so ably in Johnny Kincaid's book, of which this is an extract—

" I was conversing with a friend the day after, at the door of his tent, when we observed two ladies coming from the city, who made directly towards us ; they seemed both young, and when they came near, the elder of the two threw back her *mantilla* to address us, showing a remarkably handsome figure, with fine features ; but her sallow, sun-burnt, and careworn, though still youthful, countenance showed that in her 'the time for tender thoughts and soft endearments had fled away and gone.'

" She at once addressed us in that confident, heroic manner so characteristic of the high-bred Spanish maiden, told us who they were—the last of an ancient and honourable house—and referred to an officer high in rank in our army, who had been quartered there in the days of her prosperity, for the truth of her tale.

" Her husband, she said, was a Spanish officer in a distant part of the kingdom ; he might, or he might not, still be living. But yesterday she and this her young sister were able to live in affluence and in a handsome house ; to-day they knew not where to lay their heads, where to get a change of raiment or a morsel of bread. Her house, she said, was a wreck ; and, to show the indignities to which they had been subjected, she pointed to where the blood was still trickling down their necks, caused by the wrenching of their ear-rings through the flesh by the hands of worse than savages, who would not take the trouble to unclasp them !

" For herself, she said, she cared not ; but for the agitated and almost unconscious maiden by her side, whom she had but lately received over from the hands of her conventual instructresses, she was in despair, and knew not what to do ; and that, in the rapine and ruin which was at that moment desolating the city, she saw no security for her but the seemingly indelicate one she had adopted—of coming to the camp and throwing themselves upon the protection of any British officer who would afford it ; and so great, she said, was her faith in our national character, that she knew the appeal would not be made in vain, nor the confidence abused. Nor was it made in vain ! Nor could it be abused, for she stood by the side of an angel ! A being more transcendingly lovely I had never before seen—one more amiable I have never yet known !

" Fourteen summers had not yet passed over her youthful countenance, which was of a delicate freshness—more English than Spanish ; her face, though not perhaps rigidly beautiful, was nevertheless so remarkably handsome, and so irresistibly attractive, surmounting a figure cast in nature's fairest mould, that to look at her was to love her ; and I did love her, but I never told my love, and in the mean time another and a more impudent fellow stepped in and won her! But yet I was happy, for in him she found such a one as her loveliness and her misfortunes claimed—a man of honour, and a husband in every way worthy of her!

"That a being so young, so lovely, and so interesting, just emancipated from the gloom of a convent, unknowing of the world and to the world unknown, should thus have been wrecked on a sea of troubles, and thrown on the mercy of strangers under circumstances so dreadful, so uncontrollable, and not have sunk to rise no more, must be the wonder of every one. Yet from the moment she was thrown on her own resources, her star was in the ascendant.

"Guided by a just sense of rectitude, an innate purity of mind, a singleness of purpose which defied malice, and a soul that soared above circumstances, she became alike the adored of the camp and of the drawing-room, and eventually the admired associate of princes. She yet lives, in the affections of her gallant husband, in an elevated situation in life, a pattern to her sex, and everybody's *beau ideal* of what a wife should be." *

* *Random Shots by a Rifleman*, by Sir John Kincaid, pp. 292-296. I venture to quote the rest of Kincaid's interesting passage : "Thrown upon each other's acquaintance in a manner so interesting, it is not to be wondered at that she and I conceived a friendship for each other, which has proved as lasting as our lives—a friendship which was cemented by after-circumstances so singularly romantic that imagination may scarcely picture them ! The friendship of man is one thing —the friendship of woman another ; and those only who have been on the theatre of fierce warfare, and knowing that such a being was on the spot, watching with earnest and increasing solicitude over his safety alike with those most dear to her, can fully appreciate the additional value which it gives to one's existence.

"About a year after we became acquainted, I remember that our Battalion was one day moving down to battle, and had occasion to pass by the lone country-house in which she had been lodged. The situation was so near to the outposts, and a battle certain, I concluded that she must ere then have been removed to a place of greater security, and, big with the thought of coming events, I scarcely even looked at it as we rolled along, but just as I had passed the door, I found my

I confess myself to be the "more impudent fellow," and if any reward is due to a soldier, never was one so honoured and distinguished as I have been by the possession of this dear child (for she was little more than a child at this moment), one with a sense of honour no knight ever exceeded in the most romantic days of chivalry, an understanding superior to her years, a masculine mind with a force of character no consideration could turn from her own just sense of rectitude, and all encased in a frame of Nature's fairest and most delicate moulding, the figure of an angel, with an eye of light and an expression which then inspired me with a maddening love which, from that period to this (now thirty-three years), has never abated under many and the most trying circumstances. Thus, as good may come out of evil, this scene of devastation and

hand suddenly grasped in hers. She gave it a gentle pressure, and, without uttering a word, had rushed back into the house again, almost before I could see to whom I was indebted for a kindness so unexpected and so gratifying.

"My mind had, the moment before, been sternly occupied in calculating the difference which it makes in a man's future prospects—his killing or being killed, when 'a change came o'er the spirit of the dream,' and throughout the remainder of that long and trying day I felt a lightness of heart and buoyancy of spirit which, in such a situation, was no less new than delightful.

"I never until then felt so forcibly the beautiful description of Fitz-James's expression of feeling, after his leave-taking of Ellen, under somewhat similar circumstances—

"' And after oft the knight would say,
That not when prize of festal day
Was dealt him by the brightest fair
That e'er wore jewel in her hair,
So highly did his bosom swell
As at that simple, mute, farewell.' "

spoil yielded to me a treasure invaluable; to me who, among so many dear friends, had escaped all dangers; to me, a wild youth not meriting such reward, and, however desirous, never able to express half his gratitude to God Almighty for such signal marks of His blessing shown to so young and so thoughtless a being. From that day to this she has been my guardian angel. She has shared with me the dangers and privations, the hardships and fatigues, of a restless life of war in every quarter of the globe. No murmur has ever escaped her. Bereft of every relative, of every tie to her country but the recollection of it, united to a man of different though Christian religion, yet that man has been and is her all, on whom have hinged the closed portals of hope, happiness, and bliss; if opened, misery, destitution, and bereavement, and every loss language can depict summed up in *one* word, " *He* is lost to me." But, O my God, Thou hast kindly spared us for each other; we have, through Thy grace, been but little separated, and we have, in unison of soul, received at Thy holy altar the Blessed Sacrament of the Body and Blood of Christ.* May we, through His mediation, be still spared to each other in this life, and in the life to come be eternally united in Heaven!

After the disorganization our troops had rushed into, it became the duty of every officer to exert

---

* From the time of their first residence at the Cape in the thirties, Juana Smith conformed to the Church of England, and was in consequence disowned by her remaining Spanish relatives.

himself, and nobly did Colonel Barnard set about
the task, and ably supported was he by every
officer in the Division. We had not marched for
the north two days when our soldiers were, like
Richard, "themselves again." When the French
garrison were marched to the rear, my Brigade
furnished an escort to the next Division *en route*
to Elvas. I paraded upwards of four thousand very
orderly, fine-looking fellows. Many of the officers
praised the gallantry of our men, and all said, "Why
break ground at all with such soldiers? Had you
stormed on the rainy night of the 17th March,
you would have taken the place with half the loss."
This is creditable to us, but the Duke of Wellington
would have been by no means borne out in such an
attempt.

However, as all this writing is to show rather
my individual participation in these scenes of glory
and bloodshed, I must dwell a little upon the joy of
my marriage. I was only twenty-two, my wife just
on the verge of fourteen.* But in southern climates
Nature more early develops herself and attains
maturity. Every day was an increase of joy.
Although both of us were of the quickest tempers,
we were both ready to forgive, and both intoxicated
in happiness. All my dearest friends — Charlie
Beckwith, John Bell, Johnstone, Charlie Eeles,
Jack Molloy, etc.—were saying to themselves,
"Alas! poor Harry Smith is lost, who was the

---

* He was really twenty-four, but he seems never to have known
his own age. His wife (born 27 March, 1798) was just past fourteen.

example of a duty-officer previously. It is only natural he must neglect duty now." I assured them all that the contrary would be the case, for love would incite me to exertions in hopes of preferment, the only mode I had to look to for a comfortable maintenance; and my wife's love, aided by her good sense, would see I was never neglecting her if engaged in the performance of my duty. Conscientiously did I act up to my feeling then, and no one ever did or ever could say, I was out of my place night or day.

My duty was my duty—I gloried in it; my wife even still more so, and never did she say, "You might have been with me," or complain if I was away. On the contrary, after many a day's fatiguing march, when I sought her out in the baggage or awaiting me, her first question invariably was, "Are you sure you have done all your duty?" *Then* I admit my attention was unbounded, and we were happy—oh, how happy, often amidst scenes of distress and privation that would have appalled stouter hearts, not devoted like ours! And oh, when I reflect on God's mercy to us both! In a succession of the most brilliant battles for years I was never even wounded, and, although I say it, no man ever exposed himself in every way more as a soldier, or rode harder as a sportsman. Wonderful, most wonderful, have been my hairbreadth escapes from falls of horses under and over me all over the world.

CHAPTER IX.

CAMPAIGN OF 1812: BATTLE OF SALAMANCA—OCCU-
PATION OF MADRID—RETREAT TO SALAMANCA.

BUT to the thread of my narrative. Hardly had
we reached the frontier of Portugal [24 April,
1812] our old haunts, Ituero, Guinaldo, etc., when
our army moved on again for Spain, and fought the
Battle of Salamanca. Before this battle we had
an immense deal of marching and manœuvring.
The armies of Marmont and Wellington were close
to each other for several days, so that a trifling
occurrence would have brought on a general action,
and we were frequently under cannonade.

My wife could not ride in the least at first, and
oh, the difficulty I had! although she had frequently
ridden a donkey on her pilgrimage to Olivença,
once to avoid the siege of Badajos, and at other
times to her grandmother's at Almendrajos.*

---

* Her relations are numerous. She was in three sieges of her
native city: in one her wounded brother died in her arms. She was
educated in a convent, and is a lineal descendant of Ponce de Leon,
the Knight of Romance, and certainly she, as a female, inherits all his
heroism. Her name, Juana Maria de Los Dolores de Leon, at once
gives the idea of Hidalgo consanguinity, and she is of one of the
oldest of the notoriously old *Spanish*, not Moorish, families. After
Talavera, when the Duke's headquarters were at Badajos, and my wife
was a child, Colonel Campbell and Lord Fitzroy Somerset were

However, I had one of my saddles turned into a side-saddle most ably by a soldier of Ross's Troop of Horse Artillery, and at first made her ride a great brute of a Portuguese horse I had ; but she so rapidly improved, took such pains, had so much practice and naturally good nerves, that she soon got ashamed of her Portuguese horse, and wanted to ride my Spanish little fellow, who had so nobly carried me at Redinha and in many other fights. I always said, "When you can ride as well as you can dance and sing, you shall," for in those accomplishments she was perfect. In crossing the Tormes [21 July], the very night before the battle of Salamanca (there are quicksands in the river), her Portuguese horse was so cowardly he alarmed me, and hardly had we crossed the river when a clap of thunder, louder than anything that can be described, burst over our heads. The Portuguese horse was in such a funk, she abjured *all Portuguese*, and insisted hereafter on riding her own gallant countryman, as gallant as any Arab. He was an Andalusian, which is a thorough-bred descendant of the Moosul horse, which is literally an Arab. The next day she mounted her Tiny, and rode him ever afterwards over many an eventful field, until the end of the war at Toulouse. She

billeted in her sister's house. That was in the palmy days of their affluence, when they derived a considerable income from their olive groves. These, alas ! were all cut down by the unsparing hand of the French, and the sisters' income seriously reduced. An olive tree requires great care and cultivation, nor does it bear well until twenty or thirty years old.—H.G.S.

had him afterwards at my father's house. The affection between them was of the character of that between spaniel and master. The dear, gallant horse lived to twenty-nine years of age, and died a happy pensioner on my brother Charles's estate.

It is difficult to say who was the proudest on the morning of the battle [22 July], horse, wife, or Enrique (as I was always called). She caracoled him about among the soldiers, to their delight, for he was broken in like a Mameluke, though very difficult to ride. (The soldiers of the whole Division loved her with enthusiasm from the events so peculiar in her history, and she would laugh and talk with all, which a soldier loves. Blackguards as many of the poor gallant fellows were, there was not a man who would not have laid down his life to defend her, and among the officers she was adored, and consulted on all occasions of baggage-guard, etc.) Her attendant, who also had a led horse in case of accident, with a little tent and a funny little pair of lanterns, my dear, trusty old groom West, as the battle began, took her to the rear, much to her annoyance, and in the thunder of cannon, the pride of equestrianism was buried in anxiety for him on whom her all depended. She and West slept on the field of battle, he having made a bed for her with the green wheat he had cut just in full ear. She had to hold her horse all night, and he ate all her bed of green wheat, to her juvenile amusement; for a creature so gay and vivacious, with all her sound sense, the earth never produced.

Next morning soon after daylight she joined me on the march. I was at that time so afflicted with boils, I could hardly live on horseback. I had eleven immense ones at the time on my legs and thighs, the excruciating pain of which is not to be described. Our surgeon, old Joe Bowker, insisted on my going to Salamanca, and one particular boil on the bone of the inside of my knee proved a more irresistible argument. So to Salamanca I had to go, my brother Tom doing my duty. I stayed fourteen days at Salamanca, a time of love and excitement, although, so distressed was the army for money, we lived almost on our rations, except for a little assistance from the lady of our house in coffee, etc. Wade, Sir Lowry Cole's A.D.C., lent me one dollar out of forty which he had received to support his General (who had been severely wounded in the battle), and his staff. In such times of privation heroism is required which our countrymen little dream of.

At the end of the fourteen days I had as many boils as ever, but, boils and all, off we started, and rode some terrible distances for three or four days. We overtook the Division, to the joy of the soldiers, before we crossed the Guadarama Pass [11 Aug.]. There had been no fighting in my absence, thank God.

We soon reached the neighbourhood of Madrid. No city could be better laid out for pomp and show, and the Duke's entry [13 Aug.] was a most brilliant spectacle. My vivacious wife used to enjoy

her native capital, and in her admiration treated
London and Paris as villages in comparison. We
spent a very happy time. It was a great amusement to improve our wardrobe for the walk on the
elegant Prado of an evening, in which no love
among the Spanish beauties showed to greater
advantage than my Estremenha, or native of Estremadura. During our stay in the vicinity of Madrid
we made several agreeable acquaintances, among
others the vicar of one of the many rich villages
around Madrid, Vicalbaro, a highly educated and
clever fellow, a great sportsman and excellent shot,
with a morbid hatred to a Frenchman. Upon our
moving forward beyond Madrid as far as the
beautiful and *clean* city Alcala [23 Oct.], I was
brought in contact with the celebrated and unfortunate General Elio, whom I had known in South
America at Monte Video. He was very conver-
sational, and we had a long talk as to that colonial
war; but, as I was acting as interpreter for my friend
James Stewart, the A.Q.M.G. of our Division, who
was making arrangements of march with Elio, conversation on the past turned into plans for the
future. We moved forwards towards our right
to Arganda [27 Oct.]. At this period the Duke
had gone to Burgos, and Lord Hill commanded.
We soon felt the loss of our decided and far-seeing
chief, and we made marches and counter-marches
we were unaccustomed to. At ten at night, at
Arganda, Major-General Vandeleur received an
order from General Alten, who remained in Alcala,

to march immediately back to Alcala with the whole Division. Vandeleur sent for me and told me to order the assembly to sound. I remonstrated and prayed him to wait until two hours before day-light, for every soldier in the Division had more or less indulged in the wine for which Arganda was celebrated. The good general had been at the shrine of Bacchus too, and was uncontrollable. Blast went the assembly, and staggering to their alarm-posts went the soldiers. Such a scene of good-natured riot I had never seen in my own Division. With the Duke we generally had a sort of hint we might be wanted, and our tried soldiers would be as steady as rocks. Oh, such a dark night's march as we had back to Alcala! Vandeleur repented of his obstinacy, and well he might.

We halted the next day at Alcala. Here, al-though it was now October, it was evident to me that a long retreat to the frontier was about to be undertaken, and I got from a Spanish officer, called Labrador, his fine large Andalusian horse in ex-change for an Irish brute I had bought from General Vandeleur. He gave me three Spanish doubloons to boot, a fortune in those days, particularly to me.

These three doubloons were given to my viva-cious Spanish wife, who put them up most carefully in my portmanteau, among my few shirts. On the march the motion of the mule had shaken them out of place, the doubloons were gone, and all our fortune! Her horror, poor girl, is not to be described. She knew it was our all, and her

delight when I gave the treasure into her charge
was now more than eclipsed by the misery of the
loss. I only laughed, for in those days hardships
and privations were so common, they were missed
when comparative affluence supplied their place.

We marched [30 Oct.] to Madrid, or rather its
suburbs, where the poor inhabitants were in indescribable distress, seeing that they were again to
be abandoned to French clemency and contributions.
While our troops were halted, waiting for orders
whether to bivouac or whether to retire, to our
astonishment up came the Vicar of Vicalbaro. He
took me on one side, and told me most pathetically
that he had made himself so obnoxious to the
French, he feared to stay, and had come to crave
my protection. This I gladly promised. While I
described to him the hardships a winter retreat
would impose upon him and us, he said gallantly,
" I am young and healthy like yourselves ; what you
suffer, I can. My only fear is that I may incon-
venience you and my young countrywoman, your
wife." I laughed, and called her. She was all fun,
notwithstanding the loss of the doubloons, and
began to quiz him ; but in the midst of her raillery
he observed, as he said to me afterwards, her soul
of kindness, and the Padre was installed in my
establishment, while my old comrades laughed and
said, " Harry Smith will do, now he has a father
confessor," by which name the Padre always went—
" Harry Smith's confessor." The hour or two of
halt was occupied by the Padre in buying a pony,

G

which he soon effected, and his marching establishment, a few shirts, with an immense *capa*, or cloak, almost as much as the pony could carry.

It rained in torrents, and we marched to Aravaca, some miles to the rear of the capital, where we found Lord Hill's headquarters in possession of every hole in the village, which was a very small one. General Vandeleur, who was still suffering from his wound at Ciudad Rodrigo, found a Captain of the Waggon Train in possession of a small house. In walks the General to a nice clean little room with a cheerful fire. "Who are you, sir?" says the General. "I am Captain ——, of the Royal Waggon Train, attached to Lord Hill, and this house is given me for my quarters." "I, sir, am General Vandeleur, and am d——d glad to see you in my quarters for *five minutes.*" The poor Captain very quietly packed up his traps and went —I know not where.

I, my young wife, the Padre, all my greyhounds and dogs, about thirteen, got into a little hole about six feet square, and were glad enough to get out of the rain, for, though my wife had her little tent, that, pitched on exceedingly wet ground, was a horrid shelter for any one. Owing to the kindness of our Provost-Marshal (Mr. Stanway), I got my horses also under a kind of out-office. We marched the next day to the foot of the Guadarama Pass, where our soldiers, when dismissed in bivouac, had a fine hunt after a wild boar, which they killed. The sunshine brightened, and when I returned from a variety of duties I found the young wife as neat as a new pin in her little tent, her habit and all her things which had got wet in yesterday's rain hung out to dry. So after breakfast I proposed to decorate my person (shave I need not, for as yet that operation was unnecessary), and *the* portmanteau was opened, the delinquent from which our doubloons had escaped. Some of the shirts were wet from the rain, and in searching for a dry one, out tumbled the three doubloons, which had been shaken into the folds of the shirt by the motion of the mule, and so lost. Oh, such joy and such laughing! We were so rich. We could buy bread and chocolate and sausages and eggs through the interest of the Padre (for we found the holy friar could get things when, however much money was exhibited, it proved no talisman), and our little fortune carried us through the retreat even to Ciudad Rodrigo, where money was paid to us.

This retreat was a very severe one as to weather, and although the enemy did not actually press us, as he did the column from Burgos, we made long marches and were very broad awake, and lost some of our baggage and stores, which the wearied bullocks obliged us to abandon. On reaching Salamanca, my wife, with the foresight of age rather than youth, expended some of the doubloons in buying me two pairs of worsted stockings and a pair of worsted mits, and the same for herself, which I do believe saved her from sickness, for the rain, on the retreat from Salamanca, came in torrents.

CHAPTER X.

CAMPAIGN OF 1812 : RETREAT TO THE LINES OF TORRES VEDRAS—WINTER OF 1812-13.

THE army concentrated again under the dear Duke of Wellington, and took up its old victorious position on the Arapiles [14 Nov.], but not with the same prospects. Soult, an able fellow, had nearly double our force, and so soon as our rear was open the army was in full march on Ciudad Rodrigo. It rained in torrents, and the roads rose above the soldiers' ankles. Our supplies were *nil*, and the sufferings of the soldiers were considerable. Many compared this retreat with that of Coruña, at which I then laughed, and do now. The whole distance from Ciudad Rodrigo is only forty-four miles. On one day to Coruña we marched thirty-seven miles, fighting every yard, and the cold was intense ; on this retreat it was cold, but no *frost* in the atmosphere.

In crossing the Huebra [17 Nov.], at San Muños, the enemy pressed our rear-guard very sharply, and we had some very heavy skirmishing. Sir E. Paget, by his own obstinacy in not believing the French Dragoons had intervened upon our line

of march, was taken prisoner, and our rear-guard
(my Brigade) driven from the ford. They had to
take to the river as well as they were able, the
soldiers leaping from a steep bank into it.

The sense and strength of my wife's Spanish
horse were this day put to the test, for she had
nothing for it but to make him leap into the river
from the high bank, which the noble animal did, all
fours like a dog. The poor Padre attempted the
same, with the result that he and pony floated down
the stream, and the pony was drowned, but his
large Spanish *capa* or cloak kept him afloat, and he
was dragged out by some of our soldiers. His
holiness began now to think I had not exaggerated
the hardships of a soldier's life. When well out of
the river, he quietly asked my poor old West for a
horse I always had ready to jump on in case my own
were killed. West very quietly said, " Never lend
master's other fighting horse, not to nobody." My
wife interceded for the poor Padre, but had the same
refusal. Old West says, " We shan't march far;
the river bothered us, it will stop the French. Our
Riflemen don't mean to let those fellows over.
Night and the walk will warm you."

I, seeing the distress my poor wife was likely to
be in, had told her particularly to stay with the 52nd,
thinking they would move into bivouac, while the
Riflemen held the bed of the river where we had
crossed, to which alone my attention was drawn.
There was a ford, however, lower down the river,
to which the 52nd were suddenly ordered. It was

impassable, but in the enemy's attempt to cross, a heavy skirmish ensued, in which poor Captain Dawson was killed and forty or fifty men wounded; my wife in the thick of it, and the friar. .

As soon as the ford was ascertained impassable, I was sent to bring back the 52nd, when, to my astonishment and alarm, I found my young wife drenched with leaping in the river, as much as from the torrents of rain above. The poor Padre might have been drawn for "the Knight of the Woeful Countenance." I brought the whole into our wet and miserable bivouac, and gave some Portuguese of my Brigade a dollar for a large fire, when, cold and shivery as she was, she laughed at the Padre. We had nothing to eat that night, as our mules were sent on, and there was this young and delicate creature, in the month of November in the north of Spain, wet as a drowned rat, with nothing to eat, and no cover from the falling deluge. Not a murmur escaped her but once. I had had no sleep for three nights, our rear being in a very ticklish position. In sitting by the fire I had fallen asleep, and fell between the fire and her. She had previously been roasted on one side, a cold mud on the other. This change of temperature awoke her, and for the only time in her life did she cry and say I might have avoided it. She had just woke out of her sleep, and when cold and shivery our feelings are acute. In a moment she exclaimed, " How foolish! you must have been nice and warm, and to know that is enough for me."

I took the Padre a mule; the rain broke, the little rivulet would soon be fordable, and at daylight the next morning we expected a regular squeeze from the enemy. To amend matters, too, in place of our moving off before daylight and getting a start, we were to follow the 1st Division, and this did not move. General Alten sent repeatedly to poor dear Sir William Stewart (who gave me my commission), to represent the prospect he had of a brush which ought to be avoided, when up rides to Charlie Beckwith, our A.Q.M.G., the Honourable Arthur Upton, saying, "My *dear-e* Beckwith, you could not inform me where I could get a *paysano* (a peasant)? The 1st Division can't move; we have no guide." "Oh, d——," says Charlie, "is that it? We will do anything to get you out of our way. Come to Harry Smith. He has a paysano, *I know.*" I always had three or four poor fellows in charge of a guard, so requisite are guides with light troops. I gave him his paysano, and by this time the sun was an hour high at least. To our delight, in place of a *fight retreating*, which partakes neither of the pomp nor majesty of war, but of nothing but hard and often inglorious losses, we saw the French army dismissed, all drying their clothes, and as little in a state to attack as we were desirous of their company. We had a clear, cold, but unmolested long march, and fell in with some stores coming. Yesterday the soldier's life was one of misery, to-day all joy and elasticity!

Just as the rear-guard had moved off the ground,

I heard the voice of a soldier familiar to me calling out, "Oh, Mr. Smith!" (The Rifle soldiers ever called me "Mr. Smith.") "Don't leave me here." I rode up. As gallant a Rifleman as ever breathed, by name O'Donnell, lay there with his thigh fractured the day before by a cannon-shot. I was grieved for him. I had no means to assist him but one which I deemed it impossible he could avail himself of—the tumbril of a gun. He said, "Oh, I can ride." I galloped to Ross, who literally sent back with me a six-pounder, and took the poor fellow on the tumbril, the gunner cheerfully giving him his place. It was grievous to see poor O'Donnell hoisted up with his thigh smashed. We got him there, though, and he said, "I shall do now." He died in two hours. I shall ever feel grateful to Ross; few men could have done it, but his guns were drawn by noble horses, and he was, and is, a SOLDIER.

Over the bivouac fire this night the Padre became eloquent and sentimental. "When you told me at Madrid what were the hardships and privations of a soldier's life in retreat, pursued by a vigorous enemy, I considered I had a very correct idea; I now see I had no conception whatever. But what appears to me so extraordinary is that every one acts for himself alone. *There* you see a poor knocked-up soldier sitting in the mud, unable to move; *there* come grooms with led horses. No one asks the sick man to ride, no one sympathizes with the other's feelings—in short, every one appears

to struggle against difficulties for himself alone."
I could see the Padre had not forgotten my old
man West's refusal of my second war-horse.

On the day following [19 Nov.], the weather
was clear but bitterly cold. We reached the
suburbs of Ciudad Rodrigo, happy enough to know
that for this campaign the fighting was over.
Although some of our troops had a long march
before them into Portugal, we Light Division
gentlemen were close at home. Many of our
stoutest officers were sick, John Bell, Charlie Eeles,
etc., and we had many wounded to look after. The
Padre and my cheerful, light-hearted wife were
cooking in a little house all day long. The Padre
was a capital cook, and equally good when the food
was prepared. I went out coursing every day, and
some of our regiment fellows, notwithstanding the
"retreat" and its hardships, went out duck-shooting,
up to their middles in water, Jonathan Leach among
the rest.

My brigade was ordered into our old villages of
Alameda, Fuentes d'Oñoro, Guinaldo, and to march
viâ San Felices el chico, there to cross the Agueda.
The weather was very rainy and cold, but my
vivacious little wife was full of animation and happiness, and the Padre usually cooking.

Fuentes d'Oñoro was to be the head-quarters
of our Brigade. General Vandeleur took up his
quarters in the Curé's house, around which in the
battle had been a sanguinary conflict. I was at the
other end of the village for the sake of an excellent

stable. It belonged to the father of the beautiful Maria Josefa, who fled from her father's house with a commissary, was infamously treated by him, returned to her father's house, and was received by the good old man kindly, although with nearly a broken heart. Songs were sung about her all over Spain, and she was universally condemned, pitied, and pardoned. I put the Padre in this house, told him the tale of woe, and, to his credit, he did everything a Christian clergyman ought, to urge on the parents pardon of the ill-used penitent. Nor did he plead in vain, the poor thing was forgiven by every one but herself. The Padre requested my generous-hearted wife to see her, and this was a consolation to poor Maria Josefa worth a general action to behold.

My billet was some little distance from the stable, and while there my landlord married a second wife. The inhabitants of this part of Spain are very peculiar and primitive in their manners, dress, and customs; they are called Charras. The dress of the women is most costly, and a marriage feast exceeds any feast that I ever saw, or that has been described by Abyssinian Bruce. We had fun and much feasting for three days. One of the ceremonies is that during a dance in which the bride is, of course, the *prima donna*, her relatives and friends make her presents, which she receives while dancing in the most graceful, though rustic, attitudes. The presents are frequently considerable sums in gold, or gold and silver ornaments of singular workmanship.   All relatives and friends give something, or it is regarded as a slight.   My wife, who learned to dance the rustic measure on purpose, presented a doubloon in the most elegant and graceful manner, to the delight of her compatriots around, although, being an Estremenha, she was regarded by these primitive, but hospitable and generous, creatures, as half a foreigner.   The bride has a knife in her uplifted hand, upon it an apple, and the smaller presents are presented by cutting the apple, and placing in the cut the money or ornament.

In this part of Spain the pigs are fed most delicately; they are driven first into woods of cork trees, which produce beautiful, sweet acorns, then into woods of magnificent chestnut trees, the keeper getting into the trees and flogging down the acorns and chestnuts with an immense long whip.   The pigs thus fed yield a meat different from the usual meat of the animal.   They are of a beautiful breed, become exceedingly fat, and the season of killing them and making black puddings and sausages for the year's supply is one of continual feasting.   The peasants also cure the meat along each side of the backbone called *loma de puerco*.   This they do in a very peculiar manner with salt, red pepper, and of course a *soupçon* of garlic in a thick slice; and, notwithstanding the little garlic, when simply boiled, it is the most delicious food, for breakfast particularly, that even a French cook could boast of.

During our stay at Fuentes, many were the rides my wife took on her horse Tiny to our friends in the different villages. At last, however, an order came to our Brigade head-quarters to vacate Fuentes d'Oñoro, as it was required for a part of the head-quarters establishment not far off at Freneda, and we moved to Guinaldo, to our deep regret. The Padre a few days before had taken his departure for his living at Vicalbaro. Two most magnificent mules, and his servant, came for him. We parted with mutual regret, but I am sorry to say he only wrote to us twice afterwards, and once to ask a favour for some individual.

At this time I was sporting mad. The Duke had a capital pack of fox-hounds. James Stewart, my chum, our A.Q.M.G., had an excellent pack of harriers to which I acted as whipper-in. After a very severe run, swimming two rivers, my Anda-lusian, which produced the doubloons at Alcala, died soon after he got back to his stable. Mr. Commissary Haines, at head-quarters, had a beautiful pack of little beagles. I was too proud to look at them. I had the best greyhounds in the world,—" Moro," and some of his almost equally celebrated sons.

CHAPTER XI.

CAMPAIGN OF 1813: BATTLE OF VITTORIA.

At Guinaldo we soon saw it was requisite to prepare for another campaign, and without any previous warning whatever, we received, about twelve at night, an order to march, which we did at daylight [21 May, 1813], and marched nineteen successive days without one halt.

I commenced this campaign under very unfortunate circumstances as far as my stud was concerned. I had five capital horses, and only two fit for work. Tiny, my wife's noble little horse, had received a violent injury from the pulling down of the bullock-manger (an immensely heavy timber, with mere holes in it for the ox's muzzle), when the extreme end and sharp point fell on his off forehoof, and he was so lame he could hardly travel to Vittoria. This was an awful loss to my wife. General Vandeleur now and then mounted me, or I should have been badly off indeed. James Stewart gave me a celebrated English hunter called "Old Chap." He had picked up a nail in his hind foot, and was not fit to ride for months, and an English mare had thrown out a ring-bone. (I must observe that winter quarters to my stud was no holiday.)

The march from Guinaldo to Palencia and thence to Vittoria was exceedingly interesting; the weather delightful; supplies, the mainspring of happiness in a soldier's life, plentiful; and never was any army (although the Duke had so censured us after the retreat from Burgos) inspired with such confidence in their leader, and such dependence on their own prowess. All was cheerfulness, joy, and anticipation. On reaching Toro [2 June], we found the bridge over the Douro destroyed. The river was full and barely fordable for cavalry and baggage animals. The bridge was partially repaired, some boats collected, and by boats our artillery, baggage, and material crossed, some of the infantry in boats, some scrambling over the bridge. The Douro, a magnificent and deep flowing river, was much up for the time of year. The passage was a most animating spectacle; it would have been a difficulty to an inexperienced army. With us, we were ordered to cross, and it was a matter of fun and excitement. No halt of Divisions, the river was crossed, and the day's march completed. My wife's dear Spaniard being lame, she rode a thoroughbred mare, which I gave £140 for, an elegant animal, but it no more had the sagacity of Tiny than a cur has that of a foxhound, and the day before we reached Palencia, upon a greasy bank, the mare slipped up and fell upon my poor wife and broke a small bone in her foot. This was to me an awful accident; heretofore health and happiness facilitated all; now, but for her natural vivacity and devotion, such was the pain, she must have remained at Palencia, and we must have separated. The bare idea aroused all her energy, and she said, " Get me a mule or an ass, and put a Spanish saddle for a lady on it ; my feet will rest upon the foot-board, and go I will !" Dozens of officers were in immediate requisition, some trying mules to find a very easy one, others running from shop to shop to get a good easy and well-cushioned saddle. There was no difficulty. The word " stay behind " was the talisman to move pain, and the mule was put.in progress next morning with that success determination ever ensures, for " Where there's a will, there's a way."

The whole of the Duke's army passed this day through the narrow main street of rather a pretty city, Palencia [7 June]. From a little after daylight, until past six in the evening, there was a continued stream of men—cavalry, artillery, infantry, and baggage, without a moment's interruption the whole day. To view this torrent of life was a sight which made an indelible impression upon a beholder.

But to my wounded wife. At the end of the march, the Brigade head-quarters went, as usual, into the village near the bivouac. Oh, the ceremony of her dismounting, the quantity of officers' cloaks spread for her reception; the "Take care ! Now I'll carry the leg," of the kind-hearted doctor ! Talk of Indian attention ! Here were a set of fellows ready to lay down their lives even to alleviate momentary pain.

As we approached Burgos, the scene of previous failure, we Light, 3rd, and 4th Divisions expected the reluctant honour of besieging it, and so flushed with hope were we to meet the enemy in an open field and not behind bastions, curtains, embrasures, and defences, we fairly wished Burgos at the devil.

The day we were moving upon it [13 June] (the Duke knew it would not be defended), to our delight, one, two, three, four terrific explosions took place, and well did we know the enemy had blown Burgos to where we wished it. The universal joy was most manifest, for, if we had besieged it, former failure would have excited these crack Divisions to get into it with the determination they had ever previously evinced, but the blowing it up happily got us out of the difficulty to our hearts' content.*

My wife's foot gradually improved, and in a few days she was on her horse again, and *en route* in the column ; for the soldiers, although generally averse to be interfered with by horses on the line of march, were ever delighted to get her to ride with their Company. Seeing her again on her horse was a great relief to my mind, for, in her peculiar and isolated position, the bare surmise of our separation was horrid, and, if I must have left her behind, the fact of a true Catholic allying herself to a heretic would, among bigoted inhabitants, have secured her anything but tender attention.

---

* *Vide* Duke's letter, Nov. 23, 1812, to Lord Liverpool, in his Grace's letter to Marshal Beresford, Oct. 31, " You see what a scrape we have been in, and how well we have got out of it."—H.G.S.

Our Division at San Millan, near Vittoria [18 June], intercepted the route of one of the French Columns as it was retiring into their position at Vittoria, and had as brilliant a fight entirely of our own as any one throughout the campaign. Some of the 1st Hussars also had a severe brush. Our Division halted the next day [20th], but the army never did, from the day of breaking up its cantonments until they fought the battle of Vittoria. It was a most wonderful march, the army in great fighting order, and every man in better wind than a trained pugilist.

At the Battle of Vittoria [21 June] my Brigade, in the middle of the action, was sent to support the 7th Division, which was very hotly engaged. I was sent forward to report myself to Lord Dalhousie, who commanded. I found his lordship and his Q.M.G., Drake, an old Rifle comrade, in deep conversation. I reported pretty quick, and asked for orders (the head of my Brigade was just getting under fire). I repeated the question, "What orders, my Lord?" Drake became somewhat animated, and I heard His Lordship say, "Better to take the village," which the French held with twelve guns (I had counted by their fire), and seemed to be inclined to keep it. I roared out, "Certainly, my Lord," and off I galloped, both calling to me to come back, but, as none are so deaf as those who won't hear, I told General Vandeleur we were immediately to take the village. There was no time to lose, and the 52nd Regiment deployed into

H

line as if at Shorncliffe, while our Riflemen were
sent out in every direction, five or six deep, keeping
up a fire nothing could resist. I galloped to the
officer commanding a Battalion in the 7th Division
(the 82nd, I think). "Lord Dalhousie desires you
closely to follow this Brigade of the Light Division."
"Who are you, sir?" "Never mind that; disobey
my Lord's order at your peril." My Brigade, the
52nd in line and the swarms of Riflemen, rushed
at the village, and although the ground was intersected in its front by gardens and ditches, nothing
ever checked us until we reached the rear of the
village, where we halted to reform—the twelve
guns, tumbrils, horses, etc., standing in our possession. There never was a more impetuous onset—
nothing could withstand such a burst of determination. Before we were ready to pursue the enemy
—for we Light Division ever reformed and got
into order before a second attack, thanks to poor
General Bob Craufurd's most excellent tuition —
up came Lord Dalhousie with his Q.M.G., Drake,
to old Vandeleur, exclaiming, "Most brilliantly
achieved indeed! Where is the officer you sent
to me for orders?" "Here I am, my lord." Old
Drake knew well enough. "Upon my word, sir,
you receive and carry orders quicker than any
officer I ever saw." "You said, 'Take the village.'
My lord, there it is," I said, "guns and all." He
smiled, and old Drake burst into one of his grins,
"Well done, Harry."

We were hotly engaged all the afternoon

pursuing the French over very broad ditches. Until
we neared Vittoria to our left, there was a plain free
from ditches. The confusion of baggage, etc., was
indescribable. Our Brigade was moving rapidly
on, when such a swarm of French Cavalry rushed
out from among the baggage into our skirmishers,
opposite a company of the 2nd Battalion Rifle
Brigade, commanded by Lieutenant Tom Cochrane,
we thought they must have been swept off. Fortunately for Tom, a little rough ground and a bank
enabled him to command his Company to lie down,
and such a reception they gave the horsemen, while
some of our Company were flying to their support,
that the French fled with a severe loss. Our Riflemen were beautiful shots, and as undaunted as bulldogs. We knew so well, too, how to support each
other, that scarcely had the French Dragoons shown
themselves when Cochrane's rear was supported, and
we had such mutual confidence in this support that
we never calculated on disaster, but assumed the
boldest front and bearing.

A rather curious circumstance occurred to me
after the first heights and the key of the enemy's
central position was carried. I was standing with
Ross's Brigade of guns sharply engaged, when my
horse fell as if stone dead. I jumped off, and began
to look for the wound. I could see none, and gave
the poor animal a kick on the nose. He immediately shook his head, and as instantly jumped on
his legs, and I on his back. The artillerymen all
said it was the current of air, or, as they call it,

the wind, of one of the enemy's cannon-shot. On the attack on the village previously described, Lieutenant Northey (52nd Regiment) was not knocked off as I was, but he was knocked down by the wind of a shot, and his face as black as if he had been two hours in a pugilistic ring.

The fall of my horse had been observed by some of our soldiers as they were skirmishing forward, and a report soon prevailed that I was killed, which, in the course of the afternoon, was communicated to my poor wife, who followed close to the rear on the very field of battle, crossing the plain covered with treasure. Her old groom, West, proposed to carry off some on a led horse. She said, "Oh, West, never mind money. Let us look for your master." She had followed the 1st Brigade men, the 2nd having been detached, unobserved by her, to aid the 7th Division. After the battle, at dusk, my Brigade was ordered to join the 1st Brigade, with General Alten's head-quarters. I had lost my voice from the exertion of cheering with our men (not cheering them *on*, for they required no such example), and as I approached the 1st Brigade, to take up the ground for mine, I heard my wife's lamentations. I immediately galloped up to her, and spoke to her as well as I could, considering the loss of my voice. "Oh, then, thank God, you are not killed, only badly wounded." "Thank God," I growled, "I am neither," but, in her ecstasy of joy, this was not believed for a long while.

After putting up my Brigade. (we required no picquets, the Cavalry were far in our front in pursuit of the flying enemy) we, that is, my General and Staff, repaired to a barn, where we got in our horses and some forage, and lay down among them. It was dark; we had no lights, and sleep after such a day was as refreshing as eating, even if we had any means. At daybreak our luggage had arrived, and we were busy preparing some breakfast. Hardly did the kettle boil when " Fall in!" was the word. Just as we were jumping on our horses, my young wife, her ears being rather quick, said, " I am sure I hear some one moaning, like a wounded man." We looked round, and I saw there was a loft for hay over our barn. I immediately scrambled up with assistance, for the ladder, like Robinson Crusoe's, had been hauled up. When I reached the landing-place, such a scene met my eye! Upwards of twenty French officers, all more or less severely wounded, one poor fellow in the agony of death, and a lady, whom I recognized as Spanish, grieving over him. At first the poor fellows funked. I soon assured them of every safety and protection, and put my wife and the poor Spanish lady, her countrywoman, in communication. All we could spare, or, rather, all our breakfast, was given to the wounded, for march we must. The General sent his A.D.C. for a guard; we did all we could at the moment, and the poor fellows were grateful indeed. The Spanish lady had a most beautiful little pug dog, a thoroughbred one, with a

very extraordinary collar of bells about its neck.
She insisted upon my wife's accepting the dog as a
token of gratitude for our kindness. The little
animal was accepted immediately, and named "Vittoria"; we jumped on our horses, and parted for
ever, gratified, however, at having had it in our
power to render this slight assistance to the poor
fellows wounded and in distress. The dog became
afterwards a celebrated animal in the Division,
universally known and caressed, and the heroine of
many a little anecdote, and hereafter at Waterloo
must claim half a page to itself. It was the most
sensible little brute Nature ever produced, and it
and Tiny became most attached friends.

On this day's march our soldiers could scarcely
move—men, in such wind and health as they were
—but the fact is they had got some flocks of the
enemy's sheep, and fallen in with a lot of flour;
they had eaten till they were gorged like vultures,
and every man's haversack was laden with flour
and raw meat, all of which, except a day or two's
supply, the Generals of Brigade were obliged to
order to be thrown away. We were soon, however, close on the heels of the enemy, and the first
shot revived the power to march. The retreat of
the enemy was marked by every excess and
atrocity and villages burning in every direction.
Oh, my countrymen of England, if you had seen
the twentieth part of the horrors of war I have,
readily would you pay the war-taxes, and grumble
less at the pinching saddle of National Debt! The

seat of war is hell upon earth, even when stripped
of the atrocities committed in Spain and Portugal,
and everywhere else, I believe, except dear old
England, by the French Army.

We Light Division had the pleasure, ere we
reached Pamplona, to take the enemy's only remaining gun.*

* Cope, p. 141.

CHAPTER XII.

CAMPAIGN OF 1813: ADVANCE TO VERA.

THE night before we reached Pamplona [24 June], the enemy, rather unexpectedly to us, drove in the picquets of my Brigade in a very sharp skirmish, although we were as ever prepared, and the Division got under arms. This convinced us that the whole army, except the garrison at Pamplona, was in full retreat into France. It is a peculiar custom of the French unexpectedly to put back your picquets when they are about to retire; that is, when the ground admits no obstacle of bridge, river, or village, intervening. The object of such forward moves I have never heard satisfactorily given.

On this evening a stout French gentleman came in to our advanced post, saying he wanted to see the Duke. I took him to General Vandeleur. He dined with us, and a most jawing, facetious fellow he was. At first we regarded him as a spy, which he afterwards told General Vandeleur he was, and in the employ of the Duke. He could not proceed that night, for we did not know in the least where head-quarters were, and the night was excessively dark; so the French gentleman, whom I wished at the devil, was given in charge to *me*. If he had had any inclination to escape I defied him, for I put some of our old vigilant Riflemen around him, so that not a man could get in or out of the room I had put him in. We afterwards heard my friend was a man of great use to the Duke, and one of King Joseph's household.

The next day [25 June] we Light Division passed Pamplona, leaving it by a very intricate road to our right, and were cantoned in the village of Offala. It was necessary to keep a look-out towards Pamplona, and my General, Vandeleur, and I, rode to look where to post our picquets. I had a most athletic and active fellow with me as a guide, very talkative, and full of the battle of Vittoria. He asked me what was the name of the General before us. I said, "General Vandeleur." I heard him muttering it over to himself several times. He then ran up to the General, and entered into conversation. The General soon called me to him, for he could not speak a word [of Spanish]. "What's the fellow say?" "He is telling all he heard from the Frenchmen who were billeted in his house in the retreat. He is full of anecdote." He then looked most expressively in Vandeleur's face, and says, "Yes, they say the English fought well, but had it not been for one General *Bandelo*, the French would have gained the day." "How the devil did this fellow know?" says Vandeleur. I never undeceived the General, and he fancies to

this day his Brigade's being sent to assist the 7th
Division was the cause of the Frenchmen's remark. My guide, just like a "cute" Irishman
or American, gave me a knowing wink.

This very fellow turned out to be owner of the
house my wife and baggage and I got into—the
General's Aide-de-camp, as was often the case,
having shown her into one near the General. After
I had dressed myself, he came to me and said,
"When you dine, I have some capital wine, as much
as you and your servants like; but," he says, "come
down and look at my cellar." The fellow had been
so civil, I did not like to refuse him. We descended
by a stone staircase, he carrying a light. He had
upon his countenance a most sinister expression.
I saw something exceedingly excited him : his look
became fiend-like. He and I were alone, but such
confidence had we Englishmen in a Spaniard, and
with the best reason, that I apprehended no personal
evil. Still his appearance was very singular. When
we got to the cellar-door, he opened it, and held
the light so as to show the cellar; when, in a voice
of thunder, and with an expression of demoniacal
hatred and antipathy, pointing to the floor, he
exclaimed, "There lie four of the devils who thought
to subjugate Spain! I am a Navarrese. I was
born free from all foreign invasion, and this right
hand shall plunge this stiletto in my own heart as
it did into theirs, ere I and my countrymen are
subjugated!" brandishing his weapon like a demon.
I see the excited patriot as I write. Horror-struck

as I was, the instinct of self-preservation induced
me to admire the deed exceedingly, while my very
frame quivered and my blood was frozen, to see
the noble science of war and the honour and chivalry
of arms reduced to the practices of midnight assassins.
Upon the expression of my admiration, he cooled, and
while he was deliberately drawing wine for my dinner,
which, however strange it may be, I drank with the
gusto its flavour merited, I examined the four bodies.
They were Dragoons—four athletic, healthy-looking
fellows. As we ascended, he had perfectly recovered
the equilibrium of his vivacity and naturally good
humour. I asked him how he, single-handed, had
perpetrated this deed on four armed men (for their
swords were by their sides). " Oh, easily enough. I
pretended to love a Frenchman" (or, in his words, ' I
was an Afrancesado '), "and I proposed, after giving
them a good dinner, we should drink to the extermination of the English." He then looked at me and
ground his teeth. "The French rascals, they little
guessed what I contemplated. Well, we got into
the cellar, and drank away until I made them so
drunk, they fell, and my purpose was easily, and as
joyfully, effected." He again brandished his dagger,
and said, " Thus die all enemies to Spain." Their
horses were in his stable. When the French
Regiment marched off, he gave these to some
guerrillas in the neighbourhood. It is not difficult
to reconcile with truth the assertion of the historian
who puts down the loss of the French army, during
the Spanish war, as 400,000 men, for more men fell

in this midnight manner than by the broad-day sword, or the pestilence of climate, which in Spain, in the autumn, is excessive.

The next day we marched a short distance to a beautiful village, or town, rather,—Villalba, where we halted a day, and expected to remain three or four. It was on a Sunday afternoon, and some of the recollection of the Sunday of our youth was passing across the mind of the lover of his family and his country—the very pew at church, the old peasants in the aisle; the friendly neighbours' happy faces; the father, mother, brothers, sisters; the joys, in short, of home, for, amidst the eventful scenes of such a life, recollection will bring the past in view, and compare the blessings of peace with the horror, oh! the cruel horror, of war! In the midst of this mental soliloquy, my dear wife exclaims, "Mi Enrique, how thoughtful you look!" I dare not tell her that my thoughts reverted to my home. Hers being a desolate waste, the subject was ever prohibited, for her vivacious mind, and her years of juvenile excitement, could never control an excess of grief if the words, "your home," ever escaped my lips.

My reverie was soon aroused by the entrance of a soldier, without ceremony—for every one was ever welcome. "Sir, is the order come?" "For what?" I said. "An extra allowance of wine?" "No," he said, "for an extra allowance of marching. We are to be off directly after these French chaps, as expects to get to France without a kick from the

Light Division." I was aware he alluded to
General Clausel's division that was retiring by the
pass over the Pyrenees, called La Haca. It is most
singular, but equally true, that our soldiers knew
every move in contemplation long before any
officer. While we were in conversation, in came the
order; away went all thoughts of home, and a
momentary regret on quitting so nice a quarter was
banished in the excitement of the march.

In twenty minutes our Division was in full
march to try and intercept Clausel's Division.
That night we marched most rapidly to Tafalla,
next day to Olite, thence brought up our right
shoulder towards Sanguessa. This was a night-
march of no ordinary character to all, particularly
to me and my wife. Her Spanish horse, Tiny, was
so far recovered from his lameness that she insisted
on riding him. On a night-march we knew the road
to be difficult. In crossing the Arragon [30 June],
although the bridge was excellent, on this march
by some singular accident (it was very dark and
raining) an interval occurred in our column — a
thing unprecedented, so particular were we, *thanks
to Craufurd's instructions*—and the majority of the
Division, in place of crossing the bridge, passed the
turn and went on a league out of the direction.
My Brigade was leading. Two Battalions came all
right, and I stayed more at the head of the column
than was my wont, to watch the guides. So dark
and intricate was the road we were moving on, I proposed to the General to form up, and see that our

troops were all right. After the two first Battalions formed, I waited a short time in expectation of the next, the 2nd Battalion of the Rifle Brigade. I hallooed, seeing no column, when a voice a long way off answered. It was that of the most extraordinary character, the eccentric Colonel Wade. I galloped up, and said, "Colonel, form up your Battalion, so soon as you reach the Brigade." "By Jesus," he said, "we are soon formed; I and my bugler are alone." I, naturally somewhat excited, asked, "Where's the Regiment?" "Upon my soul, and that's what I would like to ask you." I then saw some mistake must have happened. I galloped back in the dark to the bridge, saw no column whatever, but heard voices far beyond the bridge. The column, after passing it in the dark, had discovered the error and were coming back. Meanwhile, my wife heard me hallooing and came towards me. I had dismounted, and was leading my horse a little way off the road up the left bank of the Arragon; the rain was falling in torrents, the bank of the river gave way under me, and a flash of lightning at the moment showed me I was falling into the bed of the river about thirty feet below. I had firmly hold of my bridle — the avalanche frightened my noble horse (the celebrated "Old Chap," the hunter that James Stewart gave me); he flew round and dragged me from inevitable perdition. My wife and old West were close behind at the moment, and she witnessed the whole, equally to her horror and satisfaction. Then such a tale of woe from herself. The uneven ground at night had so lamed her dear little horse, Tiny, that he could not carry her. She got off in the rain and dark, herself still excessively lame from the broken bone in the foot, and literally crawled along, until the rocky road improved, and West again put her upon her faithful Tiny. I could devote neither time nor attention to her. Day was just beginning to break. I directed her to the bivouac, and most energetically sought to collect my Brigade, which, with the daylight, I soon effected. When I got back, I found my wife sitting, holding her umbrella over General Vandeleur (who was suffering dreadfully from rheumatism in the shoulder in which he had been wounded at the storm of Ciudad Rodrigo), recounting to him her night's adventures and laughing heartily. The weather totally precluded any possibility of our molesting Clausel, and we were ordered to march to Sanguessa, which we did the following day, and Charlie Gore, General Kempt's A.D.C., gave a ball [1 July], where there was as much happiness as if we were at Almack's, and some as handsome women, the loves of girls of Sanguessa.

That night's march was the most extraordinary thing which ever occurred to our organized Light Division. We all blamed each other, but the fact is, the turn of the road to the bridge was abrupt, the night dark, the road so narrow that staff-officers could not ride up and down the flank of the column; it may be regarded as "an untoward event." From

Sanguessa we made rather long marches for the Valle of San Estevan, through a most beautiful country covered in a great measure with immense chestnut trees. After we had halted a day or two [7–14 July] in this valley, of which the beauty is not to be conceived, we marched on towards Vera by a road along the banks of the river Bidassoa. At Vera, the enemy had fortified a large house very strongly, and their picquets were upon its line. On our advance, we put back the enemy's picquets, but not without a sharp skirmish, and we held the house that afternoon.

In front of the mountain of Santa Barbara was a very steep hill, which the enemy held in force, but a dense fog of the mountains prevented us seeing each other. Colonel Barnard, with the 1st Battalion Rifle Brigade, was sent to dislodge them [15 July]. They proved to be three or four times his numbers. His attack, however, was supported, and as he himself describes it, "I hallooed the fellows off in the fog." We had a good many men and officers, however, severely wounded. The next day, or in the night, the enemy abandoned the fortified house of the large village of Vera in their front, retired behind the village, and firmly established themselves on the heights, while we occupied Vera with some sick officers, our picquets being posted beyond. The enemy's vedettes and ours for many days were within talking distance, yet we never had an alert by night or by day.

CHAPTER XIII.

CAMPAIGN OF 1813: IN THE PYRENEES—GENERAL SKERRETT—COMBAT OF VERA—FIGHT AT THE BRIDGE, AND DEATH OF CADOUX.

JUST before we reached Vera, my dear friend and General, Vandeleur, was moved to a Cavalry Brigade, and General Skerrett, a very different man, was sent to us, with a capital fellow for an A.D.C.—Captain Fane, or, as usually designated, "Ugly Tom." I, who had been accustomed to go in and out of my previous Generals' tents and quarters as my own, and either breakfast or dine as I liked, was perfectly thunderstruck when it was intimated to me I was to go only when asked ; so Tom the A.D.C. and we lived together, to the great amusement of my wife, who was always playing Tom some trick or other.

During our halt in this position, the siege of San Sebastian was going on. Soult, an able officer, who had been appointed to the command of the beaten French force, soon reorganized it, and instilled its old pride of victory, and inspired all again with the ardour and vivacity of French soldiers. The siege of San Sebastian was vigorously

I

prosecuted. Pamplona was closely invested, and, from want of provisions, must inevitably ere long surrender. Soult, therefore, had a brilliant opportunity either to raise the siege of San Sebastian, or to throw supplies in to Pamplona, or to do both, if great success attended his operations. This opportunity he ably availed himself of, by making a rapid movement to our right to the Pass of Roncesvalles of knightly fame, and obliging the Duke of Wellington to concentrate a great part of his army to protect Pamplona, or, rather, to ensure its strict blockade, while the siege of San Sebastian was for the time suspended, awaiting supplies which were on their passage from England. My Division, the Light, was kept between the two, as were Lord Dacre's "horsemen light," to "succour those that need it most," * and we had some very harassing marches, when it was discovered Soult had penetrated the Pyrenees and was resolved on a general action. This he fought on the 27th and 28th July, with the Frenchman's usual success, a good thrashing.†

The Light Division made a terrible night march on this occasion, one of the most fatiguing to the soldiers that I ever witnessed. On the Pyrenees, as on other mountains, the darkness is indescribable. We were on a narrow mountain path,

---

* "Lord Dacre, with his horsemen light.
   Shall be in rearward of the fight,
   And succour those that need it most."
                  Marmion, VI. xxiv.

† At the battles of the Pyrenees.

frequently with room only for one or two men, when a soldier of the Rifle Brigade rolled down a hill as nearly perpendicular as may be. We heard him bumping along, pack, rifle, weight of ammunition, etc., when from the bottom he sang out, " Halloa there ! Tell the Captain there's not a bit of me alive at all ; but the devil a bone have I broken ; and faith I'm thinking no soldier ever came to his ground at such a rate before. Have a care, boys, you don't follow. The breach at Badajos was nothing to the bottomless pit I'm now in."

After the battles of the Pyrenees, our Division was pushed forward with great rapidity to intercept the retreat of one of the *corps d'armée*, and General Kempt's—the 1st—Brigade had some very heavy fighting [at Jansi, 1 Aug.]; while at [Echallar], poor General Barnes, now no more, in command of a Brigade of the 7th Division, made one of the boldest and most successful attacks on five times his number, but one in which bravery and success far exceeded judgment or utility.

We moved on again, and on one of our marches came to some very nice cottages, one of which fell to the lot of myself and Tom Fane, the A.D.C. The poor peasant was a kind-hearted farmer of the mountains, his fields highly cultivated, his farmyard supplied with poultry ; every domestic comfort his situation in life demanded was his—poor fellow, he merited all. He killed some ducks for our supper, his garden supplied beautiful peas, and we had a supper royalty would have envied with our appetites. My wife had spread her cloak on the floor—she was perfectly exhausted—and was fast asleep. I awoke her, she ate a capital supper, but the next morning upbraided me and Tom Fane for not having given her anything to eat; and to this day she is unconscious of sitting at our supper-table. Judge by this anecdote what real fatigue is. The next morning we could hardly induce our host to receive payment for his eggs, his poultry, his bread, bacon, peas, milk, etc., and he would insist on giving my wife a beautiful goat in full milk, which was added to the boy Antonio's herd.* We marched with mutual feelings of newly-acquired but real friendship. Three days afterwards, we returned to the very same ground, and we again occupied our previous dear little mountain retreat, but the accursed hand of war had stamped devastation upon it. The beautiful fields of Indian corn were all reaped as forage, the poultry yard was void, the produce of our peasant's garden exhausted, his flour all consumed—in a word, he had nothing left of all his previous plenty but a few milch goats, and that night he, poor thing, supped with us from the resources of our rations and biscuit. He said the French had swept off everything the English did not require. The latter paid for everything, and gave him *bons* or receipts for the Indian corn reaped as forage, which he knew some day our commissary would take up and pay. I never pitied man more, and in the midst of his affliction it was

* See pp. 129, 130.

beautiful to observe a pious resignation and a love
for his country, when he exclaimed, " Gracias a
Dios, you have driven back the villainous French to
their own country."

> " O fortunatos nimium, sua si bona norint,
> Agricolas . . . procul discordibus armis."

We returned to our line on this side of Vera, and
the siege of San Sebastian was again vigorously
resumed. We Light Division, with the 3rd and
4th, were out of that glory, which we did not regret,
although the Duke never took the town until he
sent to these three Divisions for volunteers for
the storming party [31 Aug.]. Then we soon
took it; but in candour I should state that the
breaches were rendered more practicable than when
first stormed, the defences destroyed, and the
enemy's means of defence diminished. It was,
however, still a tough piece of work, in which we
lost some valuable officers and soldiers. The enemy
made a forward movement [the same day, 31 Aug.]
for the purpose of reinforcing the garrison, and in
the morning put back our picquets, and we anticipated
a general action. However, the whole of the enemy
moved to the Lower Bidassoa, and crossed in force.
The day was very rainy, and the river was so full
the French were compelled to retreat rapidly; in
fact, so sudden was the rise of the river, many were
obliged to retire by the bridge in our possession,
as described by Napier.

I have only, therefore, to relate an incident

which occurred between me and my new General—
who, I soon discovered, was by nature a gallant
Grenadier, and no Light Troop officer, which requires
the eye of a hawk and the power of anticipating the
enemy's intention—who was always to be found off
his horse, standing in the most exposed spot under
the enemy's fire while our Riflemen were well concealed, as stupidly composed for himself as inactive
for the welfare of his command.* When the enemy
put back our picquets in the morning, it was evidently
their intention to possess themselves of the bridge,
which was curiously placed as regarded our line of
picquets. Thus—

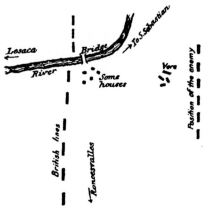

* Sir R. D. Henegan writes thus of Col. Skerrett, in describing the
defence of Tarifa: "The commanding-officer of this expedition,
although unimpeachable in the courageous bearing of a soldier, was
wanting in the bold decision which, in military practice, must often
take the lead of science and established rules."—Henegan's *Seven
Years' Campaigning* (1846), vol. i. p. 234. Colonel T. Bunbury,
Reminiscences of a Veteran, i. p. 116, gives a similar account:
"Skerrett as an individual was brave to rashness; but I should have
doubted it had I not so frequently witnessed proofs of his cool
intrepidity and contempt of danger. At the head of troops, he was
the most undecided, timid, and vacillating creature I ever met with."

We did not occupy Vera, but withdrew on our own side of it, and I saw the enemy preparing to carry the houses near the bridge in the occupation of the 2nd Battalion Rifle Brigade. I said, "General Skerrett, unless we send down the 52nd Regiment in support, the enemy will drive back the Riflemen. They cannot hold those houses against the numbers prepared to attack. Our men will fight like devils expecting to be supported, and their loss, when driven out, will be very severe." He laughed (we were standing under a heavy fire exposed) and said, "Oh, is that your opinion?" I said—most impertinently, I admit,—"And it will be yours in five minutes," for I was by no means prepared to see the faith in support, which so many fights had established, destroyed, and our gallant fellows knocked over by a stupidity heretofore not exemplified. We had scarcely time to discuss the matter when down came a thundering French column with swarms of sharpshooters, and, as I predicted, drove our people out of the houses with one fell swoop, while my General would move nothing on their flank or rear to aid them. We lost many men and some officers, and the enemy possessed the houses, and consequently, for the moment, possessed the passage of the bridge. From its situation, however, it was impossible they could maintain it, unless they put us farther back by a renewed attack on our elevated position. So I said, "You see now what you have permitted, General, and we must retake these houses, which

we ought never to have lost." He quietly said,
"I believe you are right." I could stand this no
longer, and I galloped up to Colonel Colborne, in
command of that beautiful 52nd Regiment, now Lord
Seaton, who was as angry as he soon saw I was.
"Oh, sir, it is melancholy to see this. General
Skerrett will do nothing; we must retake those
houses. I told him what would happen." "I am
glad of it, for I was angry with you." In two
seconds we retook the houses, for the enemy, seeing
our determination to hold them, was aware the
nature of the ground would not enable him to do
so unless he occupied the position we intended to
defend, and his effort was as much as not to see
whether we were in earnest, or whether, when
attacked in force, we should retire. The houses
were retaken, as I said, and the firing ceased the
whole afternoon.

The evening came on very wet. We knew that
the enemy had crossed the Bidassoa [31 Aug.], and
that his retreat would be impossible from the swollen
state of the river. We knew pretty well the Duke
would shove him into the river if he could; this
very bridge, therefore, was of the utmost importance, and no exertion should have been spared on
our part so to occupy it after dark as to prevent
the passage being seized. The rain was falling in
torrents. I proposed that the whole of the 2nd
Battalion Rifle Brigade should be posted in the
houses, the bridge should be barricaded, and the
52nd Regiment should be close at hand in support.

Skerrett positively laughed outright, ordered the whole Battalion into our position, but said, "You may leave a picquet of one officer and thirty men at the bridge." He was in the house on the heights he had previously occupied. I had a little memorandum-book in my pocket; I took it out for the first time in my life to note my General's orders. I read what he said, asking if that was his order. He said, "Yes, I have already told you so." I said most *wickedly*, "We shall repent this before daylight." He was callous to anything. I galloped down to the houses, ordered the Battalion to retire, and told my brother Tom, the Adjutant, to call to me a picquet of an officer and thirty men for the bridge. Every officer and soldier thought I was mad. Tom said, "Cadoux's company is for picquet." Up rode poor Cadoux, a noble soldier, who could scarcely believe what I said, but began to abuse me for not supporting them in the morning. I said, "Scold away, all true; but no fault of *mine*. But come, no time for jaw, the picquet!" Cadoux, noble fellow, says, "My company is so reduced this morning, I will stay with it if I may. There are about fifty men." I gladly consented, for I had great faith in Cadoux's ability and watchfulness, and I told him he might rest assured he would be attacked an hour or two before daylight. He said, "Most certainly I shall, and I will now strengthen myself, and block up the bridge as well as I can, and I will, if possible, hold the bridge until supported; so, when the attack commences, instantly send the whole

Battalion to me, and, please God, I will keep the bridge." It was then dark, and I rode as fast as I could to tell Colborne, in whom we had all complete faith and confidence. He was astonished, and read my memorandum. We agreed that, so soon as the attack commenced, his Battalion should move down the heights on the flank of the 2nd Battalion Rifle Brigade, which would rush to support Cadoux, and thus we parted, I as sulky as my hot nature would admit, knowing some disaster would befall my dear old Brigade heretofore so judiciously handled.

In the course of the night, as we were lying before the fire, I *far from asleep*, General Skerrett received a communication from General Alten to the purport " that the enemy were retiring over the swollen river; it was, therefore, to be apprehended he would before daylight endeavour to possess himself of the bridge; that every precaution must be taken to prevent him." I, now being reinforced in opinion, said, " Now, General, let me do so." As he was still as obstinate as ever, we were discussing the matter (I fear as far as I am concerned, very hotly) when the " En avant, en avant! L'Empereur récompensera le premier qu'avancera," was screeched into our very ears, and Cadoux's fire was hot as ever fifty men's was on earth. " Now," says I, " General, who is right?" *I* knew what the troops would do. My only hope was that Cadoux could keep the bridge as he anticipated. The fire of the enemy was very severe, and the rushes of his columns most determined; still Cadoux's fire was from his post. Three successive times, with half his gallant band, did he charge and drive back the enemy over the bridge, the other half remaining in the houses as support. His hope and confidence in support and the importance of his position sustained him until a melancholy shot pierced his head, and he fell lifeless from his horse.* A more gallant soul never left its mortal abode. His company at this critical moment were driven back; the French column and rear-guard crossed, and, by keeping near the bed of the river, succeeded in escaping, although the Riflemen were in support of poor Cadoux with as much rapidity as *distance* allowed, and daylight saw Colborne where he said he would be.

I was soon at the bridge. Such a scene of mortal strife from the fire of fifty men was never witnessed. The bridge was almost choked with

---

* Cope's account of Cadoux's death (pp. 149, 150), derived, he tells us, from Colonel Thomas Smith, is rather different. According to this, Skerrett sent to desire Cadoux to evacuate his post. Cadoux refused, saying that he could hold it. At 2 a.m. the French made a rush, but Cadoux, by his fire from the bridge-house, kept the head of the advancing column in check. Skerrett now peremptorily ordered Cadoux to leave the bridge-house. Cadoux could only comply, but remarked that " but few of his party would reach the camp." And as a matter of fact every officer present was either killed or wounded (Cadoux being killed), besides 11 sergeants and 48 rank and file out of a total strength of 100 men. Until the party left the bridge-house, Cadoux had not lost a man except the double sentries on the bridge, who were killed in the rush made by the French. Accordingly, while Harry Smith in the text blames Skerrett for leaving Cadoux in an almost impossible position without support, Thomas Smith's charge against Skerrett is that he recalled Cadoux when he was well able to hold his own.

the dead; the enemy's loss was enormous, and
many of his men were drowned, and all his
guns were left in the river a mile or two below
the bridge. The number of dead was so great,
the bodies were thrown into the rapid stream in
the hope that the current would carry them, but
many rocks impeded them, and when the river
subsided, we had great cause to lament our precipitancy in hurling the bodies, for the stench
soon after was awful. The Duke was awfully
annoyed, as well he might be, but, as was his
rule, never said anything when disaster could not be
amended. I have never told my tale till now.
Skerrett was a bilious fellow (a gallant Grenadier, I
must readily avow), and I hope his annoyance so
affected his liver it precipitated a step he had
desired—as his father was just dead, and he was heir
to an immense property—to retire home on sick-
leave. You may rely on it, I threw no impediment
in his way, for when he was gone, Colonel Colborne
was my Brigadier, whom we all regarded inferior to
no one but the Duke. Many is the conversation he
and I have had over the lamentable affair which
killed poor Cadoux. I really believe, had he survived, he would have held the bridge, although the
enemy attacked it in desperation, and although each
time the column was driven back, a few men in the
dark succeeded in crossing, and these fellows, all
practised soldiers, posted themselves under cover on
the banks of the river below the bridge, and caused
the loss our people sustained, that of noble Cadoux

among the rest, with impunity. Cadoux's manner was effeminate, and, as a boy, I used to quiz him.* He and I were, therefore, although not enemies, not friends, until the battle of Vittoria, when I saw him most conspicuous. He was ahead of me on his gallant war horse, which he took at Barossa with the holsters full of doubloons, as the story went. I was badly mounted that day, and my horse would not cross a brook which his was scrambling over. I leaped from my saddle over my horse's head (I was very active in those days), seized his horse by the tail, and I believe few, if any, were as soon in the middle of the Frenchmen's twelve guns as we were in support of the 7th Division. From that day we were comrades in every sense of the term, and I wept over his gallant remains with a bursting heart, as, with his Company who adored him, I consigned to the grave the last external appearance of Daniel Cadoux. His fame can never die.

The enemy retired into their previous position, as did we, and San Sebastian was ours. We were in this line for some time, daily watching the enemy making works with extraordinary vigour and diligence, which we knew ere long we should have the glory (the pleasure, to most of us) to run our heads

* In the *Recollections of Rifleman Harris* (1848), we have an account of Cadoux which tallies closely with that of the text: "I remember there was an officer named, I think, Cardo, with the Rifles. He was a great beau ; but although rather effeminate and ladylike in manners, so much so as to be remarked by the whole Regiment at that time, yet he was found to be a most gallant officer when we were engaged with the enemy in the field. He was killed whilst fighting bravely in the Pyrenees, and amongst other jewellery he wore, he had a ring on his finger worth one hundred and fifty guineas."

against, for such was the ardour and confidence of our army at this moment, that, if Lord Wellington had told us to attempt to carry the moon, we should have done it.

During the occupation of our present position, I found the Basque inhabitants on the Spanish side, and those on the French side of the Pyrenees, carried on a sort of contraband trade, and that brandy and claret were to be had. One day, therefore, upon General Skerrett's complaining to me he could get no wine or sheep, I told him I could get him both. My smugglers were immediately in requisition. They got me eight sheep and one dozen of claret. I was disappointed at the small supply—accustomed to hospitable old Vandeleur's consumption—and I told my new General. He said he was exceedingly obliged to me ; he should be glad of one sheep and two bottles of wine. It did not make a bad story through the Brigade. I and the A.D.C., Tom Fane, however, managed to consume all.

One day (the man may now be conceived) Skerrett gave a great dinner, and the *liberal* Barnard and Colborne, commanding Regiments in the Division, were asked to dine. Tom Fane and I were amused, for we knew he had but little to give them to eat and less to drink, and where were the materials to come from ? And Barnard loved a good dinner, with at least two bottles of good wine. To my astonishment, when I waited on him, as I usually did every morning, for orders, he was

dressed. I said, "Where are you going, General?"
(To me he was ever a most affable, and rather an
amusing, fellow.) He said, "To head-quarters at
Lesaca." So Tom and I supposed he would come
back laden with supplies. (At head-quarters there
was an excellent sutler, but the prices were, of
course, beyond any moderate means.) So Tom,
A.D.C., was on the look-out for his return. He
soon arrived with a bottle of sherry in each pocket
of his military blue coat, viz. two, and says, "Fane,
tell Smith, as my wine stock is not large, to be
cautious of it." Tom did tell me, and, when we
met in the dining-room, the joke was too good not
to tell such noble and liberal fellows as Barnard and
Colborne. Down we sat to, oh! such a dinner; our
soldiers in camp lived far better. So Barnard says,
"Being so near the French, we shall have plenty of
cooks in camp soon; come, Smith, a glass of wine,"
and I think we drank the pocket two bottles in
about as many minutes; when Barnard, as *funny a
fellow* and as *noble a soldier* as ever lived, says,
"Now, General, some more of this wine. We camp
fellows do not get such a treat every day." Barnard
had a French cook, taken at the battle of Salamanca,
and lived like a gentleman. "Barnard," Skerrett
says, looking like a fiend at me, "that is the last, I
very much regret to say, of an old stock" (Barnard
winked at me); "what I must now give you, I fear,
won't be so good." It was produced; it was trash
of some sort, but not wine. "No," says Barnard,
"that won't do, but let us have some brandy." We

got some execrable coffee, and here ended the only feast he ever gave while in command of my Brigade. Poor Skerrett, he soon inherited £7000 a year, not long to enjoy it. He was killed in the most brilliant, and at the same time the most unfortunate, affair that ever decorated and tarnished British laurels, at Bergen Op Zoom.

CHAPTER XIV.

CAMPAIGN OF 1813: COLONEL COLBORNE—SECOND
COMBAT OF VERA.

IN our Division, generally speaking, the officers
of each Company had a little mess of their own, an
arrangement indispensable, so much detached were
we on picquets, etc. Some of us lived most comfortably, and great interchange of hospitality existed.
We all had goats, and every mess had a boy, who
was in charge of them on the march and in quarters,
and milked them. On the march the flock of each
Regiment and Brigade assembled and moved with
their goat-herds, when each drove his master's goats
to his quarters. We observed extraordinary regularity with these goats, and upon inquiry we found
out the little fellows organized themselves into
regular guards. They had a captain, quite a little
fellow of dear old Billy Mein's (52nd Regiment);
their time of duty was as regular as our soldiers';
they had sentries with long white sticks in their
hands, and Mein's little boy held a sort of court-
martial, and would lick a boy awfully who neglected
his charge. My little boy's name was Antonio, and
when he was for guard, I have seen him turn out

K

unusually smart, with his face and hands washed. This little republic was very extraordinary, and quite true to the letter as I have drawn it. Mein's little captain told it all to my wife, who took great interest in them after she was acquainted with their organization, and the captain often consulted her. When our army was broken up after Toulouse, and all the Portuguese Corps of course marched back into Portugal, and the followers with them, we all of us gave our goats to the poor little boys to whom we had been so much indebted. My little fellow had a flock of fifteen. Many are probably great goat-proprietors now from this basis for future fortune.

Our Brigade was now commanded by Colonel Colborne, in whom we all had the most implicit confidence. I looked up to him as a man whose regard I hoped to deserve, and by whose knowledge and experience I desired to profit. He had more knowledge of ground, better understood the posting of picquets, consequently required fewer men on duty (he always strengthened every post by throwing obstacles—trees, stones, carts, etc.—on the road, to prevent a rush at night), knew better what the enemy were going to do, and more quickly anticipated his design than any officer; with that coolness and animation, under fire, no matter how hot, which marks a good huntsman when he finds his fox in his best country.

The French were now erecting works, upon a position by nature strong as one could well devise,

for the purpose of defending the Pass of Vera, and
every day Colonel Colborne and I took rides to look
at them, with a pleasant reflexion that the stronger
the works were, the greater the difficulty we should
have in turning them out—an achievement we well
knew in store for us.   On Oct. 7, the Duke resolved
to cross the Bidassoa, and push the enemy at once
into his own country, San Sebastian having been
taken.   Now had arrived the time we long had
anticipated of a regular tussle with our fortified
friends on the heights of Vera.   The Duke's dispatch,
Oct. 9, 1813, No. 837, tells the military glory of the
exploit.   My object is the record of anecdotes of
myself and my friends.   On the afternoon of the
7th, about two o'clock, we were formed for the
attack, and so soon as the head of the 4th Division
under that noble fellow, Sir Lowry Cole, appeared
in sight, we received the command to move forward.
We attacked on three different points.   Advancing
to the attack, Colborne, who had taken a liking to
me as an active fellow, says, " Now, Smith, you see
the heights above us ?"   "Well," I said, "I wish
we were there."   He laughed.   "When we are,"
he says, "and you are not knocked over, you shall
be a Brevet-Major, if my recommendation has any
weight at head-quarters."   Backed by the performance
of our Brigade, next day off he posted to Lord Fitzroy Somerset, and came back as happy as a soldier
ever is who serves his comrade.   "Well, Major
Smith, give me your hand."   I did, and my heart
too (although not as a blushing bride).   Kind-hearted

Colonel Barnard heard of this, went to Lord Fitzroy Somerset, asking for the Brevet for one of his Captains, remarking that I should be made a Major over the heads of twenty in my own Regiment. This startling fact obliged Lord Fitzroy to lay the matter before the Duke, who, I am told, said, " A pity, by G—! Colborne and the Brigade are so anxious about it, and he deserves anything. If Smith will go and serve as Brigade-Major to another Brigade, I will give him the rank after the next battle." Colborne's mortification was so great that I banished mine altogether by way of alleviating his disappointment. There was such a demonstration of justice on the part of his Grace, and so did I love the fellows whose heads I should have jumped over, that, honestly and truly, I soon forgot the affair. Colborne said, " Go and serve with another Brigade." " No," says I, "dear Colonel, not to be made of *your* rank. Here I will fight on happily, daily acquiring knowledge from your ability."

The 1st Caçadores, under poor Colonel Algeo, moved so as to threaten the enemy's left, and intercept or harass the retreat of the troops in the redoubt (which the noble 52nd were destined to carry at the point of the bayonet without one check), and the 2nd Battalion of the 95th and the 3rd Caçadores moved to the enemy's right of this redoubt for a similar purpose. This Battalion was fiercely opposed, but so soon as it succeeded in putting back the enemy, Colonel Colborne, at the head of the 52nd, with an eye like a hawk's, saw

the moment had arrived, and he gave the word
"Forward." One rush put us in possession of the
redoubt, and the Caçadores and 2nd Battalion 95th
caused the enemy great loss in his retreat to the
top of the pass where his great defence was made.
The redoubt just carried was placed on the ridge of
the ravine, and must be carried ere any advance
could be made on the actual [position].

In this attack poor Algeo was killed. He rode
a chestnut horse marked precisely as my celebrated
hunter and war-horse, "Old Chap," which I rode
on that day. My wife was looking on the fight
from the very cottage window we had occupied so
long, barely without the range of musketry, and saw
this horse gallóp to the rear, dragging for some
distance the body by the stirrup. The impulse of
the moment caused her with one shriek to rush
towards it, and so did anxiety and fright add to her
speed that my servant for some time could not
overtake her. The horse came on, when she soon
recognized it was poor Algeo's charger, not mine,
and fell senseless from emotion, but soon recovered,
to express her gratitude to Almighty God.

After this attack—and there never was a more
brilliant one—the 4th Division was well pushed up
the hill, and, so soon as our Brigade was reformed,
we prepared for the great struggle on the top of
the Pass of Vera. Colborne sent me to Sir Lowry
Cole, to tell him what he was about to attempt,
and to express his hope of a support to what he
had just so vigorously commenced. General Cole

was all animation, and said, " Rely on my support,
and you will need it, for you have a tough struggle
before you." On my return, we again advanced
with a swarm of Riflemen in skirmishing order
keeping up a murderous fire. Firing up a hill is
far more destructive than firing down, as the balls
in the latter case fly over. The 52nd Regiment,
well in hand, with their bayonets sharp and glistening in the sun (for the afternoon was beautiful), were
advanced under a most heavy fire, but, from the
cause mentioned, it was not near so destructive as
we expected. Still more to our astonishment, the
enemy did not defend their well-constructed work
as determinedly as we anticipated. Although they
stood behind their parapets until we were in the act
of leaping on them, they then gave way, and we
were almost mixed together, till they precipitated
themselves into a ravine, and fled down almost out
of sight as if by magic.

On the opposite side of this ravine, a few of the
Riflemen of General Kempt's Brigade were pushing
forward with a noble fellow, Reid, of the Engineers,
at their head. At the moment he did not know
how full of the enemy the ravine was. Colonel
Colborne and I were on horseback. We pushed on,
a little madly, I admit, followed by those who could
run fastest, until the ravine expanded and a whole
column of French were visible, but we and Reid on
the opposite side were rather ahead, while the
enemy could not see from out the ravine. The
few men who were there could not have resisted

them, and certainly could not have cut them off, had
they been aware.   Colonel Colborne, however,
galloped up to the officer at the head of the column
with the bearing of a man supported by 10,000, and
said to the officer in French, "You are cut off. Lay
down your arms."   The officer, a fine soldier-like
looking fellow, as cool as possible, says, presenting
his sword to Colonel Colborne, "There, Monsieur,
is a sword which has ever done its duty," and then
ordered his men to lay down their arms.   Colborne,
with the presence of mind which stamps the character
of a soldier, said, "Face your men to the left, and
move out of the ravine." By this means the French
soldiers were separated from their arms.   At this
moment there were up with Colborne myself,
Winterbottom, Adjutant of the 52nd Regiment, my
brother Tom, Adjutant of the 95th, and probably
ten soldiers, and about as many with Reid on the
opposite ridge. Reid wisely did not halt, but pushed
forward, which added to the Frenchman's impression
of our numbers, and Colborne turns to me, "Quick,
Smith ; what do you here ? Get a few men together,
or we are yet in a scrape."   The French having
moved from their arms, Colborne desired the officer
commanding to order them to sit down.   Our men
were rapidly coming up and forming, and, when our
strength permitted, we ordered the enemy to march
out of the ravine, and there were 22 officers and
400 men. Three pieces of cannon we had previously
carried (*vide* the Duke's dispatch, Oct. 9, 1813,
No. 837).   Colonel Colborne, myself, and others

were called madmen for our audacity. I never witnessed such presence of mind as Colborne evinced on this occasion, and when, like a *man* as he is, he returned the poor Frenchman's sword, "There," he says, "wear the sword, your pride; it is not yet disgraced." The fortune of war gave us the advantage over equal bravery.*

By this time our men had got well out of the Pyrenees into the plain of France below, and as night was rapidly approaching, I was sent on to halt them, ready for Colonel Colborne to take up his position. The prisoners were sent to the rear (what became of their arms I never knew) under charge of a Lieutenant Cargill, of the 52nd Regiment, a manly, rough young subaltern, who on his march, just at dusk, met the Duke, who says, "Halloa, sir, where did you get those fellows?" "In France. Colonel Colborne's Brigade took them." "How the devil do you know it was France?" "Because I saw a lot of our fellows coming into the column just before I left with pigs and poultry, which we had not on the Spanish side." The Duke turned hastily away without saying a word. The next morning Mr. Cargill reported this to Colonel Colborne, whom I hardly ever saw so angry. "Why, Mr. Cargill, you were not such a blockhead as to tell the Duke *that*, were you?" In very broad Scotch, "What for no? It was fact as death." It did not escape the Duke, who spoke to Colborne,

---

* Kincaid (*Random Shots*, p. 273) tells the story at second hand with his usual *esprit*.

saying, "Though your Brigade have even more than usually distinguished themselves, we must respect the property of the country." "I am fully aware of it, my lord, and can rely upon the discipline of my soldiers, but your lordship well knows in the very heat of action a little irregularity will occur." "Ah, ah!" says my lord, "stop it in future, Colborne." Nor had his Grace cause to complain of us.

This night we slept on our arms, and cold and miserable we were, for no baggage had been permitted to come to us. The next day we occupied the heights of Vera, our outposts remaining pushed forward, and head-quarters and our general hospital were established at Vera. My wife joined me very early, and I never before had seen her under such excitement, the effect of the previous day, when, as she conceived at the moment, she had seen me killed. She did not recover her usual vivacity for several days, and the report of a musket acted on her like an electric shock. We remained in this position several days.

One day I dressed myself in all my best to do a little dandy at head-quarters, to see some of my wounded comrades and officers, and to look into our hospitals. In galloping through the country, I heard a very melancholy and faint call, repeated once or twice without attracting my attention. When I turned towards it, it was repeated. I rode up and among several dead bodies of the enemy, I found the poor fellow who had called to me greatly exhausted. *Four days* had elapsed since the action, and he had both legs shot off high up. I dismounted and felt his pulse, which was still far from faint. Of course he prayed me to send succour. I promised to do so, and I proceeded to tie some of the bushes of the underwood to mark the spot, and continued to do so until I reached a mountain track leading to Vera. I now even hear the hideous moans he uttered when I turned from him, although I earnestly assured him of help. Away I galloped to the hospital, not to visit my own poor fellows, but to get a fatigue party and a stretcher, and off I set for my poor wounded enemy, whom, from the precautions taken, I easily found. Poor thing, from the belief that I had abandoned him, he was nearly exhausted. We got him on the stretcher, the party set off to the hospital, and I to my bivouac, for it was late and I was well aware the poor thing would be treated just as one of our own soldiers. I had literally forgotten the circumstance, when one day after we had advanced considerably into France, a month or five weeks after the man was picked up, a large convoy of disabled men, as an act of humanity, were sent to their own country from the rear. My Brigade was of course on the outpost, and it became my duty to go to the enemy's advanced post close to, with a letter and flag of truce. I was received as usual with great civility, and the convoy passed on. While I was talking to the French officers, a poor fellow on one of the stretchers called to me and the officer, and began a volley of thanks,

which, if it had been of musquetry, would have been
difficult to resist. I said, " I know nothing about
you, poor fellow; that will do." " I know you ; I
owe my life to you ; you fetched the party who
carried me to hospital. Both stumps were amputated; I am now doing perfectly well, and I was
treated ᵗlike one of your own soldiers." I never
saw gratitude so forcibly expressed in my life.

CHAPTER XV.

CAMPAIGN OF 1813 : BATTLE OF THE NIVELLE.

OUR Division was soon after pushed forward to
our right on a ridge somewhat in advance, and
fully looking upon the enemy's position. His right
extended from St. Jean de Luz, his left was on the
Nivelle, his centre on La Petite Rhune* and the
heights beyond that village. Our Division was in
the very centre opposite La Petite Rhune.

One morning Colonel Colborne and I were at
the advance vedette at daylight, and saw a French
picquet of an officer and fifty men come down to
occupy a piece of rising ground between our respective advanced posts, as to which the night before I
and a French staff-officer had agreed that neither
should put a picquet on it. (Such arrangements
were very commonly made.)   Colonel Colborne said,
"Gallop up to the officer, wave him back, or tell
him he shall not put a picquet there." Having
waved to no purpose, I then rode towards him and
called to him. He still moved on, so I galloped
back. Colborne fell in our picquet, ordered up a

* Cope writes *Arrhune.* The Duke's Despatches have *Rhune.*

reserve, and fired five or six shots *over the heads* of
the Frenchmen.   They then went back immediately,
and the hill became, as previously agreed, neutral
ground.   I give this anecdote to show how gentlemanlike enemies of disciplined armies can be; there
was no such courtesy between French and Spaniards.

A few days previously to Nov. 10, the Battle
of the Nivelle, the Division took ground on the
ridge of hills in our occupation, and the extreme
right of the Division became the left.   Gilmour,
commanding the 1st Battalion of the Rifles, then
in the 1st Brigade, had built a very nice little mud
hut about ten feet square with a chimney, fireplace,
and a door made of wattle and a bullock's hide.
When my wife rode up, Gilmour had just turned
out.   The night was bitterly cold; it was November
in the Pyrenees.   Gilmour says, "Jump off, and
come into *your own castle*, which I in perpetuity
bequeath to you."   When I returned from my
Brigade and new line of picquets, etc., I found my
wife as warm and as snug as possible—dinner
prepared for me and Tom Fane, our horses all
bivouacked, our cold tent pitched, and our servants
established in it; all was comfort, happiness, and
joy, every want supplied, every care banished.
At night we retired to our nuptial couch, a hard
mattress on the floor, when a sudden storm of rain
came on.   In ten seconds it came down through
the roof of our black-earth sods, and, literally in a
moment, we were drenched to the skin and as
black as chimney-sweepers.   The buoyant spirits

of my wife, and the ridiculous position we were in, made her laugh herself warm. We turned the servants out of our tent, and never enjoyed the late comforts of our castle again.

The enemy, not considering this ground strong enough, turned to it with a vigour I have rarely witnessed, to fortify it by every means art could devise. Every day, before the position was attacked, Colonel Colborne and I went to look at their progress; the Duke himself would come to our outpost, and continue walking there a long time. One day he stayed unusually long. He turns to Colborne, "These fellows think themselves invulnerable, but I will beat them out, and with great ease." "That we shall beat them," says Colborne, "when your lordship attacks, I have no doubt, but for the ease——" "Ah, Colborne, with your local knowledge only, you are perfectly right; it appears difficult, but the enemy have not men to man the works and lines they occupy. They dare not concentrate a sufficient body to resist the attacks I shall make upon them. I can pour a greater force on certain points than they can concentrate to resist me." "Now I see it, my lord," says Colborne. The Duke was lying down, and began a very earnest conversation. General Alten, Kempt, Colborne, I, and other staff-officers were preparing to leave the Duke, when he says, "Oh, lie still." After he had conversed for some time with Sir G. Murray, Murray took out of his sabretache his writing-materials, and began to write the plan of attack for the whole army. When it was finished, so clearly had he understood the Duke, I do not think he erased one word. He says, "My lord, is this your desire?" It was one of the most interesting scenes I have ever witnessed. As Murray read, the Duke's eye was directed with his telescope to the spot in question. He never asked Sir G. Murray one question, but the muscles of his face evinced lines of the deepest thought. When Sir G. Murray had finished, the Duke smiled and said, "Ah, Murray, this will put us in possession of the fellows' lines. Shall we be ready to-morrow?" "I fear not, my lord, but next day." "Now, Alten," says the Duke, "if, during the night previous to the attack, the Light Division could be formed on this very ground, so as to rush at La Petite Rhune just as day dawned, it would be of vast importance and save great loss, and by thus precipitating yourselves on the right of the works of La Petite Rhune, you would certainly carry them." This Petite Rhune was well occupied both by men and works, and a tough affair was in prospect. General Alten says, "I 'dink' I can, my lord." Kempt says, "My Brigade has a road. There can be no difficulty, my lord." Colborne says, "For me there is no road, but Smith and I both know every bush and every stone. We have studied what we have daily expected, and in the darkest night we can lead the Brigade to this very spot." I was proud enough at thus being associated, but no credit was due to me. "Depend on me, my lord," says

Colborne. "Well then, Alten, when you receive your orders as to the attack, let it be so."

Just before starting on this night's march, [9 Nov.], having had many military arrangements to make before I got on my horse, I had got a short distance when I remarked that, although I knew a proper tough fight was in hand, I had forgotten to bid my "goodbye" to my wife, which habit (on my part, at least) had rendered about as formal as if going to London out of the country. Her feelings were acute enough on such occasions, so I went into my hut, and avowed my neglect. She looked very sad, and I said, "Hallo, what's the matter?" "You or your horse will be killed to-morrow." I laughed and said, "Well, of two such chances, I hope it may be the horse." We parted, but she was very sad indeed.

As we started for our position before the great, the important day [Battle of Nivelle, 10 Nov.], the night was very dark. We had no road, and positively nothing to guide us but knowing the bushes and stones over a mountain ridge. Colborne stayed near the Brigade, and sent me on from spot to spot which we both knew, when he would come up to me and satisfy himself that I was right. I then went on again. In this manner we crept up with our Brigade to our advanced picquet within a hundred and fifty yards of the enemy. We afterwards found Kempt's Brigade close to our right, equally successfully posted. When Colborne and I rode up to our most advanced picquet, of course by the rear, we found, to the delight of us both, the Sergeant, Crowther, and his men, all sitting round a fire, as alert as if on sentry themselves, with their rifles between their legs, the sentry a few paces in their front. We had crept up by ourselves. Without any agitation, they stood up very quietly to reconnoitre us, when Colborne spoke, and commended their vigilance. [I and] Tom Fane, Skerrett's A.D.C., who nobly stayed with me rather than go to the rear, lay down for about two hours, when I could sleep, but Tom told me he could not. He had had a small flask of brandy, but, what with the cold and the necessity of keeping it out, the brandy was exhausted. About an hour before daylight, by some accident, a soldier's musket went off. It was a most anxious moment, for we thought the enemy had discovered us, and, if they had not, such shots might be repeated, and they would; but most fortunately all was still. I never saw Colborne so excited as he was for the moment. The anxious moment of appearing day arrived. We fell in, and our attack was made on the enemy's position in seven columns, nor did we ever meet a check, but carried the enemy's works, the tents all standing, by one fell swoop of irresistible victory. Napier, the author of the *History of the Peninsular War*, at the head of the 43rd, had his pantaloons torn by the ball, and singed by the fire, of one of the enemy from the parapet of their works. Such was the attack and such the resistance, that a few prisoners whom we took declared that they and their officers were

L

perfectly thunderstruck, for they had no conception
any force was near them. The 4th Division had
some heavy fighting on our right. *Vide* Napier and
the Duke's despatch.* Ours was the most beautiful
attack ever made in the history of war.

The key of the enemy's position was in our
hands, and the great line was our next immediate
object. We were speedily reformed, and ready for
our attack on the enemy's line-position and strong
field fortifications. In descending La Petite Rhune,
we were much exposed to the enemy's fire, and when
we got to the foot of the hill we were about to
attack, we had to cross a road enfiladed very
judiciously by the enemy, which caused some loss.
We promptly stormed the enemy's works and as
promptly carried them. I never saw our men fight
with such lively pluck ; they were irresistible ; and
we saw the other Divisions equally successful, the
enemy flying in every direction. Our Riflemen
were pressing them in their own style, for the
French themselves are terrific in pursuit, when poor
dear gallant (Sir Andrew) Barnard was knocked off
his horse by a musket-ball through his lungs.†
When Johnny Kincaid (the author), his adjutant,

---

* St. Pé, Nov. 13, 1813. No. 847.

† Cope's account (p. 155) represents Barnard as falling wounded
in the attack on the redoubt described in the text below. But he
seems here to have read George Simmons's rather carelessly. Though
Simmons, in his Journal for Nov. 10, says Barnard was wounded
"towards the end of this day's fighting" (p. 321), in his letter of
Dec. 7, he makes it clear that it was before the final attack on the
redoubt ; in fact, as Barnard was " reconnoitring how to move to the
best advantage " (p. 326). There is no discrepancy between this and
the text above.

got up to him, he was nearly choked by blood in
his mouth. They washed it out for him, and he
recovered so as to give particular orders about a
pocket-book and some papers he wished sent to his
brother. He did not want assistance ; the soldiers
loved him ; he was borne off to the rear, and, when
examined by Assistant-Surgeon Robson, it was found
that the ball had not passed through, but was
perceptible to the touch. The surgeon had him
held up, so that when he made a bold incision to let
the ball out, its own weight would prevent its being
repelled into the cavity of the chest. The ball was
boldly and judiciously extracted, no fever came on,
and in three weeks Barnard was at the head of a
Brigade, with one wound still open, and in the
passage of the Gave d'Oleron he plunged into the
water, and saved the life of a soldier floating down
the river.

But to the fight. Everything was carried
apparently, and our Division was halted. Some
sharp skirmishing was going on, and Colborne and
I were standing with the 52nd Regiment, again
ready for anything, on a neck of land which conducted to a strong-looking star redoubt, the only
work the enemy still held, when Charlie Beckwith,
the A.Q.M.G. of our Division, came up with orders
from General Alten to move on. " What, Charlie,
to attack that redoubt ? Why, if we leave it to our
right or left, it must fall, as a matter of course ; our
whole army will be beyond it in twenty minutes."
" I don't know ; your orders are to move on." " Am

I to attack the redoubt?" says Colborne. "Your orders are to move on," and off he galloped. Colborne turns to me, and says, "What an evasive order!" "Oh, sir," says I, "let *us* take the last of their works; it will be the operation of a few minutes," and on we went in a column of companies. As we neared the enemy, Colborne's brilliant eye saw they were going to hold it, for it was a closed work, and he says, "Smith, they do not mean to go until fairly driven out; come, let us get off our horses." I was just mounted on a beautiful thoroughbred mare, my "Old Chap" horse being somewhat done, and I really believed anything like *fighting* was all over. I said nothing, but sat still, and on we went with a hurrah which we meant should succeed, but which the garrison intended should do no such thing. My horse was struck within twenty yards of the ditch, and I turned her round so that I might jump off, placing her between me and the fire, which was very hot. As I was jumping off, another shot struck her, and she fell upon me with a crash, which I thought had squeezed me as flat as a thread-paper, her blood, like a fountain, pouring into my face. The 52nd were not beat back, but swerved from the redoubt into a ravine, for they could not carry it.* While lying under

* It is difficult to reconcile this story with that told by Colonel Gawler (quoted by Leeke, *Lord Seaton's Regiment at Waterloo*, vol. ii. p. 365). Speaking of the check received by Colborne and the 52nd in their advance on the redoubt, he goes on: "At this moment an interesting episode occurred. Baron Alten, seeing from the lower ridge the desperate nature of the effort, endeavoured to send an order to prevent further attempts. It was confided to the Brigade-Major,

my horse, I saw one of the enemy jump on the
parapet of the works in an undaunted manner and
in defiance of our attack, when suddenly he started
straight up into the air, really a considerable height,
and fell headlong into the ditch.   A ball had struck
him in the forehead, I suppose—the fire of our
skirmishers was very heavy on the redoubt.   Our
whole army was actually passing to the rear of the
redoubt.   Colborne, in the most gallant manner,
jumped on his horse, rode up to the ditch under the
fire of the enemy, which, however, slackened as he
loudly summoned the garrison to surrender.   The
French officer, equally plucky, said, " Retire, sir, or
I will shoot you !" Colborne deliberately addressed
the men.   " If a shot is fired, now that you are
surrounded by our army, we will put every man to
the sword."   By this time I succeeded in getting
some soldiers, by calling to them, to drag me from
under my horse, when they exclaimed, " Well, d—
my eyes if our old Brigade-Major is killed, after all."
" Come, pull away," I said ; " I am not even wounded,
only squeezed."   " Why, you are as bloody as a
butcher."   I ran to Colborne just as he had finished
his speech.   He took a little bit of paper out, wrote
on it, " I surrender unconditionally," and gave it to
me to give the French officer, who laughed at the

Harry Smith. Trusting to the shifting character of the mark of a
horseman in motion, he tried the desperate venture ; but it was
impossible ; no single living creature could reach the 52nd under the
concentrated fire from the forts. The horse was soon brought down,
and Captain Smith had to limit his triumph to carrying off his good
and precious English saddle, which he performed with his accustomed
coolness, to the amusement of observing friends and enemies."

state of blood I was in. He signed it, and Colborne sent me to the Duke. When I rode up (on a horse just lent me), his Grace says, "Who are you?" "The Brigade-Major, 2nd Rifle Brigade." "Hullo, Smith, are you badly wounded?" "Not at all, sir; it is my horse's blood." "Well." I gave him the paper. "Tell Colborne I approve." The garrison began to march out just as my Brigade were again moved on, and General Downie was left to receive it with his Spaniards. The garrison was composed of the whole of the French 88th Regiment, complete in every respect. The Duke was sorry we had attacked, for the 52nd lost many men, and it never was the Duke's intention, as he saw what Colborne had previously observed. Some discussion afterwards took place as to the order Colborne received. However, I think now, as I did then, *move on* implied *attack*.

This was a most brilliant day's fighting, and showed how irresistible our army was. As the Duke foretold, the enemy had not men enough. We were never opposed to a formed body. The whole army was in occupation of their works, and when we penetrated, retired. A proclamation had been issued to show the French inhabitants we made war on their army, not on them, and never in an enemy's country was such rigid discipline maintained as by the British Army. It is scarcely to be credited. The day after the battle our baggage moved up, and my wife joined me, horror-struck at the state of my cocked hat, clothes, and only half-washed face. She would not believe I was not awfully wounded, and then reminded me of her prophecy, that either I or my horse would be killed the following day.

A curious coincidence occurred in respect to this horse. Shortly before the Battle of Salamanca [22 July, 1812] a great friend of mine, Lindsay,* of the 11th Dragoons, came and prayed me to take it in exchange for a magnificent brown mare I had bought from Charlie Rowan ; he had often tempted me, but I resisted, but upon this occasion I yielded, so earnest was he for a Dragoon's charger ; and he gave me sixty guineas to boot. In a few months he was killed off my gallant mare on the Bridge of Tudela on the Douro, and now his mare was killed under me as described. Lord Fitzroy Somerset bought his mare at the sale ; his lordship afterwards sold her to me, and she went with me to Washington. I brought her back, gave her to a brother, and she bred many foals afterwards.

* Query, Lindsell ? See W. Tomkinson, *Diary of a Cavalry Officer* (1894), p. 195.

CHAPTER XVI.

COMBAT OF THE 10TH DECEMBER—HARRY SMITH'S
DREAM AND THE DEATH OF HIS MOTHER.

THE following day we moved into a most beautiful country, intersected with hedgerows, and
the finest and sweetest second crop of hay I ever
saw, which our horses rejoiced in. We took up our
posts in front of Arbonne [15 Nov.], and the
following day had a sharp skirmish at our advanced
posts. We halted here a day or two, and then
moved on to a line more approaching Bayonne.
The first Brigade occupied the Chateau d'Arcangues
[17 Nov.], of which Johnny Kincaid recounts
some anecdotes; the second the Chateau of Castilleur, where Colonel Colborne packed the 52nd
Regiment as close as cards ; and the 2nd Battalion,
95th Regiment, and the 1st and 3rd Caçadores also
had cover. Our posts were here very close upon
each other, and we had far more skirmishing and
alarms than usual.

Upon the morning of the 9th December, the 1st
and 7th Divisions came close up to our rear, which
led us to suppose something was going on. The
enemy in our front were alarmed, and stood to their

arms.   Shortly after these Divisions moved to our right, for the purpose of crossing the river [Nive], and our Division moved on to drive back the enemy's picquets in the direction of Bayonne.   To occupy his attention, our Riflemen formed up before the firing commenced close to the enemy's strongest post, on the high-road to Bayonne, where we had been watching each other for several days.   When I and Beckwith, the A.Q.M.G., rode up and ordered our people to advance, not a shot was fired.   The French saw we were going to attack, but did not withdraw their picquet.   We beckoned to them to do so, but they would not take the hint.   We then actually fired some shots over their heads.   There was positively a reluctance on our part to shoot any man in so cold-blooded a manner.   The moment a shot was fired the affair became general, and we drove in the French picquets, who rapidly retired, and we had little fighting all day.   In the evening, having effected the demonstration required, the Division retired to its old ground, and we resumed our usual line of picquets.

On the following morning [10 Dec.], having a presentiment the enemy would create a considerable diversion upon the left of our army, I was with our most advanced picquets before daylight.   I had not been there many minutes, when I was joined by Beckwith, and soon after up came Colborne. We said, "The enemy are going to attack us." Colborne said, "No; they are only going to resume their ordinary posts in our front."   I said, "But look at the body in our immediate front, and a column far off, evidently moving on the 1st Division," which was on the extreme left.   It was evident we should be attacked immediately, and I said so, but Colborne asserted it was no such thing.   I prayed him to allow me to order my Brigade under arms.   At last he consented, and, although I rode at the utmost speed, our troops were barely out in time, so furiously did the French drive us back.   They took the Chateau of Castilleur from us, making at the same time a heavy attack on that of Arcangues.   Much of our baggage fell into the enemy's hands, although they could not carry it off.   My wife had barely time to slip on her habit and jump upon her horse; her Vittoria pug-dog in the scuffle was left behind, so sharp was the fire on the Chateau.   A bugler of the 52nd Regiment, however, knew pug, whipped him up, and put him in his haversack.   This was nearer a surprise than anything we had ever experienced.   For some time the enemy possessed our quarters and bivouac, and—what was of great importance to Tom Fane—rifled his portmanteau. They also carried off a goose which was fattening for our Christmas dinner.   We soon repaid our friends with interest and retook our position, but it was one of as heavy attacks as I have ever witnessed.

In the afternoon of that day, the enemy made a most vigorous attack on Sir J. Hope, particularly at the Mayor's House of Biaritz,* sharply skirmishing

---

* So in the Duke's despatch.   But query, Barrouilhet?   See Napier, Bk. xxiii. ch. ii., and the plan in Sir H. E. Maxwell's *Life of Wellington*, i. p. 358

with us at the same time to occupy our attention. I thought then, and I think now, if my
Brigade had been moved on the left of the attack
on Sir J. Hope, it would have caused the enemy
great loss, as his flank was exposed, but the Duke
of Wellington knew better, and never attempted
hazardous and little affairs, but ever played a great
and safe game.

That evening the Regiments of Nassau and
Frankfort walked over to us from the French lines
into those of the 7th Division at Arbonne. Colonel
Beyring,* Count Alten's A.D.C., was said to have
been for some time with them, and it was evident
the Duke knew about their intention.

Upon the 11th [Dec.] we had some partial
skirmishing. The 2nd Battalion Rifle Brigade
struck their tents for the purpose of moving their
ground. The enemy were most alarmed, and took
up their ground to receive us. That night, when
our armies were dismissed, rations were served out.
In my life I never heard such a row as among the
French when preparing to cook. I was posting the
night's sentries, when I saw a French officer doing
the same. I went towards him, and we civilly
greeted each other. I said I wished to speak to
him. He came up with the greatest confidence and
good humour. I showed him my vedette, and then
remarked that his was too far in advance and might
create an alarm at night when relieving. He said

* Query, Baring? The name Beyring seems not to occur in the
Army Lists of 1813, 1814.

he did not see that, but to please me, if I would point out where I wished he should be, he would immediately move him—which he did.   He presented his little flask of excellent French brandy, of which I took a sup, and we parted in perfect amity.

When I returned to Colborne, who was in the Chateau, I found him lying asleep before a fire just as he had got off his horse.   I did not awake him, nor had I anything to eat.   Sleep at night readily supplies the place of food, and hunger at night on that account is not nearly so acute and painful as in the morning, when your day's work is before you. Down I lay, without one thought in the world, from exhaustion.   I had a long dream, its purport that the enemy had attacked my father's house (the front of which opened to the street, the back into a beautiful garden, by what we children called "The Black Door").   My father had my mother in his arms; I saw them as plainly as ever I did in my life, he carrying her through the Black Door, at the moment calling out, "Now, some one shut the door; she is safe and rescued."   At the instant I sprang on my feet, and in our usual military words in cases of alarm, roared out in a voice of thunder, "Stand to your arms."   Colborne was on his feet like a shot, the light of the fire showed me the room and my delusion, and I said, "Oh, sir, I beg your pardon; I have been dreaming."   He said, in his noble way, "Never mind, it is near daylight, and it shows that, asleep or awake, you are intent on your duty."   He

lay down, and was asleep in a moment. I never felt
so oppressed in my life, so vividly was depicted to
my mind the scene described, and I took out of my
pocket a little roster of duties and picquets bound in
calf-skin, and noted down the hour and particulars
of my dream. In a few days I received a letter
from my afflicted father,* telling me my mother died
on Sunday morning, Dec. 12, at one o'clock, at the
very moment I cried out, "Stand to your arms."
Such is the fact. When I lay down, I was tired
and exhausted, as before expressed. I had not a
thought in the world of home or anything, nor was
I prepared for the probability of the event. I
presume to make no remarks on such intimations
from God alone, but the whole day I was heavy
and oppressed, nor did I ever shake off the vivid
impression until the receipt of the letter put me in
possession of the loss I had sustained.

Her dying moments were perfectly composed;
to the last she blessed her two sons engaged in
the wars of their country, and died saying, " Would
I could have seen them after their dangers and
good conduct!" Among all our relations and friends
we receive kindness and attention and unbounded
love, but the love of a mother is distinct in character; youth in distress turns to the mother for
sympathy and pardon; in joy it desires to impart
its feeling to the mother, who participates in it
with the warmth of a mother's heart. The mother
is the friend, the counsellor, the pardoner of offences,

---

* See Appendix II. The *hour* of the death is not stated in the letter.

and, happen what may, the mother ever clings
to her offspring. When I first parted from my
mother to join my Regiment, the French Army was
assembled at Boulogne, and every day was full of
news that the French were coming. We dined
early that day, I and my father, who was kindly
to accompany me to Brabourne Lees, in Kent. At
dinner I held up manfully. Then I ran to the
stable to part with a beautiful little horse I
had reared almost from a foal—he was thoroughbred, and carried me hunting in such a style that
no one could beat me. I threw my arms round
Jack's neck, and had a good cry. I saw my poor
mother observed what I had been doing, and a
smile of approbation curled upon her placid lip.
The awful moment now approached : the buggy was
at the door. I parted with my dear brothers and
sisters (five boys and five girls) tolerably well, my
poor mother glad to observe in me a force of
character which *she hoped* in greater and more
eventful scenes I might evince. It came next to
her turn. She seized me in her arms, and wept
awfully. Suddenly, with an effort I shall never
forget, her tears were dried, she held me at arm's
length, and, gazing at me most intently, said, " I
have two favours to ask of you : one is that you
never enter a public billiard-room ; the next—our
country is at war—if ever you meet your enemy,
remember you are born a true Englishman. Now,
God bless and preserve you, which I hope He will,
and listen to the constant, the fervent prayers, I

will offer up for your welfare." I exclaimed, "Dear
mother, I promise!" God knows the first request
I have honestly fulfilled, the latter I hope I have—
at least, my superiors and comrades ever gave me
credit for a bold and courageous bearing. I returned to her beloved embrace after South America,
and got a commission for my brother Tom, and
again to her nearly naked and a skeleton after the
retreat to Coruña. I was covered with vermin,
and had no clothes but those on my back. *To her
alone* did I impart what, although I felt no disgrace, I did not want to be known. She dressed
me, and put me in a hot bath, and we preserved
our secret mutually inviolate. I soon again left her
for Talavera, restored to health by her care, never
to see her again, but our intercourse by letters was
constant. The last she received from me was after
we had carried the heights of Vera in such a brilliant
manner, and it told her that for my conduct I was
promised the brevet rank of Major. May every
soldier obey the fifth commandment as I did! I
never was in a situation of appalling death, mortality,
and danger, but my mother's words rang in my
ears, " Remember you were born an Englishman."
My dear wife participated and sympathized in all
my grief, for I admit it was excessive, saying ever,
" I have lost father and mother, and my brother
died in my arms of his wounds. Your home and
relatives you have still left, while I live alone for
you,—my all, my home, my kindred."

The morning after my dream [12 Dec.] I was

very early at our advanced posts, and I saw some
French soldiers coming on in a very unusual manner
to attack us, while the mass of their force were dismissed in bivouac. The 1st Caçadores had the
advance. I never saw the French so daring since
the retreat to Coruña, and they were most excellent shots, and actually astonished our Caçadores.
Colborne, hearing a smart firing, rode up, and
stopped in the road opposite one of the barricades
of our picquets. I said, " I don't know what the
devil we have got in our front to-day. Don't stand
there, you will be shot in a moment!" He laughed,
but would not move. In a second a ball went
through his cap just above his noble head. He
moved then and laughed. "Look at the fellows,"
he says, "how viciously they come on ; it is evident
it is no general attack, for the troops in their
bivouac are not under arms. They want this post."
"Which," says I, "they will have in ten minutes,
unless I bring up the 2nd Battalion Rifle Brigade,"
for our Caçadores were evidently not equal to their
task. Colborne says, "Fetch them!" In a very
short time our Riflemen came up. By this time
the enemy had driven in everything beyond the
barricade, and were prepared to assault it. Our
95th fellows had a few men wounded as they were
coming up the road, before they could be extended,
which made them as savage as the enemy, who
were capering about the fields in our front as if
drunk. Our fellows turned to, and soon brought
them to repent any pranks or exposure. We took

a few prisoners, and ascertained the Regiment was the 32nd Voltigeurs, a crack corps of Suchet's army which had joined the night before, when we heard all the noise going on in the bivouac. These gentlemen had ever previously been venturous and laughed at the tales of British prowess; that morning's lesson, however, seemed to have made converts of them, for I never after observed any extra feats of dancing; but Colborne and all of us were perfectly astonished when the fact was known, and our 2nd Battalion 95th Regiment were rather elated in having thus shown themselves such able instructors.

We were very much on the alert all day, and a few shots were exchanged. At night our picquets were strengthened, for we were not aware if our friends, the new Voltigeurs, intended a fresh prank. After these three days' fighting and vigilance, the enemy withdrew close to Bayonne, their and our advanced posts being nearly as before. Notwithstanding the loss of our goose, we had a capital Christmas dinner, at which, of course, we had the Commissary of the Brigade, and induced him to find us champagne, which many commissaries were able to do.

M

CHAPTER XVII.

CAMPAIGN OF 1814 : BATTLE OF ORTHEZ—ANECDOTE
OF JUANA SMITH.

FROM the Chateau of Castilleur we moved more
into the mountains to the rear and to our left of
Ustaritz, where we never saw the enemy [Jan.
1814]. Our time was spent in shooting, and ex-
ploring the mountains. While we were in this
position forage was very scarce, and we chopped
up the furze-bushes very small by way of hay.
It is astonishing how it agreed with the horses.
The natives use it in the same way for their cattle.

We remained in this position until the end of
February, when we moved, reaching Orthez on the
26th. Here our Division had one of the sharpest
skirmishes in a town which I ever saw. Orthez is
situated on both sides of the Gave de Pau and has
a bridge, which the enemy held with great jealousy.
On the afternoon of this day, the Duke and his
head-quarters came up. It was his intention to
have fought the battle that afternoon, had the 3rd
Division been able to reach its position in time. I
heard the Duke say, " Very well, Murray, if the
Division does not arrive in time, we must delay the

attack till to-morrow. However, I must have a
sleep."   He folded his little white cloak round him,
and lay down, saying, "Call me in time, Murray."
Murray awoke the Duke, saying, "It is too late
to-day, my Lord." "Very well, then, my orders
for to-morrow hold good."

At dark we withdrew all our posts out of
Orthez but a picquet near the bridge in the town,
and at daylight [27 Feb.] we crossed by a pontoon bridge below Orthez, and marched over
difficult ground. We saw the enemy very strongly
posted, both as regards the elevation and the
nature of the ground, which was intersected by
large banks and ditches, while the fences of the field
were most admirably calculated for vigorous defence. As we were moving on the right of the 3rd
Division, Sir Thomas Picton, who was ever ready
to find fault with the Light, rode up to Colonel
Barnard. "Who the devil are you?" knowing
Barnard intimately. "We are the Light Division."
"If you are Light, sir, I wish you would move a
little quicker," said in his most bitter and sarcastic
tone. Barnard says very cool, "Alten commands.
But the march of infantry is quick time, and you
cannot accelerate the pace of the head of the
column without doing an injury to the whole.
Wherever the 3rd Division are, Sir Thomas, we
will be in our places, depend on it."

We were soon engaged, but less for some time
than the troops to our right and left. I never saw
the French fight so hard as this day, and we were

actually making no advance, when the Duke came up, and ordered the 52nd Regiment to form line and advance. The Battalion was upwards of seven hundred strong. It deployed into line like clockwork, and moved on, supported by clouds of sharpshooters. It was the most majestic advance I ever saw. The French, seeing this line advance so steadily, were appalled ; their fire, which at first was terrific, gradually decreased as we neared. The Divisions on our right and left also moved on. The battle was won.

In this advance the 52nd suffered considerably. The present Duke of Richmond, then Lord March, a Captain in the corps, received a severe wound in the side ; the ball still annoys him. The Duke himself also got a crack on his knee, which lamed him for several days. When Lord March lay on the ground after the attack, I went to bring up Maling, Surgeon of the 52nd Regiment. As soon as he arrived, to my horror, he poked his forefinger into the wound to trace the course of the ball. At this moment up rode Lord Fitzroy Somerset, and Lord March's brother, Lord George Lennox, awfully affected, believing the wound mortal. Lord March said, "Maling, tell me if I am mortally wounded, because I have something I wish to impart to George." Maling said, "If you will be quiet, you will do very well." Maling did not think so. However, Lord March made a miraculous recovery. I never knew a finer young fellow, braver or cooler. In those days, he would not have

opposed his kind patron, the Duke, as he did
subsequently. That every peer and every other
man should speak out his mind according to his
conscience, I earnestly desire ; but, as Duke of
Richmond, he opposed the Duke of Wellington
politically in a manner rather partaking of personal
hostility than political consistency.* Every admirer
of Lord March in the army, and he had many,
lamented the course he pursued.

But to the fight. We drove the enemy in great
confusion before us. On this occasion, I literally
lost a Battalion of my Brigade, the 1st Caçadores,
for two days, they got so mixed with the 6th
Division. The night I found them, after much
diligence, I and my Brigadier, Barnard, got into a
little sort of inn, kept by an old soldier disabled in
Bonaparte's Italian campaigns. He did not require
to be told the wants of a soldier, but from habit and
sympathy turned to like a "good 'un" to cook us
some dinner. As he was hard at work, he said to
Barnard, " Ah, the French are not always victorious,
and I see war now is [not ?] what it was when I
served. The Cavalry give way first, then come
the Artillery, and then follow the Infantry in disorder." He became in the course of the evening
very eloquent over his own wine, and told us some

* Charles, from 1819 5th Duke of Richmond, after the introduction
of the Catholic Emancipation Bill became a vigorous opponent of
Wellington. Though reckoned an ultra-Tory, he joined the Reform
Ministry in 1830, and afterwards supported Lord Melbourne. On the
other hand, in 1845-6 (after the date when the remarks in the text
were written), he was a leader of the opposition to corn-law abolition.
He died within a few days of Sir Harry Smith, on 21st October, 1860.

very amusing stories. The next morning, when Barnard paid him for everything we had consumed, he was perfectly thunderstruck. I shall never forget his astonishment or his " Eh bien! monsieur, comme vous voulez."

The baggage reached us early the following day [1 March], and in the afternoon we forded the Adour, which was deep, rapid, and broad. My wife had ridden over the field of battle, and described it as covered with dead, dying, and wounded. She observed an extraordinary number of wounds in the head. These were due to the fact that, owing to the cover of the high banks before described, the head only was vulnerable or exposed. She saw one fine fellow of an Artilleryman with both his arms shot off, which he said occurred while he was ramming down the cartridge into his own gun. She offered him all she had in the eating or drinking way, but he most disdainfully refused all.

The same afternoon we made a long and rapid march on Mont de Marsan, where a Division of Cavalry and Marshal Beresford and his headquarters preceded us. We did not reach Mont de Marsan until some hours after dark. We were ordered to take up quarters for the night, but so full of Cavalry and head-quarters was the place, and all scattered over the town, not collected, as we Light Division used to be by streets and regiments as if on parade, we had great difficulty in getting in anywhere.

The night was showery, with sleet drifting, frosty and excessively cold. My poor wife was almost perished. We at last got her into a comfortable little house, where the poor Frenchwoman, a widow, lighted a fire, and in about half an hour produced some bouillon in a very handsome Sèvres slop-basin, saying this had been a present to her many years ago on the day of her marriage, and that it had never been used since her husband's death. She, therefore, wished my wife to know how happy she was to wait on the nation who was freeing France of an usurper. The widow was a true " Royaliste," and we were both most grateful to the poor woman. The next day we were ordered back to St. Sever, on the high-road to Toulouse, and parted with our widow with all mutual concern and gratitude, our baggage being left to follow. We had a very showery, frosty, and miserable long march over an execrable road, after which we and Barnard got into a little cottage on the roadside. At daylight the following morning we were expecting to move, but, having received no order, we turned to to breakfast, my wife relating to Barnard the kindness she had received the previous night and the history of the basin. To our horror in came my servant, Joe Kitchen, with the identical slop-basin full of milk. The tears rolled down my wife's cheeks. Barnard got in a storming passion. I said, " How dare you, sir, do anything of the sort?" (he was an excellent servant.) " Lord, sir," he says, " why, the French soldiers would have carried off *the widow,* an' she had been young, and I thought it would be so nice for the goat's milk in the morning; she was very angry, though, 'cos I took it."

Barnard got on his horse, and rode to head-quarters. About ten o'clock he came back and said the Duke told him the army would not march until to-morrow. My wife immediately sent for the trusty groom, old West, and said, " Bring my horse and yours too, and a feed of corn in your haversack." She said to me, " I am going to see an officer who was wounded the day before yesterday, and if I am not back until late, do not be alarmed." Young as she was, I never controlled her desire on such occasions, having perfect confidence in her superior sense and seeing her frequently visit our wounded or sick. I went to my Brigade, having various duties, just before she started. It became dark, she had not returned, but Barnard would wait dinner for her, saying, " She will be in directly." She did arrive soon, very cold and splashed from hard riding on a very dirty, deep, and wet road. She laughed and said, " Well, why did you wait dinner? Order it; I shall soon have my habit off." Barnard and I exclaimed with one voice, " *Where have you been?*" " Oh," she says, " do not be angry, I am not taken prisoner, as you see. I have been to Mont de Marsan, to take back the poor widow's basin." I never saw a warm-hearted fellow so delighted as Barnard. " Well done, Juana, you are a heroine. The Maid of Saragossa is nothing to you." She said the widow cried exceedingly with

joy, but insisted on her now keeping the basin for
the milk, which my wife would on no account do.
She had ridden that day thirty miles and had every
reason to expect to meet a French patrol. I said,
"Were you not afraid of being taken prisoner?"
"No, I and West kept a good look-out, and no
French dragoon could catch me on my Spanish
horse, Tiny." She was tired from the excessive
cold, but the merit of her act sustained her as
much as it inspired us with admiration. The
story soon got wind, and the next day every
officer in the Division loaded her with praise. It ·
was a kind and noble act which few men, much
less a delicate girl of sixteen, would have done
under all the circumstances. Our worthy friend,
Bob Digby, of the 52nd Regiment, Barnard's
A.D.C., overhearing my wife's orders to West, after
she had started, most kindly followed and joined
my wife on the road, for, as he said, he was alarmed
lest she should fall in with a patrol.

CHAPTER XVIII.

CAMPAIGN OF 1814: AT GÉE, NEAR AIRE—BATTLE OF
TARBES—BATTLE OF TOULOUSE—END OF THE WAR.

ON our advance [9 March, etc.], we were for
some days at a village called Gée, near Aire,
where the 2nd Division, under Sir W. Stewart, had
a brilliant little affair.

But I must first interpose an anecdote. One of
his A.D.C.'s, his nephew, Lord Charles Spencer, a
Lieutenant of the 95th Regiment, was mounted on
a very valuable horse which he had paid more for
than he could afford, contrary to the advice of Sir
William. In driving the French through the town,
Lord Charles's horse was shot on the bank of a
large pond, into which he himself was thrown head
foremost. (The fire at this moment was very heavy,
and in a street more balls take effect than in the
open.) Sir William very quietly says, " Ha, there
goes my poor nephew and all his fortune," alluding
to the price he paid for his horse.

I have often heard Colonel Colborne (Lord
Seaton) affirm that if he were asked to name the
bravest man he had ever seen (and *no one* was a

better judge), he should name Sir William Stewart.
Although he gave me my commission, I never saw
him under fire.   If he exceeded in bravery my dear
friend, Sir Edward Pakenham, he was gallant
indeed.   Pakenham's bravery was of that animated,
intrepid cast that he applied his mind vigorously at
the moment to the position of his own troops as
well as to that of the enemy, and by judicious foresight ensured success, but he never avoided a fight
of any sort.

The village of Gée was to the right of the
high-road to Toulouse, the River [Adour] running to
our right.   The Cavalry were posted on the main
road, their advance vedettes looking on to the
village of [Tarsac?] where the enemy were very
alert and obstinate in resisting our approach.

On the day the army advanced,* the French
Cavalry made a fierce resistance in the village, and
when driven out, made some desperate charges on the
chaussée, in one of which the officer in command was
cut down while gallantly leading his Squadron. An
officer of our 15th Hussars (I think Booth), having
admired his gallant bearing, dismounted to his
assistance. He said he believed he was not mortally wounded, and he requested to be carried to
the Chateau in the village he had so gallantly
fought for, where his father and family resided.
This peculiar tale may be relied on, like everything

---

* According to G. Simmons' diary (p. 340), this attack on the French
Cavalry took place on 16th March, two days before the advance of the
Division.   Simmons says the French captain "died soon after."

else, as I hope, which I have asserted.   For several
days it was the usual topic of conversation, and
when any one came from the rear, inquiry was
always made if the French Captain who was
wounded and in his father's house, (we never knew
his name), was doing well. We learnt afterwards
that he perfectly recovered, but the sword wound
had stamped him with a deep scar.

At Gée we had several alerts, and our baggage
for some successive days was loaded for hours.   On
one of these occasions the old housekeeper of a large
house which Barnard occupied, and whom he had
paid for many a fat fowl and fish out of tanks, etc.,
came into the room where my wife remained waiting to join the troops, seized my wife and vowed
she would put her to death, grasping her with
a fiend-like strength.   Fortunately, at this moment
my servant returned to say the Division were not
to march, and rescued my poor affrighted and delicate wife.   We afterwards learnt that this violent
woman, if anything excited her, was afflicted with
temporary insanity, and she had been put in a rage
below, and came up to vent her spleen on my poor
wife.   We were in this house for two or three days
after, but my wife had been so alarmed she would
never allow her servant to quit her.   The latter was
a powerful woman of the 52nd, rejoicing in the name
of Jenny Bates.

While in this village, Charlie Beckwith, the
Q.M.G., came to me and said, "Harry, I want a
Company for picquet immediately."   I named the

Corps, 1st Battalion 95th, who had one ready
accoutred in waiting, as we always had in positions
subject to alerts. It was out in five minutes, and
Charlie Beckwith marched to point out where the
officer commanding was to post it. I invariably
went out with every picquet when possible. On
this occasion I had other duty. In the afternoon
I got on my horse to look for my picquet. I met
Charlie Beckwith in the village. He said, " I will
ride with you." We did not find the picquet where
we expected—on our side of a bridge (beyond which
was a comfortable village). Having heard no firing,
we were not alarmed for the safety of the Company,
still we could not find it. We rode to the bridge,
the object of the officer's watch, saying, " There will
surely be a sentry upon it." We rode up and found
one certainly, but on the enemy's side. We asked
where the Company was. The vedette was an Irishman. " By Jasus, the Captain's the boy. It was so
rainy and cold on the plain, he harboured us all comfortably, like the man that he is, in the village."
The French were in the habit of patrolling into this
village in force, and, although the Captain had so
posted himself as I do believe he would have been
able to hold his own until the Division came up, it
would have cost us a fight to rescue him from the
far side of the bridge, which he ought never to have
crossed. So the Captain got a blowing-up, and the
Company had to make their fires in a cold, wet, and
miserable bivouac. I never had a picquet out from
the Brigade without visiting it so as to judge how

it was posted, and how to withdraw it either at night or in case of abrupt necessity.

We had also a sharp skirmish at Vic Begorre, but the brunt of it fell on the 3rd Division, where one of the most able officers got himself killed where he had no business to be—Major Sturgeon, of the Staff. I hold nothing to be more unsoldierlike than for officers well mounted to come galloping in among our skirmishers. The officers of companies have always some little exertion to restrain impetuosity, and your galloping gentlemen set our men wild sometimes. We Light Division, while ever conspicuous for undaunted bravery, prided ourselves upon destroying the enemy and preserving ourselves; for good, light troops, like deer-stalkers, may effect feats of heroism by stratagem, ability, and cool daring.

At Tarbes [20 March] we fell in with the enemy, strongly posted, but evidently only a rearguard in force. The Duke made immediate dispositions to attack them, and so mixed up did we appear, that we concluded a large number of the enemy must be cut off. The Light Division, however, alone succeeded in getting up with them. Our three Battalions of the 95th were most sharply engaged. Three successive times the enemy, with greatly superior force, endeavoured to drive them off a hill, but the loss of the enemy from the fire of our Rifles was so great that one could not believe one's eyes. I certainly had never seen the dead lie so thick, nor ever did, except subsequently at Waterloo. Barnard even asked the Duke to ride over the hill and see the sight, which he consented to do, saying, "Well, Barnard, to please you, I will go, but I require no novel proof of the destructive fire of your Rifles."

At this period we lived capitally. It was delightful to see one of our soldiers with a piece of cold bacon, slicing it over his bread like an English haymaker.

We had at this time exceedingly wet weather. Notwithstanding the fulness of the Garonne, however, after a feint or two and some skilful demonstrations to deceive the enemy, the Duke succeeded [4 April] in throwing over the 3rd, 4th, and 6th Divisions with as much ease as he had previously overcome what seemed to others insurmountable difficulties. These Divisions were strongly posted under Marshal Beresford as a *tête du pont*. They were barely established on the opposite side when such a torrent of rain fell, our bridge could not stem the flood. It was hauled to the shore, and, of course, our communication cut off. Marshal Beresford had every reason to apprehend an attack, for the enemy, being in his own country, possessed perfect information, and would know the moment the bridge was impassable. The Marshal wrote very strongly to the Duke, who was ferried over in a little boat with one or two of his Staff, while their horses swam across. His Grace quickly but narrowly examined the position, which was excellent, behind a very difficult ravine. "Beresford," said the Duke, "you are safe enough; two such

armies as Soult's could make no impression on you.
Be assured, he is too clever a General to attempt
to drive you into the river." Our Division was
immediately opposite the bridge, but on the left,
or opposite bank, to the Marshal. The river soon
subsided sufficiently to enable us to relay the bridge,
and at daylight on the 10th of April the Light Division crossed, followed by the remainder of the army,
except Lord Hill's corps, which was posted on the
Pyrenees side of Toulouse. It was evidently the
Duke's intention to attack Soult's position this day.
Nor were we long on the march before each general
officer had his point of rendezvous designated.

The battle of Toulouse [10 April] has been so
often fought and refought, I shall only make two
or three remarks. Sir Thomas Picton, as usual,
attacked when he ought not, and lost men. The
Spaniards made three attacks on a very important
part of the enemy's position defended by a strong
redoubt. The first was a very courageous though
unsuccessful attack; the second, a most gallant,
heavy, and persevering one, and had my dear old
Light Division been pushed forward on the right of
the Spaniards in place of remaining inactive, that
attack of the Spaniards would have succeeded. I
said so at the moment. The third attempt of the
Spaniards was naturally, after two such repulses, a
very poor one. At this period, about two o'clock
in the afternoon, the Duke's Staff began to look
grave, and all had some little disaster to report to
His Grace, who says, " Ha, by God, this won't do;

I must try something else." We then saw the heads of the 4th and 6th Divisions coming into action immediately on the right flank of the enemy, having been conducted to that particular and vulnerable spot by that gallant, able, and accomplished soldier, my dear friend, John Bell, A.Q.M.G., 4th Division.

I must record an anecdote of John. He was mounted on a noble English hunter, but the most violent and difficult horse to manage I ever rode to hounds, and would of course, in a fight, be equally so. This animal knew by the mode in which she was mounted whether her rider was an artist or not, and in a moment would throw her rider down by way of fun. Colonel Achmuty, a noble fellow, would ride John Bell's horse awkwardly, and she would then plunge like a devil, but if *ridden*, she was as quiet as possible. John Bell had on this horse a very large and high-peaked Hussar saddle, with his cloak strapped on the pique before, a favourite mode of General Robert Craufurd, who indeed gave Bell the identical saddle. Over this pique Craufurd's black muzzle could barely be discovered (he was a short man), so entrenched was he. In conducting their Divisions, the Staff officers moved on small roads through a country intersected by deep and broad ditches full of water. Many of them attempted to ride on the flanks, but no one succeeded but Bell on his fiery horse. At one ditch John Bell was fairly pitched over the pique on to the neck of his horse, a powerful mare six feet high. "Oh,"

N

says John, in telling this story, "Ah, to get there was extraordinary, but wait! The horse tossed up her head, and by some violent exertion pitched me over the pique back again to my saddle." "Oh, John!" I exclaimed, "how is that possible?" "With that, Harry, I have nothing to do."

But to the fight. The 4th and 6th Divisions were brought up in most gallant style, carrying redoubt after redoubt, which were ably defended by the enemy. It was the heaviest fighting I ever looked at, slow owing to the redoubts. The ground was gained step by step, and so was the battle of Toulouse. Our Cavalry lost a brilliant opportunity of distinguishing themselves and punishing the rearguard of the French.

This battle appeared to me then, and does the more I reflect on it, the only battle the Duke ever fought without a weight of attack and general support. It was no fault of the Duke's. There are fortunate days in war as in other things. Our attacks were commenced by that of the 3rd Division; then came those of the Spaniards, in which the Light Division did not support as the 4th Division supported us at the heights of Vera. Thus, until the afternoon, we literally had done rather worse than nothing. The success of this battle is to be attributed mainly to the 4th and 6th Divisions, but I will ever assert that the second attack was most heavy and energetic, and would have succeeded if my dear old Division had been shoved up. As a whole, the French lost a great number of men and were thoroughly defeated. The French have now agitated a claim to the victory, which they are as much borne out in as they would be in claiming the victory at Waterloo.

The next day [11 March] various were the reports flying about camp as to peace, etc. In the afternoon I was posting a picquet, and in riding forward no nearer than usual to a French sentry, the fellow most deliberately fired at me. I took off my cocked hat and made him a low bow. The fellow, in place of reloading his musket, presented arms to me, evidently ashamed of what he had done.

Peace was soon made known. The French moved out of Toulouse, and we occupied it. (The most slippery pavement to ride over in Europe is that of the streets of Toulouse.) My Division was most comfortably cantoned in the suburbs. I and my wife, and two or three of my dear old Rifle comrades—Jack Molloy and young Johnstone (not the Rifle hero of Badajos and Ciudad Rodrigo, old Willie)—had a delightfully furnished château. We got a French cook, and were as extravagant and wanton in our ideas as lawless sailors just landed from a long cruise. The feeling of no war, no picquets, no alerts, no apprehension of being turned out, was so novel after six years' perpetual and vigilant war, it is impossible to describe the sensation. Still, it was one of momentary anxiety, seeing around us the promptitude, the watchfulness, the readiness with which we could move and be in a state of defence or attack. It was so novel that at first it was positively painful—at least, I can answer for myself in this feeling. I frequently deemed the old Division in danger, who had never even lost a picquet, or, to my recollection, a sentry, after so many years' outpost duty.

We had one melancholy duty to wind up our period of war—the funeral of poor Colonel Coghlan, 61st Regiment. The officers of the army attended, the Duke himself as chief mourner. Many is the gallant fellow we had all seen left on the field or with some trifling ceremony consigned to his long home; but this funeral, in the midst of a populous city, in a graveyard, after a ceremony in a Protestant chapel, where the corpse was placed, in the custom of our home and infancy, while the service was read by a clergyman, after death in the last battle, and nearly at the end of it, too—all so tended to excite our comrade-like feelings, it positively depressed us all, for the love a soldier bears another tried and gallant soldier is more than fraternal.

Toulouse, a royalist city, soon rushed into the extravagant and vivacious joy of France. We had theatres, balls, fêtes, etc., until the army moved into regular cantonments. There we had plenty of room and quarters, no squabbling about the shade of a tree in bivouac, or your stable being previously occupied by cavalry or artillery horses. Abundance of food, drink, and raiment, and the indolence of repose, succeeded the energetic and exciting occupation of relentless and cruel war. I had a safeguard

in a lovely young wife; but most of our gallant
fellows were really in love, or fancied themselves
so, and such had been the drain by conscription of
the male population, you never saw a young Frenchman. The rich and fertile fields in this part of
France were cultivated by female exertion.

My Division went to Castel Sarrasin [towards
the end of April]. This place is situated on the
Tarne, which divides it from Marsac, where were
a body of French troops; but, as they seldom
came to visit us, we seldom encroached upon
them, for the Napoleonist officers were brutally
sulky and so uncivil, John Bull could not put
up with it with impunity. This part of France
is a garden, and the views, trees, beautiful rivers,
etc., and the idleness rendered it a perfect Elysium.
I say "idleness;"—because it was so totally novel,
it was amusing. Fortunately—for we were *nine
months* in arrear of pay—money was so scarce
that a trifle of ready money produced a great
deal. Among the rich inhabitants money was never
seen, any more than young men. Rents were
paid in produce, wages in kind, purchases made by
barter. Oh, dear John Bull, grumbling, still liberal
John Bull, had you witnessed, felt, and suffered all
this, and then had the best rooms in your house
occupied by soldiers (for, however orderly, there is
much riot and fun ever going on amongst them),
you would now wear the yoke of the national debt
as a light burden !

CHAPTER XIX.

HARRY SMITH PARTS FROM HIS WIFE BEFORE START-
ING FOR THE WAR IN AMERICA.

My happiness of indolence and repose was doomed
to be of short duration, for on the 28th of
August I was in the Battle of Bladensburg, and at
the capture of the American capital, Washington,
some thousands of miles distant. Colborne, my
ever dear, considerate friend, then in command
of his gallant Corps, the 52nd, sent for me, and
said, "You have been so unlucky, after all your
gallant and important service, in not getting your
Majority, you must not be idle. There is a force,
a considerable one, going to America. You must
go. To-morrow we will ride to Toulouse to head-
quarters ; send a horse on to-night—it is only thirty-
four miles—we will go there and breakfast, and ride
back to dinner." I said, very gratefully, "Thank
you, sir ; I will be ready. This is a kind act of
yours ;" but as I knew I must leave behind my
young, fond and devoted wife, my heart was ready
to burst, and all my visions for our mutual happiness were banished in search of the bubble reputation. I shall never forget her frenzied grief when,

with a sort of despair, I imparted the inevitable
separation that we were doomed to suffer, after all
our escapes, fatigue, and privation; but a sense of
duty surmounted all these domestic feelings, and
daylight saw me and dear Colborne full gallop
thirty-four miles to breakfast. We were back again
at Castel Sarrasin by four in the afternoon, after
a little canter of sixty-eight miles, not regarded as
any act of prowess, but just a ride. In those days
there were men.

On our arrival in Toulouse, we found my name
rather high up—the third, I think—on the list of
Majors of Brigade in the A.G.'s office desirous to
serve in America. We asked kind old Darling
who had put my name down. He said, "Colonel
Elley," afterwards Sir John. He had known my
family in early life, and was ever paternally kind
to me. He had asked my ever dear friend, General
Sir Edward Pakenham, to do so, which he readily
did. Colborne then said, "My old friend Ross, who
commanded the 20th Regiment while I was Captain
of the Light Company, is going. I will go and
ask him to take you as his Major of Brigade."
Ross knew me on the retreat to Coruña, and the
affair, in a military point of view, was satisfactorily
settled. But oh! the heaviness of my heart when
I had to impart the separation now decided on to
my affectionate young wife of seventeen years old!
She bore it, as she did everything, when the energies
of her powerful mind were called forth, exclaiming,
" It is for your advantage, and neither of us must

repine. All your friends have been so kind in arranging the prospect before you so satisfactorily." At the word "friends" she burst into a flood of tears, which relieved her, exclaiming, "You have friends everywhere. I must be expatriated, separated from relations, go among strangers, while I lose the only thing on earth my life hangs on and clings to!"

Preparation was speedily made for our journey down the Garonne, which we performed in a small boat, accompanied by our kind friend Digby. My wife was to accompany me to Bordeaux, there to embark for England with my brother Tom, who had recently suffered excessively in the extraction of the ball he had received in his knee five years previously at the Coa. The great difficulty I had was to get my regimental pay (nine months being due to me), and I only did so through the kindness of our acting-paymaster, Captain Stewart, and every officer readily saying, "Oh, give us so much less the first issue, and let Smith have what would otherwise come to us." Such an act, I say, testifies to the mutual friendship and liberality we acquired amidst scenes of glory, hardship, and privation.

Before I left my old Brigade, the 52nd Regiment, the 95th Regiment (Rifle Brigade now), the 1st and 3rd Caçadores,[*] with whom I had been so many

* The 3rd Caçadores at this period were commanded by a fine gallant soldier and a good fellow, but as he rejoiced in a name of unusual length—Senhor Manuel Terçeira Caetano Pinto de Silvuica y Souza—we gave him the much shorter appellation of "Jack Nasty Face," for he was an ugly dog, though a very good officer.—H.G.S.

eventful years associated—and I may say, most happily—all gave me a parting dinner, including the good fellows, the Portuguese, whom I never had any chance of seeing again. Our farewell dinner partook of every feeling of excitement. The private soldiers, too, were most affectionate, and I separated from all as from my home. The Portuguese are a brave, kind-hearted people, and most susceptible of kindness. We had also ten men a Company in our British Regiments, Spaniards, many of them the most daring of sharpshooters in our corps, who nobly regained the distinction attached to the name of the Spanish infantry in Charles V.'s time. I never saw better, more orderly, perfectly sober soldiers in my life, and as vedettes the old German Hussar did not exceed them. The 52nd Regiment I was as much attached to as my own corps, with every reason.

My old 1st Battalion embarked at Dover just before Talavera, 1050 rank and file. During the war only 100 men joined us. We were now reduced to about 500. There was scarcely a man who had not been wounded. There was scarcely one whose knowledge of his duty as an outpost soldier was not brought to a state of perfection, and when they were told they must not drink, a drunken man was a rare occurrence indeed, as rare as a sober one when we dare give a little latitude. My old Brigade was equal to turn the tide of victory (as it did at Orthez) any day.

It was early in May when we left Castel Sarrasin, where we had been happy (oh, most happy!) for a month—an *age* in the erratic life we had been leading. We were quartered in the house of a Madame La Rivière, an excellent and motherly woman, a widow with a large family and only one son spared to her—the rest had perished as soldiers. Never was there a more happy and cheerful family, and never did mother endeavour to soothe the acute feelings of a daughter more than did this good lady those of my poor wife. We often afterwards heard of her in Paris in 1815.

Our voyage down the Garonne in our little skiff was delightful. We anchored every night. In youth everything is novel and exciting, and our voyage was such a change after marching! The beauties of the scenery, and the drooping foliage on the banks of the river, added to our enjoyment. We landed each night at some town or village, and ever found a comfortable inn which could give us a dinner. After such privations as ours, the delight of being able to order dinner at an inn is not to be believed. On reaching Bordeaux, the most beautiful city I was ever in, I found I had only three or four days to prepare to reach the fleet and the troops embarked in the Gironde (a continuation of the Garonne), and that I was to embark on board his Majesty's ship the *Royal Oak*, 74, Rear-Admiral Malcolm, for the troops under General Ross were destined for a peculiar and separate service in America. I did, of course, all I could to draw the attention of my poor wife from the approaching separation. There was a theatre, various spectacles,

sights, etc., but all endeavour was vain to relieve
the mind one instant from the awful thought of that
one word "separation."   Digby was most kind to
her.   He had an excellent private servant, who was
to embark with her for London.   My brother Tom
was to her all a brother could be, and in the transport she was to proceed in were several old and
dear Rifle friends going to England from wounds.
I wished her to go to London for some time before
going down to my father's, for the benefit of masters
to learn English, etc.—for not a word could she
speak but her own language, French, and Portuguese,—and to every wish she readily assented.

Time rolls rapidly on to the goal of grief, and
the afternoon arrived when I must ride twenty
miles on my road for embarcation.   Many a year
has now gone by, still the recollection of that
afternoon is as fresh in my memory as it was
painful at the moment—oh, how painful !   To see
that being whose devotedness in the field of three
years' eventful war, in a life of such hardship at the
tender age of fourteen, had been the subject of
wonder to the whole community, in a state bordering on despair, possessing, as she did, the strong
and enthusiastic feelings of her country-women—
who love with a force cooler latitudes cannot boast
of—*this* was to me an awful trial, and although she
had every prospect of care and kindness, to be
separated conveyed to the sensitive mind of youth
(for I was only twenty-four *) every anguish and

* He was nearly twenty-seven. See p. 1 *n*.

horror that is to be imagined.   I left her insensible
and in a faint.   God only knows the number of
staggering and appalling dangers I had faced ; but,
thank the Almighty, I never was unmanned until
now, and I leaped on my horse by that impulse
which guides the soldier to do his duty.

I had a long ride before me on the noble mare
destined to embark with me.   On my way I
reached a village where I received the attention
of a kind old lady, who from her age had been
exempt from having any troops quartered on her ;
but, the village being full of Rifle Brigade, Artillery, and Light Division fellows, the poor old lady
was saddled with me.   The Artillery readily took
charge of my horse.   The kind old grandmamma
showed me into a neat little bedroom and left me.
I threw myself on the bed as one *alone* in all the
wide world, a feeling never before experienced,
when my eye caught some prints on the wall.
What should they be but pictures in representation
of the *Sorrows of Werther*, and, strange though it
be, they had the contrary effect upon me to that
which at the first glance I anticipated.   They roused
me from my sort of lethargy of grief and inspired a
hope which never after abandoned me.   The good
lady had a nice little supper of *côtelettes de mouton*,
and the most beautiful strawberries I ever saw, and
she opened a bottle of excellent wine.   To gratify
her I swallowed by force all I could, for her kindness was maternal.

We soon parted for ever, for I was on horseback

before daylight, *en route* to Pauillac, a village on the Garonne, where we were to embark. On my ride, just at grey daylight, I saw something walking in the air. "It is like a man," I said, "certainly, only that men do not walk in the air." It advanced towards me with apparently rapid strides, and in the excited state of mind I was in, I really believed I was deluded, and ought not to believe *what I saw.* Suspense was intolerable, and I galloped up to it. As I neared my aeronaut, I found it a man walking on stilts about twenty-five feet high. In the imperfect light and the distance, of course the stilts were invisible. The phenomenon was accounted for, and my momentary credulity in I did not know what called to mind stories I had heard recounted, evidently the results of heated imaginations. This walking on stilts is very general in the deep sands of this country.

On reaching Pauillac, I found my trusty old groom West waiting for me. He led me to a comfortable billet, where my portmanteau, all my worldly property, and my second horse, which was to embark with me, were reported "All right, sir." Old West did not ask after " Mrs.," but he looked at me a thousand inquiries, to which I shook my head. I found a note for me at our military post-office from dear little Digby, as consolatory as I could expect.

I was detained two days at Pauillac, in the house of another widow, an elderly lady (all women in France of moderate or certain age were widows

at this period). One morning I heard a most
extraordinary shout of joyful exclamation, so much
so I ran into the room adjoining the one I was
sitting in. The poor old woman says, "Oh, come
in and witness my happiness!" She was locked in
the arms of a big, stout-looking, well-whiskered
Frenchman. "Here is my son, oh! my long-lost
son, who has been a [prisoner] in England from the
beginning of the war." The poor fellow was a
sous-officier in a man-of-war, and, having been taken
early in the war off Boulogne, for years he had
been in those accursed monsters of inhuman invention, "the hulks," a prisoner. He made no
complaint. He said England had no other place to
keep their prisoners, that they were well fed when
fed by the English, but when, by an arrangement
with France at her own request, that Government
fed them, they were half starved. The widow gave
a great dinner-party at two o'clock, to which I was
of course invited. The poor old lady said, " Now
let us drink some of this wine: it was made the
year my poor son was taken prisoner. I vowed it
should never be opened until he was restored to
me, and this day I have broached the cask." The
wine was excellent. If all the wine-growers had
sons taken prisoners, and kept it thus until their
release, the world would be well supplied with good
wine in place of bad. Poor family! it was delightful to witness their happiness, while I could
but meditate on the contrast between it and my
wretchedness. But I lived in hope.

CHAPTER XX.

VOYAGE TO BERMUDA—RENDEZVOUS IN THE CHESA-
PEAKE—BATTLE OF BLADENSBURG AND CAPTURE
OF WASHINGTON — HARRY SMITH SENT HOME
WITH DISPATCHES.

THAT afternoon, after seeing my horses off, I
embarked in a boat, and I and all my personal
property, my one portmanteau, reached the *Royal
Oak*, at her anchorage a few miles below, about
eight o'clock. I found General Ross had not
arrived, but was hourly expected. We soldiers had
heard such accounts of the etiquette required in a
man-of-war, the rigidity with which it was exacted,
etc., that I was half afraid of doing wrong in anything I said or did. When I reached the quarters,
the officer of the watch asked my name, and then, in
the most gentlemanlike and unaffected manner, the
lieutenant of the watch, Holmes (with whom I afterwards became very intimate), showed me aft into
the Admiral's cabin. Here I saw wine, water,
spirits, etc., and at the end of the table sat the finest-
looking specimen of an English sailor I ever saw.
This was Admiral Malcolm, and near him sat
Captain Dick, an exceedingly stout man, a regular

representation of John Bull. They both rose immediately, and welcomed me on board in such an honest and hospitable manner, that I soon discovered the etiquette consisted in nothing but a marked endeavour to make us all happy. The fact is that Army and Navy had recently changed places. When I joined the Army, it was just at a time when our Navy, after a series of brilliant victories, had destroyed at Trafalgar the navy of the world. Nine years had elapsed, and the glories of the Army were so fully appreciated by our gallant brothers of the sea service, we were now by them regarded as the heroes whom I well recollect I thought them to be in 1805.

The Admiral says, "Come, sit down and have a glass of grog." I was so absorbed in the thought that this large floating ship was to bear me away from all I held so dear, that down I sat, and seized a bottle (gin, I believe), filled a tumbler half full, and then added some water. "Well done!" says the Admiral. "I have been at sea, man and boy, these forty years, but d—— me, if I ever saw a stiffer glass of grog than that in my life." He afterwards showed me my cabin, telling me he was punctual in his hours. "I breakfast at eight, dine at three, have tea in the evening, and grog at night, as you see; and if you are thirsty or want anything, my steward's name is Stewart, a Scotchman like myself—tell the Marine at the cabin door to call him and desire him to bring you everything you want." I shall never forget the kindness I received on board the *Royal Oak*, and subsequently on board the *Menelaus* (commanded by poor Sir Peter Parker), and from every ship and every sailor with whom I became associated. Our Navy are noble fellows, and their discipline and the respect on board for rank are a bright example to the more familiar habits of our Army.

General Ross arrived next morning, with his A.D.C., Tom Falls, a Captain in the 20th, and Lieut. De Lacy Evans (subsequently of great notoriety), both as good-hearted fellows as ever wore a sword. The fleet sailed in the afternoon. The troops all embarked in men-of-war, with the lower-deck guns out. We had on board a Company of Artillery; otherwise the force consisted of the 4th Regiment, the 44th, and the 85th. We had a very slow but beautiful passage to St. Michael's, one of the Western Islands, where, as Admiral Malcolm said, "that d——d fellow Clavering, the Duke of York's enemy, had the impudence to call on me," and we embarked live bullocks, fruit, and vegetables.

The parts capable of cultivation in this island are most fertile, and the inhabitants (all Portuguese) looked cheerful and happy. I could then speak Portuguese like a native. One day on shore I walked into a large draper's shop, where I was quite struck by the resemblance of the man behind the counter to my old clerk, Sergeant Manuel. After some little conversation, I discovered he actually was his brother. At first I doubted it, but he fetched me a bundle of letters in which my name frequently appeared. It was an extraordinary rencontre, and my friend Señor Manuel's attention to me was very "gostozo" indeed.

We sailed for Bermuda in a few days. It was a long passage, but we had fine weather until we neared Bermuda, when we fell in with a violent thunderstorm, which carried away the mizen top-mast of the *Royal Oak.*

Much of my time was spent with my friend Holmes, and many is the time I have walked the quarter-deck with him. In any state of grief or excitement, some one who participates and sympathizes in your feeling is always sought for, and this warm-hearted fellow fully entered into all I must feel at the fate of my wife—a foreigner in a foreign land, to whom, though surrounded by many kind friends, everything was strange, everything brought home the absence of that being on whom her life depended.

On reaching Bermuda we found the 21st Regiment awaiting us, and a communication from the Admiral, Cochrane, Commander-in-chief of the Navy (who commanded on the coast of America 170 Pennons of all descriptions), that a Battalion of Marines was organized under Colonel Malcolm, the Admiral's brother, upwards of 800 strong, so that General Ross's force became respectable. The Admiral proposed to *rendezvous* in Chesapeake Bay so soon as possible.

Ross organized his force into three Brigades,

one commanded by Colonel Thornton, the second
by Colonel Brooke, the third, which comprised all
Naval auxiliaries, by Colonel Malcolm. A Brigade-
Major was appointed to each. I was put in orders
Deputy Adjutant-General; Evans, Deputy Quartermaster-General. The price of things on this spot
in the ocean was enormous; I, Evans, Macdougall,
of the 85th, Holmes of the Navy, etc., dined on
shore at the inn one day, and were charged fifteen
Spanish dollars for a miserable turkey; but the
excellent fish called a "groper" made up for the
price of the turkey.

General Ross left the troops here, and proceeded
to join the Naval Commander-in-chief in a frigate.
I was the only Staff officer left with Admiral Malcolm,
who was quite as much a soldier in heart as a
sailor; he prided himself very much on having
brought home the Duke of Wellington (when
Sir A. Wellesley) from India, and he landed his
army at Mondego Bay, before Vimiera. I never
saw a man sleep so little : four hours a night was
plenty, and half that time he would talk aloud in
his sleep, and if you talked with him would answer
correctly, although next morning he recollected
nothing.

To get from the anchorage at Bermuda is
difficult, and the wind was contrary, and appeared
so likely to continue so, that the Admiral resolved
on the boldest thing that was ever attempted, viz.
to take the whole fleet through the North-east
Passage—a thing never done but by one single

frigate. There was only one man in the island who would undertake to pilot the 74 *Royal Oak* through. The passage is most intricate, and the pilot directs the helmsman by ocular demonstration, that is, by looking into the water at the rocks. It was the most extraordinary thing ever seen, the rocks visible under water all round the ship. Our pilot, a gentleman, said there was only one part of the passage which gave him any apprehension. There was a turn in it, and he was afraid the *Royal Oak* was so long her bows would touch. When her rudder was clear, on my honour, there appeared not a foot to spare. The breeze was very light; at one period, for half an hour, it almost died away. The only expression the Admiral was heard to make use of was, "Well, if the breeze fails us, it will be a good turn I have done the Yankees." He certainly was a man of iron nerves. The fleet all got through without one ship touching. The Admiral's tender, a small sloop, ran on a rock, but was got off without injury.

At night, after the fleet was well clear (and the bold attempt was of every importance to the success of our expedition, which, as we now began to observe, evidently meditated the capture of Washington), we had rather a good passage to the mouth of the Chesapeake, where we met the Admiral Chief in Command and General Ross. We did not anchor, having a leading wind to take us up the bay. We were going ten knots when the frigate struck on the tail of a bank, with a crash like an earthquake; she got over, however, without injury. We anchored off the mouth of the Patuxen, the river which leads to Washington.

Next day all the Staff were assembled on board the *Tonnant*, and all the Admirals came on board. We had present—Sir A. Cochrane, Admiral Cockburn (of great renown on the American coast), Admiral Malcolm, Admiral Codrington, Captain of the Fleet, and, if I recollect right, Sir T. Hardy, but he left us next day. After much discussion and poring over bad maps, it was resolved the force should sail up the serpentine and wooded Patuxen in the frigates and smaller vessels. This we did, and it was one of the most beautiful sights the eye could behold. The course of the large river was very tortuous, the country covered with immense forest trees; thus, to look back, the appearance was that of a large fleet stalking through a wood. We went up as far as we could, and the Navy having very dexterously and gallantly burned and destroyed Commodore Barney's flotilla, which was drawn up to oppose our passage [19, 20 Aug.], the army was landed about thirty-six miles from Washington. I cannot say my dear friend General Ross inspired me with the opinion he was the officer Colborne regarded him as being. He was very cautious in responsibility—awfully so, and lacked that dashing enterprise so essential to carry a place by a *coup de main*. He died the death of a gallant soldier, as he was, and friendship for the man must honour the manes of the brave.

We fell in with the enemy on our second day's
march, well posted on the eastern bank. We were
told that the only approach to their position was by a
bridge through the village of Bladensburg. The
day we landed, a most awful spectacle of a man
named Calder came in to give us information.
He was given in my charge, the secret service
department having been confided to me. The
poor wretch was covered with leprosy, and I really
believe was induced to turn traitor to his country
in the hope of receiving medical [aid] from our
surgeons, in the miserable state of disease he was
in. If such was his object, he is partly to be pardoned. He was a very shrewd, intelligent fellow,
and of the utmost use to us. He was afterwards
joined by a young man of the name of Brown, as
healthy a looking fellow as he was the reverse,
who was very useful to us as a guide and as a
scout.

When the head of the Light Brigade reached
the rising ground, above the bridge, Colonel
Thornton immediately proposed to attack, which
astonished me [Battle of Bladensburg, 24 Aug.].
We old Light Division always took a good
look before we struck, that we might find a vulnerable part. I was saying to General Ross we
should make a feint at least on the enemy's left
flank, which rested on the river higher up, and
I was in the act of pointing out the position, guns,
etc., when Colonel Thornton again proposed to
move on. I positively laughed at him. He got

furiously angry with me; when, to my horror and astonishment, General Ross consented to this isolated and premature attack. "Heavens!" says I, "if Colborne was to see this!" and I could not refrain from saying, "General Ross, neither of the other Brigades can be up in time to support this mad attack, and if the enemy fight, Thornton's Brigade must be repulsed." It happened just as I said. Thornton advanced, under no cloud of sharpshooters, such as we Light Division should have had, to make the enemy unsteady and render their fire ill-directed. They were strongly posted behind redoubts and in houses, and reserved their fire until Thornton was within fifty yards. Thornton was knocked over, and Brown, commanding the 85th Light Infantry, and Captain Hamilton, a noble fellow from the 52nd, were killed, and the attack repulsed. "There," says I, "there is the art of war and all we have learned under the Duke given in full to the enemy!" Thornton's Brigade was ordered to hold its own until the arrival of the Brigade consisting of the 4th and 44th under Brooke, many men having dropped down dead on the march from the heat, being fat and in bad wind from having been so long on board. As the Brigades closed up, General Ross says, "Now, Smith, do you stop and bring into action the other two Brigades as fast as possible." "Upon what points, sir?" He galloped to the head of Thornton's people, and said, "Come on, my boys," and was the foremost man until the victory was complete. He had two horses shot

under him, and was shot in the clothes in two or
three places. I fed the fight for him with every
possible vigour. Suffice it to say we licked the
Yankees and took all their guns, with a loss of
upwards of 300 men, whereas Colborne would have
done the same thing with probably a loss of 40 or
50, and we entered Washington for the barbarous
purpose of destroying the city. Admiral Cockburn
would have burnt the whole, but Ross would only
consent to the burning of the public buildings. I
had no objection to burn arsenals, dockyards, frigates
building, stores, barracks, etc., but well do I recollect that, fresh from the Duke's humane warfare
in the South of France, we were horrified at the
order to burn the elegant Houses of Parliament and
the President's house. In the latter, however, we
found a supper all ready, which was sufficiently
cooked without more fire, and which many of us
speedily consumed, unaided by the fiery elements,
and drank some very good wine also.* I shall
never forget the destructive majesty of the flames
as the torches were applied to beds, curtains, etc.
Our sailors were artists at the work. Thus was
fought the Battle of Bladensburg, which wrested
from the Americans their capital Washington, and
burnt its Capitol and other buildings with the

---

* Ross wrote, "So unexpected was our entry and capture of
Washington, and so confident was Madison of the defeat of our
troops, that he had prepared a supper for the expected conquerors;
and when our advanced party entered the President's house, they
found a table laid with forty covers" (*Dictionary of National Biography*, "Ross").

ruthless firebrand of the Red Savages of the woods. Neither our Admirals nor the Government at home were satisfied that we had not allowed the work of destruction to progress, as it was considered the total annihilation of Washington would have removed the seat of government to New York, and the Northern and Federal States were adverse to the war with England.

We remained two days, or rather nights, at Washington, and retired on the third night in a most injudicious manner. I had been out in the camp, and when I returned after dark, General Ross says, " I have ordered the army to march at night." " To-night ? " I said. " I hope not, sir. The road you well know, for four miles to Bladensburg, is excellent, and wide enough to march with a front of subdivisions. After that we have to move through woods by a track, not a road. Let us move so as to reach Bladensburg by daylight. Our men will have a night's rest, and be refreshed after the battle. I have also to load all the wounded, and to issue flour, which I have also caused to be collected." (I had seized in Washington everything in the shape of transport, and Baxter, the Staff Surgeon, brought away every wounded man who could travel.) General Ross said, " I have made the arrangement with Evans, and we must march." I muttered to myself, " Oh, for dear John Colborne ! "

We started at nine, and marched rapidly and in good order to Bladensburg, where we halted for about an hour to load the wounded. The barrels of flour were arranged in the streets, the heads knocked in, and every soldier told to take some. Soldiers are greedy fellows, and many filled their haversacks. During a tedious night's march through woods as dark as chaos, they found the flour far from agreeable to carry and threw it away by degrees. If it had not been for the flour thus marking the track, the whole column would have lost its road. Such a scene of intolerable and unnecessary confusion I never witnessed. At daylight we were still not three miles from Bladensburg. Our soldiers were dead done, and so fatigued, there was nothing for it but to halt and bring into play the flour, which was soon set about, while we Staff were looking out like a Lieutenant of the Navy in chase, to see the Yankees come down upon us with showers of sharpshooters. Thanks to their kind consideration they abstained from doing so, but we were very much in their power.

I now began to see how it was that our Light Division gentlemen received so much credit in the army of the dear Duke. I recommend every officer in command to avoid a night march as he would the devil, unless on a good road, and even thus every precaution must be taken by all staff officers to keep up the communications, or regularity cannot be ensured. I have seen many night marches, but I never yet saw time gained, or anything, beyond the evil of fatiguing your men and defeating your own object. You may move before daylight, *i.e.* an hour or two, if the nights are light. By this means, about the time the column requires collection, daylight enables you to do it. You have got a start of your enemy, your men are in full vigour either to march rapidly or, in case of difficulty, to fight. But avoid night marches. However, owing to their want of knowledge of the art of war, the enemy on this occasion allowed us to get to our boats perfectly unmolested.

On one of the days we were near Washington a storm came on, a regular hurricane. It did not last more than twenty minutes, but it was accompanied by a deluge of rain and such a gale that it blew down all our piles of arms and blew the drums out of camp. I never witnessed such a scene as I saw for a few minutes. It resembled the storm in Belshazzar's feast,* and we learnt that even in the river, sheltered by the woods, several of our ships at anchor had been cast on their beam ends.

We gave out we were going to Annapolis, and thence to Baltimore to re-act the conflagration of Washington, and the bait took. Some American gentlemen came in under a flag of truce, evidently to have a look at us, but avowedly to ask how private property had been respected. Their observations were frustrated by our vigilance. I was sent out to receive them, and nothing could

* The biblical account of Belshazzar's feast (Daniel v.) does not mention a storm. Sir H. Smith's mental picture was no doubt derived from engravings of Martin's representation of the scene.

exceed their gentlemanlike deportment. I loaded them with questions about roads, resources, force, etc., etc., at Annapolis and Baltimore. It was evident they took the bait, for that night we heard their army was off in full force to Annapolis, leaving us quietly to get down to our ships. We made arrangements for the care and provisioning of the wounded we had left at Bladensburg, and the attention and care they received from the Americans became the character of a civilized nation.

We reached our landing-place unmolested, and at our leisure embarked our army, which began to suffer very much from dysentery. A long sea voyage is the worst possible preparation for long and fatiguing marches. The men are fat, in no exercise, have lost the habit of wearing their accoutrements, packs, etc.—in short, they are not the same army they were on embarcation. Before our men left the Gironde, thirty miles a day would have been nothing to them.

General Ross, just before we went on board, sent for me (there never was a more kind or gallant soldier), and said, "Smith, the sooner I get my dispatch home the better. As you know, it is nearly ready, and as poor Falls, my A.D.C., is too unwell, it is my intention you should be the bearer of my dispatches, and that Falls should go home for the benefit of his health." This most unexpected arrangement set me on the *qui vive* indeed. I had not been in England for seven years. Wife, home, country, all rushed in my mind at once. The

General said, " A frigate is already ordered by the Admiral."

This day my information man, Calder the Leper, came to me, and told me that Brown had been taken and would be hung. I was much distressed. Although one cannot admire a traitor to his country, yet I was some degree of gratitude in his debt, and I said, " Well, Calder, but can we do nothing to save him ? " " Well, now I calculate that's not to be denied, and if I hear General Ross say, ' If I catch that rascal Brown, I will hang him like carrion,' he may be saved, for I would go at once among our people (they will not injure me), and I will swear I heard General Ross say so." I immediately went to the General. On the first view of the thing, his noble nature revolted at making an assertion he never intended to abide by. At length, however, to save the poor wretch's life, he consented, and in course of a desultory conversation with Calder, dovetailed the words required into it. I saw Calder catch at it. When he left the General's tent, he said to me, " Well, now, I calculate Brown may yet live many years." He left us that night with a purse of money and a long string of medical instructions for the benefit of his health from one of our surgeons. " Ah," says he, " this will save *me* " (meaning the medical advice) ; " I can save Brown." I had an hieroglyphical note from him brought by a slave, just before I sailed [30 ? Aug. 1814], to say " All's right, you may reckon." I told this story afterwards to the Prince Regent. He was exceedingly amused.

The *Iphigenia* frigate, Captain King, was to take me home, and Captain Wainwright of the *Tonnant* was to be the bearer of the naval dispatches. Sir Alexander Cochrane, Admiral Cockburn, and Evans, burning with ambition, had urged General Ross to move on Baltimore. The General was against it, and kindly asked my opinion. I opposed it, not by opinions or argument, but by a simple statement of facts.

" 1. We have, by a ruse, induced the enemy to concentrate all his means at Baltimore.

" 2. A *coup de main* like the conflagration of Washington may be effected once during a war, but can rarely be repeated.

" 3. The approach to Baltimore Harbour will be effectually obstructed." "Oh," says the General, "so the Admirals say; but they say that in one hour they would open the passage." I laughed. "It is easier said than done, you will see, General." (The passage defied their exertions when tested.)

" 4. Your whole army is a handful of men, and the half of them are sick from dysentery.

" 5. Your success in the attack on Washington is extraordinary, and will have a general effect. Your success on Baltimore would add little to that effect, admitting you were successful, which I again repeat I doubt, while a reverse before Baltimore would restore the Americans' confidence in their own power, and wipe away the stain of their previous discomfiture."

General Ross says, "I agree with you. Such is my decided opinion." "Then, sir, may I tell Lord Bathurst you will not go to Baltimore?" He said, "Yes." I was delighted, for I had a presentiment of disaster, founded on what I have stated.

The day we were to sail in the *Iphigenia*, as I left the *Tonnant*, kind-hearted General Ross, whom I loved as a brother, accompanied me to the gang-way. His most sensible and amiable wife was at Bath. I promised to go there the moment I had delivered my dispatches, and of course I was charged with a variety of messages. In the warmth of a generous heart he shook my hand, and said, "A pleasant voyage, dear Smith, and thank you heartily for all your exertions and the assistance you have afforded me. I can ill spare you." My answer was, "Dear friend, I will soon be back to you, and may I assure Lord Bathurst you will not attempt Baltimore?" "*You may*." These were the last words I ever heard that gallant soul utter. He was over-ruled: attempted Baltimore [12 Sept. 1814], failed, and lost his noble life. A more gallant and amiable man never existed, and one who, in the continuance of command, would have become a General of great ability. But few men, who from a Regiment to a Brigade are suddenly pushed into supreme authority and have a variety of conflicting considerations to cope with—Navy,

Army, country, resources, etc., are at the outset perfectly at home.

The *Iphigenia* had a most extraordinary passage from the Chesapeake to our anchorage at Spithead. We were only twenty-one days. The kindness I received from Captain King I shall never forget. The rapidity of our voyage was consonant to my feelings and in perfect accordance with my character.

CHAPTER XXI.

HARRY SMITH ONCE MORE IN ENGLAND—REUNION
WITH HIS WIFE IN LONDON—INTERVIEW WITH THE
PRINCE REGENT—DINNER AT LORD BATHURST'S—
A JOURNEY TO BATH—HARRY SMITH INTRODUCES
HIS WIFE TO HIS FATHER—VISIT TO WHITTLESEY
—HE RECEIVES ORDERS TO RETURN TO AMERICA
UNDER SIR EDWARD PAKENHAM.

WAINWRIGHT and I started from the George Inn,
Portsmouth, which I well knew, with four horses at
five o'clock. I do not know what he considered
himself, but I was of opinion that, as the bearer of
dispatches to Government, I was one of the greatest
men in England. Just before we started, our outfit
merchant and general agent, tailor, etc., by name
Meyers, who had been very civil to me going out
to South America, begged to speak to me. He
said, " I find the *Iphigenia* is from America, from
the Chesapeake: that little box under your arm
contains, I see, dispatches." " Well," I said, " what
of that?" " If you will tell me their general
purport, whether *good news* or *bad*, I will make
it worth your while, and you may secure some
pounds for a refit." At first I felt inclined to

P

knock him down. On a moment's reflexion I thought, "every one to his trade," so I compromised my feelings of indignation in rather a high tone of voice, and with " I'd see you d—— first; but of what use would such general information be to you ? " He, a knowing fellow, began to think *the pounds* were in my thoughts, so he readily said, " I could get a man on horseback in London two hours before you, and good news or bad on 'Change' is my object. Now do you understand ? " I said, " Perfectly, and when I return to America I shall expect a capital outfit from you for all the valuable information I have afforded you. Good-bye, Meyers."

Oh ! the delight of that journey. I made the boys drive a furiously good pace. D—— me, if I had rather be beating off a leeshore in a gale, tide against me ! The very hedgerows, the houses, the farms, the cattle, the healthy population all neatly clothed, all in occupation ; no naked slaves, no burned villages, no starving, wretched inhabitants, no trace of damnable and accursed war ! For seven years, an immense period in early life, I had viewed nothing beyond the seat of a war, a *glorious* war, I admit, but in that glory, death in its most various shapes, misery of nations, hardships, privations, wounds, and sickness, and their concomitants. The wild excitement bears a soldier happily through. My career had been a most fortunate one. Still the contrast around me was as striking as the first appearance of a white and clothed man

to a naked savage. The happy feeling of being in
my native land once more, in health and in possession of every limb, excited a maddening sensation
of doubt, anxiety, hope, and dread, all summed up
in this—"Does your young wife live? Is she
well?" Oh! the pain, the hope, the fear, and the
faith in Almighty God, who had so wonderfully
protected me, must have turned the brain if endur-
ance had continued, for I had never heard of her
since we parted.

At twelve o'clock we were in London, and
drove to Downing Street, where I lodged my dispatches; then we sought out a bivouac, I and poor
Falls. The navy man was off to the Admiralty.
Every inn was full near Downing Street, at least
where I desired to be. At last we got to the
Salopian Coffee-house in Parliament Street. The
waiter said, "One spare bedroom, sir; nothing
more." "Oh, plenty!" we said. We had been
feasting on the road on that indigenous-to-England
luxury of bread, butter, cream, and tea. All we
wanted was an hour or two's sleep, for, at that time
of night, as to finding any one, we might as well
have been back in America! The chambermaid
said, "Only one room, sir." "Plenty," we said.
"But only one bed, gentlemen!" "Plenty," we
said. "Bring up the portmanteau, West." When
we got to the room and proceeded (West and I) to
divide this copious bed into two by hauling half
the clothes on the floor, according to our custom
of seven years, the astonishment of the poor

chambermaid is not to be described. We bundled her out and were asleep before a minute.

By daylight I was in a hackney coach, and drove to the British (the Scotch) barracks of my old Rifle comrades. There I asked the porter the name of any officer he knew. At last he stammered out some. "Colonel Ross? What regiment?" says I. "He had a green jacket when he came up." I knew it was my dear friend John Ross. "Where is the room?" I said. "Oh, don't disturb the gentleman, sir; he is only just gone to bed." Says I, "My friend, I have often turned him out, and he shall quickly be broad awake now." He showed the room. In I bolted. "Halloa, Ross, stand to your arms." "Who the devil are you?" "Harry Smith," I said; "fall in." Our joy was mutual. "Well, but quiet, John; is my wife alive and well?" "All right, thank God, Harry, in every respect as you would wish. I was with her yesterday." "Where, John? where?" "In Panton Square, No. 11." It is difficult to decide whether excess of joy or of grief is the most difficult to bear; but seven years' fields of blood had not seared my heart or blunted my naturally very acute feelings, and I burst into a flood of tears. "Oh, thank Almighty God." Soon I was in Panton Square, with my hand on the window of the coach, looking for the number, when I heard a shriek, "Oh Dios, la mano de mi Enrique!" Never shall I forget that shriek; never shall I forget the effusion of our gratitude to God, as we held each other

in an embrace of love few can ever have known,
cemented by every peculiarity of our union and the
eventful scenes of our lives. Oh! you who enter
into holy wedlock for the sake of connexions—tame,
cool, amiable, good, I admit—you cannot feel what
we did. That moment of our lives was worth the
whole of your apathetic ones for years. We were
unbounded in love for each other, and in gratitude
to God for all His mercies. Poor little Pug was, in
her way, as delighted to see me as her more happy
mistress, and many an anecdote was told me of
her assisting by moaning pitifully when my wife
grieved aloud, as she was sometimes induced to do.

This happy reunion effected, I was off to Downing Street, where my Lord Bathurst received me in
the kindest manner, and said, "The intelligence
you bring is of such importance, the Prince Regent
desires to see you. We will go immediately." I
said, "My Lord, be so good as to allow me to take
the map I brought you." "It is here." And off we
started to Carlton House. We were shown into a
large room where Lord Bathurst fortunately left me
for half an hour, which enabled me somewhat to
allay my excited imagination and return to the
battlefields. I was soon deep in thought, when
a sort of modesty came over me at the idea of
approaching England's (*actual*) king. I gave my
head a toss, saying, "I never quailed before the
dear Duke of Wellington, with his piercing eye, nor
will I now, and General Ross begged of me to
talk;" for His Royal Highness, the story went,

complained that "the bearer of dispatches will never talk." Johnny Kincaid says I was an "impudent fellow." At any rate, I determined, if I saw His Royal Highness really desired me to be communicative, I would not be unready. While I was forming all sorts of plans for both attack and defence, in came Lord Bathurst: "The Prince will see you." So I said, "My Lord, if we were in camp, I could take your Lordship all about, but I know nothing of the etiquette of a court." So he says, "Oh, just behave as you would to any gentleman; His Highness's manner will soon put you at ease. Call him 'Sir,' and do not turn your back on him." "No," says I, "my Lord, I know that; and my profession is one of 'show a good front.'" In we went to the Prince's dressing-room, full of every sort of article of dress, perfumes, snuff-boxes, wigs, every variety of article, I do believe, that London could produce. His Highness rose in the most gracious manner, and welcomed me to his presence by saying, "General Ross strongly recommended you to my notice * as an officer who can afford me every information of the service you come to report, the importance of which is marked by the firing of the Parliament and Tower guns you now hear." I

* "FROM MAJOR-GENERAL ROSS TO EARL BATHURST.

"*Tonnant* in the Patuxent, Aug. 30, 1814.

"Captain Smith, assistant adjutant-general to the troops, who will have the honor to deliver this dispatch, I beg leave to recommend to your lordship's protection, as an officer of much merit and great promise, and capable of affording any further information that may be requisite" (Given in W. James's *Military Occurrences of the Late War* (1818), ii. p. 498).

could not refrain from smiling within myself at
Harry Smith of the Light Division sitting with the
Prince Regent, and all London in an uproar at the
news he brought. I was perfectly thunderstruck at
the military questions the Prince asked me. He
opened a map of America, and then referred to the
plan of Washington I had brought home, with the
public buildings burnt marked in red. He asked
the name of each, and in his heart I fancied I saw
he thought it a barbarian act. On all other topics
he spoke out. I said it was to be regretted a
sufficient force had not been sent to hold Washington. His Highness said, "What do you call a
sufficient force?" I said, "14,000 men." He
very shrewdly asked on what I based such an
opinion. I talked of Navy, of population, etc., and
perfectly satisfied His Highness I did not give
an opinion at random. He asked a variety of
questions, and laughed exceedingly when I told
him the anecdote of Calder's promising to save
Brown. When I got up to leave the room, and
was backing out, His Highness rather followed me,
and asked if I were any relation of his friend, Sir
—— Smith, in Shropshire. I said, "No." He
then said, "I and the country are obliged to you
all. Ross's recommendations will not be forgotten,
and, Bathurst, don't forget this officer's promotion."
It was the most gentlemanlike and affable interview
I could possibly imagine.

That evening I was to dine at Lord Bathurst's
at Putney. I never met a more amiable-mannered

man than Lord Bathurst; and his secretary, Punch Greville,* volunteered to drive me out in his tilbury. When I got into the drawing-room, who should be there but my dear friend Lord Fitzroy Somerset? He had been recently married. At dinner I sat between Lady Fitzroy and an elderly gentleman whose name I did not know, and, as the party was small, and I the lion, every one induced me to talk. Lord Fitzroy and I across the table got back into Spain; and, of course, as I regarded the Duke of Wellington as something elevated beyond any human being, and I was in high spirits, I did not hesitate to launch forth our opinion of him. The elderly gentleman who sat next me said, "I am very glad to hear you speak in such raptures of the Duke. He is my brother." I laughed, and said, "I have not exceeded in anything, to the best of my judgment." After dinner Lord Fitzroy Somerset and I had a long talk. He had travelled after Toulouse, in a little carriage from Bordeaux to Cadiz with the Duke, and their conversation frequently turned on the Army. Fresh are the words on my mind at this moment. "The Duke often said to me, 'The Light, 3rd and 4th Divisions were the *élite* of my army, but the Light had this peculiar perfection. No matter what was the arduous service they were employed on, when I rode up next day, I still found a *Division*. They never lost one half the men other Divisions did.'" I was delighted,

* Charles Cavendish Fulke Greville (1794-1865), Clerk to the Privy Council from 1821; author of the *Greville Memoirs;* known to his friends as Punch, or the Gruncher (*Dict. Nat. Biog.*).

for this was what we so prided ourselves on. I
have often heard our soldiers bullying one another
about the number such a Company had lost, always
attaching discredit to the loss. It was a peculiar
feeling, and one which actuated them throughout
the war, combined with the most undaunted bravery
and stratagem as sharpshooters.

But I must revert to domestic matters. My
wife had refused all the entreaties of my family to
leave London before my return. She availed herself
of masters, and saw so many friends daily. She
had a forcible impression that I should not be long
away. We started for Bath, and I wrote to my
father to come to London in a few days, and we
would return with him to Whittlesea. We found
poor Mrs. Ross in the highest spirits at the achievement of our arms under her husband. Poor thing!
at that very moment of her excessive happiness he
was in a soldier's bloody grave. The delight of
our journey to and from Bath is not to be described.
Everything was modern, novel, and amusing to my
wife: every trifle called forth a comparison with
Spain, although she admitted that there was no comparison between our inns and the Spanish *posadas*,
so accurately described in *Gil Blas*. No brutal railroads in those days, where all are flying prisoners.
We dined where we liked ; we did as we liked. At
the last stage back into London, my wife, in looking at
a newspaper (for she began to read English far better
than she spoke), saw my promotion to the rank of
Major—"The reward," she said, "of our separation."

On arrival in London we found my father had
arrived from the country. I had not seen him for
seven years. In this period *he* had been deprived
of his devoted wife, leaving him eleven children,
I, of a mother; for everything that word comprises
in its most comprehensive sense I had lost. Our
pleasure at meeting, as may be supposed, was
excessive, while we mingled our tears for the
departed. As my wife had just come off a journey,
and it was late in the afternoon, I would not show
her to my father until she was dressed for dinner:
a little bit of vanity and deception on my part, for I
led him to believe she was of the stiff Spanish school,
as stately as a swan and about as proud as a
peacock. She liked the fun of the deception, and
promised to dress in full Spanish costume, and act
up to the supposition. In she came, looking—oh!
if I could but describe her! but in place of acting
either the swan or the peacock, she bounded into
my father's arms, who cried like a child, between
joy, admiration, astonishment and delight at seeing
so young and beautiful a creature who had gone
through so much, and showed a heart evidently
framed for love. She was now nearly eighteen, but
a woman—not a girl, and certainly a person of most
distinguished appearance, especially in her Spanish
costume; not handsome, if beauty depends on
regularity of features, for she had the dark com-
plexion of the fairer part of her countrywomen, but
with a colour beneath the clearest skin of olive which
gave a lustre to her countenance—a countenance

illumined by a pair of dark eyes possessing all
the fire of a vivid imagination, and an expression
which required not the use of speech. Her figure
was beautiful, and never was any costume so
calculated to exhibit it in perfection and in all its
graces as that of her native land. She had a profusion of the darkest brown hair; teeth, though not
regular, as white as pearls; with a voice most silvery
and sweet in conversation, and she would sing the
melancholy airs and songs of constancy of her
country (so celebrated for them) with a power and
depth of voice and feeling peculiar to Spain. Her
foot and ankle were truly Spanish. She danced
beautifully. Thus it was that the natural grace of
her figure and carriage was developed, while the
incomparable elegance and simplicity of her manner
was a thing not to be forgotten, rarely to be met
with. Her pronunciation of English at this period
was most fascinating, and when she wanted a word,
the brilliancy and expression of the eye would supply
it. It flashed perpetually as she spoke, and filled up
the intervals her slight knowledge of our language
could not supply. She was animated and intelligent,
with a touching tone of confidence and gentleness
which made the hearer a willing listener to her
words, but still her meaning was supplied by her
vivid countenance. Such was the being my affectionate and kind-hearted father held locked in his
paternal embrace, the faithful wife of his son. They
were ever afterwards friends in every sense of the
word, and, as he was the best and boldest horseman

I ever saw in my life, and she could ride beautifully
and any horse, they were inseparable.   Poor " Old
Chap," my war horse, which, together with her
Andalusian " Tiny," I had sent to him, was dead,
but, the morning after our arrival at Whittlesea, we
were taken to the stall.   There was Tiny in *such*
condition !   The meeting between my wife and the
horse was, as she said, that of compatriots in a
foreign land.   It was rendered still more amusing
by the little pug and horse equally recognizing each
other, for many a day had Tiny carried Pug.   (My
dear little thorough-bred horse I had so cried
over* was still alive and fresh, but alas! I had
grown out of his memory.   He was standing in the
next stall, and had acquired the name of " Old
Jack.")   My wife let Tiny loose, to the alarm of my
father, who expected to see him fly off full speed
into his garden, which he prided himself on considerably.   To his astonishment, and to mine too
(for my father told me the groom could barely lead
him), she says, " Now don't make a noise, and he
will follow me like a dog," which he did into the
drawing-room, occasionally licking her hand or face
when she allowed him.   The saddle, however, was
soon on him, and, as if proud to show off that he
was broken in like a Mameluke's, she figured him
so that few Mamelukes, jerreed † in hand, could
have touched her with effect.

* See p. 158.
† Byron, *The Giaour :*

"Swift as the hurled on high jerreed,
  Springs to the touch his startled steed."

In the midst of [happiness] I had the most melancholy visit to pay to my mother's tomb. If ever souls on earth could commune, I was so fascinated by the hallowed spot, which contained all which I so adored from my infancy, my consoler, my counsellor, my guide to the holy hill of God, I really believed I heard her speak when I prayed over her head and again vowed my promises at parting. Oh! that she could have lived to know my elevation, my being the bearer of dispatches to our King, that she could have seen my wife, that she could have shared, Heaven bless her, in the happiness of her children around! This one blank was for the moment all I lacked. I consoled myself that while we were revelling on earth with every uncertainty before us, she, my mother, was in heaven, where I dare firmly believe she is, for God is gracious and bountiful.

On my return from that hallowed and sacred spot, I found letters from the Horse Guards. The first was to order me to London immediately, the next was to tell me what I little anticipated. General Ross, contrary to his own opinion and his promise, had attempted Baltimore [12 Sept.], failed, as I anticipated, and lost his gallant life from not following the dictates of his own good sense and ability. My dear friend Sir Edward Pakenham was appointed to succeed him. I was appointed A.A.G. to the increased force going out! I had been nearly three weeks under the paternal and hospitable roof—my only holiday for years—when that blighting word "separation" was again to be imparted to my faithful and adoring wife; and, cut off from all social ties of happiness and endearment, I was again immediately, in the very middle of winter, to encounter the stormy Atlantic and all the horrors of war in the distance. It is only a repetition of the former tale to talk of my poor wife's distress. It was agreed she was to accompany me to London, and my father was to bring her back; and twenty-four hours later, while brothers and sisters re-echoed each others' promises, and indeed feelings, of affection, we started back to London, with hearts as heavy as they were light coming down. I little thought then of what I had to go through, witness, and endure, but, if I had, my task would still have been to affect a cheerfulness in the prospect of more promotion which, I avow candidly, I did not feel. However, I was a soldier, and as much wedded to my profession and a sense of duty as any man, so I lit up my torch of hope and did all in my power to cheer and comfort her I so loved.

On our arrival in London I immediately went to poor dear Sir Edward Pakenham, who was delighted to see me, and said that we must be in Portsmouth in a few days, and that the *Statira* frigate was waiting for us. I then sought out Macdougall of the 85th, who before I left the Army had been acting, in place of sick Falls, as A.D.C. to poor Ross, and I readily learned all that occurred before the service lost that gallant soldier. My firm and faithful friend John Robb, surgeon of the 95th when I joined, was appointed Inspector-General of Hospitals, and he and I agreed to send our baggage by coach, and go down together to Portsmouth in a post chaise on Sunday afternoon, for the *Statira* was to sail on Monday.   Old West was started off per coach, and at three o'clock on Sunday, the — November, the horrible scene of parting was again to be endured.   It was less painful to me than the first, I admit, for my dear wife was now known and beloved by all my family; but to her the dread of separation, and separation for the exploits of war, was as painful as before, and, when I tore myself from her, which I was literally obliged to do, that heart must be hard indeed that was not, as mine was, ready to break.   I can see her now, with her head resting on the chimney-piece (as I left the room, and took a farewell glance) in a state bordering on despair.   My father, too, was awfully overcome.

In a few minutes I was rolling on my road to Portsmouth, deeply absorbed, I admit, but my companion Robb was a man of strong mind, of whom I had a high opinion, and not to appear desponding before him, I exerted all my energy and began to talk of my plans on my return.   Robb said—the only thing I ever heard him say that I thought would have been as well unsaid—"Oh, that's capital! a fellow going out to be killed by an American Rifleman, talking of what he will do when he comes back!"   Now, such is the perversity of human nature, this so put up my blood, that grief and anguish were mitigated in a determined spirit of opposition.

We arrived at the George at twelve at night, and found West, who reported all right. We found an order directing us to be on board by ten o'clock, as the ship would get under weigh at twelve, and we knew that our men of war are punctual fellows.

The next morning, at breakfast, we directed old West to parade our portmanteaus. My kit had increased just double, viz. I had now *two* portmanteaus. " Here they are, sir," says West. " Why, that is not mine, West!" He overhauled it, and soon agreed with me. We went to the coach; there was no other. So I opened it, and, to my horror, in place of my things, it contained the dirty linen of a Frenchman and his silk stockings and evening pantaloons, etc., etc. Upon a little inquiry from poor old West, we learned that two coaches were loading at the same time, one for Dover, the other for Portsmouth. It was evident, therefore, my red coats were in company with my French friend. In my portmanteau were all my boots, my uniform, and my flannel waistcoats. We were to embark immediately, and I had nothing for it but to go to my *friend,* and tell him, " Now's the time for the outfit: I have lost my portmanteau." He very kindly undertook to write to Charing Cross and send back the Frenchman's, and in three weeks after the failure at New Orleans my portmanteau

* See p. 209.

was sent out to me by my dear friend John Bell. It is a very odd coincidence that, on my first going abroad to South America, I lost my kit and all my large stock of silver given me by my poor mother —some teaspoons, etc.   On that occasion I never recovered anything.

CHAPTER XXII.

SAILS WITH SIR EDWARD PAKENHAM ON THE EXPE-
DITION AGAINST NEW ORLEANS—REVERSE OF
8 JANUARY, 1815, AND DEATH OF PAKENHAM—
SIR JOHN LAMBERT SUCCEEDS TO THE COMMAND,
APPOINTS HARRY SMITH HIS MILITARY SECRETARY,
AND WITHDRAWS THE FORCE.

WE soon reached our frigate, and oh, so crowded
as she was!—Sir Edward Pakenham and all his
Staff, the Commanders of the Engineers and Artillerymen with their Staff, and about thirty pas-
sengers! The most of us slept in cots in the
steerage. Young D'Este, the real Duke of Sussex,*
was a fund of great amusement, the most gentlemanlike, kind-hearted young fellow possible, affable
to a degree, and most unpretending; but he had a
thirst for obtaining information, I never beheld
before. Consequently he laid himself open to some
very peculiar replies to his queries. He proved
himself on shore, like all the royal family, a gallant

* Augustus Frederick (b. 1794), only son of Augustus Frederick,
Duke of Sussex (son of George III.), by his marriage with Lady
Augusta Murray. The two children of this marriage, when disinherited
by the Royal Marriage Act, took the name D'Este.

and intrepid soldier, and the best shot with a rifle
for a youth that I have almost ever seen.   He
attached himself passionately to me on board and on
shore, and if he ever became Elector of Hanover, I
was to have been his Secretary.

We had a very agreeable party of gallant old
Peninsular soldiers, and dear Sir Edward was one
of the most amusing persons imaginable—a high-
minded and chivalrous fellow in every idea, and,
to our astonishment, very devoutly inclined ; and
Major Gibbs, who was afterwards killed on the
same day as Sir Edward, was a noble fellow.

The *Statira* was a noble frigate ; she had a
full complement of men, and was in crack order,
having every individual on board but the individual
who had put her in—that Irish Captain Stackpoole,
of duelling celebrity, who had very shortly before
been shot in the West Indies by a Lieutenant of
another ship. on whom he saddled a quarrel originating in an occurrence when both were middies.
The Lieutenant denied all recollection of it to no
purpose.   Stackpoole insisted on his going out.
The Lieutenant, it was said, had never fired a pistol
in his life, but at the first shot Stackpoole fell dead.
I never saw a body of officers and men more
attached than these were to their last Captain.
Every one had some anecdote of his kindness and
ability as a seaman.   The propensity which cost
him his life can be attributed, I am firmly of opinion,
to nothing but a strain of insanity upon that particular subject alone.   His prowess as a shot with a

pistol, it was asserted, was inconceivable, but "the battle is not always to the strong."

On this voyage I had two opportunities of writing to my wife, or, rather, sending her the sheets of a sort of journal which she made me promise to keep. Our Captain, Swaine, a neighbour of mine in Cambridgeshire, was of the old school, and made everything snug at night by shortening sail, to the great amusement of poor Stackpoole's crew, accustomed to carry on night and day. But for this, we should have been off the mouth of the Mississippi at the time when Sir Edward was informed a fleet and his army would rendezvous for an assault on New Orleans. As it was, we did [not] reach the fleet until [25 Dec.] three days after the landing had been effected, and our army under Major-General Sir J. Keane, now Lord Keane (as noble a soldier as our country ever produced) had sustained a sharp night-attack. Stovin, the A.G., had been shot through the neck, and I was at the head of the department.

I never served under a man whose good opinion I was so desirous of having as Sir Edward Pakenham, and proud was I to find I daily succeeded. I was always with him, and usually lay in my cloak in his room. The second day after we reached General Keane [28 Dec.], the army was moved up to reconnoitre the enemy's position, or to attack, if we saw it practicable. I was that day delighted with Sir Edward : he evinced an animation, a knowledge of ground, of his own resources and the

strength of the enemy's position, which reminded us
of his brother-in-law, *our Duke.* The Staff were
very near the enemy's line, when I saw some riflemen evidently creeping down and not farther off
than a hundred yards, and so I very abruptly said,
" Ride away, Sir Edward, behind this bank, or you
will be shot in a second. By your action you will
be recognized as the Commander-in-Chief, and
some riflemen are now going to fire." The
American riflemen are very slow, though the most
excellent shots. My manner was so impressive he
came away. As we were returning that evening he
called me to him, and said, " You gentlemen of the
Craufurd school" (he was very fond of our old Light
Division) "are very abrupt and peremptory in your
manner to your Generals. Would you have spoken
to Craufurd as you did to me to-day ? " I said,
" Most certainly, for if I had not, and one of us had
been killed or wounded, and he became aware I
observed what I did when I spoke to you, he would
have blown me up as I deserved. He taught us
to do so." How my dear friend Sir Edward
laughed !

We soon found that, with our present force, the
enemy's position was impregnable. A Brigade was,
however, daily expected, under Sir J. Lambert. While
we were looking out with our telescopes, Sir Edward
turned very abruptly to me, and said, " Now for a
Light Division [opinion]. What do you say, Smith,
as to the practicability of an attack on the enemy's
line ? " I replied, " His position is strong—his left

being on an impracticable morass, his right on the
Mississippi; the ground is a dead flat, intersected
with ditches which will impede our troops. The
enemy has, literally, a breastwork, and plenty of
men upon it, and their fire will sweep the plain with
unerring precision, causing us great loss; for we can
produce no fire, flank or otherwise, to render them
uneasy or unsteady. As yet, the enemy has not
occupied the opposite bank of the river. He has
two armed vessels in the river. We must destroy
these as soon as possible, possess the right bank of
the Mississippi, enfilade the enemy's position with
our fire (the width of the river being only from
seven to eight hundred yards), and, so soon as we
open a fire from the right bank, we should storm
the work in two, three, or more columns." "You
Rifle gentlemen have learnt something, I do believe."
I did not know at the time whether he said this in
jest or not, for he was a most light-hearted fellow;
but, when we got back to the house we put up in,
he sent for me. He had a plan of the works and
position of the enemy before him, and said, " Smith,
I entirely [concur] in all you said in the field to-day.
In the meanwhile, we must facilitate our communications by roads in our rear, etc. I will erect
batteries and destroy the ships, and, when the
batteries are complete, they shall open on the
enemy. If they can destroy the enemy's defence
in any part, or silence the fire of his batteries, the
army shall storm at once. Lambert's arrival is very
uncertain." I remarked, if Lambert's arrival was

so uncertain, we had no alternative, and under any circumstances the ships must be destroyed and batteries erected, whether Lambert's force arrived or not.

We succeeded in destroying one ship—we *might have* destroyed both. We erected several batteries, their defences principally sugar-casks,—for here on the plain, on the banks of the Mississippi, if you dug eight inches, water followed: hence to erect batteries with earth was impracticable, and we had not sufficient sand-bags. The defences of our batteries, therefore, were reported complete on the night of the 31st December. The army was formed into two columns of attack—one threatening the right flank, the other the left, and a party was hid in the reeds in the morass on the enemy's left flank with orders to penetrate, if possible, and disturb the enemy's left.

At daybreak on the 1st of January, 1815, our troops were formed, and our batteries opened. They had not the slightest effect on the enemy. On the contrary, his shot went through the imperfect defence, caused our noble artillerymen great loss, and silenced our batteries. Hence there was no attack, and Sir Edward still more strenuously adhered to the necessity of occupying the right bank of the river. The troops were withdrawn, except such strong picquets as were left to protect the guns in the [batteries].

Poor Sir Edward was much mortified at being obliged to retire the army from a second demonstration and disposition to attack, but there was nothing for it. It came on to rain in the evening, and was both wet and cold. Sir Edward slept in a little house in advance of his usual quarters. He told me to stay with him, and all his Staff to return to the usual house. He said, "Smith, those guns must be brought back; go and do it." I said, "It will require a great many men." "Well," he says, "take 600 from Gibbs's Brigade." Off I started. The soldiers were sulky, and neither the 21st nor the 44th were distinguished for discipline—certainly not of the sort I had been accustomed to. After every exertion I could induce them to make, I saw I had no chance of success—to my mortification, for to return and say to Sir Edward I could not effect it, was as bad as the loss of a leg. However, the night was wearing, and my alternative decided; so I told him as quietly as I could. He saw I was mortified, and said nothing, but jumped up in his cloak, and says, "Be so good as to order my horse, and go on and turn out Gibbs's whole Brigade quietly." They were under arms by the time he arrived, and by dint of exertion and his saying, "I am Sir Edward Pakenham, etc., and Commander-in-Chief," as well as using every expression to induce officers and soldiers to exertion, just as daylight appeared he had completed the task, and the Brigade returned to its ground. As we were riding back Sir Edward said, "You see, Smith, exertion and determination will effect anything." I was cruelly mortified, and said, "Your excitement, your name, your energy, as Commander-in-Chief with a whole Brigade, most certainly has done that which I failed in with 600 men, but I assure you, Sir Edward, I did all I could." His noble heart at once observed my misery. He said, " I admire your mortification; it shows your zeal. Why *I* barely effected, with all the exertion of the Commander-in-Chief, and, as you say, a Brigade, what I expected you to do with one-fourth of the men!" He might have added, "and I did with some of the guns what you dare not even recommend to me." Oh, how I was comforted! To fall in his estimation would have been worse than death by far.

In a day or two we had information that Lambert's Brigade, the 7th Fusiliers and the 43rd Foot, [had arrived]. Two such Corps would turn the tide of a general action. We were rejoiced! Sir Edward then made preparations to cross the river, and so to widen a little stream as to get the boats into the Mississippi. The story has been too often told to repeat. Lambert's Brigade landed, and, upon a representation made to Sir Edward by Major Sir G. Tylden, who was an Assistant Adjutant-General like myself, but a senior officer (as kind a fellow as ever lived), that, in Stovin's incapacity from his wound, he must be at the head of the Adjutant-General's Department, Sir Edward sent for me. "Smith," he said, "it was my intention you should have remained with me, Tylden with Lambert; but he claims his right as senior officer. You would not wish me to do an unjust thing when the claim is preferred?" I said, with my heart in my mouth, "Certainly not, sir." (I do believe I was more attached to Sir Edward, as a soldier, than I was to John Colborne, *if possible*.) "You must, therefore, go to Lambert. I will [enter] this arrangement in Orders; but, rely on it, I shall find enough for you and him to do too."

The night of the 7th January, the rivulet (or bayou, as then called) was reported dammed, and the boats above the dam ready for the banks of the Mississippi to be cut. The water within the banks was higher than the level of the water in the bayou, consequently so much water must be let into the bayou as to provide for the level. In the meanwhile, the enemy had not been asleep. They had been apprised of our operations to establish ourselves on the right bank; they had landed the guns from the second ship (which we ought to have destroyed), and were respectably in possession of that which we must turn them out of. Sir Edward Pakenham went to inspect the bayou, the boats, etc. I heard him say to the engineer, "Are you satisfied the dam will bear the weight of water which will be upon it when the banks of the river are cut?" He said, "Perfectly." "I should be far more so if a second dam was constructed." The engineer was positive. After dark the banks were cut, the dam went as Sir Edward seemed to anticipate, and the delay in repairing it prevented the boats being got into the river in time for the troops under Colonel Thornton of the 85th to reach their ground and make a simultaneous attack with the main body, according to the plan arranged. Sir John Lambert's Brigade, the *élite* 7th Fusiliers and 43rd, were in reserve. Sir Edward said, " Those fellows would storm anything, but, indeed, so will the others, and when we are in New Orleans, I can depend upon Lambert's Reserve." We were all formed in three columns [8 Jan.], about 6000 British soldiers and some sailors: a column under Colonel Renny of the 21st were destined to proceed on the banks of the river and right of the enemy, and carry a powerful battery which enfiladed the whole position : General Keane's Brigade was to assail the enemy's right-central position : General Gibbs's Brigade to attack well upon the enemy's left : General Lambert's Brigade to be in reserve nearer Gibbs's Brigade than Keane's.

About half an hour before daylight, while I was with General Lambert's column, standing ready, Sir Edward Pakenham sent for me. I was soon with him. He was greatly agitated. " Smith, most Commanders-in-Chief have many difficulties to contend with, but surely none like mine. The dam, as you heard me say it would, gave way, and Thornton's people will be of no use whatever to the general attack." I said, " So impressed have you ever been, so obvious is it in every military point of view, we should possess the right bank of the river, and thus enfilade and divert the attention of the enemy ; there is still time before daylight to retire the columns now. We are under the enemy's fire so soon as discovered." He says, "This may be, but I have twice deferred the attack. We are strong in numbers now comparatively. It will cost more men, and the assault must be made." I again urged delay. While we were talking, the streaks of daylight began to appear, although the morning was dull, close, and heavy, the clouds almost touching the ground. He said, "Smith, order the rocket to be fired." I again ventured to plead the cause of delay. He said, and very justly, "It is now too late : the columns would be visible to the enemy before they could move out of fire, and would lose more men than it is to be hoped they will in the attack. Fire the rocket, I say, and go to Lambert." This was done. I had reached Lambert just as the stillness of death and anticipation (for I really believe the enemy was aware of our proximity to their position) [was broken by the firing of the rocket]. The rocket was hardly in the air before a rush of our troops was met by the most murderous and destructive fire of all arms ever poured upon column. Sir Edward Pakenham galloped past me with all his Staff, saying, "That's a terrific fire, Lambert." I knew nothing of my General then, except that he was a most gentlemanlike, amiable fellow, and I had seen him lead his Brigade at Toulouse in the order of a review of his Household Troops in Hyde Park.* I said, "In twenty-five

* Sir J. Lambert was always in the Guards, and prided himself on being Adjutant of the Grenadier Guards, as his eldest son now is.— H.G.S. (1844).

minutes, General, you will command the Army.
Sir Edward Pakenham will be wounded and
incapable, or killed. The troops do not get on a
step. He will be at the head of the first Brigade
he comes to, and what I say will occur." A few
seconds verified my words. Tylden came wildly up
to tell the melancholy truth, saying, "Sir Edward
Pakenham is killed. You command the Army, and
your Brigade must move on immediately." I said,
"If Sir Edward Pakenham is killed, Sir John
Lambert commands, and will judge of what is to be
done." I saw the attack had irretrievably failed.
The troops were beat back, and going at a tolerable
pace too; so much so, I thought the enemy had
made a sortie in pursuit, as so overpowering a
superiority of numbers would have induced the
French to do. "May I order your Brigade, sir, to
form line to cover a most irregular retreat, to apply
no other term to it, until you see what has actually
occurred to the attacking columns?" He assented,
and sent me and other Staff Officers in different
directions to ascertain our condition. It was
(summed up in few words) that every attack had
failed; the Commander-in-Chief and General Gibbs
and Colonel Renny killed; General Keane, most
severely wounded; and the columns literally
destroyed. The column for the right bank were
seen to be still in their boats, and not the slightest
impression had been made on the enemy.

Never since Buenos Ayres had I witnessed a
reverse, and the sight to our eyes, which had

looked on victory so often, was appalling indeed. Lambert desired me, and every Staff Officer he could get hold of, to go and reform the troops, no very easy matter in some cases. However, far to the rear, they (or, rather, what were left) were formed up, Sir John meanwhile wondering whether, under all the circumstances, he ought to attack. He very judiciously saw that was impossible, and he withdrew the troops from under a most murderous fire of round shot. Soon after this we heard the attack on the right bank, which succeeded easily enough. The extent of our loss was ascertained : one-third.

The Admirals came to the outlying picquet-house with faces as long as a flying jib: a sort of Council of War was held. I had been among the troops to find out how the pluck of our soldiers [stood]. Those who had received such an awful beating and been so destroyed were far from desirous to storm again. The 7th and 43rd, whose loss had been trifling, were ready for anything, but their veteran and experienced eyes told them affairs were desperate. One Admiral, Coddrington, whose duty as Captain of the Field was to have seen it supplied with provisions, said, " The troops must attack or the whole will be starved." I rather saucily said, " Kill plenty more, Admiral ; fewer rations will be required." A variety of opinions were agitated. I could observe what was passing in Sir J. Lambert's mind by the two or three remarks he made. So up I jumped, and said,

"General, the army are in no state to renew the attack. If success now attended so desperate an attempt, we should have no troops to occupy New Orleans ; our success even would defeat our object, and, to take an extreme view, which every soldier is bound to do, our whole army might be the sacrifice of so injudicious an assault." A thick fog was coming on. I said, "We know the enemy are three times our number. They will endeavour immediately to cut off our troops on the right bank, and we may expect an attack in our front. The fog favours us, and Thornton's people ought to be brought back and brought into our line. The army is secure, and no farther disaster is to be apprehended." The General was fully of my opinion, as was every officer of experience. I think my noble friend, "fighting MacDougall," was the only one for a new fight. That able officer, Sir A. Dickson, was sent to retire Thornton, and, thanks to the fog, he succeeded in doing so unmolested, though, at the very time our people were crossing the river, a powerful body of the enemy (as I had supposed they would) were crossing to dislodge Thornton ; and the woods on the right bank so favoured their species of warfare, that Thornton would have met the fate he did at Bladensburg but for Lambert's cool judgment. This was my view of the position then, and it is now.

The number of wounded was three times what the Inspector-General Robb was told to calculate on, but never did officer meet the difficulties of his position with greater energy, or display greater resources within himself. He was ably assisted in the arrangements of boats, etc., by that able sailor, Admiral Malcolm, and I firmly assert not a wounded soldier was neglected.

Late in the afternoon I was sent to the enemy with a flag of truce, and a letter to General Jackson, with a request to be allowed to bury the dead and bring in the wounded lying between our respective positions. The Americans were not accustomed to the civility of war, like our old *associates* the French, and I was a long time before I could induce them to receive me. They fired on me with cannon and musketry, which excited my choler somewhat, for a round shot tore away the ground under my right foot, which it would have been a bore indeed to have lost under such circumstances. However, they did receive me at last, and the reply from General Jackson was a very courteous one.

After the delivery of the reply to General Lambert, I was again sent out with a fatigue party —a pretty large one too—with entrenching tools to bury the dead, and some surgeons to examine and bring off the wounded. I was received by a rough fellow—a Colonel Butler, Jackson's Adjutant-General. He had a drawn sword, and no scabbard. I soon saw the man I had to deal with. I outrode the surgeon, and I apologized for keeping him waiting; so he said, " Why now, I calculate as your doctors are tired; they have plenty to do to-day."

There was an awful spectacle of dead, dying, and wounded around us. "*Do?*" says I, "why this is nothing to us Wellington fellows! The next brush we have with you, you shall see how a Brigade of the Peninsular army (arrived yesterday) will serve you fellows out with the bayonet. They will lie piled on one another like round shot, if they will only stand." "Well, I calculate you must get at 'em first." "But," says I, "what do you carry a drawn sword for?" "Because I reckon a scabbard of no use so long as one of you Britishers is on our soil. We don't wish to shoot you, but we must, if you molest our property; we have thrown away the scabbard."

By this time our surgeon had arrived. There were some awful wounds from cannon shot, and I dug an immense hole, and threw nearly two hundred bodies into it. To the credit of the Americans not an article of clothing had been taken from our dead except the shoes. Every body was straightened, and the great toes tied together with a piece of string. A more appalling spectacle cannot well be conceived than this common grave, the bodies hurled in as fast as we could bring them. The Colonel, Butler, was very sulky if I tried to get near the works. This scene was not more than about eighty yards away from them, and, had our fellows rushed on, they would not have lost one half, and victory would have been ours. I may safely say there was not a vital part of man in which I did not observe a mortal wound, in many bodies there were three

R

or four such ; some were without heads ; there were
others, poor fellows, whom I recognized. In this part
of America there were many Spaniards and Frenchmen. Several soldiers and officers gathered round
me, and I addressed them in their own language.
Colonel Butler became furious, but I would not
desist for the moment, and said, " The next time
we meet, Colonel, I hope to receive you to bury
your dead." "Well, I calculate you have been on
that duty to-day," he said. God only knows I
had, with a heavy heart. It was apparently light
enough before him, but the effort was a violent
one.

At night it was General Lambert's intention to
withdraw his line more out of cannon shot, for we
were on a perfect plain, not a mound as cover, and
I and D'Este (His Royal Highness, as I used to
call him) were sent to bring back Blakeney's Brigade.
Blakeney was as anxious a soldier in the dark as
he was noble and gallant when he saw his enemy.
He would fain induce me to believe I did not know
my road. I got all right, though, with the aid of
D'Este, who, if the war had lasted, would have made
as able a soldier as his ancestor George the Second.
I did not regard myself, though, as Marlborough, who
was little employed on any retiring duty.

That night I lay down in my cloak, in General
Lambert's room, at twelve o'clock, so done that all
care or thought was banished in sleep. Before daylight [9 Jan.] I awoke to the horror of the loss of the
man I so loved, admired, and esteemed, and to the

feelings of a soldier under such melancholy circumstances. Those feelings could be but momentary. It was my duty to jump on my horse and see what was going on at our post, which I did, after returning Almighty God thanks. Thence to the hospital to render the Inspector whatever aid he required in orderlies, etc. Robb deserved and received the highest encomiums for the arrangements, which secured every care to our wounded.

In returning from the outposts, I met General Lambert. Upon my assuring him everything was perfectly quiet, he said, "I will now ride to the hospital." "I was just going there, sir, and will ride with you." The General said, "You must have been pretty well done last night, for I did not see you when I lay down." "Yes, I had a long day, but we Light Division fellows are used to it." "Smith, that most amiable man and cool and collected soldier, Secretary Wylly, will take home the dispatches of the melancholy disaster, and of the loss of his General and patron, and I offer for your acceptance my Military Secretaryship." I laughed, and said, "Me, sir! I write the most illegible and detestable scrawl in the world." "You can, therefore," he mildly said, "the more readily decipher mine. Poor Pakenham was much attached to you, and strongly recommended you to me." I had borne up well on my loss before, but I now burst into a flood of tears, with—"God rest his gallant soul." From that moment to the present, dear General Lambert has ever treated me as one of

his own family. Our lamented General's remains
were put in a cask of spirits and taken home by his
Military Secretary, Wylly, who sailed in a few days
with dispatches of no ordinary character—a record
of lamentable disaster, and anything but honour to
our military fame.

It was resolved to re-embark the army, and
abandon the idea of further operations against the
city of New Orleans, for the enemy had greatly
added to his strength in men and works on both
banks of the river.   This decision was come to
although we were expecting reinforcements, the
40th and 27th Regiments, and that noble soldier,
Sir Manley Power. The enemy continually cannon-
aded our position, and caused us some loss. We
were obliged, however, to maintain an advance
position to cover effectually the embarcation of all
the impedimenta, etc., invariably giving out as a
ruse that we were only disencumbering ourselves
of wounded, sick, etc.

I was sent in, also, with a flag of truce to
propose an exchange of prisoners. Two Companies
of the 21st Regiment and many of our Riflemen
had crowned the works, and, not being supported
by the rush of the column, of course were taken
prisoners. (It was all very well to victimize * old
Mullins †; the fascines, ladders, etc., could have been
supplied by one word which I will not name,‡ or

---

* *I.e.* make a scapegoat of.

† Colonel Mullins was blamed for not having the ladders and
fascines ready.

‡ Pluck?

how could these two Companies have mounted the works ?) Similarly we had several men of theirs taken the night the enemy attacked General Keane.*

In the negotiations for this exchange I was always met by a Mr. Lushington, General Jackson's Military Secretary, a perfect gentleman, and a very able man. He was well known in London, having been Under Secretary of the Legation. I never had to deal with a more liberal and clear-headed man. His education had not been military, however, and in conversation, by questions, etc., I always induced him to believe we had no intention of abandoning our attempts. On the afternoon when our prisoners were mutually delivered, I said, "We shall soon meet in New Orleans, and after that in London." He was evidently impressed with the idea that we meant to attack again, and I led him to the supposition that a night attack would succeed best. We parted excellent friends, and shook hands, and many notes of courtesy passed between us afterwards.

So soon as it was dark [18 Jan.] our troops began to move off, and about twelve o'clock all were well off the ground, and the picquets were

---

* After that attack I have always been of opinion that General Keane should have occupied the narrow neck of land behind the deep ditch which ran across from the river to the morass, and was afterwards (but then not at all) so strongly fortified by the enemy. I admit there were many, very many objections, but I still maintain there were more important reasons for its occupation, since our Army had been shoved into such a position, for, to begin from the beginning, it ought never to have gone there.--H.G.S.

retired. As we were so engaged, the enemy heard us, and in a moment opened a fire along their line, evidently under the belief that our night attack was actually about to be made. We retired, up to our necks in mud, through a swamp to our boats, and the troops and stores, etc. were all embarked in three days without interruption, or any attempt whatever, on the part of the enemy.

Thus ended the second awful disaster in America it had been my lot to be associated with—Buenos Ayres and New Orleans. In the circumstances of both, many military errors may be traced. But in the case of Buenos Ayres, White-lock is more abused than he merits. General Leveson-Gower was the great culprit; an overbearing, disobedient man, whose first disobedience, like Adam's, entailed the misfortune. He was ordered, when advancing on Buenos Ayres, not to engage the enemy before it was invested. He did engage, beat them, and might, in the *melée*, have possessed the city. That he neglected, and he ought to have been dismissed our service, probably with greater justice than Whitelock, whose orders were wantonly disobeyed, and the Church of San Domingo shamefully surrendered. Had it been held, as it might, it would have enabled Whitelock, from the base of his other success, to have made an attempt either to rescue the force in San Domingo, or again to have moved against the city. Whitelock's plan of attack was injudicious, too many columns, no weight and ensemble, and when he knew the city was fortified at every street, he should have effected regular lodgments and pushed forward from their base. The troops behaved most gallantly.

Poor dear Sir Edward Pakenham, a hero, a soldier, a man of ability in every sense of the word, had to contend with every imaginable difficulty, starting with the most unwise and difficult position in which he found the Army. By perseverance, determination, and that gallant bearing which so insures confidence, he overcame all but one, which he never anticipated, a check to the advance of British soldiers when they ought to have rushed forward. There was no want of example on the part of officers. The fire, I admit, was the most murderous I ever beheld before or since; still two Companies were successful in the assault, and had our heaviest column rushed forward in place of halting to fire under a fire fifty times superior, our national honour would not have been tarnished, but have gained fresh lustre, and one of the ablest generals England ever produced saved to his country and his friends.

In General Lambert's dispatches he was good enough to mention me.*

---

* "From MAJOR-GENERAL LAMBERT to EARL BATHURST.

"His Majesty's Ship *Tonnant*, off Chandeleur's Island,
"January 28, 1815.

"Major Smith, of the 95th Regiment, now acting as Military Secretary, is so well known for his zeal and talents, that I can with great truth say that I think he possesses every qualification to render him hereafter one of the brightest ornaments of his profession."

CHAPTER XXIII.

CAPTURE OF FORT BOWYER—DISEMBARCATION ON ILE DAUPHINE—END OF THE AMERICAN WAR— VISIT TO HAVANA AND RETURN-VOYAGE TO ENGLAND—NEWS OF NAPOLEON'S RETURN TO POWER — HARRY SMITH AT HIS HOME AT WHITTLESEY.

AFTER the Army was somewhat refreshed, an attempt on Mobile was resolved on, for which purpose the fleet went down to the mouth of Mobile Bay. Here there was a wooden fort of some strength, Fort Bowyer, which some time previously had sunk one of two small craft of our men-of-war which were attempting to silence it. It was necessary that this fort should be reduced in order to open the passage of the bay. It was erected on a narrow neck of land easily invested, and required only a part of the army to besiege it. It was regularly approached, and when our breaching batteries were prepared to burn or blow it to the devil, I was sent to summon it to surrender. The Americans have no particular respect for flags of truce, and all my Rifle education was required to protect myself from being rifled and to procure a

reception of my flag.   After some little time I was
received, and, upon my particular request, admitted
into the fort, to the presence of Major Lawrence,
who commanded, with five Companies, I think, of
the 2nd Regiment.   I kept a sharp look-out on the
defences, etc., which would not have resisted our
fire an hour.   The Major was as civil as a vulgar
fellow can be.   I gave him my version of his
position, and cheered him on the ability he had
displayed.   He said, " Well, now, I calculate you
are not far out in your reckoning.   What do you
advise me to do ?   You, I suppose, are one of
Wellington's men, and understand the rules in
these cases."   " This," I said, " belongs to the rule
that the weakest goes to the wall, and if you do not
surrender at discretion in one hour, we, being the
stronger, will blow up the fort and burn your
wooden walls about your ears.   All I can say is,
you have done your duty to your country, and no
soldier can do more, or resist the overpowering
force of circumstances."   " Well, if you were in
my situation, you would surrender, would you ? "
" Yes, to be sure."   " Well, go and tell your
General I will surrender to-morrow at this hour,
provided I am allowed to march out with my arms
and ground them outside the fort."   " No," I said,
" I will take no such message back.   My General,
in humanity, offers you terms such as he can alone
accept, and the blood of your soldiers be on your
own head."   He said, " Well, now, don't be hasty."
I could see the Major had some hidden object in

view. I said, therefore, "Now, I tell you what message I will carry to my General. You open the gates, and one of our Companies will take possession of it immediately, and a body of troops shall move up close to its support; then you may remain inside the fort until to-morrow at this hour, and ground your arms on the glacis." I took out pen and ink, wrote down my proposition, and said, "There, now, sign directly and I go." He was very obstinate, and I rose to go, when he said, "Well, now, you are hard upon me in distress." "The devil I am," I said. "We might have blown you into the water, as you did our craft, without a summons. Good-bye." "Well, then, give me the pen. If I must, so be it;" and he signed. His terms were accepted, and the 4th Light Company took possession of the gate, with orders to rush in in case of alarm. A supporting column of four hundred men were bivouacked close at hand with the same orders, while every precaution was taken, so that, if any descent were made from Mobile, we should be prepared, for, by the Major's manner and look under his eyebrows, I could see there was no little cunning in his composition. We afterwards learned that a force was embarked at Mobile, and was to have made a descent *that very night*, but the wind prevented them. We were, however, perfectly prepared, and Fort Bowyer was ours.

The next day [12 Feb.] the Major marched out and grounded his arms. He was himself received very kindly on board the *Tonnant*, and his officers were disposed of in the Fleet. The fellows looked very like French soldiers, for their uniforms were the same, and much of the same cut as to buttons, belts, and pipe-clay.

In a few days after the capture of this fort the *Brazen* sloop-of-war arrived with dispatches [14 Feb.]. The preliminaries of peace were signed, and only awaited the ratification of the President, and until this was or was not effected, hostilities were to cease. We were all happy enough, for we Peninsular soldiers saw that neither fame nor any military distinction could be acquired in this species of milito-nautico-guerilla-plundering-warfare. I got a letter from my dear wife, who was in health and composure, with my family all in love with her, and praying of course for my safe return, which she anticipated would not be delayed, as peace was certain. I for my part was very ready to return, and I thanked Almighty God from my heart that such fair prospects were again before me, after such another series of wonderful escapes.

Pending the ratification, it was resolved to disembark the whole army on a large island at the entrance of Mobile Bay, called Isle Dauphine.* This was done. At first we had great

* Cope's order of events (p. 192) is as follows : Disembarcation of troops on Ile Dauphine, Feb. 8 ; surrender of Fort Bowyer, Feb. 11 ; arrival of news of the preliminaries of peace, Feb. 14. According to the text, the disembarcation on Ile Dauphine would appear to have followed the peace-news. There is no inconsistency, however. Only one Brigade (the 4th, 21st, and 44th Regiments) was employed in reducing Fort Bowyer. This Brigade disembarked on Ile Dauphine after the capture of the Fort, the rest of the army having disembarked previously.

difficulty in getting anything like fresh provisions; but, as the sea abounded with fish, each regiment rigged out a net, and obtained a plentiful supply. Then our biscuit ran short. We had abundance of flour, but this began to act on the men and produce dysentery. The want of ovens alone prevented our making bread. This subject engrossed my attention for a whole day, but on awakening one morning a sort of vision dictated to me, "There are plenty of oyster-shells, and there is sand. Burn the former and make mortar, and construct ovens." So I sent on board to Admiral Malcolm to send me a lot of hoops of barrels by way of a framework for my arch. There was plenty of wood, the shells were burning, the mortar soon made, my arch constructed, and by three o'clock there was a slow fire in a very good oven on the ground. The baker was summoned, and the paste was made, ready to bake at daylight. The Admiral, dear Malcolm, and our Generals were invited to breakfast, but I did not tell even Sir John Lambert why I had asked a breakfast-party. He only laughed and said, "I wish I could give them a good one!" Oh, the anxiety with which I and my baker watched the progress of our exertions! We heard the men-of-war's bells strike eight o'clock. My breakfast-party was assembled. I had an unusual quantity of salt beef and biscuit on the table, the party was ready to fall to, when in I marched at the head of a column of loaves and rolls, all piping hot and as light as bread should be.

The astonishment of the Admiral was beyond all belief, and he uttered a volley of monosyllables at the idea of a soldier inventing anything. Oh, how we laughed and ate new bread, which we hadn't seen for some time! At first the Admiral thought I must have induced his steward to bake me the bread as a joke, when I turned to Sir John and said, " Now, sir, by this time to-morrow every Company shall have three ovens, and every man his pound and a half of bread." I had sent for the Quartermasters of Corps ; some started difficulties, but I soon removed them. One said, "Where are we to get all the hoops ? " This was, I admit, a puzzle. I proposed to make the arch for the mortar of wood, when a very quick fellow, Hogan, Quartermaster of the Fusiliers, said, " I have it : make a bank of sand, plaster over it ; make your oven ; when complete, scratch the sand out." In a camp everything gets wind, and Harry Smith's ovens were soon in operation all over the island. There were plenty of workmen, and the morrow produced the bread.

The officers erected a theatre, and we had great fun in various demi-savage ways. Bell, the Quartermaster-General, dear noble fellow, arrived, and a Major Cooper, and, of some importance to me, my stray portmanteau. I was half asleep one morning, rather later than usual, having been writing the greater part of the night, when I heard old West say, " Sir, sir." " What's the matter ? " " Thank the Lord, you're alive."

"What do you mean, you old ass?" "Why, a navigator has been going round and round your tent all night; here's a regular road about the tent." He meant an alligator, of which there were a great many on the island. The young ones our soldiers used to eat. I tasted a bit once; the meat was white, and the flavour like coarsely-fed pork.

In this very tent I was writing some very important documents for my General; the sandflies had now begun to be very troublesome, and that day they were positively painful. I ever hated tobacco, but a thought struck me, a good volume of smoke would keep the little devils off me. I called my orderly, a soldier of the 43rd, and told old West, who chawed a pound a day at least, to give him plenty of tobacco, and he was to make what smoke he could, for of two evils this was by far the least. The old Peninsular soldiers off parade were all perfectly at home with their officers, and he puffed away for a long time while I was writing, he being under my table. After a time he put his head out with a knowing look, and said, "If you please, sir, this is drier work than in front of Salamanca, where water was not to be had, and what's more, no grog neither." I desired West to bring him both rum and water. "Now, your honour, if you can write as long as I can smoke, you'll write the history of the world, and I will kill all the midges."

The ratification at length arrived [5 March], and the army was prepared to embark. Sir John Lambert, Baynes his Aide-de-camp, and I were to go home in the *Brazen* sloop-of-war, with a Captain Stirling, now Sir James, who was ultimately the founder of the Swan River Settlement. A more perfect gentleman or active sailor never existed : we have been faithful friends ever since. As many wounded as the *Brazen* could carry were embarked, and we weighed with one of our noble men-of-war.

As soon as the word was given, we sailed to the Havannah for fresh provisions. We spent a merry week there, when Stirling and I were inseparable. We were all *fêted* at the house of a Mr. Drake, nominally a wealthy merchant, but actually in every respect a prince. I never saw a man live so superbly. He put carriages at our disposal ; one for Sir John Lambert, and one for me and Stirling. He was married to a Spanish woman, a very ladylike person, who played and sang beautifully. I could speak Spanish perfectly, and the compatriot connexion I told her and her maiden sisters of made us friends at once. My spare time, however, was spent in the house of the Governor, Assuduco, who had a daughter so like my wife in age, figure, etc., and speaking English about as much as she could, I was never so much amused as in her society ; and my wife and she corresponded afterwards. We stayed in the Havannah a week, and the public drives brought us all back again to the Prado of Madrid. Although the beauty of the ladies of the capital was wanting, the costumes were equally elegant.

The celebrated Woodville, the cigar manufacturer, asked us to a public breakfast at his house, four or five miles out of the city. He was about six feet two, as powerful a man as I ever saw ; his hair in profusion, but as white as snow ; the picture of health, with a voice like thunder. He was rough, but hospitable, and after breakfast showed us the various processes of his manufactory, and the number of hands each went through. "Now," says he, "Sir John, I have another sight to show you, which few men can boast of.". With his fingers in his mouth, he gave a whistle as loud as a bugle, when out ran from every direction a lot of children, of a variety of shades of colour, all looking happy and healthy. Not one appeared above twelve or thirteen. "Ah," he said, "report says, and I believe it, they are every one of them my children." "Count them," he said to me. I did ; there were forty-one. I thought Stirling and I would have died of laughing. Sir John Lambert, one of the most amiable and moral men in the world, said so mildly, "A very large family indeed, Mr. Woodville," that it set Stirling and me off again, and the old patriarch joined in the laugh, with, "Ah, the seed of Abraham would people the earth indeed, if every one of his descendants could show *my* family."

After a week of great amusement we sailed from Havana. The harbour and entrance are perfectly beautiful : the works most formidable, but the Spaniards would not let us inside. Sailing into the harbour is like entering a large gateway ; the sails are almost within reach of the Moro rock, and there is a swell setting into the harbour, which gives the ship a motion, as if every wave would dash her on the Moro.

In the Gulf of Florida we encountered a most terrific gale, wind and current at variance, and oh, such a sea! We lay to for forty-eight hours; we could not cook, and the main deck was flooded. Sir John and I never got out of our cots : he perfectly good-humoured on all occasions, and always convincing himself, and endeavouring to convince us, that the gale was abating. The third morning Stirling came to my cot. "Come, turn out; you will see how I manage my craft. I am going to make sail, and our lubberly cut may set us on our beam-ends, or sink us altogether." A delightful prospect, indeed. He was and is a noble seaman, all animation, and he was so clear and decided in his orders ! Sail was made amid waves mountains high, and the *Brazen*, as impudent a craft as ever spurned the mighty billows, so beautifully was she managed and steered, rode over or evaded seas apparently overwhelming; and Stirling, in the pride of his sailor's heart, says, "There, now, what would you give to be a sailor ?" It really was a sight worth looking at—a little bit of human construction stemming and resisting the power of the mighty deep.

As we neared the mouth of the British Channel, we had, of course, the usual thick weather, when a strange sail was reported. It was now blowing a fresh breeze; in a few minutes we spoke her, but

s

did not make her haul her main-topsail, being a bit of a merchantman. Stirling hailed as we shot past. "Where are you from?" "Portsmouth." "Any news?" "No, none." The ship was almost out of sight, when we heard, "Ho! Bonapart*er's* back again on the throne of France." Such a hurrah as I set up, tossing my hat over my head! "I will be a Lieutenant-Colonel yet before the year's out!" Sir John Lambert said, "Really, Smith, you are so vivacious! How is it possible? It cannot be." He had such faith in the arrangements of our government, he wouldn't believe it. I said, "Depend upon it, it's truth; a beast like that skipper never could have invented it, when he did not even regard it as news: 'No, no news; only Bonaparte's back again on the throne of France.' Depend on it, it's true." "No, Smith, no." Stirling believed it, and oh, how he carried on! We were soon at Spithead, when all the men-of-war, the bustle, the general appearance, told us, before we could either see telegraphic communication or speak any one, where "Bonaparter" was.

We anchored about three o'clock, went on shore immediately, and shortly after were at dinner in the George. Old West had brought from the Havannah two pups of little white curly dogs, a dog and bitch, which he said were "a present for missus." They are very much esteemed in England, these Havana lapdogs; not much in *my* way.

The charm of novelty which I experienced on my former visit to England after seven years'

absence, was much worn off, and I thought of
nothing but home.   Sir John and I started for
London in a chaise at night, and got only as far
as Guildford.   I soon found our rate of progression
would not do, and I asked his leave to set off home.
At that time he was not aware of all my tale.   I
never saw his affectionate heart angry before; he
positively scolded me, and said, "I will report our
arrival; write to me, that I may know your address,
for I shall most probably very soon want you again."
My wife and Sir John were afterwards the greatest
friends.

So Mr. West and I got a chaise, and off we
started, and got to London on a Sunday, the most
melancholy place on that day on earth.   I drove
to my old lodgings, where I had last parted from
my wife.   They could assure me she was well, as
she had very lately ordered a new riding-habit.
So I ordered a post-chaise, and ran from Panton
Square to Weeks' in the Haymarket, and bought
a superb dressing-case and a heavy gold chain; I
had brought a lot of Spanish books from the
Havannah.   So on this occasion I did not return to
my home naked and penniless, as from Coruña.

I got to Waltham Cross about twelve o'clock.
I soon found a pair of horses was far too slow for
my galloping ideas; so I got four, and we galloped
along then as fast as I could wish.   I rattled away
to the Falcon Inn in my native place, Whittlesea;
for I dare not drive to my father's house.   I sent
quietly for him, and he was with me in a moment.

me again to the war, but nothing affected us *when united;* the word "separation" away, all was smooth. All was now excitement, joy, hope and animation, and preparation of riding-habits, tents, canteens, etc., my sisters thinking of all sorts of things for my wife's comfort, which we could as well have carried as our parish church. My youngest brother but one, Charles, was to go with me to join the 1st Battalion Rifle Brigade, as a Volunteer,* and his departure added to the excitement. I never was more happy in all my life; not a thought of the future (though God knows we had enough before us), for my wife was going and all the agony of parting was spared.

I immediately set to work to buy a real good stud. Two horses I bought at Newmarket, and two in my native place; and as Tiny the faithful was voted too old, as was the mare I had with me in Spain and Washington, I bought for my wife, from a brother, a mare of great celebrity, bred by my father, a perfect horse for a lady who was an equestrian artist.

In a few days I had a kind letter from Sir John

* " During the Peninsular War, and how long before I know not, it was very occasionally permitted to young men who had difficulty in getting a commission, with the consent of the commanding officer, to join some regiment on service before the enemy. In action the Volunteer acted as a private soldier, carrying his musket and wearing his cross-belts like any other man. After a campaign or two, or after having distinguished himself at the storming of some town or fortress, he would probably obtain a commission. He messed with the officers of the company to which he was attached. His dress was the same as that of an officer, except that, instead of wings or epaulettes, he wore shoulder-straps of silver or gold, to confine the cross-belts."— W. Leeke, *Lord Seaton's Regiment at Waterloo* (1866), vol. i. p. 6.

Lambert, saying I was appointed his Major of Brigade; and as he was to proceed to Ghent in Flanders, recommending me, being in Cambridge-shire, to proceed *viâ* Harwich for Ostend, as I must find my own passage unless I went on a transport. West was therefore despatched with my four horses *viâ* Newmarket for Harwich, and I intended so to start as to be there the day my horses would arrive.

The evening before we started, my father, wife, sisters, myself, and brothers had a long ride. On returning, at the end of the town, there was a new stiff rail, with a ditch on each side. I was riding my dear old mare, that had been at Washington, etc., and off whose back poor Lindsay had been killed;* she was an elegant fencer, and as bold as in battle. I said to my sisters, " I will have one more leap on my war-horse." I rode her at it. Whether she had grown old, or did not measure her leap, I don't know, but over she rolled. One of my legs was across the new and narrow ditch, her shoulder right upon it; I could not pull it from under her. I expected every moment, if she struggled, to feel my leg broken, and there was an end to my Brigade Majorship! I passed a hand down, until I got short hold of the curb, and gave her a snatch with all my force. She made an effort, and I drew my leg out, more faint than subsequently in the most sanguinary conflict of the whole war. I never felt more grate-ful for an escape.

* See p. 151.

CHAPTER XXIV.

HARRY SMITH AND HIS WIFE START TOGETHER FOR
THE WATERLOO CAMPAIGN—GHENT—BATTLE OF
WATERLOO.

MY wife and I and my brother Charles were to
start in a chaise at three o'clock the next morning.
I never saw my poor father suffer so much as at
thus parting from three of us at once, and feeling
that his companion, my wife, was lost to him. He
said, " Napoleon and Wellington will meet, a battle
will ensue of a kind never before heard of, and I
cannot expect to see you all again."

We reached Harwich in the afternoon, found
West, his horses, and all our things right, and went
to the Black Bull, from whence I had embarked
years before for Gottenburgh. There we found my
old acquaintance, the landlord, Mr. Briton, a man
as civil as full of information. He said I had no
chance of embarking at Harwich, unless I freighted
a small craft that he would look out, and fitted it up
for my horses.

Next day I came to terms with the skipper of a
sloop of a few tons' burden, himself and a boy the
crew. I couldn't help thinking of the 74's and

frigates in which I had been flying over the ocean.
We measured it, and found there was just room for
the horses, and a hole aft, called a cabin, for my wife
and self and brother.   I did not intend to embark
the horses till the wind was fair—a fortunate plan,
for I was detained in the Black Bull by foul
winds for a fortnight.   The wind becoming fair, in
the afternoon we embarked all our traps.   Mr.
Briton amply provided us with provisions and
forage, and brought his bill for myself, wife, brother,
two grooms, five horses, lady's maid, sea stock, etc.
I expected it to be fifty or sixty pounds ; it was
twenty-four and some shillings, and we had lived on
the fat of the land, for having been half-starved so
many years, when once in the flesh-pots of England,
we revelled in a plenty which we could scarcely
fancy would last.

A gentle breeze carried us over to Ostend in
twenty-four hours, where we landed our horses by
slinging them and dropping them into the sea to
swim ashore.   My wife's noble mare, which we
called the " Brass Mare " after her son of that ilk,
when in the slings and in sight of the shore, neighed
most gallantly, and my wife declared it an omen of
brilliant success.   We went to the great inn of
Ostend.   The difference between it and our late
bivouac, the Black Bull, is not to be described.
I found an English horse-dealer there.   I bought
two mules of him and a stout Flanders pony for
our baggage, and in three days we were *en route* for
Ghent, stopping one night at Bruges, where was an

excellent inn, and the best Burgundy I had drunk up to that hour. My wife was delighted to be once more in campaigning trim.

When we reached Ghent we found Sir John Lambert had reached it the day before. Louis XVIII. was there, his Court and idlers, and Ghent was in as great a state of excitement as if the Duke of Marlborough was again approaching. I found our Brigade were all New Orleans Regiments—three of the best regiments of the old Army of the Peninsula, the 4th, 27th, and 40th, and the 81st in garrison at Brussels. We were ordered to be in perfect readiness to take the field with the warning * we had been so many years accustomed to.

Louis held a Court while we were there. I was near the door he entered by. He was very in-active, but impressive in manner. He laid his hand on my shoulder to support himself. His great topic of conversation was how delighted he was to see us, and how much he was indebted to our nation. A more benign countenance I never beheld, nor did his subsequent reign belie the benignity of his expression.

While at Ghent I waited on Sir John Lambert every morning just after breakfast for orders. On one occasion we heard a voice thundering in the passage to him, "Hallo there, where the devil's the door?" I went out, and to my astonishment saw our noble friend Admiral Malcolm. "Why, where the devil has Lambert stowed himself? The

* See p. 80.

house is as dark as a sheer hulk." He was delighted to see us, and sang out, "Come, bear a hand and get me some breakfast; no regular hours on shore as in the *Royal Oak*." He had been appointed to the command of the coast. He was very much attached to the Duke. During our stay at Ghent we had Brigade parades almost every day, and my General, an ex-Adjutant of the Guards, was most particular in all guard mountings, sentries, and all the correct minutiæ of garrison. The three regiments were in beautiful fighting trim, although the headquarters ship with the Grenadiers, the 27th, had not arrived from America. Poor 27th! in a few days they had not two hundred men in the ranks.

As we anticipated, our march from Ghent was very sudden. In an hour after the order arrived we moved *en route* for Brussels. We reached Asche on the afternoon of the 16th June. The rapid and continuous firing at Quatre Bras, as audible as if we were in the fight, put us in mind of old times, as well as on the *qui vive*. We expected an order every moment to move on. We believed the firing to be at Fleurus. As we approached Brussels the next day [17 June], we met an orderly with a letter from that gallant fellow De Lancey, Q.M.G., to direct us to move on Quatre Bras.

In the afternoon, after we passed Brussels, the scene of confusion, the flying of army, baggage, etc., was an awful novelty to us. We were directed by a subsequent order to halt at the village of Epinay, on the Brussels side of the forest of Soignies, a report having reached his Grace that the enemy's cavalry were threatening our communication with Brussels (as we understood, at least). The whole afternoon we were in a continued state of excitement. Once some rascals of the Cumberland Hussars, a new Corps of Hanoverians (not of the style of our noble and gallant old comrades, the 1st Hussars), came galloping in, declaring they were pursued by Frenchmen. Our bugles were blowing in all directions, and our troops running to their alarm-posts in front of the village. I went to report to Sir John Lambert, who was just sitting quietly down to dinner with my wife and his A.D.C. He says very coolly, "Let the troops——; this is all nonsense ; there is not a French soldier in the rear of his Grace, depend on it, and sit down to dinner." I set off, though, and galloped to the front, where a long line of baggage was leisurely retiring. This was a sufficient indication that the alarm was false, and I dismissed the troops and started for the *débris* of a magnificent turbot which the General's butler had brought out of Brussels. This was in the afternoon.

Such a thunderstorm and deluge of rain now came on, it drenched all that was exposed to it, and in a few minutes rendered the country deep in mud and the roads very bad. All night our baggage kept retiring through the village.

In the course of the night, Lambert's Brigade were ordered to move up to the position the Duke had taken up in front of the forest of Soignies, and our march was very much impeded by waggons upset, baggage thrown down, etc. [18 June]. We met Sir George Scovell, an A.Q.M.G. at head-quarters, who said he was sent by the Duke to see the rear was clear, that it was choked between this and the Army, and the Duke expected to be attacked immediately; our Brigade must clear the road before we moved on. Our men were on fire at the idea of having to remain and clear a road when an attack was momentarily expected, and an hour would bring us to the position. The wand of a magician, with all his spells and incantations, could not have effected a clear course sooner than our 3000 soldiers of the old school.

This effected, General Lambert sent me on to the Duke for orders. I was to find the Duke him-self, and receive orders from no other person. About 11 o'clock I found his Grace and all his staff near Hougoumont. The day was beautiful after the storm, although the country was very heavy. When I rode up, he said, "Hallo, Smith, where are you from last?" "From General Lambert's Brigade, and they from America." "What have you got?" "The 4th, the 27th, and the 40th; the 81st remain in Brussels." "Ah, I know, I know; but the others, are they in good order?" "Ex-cellent, my lord, and very strong." "That's all right, for I shall soon want every man." One of his staff said, "I do not think they will attack to-day." "Nonsense," said the Duke. "The columns are already forming, and I think I have

discerned where the weight of the attack will be
made. I shall be attacked before an hour. Do
you know anything of my position, Smith?"
"Nothing, my lord, beyond what I see—the general
line, and right and left." "Go back and halt
Lambert's Brigade at the junction of the two great
roads from Genappe and Nivelles. Did you
observe their junction as you rode up?" "Particularly, my lord." "Having halted the head of the
Brigade and told Lambert what I desire, ride to
the left of the position. On the extreme left is
the Nassau Brigade *—those fellows who came over
to us at Arbonne, you recollect.† Between them
and Picton's Division (now the 5th) I shall most
probably require Lambert. There is already
there a Brigade of newly-raised Hanoverians,
which Lambert will give orders to, as they and
your Brigade form the 6th Division. You are the
only British Staff Officer with it. Find out, therefore, the best and shortest road from where
Lambert is now halted to the left of Picton and
the right of the Nassau troops. Do you understand?" "Perfectly, my lord." I had barely
turned from his Grace when he called me back.
" Now, clearly understand that when Lambert is
ordered to move from the fork of the two roads
where he is now halted, you are prepared to conduct him to Picton's left." It was delightful to
see his Grace that morning on his noble horse

* The Regiment of Orange Nassau held Smohain and La Haye,
and part of the second Regiment of Nassau the farm of Papelotte.
† See p. 155.

Copenhagen—in high spirits and very animated, but so cool and so clear in the issue of his orders, it was impossible not fully to comprehend what he said; delightful also to observe what his wonderful eye anticipated, while some of his staff were of opinion the attack was not in progress.

I had hardly got back to Lambert, after reconnoitring the country and preparing myself to conduct the troops, when the Battle of Waterloo commenced. We soon saw that where we should be moved to, the weight of the attack on Picton would be resisted by none but British soldiers. For a few seconds, while every regiment was forming square, and the charge of Ponsonby's Brigade going on (which the rising ground in our front prevented us seeing), it looked as if the formation was preparatory to a retreat. Many of the rabble of Dutch troops were flying towards us, and, to add to the confusion, soon after came a party of dragoons, bringing with them three eagles and some prisoners. I said to General Lambert, "We shall have a proper brush immediately, for it looks as if our left will be immediately turned, and the brunt of the charge will fall on us." At this moment we were ordered to move to the very spot where the Duke, *early in the morning*, had expected we should be required. Picton had been killed, Sir James Kempt commanded on the left of the road to Genappe, near La Haye Sainte; his Division had been already severely handled, and we took their position, my old Battalion of Riflemen remaining with us.

The Battle of Waterloo has been too often described, and nonsense enough written about the Crisis,* for me to add to it. Every moment was a crisis, and the controversialists had better have left the discussion on the battle-field. Every Staff officer had two or three (and one four) horses shot under him. I had one wounded in six, another in seven places, but not seriously injured. The fire was terrific, especially of cannon.

Late in the day, when the enemy had made his last great effort on our centre, the field was so enveloped in smoke that nothing was discernible. The firing ceased on both sides, and we on the left knew that one party or the other was beaten. This was the most anxious moment of my life. In a few seconds we saw the red-coats in the centre, as stiff as rocks, and the French columns retiring rapidly, and there was such a British shout as rent the air. We all felt then to whom the day belonged. It was time the "Crisis" should arrive, for we had been at work some hours, and the hand of death had been most unsparing. One Regiment, the 27th, had only two officers left—Major Hume, who commanded from the beginning of the battle, and

---

* In 1833, Major G. Gawler, of the 52nd, published *The Crisis of Waterloo*, in which he claimed for his regiment the honour of having by their flank-attack defeated the Imperial Guards in their last charge, an honour generally given to the Guards. His contention was supported by Rev. W. Leeke in *Lord Seaton's Regiment at Waterloo* (1866).

another—and they were both wounded, and only a hundred and twenty soldiers were left with them.

At this moment I saw the Duke, with only one Staff officer remaining, galloping furiously to the left. I rode on to meet him. "Who commands here?" "Generals Kempt and Lambert, my lord." "Desire them to get into a column of companies of Battalions, and move on immediately." I said, "In which direction, my lord?" "Right ahead, to be sure." I never saw his Grace so animated. The *Crisis* was general, from one end of the line to the other.

That evening at dark we halted, literally on the ground we stood on; not a picquet was required, and our whole cavalry in pursuit. Then came the dreadful tale of killed and wounded; it was enormous, and every moment the loss of a dear friend was announced. To my wonder, my astonishment, and to my gratitude to Almighty God, I and my two brothers—Tom, the Adjutant of the 2nd Battalion Rifle Brigade, who had, during the day, attracted the Duke's attention by his gallantry, and Charles, in the 1st Battalion, who had been fighting for two days—were all safe and unhurt, except that Charles had a slight wound in the neck. In the thunderstorm the previous evening he had tied a large silk handkerchief over his stock; he forgot to take it off, and probably owed his life to so trifling a circumstance. There was not an instance throughout the Army of *two* brothers in the field escaping.* We

* There was one case at least : John Luard, Lieutenant, 16th Light Dragoons, and George Luard, Captain, 18th Hussars.

were three, and I could hardly credit my own eyes. We had nothing to eat or drink. I had some tea in my writing-case, but no sugar. It had been carried by an orderly, although in the ranks. He found me out after the battle, and I made some tea in a soldier's tin for Sir James Kempt, Sir John Lambert, and myself; and while we were thus regaling, up came my brother, of whose safety I was not aware.

Captain McCulloch of the 95th Regiment wished to see me. He was a dear friend whom I had not seen since he was awfully wounded at Foz d'Aruz [Foz de Aronce] on Massena's retreat, after having had seven sabre-wounds at the Coa, in Massena's advance, and been taken prisoner. He was in a cottage near, awfully wounded. I found him lying in great agony, but very composed. " Oh, Harry, so long since we have met, and now again under such painful circumstances; but, thank God, you and Tom are all right." I had brought all my remaining tea, which he ravenously swallowed. The ball had dreadfully broken the elbow of the sound arm, and had passed right through the fleshy part of his back, while the broken bone of the arm previously shattered at Foz d'Aruz was still exfoliating, and very painful even after a lapse of years. I got hold of a surgeon, and his arm was immediately amputated. When dressed, he lay upon the stump, as this was less painful than the old exfoliating wound, and on his back he could not lie. He recovered, but was never afterwards able to feed

T

himself or put on his hat, and died, Heaven help him, suddenly of dysentery.

No one, but those who have witnessed the awful scene, knows the horrors of a field of battle—the piles of the dead, the groans of the dying, the agony of those dreadfully wounded, to whom frequently no assistance can be rendered at the moment ; some still in perfect possession of their intellect, game to the last, regarding their recovery as more than probable, while the clammy perspiration of death has already pounced upon its victim; others, again, perfectly sensible of their dissolution, breathing into your keeping the feelings and expressions of their last moments—messages to father, mother, wife, or dearest relatives.   Well might Walter Scott say—

> " Thou canst not name one tender tie
> But here dissolved its relics lie."

Often have I myself, tired and exhausted in such scenes, almost regretted the life I have adopted, in which one never knows at any moment how near or distant one's own turn may be. In such dejection you sink into a profound sleep, and you stand up next morning in fresh spirits. Your country's calls, your excitement, honour and glory, again impel, and undauntedly and cheerfully you expose that life which the night before you fancied was of value. A soldier's life is one continued scene of excitement, hope, anticipation ; fear for himself he never knows, though the loss of his comrade pierces his heart.

Before daylight next morning [19 June] a Staff officer whose name I now forget, rode up to where we were all lying, and told us of the complete *déroute* of the French, and the vigorous pursuit of the Prussians, and that it was probable that our Division would not move for some hours. At daylight I was on horseback, with a heart of gratitude as became me, and anxious to let my wife know I was all right. I took a party of each Regiment of my Division with me, and went back to the field; for I was now established as Assistant-Quartermaster-General.

I had been over many a field of battle, but with the exception of one spot at New Orleans, and the breach of Badajos, I had never seen anything to be compared with what I saw. At Waterloo the *whole* field from right to left was a mass of dead bodies. In one spot, to the right of La Haye Sainte, the French Cuirassiers were literally piled on each other; many soldiers not wounded lying under their horses; others, fearfully wounded, occasionally with their horses struggling upon their wounded bodies. The sight was sickening, and I had no means or power to assist them. Imperative duty compelled me to the field of my comrades, where I had plenty to do to assist many who had been left out all night; some had been believed to be dead, but the spark of life had returned. All over the field you saw officers, and as many soldiers as were permitted to leave the ranks, leaning and weeping over some dead or dying brother or comrade. The battle was fought on a Sunday, the 18th June, and I repeated to myself a verse from the Psalms of that day—91st Psalm, 7th verse: "A thousand shall fall beside thee, and ten thousand at thy right hand, but it shall not come nigh thee." I blessed Almighty God our Duke was spared, and galloped to my General, whom I found with some breakfast awaiting my arrival.

So many accounts and descriptions have been given of the Battle of Waterloo, I shall only make one or two observations. To those who say the ultimate success of the day was achieved by the arrival of the Prussians, I observe that the Prussians were part of the whole on which his Grace calculated, as much as on the co-operation of one of his own Divisions; that they ought to have been in the field much sooner, and by their late arrival seriously endangered his Grace's left flank; and had Napoleon pushed the weight of his attack and precipitated irresistible numbers on our left, he would have forced the Duke to throw back his left and break our communication with the Prussians. The Duke's army was a heterogeneous mass, not the old Peninsular veterans; young 2nd Battalions most of them, others intermixed with the rabble of our allied army. Thus the Duke could not have counter-manœuvred on his left, as he would have been able with his old army; and we had one Division under Colville far away to our right.

Napoleon fought the battle badly; his attacks were not simultaneous, but partial and isolated, and enabled the Duke to repel each by a concentration. His cavalry was sacrificed early in the day. If

Napoleon did not desire to turn our left flank, and the battle is to be regarded as a fight hand to hand, he fought it badly.

By a general attack upon our line with his overpowering force of artillery, followed up by his infantry, he might have put *hors-de-combat* far more of our army than he did. His cavalry would have been fresh, and had he employed this devoted and gallant auxiliary late in the day as he did early, his attempts to defeat us would have been far more formidable.

His artillery and cavalry behaved most nobly, but I maintain his infantry did not. In proof, I will record one example. On the left, in front of the 5th Division, 25,000 of the Young Guard attacked in column. Picton was just killed, and Kempt commanded. It is true this column advanced under a galling fire, but it succeeded in reaching the spot where it intended to deploy. Kempt ordered the Battalion immediately opposite the head of the column to charge. It was a poor miserable Battalion compared with some of ours, yet did it dash like British soldiers at the column, which went about. Then it was that Ponsonby's Brigade got in among them, and took eagles and prisoners.

As a battle of science, it was demonstrative of no manœuvre. It was no Salamanca or Vittoria, where science was so beautifully exemplified: it was as a stand-up fight between two pugilists, "mill away" till one is beaten. The Battle of Waterloo, with all its political glory, has destroyed the field movement of the British Army, so scientifically laid down by Dundas, so improved on by that hero of war and of drill, Sir John Moore. All that light-troop duty which he taught, by which the world through the medium of the Spanish War was saved, is now replaced by the most heavy of manœuvres, by squares, centre formations, and moving in masses, which require time to collect and equal time to extend; and all because the Prussians and Russians did not know how to move quicker, we, forsooth, must adopt their ways, although Picton's Division at Quatre Bras nobly showed that British infantry can resist cavalry in any shape. It is true the Buffs were awfully mauled at Albuera, but what did my kind patron, Sir William Stewart, order them to do? They were in open column of companies right in front, and it was necessary at once to deploy into line, which Sir William with his light 95th had been accustomed to do on any company: he orders them, therefore, to deploy on the Grenadiers; by this the right would become the left, what in common parlance is termed "clubbed;" and while he was doing this, he kept advancing the Grenadiers. It is impossible to imagine a battalion in a more helpless position, and it never can be cited as any criterion that a battalion must be in squares to resist cavalry. At the Battle of Fuentes d'Oñoro, the overwhelming French cavalry, having rapidly put back our very inferior force, were upon a regiment of infantry of the 7th Division, to the right of the Light

Division, before either were aware. The French advance of the Chasseurs Britanniques, I think (it was *one* of the mongrels, as we called those corps, anyhow), was imposing, heavy, and rapid (I was close to the left of our infantry at the time), but it made not the slightest impression on the regiment in line; on the contrary, the Chasseurs were repulsed with facility and loss.

But to return to our narrative. A party was sent to bury the dead of each regiment as far as possible. For the Rifle Brigade, my brother Charles was for the duty. In gathering the dead bodies, he saw among the dead of our soldiers the body of a French officer of delicate mould and appearance. On examining it, he found it was that of a delicate, young, and handsome female. My story ends here, but such is the fact. What were the circumstances of devotion, passion, or patriotism which led to such heroism, is, and ever will be, to me a mystery. Love, depend upon it.

That afternoon we moved forward by the Nivelles road. I had to go into my General's room. I was not aware he was there, and entered abruptly. He was changing his shirt, when I saw he had received a most violent contusion on his right arm. It was fearfully swelled (in those days our coat-sleeves were made very large), and as black as ebony from the shoulder to the wrist. "My dear General," I said, "what an arm! I did not know you had been wounded." "No, nor you never would, if accident had not shown you." He made me promise to say nothing, about which I compromised by saying, "To no one but to a surgeon, whom you must see. An arm in that state, if inflammation succeed, might slough, and you would lose it." The General would not see a surgeon, and thank God he got well.

But turn we now to the poor wife. I left her at daylight on the 18th, prepared to get on her horse and go to Brussels, to await the result of the storm of war which I had prepared her for. Her tale of wonder must form a separate and distinct narrative.

CHAPTER XXV.

JUANA'S STORY.[*]

WHEN the troops had moved forward on the morning of the 18th June, I, as you directed, got on my horse and went to Brussels, intending to await the result of the pending battle. On arrival I found my baggage and servant in the great square, and an order had just arrived for the whole of the baggage of the army to move on the road towards Antwerp, and afterwards to cross the canal about five miles from Brussels, at a village on the Antwerp side. On reaching the village I dismounted, the baggage was unloaded, and West was endeavouring to get something for me to eat in the inn. It was about five o'clock. Suddenly an alarm was given that the enemy was upon us. West brought my mare to the door as quickly as I could run downstairs, but from the noise, confusion, and everything, my horse was perfectly frantic. West succeeded in tossing me up, but my little pug, Vitty, was still below. I said, "Now, West, give me my dog;" when, as he put her into my lap,

---

[*] The MS. is in Harry Smith's hand, and the wording is probably his.

I dropped my reins. West, knowing I always gathered up my reins before I jumped up, let go, and off flew the mare with such speed that, with the dog in my lap, it was all I could do for some time to keep my seat. I had the snaffle rein in my hand, but I could not restrain her; the curb rein was flying loose, and I couldn't stoop to get hold of it. She flew with me through the streets of Malines, across a bridge over the river, the road full of horses and baggage, still flying away, away, until I was perfectly out of breath. I saw a waggon upset lying immediately before me across the road, and I knew that if I could not turn her on one side, I must inevitably be knocked to pieces. The mare would not answer my snaffle rein, and I felt her charge the waggon as at a fence to leap it. The height was beyond the spring of my horse. As the animal endeavoured to leap, the loose curb rein caught. This brought her at once to a halt, and I was precipitated on her head, pug and all. I had come at this rate eight miles, over a road covered with mud and dirt. The mare was as much out of breath as I was. I managed to get back into the saddle, and felt that now was my only chance to get hold of the curb. I succeeded in doing so, and we were then on terms of equality.

Having righted my habit, I looked back and saw some five or six men on horseback, whom of course I construed into French Dragoons, although, if I had considered a moment, I should have known that no Dragoon could have come the pace *I* did;

but I was so exhausted, I exclaimed, "Well, if I am to be taken, I had better at once surrender." The first horseman proved to be one of my servants, riding one of the Newmarket horses, having taken the animal from West against his orders. The others were a Commissary, an officer of the Hanoverian Rifles, and an officer, I regret to say, of our own Hussars. I addressed myself to the Hussar, who appeared the oldest of the party. "Pray, sir, is there any danger?" (I had forgotten almost all the little English I knew in my excitement.) "Danger, mum! When I left Brussels the French were in pursuit down the hill." "Oh, sir, what shall I do?" "Come on to Antwerp with me." He never pulled up. During the whole conversation we were full gallop. One of the party says, "You deserve no pity. You may well be fatigued carrying that dog. Throw it down." I was very angry, and said I should deserve no pity if I did.

Our pace soon brought us to Antwerp, where the Hussar was very civil, and tried to get me a room in one of the hotels. This he soon found was impossible, as all the English visitors at Brussels had fled there. We must now go to the Hôtel de Ville and try for a billet. Whilst standing there, the officer having gone inside, I was an object of curious attention. I was wet from head to foot with the black mud of the high-road. On my face the mud had dried, and a flood of tears chasing each other through it down my cheeks must have

given me an odd appearance indeed. While standing on horseback there, an officer of the English
garrison, whom I did not know (he must have
learnt my name from my servant) addressed me by
name. "Mrs. Smith, you are in such a terrible
plight, and such is the difficulty of your getting
in anywhere, if you will come with me, I will conduct you to Colonel Craufurd, the Commandant of
the Citadel; his wife and daughters are most kind
and amiable people, and readily, I know, would they
contribute with happiness anything to your comfort." My situation was not one to stand on
delicacy. I therefore promptly accepted this offer,
leaving my kind Hussar in the Hôtel de Ville.
When I arrived, nothing could exceed the kindness
of all, which was as striking at the moment as it
seems to me now. I was stripped from a weight
of mud which, with my long riding-habit, I could
hardly move under. A shower of hot water again
showed my features, and I was put in the clothes
of good Mrs. Craufurd, a very tall woman; and in
these comfortable dry clothes I was nearly as
much lost as in the case of mud I had been washed
out of.

The hospitality of this night ought to have
soothed me, but the agony of hope, doubt, and fear
I was in absorbed every other feeling, although
I was so sensible of kindness.

The next day [19 June] the officer who had
so kindly brought me to Colonel Craufurd came to
tell me a great quantity of baggage was momentarily

arriving: could I give him any directions or clue to find mine? In about an hour he returned with my spare horses, old trusty West, who had never left anything behind, my baggage, and my maid.

In the afternoon we heard of the battle having been fought and won, but no news of my husband. So, contrary to the wishes of my kind host and hostess, I ordered my horse to be ready at three o'clock in the morning to rejoin my husband, whatever shape fate had reduced him to. It was all I could do to resist the importunity of those kind people who wished me to remain. But at three o'clock [20 June] West and I were on horseback, desiring baggage, servants, and horses to follow. In conversation with West, I ascertained that at the village we fled from, my mattrass, and in it my dressing-case (bought on a Sunday at Weeks' *) with all my fortune, two Napoleons, had been left in the inn. When I arrived, I asked the landlord of the little wretched inn about it. He pretended he knew nothing, but old cunning West got information in the stable-yard, and gave a boy five francs to conduct him to the hayloft where my treasure was. West soon transported what he called *ours* to me, and upon opening it, I found my important dressing-case there untouched. I had something in the shape of breakfast. In the mean time my servants had arrived, the lost mattrass was restored to the baggage, and West and I, in light

* See p. 259.

marching order, started for Brussels. We were only five miles away, and arrived by seven in the morning.

Seeing some of our Rifle soldiers, with an eagerness which may be imagined, I asked after my husband, when to my horror they told me that Brigade-Major Smith of the 95th was killed. It was now my turn to ask the "Brass Mare" to gallop, and in a state approaching desperation I urged her to the utmost speed for the field of battle to seek my husband's corpse. The road from Brussels to the field almost maddened me, with wounded men and horses, and corpses borne forward to Brussels for interment, expecting as I was every moment to see that of my husband, knowing how he was beloved by officers and soldiers. The road was nearly choked which was to lead me to the completion, as I hoped, of my life; to die on the body of the only thing I had on earth to love, and which I loved with a faithfulness which few can or ever did feel, and none ever exceeded. In my agony of woe, which of course increased as my expectations were not realized (it was now Tuesday), I approached the awful field of Sunday's carnage, in mad search of Enrique. I saw signs of newly dug graves, and then I imagined to myself, "O God, he has been buried, and I shall never again behold him!" How can I describe my suspense, the horror of my sensations, my growing despair, the scene of carnage around me? From a distance I saw a figure lying; I shrieked,

"Oh, there he is!" I galloped on. "No, it is not he! Find him I will, but whither shall I turn?" O ye in peaceful homes, with every comfort around you, you wonder how I did not sink under my afflictions, a foreigner in a strange land, thus at once bereft of my all! I will tell you. Educated in a convent, I was taught to appeal to God through Jesus Christ. In this my trouble I did so. At this moment, as a guardian angel, a dear and mutual friend, Charlie Gore, A.D.C. to Sir James Kempt, appeared to me. In my agony and hope, hope alone of finding the body, I exclaimed, "Oh, where is he? Where is my Enrique?" "Why, near Bavay by this time, as well as ever he was in his life; not wounded even, nor either of his brothers." "Oh, dear Charlie Gore, why thus deceive me? The soldiers tell me Brigade-Major Smith is killed. Oh, my Enrique!" "Dearest Juana, believe me; it is poor Charles Smyth, Pack's Brigade-Major. I swear to you, on my honour, I left Harry riding Lochinvar in perfect health, but very anxious about you." "Oh, may I believe you, Charlie! my heart will burst." "Why should you doubt me?" "Then God has heard my prayer!" This sudden transition from my depth of grief and maddening despair was enough to turn my brain, but Almighty God sustained me. Gore told me he had returned to Brussels to see poor Charlie Beckwith, who had lost, or must lose, his leg; and that he was then in the act of looking for the grave of our mutual friend, poor Charlie Eeles. Gore said,

" I am now going to Mons : can you muster strength to ride with me there ? " I said, " Strength ? yes, for anything now ! " and we reached Mons at twelve o'clock at night. I had been on the same horse since three in the morning, and had ridden a distance from point to point of sixty miles ; and after all the agony, despair, relief, and happiness I had gone through in one day, I ate something, and lay down until daylight next morning [21 June], when I rapidly pushed on to Bavay, on my really wonderful thoroughbred mare.

I first met Sir John. Lambert, who showed me where Enrique was to be found. Until I saw him, I could not persuade myself he was well, such a hold had my previous horror taken of my every thought and feeling. Soon, O gracious God, I sank into his embrace, exhausted, fatigued, happy, and grateful—oh, how grateful !—to God who had protected him, and sustained my reason through such scenes of carnage, horror, dread, and belief in my bereavement.

[*Narrative resumed.*]

I was afterwards told all this, and I could not but reflect on what we had all gone through since the morning we had parted with my father, and how his prediction of a terrific struggle had been verified. Our adventures formed the subject of a long letter, and from him came one soon after.

" Never did I receive two letters with such

pleasure as your two last after the glorious Battle of Waterloo. For three of you, my sons, to have been so hotly engaged, and to have come off unhurt, must not have been chance or fate ; but Providence seems to have watched over you all and protected you. How grateful ought we all to be to the Almighty God ! I assure you my prayers have ever been offered up to the Throne of Grace for the protection of you all, and a safe return to England."

This letter is now on my table before me, fresh as when written,[*] while the author, God bless him, has mixed with the earth to which all must return. He lived to the age of 87, and died in Sept. 1843, a strong and healthy man until within a few months of his dissolution. It is difficult to say whether he was the more proud of having three sons at Waterloo, or grateful to Almighty God for their preservation.

* See Appendix II., pp. 708, 709.

CHAPTER XXVI.

OUR march to Paris was unaccompanied by anything to relate except that I had a gallop round Mons and a good look on Malplaquet, but could picture to myself no position, while I felt as a soldier standing on the classic ground of the gallant achievements of my country and our former army of heroes (for I regard Marlborough and Wellington as the greatest men England or the world ever produced). But the latter days of Wellington are as conspicuous for ability and energy as the days of his youth. Poor Marlborough dwindled into imbecility, and became a miser. To Wellington his country has ever been enthusiastically grateful, while Marlborough, by ill-treatment, was driven into voluntary banishment. Although I love

Wellington with a fervour which cannot be exceeded, I pray my God he may never outlive his mental faculties, but leave this world and the country and cause he has so eminently served while that world and country are still in admiration and wonder. Alava, the Spanish General, so attached and devoted to the Duke (by-the-bye, he was a Captain of a Spanish battleship or frigate, I forget which), told me and Juana two years after the Battle of Waterloo that the night after that eventful day, the Duke got back to his quarters at Waterloo about nine or ten at night. The table was laid for the usual number, while none appeared of the many of his staff but Alava and Fremantle. The Duke said very little, ate hastily and heartily, but every time the door opened he gave a searching look, evidently in the hope of some of his valuable staff approaching. When he had finished eating, he held up both hands in an imploring attitude and said, " The hand of Almighty God has been upon me this day," jumped up, went to his couch, and was asleep in a moment. At this period he was not aware of the extent of his wonderful victory.

When we approached the capital, we found the French army strongly posted in a position near St. Denis and the previously shamefully abandoned post of Mont Martre. From this position we expected to have to drive them, but a day or two's suspense relieved us. In a day or two we went to see the *entrée* of Louis into Paris—a humble spectacle indeed compared to the magnitude of the struggle that brought it about.

Lieut.-General Sir Lowry Cole had now arrived to take the command of the 6th Division, previously under Lambert. The 5th, 6th, and Brunswickers composed the Reserve, about 17,000, Sir James Kempt, the senior General, commanding; whose Quartermaster-General, Sir William Gomm, gave all orders for marching, bivouac, etc. Now it became my province to do so, and I never felt more proud than in having the movement and arrangement of march of 17,000 soldiers.

Our army was in the environs of Paris, the 5th Division at Clichy, the 6th at Neuilly, the Brunswickers near Clichy. The house I and my wife occupied in the town of Neuilly we found was a sort of country residence belonging to a nice old lady in Paris. There was a beautiful and most productive garden, and an establishment of regular gardeners. When I sent for the head man and desired him to take to his mistress the vegetables he was accustomed to send her, and to obey her orders, whatever they were, he was thunderstruck. I said, " If the garden is not kept in real good order, then I will show you what an Englishman is." The poor old lady, hearing this, came out to thank us, and we often dined with her in Paris. She lived in great style, and was of use to my wife in showing her milliners, etc., for a refit *à la mode* was necessary.

Our life was now one of continued pleasure and excitement—nothing but parties at night and races

by day. At these I was steward. The crowd of
foreign officers being very unruly in riding in after
the race-horses, I put some proper fellows of soldiers
at the distance-post (who, having resisted many a
charge of French cavalry, cared little for an unarmed
galloping man), with orders to run the rope across
to stop this disorder. My orders were obeyed, as
I expected, and that gallant hero, Marshal Blucher,
not seeing the rope, rode his horse full speed against
it and fell, and in the crash the noble old fellow
broke his collar-bone, to my annoyance and distress.

While one day walking in my garden at Neuilly,
my old friend Tom Fane, who had come to Paris
as one of the sight-seers, came full gallop up to
me and Juana, " Hurrah, Harry, the *Gazette* has
arrived! You are Lieutenant-Colonel, and here is
a case for you; it has some order in it, I think.
I found it at the Military Secretary's office, and,
being to your address, brought it. Let me open
it." It was the Order of Companion of the Bath,
which pleased poor Tom more than it did me.
Thus again had I and Juana cause to be grateful
to Almighty God, not only for perfect safety, but for
worldly distinction and promotion. It was barely
fourteen months since the Battle of Toulouse. I
had crossed the Atlantic to and from America four
times; fought a gallant action, and captured the
metropolis of that world; brought home dispatches,
and received £500; was in communication with
ministers, and honoured by a long audience of His
Royal Highness the Prince Regent; again went

out; again was under fire for three weeks, and in the sanguinary disaster at New Orleans; was in the Battle of Waterloo, and had been promoted from Captain to Lieut.-Colonel and Companion of the Bath; without a wound; restored to my wife in health and contentment, and nothing to distress or annoy me beyond the loss and wounds of so many gallant and dear friends. Cold must that heart be which could not feel to its inmost core God Almighty's providence.

While in our cantonments around Paris we had frequent reviews with Emperors, Kings, etc., as spectators, and nothing could exceed the style and bearing of our army. The conduct, too, was exemplary. The taking down of the horses from Venice, from the Place du Carrousel; the execution of poor Ney, that hero of reality, not romance; the desire of Blucher to destroy the bridge of Jena, which the Duke of Wellington prevented; the escape of La Vallette, etc., kept us all in a state of excitement, while the lions of Paris, then the *entrepôt* of every article of value in the arts, afforded daily occupation. Not a valuable picture in Europe but was in the Place du Carrousel. It was my delight to stand, often an hour at a time, looking at Paul Potter's small painting of the bull and the peasant behind the tree, and I have been so fascinated I have expected the bull to charge.

In the autumn [1815] it became necessary to move the army into more permanent quarters, and my Division, the 6th, was sent to St. Germain,

that magnificent and ancient resort of former
kings. The woods were in perfect order, and cut
into beautiful *foci* and avenues like radii of circles,
for hunting in the French style. The Duke de Berri
had hounds, and was passionately fond of the sport.
The stag was turned out, there were relays of
hounds in couples, and huntsmen of various de-
nominations with large French horns, all in a
costume de chasse, with large cocked hats and a
couteau de chasse by their sides. The carriages,
full of ladies of the court and others, assembled
in one of the *foci*, or centres, from which the
avenues radiated. When the stag crossed into
another part of the wood, the carriages galloped
to the "*focus*" of that part of the forest where the
hunt was now going on, and such a crash of horns
as there was to denote that the stag had changed
his direction! The Duke went galloping up and
down the avenues, changing very frequently from
one fat brute of a horse to another. My wife and
I, who went out every day and galloped after the
Duke, an ill-tempered fellow, up and down the
avenues, were barely able to keep our real good
hunters warm. It was, however, capital fun,
although foreign to our ideas of hunting. I
always fancied myself a figure in a tapestry, hunting being a favourite subject for that kind of
delineation.

At the *mort* (or death), or when the stag was at
bay, there was always a great row of horns and
shouting, but *no dog-language*. On one occasion

the stag, a noble animal, was at bay, and fiercely contending with the hounds. The Duke de Berri jumped off his horse and drew his *couteau de chasse*, making great demonstration of going up to the stag, while his courtiers were screeching, "Oh, monsieur, monsieur, prenez garde, pour l'amour de Dieu." He reminded me of the Irish hero, "Hold me, Jim; you know my *temper*," for the Duke had no real idea of doing anything of the sort, although, when the poor noble animal had been shot by some of the *piqueurs*, the Duke then ran in *valorously* and dipped his *couteau* in the beautiful animal's chest. For this feat a lot of us were determined to play the Duke a trick, and the next hunting-day we contrived to break down the paling of the forest and to induce the stag to bolt. We succeeded to our hearts' content, and away into the open went stag safe enough, the hounds in no wind after him. The Duke and all his equipage were soon planted, and he was in a furious passion. The *couteau de chasse* was not required that day.

The most ridiculous thing is that they do not let the hounds "tear him and eat him" while their blood is up. The stag is taken to the kennel and skinned, and all the meat cut into small pieces and put again into the hide, and the hounds then, in this cold-blooded way, rush at a *mess*, instead of the whole pack, in a state of excitement, falling on the hunted animal reeking with fatigue.

We were all amused one day at observing a

man elegantly mounted on an English horse in
the full costume of the French *chasse* (*couteau,*
etc.), when who should this be but our own dear
Duke! He looked so neat and smart, and we
had such a laugh. He himself had a beautiful
pack of hounds and some boxed stags, which gave
runs sometimes, but he was not of the age for a
sportsman.

About this time I and Will Havelock set on
foot a pack of foxhounds. We sent to England
for hounds. The numbers of our pack being
thirteen couple, we sent to Brussels for [five
couple more] from the Prince of Orange's establishment. This pack afterwards became a capital
one.

On the conclusion of the treaty between the
Allied Powers and France, by which an Army of
Occupation was designated to remain on the
northern boundary of France for three or five
years, the large armies (except their quota of
the contingent) marched back to their respective
countries. Of the British Army four Divisions
alone were to remain. Mine was reduced, and
being no longer on the staff, I joined my regiment. Some of my old comrades said to Charlie
Beckwith, who had also joined, "Now, how will
Harry Smith, after a career of such extended
authority, like to come back to the command of
a Company?" Charlie says (for he loved me),
"In the execution of his duty and care of his
Company he will be an example to us all."

My corps was moved again into the environs of Paris preparatory to its march to the north. I was now visited by the deepest distress and grief, for three days expecting the death of all I loved and cherished—my dear wife. Nothing but vigour of mind and a good constitution saved her. I had encountered many previous difficulties, dahgers, and disasters, but never aught like this. God in His continued mercy spared her to me. Praised be His Name.

She was scarcely fit to move when we marched from Paris to Louvres [16 Jan. 1816] and an adjacent village. My Company went to Vernais. We were again under Sir John Lambert, who had been moved from one Brigade to another. My wife drove herself in my tilbury; I marched with my men. We had a large cold château as a quarter, with a very civil landlord. I had with me the hounds—eighteen couple. He put them up most kindly, and appeared delighted—so much so that I had no delicacy in asking him to get me a dead horse or to buy a dying brute for a few shillings. To my astonishment, he regarded the request as a direct insult. It was all I could do to make him understand I had no idea of offending. He was with difficulty appeased, but I saw he never forgot the dead horse, any more than the Antiquary's nephew the "*phoca* or seal."

From hence we marched to Cambray, around which place and Valenciennes the greater part of the army was to be cantoned. Three fortresses

were to be garrisoned by us. The Duke's head-
quarters were to be at Cambray. One day Major
Balvaird came to me. He was my commanding
officer (I being only a *Brevet* Lieut.-Colonel
and *Captain* under his command). He was an
excellent fellow, and as gallant a soldier as ever
lived, a bosom friend, and a Scotchman with a
beautiful accent. "Weel, Harry, mi mon, the
deevil is in it. I have an order to send a Captain
to the depôt at Shorncliffe. You are the first for
my duty, my lad. You canna be more hurt at being
ordered than I am to order you. So be prepared.
There is a just ane chance for you, but you must be
prepared." My mortification was excessive, for
with my habits, hounds, horses, and wife, etc., the
income I should get in England was not at all to
my desire. However, I said nothing to my wife,
always hoping something might turn up.

On the march one night my Company was in a
wretched little village, my quarters a miserable dirty
little farmhouse. On any other occasion I should
have cared more than my wife herself, but she was
still very delicate, and I was awfully afraid of a
relapse. It was February, and the cold very severe.
In watching her, I did not go to sleep until just
before it was time to jump up and march, when I
had a curious dream that the Duke of Wellington
sent for me and said, "Smith, I have two staff-
appointments to give away, you shall have one,"
and that as I went out, poor Felton Hervey, the
Military Secretary, said, "You are a lucky fellow,

Harry, for the one you are to have is the most preferable by far." I told my wife this dream, and said, " Mark my words if it does not turn out to be true."

On reaching our cantonment at Bourlon, a little beyond Cambray, I had just put up my Company when General Lambert sent for me. " Smith," he says, " I am ordered to send a field officer to Cambray, who, in conjunction with an officer of Engineers, is to take over Cambray, its guns, stores, etc., from the French Commander and Engineers. It may lead to something further. I therefore wish you to start at daylight; the duty is important." *His* wish was *my* law. Off I started. I had scarcely completed the transfer when the General Orders were put into my hand in which I saw I was appointed Major de Place, or Town-Major of Cambray, and Charlie Beckwith Major de Place of Valenciennes, each with the pay or allowance of Assistant Quartermaster-General, to which department we were to report. Thus my dream was verified, for, as Cambray was headquarters, and I had none of that horrid duty, billeting on the inhabitants, which was attached to Valenciennes (the headquarters A.Q.M.G. being desired to do it), I was given the better place of the two, as Hervey said in my dream.

CHAPTER XXVII.

CAMBRAY, 1816–1818—SPORT AND GAIETY—THE DUKE
    OF WELLINGTON—HARRY SMITH RECEIVES A VISIT
    FROM HIS FATHER.

SOON after our establishment at Cambray, I received a note from one of His Grace's Aides-de-Camp. "The Duke desires you will come to him immediately, and bring with you the sheet of Cassini's map of the environs of Cambray." Fortunately I had this map. I asked myself what in the name of wonder the Duke could want. Off I cut. "Well, Smith, got the map?" I opened it. "Now, where is my château?" "Here, my lord." "Ah, the coverts are very well shown here. Are there foxes in all these?" "Yes, my lord, too many in every one." "Well, then, hounds must always know their own country"—he drew his finger as a line across the map. "Now, your hounds hunt that side, mine this."

On one occasion, when Lord Castlereagh was staying with His Grace, the former wanted to see some coursing in France, and about 2 o'clock in the afternoon the Duke sent for me to bring some greyhounds. We went out, and were lucky in finding, and killed a brace. I never saw a man in such spirits as the Duke. He rode like a whipper-in.

I once trained some greyhounds for the Duke, almost puppies, against some of the same age which that noble fellow, Sir Edward Barnes had bred. We were to meet near the Duke's château, where there were plenty of hares. We had great sport to beat Sir Edward every match. My wife rode her "Brass" seventeen miles before we looked for a hare. The Duke made her one of his umpires. She rode every course, and back again at night.

Poor Felton Hervey was prejudiced against Spanish greyhounds, and he and the present Duke of Richmond got out some English hounds to the Peninsula to beat my celebrated "Moro," which Harry Mellish, a gallant hero alike as soldier and sportsman, declared the best dog he ever saw in his life. Of course the English dogs had no chance.

While at Cambray I had two dogs, sons of the "Moro," and we had a great coursing party—the Duke of Wellington, Lord Hill (who had beautiful English greyhounds), Sir Hussey Vivian, etc. We were near the Duke's château, where there were plenty of right good hares. Hervey objected to my Spaniards running. We had been coursing all day and not a hare was killed, so I rode up to the Duke and said, "My lord, this won't do. A hare must be killed to go to the château." The Duke said, "Ah! but how?" "My Spaniards should kill you a hare, my lord." The sun was

almost down. Felton Hervey says, "Lord Hill's
'Laura' and 'Rattler' shall get a hare. We will put
them in slips ; Smith shall call 'Loo,' and if they
don't kill their hare, then let the Moro blood try,
and I will halloo them out of their slips." At it we
went. A hare jumped up under the nose of Lord
Hill's dogs. I hallooed. The hare hadn't twenty
yards' law. "Ah," says the Duke, "you gave the
hare no chance." "Plenty, my lord. They won't
kill her." After a terrific course she fairly beat
them. Hervey was very angry. It was nearly
dark, when hares run like devils. My dogs, two
brothers, were in the slips. So late in the evening
hares are sly. One jumped up sixty yards off,
and Hervey hallooed. The honesty of the field
went with me, and all sung out, "Shame, Hervey !
your dogs were close to their hare." "Never mind,"
I said. "My lord, you shall have the hare." I was
on that wonderful horse Lochinvar, and never did
I so ask him to go along. My dogs soon closed
with their hare, when I knew, if they once turned
her with such a law, she was ours. We had a
terrific course, and killed her in a bank, within three
yards of a covert where she would have been safe.
I galloped back in triumph with my hare, for not
a horse could live with Lochinvar, and I threw the
hare down at his Grace's feet. Hervey was furious,
and insisted that I and Lochinvar acted third greyhound. I did not, and I gained accordingly. The
Duke laughed, and turned round to go home, saying,
"Thank you for the hare, Smith. We should have

gone home without one but for your Spanish greyhounds."

Coming home from riding one afternoon, I overtook the Duke on the bank of the canal, all alone. When I rode up I must either pass him, or saddle myself on him as companion, neither of which etiquette or delicacy tolerated. After my usual salutation, the Duke, with his brilliant imagination in trifles as well as things of moment, said, " If not in a hurry, ride home with me." After a little talk about hounds, greyhounds, etc., he said, " What! no dogs with you?" I said, " On Sundays, my lord, I never take them out." "Very proper," he said, " although I fear in our late struggle we respected Sunday but little. All our great battles were fought on that holy day which ought to be." " Yes," said I, "my lord, so was Trafalgar, and so was that dire disaster, New Orleans." "Was it?" he said. " You were there, were you not?" " Indeed was I, my lord." His Grace never mentioned dear Sir Edward Pakenham, and of course I never did, although my heart was full of him. "Tell me all about it." I did so. "What! the troops stood and fired in column, did they? What corps?" I named them. " Ah," he said, " they had not been accustomed to victory, but it was quite right to keep two such corps as the 7th Fusiliers and the 43rd in reserve." "We ought not to have landed where we did, my lord." "Certainly not," he said. " I was consulted about those lakes, and I immediately asked, 'Is there navigation there for

purposes of trade ?' When I was answered 'No,'
I said, 'Then it is injudicious to use them to land
an army, and craft of any size will never get up
to land the troops.'"

I had received and carried many orders from
his Grace, but of course never held a military conversation with him before. I was never so struck
as by the pointed questions he asked and the more
rapid questions my answers elicited. In half an
hour's ride he was perfectly acquainted with all
I could tell him, and said, " I am glad I have had
this conversation with you. It agrees as nearly
as may be with the opinion I had previously formed.
If you are not engaged, you and Juana come and
dine with me to-day. Her friend Alava will be
there." I was as proud as may be, because I knew
by this his Grace was satisfied with my explanation.
How I longed to tell him how I loved and admired
his brother-in-law, Sir Edward Pakenham! But
although I talked of "the General," I never made
use of the magic word (to me at least) "Pakenham."

One night, at a great ball at the Duke's, the
Prince and Princess Narinska were present, and a
lot of Russian and Cossack officers. The Princess
was the only Russian lady, a very beautiful and
accomplished woman. The Duke wished that the
mazurka should be danced in compliment to her,
but none of our ladies would stand up with the
Princess. So the Duke came up to my wife, and
took her hand : " Come, Juana, now for the Russian
fandango ; you will soon catch the step." A young

x

Russian came forward as her partner. The Princess danced elegantly, and the Duke was as anxious as I was that Juana should acquit herself well. She did, and he was as pleased as possible.

The Duke was in great spirits in those days, and whenever he was surrounded by Emperors and Kings he showed himself the great man that he was. His attention to them was most marked, but we ever observed that his Grace felt he was the representative of our King and country, and we could see the majesty and still the delicacy with which he conducted himself.

On one occasion the King of Prussia begged to see as many of the British Army by themselves as could be collected, and the majority were assembled not far from the pillar erected by the French in honour of the victory of [Denain *], and which was equally in honour of the Duke of Marlborough. (The French never gained a battle until [Marlborough] was so madly taken away by the intrigues of the British Government.) The King arrived much before his time, and our troops were not formed

---

* Battle of Denain, 24 July, 1712. Denain is only about five miles from Cambray. Marlborough was removed from the command of the armies of the Grand Alliance by the intrigues of Oxford and St. John in order to force the allies into the peace of Utrecht. The withdrawal of the British troops in the field a little later was immediately followed by the first really serious defeat sustained by the allies in the central field of the war since Marlborough had assumed the command ; Villars cutting up and annihilating an isolated force of 8000 men under the Earl of Albemarle, who were holding a bridge across the Scheldt at Denain to cover Eugene's force besieging Landrécy. For the clearing up of this passage (left incomplete in the MS.) I am indebted to my colleague, Mr. H. W. Appleton, M.A.

to receive him. The Duke's quick eye detected his
approach in the distance, and he says, " Hallo,
Fremantle, there he is ! He will be upon us before
we are ready, and we can't keep him back with
picquets. Ride up and make him take a long détour
until you see we are ready, although a few minutes
will suffice us." Our troops were in position like
lightning, and it was beautiful to see the Duke so
animated, so cool, so proud of his Army and the
rapidity with which we all moved to act up to his
wishes. He was altogether very popular with his
Army, but not so much so as after Toulouse. He
felt that everything that occurred at his head-
quarters must be a precedent for the guidance of all
the Armies he was in command of, and he was
frequently rigid, as it seemed, to extremes, particularly in all cases of disputes between officers
and the French inhabitants. At Cambray it was
part of my duty to receive all complaints, and,
generally speaking, our own people were the
aggressors. When the French were, his Grace
demanded that *their* authorities should make an
equal example. This correct principle of action
was as highly extolled by all thinking men as it
deserved, especially as the French had degraded
themselves all over the world (except in dear old
England which we protected) by acts of cruelty,
oppression, and tyranny towards the inhabitants.
The Duke said, " We are Englishmen and pride
ourselves on our deportment, and that pride shall
not be injured in my keeping." On parting with

his Army, he thanked the British contingent after
all the others. "He begs them to accept his best
acknowledgments for the example they have given
to others by their own good conduct, and for the
support and assistance they have invariably afforded
him to maintain the discipline of the Army." This
I thought at the time, and I do so more now, was
the highest compliment his Grace could pay us.
We had saved Europe, and now we were thanked
for our conduct in quarters, when in occupation
of the country of our enemy, who had been the
oppressors of the world; although, as good does
come out of evil, so has Europe been wonderfully
improved owing to the liberal principles moderately
derived from the madness of French democracy.

Our life in Cambray was one excess of gaiety.
My dear old friend and commander, Sir Andrew
Barnard, had been appointed Commandant, so that,
surrounded by my old generals, friends, and comrades, I was at home at once. We were both
young; my wife was beautiful. We were fêted
and petted by every one. I was the huntsman of a
magnificent pack of hounds, steward of races, riding
steeplechases, etc. My wife was taken the greatest
notice of by every one, especially by the Duke,
who, having known her as a child, always called
her his Spanish heroine, Juana. She rode beautifully hunting, was the best of waltzers, and sang
melodiously. We were surrounded by the best
society. All England's nobility poured forth to
see the lion of the day, the Duke's headquarters.

No wonder that in the midst of this gaiety and in this land of plenty, after the life of hardship and privation which we had led, we should have been somewhat intoxicated by the scene around us, and I spent a lot of money which, had I saved it prudently, would have now nearly accumulated to a fortune. I had prize-money for the Peninsula, for Washington, and for Waterloo paid at this period. I had money left me by my grandmother. All went as fast as I could get it.

In 1817, I and a friend went to look over the field of Waterloo. The wood of Hougoumont had been cut down, which very much altered the appearance of the ground, as did the want of troops, etc. To those unaccustomed to look at ground with and without troops, the difference cannot well be explained. I trod, however, upon this immortal field with a thrilling sensation of gratitude to Almighty God, first for personal safety and for the additional honour and glory my country's Army had acquired there, and next for the beneficial results to Europe ensured by the achievement of that wonderful battle. The left of the position as well as the centre was as during the battle, with the exception of the many tombs and monuments erected to mark the spots where lay interred so many gallant spirits, and many is the burning tear I shed over the mounds of some of my dearest friends, many of England's brightest sons and rising soldiers. No one can feel what a soldier does on such a spot, especially one who was in the midst of the strife. But nothing struck me so forcibly as the small extent of the field. It appeared impossible that so many thousands of troops could have contended on so constricted a space, the one spot on earth which decided the fate of Emperors and Kings, and the future destiny of nations.

Every year we had a grand review of the whole Army of the contingencies. One year the Duke of Kent was the Review-Marshal. The last year of occupation, viz. the third, we had an immense sham-fight, which ended on the heights of Fimare, where the Army passed in review [23 Oct.] the Emperor of Russia, King of Prussia, the Grand Duke Constantine, the Grand Duke Michael, etc. In the course of the day the Duke, riding with their Majesties, saw Juana. He called her up and presented her to the Emperor of Russia, "Voilà, Sire, ma petite guerrière espagnole qui a fait la guerre avec son mari comme la héroine de Saragosse." The Emperor shook her hands, and asked her to ride for some time with him as she spoke French fluently, when he put a variety of questions to her about the war in Spain, all of which she could answer as intelligently as most officers. At night she danced with the Grand Duke Michael, an excellent waltzer. When the Emperor's courtiers observed the attention paid by the Emperor to my wife, they sought out the husband. I was in my Rifle uniform. One fellow said, "Are you aware to whom Madame has had

the honour to be presented?"   "To be sure," I
said, saucily, "and by *whom*—the greatest man in
the world."

That night, riding into Valenciennes on the
pavé, both sides of the road being covered with
troops marching to their cantonments, it was very
cold, and I was clapping my hands on my shoulders,
à l'anglaise, when my wife says, "You have lost
your Star of the Bath."   I had felt something catch
in the lace of my sleeve, so I turned back.   A
column of Russian Cuirassiers were marching over
the ground I had traversed, and the sides of the
road being excessively dusty, I said to myself,
"What nonsense!   I can never find it," and was
in the act of turning back to my wife, when a flat-
footed dickey dragoon horse, having set his hollow
foot upon it, tossed it under my horse's nose out
of the dust upon the *pavé*.   It is a most ridiculous
occurrence to record, but my astonishment at the
time was excessive.   The star was bruised by the
horse's foot, in which shape I wore it twenty-nine
years.

The period of occupation was now reduced to
three years, and the Army was prepared to withdraw—to *our* mortification, for we should have
been delighted with two years more.   It was now,
on winding up my private accounts which had
been miserably neglected, I discovered my money
was far exceeded by my debts.   I therefore, as
one of my auxiliaries, put up to raffle, for 250
napoleons, a celebrated thoroughbred horse, the

Young Lochinvar, by Grouse, out of Dab Chick,
Vandyke's dam. This horse I had bought for a
large sum in my native town, just before the Battle
of Waterloo, from a gentleman who had bought
him at Newmarket for an immense price and
whose circumstances compelled him to become a
bankrupt. My father was aware of his pending
situation, and just on the eve of it bought
Lochinvar. I had ridden him hunting three years;
he was the only horse in the Army that was never
planted in the deep fields of France. As a horse
he was as celebrated as His Grace was as a
General, 16 hands high and equal to 14 stone.
It went to my heart to part with him. My wife
said, "Oh, I will have a ticket." "Oh, nonsense,
it is only throwing five napoleons away." However, she had her own way, as wives always have
(especially Spanish wives), and, by another piece
of my continued good luck, her ticket won the
horse, and I had Lochinvar in my stable, while the
245 napoleons readily found claimants. It was
a piece of fortune I was very grateful for. I
loved the horse, and he carried me in that stiff
county of Kent afterwards, as he had ever done
elsewhere.

From the day on which I presented my billet
to my landlord in Cambray, I was much struck
with his manly bearing and open conduct. He
was a man of a large family, a Monsieur Watin,
and his brother, also with a family, resided with
him. He showed me all his house and his stables

(he had built a kitchen and servants' rooms for any
one who should be quartered on him). He said,
"In this life, happiness is not to be attained, but
it must not be impeded. I am aware of the way
French officers behave in quarters. I hear you
English are less *exigeant.* This part of the house
I reserve for myself and my brother, the rest I
give to you." And I certainly had the best, for
he only reserved to himself one sitting-room. I
said, "I have more than enough." "No, no," he
said, "when you give a soirée you shall have this
too." I was three years in his house, and I never
had a word with either him or any member of his
family. On the contrary, nothing could be more
amicable. In the course of the second year my
father came and paid me a visit for near three
months. Never was man more happy and delighted. He was fond of field sports and of
flowers. The Bishop of Cambray had a magnificent garden, and many an hour did my father
spend there. When he arrived, of course I begged
him to tell us what he liked best at table. "Oh,
anything," he says, "only take care your French
cook does not make the pastry with oil, which I
know they do, but with butter." I had an excellent
cook, and I told him to be careful about his pastry,
which was, of course, made with oil. Every day
my father praised the pastry. After some weeks
I let him into the secret. "Ah," says he, "such
through life is prejudice." He was far from dis-
liking French wines. The day he left us—"Well

it is very true that you and the poor man of the
house live very friendly, but you have the whole
nearly. I shall go home now and pay my taxes
with delight. Even were they double, readily
would I pay rather than have such a fellow as you
and your establishment quartered on me!" Poor
dear father! I had been your pet son. Everything I practised that was manly, you taught me,
and to my equestrian powers and activity, which
first brought me into notice, did I owe my rapid
rise in the service.

The day having at length arrived when we were
to leave Cambray, [27 Oct. ?] Sir Andrew Barnard
and I were asked to at least twenty breakfasts. My
first was with the family on whom we were billeted,
and if they had been our nearest relations no greater
feeling could have been evinced. Monsieur Watin
was a great carpenter. To him I gave a capital
chest of tools, to his brother, who was a sports
man (in his way), I gave one of Manton's double-
barrelled guns, and my wife made many presents
to the female part of the family. Then came my
nineteen breakfasts with Barnard. We positively
sat down a few minutes with all our hosts and ate
something ; both of us laughing and saying, " We
have been together in situations when the sight of
such breakfasts would have been far from objectionable, but ' enough is as good as a feast.'" I never
was so tired of the sight of food. I felt as though
I never could feel the sensation of hunger again.
All this attention, however, was very gratifying,

and upon parting with our worthy family, as our
carriage drove through the streets, there was nothing
but waving of handkerchiefs and adieus. The
garrison had marched two days before. The most
complimentary letter I ever read was addressed
to the Commandant Barnard by the Mayor, a
Monsieur Bethune, a Bonapartist too, to the purport that, although every Frenchman must rejoice
at the cessation of the foreign occupation of his
country, as individuals he and all the city would
and must ever remember the English with gratitude for their generosity and liberality, and for
the impartial justice ever shown by Barnard
during his three years' Commandantship. In a
French fortress the Commandant has far more
authority than the Prime Minister in England.
Thus we parted from Cambray, where we had had
three years' gaiety amidst the wealth and aristocracy
of England, in the country of an enemy that had
contended and struggled to subdue our own in a
most sanguinary war by sea and land, lasting with
but little intermission from 1798 to 1815. The
garrison of Cambray was composed of a Brigade of
Guards,—the 1st Battalion Grenadiers under Colonel
the Hon. William Stewart, and the Coldstreams
under Colonel Woodford. I never before or since
served with such correct soldiers, and they had the
very best non-commissioned officers. There were
peculiarities in the mode in which the officers
performed their duties, but, according to their own
rules, it was a lesson of rectitude, zeal, honour,

and manliness. 1 quite agree with Johnny Kincaid that the officers in our Army who come from our aristocracy are ever most zealous as officers, and certainly most agreeable as companions, and I have now served with most corps of the Army, Hussars, Guards, Infantry, etc.

CHAPTER XXVIII.

RETURN TO ENGLAND (1818)—HARRY SMITH REJOINS HIS REGIMENT—SHORNCLIFFE—GOSPORT—DISCHARGE OF THE PENINSULAR VETERANS.

ON reaching Calais I could not avoid calling to memory the British possession of that celebrated fortress, for so many years the bone of contention and strife. All was bustle and embarcation. We embarked in a small vessel [31 Oct. ?], and the wind obliged us to go to Ramsgate. The London Custom House had provided for baggage to be examined at Ramsgate as well as at Dover, and nothing could be more liberal and gentlemanlike than the Custom House officers (of course acting under instructions). My wife had an immense box of French dresses which, being all extended on account of the large flounces then worn, required great room. While I was passing my baggage, one of the officers said, "And that large box—what does it contain?" I said, "My wife's dresses." "I have not the least doubt of it, sir, as you say so, sir; but I declare I never saw such a box of ladies' dresses in my life before." Then came her guitar. "What is this?" "Oh, hand it along, it's naught but a fiddle."

The celebrated Cavalry officer, Sir John Elley, a very tall, bony, and manly figure of a man, with grim-visaged war depicted in his countenance, with whiskers, moustaches, etc. like a French Pioneer, came over to Dover during the time of our occupation of France. He was walking on the path, with his celebrated sword belted under his *surtout*. As the hooking up of the sword gave the coat-flap the appearance of having something large concealed under it, a lower order of Custom officer ran after him, rudely calling, "I say, you officer, you! stop, stop, I say! What's that under your coat?" Sir John turned round, and drawing his weapon of defence in many a bloody fight, to the astonishment of the John Bulls, roared out through his moustache in a voice of thunder, "That which I will run through your d——d guts, if you are impertinent to me!"

My Regiment was at Shorncliffe, and thither I and my wife proceeded, parting with many friends of the Guards, some of whom she has never seen since. I was given an entirely new Company, that is, one composed of recruits. I interceded with Colonel Norcott, however, to give me a few of my dear old comrades into each squad, and with their help and example I soon inspired the rest with the feelings of soldiers. There was a pack of hounds too in the neighbourhood, and though it is a stiff, bad country, fox-hunting is fox-hunting in any shape, and I had two noble hunters, Lochinvar and a celebrated mare, besides the " Brass Mare" for my wife. My whole income at the moment was my pay, 12s. 6d. a day. One day, after a capital run with the hounds, Mr. Deedes asked me to dine with him, and I had a post-chaise to go in to dinner, which cost me 17s. Thus—

> " How happy's the soldier who lives on his pay,
>   And spends half-a-crown out of sixpence a day ! "

My Battalion was ordered to Gosport, and soon after at Shorncliffe, which had been the depôt of the Regiment during the whole war, not a Rifleman was left. I marched [about Dec. 24–28] in command of the Headquarters Division, all our old soldiers. Neither they nor I could help remarking the country as a difficult one to make war in. You would hear the men, " I say, Bill, look at that wood on the hill there and those hedgerows before it. I think we could keep that ourselves against half Soult's Army. Ah, I had rather keep it than attack it ! But, Lord, the war's all over now."

When I first joined at Shorncliffe we heard of nothing but "the French are coming over." We have been in among *them*, I take it, since. They never could have got to London through such a stiff country. We would have destroyed the roads and cut down the trees to make those d——d things they used to do—*abattis* * ; besides, where

---

* "Few good riders haggle at a ditch, but an abattis of trees, with their trunks towards their friends, and their branches spread out towards the foe, is a less manageable obstacle."—H. Havelock, in his account of his brother W. H. (Buist's *Annals of India for* 1848).

would be the use of all their capering cavalry, etc. ?

During this march, when the men were billeted in the inns and scattered over the country, I could not divest myself of the feeling of insecurity I had acquired after so many years' precautionary habits ; and although I repeated to myself a hundred times daily, "You are in England," the thought would arise, "You are in the power of your enemy." Before dismissing the men, I always told them the hour I should march in the morning, and men who were billeted either ahead or on the sides of the road were to join their Companies as I arrived. During the whole march I never had a man absent or irregular. Such a band of practised and educated soldiers may never again traverse England.

My wife posted from Shorncliffe into Sussex—to Beauport, Sir John Lambert's temporary seat, where the kind family insisted on her staying until I came to fetch her to Gosport, which I did soon after. On arrival at Gosport we were led to believe we should be a year or two there, and we began to (what is called) make ourselves comfortable.

We had a great number of guards and sentries literally over nothing. One night, however, on visiting the different guards and counting them, I found every man present. I asked, "What! no man on sentry ?" "Oh no, sir; the 86th, whom we relieved, say they always bring in all sentries at night." "Why, this is a new way—new to us." "Certainly," the sergeants said.

The following day I and two or three officers went to inspect every sentry's post. We found some with orders "to see that no one took that gun away" (a 32-pounder dismounted), one "to see as them goats did not leave the rampart." He was one of our soldiers, and I said, "Confound you, did you take such an order from a storekeeper?" He said, "Why, I hardly look on it as a *horder*, only civil-like of me; and you know, sir, goats were worth looking after at Dough Boy Hill" (near Almaraz, so called from our having nothing to eat for three weeks but dough and goats' flesh, and very little of either).* I represented all this to Lord Howard of Effingham, who very readily entertained the report, and sentries were all taken off, where not required. Colonel Norcott soon after joined.

While we were here 300 of our oldest and best soldiers were discharged. Every one came to say farewell to my wife; and there was a touching parting between officers and soldiers, now about to be dispersed through Great Britain, after so many years' association under such eventful circumstances. There was not one who could not relate some act of mutual kindness and reciprocity of feeling in connexion with the many memorable events in which they had taken part. I and many of the officers marched several miles on the road with these noble fellows. In the Barrack Square they had prayed me to give them the word of command

* See p. 19, bottom.

Y

to march off. " Sure," says an Irishman, "it's the last after the thousand your honour has given us." I did so; but when the moment arrived to part every man's tears were chasing each other down his bronzed and veteran cheeks. They grasped their officers' hands,—"God bless your honour!" then such a shout and cheer. Such feelings in times of peace are not, cannot be acquired. My faithful old West was of the party; but he parted from me and his mistress in our house. Poor faithful, noble fellow, as gallant as a lion, he had been with me from Vimiera and Coruña until 1819.

The 18th June, the first anniversary of the Battle of Waterloo which we had spent in England, was such a day throughout the Regiment, with dinners for the soldiers, non-commissioned officers, wives and children. Among the officers there was such a jubilee of mirth, mingled with grief for our lost comrades, as must be conceived, for never was there a Regiment in which harmony and unanimity were more perfect.

In the autumn the manufacturing districts, Glasgow, Manchester, Birmingham, etc., became much disturbed, and our soldiers, who invariably know everything first, insisted on it we should go to Glasgow. My Company was out at target practice with others, when we heard the assembly sound. "Hurrah for Glasgow!" said the men. We all marched home, and found we were to embark on board a man-of-war immediately. By four o'clock that afternoon [18 Sept.] we were all on board the *Liffey*. Sir James Kempt had succeeded Lord Howard of Effingham in the command at Portsmouth, and proud he was to see one of his old Battalions in peace the same ready soldiers they were in war. My wife remained behind to go in the *Spartan* frigate, which had been recently fitted up for the Duchess of Kent. The Captain put her up superbly, and she reached Leith Roads in time to join my Company on the march.[*]

[*] The 1st Battalion landed at Leith on 27th Sept. (Cope, p. 217.)

CHAPTER XXIX.

GLASGOW (1819–1825)—RADICAL DISTURBANCES—
HARRY SMITH ONCE MORE ON THE STAFF AS
MAJOR OF BRIGADE—GEORGE IV.'S VISIT TO
EDINBURGH—HARRY SMITH REVISITS PARIS—HE
REJOINS HIS REGIMENT IN IRELAND.

GLASGOW at this season of the year, October, is
a most melancholy, dirty, smoky city, particularly
the end in which the barracks are placed; and
such was the state of the city, my wife had to live
in barracks and we were again shut up in one
room, as during the war. When matters approached
the worst, I sent my wife to Edinburgh, where
she received every kindness and hospitality. There
was living there then Mrs. Beckwith, who had
campaigned with her husband in Prince Ferdinand
of Brunswick's time. She was then ninety-four,
and lived afterwards to upwards of a hundred, the
mother of Sir George Beckwith, my dear Sir
Sydney, and several other sons. She was in full
possession of her intellect, and was delighted to
talk of war with my wife. The latter said one
day, "I am afraid I do not speak English well
enough to explain myself." "Not speak well

enough! Why?"   "Because I am a Spaniard,
and have only recently learned to speak English."
"A Spaniard?   Stand up, and let me look at your
feet and ankles, for I have always heard your
countrywomen celebrated for their neatness."   My
wife was still in heart a Spaniard, and as particular
as ever in shoes and stockings, and the poor old
lady was delighted. After talking for a certain time,
she used to say, "Now go; I am tired."

Our duty in Glasgow was very laborious and
irksome. We had neither enemy nor friends: a
sort of *Bellum in Pace*, which we old campaigners
did not understand. But, although constantly insulted by the mob in the streets, either individually
or in a body, our deportment was so mild that we
soon gained rather the respect than otherwise of
the misguided and half-starved weavers. They had
many old soldiers amongst them, and had organized
themselves into sixteen Battalions.   Many of
these old soldiers I knew; one was a Rifleman—
an old comrade who had lost his arm at New
Orleans—and from him I ascertained their perfect
organization. They had a General, or Central,
Committee of Delegates ("a House of Lords"), and
each district had a committee, who sent a delegate
to the Central Committee. The regiments were
formed by streets, so that in case of a turn-out
they could parade—"Ah, just as we did in the
towns of Spain and France," * my comrade said.

One day my Company was sent out with twenty

* See p. 166, bottom.

of the 7th Hussars, just before daylight, to arrest a party of delegates. We had magistrates, etc. with us, and succeeded in arresting every man. I saw a violent storm of mob assembling. I put the prisoners in the centre of my Company, under the command of my subaltern, Henry Havelock,* now a hero of Burma, Afghanistan, and Maharajpore celebrity, a clever, sharp fellow, and said, " Move you on collected to the barracks, and I will cover you with the Hussars." On my word, they were violent, and the Hussars, with the flat of their swords, as I particularly directed, did make the heads of some ache, while brickbats, stones, etc. were flying among us half as bad as grapeshot. The magistrates were horridly timid and frightened lest I should

---

* Henry Havelock, writing to his old Captain, then Major-General Smith, Oct. 3, 1840, refers perhaps to the events of this day. [Was it April 2, 1820 ? See Cope, p. 220.] " I feel that it is time I ought to be trying to ascend the ladder, if ever, for as the *Battle of Glasgow Green* was fought in 1820, I fear I must now be not very far from forty-six." It is perhaps not the least of Harry Smith's services to his country that he incited his subaltern, Henry Havelock, to make a serious study of the science of his profession. Havelock writes to him Sept. 5, 1840, as his " master," and writes of him on Oct. 2, 1847 (after his appointment to the Governorship of the Cape) : " When I was a boy, he was one of the few people that ever took the trouble to teach me anything ; and while all the rest around me would have persuaded me that English soldiering consisted in blackening and whitening belts with patent varnish and pipe-clay, and getting every kind of mercenary manoeuvre, he pointed my mind to the nobler part of our glorious profession. As a public man I shall ever acknowledge his merits. He is an excellent soldier—one of the few now extant among us who have set themselves to comprehend the higher portions of the art. He has a natural talent for war, and it has been improved by the constant reflection of years, and much experience. There is no species of business which Harry Smith's mental tact will not enable him to grasp."—Marshman's *Memoirs of Sir H. Havelock* (1867), pp. 66, 165.

order the troops to fire. I said, "You command," which in those days they did, nor could the officer fire, according to law, without their order.

The Commander-in-Chief in Scotland, Major-General Sir T. Bradford, was then in Glasgow, and also Sir W. Rae, the Lord-Advocate. Officers who had been on duty were to report direct to the Commander-in-Chief. This I did, and hardly was my report received, when I was sent for to the Inn where these authorities were. Sir Thomas, ever a kind friend to me, met me at the door of the room where they were, and said, "Smith, the Lord-Advocate is most annoyed that you permitted His Majesty's troops to be insulted this morning with impunity, and desires to speak with you." Sir W. Rae, although afterwards I found him a capital fellow, was dictatorial in his manner, and violent and pompous in his address. He sat when I advanced towards him. I saw by his eye what was coming, and my blood was as hot as his; and the thought rushed into my mind, "What! to be rowed by this man, who have ever been approved of by *the Duke!*"

"Pray, sir, are you the officer who allowed His Majesty's troops to be insulted in such a manner, with arms in their hands? *I am surprised, sir.* Why did you thus tamely act?" So I replied, quite as dictatorially as my lord, "Because, my lord, I was acting under the officers of the law, the magistrates, of whom you are the Commander-in-Chief. They would not act, and I did not desire

to bring upon my head either the blood of my
foolish and misguided countrymen, or the odium
of the Manchester magistrates." (An affair of
Yeomanry * had lately occurred.) "I brought off
every prisoner; but, my lord, since that is your
feeling, give me a written order to march through
Glasgow with the same party of soldiers and my
prisoners. A mob will soon attempt the rescue,
and d—— me, my lord, but I will shoot all
Glasgow to please you." I saw Sir Thomas Bradford biting his lips, and looking at me as much as
to say, "Gently, Smith." I turned on my heel,
and said, "Good morning, my lord."

From that day the Lord-Advocate took a great
fancy to me, and gave me some of the most laborious
night-marches I ever made, especially one to Galston
New Mills and Kilmarnock. It was so dark (and
an *ignis fatuus* dancing before us to make it
worse), I had a 6-pounder upset over a bridge.
Throughout my previous services I never had
more arduous duties than on this occasion.

A Battalion of Volunteer Riflemen were organized
here,† all young gentlemen, under the superin-

* "Peterloo," 16 August, 1819. It is amusing to contrast the
soldierly reference to an " affair of Yeomanry," with Shelley's *Masque
of Anarchy*, called forth by the same occurrence.

† " In 1819 and onwards for a few years, when the country was
supposed to be in danger from a rising of the " Radicals," and there was
certainly a good deal of disaffection, Glasgow was the centre of the agitation. In these circumstances it was resolved to re-embody the " Glasgow
Volunteer Sharpshooters," a Corps which in 1808 had made way for
the " Local Militia." This was accordingly done, the senior surviving
officer of the old corps, the well known Samuel Hunter, of the " Glasgow
Herald," being appointed Lieut.-Colonel Commandant, and Robert

tendence of my old Regiment, now called the Rifle Brigade.* This corps more nearly deserved the comprehensive appellation "soldiers" than any corps ever did, except those of the line. Their Colonel, Sam Hunter, walked twenty-two stone, an enormous man, with a capacity of mind fully proportioned to his corporeal stature. Many are the arduous duties I exacted of these Volunteers, and they were executed with cheerfulness and prompt obedience.

Sir Hussey Vivian came down to command, bringing with him as his Major-of-Brigade, my friend, (now Sir) De Lacy Evans. Evans did not wish to serve, but to study in London to prepare himself to be a senator, and he kindly went to the Horse Guards and said, "If my appointment is filled up by Harry Smith of the Rifles, I will resign." This arrangement was readily assented to, and I was again on the Staff, where I remained until 1825.

I had occasionally the most disagreeable duty, and always a difficulty to resist the importunity of the kindest hospitality that ever I and my wife received in this world. Immediately after I was

Douglas Alston, the Major. Colonel Hunter retired in 1822, and Major Alston became Colonel.

Colonel Alston was a capital officer, and the regiment, in appearance, discipline and drill, a very fine one. Some of the older citizens of Glasgow must still remember the grand reviews on the green, in which the Sharpshooters and Regulars took part under the command of Colonel Smith, afterwards Sir H. Smith, the hero of Aliwal."—*The Old Country Houses of the Old Glasgow Gentry*, 2nd edit., p. 6.

* "By an order dated 'Horse Guards, Feb. 16, 1816,' the 95th was removed from the regiments of the line, and styled *The Rifle Brigade*."—Cope, p. 214.

appointed Major-of-Brigade, Major-General (now Sir T.) Reynell was appointed to command the district of Glasgow and the West of Scotland in place of Sir Hussey Vivian. In a year, as affairs in Glasgow assumed a more tranquil appearance, Queen Caroline's trial being finished and Her Majesty's death having occurred, Major-General Reynell was removed from the Staff of Glasgow, and went out in the *Glasgow* frigate to the East Indies to a command in Bengal, but I, the Major-of-Brigade, was kept on. My orders were to report direct to the Commander-in-Chief, Sir T. Bradford, in Edinburgh, and to receive no orders from any one but himself; and I could give any orders in his name which the exigencies of the moment required. Of course I was very cautious, fully aware of the delicacy of my position as regarded my senior officers, some of whom were very jealous of the authority vested in me, although personally I had never had a controversial word with them.

A great part of my duty in the summer was to inspect the various Corps of Yeomanry throughout the Western District, a most delightful duty. I was treated *en prince* by the Duke of Montrose, Lord Glasgow, Lord Douglas, Lord-Lieutenants of counties, Lord Blantyre, etc. The officers of the Corps of Yeomanry, too, all belonged to the aristocracy of the country, and their houses were open as their hospitable hearts.

In 1820 I had with me Sir John Hope's and Lord Elcho's Troops of the Edinburgh Light Horse,

consisting entirely of gentlemen of the highest class
in Scotland, and we were employed upon some
very arduous duty together. I have seen these
gentlemen after a long, heavy, and wet night's march,
every one dressing his own horse, feeding him, etc.,
like a German Hussar, ere they thought of anything
for themselves. One of the Troop, Corporal Menzies,
is now a Judge at the Cape, my most intimate
friend, and many is the laugh we have had at his
military experiences.

When we see the gentlemen of the country thus
devoted to it, we need have little fear of its continued prosperity. In my opinion there is no system
which can be adopted of such importance to our
country as the yearly calling-out of the Yeomanry
for a few days' exercise. It brings the educated
aristocracy in contact with the less favoured in life,
the cultivators of the soil,—landlords with tenants.
It shows the latter in their true character—honest,
manly, and liberal fellows, and teaches them to look
up to their superiors, while it also shows the former
what a noble set of men their tenants are, obedient,
but as proud as an English yeoman ought to be,
and that, thus engaged in the defence of our country
and in the maintenance of our rights as British
subjects, they are to be treated with the respect
due to every individual of the social compact.

When His Majesty George IV. paid a visit to
Edinburgh [15–27 Aug. 1822], I was ordered thither,
and sent to Dalkeith (where His Majesty was to
reside in the palace of the Duke of Buccleugh) to

superintend the guards and escorts, etc., for his Majesty's state (his *protection* was in the safe custody of the hearts of his loyal people); and when Sir Walter Scott and the Commander-in-Chief, Sir Thomas Bradford, had planned all the various processions, the organization and conduct of them was given to me, and His Majesty was kind enough to say they were conducted to his royal satisfaction. He never once was delayed in the streets by a check, thanks to the lesson I learnt in the Light Division how to regulate the march of a column.

Early every day I went, as I was ordered, to the palace to receive orders through the Gold Stick. The morning His Majesty was to leave Dalkeith, he sent for me to express his approbation of all I had done, and as I left the apartment Sir William Knighton followed me, and asked me, by the king's command, if there was anything I desired. I was so young a Lieutenant-Colonel, only of eight years' standing, with hundreds senior to me, that I neither desired to ask such an exorbitant thing as to be Aide-de-Camp to His Majesty, nor felt any inclination, on account of such pacific services, to be exalted above so many of my more meritorious comrades. Knighthood I would not accept, so I very quietly said, " I will ask a great favour of His Majesty—to give Sir Thomas Bradford's Aide-de-Camp the rank of Lieutenant-Colonel." Sir William said, " If the Commander-in-Chief will write me a note, it shall be done," and thus as good a fellow as ever lived got his rank. There is much honour

attached to the charge of royalty, and as many of
my old comrades were about the king, Barnard,
Vivian, etc., I spent a most agreeable time, but the
expense for myself and my wife was enormous. It
cost me upwards of a year's income in new uniforms,
court dresses, etc. His Majesty particularly admired
my wife's riding.

Never was the old adage of "like master, like
man" more exemplified than in the royal household.
In the organization of the processions, etc. I was
frequently engaged with the servants, coachmen,
footmen, etc. I never saw such obedient, willing,
and respectful fellows in my life; and I never had
to express more than a wish, to have any order
implicitly, readily, and agreeably obeyed. Accustomed to the obedience of soldiers, I was particularly
struck with equally obedient deportment on the
part of those whom imagination had led me to
believe to be a set of troublesome fellows. George
IV. was a gentleman, and from His Noble Majesty
was derived a "*ton*" which spread throughout his
court and his household, an example and honour to
the great nation he ruled.

In 1824 my gallant friend, Macdougall, requested me to accompany him to Paris to arrange
a little matter of delicacy with a gentleman who had
ill-used a lady, a great friend of Mac's family. We
soon arranged that matter, the gentleman being one
in fact, as well as in name, and acting as well as
any could under the circumstances. Ten years had
now elapsed since my first acquaintance with the

south of France, and six since I had quitted
Cambray. We landed at Boulogne, and had a long
journey to Paris by *diligence,* that renowned and
cumbrous and slow machine now replaced by the flying steam-coaches. Our *diligence* adventures were
numerous but not unusual. But my new visit to
France, and entry into Paris, forcibly brought
to mind the immense Armies assembled around
us in 1815,—the streets filled with uniforms of
every civilized nation, the public resorts ornamented
with the spoil of every nation in Europe except
Great Britain!

Paris was now a quiet city, much like any other,
and the only thing which attracted my attention
was the number of drunken soldiers in the streets.
In London such a thing is of rare occurrence indeed.
But it appeared to me that the French Army had
acquired some of those habits of the English which
we would willingly resign to them in perpetuity.
I visited my old quarters at Neuilly. My good old
landlady was no more. Imagination aroused a
variety of feelings closely cemented with the past,
while the present showed Paris aiming at English
habits, just as London was rapidly acquiring French
manners. In the streets of Paris we saw young
dandies driving tilburys in the last style, with
grooms in brown top-boots. To speak English
was becoming fashionable, whereas formerly any
Frenchman attempting to speak English was regarded as a Bourbonist, or an enemy to the blood-
acquired liberties of his country. We left France

now certainly flourishing, and speedily returned to our own land of fair and handsome faces, well-fed inhabitants, richly cultivated and enclosed fields. And oh, my countrymen, had you seen as many countries as I now have, and been banished so many years from your own, then would you bless that land of happiness and liberty which gave you birth, that land which was exempt from the horror of war through the ability of your statesmen, the blood of your sailors and soldiers, and the patriotism of the people !

During my residence in Glasgow, I twice went over to the Isle of Man, in expectation of succeeding to the Government of the House of Keys. The Governor was very ill, and desirous to retire. He got well, and forgot his former inclinations.

In 1825, such was the tranquillity in this immense manufacturing district, I was put off the Staff, and received from the Lord-Provost, Town Councillors, and Municipality every demonstration of their gratitude for the efficient aid I had afforded them to maintain tranquillity and subdue riots, mobs, and popular ebullitions.*   My answer was, that the only merit I claimed was that in the service of my country and in the execution of this duty on very trying and most irritating occasions for five years, not a drop of my deluded countrymen's blood had been shed, though it was often indeed difficult in the extreme to avoid it.

The parting of myself and wife from our

* He was now admitted to the Freedom of the City of Glasgow.

numerous and most hospitable and kind friends in Glasgow, and the whole of the West of Scotland, is not to be described. My principal quarters I may say were Elderslie House,* where the most amiable and numerous family were ever to us a source of happiness, Harhead, Lord Glasgow's, and Cumbernauld House, Admiral Fleming's, whose wife was a county-woman of mine; but to name these houses in particular is hardly fair, for throughout the country we received equal hospitality. Certainly the happiest five years of my life were spent in Scotland, amidst the society of such people. Books were to be had of every description, intellectual conversation was ever enjoyed, and amidst the learned professors of the colleges I have spent some of the most agreeable evenings.

I was to join my Corps in Belfast, and as we went down the Clyde in the steamer, the inmates of every seat on its banks were assembled to wave us, alas! a *last* farewell, for many of those dear and valued friends are now in the silent grave. Glasgow, with all your smoke, your riots, mobs, and disaffections, I look back to you with perfect happiness, and I love the Scotch nation with a similar degree of patriotism to that with which I have fought for my native land, the words of my dear mother ever ringing in my ears, " Remember, if ever you fight for your country, you were born an Englishman."

Belfast, although then a flourishing city, showed

---

* Then the seat of Archibald Speirs, Esq. His family consisted of five sons and nine daughters.—*The Old Country Houses of the Old Glasgow Gentry*, 2nd edit. pp. 95, 96.

a great contrast to Glasgow in regard to the appearance of its population, although the gentlemen were as hospitable as possible, and most enthusiastic sportsmen, and, as I could ride a bit, I was soon at home among them. I was soon, however, ordered to Downpatrick, where my Company and two others were quartered. I was received by my dear old Regiment with every demonstration of affection, and spent a few months most happily at this little town of Downpatrick, among very amiable and kind people. The peasantry there were my delight, such light-hearted, kind creatures I never saw, and as liberal as primitive Christians. Not a day I had not sent me presents of eggs and butter, etc. It was painful occasionally to accept them, but as I saw that refusal created pain, I had no alternative. There were many of our old Light Division soldiers discharged and living in this neighbourhood, and every market day (Saturday) a re-enacting of old times was imposed on my patience. One, a noble soldier of the 43rd, celebrated every anniversary of a battle by getting gloriously drunk. On one occasion he was drunk without this exciting cause. I said, " Come, come, Murphy, this is too bad ; to-day is no anniversary." " Maybe not, your honour, but, by Jasus, there are so many it is hard to remember them all, and the life's blood of me would dry up, if I missed the ' cilibration ' of one of 'em—so it's safest to get drunk when you can."

CHAPTER XXX.

SHORTLY after this, my Corps was ordered to embark at Belfast [30 July] for Nova Scotia on board three transports, the *Arab,* the [*Speke* *], and the *Joseph Green.* I had the command of two Companies and a half in the last ship. When we arrived on board, with the quantity of baggage, etc., the ship was in a wild-looking state. The Captain and the agent came to me and said, "We are ordered to go to sea to-morrow, but this is impossible from the state of the ship ; it is of no consequence, if you would give us a certificate to this effect ; the day after to-morrow will do quite as well." "The devil it will," says I, "when you are ordered. Have you everything belonging to the ship's stores on

* I supply this name from Cope, p. 226.

board ?"   " Everything." Johnny Kincaid was my
subaltern, so I said, " Johnny, at daybreak in the
morning turn out all hands, and prepare a certificate
for my signature at eight o'clock if required."
Eight o'clock arrived, and no man-of-war's decks
were ever more ready for action—our baggage all
stored below, our soldiers' arms and everything else
arranged, and I told the Captain, " Now, you see,
I need sign no certificate. We Riflemen obey
orders and do not start difficulties."   We were
under way in no time.   This Captain Lumsden
was an excellent fellow; some years after he took
Sir James Stirling out as Governor to Swan River
and touched at the Cape, when I had an opportunity of returning some of his many acts of
kindness.

Our voyage was much like other voyages across
the Atlantic, but an odd circumstance occurred.
Although each ship sailed from Belfast separately
and at an interval of two days, mine the last, we
were all three sailing into Halifax Harbour the
same day [1 Sept. ?], in the very order in which we
left Belfast, and anchored within a few hours of
each other. Our dear old friend, Sir James Kempt,
the Governor there, was delighted with this odd
re-union, and laughed and said, " I see my old
comrades, whether separated by sea or land, get
together in the old way, however distantly extended."   In Halifax we were soon found by our
other dear old friends, the 52nd Regiment. They
had more old soldiers in their ranks than we had,

having embarked for America two or three years before us; and oh, the greeting with us all, and the happiness of the old soldiers at meeting my wife again! They were inquiring after her horse Tiny, her dog, etc., and expecting all were alive as when we had parted at Bordeaux in 1814.

If ever happiness existed in this world, we may claim it for Halifax when the Government was administered by Sir James Kempt. Society, by the force of his example, was the most agreeable thing imaginable. Government House was princely in its style; we had private theatricals, races, sham-fights, regattas, and among all our varied amusements (to which were added in the winter four-in-hand and tandem driving-clubs, and picnics at the Half-way House), harmony the most perfect prevailed between civilians and officers, soldiers and sailors. (Our noble fellows of the Navy were commanded by Admiral Lake.)

We had a great re-union of Governors there one year; Lord Dalhousie, Governor-General of North America, Sir James Kempt, Governor of Nova Scotia, General Sir John Keane, Governor of Jamaica, Sir Howard Douglas, Governor of New Brunswick, and Colonel Reid, Governor of Prince Edward's Island—a regular court of magnates—and never were people more happy than all. For some time I had the command of the Regiment, Colonel Norcott that of the Garrison. I afterwards accepted an unattached half-pay majority, expecting to be brought in again, and I was appointed A.D.C. to

my dear and valued friend, Sir James Kempt. I
thus learned much of the administration of a Government, which was afterwards of the greatest possible
use to me when administering a Government myself. I had often witnessed Sir J. Kempt's ability
as a soldier; but I cannot avoid saying he perfectly
astonished me and all who knew him as a statesman
and a ruler. Evincing such temper, such a clear-
ness of judgment, such discretion and most uncompromising justice, he soon carried with him the
Colony. The House of Assembly, and even the
Whig opposition, admired his talent and never
opposed any of his great acts, while, by his amiable
manners and kind, though unostentatious, hospitality,
society was cemented, and indeed, what the word
implies, *social.*

The day I was gazetted out, my old Company
came in a body to ask me to allow them to give me
a dinner, "that is, we don't expect your honour
to sit down with us, but we will have a dinner, and
you will drink with us a parting glass." I readily
consented, and sat down with them, too, for a few
minutes. Old Johnny Kincaid, who succeeded
me as Captain, and my subalterns, were present,
and the parting glass was drunk with that mutual
feeling of strong affection which exists between
officers and soldiers. I was a most rigid disciplinarian, but good conduct was as much distinguished
by me as bad was visited, and I carried all with me.

I was not long permitted to enjoy this comparative repose, but was appointed [23 Nov.]

Deputy Quartermaster-General in Jamaica. I
speedily prepared to join, taking a passage on
board a little brig for ourselves and our horses. I
had a farewell dinner given me by the Governor
and by the Admiral, and many of the kind inhabitants, and by every Regimental Mess, while
the Regimental Order issued by Colonel Norcott
speaks for itself.*

I had served twenty-five [twenty-one ?] years in
this Corps during the most eventful periods. It
had never been on service but I was fighting with
some portion of it. No officer had ever posted it so
often on outlying picquet, and I had fought where

* " Colonel Norcott feels himself bound by every principle of public
and private duty to express to Lieutenant-Colonel Smith and the
officers and battalion at large his most sincere and deep regret
for the loss of an officer who has served for twenty-two years with
such indefatigable zeal, distinguished bravery, and merit, and now
retires from its active duties on promotion and an appointment on the
staff in Jamaica, but to resume in that situation the same persevering
devotion to his profession, his king, and country.

" The Colonel knows how truly every officer in the Brigade participates his feelings and sentiments, and is assured of the lively and
warm wishes of every non-commissioned officer and soldier for the
welfare of one who, with every attribute of as good and as gallant an
officer as ever lived, invariably united the most kind and peculiar
interest for the comfort and happiness of the soldier.

" At the particular request of this officer, it affords the Colonel
much pleasure to release from confinement to barracks, and punishments of every description, all soldiers now under their sentences ;
he only hopes, and is ready to believe, that they will prove sensible
and grateful for Colonel Smith's kindness, shown up to the very last
moment he remains amongst them, in addition to every noble and
honourable feeling which all soldiers ought to show in the performance
of their duty and conduct on every occasion, by a determination to
relinquish every habit tending to injure the good of the service, their
corps, and individual respectability, comfort, happiness, and future
welfare.

" A. NORCOTT, *Colonel.*

" Halifax, Nova Scotia, June 4, [? Jan.] 1827."

it had not been ; thus were severed no ordinary or transient ties.

The day we were to leave we can never forget. Sir James Kempt sent for me to his private room. I saw his warm heart was full. He said, " Harry, I am going to exact a promise of you. The climate you are going to is one where life and death so rapidly change places, it would be folly to rush into unnecessary danger, by exposing yourself to the effects of the sun or leading that life of violent exercise you have ever done. My desire, therefore, is your promise never to go out snipe-shooting or to ride any more races, in a tropical climate at least." Of course I promised. He then said, holding a letter in his hand, " Here are some notes for your guidance in Jamaica, and as you have paid three times more for your passage [than the allowance ?], there is a note enclosed which makes up the difference." The tears rolled down his gallant cheeks, and I left the room in the deepest affliction.

On descending to the ball-room I found every gentleman of Halifax and every officer of the garrison awaiting to accompany us on board. Sir James, taking my wife under his arm, led the procession.

As I was with Sir James, three non-commissioned officers, one Rifles, one 52nd, and one 74th, came up and begged to speak to me. They said, " Your Honour, the whole garrison are turned out and in column in the street. There's the head of it to carry your Honour on board." By Jupiter, there

they were, sure enough, in a column of sixes, one
file Rifles, one 52nd, one 74th. They had a chair
in which they seated me, and carried me after the
procession of officers on board. These compli-
ments *at the time* are impressive, but when we look
back remind us of the pain of parting, and that
many who were then most loud in their shouts of
parting acclamation are long ago mingled with the
mortal dust we shall all add to. The little brig was
weighed immediately. All officers who had sailing
boats accompanied us to the mouth of the harbour,
and thus we parted from faithful friends, veteran
comrades, and three of the most renowned Regiments of the Duke's old Army, and in a few hours
found ourselves alone on the wide Atlantic, with a
crew of one captain and seven sailors, and one
quadrant the only nautical instrument on board.
But as we were all in all to each other, so were we
still in possession of the world. This quadrant the
captain would leave about the deck in a careless
manner when taking his observations. I almost
worshipped it, and therefore watched over it accordingly. We had a very favourable passage, and
dined every day on deck but one (for our cabin was
not that of the *Royal Oak*), and ourselves and
horses reached Jamaica in twenty-eight days all
right. Soon after we landed, the crew, all but one
man, an old German carpenter, died of yellow fever,
and in the harbour commenced one of those awful
visitations to the island which sweep off hundreds.

We landed at Kingston, where Sir J. Keane's

house was prepared for us. The Governor was at Spanish Town, but came in with his generous warmth of heart next day to entertain us. Our worthy friend, Admiral Fleming, of Cumbernauld House,* was in naval command. Mrs. Fleming was with him, so that, although in a new world, we were among faithful old friends.

As Quartermaster-General, my first attention was directed to the barrack accommodation, furniture, utensils, etc. The barracks at Upper Park was a Royal Establishment in every respect; the buildings were most beautifully provided, capacious, and built on arches with a current of air passing beneath; they had a bath-room, etc. The barracks in every other quarter of the island were Colonial Establishments, the buildings at many execrable, and the barrack furniture, bedding, etc., horrible. The soldier's bed was a blanket, though the very touch of a blanket in a tropical climate is disagreeable; and this, laid on the floor, was his all : a wooden floor certainly, but full of bugs, fleas, etc., to an incredible extent. So soon as I laid my report before Sir John Keane, he was most desirous to effect an improvement. We turned to and framed a statement to the Horse Guards (the Duke was then Commander-in-Chief), and in a few months every soldier had a bed, sheets, iron bedstead, etc., and every other requisite.

Still the troops did not escape the yellow fever, of which the seeds, as usual in its visitations, had

* See p. 336.

first germinated among the shipping (where the mortality was fearful). The disease spread to our troops—first to the Artillery at Port Royal, then to the 84th at Fort Augustus, next to the 22nd Regiment at Stony Hill (in both cases to an appalling extent), then partially to the 33rd Regiment at Upper Park Camp, the Royal Barracks. In about six weeks we buried 22 officers and 668 soldiers, out of the 22nd and 84th Regiments principally. Sir John (now Lord) Keane was up the country, and I had a *carte blanche* to do what I thought best. I therefore, in conjunction with the Acting Inspector-General of Hospitals, resolved to move the 84th from Fort Augustus to a bivouac at Stony Hill. Tents were sent up and huts were in progress. So soon as they were ready I marched the corps, and from that day the yellow fever ceased; there was only one admission afterwards. The day previously to the march of the poor 84th, I went down to Fort Augustus and paraded the Regiment. Only two subalterns were fit for duty, and although only sixty men were in hospital, seventeen died that day. The admissions into hospital were not so great in proportion as the mortality, one in four being the average of deaths. The Regiment was in a perfect state of despondency (it consisted like the 22nd Regiment, of young fresh soldiers recently arrived from England); but I cheered them up. I wheeled them into line a time or two, formed close column, and told them, whether a soldier died by yellow fever or on the battle-field, it was all in the service of his country ; that I should move them to a healthy spot the next day where they would leave the yellow fever behind, and now three cheers for his Majesty! The poor fellows were all alive again in no time. When we consider that every officer but two was sick, that already upwards of two hundred out of six hundred of their comrades had been buried, when death in this passive shape lay hold of them, it is not to be wondered at that a young (or any) Regiment should be appalled.

In Jamaica, while this yellow fever was raging, I have ridden thirty-five miles in the sun and gone sixteen miles in an open boat in one day, and been for a long time in the wards of different hospitals, where sickness and death in every stage was progressing around me. It is an awful sight to the afflicted patients in the large wards of a hospital, reduced by sickness to the excess of debility, to see the men on either side probably dead or dying, and there is no remedy and very little power of at all alleviating such a calamity. Many a man who would live if in a solitary room, dies from the power of imagination on the debilitated frame. Then, again, when a man has lost the fever, the surgeon is obliged to discharge him, because he requires the accommodation for recent admissions. He goes to his Company, his appetite has somewhat recovered, he eats heartily, a relapse ensues, he goes to hospital and dies to a certainty. It is rarely indeed that a case of relapse recovers. To obviate this, I established convalescent hospitals. I had various difficulties to contend with, but the success of the institution was an ample reward for labour, and established a precedent since equally advantageously acted on.

Nothing can be more capricious than these epidemics in tropical climates. On the very day twelvemonth that I paraded the 84th and seventeen men died, Sir John Keane made his half-yearly inspection of the corps at the same place, Fort Augustus. There was not a man in hospital and only one man out of the ranks; he paraded in the rear of his Company, being lame from a fractured leg.

The poor 22nd Regiment at Stony Hill suffered equally with the 84th; the Colonel, the Major, the Paymaster, and five officers died in a few days. The Adjutant's room, next the Orderly room, possessed the mortal seeds of the yellow fever. Every one who sat to write in the room was knocked down and died in a few days; in consequence I prohibited the use of it. Major Stewart, a most excellent officer, though not obedient in this instance, treated the prohibition slightingly, wrote there *two* days, on the fifth he was buried.

In a short time this fearful epidemic disappeared, and the troops, five regiments in all on the island, were healthy. Sir John Keane proposed a tour of inspection throughout the island. He was to sail in his yacht, landing every night. I, having a terrestrial turn, drove my wife four-in-hand. The daughter of the Receiver-General, Miss Stevenson, accompanied us, the beauty of the island.

A very curious appearance presents itself nearly
all round Jamaica. The coast is very bold, and
ships to load sugar are navigated through sunken
rocks within a few yards of the very shore. At
a distance the ships look as if *on* shore, but they
ride in perfect safety, the sunken rocks forming the
protection of the harbour. To all these spots a road
is made from the adjacent sugar estates, called a
barcadero, from the Spanish *embarcaro,* "to embark."

The hospitality of the superb mansions we
stopped at, the fortunate union with Sir John every
night—for the sea-breeze blows so regularly he
could calculate his arrival as by land—made this one
of the most pleasant tours I ever made. Nothing
can be more picturesque than the whole island, and
its fertility exceeds anything I have ever seen; while
its population (slaves) were more happy, better
fed, less worked, and better provided for in sickness
than any peasants throughout the many parts of
the world in which I have been. Slavery there
was merely nominal; the young were educated to
a necessary extent, the able-bodied lightly worked,
the sick comforted, the aged provided for. All had
little huts, some very comfortable, according to the
turn and industry of the occupants. All had a nice
garden, and all were well fed.

After our tour we went to live in the Liguanea
Mountains, in Admiral Fleming's Pen (as a country
residence is there called); a most delightful spot,
the climate luxurious, though enervating if you
descend into the plains, which I did to my office

regularly twice a week. In these hills you have constant thunder-showers; hence the gardens produce every European vegetable as good as in Covent Garden, and the fruits are unequalled.

While in this happy retreat, I received a note one evening from my worthy friend, Lord Fitzroy Somerset, to say *the Duke*, having been pleased with my exertions in Jamaica, had appointed me [24 July] to succeed my old friend John Bell (recently made Colonial Secretary) as Deputy-Quartermaster-General at the Cape of Good Hope. I never received any official communication of my appointment, and in forty-eight hours, bag and baggage, I was on board the *Slany* man-of-war, and under way for Nassau to Admiral Fleming, in the hope of some ship being ordered to proceed direct for the Cape, or to some intermediate port from whence I could take a fresh departure for my destination.

I was very fortunate in disposing of my furniture, carriage, buggy, horses, etc., particularly the latter, which I had brought from Halifax. They sold for three times what I had paid for them. They have an excellent breed of thoroughbred horses on the island, excessively dear, but for carriages the American horses are preferred.

Without egotism, our departure from Jamaica was as gratifying to us both as that from Halifax. Nothing could exceed the kindness of a vast number of friends, and I had a letter from every officer commanding a regiment.

CHAPTER XXXI.

AFTER STAYING THREE WEEKS AT NASSAU, HARRY
SMITH AND HIS WIFE SAIL FOR ENGLAND, AND
AFTER A MISERABLE VOYAGE LAND AT LIVERPOOL
—HE VISITS LONDON AND WHITTLESEY, AND
LEAVES ENGLAND (1829), NOT TO RETURN TILL
1847.

WE sailed in that, to appearance, heavenly
climate with a fresh sea-breeze, and as the magnificent Blue Mountains of Jamaica receded, the appearance of an island towering from the sea into
the very heavens became as it were a speck on the
mighty ocean. On our way to Nassau we passed
New Providence—the first land discovered by
Columbus, the joyful realization of his anticipations
and the fruit of his wonderful perseverance. The
transparency of the water in all the harbours of these
islands is very singular. At the depth of many
fathoms you see your anchor, cable, fish, etc., at the
bottom as distinctly as if no water intervened. A
sixpence may be discovered at a depth of twenty
fathoms.

On arrival at Nassau we found Admiral Fleming
away on a cruise. It was supposed he had gone to

Halifax.   So, there being no chance of a man-of-war, we had to await the arrival of a brig called the *Euphemia*, which was daily expected, and which would sail again for Liverpool so soon as her cargo was landed and a fresh one shipped.

General Sir Lewis Grant was the Governor, and for three weeks he and his staff put Government House at our command in every way, and did all in their power to render our visit delightful, and to provide my wife with every little amusement the island afforded.   The island of Nassau is a coral formation, but many parts of it are exceedingly fertile.   The wells, which produce most excellent fresh water, rise and fall with the tide.

On the arrival of the *Euphemia* our passage was soon arranged, but I could have only half the stern (and only) cabin partitioned off with canvas during the night (the other half being already engaged for two officers of the West Indian Regiments), and a small mate's cabin for my wife's maid.   The prospect before my poor wife was miserable enough, and we were afraid that in a three weeks' voyage we should not always have a fair wind, but her buoyant spirits laughed at the ideal distress.

We soon left the hospitable Governor and the happy island of Nassau.   Luckily, I put on board ship goats and dry stock of every description, although the captain (a well-spoken, smart-looking young Scotchman, married to a Liverpool woman, on board with him) engaged to find us capitally Our misery soon began.   The ship sailed like a witch, but we were constantly in a terrific storm, with the little cabin battened down, no means of cooking, and but little to cook if we had the means, and we should have been literally starved but for the things I fortunately shipped. We were upwards of thirty days at sea. Our captain assured me he had a timekeeper on board, and so he had, but he knew no more how to use it than I did. We had to lay to for forty-eight hours, during which we shipped a sea which swept the boats, caboose, binnacles, etc., clean off the deck. It was December, and as we approached Liverpool the weather was excessively cold, the sailors were frost-bitten in the hands, and the captain had not a glass of grog on board for them. I was, luckily, able to broach for them a small cask of peculiarly good rum of great antiquity, which I was taking as a present to an old Glasgow friend. In the midst of all these miseries, we fortunately fell in with a little Irish smack, which put us into the Bristol Channel, for my skipper knew no more where he was than the ship did, the weather having been very cloudy, no observations taken, and he and his mate execrable navigators. We made the Tuskar Light most accidentally, and then the previously cast-down fellow was all elevation. We got hold soon after of a Liverpool pilot. This was no small relief to me, who, although I said nothing, saw what an ignorant brute we were in the care of. He had neither candles nor oil, and the very binnacle light was supplied from my wax candles. He said he was never before more than three weeks on the voyage, and his store (a pretty misnomer) was laid in only for that period. For the last two days the sailors had no biscuit, and three days more would have exhausted meat, flour, and water. The fellow was a capital seaman on deck, and managed the beautifully-sailing brig most skilfully, and whenever he did get a start of wind, as he termed it, he carried on like a man.

We reached our anchorage in the Mersey long after dark, so beautifully lighted is the approach, and lay at anchor all night in a strong north-east wind, cold enough to cut off our tropical noses. We left our dirty, miserable, exhausted, and stinking brig, and landed as soon as we could the next morning, about five o'clock, in a state of the most abject filth and misery.

We went to the Adelphi Hotel, where in a moment we were surrounded by every luxury and attendance our wealthy country so sumptuously affords. The sudden transition from a state of dire misery into such Elysian Fields is not to be described by me, or forgotten by myself and wife. It was like a miracle. No complaint ever escaped her while on board, but after baths and every imaginable want had been supplied in one of the best of English inns, she then exclaimed, " I hope we may never again experience such a month of wretchedness, misery, and tempest ; and if we must, that we may bear it equally well (for it was a heavy task), be equally protected by Divine Providence, and as happily situated after it as at this moment."

The next day I made every inquiry about ships, and found a very fine brig, the *Ontario*, bound for Calcutta without a passenger. She was to sail in a fortnight. The captain offered to take me, provided the underwriters would allow him to go into Table Bay without an additional premium; and this they assented to, the season of the year being favourable.

My wife stayed at Liverpool, and I started for London, to make a few arrangements for our voyage and to thank Lord Fitzroy Somerset and the Duke. While I was with Lord Fitzroy Somerset, who was delighted to see me, he said, "Hardinge, the Secretary at War, wants to see you." I offered to go, but he said, "No, he will come, he told me, if I would let him know when you are here." That able soldier and Secretary at War and statesman (now Governor-General of India) was soon with us, and made as useful and practical inquiries about barracks, etc., in Jamaica as if he had been there. I then parted with these two of the Duke's staff with a full heart, and went to Downing Street.

The Duke was just appointed First Lord of the Treasury. I found my old friend and brother staff-officer with Sir John Lambert, Greville * (as good a

---

* Algernon Frederick Greville (1798–1864), younger brother of the author of the *Greville Memoirs* (see p. 216), after being present as an ensign at Quatre Bras and Waterloo, served as aide-de-camp during the occupation of France, first to Sir John Lambert and afterwards to the Duke of Wellington. When the Duke became Commander-in-Chief, January, 1827, Greville became his private secretary and continued so during the Duke's premiership.

fellow as ever breathed), the Duke's private secretary. Greville was delighted to see me, and expected his Grace every moment. He said the Duke as Prime Minister was as light-hearted and as lively as when comparatively idle at Cambray, that no great question seemed to stagger him, and the facility with which all business progressed under his conduct was truly wonderful. Greville added, " I will give you an anecdote. The Duke is very fond of walking from Apsley House to Downing Street, and we go through the Park, from which a small door opens into the Prime Minister's office. We arrive regularly at ten, and the porter is ready to open and close the door. One day we were rather late, and the porter looked like a weary sentry and was moving very slow. The Duke observed this, and in his usual emphatic manner said, 'Greville, look at that careless fellow; I will turn his flank, by G——.' The Duke watched his opportunity, slipped in unperceived, and says to the porter, ' Hallo, you sir, a pretty *look-out* this!' and laughed, and enjoyed the feat, as much as he did when he played the same flank-turning game in war." This little anecdote depicts the character of the man of mind, free, unshackled from thought until the question is brought before him, and then his powerful mind is absorbed in it, and in it solely.

I waited until three, when I was obliged to go, as I was to dine with Sir John Lambert, and leave town for my father's in Cambridgeshire by seven o'clock. I was a few hours with my dear sister,

Mrs. Sargant, and then dined in my travelling costume. Dear, warm-hearted Sir John Lambert had all his family to bid me farewell. O what a happy and united family of brothers and sisters! and his own children were perfectly beautiful.

At daylight the next day I was in my native place, Whittlesea. O home, our happy home! how altered! I stayed in the house of my third Waterloo brother, now settled as Captain of the Troop of Cavalry, magistrate, etc.; but I could not remain more than forty-eight hours, when I was again on my road back to London. Here I stayed a few hours with my sister, and then off to Liverpool to join my lonely wife, a total stranger and a foreigner in a great, commercial city!

My baggage, by the kind and civil attention of the Custom-house officers, was transferred from one brig to the other without the usual and laborious ordeal of landing. My new things arrived from London, and in a few days we were summoned to embark. It was daybreak, and the brig was floating in dock ready for the gates to be opened. We were soon on board; I had taken a little shore-boat to row me the few yards across. After paying my outfit, my bill at the inn, passage, insurance of baggage, etc., the last remains of my money was half a crown. "There," says I, "my friend!" "Lord, sir, my fare is only threepence." "Keep it," says I, "and drink the health of a man banished from his native land." The fellow stared at me at first as if looking at a convict. At last, in that

manner so peculiarly English, he made up his mind,
" He must be a gentleman." " I'll drink to your
Honour's health, depend on it, and success attend
you wherever you go." My friend and his boat
were the farewell to my native land. It was then
January, 1829 ; this is 1844, and I have never been
home since.

CHAPTER XXXII.

VOYAGE TO THE CAPE — MILITARY DUTIES AND
SPORT, 1829–1834 — SIR BENJAMIN D'URBAN
SUCCEEDS SIR LOWRY COLE AS GOVERNOR OF
THE COLONY.

THE stormy element, as if to atone for the violence
with which it treated us on our voyage from Nassau,
now behaved most moderately. We had a strong
breeze across the Bay of Biscay, but as it was abaft
the beam we did not feel it, and our whole passage
was one of fine and moderate weather. This was
very fortunate, as the brig was so heavily laden, that
at the beginning of the voyage her main chains
were positively under water. We were well found
in everything, and had the whole after-cabin to
ourselves. The captain was an able navigator,
both nautical and astronomical. He gave me a list
of his stock on board, and requested me to manage
dinner, etc., saying, " There is, I think, plenty, so
that if we live badly you will be to blame ; but the
brig is deep and no great sailer at any time, so

calculate on a three months' passage, to make sure."

The captain was a most excellent and kind-hearted man, a regular British tar. During the war he had been in the Navy, and prided himself on having been the coxswain of Captain Seymour on a frigate whose name I forget. "Lord, Sir," he would say, "he was a proper taut hand, but a real gentleman."

During the whole voyage our captain, who had a studious turn for mathematics and astronomy, was always hard at work, and highly delighted to explain the methods of his nautical calculations. He would exclaim, "Oh! if I had been so lucky as to have had a real education, I think I should have made a mathematician and astronomer." He was a large powerful man, and had a forehead as clear and as prominent as that of Dr. Chalmers.

Our voyage was more fortunate than the captain had anticipated, and in eleven weeks we anchored in Table Bay. I had never been at the Cape before, but I had heard much of it from part of my Corps which touched there years before [March, 1807] on their way to Buenos Ayres, and as I had read every book about it which I could lay my hands on, I was scarcely in a foreign land. As soon as I landed, I found that the Governor, my old and noble General, Sir Lowry Cole, was not at Government House, but residing in the country. I then went to look for my dear old friend John Bell and his noble wife, Lady Catherine. They were in

an excellent house of their own, and as rejoiced to
see me as I was to see them. John and My Lady
would hear of nothing but our putting up with them,
Johnny saying, "Harry, you and I and Juana have
fared more sparingly together than we will now."
The carriage was ordered, and John and I went on
board to bring the wife ashore, all delighted at our
happy union after an absence of years.

Next day John and I drove out in his buggy
to breakfast with the Governor. He and Lady
Frances, that noble and accomplished woman, were
delighted to see me, but oh, how she was altered!
When I first knew her in 1815, a few days after
her marriage, she was in the prime of life, a full-
blown beautiful woman, and the most interesting I
ever knew. As soon, however, as my old recollection of her was somewhat subdued, I found her
ladyship everything I had a right to expect, the
mother of six beautiful children, whose education
she conducted herself, and my gallant General all
kindness and hospitality.

He and I had a long walk in the garden, when
he said, "I shall appoint you Commandant of the
Garrison. You are *ex officio*, as second in command
to me, the senior Member of Council, and, if any
accident happened to me, the administration of the
government would devolve on you—John Bell, your
senior officer, being Colonial Secretary and holding
no military position."

No man was ever more happily placed than I
was. The quarter in Cape Castle forming the

residence of the Governor was excellent, with a little square in the rear with capital stables and out-offices. The garrison consisted of one company of Artillery, the 72nd Highlanders, a magnificent corps, and the 98th, very highly organized, considering the short period they had been raised.

My first object was to visit and reduce the guards, which I soon did very considerably on a representation to the Governor. The next was to do away with guards over convicts working on the road. This could not be effected at once, but such a friend to the soldier as Sir Lowry was, readily received my various representations of the ill effects on discipline of these guards, and, so soon as arrangements could be made, these were also abolished. The next guard to dispose of was one of one sergeant, one corporal, and six privates at the Observatory, four miles from Cape Town, and it was not long before the building, or the star-gazers, discovered that their celestial pursuits could be carried on without the aid terrestrial of soldiers.

Some months after my arrival, the Kafirs being on the eve of an outbreak, the Governor, Sir Lowry Cole, went to the frontier. He requested me to remain at Cape Town unless a war began, when I was immediately to join. I frequently had the troops bivouacked, and taught them to cook in camp, piquets, etc., and every other camp duty. On one occasion I had ball cartridges, every company at its target, and I had out two six-pounders with their target. I manœuvred the troops, so moving the

targets as to be in their front, and I never saw half
so good target practice with muskets before. The
men were delighted and emulous beyond measure.
The six-pounders, too, made excellent shots, and I
had not a single casualty.

About this time that noble fellow, General
Lord Dalhousie, arrived on his way out to India as
Commander-in-Chief. I gave him a capital sham
fight, concluding by storming Fort Amsterdam, at
which he was highly amused. I knew his Lordship
in America,* and we then and now had many a laugh
at our performances at Vittoria, previously related.

The Kafir war ended in patching up old
treaties, and the Governor returned. About this
time I acted as Military Secretary and Deputy
Adjutant-General, holding the appointments of
Deputy Quartermaster-General and Commandant;
and ultimately the appointments of Deputy Adjutant-
General and Deputy Quartermaster General were
blended, and I held both, being called Deputy
Quartermaster-General.

Horses at the Cape are excellent. The breed
had been much improved by Lord Charles Somerset,
the former Governor, by the importation of some
mares and several of the highest-bred English
thoroughbred sires. I soon had a most beautiful
stud. The sporting butcher Van Reenen had an
excellent pack of fox-hounds, which he virtually
allowed me to hunt, and many is the capital run we
had, but over the most breakneck country that

* See pp. 340 and 97, 98.

hounds ever crossed—sands covered with the most beautiful variety of the *erica*, or heath, and barren hills of driftsands. These are dug up by moles literally as big as rabbits. Their ordinary holes on hills and under-excavations no good hunter will fall in, but in their breeding-holes I defy any horse to avoid going heels over head, if his fore-legs come on them, although many old experienced hunters know them and jump over. I had one little horse not fourteen hands, descended from Arabs; he never gave me a fall, and I never failed to bring the brush to his stable when I rode him; but with all other horses I have had some awful falls, particularly after rain, when the sand is saturated with water and very heavy. Falls of this description are far more serious than rolling over our fences at home, where activity enables you to get away from your horse, as he is some seconds or so coming down, but in a mole-hole you fall like a shot, the horse's head first coming to the ground, next yours, and he rolls right over you. When a horse's hind legs go into a breeding-earth the sensation is awful, and how the noble animals escape without breaking their backs remains one of the wonders.

Every shooting-season I made a capital excursion, first to my sporting friend's, Proctor's. He was a retired officer of the 21st Dragoons, a capital sportsman, an excellent farmer, a good judge of a horse, and a better one of how to sell him to those whom he saw he could make money of. He had a family of thirteen children; his wife was a Dutch lady, still good-looking. My wife always accompanied me, as well as my friend Bob Baillie, of the 72nd Regiment, who was subsequently celebrated in the sporting magazines as a rider. We started with an immense waggon, eight horses, every description of commissariat stores, greyhounds, pointers, setters, retrievers, terriers, spaniels, and, under Proctor's guidance, we had capital sport.

The partridge-shooting was nearly as good as grouse-shooting; the bird, called the grey partridge, very much resembled the grouse, and was a noble sporting bird. There is also the red partridge, large, but stupid to shoot. The best sport with them is to ride them down with spaniels. There are several sorts of antelopes, which lie in the bushes and jump up under your feet as hares do. These you shoot with buck-shot. Near Cape Town there is only one sort of antelope "on the look-out" like our fallow deer, grey, very handsome, and fleet, called by the Dutch the rhee-bok. On the frontier and in the interior there are a great variety of this gazing-deer, the most remarkable being the springbok, which is exceedingly swift, parti-coloured or pied, and they almost fly from you. They have the power of expanding their long hair on the top of the back, like opening and shutting a fan. The bonte-bok is in very large herds. These you are prohibited to shoot without a special authority from Government, and the number even which you may shoot is limited.

The variety of modes of shooting these antelopes

is highly amusing. To shoot the eland, the largest species, as big as a two-year-old heifer, you go full speed in a waggon over ground so rough that, what with the speed, you can hardly hold on and preserve your guns. The animals, hearing all the noise, stop to gaze. The waggon is instantly pulled up, and you fire balls. After such a jolting, he is a steady fellow who fires with any precision.

You have pheasants, too, inmates of very stiff and thorny-bushed ravines ; they afford good sport, but you must shoot them dead, or you will never find them. There are also several species of the bustard genus, but near Cape Town only the black and grey khoran, so called. On the frontier you have the ordinary bustard, a noble bird and excellent eating, weighing from 9 to 12 lbs., and a species of great bustard, weighing from 20 to 25 lbs. The latter is eatable, but coarse. These you shoot with balls. On the frontier, too, you have buffaloes, elephants, lions, camelopards, ostriches, etc., so well described by Major Harris that it is impossible to add to his faithful account.

Coursing at the Cape is not good. I pursued it much for the sake of hunting four or five couple of spaniels. Hares there never sit in the open as in Europe, but in low stunted bushes—half rabbits. However, this sort of coursing with the spaniels and greyhounds teaches your horse to become a hunter, and by rushing him after hares, he well learns how to tumble or to avoid tumbles.

In the course of our sporting tour, I used to

visit the breeding establishments (then called kraals) of all the great breeders, I think, Melk, Kotze, Proctor, Van Reenen, Van der Byl, etc. Melk has six hundred mares, all running out in unenclosed fields. With such an establishment you would expect that he could show you three or four hundred one, two, and three year olds (for they are all sold by this age). He can never show more than seventy or eighty colts of the year, and the rest of the breeders can show no higher proportion. The thoroughbred mares are invariably in miserable condition, the cock-tails fat and sleek. Many of the mares, etc., are afflicted with a disease from an accumulation of sand in their stomachs and intestines.

It was thought far beneath the dignity of a gentleman at the Cape to ride or drive mares, but seeing that the mares were far finer and larger than the horses, and one-fifth of the price, I bought from Proctor two immense mares, as like English hunters as possible, for £45; a thoroughbred mare, 16 hands high, four years old, for my wife (a beautiful creature which very much delighted Lord Dalhousie); and another thoroughbred mare, 15½. They were the four finest horses in Cape Town. One of the carriage mares ruptured her bladder in the carriage, and died in a few hours. The large thoroughbred got a most tremendous fall out hunting, nearly broke my neck, and was chest-foundered ever afterwards. The other two I sold remarkably well. By some accident I never set up mares in my establishment again, but I was never so elegantly horsed.

What with my military duties and those of
Council, I led a far from idle life, and there is an
elasticity in the atmosphere at the Cape which
conduces to a desire to take violent rides.   The sun
never heats you.   I have ridden 140 miles in thirty
hours to go to look at a horse or buy one, or to
look at a particular line of country.   I have been
out shooting in the middle of the summer from daylight to dark, the sun like a furnace, the pummel of
the saddle like a red-hot poker, your gun-barrel,
after a few rapid shots, so heated you almost fear to
reload, then come home at night (or slept out in
the fields, if you like) and eaten a right good dinner,
not in any way heated, and without either headache
or cold.   An exposure of this sort to the sun of
India would probably cause a roaring fever or
death.

This is the sort of life which I and my wife lived
from 1829 to the end of 1834, enjoying the greatest
kindness and hospitality, and living in happiness and
sociability with every one.   We had lost our dear
kind friends, Sir Lowry and Lady Frances Cole,
but he was succeeded as Governor and Commander
in-Chief, early in 1834, by a most amiable man,
Sir Benjamin D'Urban, the most educated and
accomplished soldier I have ever served with.*

* For an interesting memorandum on the diet and treatment of
military prisoners, submitted by Harry Smith to Sir B. D'Urban in
1834, see Appendix III.

CHAPTER XXXIII.

OUTBREAK OF A KAFIR WAR—HARRY SMITH'S HIS-
TORIC RIDE TO GRAHAMSTOWN—ON HIS ARRIVAL
HE PROCLAIMS MARTIAL LAW—PROVIDES FOR THE
DEFENCE OF THE TOWN—ATTACKS THE KAFIRS
AND RESCUES SEVEN MISSIONARIES.*

THE Kafir tribes, which for many months had
been greatly agitated and excited, at length burst
into the Colony in what was for the moment an irresistible rush, carrying with them fire, sword, devastation, and cold-blooded murder, and spoiling the
fertile estates and farms like a mountain avalanche.
Such were the reports received from the Civil Commissioners and the Commandant of the troops. His
Excellency Sir B. D'Urban determined to dispatch
me immediately, with full powers civil and military to
adopt whatever measures I found requisite, while
he would himself follow as soon as possible. His
Excellency told me a sloop of war was ready to take
me to Algoa Bay. I, however, preferred riding
post, and the horses were laid for me for a seven
days' ride, 600 miles. It was needless to start until
the horses were on the road, so I had two days † to

* With this and the four following chapters, compare Appendix II.
† This disposes of part of H. Cloete's dramatic story, which, however, should be compared (*Great Boer Trek*, pp. 78, 79).

2 B

make arrangements, and to ship military stores of every description, ordnance, etc. One half of the 72nd Regiment was to proceed in waggons, the other by sea.

On the night of the 31st December [1834], I dined with Sir B. D'Urban at Cape Town (my own dear little cottage at Rondebosch being four miles off), and after dinner His Excellency and I had a long conversation. I fully ascertained his views and desires, and then made a resolution in my own mind never to swerve from his principles where circumstances admitted of their application. He on his part was most frank, honest, and decided, saying, "You now understand me thoroughly. Rely on my support in every way, and my perfect readiness to bear all the responsibility."

I parted with this noble soldier and able statesman at half-past twelve, drove out to my cottage, and lay down for three hours. I then started with a single Hottentot for a ride of 90 miles the first day [1st January, 1835], the heat raging like a furnace. My orders, warrants, etc., were sewn in my jacket by my own dear wife. From the anxiety and exertion of the previous day's running about Cape Town from store to store, and the little sleep I had had, as I rode the first 25 miles to the first change of horses I was half tired, but I got a cup of tea at the post-house, and never felt fagged again.

I arrived at Caledon at one o'clock, when it was threatening a heavy thunderstorm. I had then 25 miles to ride. The storm came on violently, the rain poured behind me, but I reached my stage, Field Cornet Leroze, by three, perfectly dry.

The next day I started before daylight, and got to Swellendam to breakfast. I had two heavy, lazy brutes of horses. In Swellendam I wrote letters of instructions to that able fellow the Civil Commissioner, Harry Rivers, and I then started for an additional ride of 70 miles. I found the Buffeljagts river out. My first horse from Swellendam had a 20-miles stage, but through having to go up the river to ford, this noble little four-year-old had 30 miles, which he did, crossing the river too, in two hours and twenty minutes. I was so pleased with him, I wrote to Rivers to buy him and bring him up with the burghers. He bought him for £18 5s. I afterwards rode him very hard for two years, and sold him to Sir George Napier for £50. This day was excessively hot. I reached my stage at three o'clock.

I started the next day for George, with a long ride of 100 miles before me. At the second stage I found no horses and was kept waiting one hour. I got to a Field Cornet's where there was a great assembly of burghers enrolling their names for service, and a great dinner prepared at twelve o'clock, at which I was fool enough to eat, the remainder of my ride to George being rendered thereby a great exertion. Unfortunately, after a ride of 100 miles, I found all the civil authorities and inhabitants prepared to receive me, a ceremony I could readily have dispensed with. I soon got rid of these well-meant attentions, had a hot bath, lay down, and dictated letters to the Civil Commissioner, Mynheer de Bergh, until eleven at night.

I was off before daylight with a tremendous ride before me, over mountains, etc., etc. About halfway I met the mail from Grahamstown, and such a task as I had to open it! Not till I had opened the last bag did I find the packet of letters I wanted from the Commandant and the Civil Commissioner, Grahamstown. Their descriptions of disaster, murders, and devastations were awful; the Commandant talked of the troops being obliged to evacuate Grahamstown. I made comments on all these letters, and resolved to reach Grahamstown in two days. The heat to-day and the exertion of opening the letter-bags were fatiguing. On my arrival at my stage, I got hold of the Field Commandant Rademeyer, and sent on expresses all night to have the horses ready a day before they were ordered, being determined to reach Uitenhage the next night (the fifth from Cape Town),—500 miles.

Off two hours before daylight. One river, so tortuous is its bed, I had to cross seven times. I galloped through, and was as wet for hours as if I had been swimming, with a sun on me like a furnace. About halfway to Uitenhage, the heat was so excessive my horse knocked up, and no belabouring would make him move. About half a mile off I saw a sort of camp, went up, and found

a Dutch farmer with his family, herds, flocks, etc.,
fleeing from the scene of devastation. I told him
who I was, where and what I was going for, and
asked him to horse me to the next stage, about
seven miles. To my astonishment (for nothing can
exceed the kindness and hospitality of the Dutch
Boers on ordinary occasions), he first started a
difficulty, and then positively refused, which soon
set my blood boiling. He was holding a nice-
looking horse all ready saddled, so I knocked him
down, though half as big again as myself, jumped
on his horse, and rode off. I then had a large river
to cross by ferry, and horses were waiting for me.
The Boer came up, and was very civil, making all
sorts of apologies, saying until he spoke to the
guide who *followed* me, he did not believe that in
that lone condition I could be the officer I represented myself. The passion, the knocking him
down, the heat, etc., was very fatiguing, and I reached
Uitenhage at five o'clock, having been beating
grass-fed post-horses from three in the morning
until that hour, and ridden over some very bad and
mountainous roads, 140 miles. To my horror, the
Civil Commissioner (though a very worthy, good
man) had all the town turned out to receive me,
and a large dinner-party to *refresh* me, while I
wanted repose. To add to this, a Colonel Cuyler,
an officer retired on half-pay, of great experience
and abilities on this frontier, waited on me. He
was very communicative, of great use to me, but,
being as deaf as a beetle, the exertion of calling

loud enough for him to hear (although naturally
I have a very powerful voice) I cannot describe. I
had a wash, went to the great dinner—I dare not
eat, quite to the astonishment of my host—soon
retired, got hold of his secretary, and lay on my
back dictating letters until twelve o'clock, when,
fairly exhausted, I fell asleep.

Off again next morning for Grahamstown. If
the previous day's work had been excessive, it was
short of what I this day encountered from the
wretched brutes of knocked-up horses laid for me.
About half way I found the country in the wildest
state of alarm, herds, flocks, families, etc., fleeing like
the Israelites. Everything that moved near a bush
was a Kafir. I was forced to have an escort of
burghers on tired horses, and oh, such a day's
work, until I got within ten miles of Grahamstown !
There I found awaiting me a neat clipping little
hack of Colonel Somerset's (such as he is celebrated
for) and an escort of six Cape Mounted Rifles. I
shall never forget the luxury of getting on this little
horse, a positive redemption from an abject state of
misery and labour. In ten minutes I was perfectly
revived, and in forty minutes was close to the barrier
of Grahamstown, fresh enough to have fought a
general action, after a ride of 600 miles in six days
over mountains and execrable roads, on Dutch horses
living in the fields without a grain of corn. I performed each day's work at the rate of fourteen miles
an hour, and I had not the slightest scratch even on
my skin.

If it be taken into consideration that there was no previous training, that I started without sleep almost and after two days' excessive fatigue of mind and body in Cape Town, embarking stores, troops, etc., the little sleep I had on the journey from being obliged to dictate letters and give orders, the excessive heat, the roads, the horses, then it must be admitted a performance of no ordinary exertion for a man who, when it was over, was ready and required to use every energy of mind and body.

On reaching the barricaded streets, I had the greatest difficulty to ride in. I found Colonel Somerset parading the night duties. Consternation was depicted on every countenance I met, on some despair, every man carrying a gun, some pistols and swords too. It would have been ludicrous in any other situation than mine, but people desponding would not have been prepossessed in my favour by my laughing at them, so I refrained, although much disposed to do so. I just took a look at the mode adopted to defend Grahamstown. There were all sorts of works, barricades, etc., some three deep, and such was the consternation, an alarm, in the dark especially, would have set one half of the people shooting the other. I at once observed that this defensive system would never restore the lost confidence, and I resolved, after I had received reports and assumed the command, to proclaim martial law, and act on the initiative in every respect.

I rode to Somerset's, where I was treated *en*

prince. I sent for the Civil Commissioner, Captain
Campbell, and from him learned the exact state of
the country—that despondency did exist to a fearful
extent, originating from the sight of the horrors perpetrated by the remorseless enemy, but any vigorous
steps and arbitrary authority boldly exerted would
still ensure a rallying-point for all. I said, "Very
well; I clearly see my way. At as early an hour as
possible to-morrow morning I shall declare martial
law, and woe betide the man who is not as obedient
as a soldier. Be so good as to prepare the necessary
document and copies to be printed for my signature.
I will be with you soon after daylight in your office,
where I shall take up my abode." I was there
according to my appointment, and found everything
ready upon this and every other occasion when I
required the services of this able public officer. No
man was ever better seconded and supported in
every way than I was by Captain Campbell. I
learnt the number of regular troops to be a little
above 700, the civil force under arms 850, then
occupying Grahamstown, Fort Beaufort, the connecting post of Hermanus Kraal (the civil force
being at the Kat River Settlement, a location of
Hottentots, where Captain Armstrong with a troop
of Cape Mounted Rifles acted in a civil and
military capacity). Fort Willshire had been most
shamefully abandoned. I received a report that a
body of 200 Burghers of the Graaf Reinet district,
under their Civil Commissioner Ryneveld, was
approaching. I knew the front of the 72nd Regiment

in waggons would reach me in a day or two. I
resolved, therefore, as soon as possible to make an
inroad into the heart of the enemy's country in one
direction, reoccupy Fort Willshire, and thence march
to rescue the missionaries who were assembled in
one house, " Lonsdale," in Kafirland, and whose
safety could not be calculated on for one moment.
I then directed the population of Grahamstown,
so soon as martial law was proclaimed, to be formed
into a Corps of Volunteers, and I would issue them
arms. The church in the square in Grahamstown
being occupied as a military post and a council
chamber, I desired the principal gentlemen to
assemble, to name their own officers, etc., and to
submit them for my approval, and told them that
they and the organization of the corps should be
instantly gazetted.

This was in progress, when there were so many
speakers and so few actors, the Civil Commissioner
recommended me to go to the meeting. I deemed
this a good opportunity to display my authority,
which I was resolved on doing most arbitrarily on
such a momentous occasion.

When I went in, there was a considerable
assembly of very respectable-looking men. I asked
what was the cause of delay in executing my
demands ? One gentleman, a leader in what was
called the Committee of Safety, which I very soon
complimentarily dissolved, stood up and began to
enter into argument and discussion. I exclaimed in
a voice of thunder, " I am not sent here to argue,

but to command. You are now under martial law, and the first gentleman, I care not who he may be, who does not promptly and implicitly obey my command, he shall not even dare to give an opinion ; I will try him by a court martial and punish him in five minutes."

This sally most completely established my authority, and I never met with any opposition afterwards ; on the contrary, a desire on the part of all to meet my wishes. The corps were formed, officers gazetted. As we issued, and on parade that evening, I gave the command, as was promised, to Captain Sparks of the 49th Regiment, on leave of absence with his family at Grahamstown.

My attention was next turned to the defence of Grahamstown. I found that the officer in command of the 75th Regiment had taken great care of the barracks, distant half a mile or more, but that he was averse to detaching troops to the defence of Grahamstown. This I soon settled, opened all the barricades, established fresh alarm posts, and at once showed the alarmed inhabitants that defence should consist in military resources and military vigilance, and not in being cooped up behind doors, windows, and barricades three deep, from which they would shoot each other. That evening, the first after I assumed the command, the aspect of affairs had changed. Men moved like men, and felt that their safety consisted in energetic obedience.

The next day two hundred Graaf Reinet
burghers arrived. I despatched some of them and
Colonel Somerset with a force to the rear to improve our communication with Algoa Bay, which
was interrupted, and I prepared a force of three
hundred men to invade the kraal of the Kafir chief
Eno, and, if possible, to seize that double-faced old
murderer and breaker of treaties. This command I
gave to an old brother Rifleman, Major William Cox,
then in the 75th Regiment, a soldier by experience,
nature, and courage, the most useful and active
officer under my command. I never expected they
would seize old Eno—he had a very narrow escape,
though—but, as I anticipated, the object of my
inroad was completely achieved, and from that
moment all the invading Kafirs rapidly withdrew
from the Colony. It also showed the Kafirs that
the Hottentots would fight against them, which
previously they had disbelieved.

A party of the 72nd Regiment having arrived, I
immediately reoccupied Fort Willshire.

My next object was to rescue the missionaries
from the very heart of Kafirland, where seven of
them (I think) with their families expected momentarily to have their throats cut. I again employed
my old brother Rifleman, Major Cox, who succeeded
to the utmost of my most sanguine expectations and
brought off every British subject.

After [leaving] his command at Fort Willshire,
and [the missionaries] were in perfect security, he
pushed on to Grahamstown to report his success.

When he reached the Fish River he found it full, and swam across, leading his horse in his hand, like a gallant fellow as he is. On reaching me, he found that Sir B. D'Urban, the Governor, had arrived; and highly delighted Cox and I were that the last act of mine before resigning the command was one of brilliant success and an achievement of no ordinary enterprise. The Governor was as pleased as we were. This rescue of the missionaries was the best thing I ever did during the war, but one which these holy gentlemen and their Societies never acknowledged as they ought, though always ready to *censure.* "Charity is a comprehensive word."

The day after the arrival of the Governor he issued a General Order, of which the following is an extract :—

"Headquarters, Grahamstown,
"Frontier of the Cape of Good Hope, 22 Jan. 1835.

"The Commander-in-Chief desires to offer Colonel Smith the expression at once of his unqualified appro-
.bation and of his warmest thanks for the important services which he has rendered to the King and to the Colony during the period of his commanding the forces on the Frontier District.

"The unparalleled rapidity with which he rode from Cape Town to Grahamstown, a distance of 600 miles, accomplishing it in less than six days; his indefatigable and most able exertion from the moment of his arrival to expel the savage enemy from the ground their unexpected and treacherous invasion had gained—to afford protection

and support to the inhabitants ; to restore confidence and
to organize the armed population, and combine the
resources of the country—have been beyond all praise,
and justly entitle him to the grateful acknowledgments
of the Colony and of the Commander-in-Chief." *

* The following characteristic story of Harry Smith about this
time is told by Mr. H. A. Bryden in *Temple Bar*, April, 1902. " In
the Kafir War, when irregular troops were much employed, odd scenes
occasionally happened. A corps of Grahamstown Volunteers was
drawn up and paraded before Colonel Smith, then Chief of the Staff.
As he passed down the ranks, one of the men touched his hat. ' None
of your d—d politeness in the ranks, sir,' was the response."

CHAPTER XXXIV.

HARRY SMITH CHIEF OF THE STAFF UNDER SIR BENJAMIN D'URBAN—HE MAKES TWO FORAYS INTO THE FISH RIVER BUSH AND ONE INTO THE UM- DIZINI BUSH—THE FORCE UNDER SIR B. D'URBAN MARCHES FROM FORT WILLSHIRE TO THE POORTS OF THE BUFFALO, FROM WHENCE HARRY SMITH MAKES ANOTHER FORAY.

My duty now, although not of so directly re- sponsible a nature, was laborious and active in the extreme in conformity to the General Orders which follow :—

"Colonel Smith will, for the present, resume his duties as Deputy Quartermaster-General and acting Deputy Adjutant-General of the forces, and, in this capacity as Chief of the Staff, will take charge of the organization of a force to be prepared for active operations ; for carrying which into effect he is hereby authorized to make requisi- tions upon the competent departments, and to approve all requisitions and contracts, which approvals will be then sufficient warrant for the corresponding issues and pur- chases ; and he will be so good as to make a daily report of the progress of this service to the Commander-in-Chief."

In the progress of these arduous services, I

organized two corps of Hottentots, consisting of every loose vagabond I could lay my hand on, called the 1st and 2nd Battalion Hottentot Infantry. They consisted of four Companies each, 100 men to a Company. It is scarcely to be credited how rapidly these men trained as soldiers. No nation in the world, with the exception of the inhabitants of the South of France, have such a natural turn to become soldiers as the Hottentots.

In the various operations I had carried on, I had never been able to give a command to Lieut.-Colonel Z—— of the — Regiment, who had been active and useful under me, but I promised him that, as soon as I possibly could do so, he should have one. I ascertained that a considerable body of Kafirs, cattle, etc., were concentrated in the dense fastnesses of the Fish River bush, from which it was necessary to dislodge them before the advance of the invading force. I laid my plan before Sir Benjamin D'Urban, who fully approved of it, and as I wished, he consented that Colonel Z—— should have the command of the troops to effect this service. I sent for the Colonel, and he was delighted. I said, "Now, make your own arrangements. You know the country; you know the desire I have had to give you a command, and I should be sorry if I did not everything in my power to make it agreeable."

All was arranged, and Z—— and his expedition marched. I was under no apprehension of its success, and my mind was devoted to the eternal subject of organization of Boers, Hottentots, waggons, etc.,

when most unexpectedly Colonel Z—— returned
to headquarters, and I could observe by his manner
victory was not the subject.   He of course never
acknowledged reverse; said he had not sufficient
troops, etc., and that to dislodge the savages, as
he always termed them, more must be employed.
" But," I said, "how came you to leave your
command?"   "Oh, I thought I could best explain
matters myself."   "Well," I said, " come to the
Commander-in-Chief."

His Excellency received him very coldly, being
exceedingly offended at his leaving his troops, especially under the circumstances.   When Colonel
Z—— went, Sir Benjamin D'Urban broke out
and said, "G——, he has had a licking, and what
the devil made him leave his troops?   Smith,"
says Sir B., "this check must be immediately repaired, and you must go yourself.   Take with you
what you deem sufficient, and lose no time."

I certainly did not, for that afternoon some
more infantry were on the march.   In the course of
the day Jim Cox came to me from Z——, describing how hurt he was that I had to command.   I
positively laughed at the idea of such a command
adding to anything but my labours, and I said,
" Willingly will I go to Sir Benjamin D'Urban and
tell him Z—— is hurt and in some degree
imputes to me the arrangement."   The only time
Sir Benjamin D'Urban was ever angry with me was
on this occasion. " I have decided on what I consider
the service demands, and I little expected any

remonstrances from you, Smith." I said quietly, " It was only to serve another, sir." " Yes, at the risk of the public service." Z——— was furious. He was ordered to rejoin his former command.

So soon as I reached the troops on the banks of the river, I reconnoitred the enemy's position, rendered extraordinarily strong from dense bush, almost impenetrable to any but a creeping Kafir, ravines, mountains, etc. I found it necessary to attack at three points, and disposed of my troops accordingly, giving the command of the right and cavalry division to Colonel Somerset, and the left to Colonel Z——, while I remained with the centre.

The river was up, and prevented me crossing for three days. The heat on its banks was intense. I determined, however, that so soon as the river was practicable, I would attack and that my infantry should penetrate the thickets while the cavalry should intercept the retreat of the enemy and their cattle. The evening before the attack, when I gave Colonel Z—— his orders, he said, " Any further orders ?" I said, " None." He laughed in a very satirical manner. " Ah, ah, catch a Kafir with infantry." I said, " Yes, Colonel, I intend it, and *you shall too*." Our success exceeded my most sanguine expectations.

Such was the extent of the country, that a considerable part of it I had not been able to penetrate. I was resolved, therefore, to make a second attempt, which I was not long about.

2 O

The evening previous to a long march for the different columns to gain their ground, I received an application from Colonel Z—— for permission to return to Grahamstown. I was thunderstruck, but of course said, "Go when you like"; and I had to send Major Gregory, an excellent officer, thirty miles to take the command of Z——'s force, which he reached just in time for it to commence its march. On my second attempt I completely scoured the holds and fastnesses of the Kafirs, namely, "the dense and extensive thorny ravines, etc., of the great Fish River bush," which they had deemed impenetrable, and which in no previous war had they ever been driven from. The Kafirs never again occupied this bush permanently, although a brilliant affair subsequently occurred [9th March] between some Boers under Field Commandant Rademeyer and a large body of them.* Thus Kafirs were caught by infantry, and we secured a considerable quantity of cattle, upwards of 5000, for which the savage fights desperately. The nature of this bush service requires the most practised light troops, and the advantage I derived from the service of my old comrade Cox is not to be described.

After this I brought my two battalions of Hottentots into play. The enemy in this bush had about thirty renegade Hottentots, many of them runaway servants who had deserted with their masters' double-barrelled fowling-pieces. I never

---

* Cp. for this incident, and the whole history of the war, Sir J. E. Alexander's *Narrative of a Voyage, etc.* London, 1837.

had more difficulty to dislodge a few men in my life, and these fellows caused me a loss of some valuable men.

Sir Benjamin D'Urban was highly gratified with my success, and issued a very complimentary General Order to that effect.*

Soon after this I went to Fort Willshire, to prepare the camp for the rendezvous of the army under Sir Benjamin D'Urban in person, and, the troops being much in want of cattle from the country having been so driven, spoiled, and devastated, I resolved to make an inroad into Kafirland to a dense bush (as it is in this country called) beyond the Umdizini, where I was led to believe a considerable quantity of Kafirs and cattle were collected. The distance from my camp was thirty-five miles, and I had the rapid Keiskamma River to cross. I marched at one o'clock in the morning, with a corps of mounted men, principally composed of the Swellendam Burghers or Yeomanry, under a veteran old Commandant who had made seven Kafir campaigns. My inroad was perfectly successful, and I reached my bivouac at nine the following night, having marched a distance from point to point of 70 miles, exclusive of operations in the bush. I brought with me upwards of 2000 head of fat cattle, which were most acceptable for the consumption of our troops.

In a few days the Commander-in-Chief reached the camp [31 March] at Fort Willshire, and the troops were all ready for the field, and as highly

---

* Given by Alexander, vol. ii. p. 14.

organized as such a mob of armed inhabitants could
be. Our train of commissariat waggons, each with
twenty oxen in it, was immense. With the head-
quarters column alone we had 170 occupying about
two miles. From the length of these teams, I
expected great difficulty with them, and certainly
took every pains to regulate and divide them into
divisions, departments, etc., appointing a captain
over the whole. To my astonishment, so excellent were the bullocks, I never had the slightest
trouble, and they could march over any country
whatever with the troops.

From Fort Willshire we marched to a position at
the foot of what are termed the Poorts of the Buffalo,
very high wooded ridges, high up the river of this
name, and, as we were obliged to halt there for our
left column to get into its line, I requested Sir
Benjamin D'Urban to allow me to conduct a patrol
into this bush. He consented; and I had the
prettiest affair by far of any during the war, and the
most like a fight.

I took with me a detachment of the 72nd
Highlanders, under Captain Murray, my faithful
attendant always; one of the Hottentot Battalions;
and my Corps of Mounted Guides, gentlemen of the
country and merchants who had traded all over
Kafirland and knew the country perfectly. Never
was there a more useful body. The Hottentot
Battalion had a considerable *détour* to make, and I
wished to occupy a ridge to support and to observe
their movement. In attempting this, I was opposed

by a considerable body of Kafirs posted on a sort
of natural castle of rocks, steep and scarped by
nature, and so well did the Kafirs maintain themselves, wounding Murray and several of his men,
that I had to turn them ere they were dislodged.*
In the meanwhile, the Hottentot Battalion, hearing
the firing and seeing the bush full of cattle, came
flying on and drove the Kafirs in every direction,
killing many. We captured upwards of four thousand
cattle. The care of these cattle and the sending
them to the rear were a very laborious and arduous
duty.

* Writing of this to his wife, on the 7th April, he says, "Well,
yesterday, alma mia, was the anniversary of that which led to our
blessed union, and, after my check at the natural fortress, which, by
Jupiter, was very strong—inaccessible, in short—I thought to myself,
'Well, this day so and so many years ago, I had a good licking in
Badajos breaches, and the old Duke tried something else.' So the
blood rushed into my heart again as gay as ever. 'By G—d, I'll have
them out yet.' I had no information but my spyglass, and I made a
détour, and was lucky in hitting off the plan to approach."

CHAPTER XXXV.

OVER THE KEI INTO HINTZA'S TERRITORY—WAR
DECLARED AGAINST HINTZA—HIS KRAAL BEING
DESTROYED THE CHIEF COMES IN, AND AGREES TO
THE TERMS OF PEACE—HE REMAINS AS A HOSTAGE
WITH THE BRITISH FORCE, WHICH MARCHES BACK
TO THE KEI—HARRY SMITH MARCHES UNDER
HINTZA'S GUIDANCE INTO HIS TERRITORY TO RE-
COVER THE STOLEN CATTLE—NEAR THE XABECCA
HINTZA TRIES TO ESCAPE, AND IS SHOT.

FROM the Poorts of the Buffalo we marched up
to the Kei, the right bank of which was the great
chief Hintza's territory. Every overture of a
pacific character had been made this chief, but no
satisfactory, nor indeed decided, answer could be
obtained. It was, in the first instance, ordered that
we should cross the river without committing any act
of hostility, but our sentries and picquets were to be
most watchful and vigilant, our avowed object being
to recover the cattle which had been so treacherously
stolen out of the colony and driven into Hintza's
country, and from which he would undoubtedly take
a considerable duty. The troops marched on to

the missionary station of Butterworth, close to one of Hintza's great kraals.

The army remained here some days, constantly receiving shuffling messages from Hintza. Here the whole of the Fingoes in Hintza's territories threw themselves on the protection of the Governor. These Fingoes were once a powerful nation, but, being defeated in war, fled to Hintza's territories for protection, which he promised. However, so soon as they were dispersed and powerless, he and his chieftains seized all their cattle, and reduced the whole to the most abject state of slavery. These were the remains of eight powerful nations.[*]

After a day or two's shuffling, Hintza sent into camp his Prime Minister, Kuba, a sharp wolf-like looking fellow, with the cunning of Satan. I would back him eating beef-steaks against any devil. After the Governor had given Kuba several audiences and patiently heard all he had to urge in extenuation of Hintza's evasive conduct, it was evident he had not the slightest intention of restoring the cattle, or making any reparation for the murder of British subjects early in the war, the destruction of the missionary station at Butterworth, etc. Accordingly, war was formally declared.

At ten o'clock our tents were struck, and the army marched [24 April]. A mounted patrol of three hundred cavalry were given to me, and some Fingoes. I made a most rapid march on another of Hintza's kraals, where his great wife Nomsa

---

[*] Alexander, vol. ii. p. 99.

frequently resided. I reached it just before dark, and had a smart brush with the enemy and took a lot of cattle. The next morning at daylight I pushed forward to the bed of the Upper Kei, where information led me to believe a considerable quantity of colonial cattle were secreted. I had a tremendous march this day, and the heat on the banks of the river was excessive. At dark this night I had captured 14,000 head of cattle, principally colonial. I ascertained some months afterwards that these were Macomo's booty. The next day I joined the headquarters column to get rid of my cattle and to get some fresh troops.

At daylight the following day I crossed the rocky bed of the T'somo, very deep and rapid, and made a most precipitate march on Hintza's kraal. He was not there, but many of his followers were ; his cattle were all driven off. I immediately burnt his kraal—in Kafirland regarded as the possession of his territory—the only kraal I burnt in his country.

The rapidity of these inroads, the extraordinary extent of country traversed by the troops with me, the burning of Hintza's kraal, were viewed by Hintza with the utmost surprise and consternation, and this chief, who had treated with the utmost evasion and contempt all previous overtures, on the day after his kraal was burnt came into our camp with his son and court, a humble suppliant for peace and mercy. A few years before, a detachment of troops under Colonel Somerset had been sent to assist him against his enemies, and saved him from destruction. He therefore rode into our camp in an undaunted manner. (The poor savage always buries the past in oblivion, and regards the present only. He has not the most distant idea of right or wrong as regards his line of conduct. Self-interest is his controlling impulse, and desire stands for law and rectitude.) The Governor, Sir B. D'Urban, recorded on paper, in a clear and strong manner, all the grievances he had to complain of, and the redress which he sought and would have. Hintza, with about fifty followers, was immediately prepared to enter into treaty. Kuba was not with him, but he had another of his councillors, a man of great repute, Umtini. As the interpreter translated the Governor's statement paragraph by paragraph, Hintza acknowledged everything. The demand was made for restitution of cattle stolen and redress for all other grievances. Hintza asked to have till next day to consider it, which was granted.

That night he dined with me, while a bullock was given for a feast to his followers, one of whom acted as butcher. The slaughtering is done with great ceremony, but it is horrible to behold. The ox is thrown on his back. The butcher then makes an incision between the chest and the abdomen, through which protrudes immediately a considerable portion of the omentum. This is cut off for the great man of the party as the most acceptable relish. The butcher then introduces his

hand and arm up to the very shoulder into the
incision, gets hold of the heart and turns it, the
animal giving a terrific roar of excruciating pain
which is really appalling. But he is dead in a
moment, the circulation being stopped by the
twisting of the blood-vessels. By this method of
slaying the animal, all the blood is preserved in
the meat, which the Kafir thinks adds to its flavour
and nutritious power.*

Hintza, Umtini, myself, and the interpreter were
together four hours. I was never more astonished
than by the ability with which Hintza argued on
every point and by the shrewd and cautious
opinions expressed by Umtini. The interpreter,
Mr. Shepstone,† a very clever youth of nineteen,
was the son of a missionary. He had been born
among the Kafirs, and the language was as familiar
to him as that of his father. He was the only
interpreter we had who could convey your meaning
in the Kafir idiom and in conformity to their usages
and knowledge of men and things. After all this
discussion, Hintza said, "Well, I shall agree to-
morrow to the Governor's demands in every
respect." He then left me, having eaten enough for
seven men. I walked with him to his people, where
the protruding omentum of the slaughtered bullock
was prepared for him. Curiosity induced me to
remain. He ate every bit of this fat fried lightly;
there could not have been less than four pounds.

* The slaying of the ox on this occasion is also described by
Alexander, vol. ii. p. 132.

† Afterwards Sir Theophilus Shepstone.

The next day a sort of court was held, and Hintza formally accepted the conditions of peace offered by his Excellency. Peace was therefore proclaimed, and Hintza went through the ceremony of despatching messengers in all directions to collect the quota of cattle he was to furnish, as well as to bring to headquarters the colonial cattle.

On one of my predatory expeditions I had taken a great chief, by name Maquay. My A.D.C., Balfour, seized him and saved his life, and he was a prisoner in our camp, and I had several others. I now released them all, being very glad to get rid of their custody. If ever a savage can feel any sensation approaching to gratitude, this chief Maquay did when I gave him his liberty. He thanked me for his life, while he frankly acknowledged that, under similar circumstances, he should have taken mine.

Hintza's promises were so strong that the army commenced its march [May 2] towards the ford of the Kei, since called Smith's Tower, there to remain until the conditions of the treaty were fulfilled. A deluge of rain detained us some days. In daily expectation of the arrival of the cattle, the army was as well in one camp as another. Hintza remained with us, which gave us every confidence. When pressed to name hostages, he said, "Oh, I shall willingly remain myself." This act of frankness was evidently intended as a cloak, and he meditated his escape. He was frequently asking me leave to ride out to meet his people bringing in cattle. This I usually refused. One fine sunny day he so pressed

me that I asked the Governor's permission, saying
that I would provide for his security.   Sir Benjamin
D'Urban said, " Depend on it, he meditates his
escape"; for some days over the period stipulated
had elapsed, and not an article of the treaty
acted on.

I sent with Hintza a well-mounted escort of the
Cape Corps under a Lieut. Wade, a smart, active
and well-mounted officer.   I directed him to examine
his pistols in Hintza's presence, and the escort their
carbines, and to be most vigilant.   Hintza endeavoured to lead him into intricate ground, but
Wade was far too sharp a fellow, and said, " Hintza,
riding about in this way is all folly.   I shall take
you back to camp."   That very day Hintza's and
Boku his brother's people had commenced a
general massacre of all the Fingoes near them who,
in virtue of the treaty of peace, had wandered from
the camp.   The Governor, seeing the treachery and
the absolute want of all faith, became exceedingly
indignant, and threatened to hang Hintza himself,
and Kreili his son, and Boku his brother, if an
instant cessation of this carnage did not take place.
The fellows funked, and immediately sent messengers
scampering in every direction.

The same night, Hintza's sort of confidential
man, a notorious thief and spy, came to me requesting a private audience.   I said, " Let him come in."
The sergeant of my escort, who always had his double-
barrelled carbine in his hand, made me a sign he
would be at hand.   I then, alone with the fellow (a

copper-coloured half-Hottentot, half-Kafir, a strong
athletic fellow), said in Dutch, which he spoke perfectly, " Well, what do you want ? " He began to
abuse Hintza, saying he was a robber, a traitor to
his own people and to us (I saw by the rascal's eye
there was mischief in it), and that he wished to serve
me. " You scoundrel," I said, " you have been
well treated by Hintza ; you now wish to desert him
because you think he is in difficulties. I will show
you how Englishmen treat runaway servants." I
called Japps, and desired him to give the fellow a
good flogging and kick him into Hintza's camp.
Japps was not long in obeying my orders, and soon
came back with a large clasp-knife in his hand.
" There," says he, " this fell from under the rascal's
arm, and he has confessed Hintza sent him to
murder you." *

We moved our camp from the bed of the Kei
on the road. The Governor began to think Hintza
had no intention whatever of fulfilling his promises,
but he did not desire to bring him over the Kei a
prisoner, which would have been regarded throughout his country as an insult ; he therefore proposed
that two of his comrades should remain as hostages.
Hintza would only offer two common men. The
Governor then said, " Hintza, I shall keep Kreili and
Boku." This startled Hintza exceedingly, and he
renewed a proposal to me which he had often made,
that if I would go with him and take troops, he
would himself speedily collect the cattle. After all

* Alexander, vol. ii. p. 147.

our marches and exertions, it was as annoying as unsatisfactory to recross the Kei without the redemption of the colonial cattle. I therefore rather urged this proposal on the consideration of his Excellency, who was always of opinion that Hintza was playing false and that his liberty was his sole consideration. "However," his Excellency said, "it is a chance in our favour; you may go with him, but, depend on it, you have undertaken a laborious task."

I prepared, therefore, to march immediately, while the Governor intended to cross over the Fingoes—an operation something resembling the flight of the Israelites out of Egypt—and then to pass the troops. I took with me—

50 Cape Rifles, under an old Peninsular officer, a Captain Ross.

2 Companies 72nd Regiment, under Captain Murray, who had now perfectly recovered from his wound.

3 Companies 1st Battalion Hottentots.

15 of the Corps of Guides.

My A.D.C., Balfour, and my worthy friend Major White, the Q.M.G. of the Burgher force.

Some commissariat stores of bread, flour, and spirits packed on oxen.

Hintza had been treated by me with every possible kindness, and always affected to acknowledge it. He had been loaded with presents by the Governor, and I candidly admit I had a feeling of kindness towards the chief daily growing upon me, which I could not account for.

We were all soon *en route* [10 May]. The troops had a very long, steep, and winding road, the ascent from the bed of the Kei to the tableland. Hintza, I, my A.D.C., and interpreter, with my escort of Guides, rode on, dismounted, and sat looking at the troops climbing the ascent. Hintza said to the interpreter, " Ask the Colonel in what position I now stand as regards myself and my subjects." I was very glad he put this question, and in very deliberate terms and in an impressive manner I thus expressed myself through the interpreter : " Hintza, you have lived with me now nine days ; you call yourself my son, and you say you are sensible of my kindness. Now, I am responsible to my King and to my Governor for your safe custody. Clearly understand that you have requested that the troops under my command should accompany you to enable you to fulfil the treaty of peace you have entered into. You voluntarily placed yourself in our hands as a hostage ; you are, however, to look upon me as having full power over you, and if you attempt to escape, you will assuredly be shot.* I consider my nation at peace with yours, and I shall not molest your subjects provided they are peaceable. When they bring the cattle according to your command, I shall select the bullocks and return the cows and calves to them."

Hintza replied that he came out to fulfil his

* The same speech is quoted by Alexander, vol. ii. p. 160.

treaty of peace, and with no intention to escape, and
that the fact of his son's being in our hands was a
sufficient guarantee of his sincerity.   I replied most
emphatically, "Very well, Hintza; act up to this, and
I am your friend.   Again I tell you, *if you attempt
to escape, you will be shot.*"

Notwithstanding these specious professions, that
very afternoon my suspicions were aroused.   I
observed two Kafirs coming towards us with five
head of cattle.   On seeing us, they stopped, and
Hintza, without asking my leave, sent a mounted
man to them—as he said, to bring them in; but, in
place of that, the messenger and the others went
off together.   My officer, Mr. Southey of the Corps
of Guides, attached much importance to this little
circumstance.   On closely questioning Hintza, I
received from him such evasive replies I began to
think there must be some little act of treachery, and
I pressed him to define the route which he proposed
I should take.   I could never get more from him
than "We are going right."

I knew any chance of success in my expedition
depended on the rapidity of my march, for the
Kafirs themselves would drive the surrounding
country as we approached.   I marched, therefore, till
dark, having crossed the Guadan Hills that night.
Before daylight the next morning [11 May] I was
again *en route*, and reached the Guanga late in the
afternoon.   There I bivouacked and my men cooked.
Hintza always ate with me, and, with his councillor
Umtini, lay near me at night.   I kept a very Light

Division watch over him. After eating, I said, "Now, Hintza, we are a long way in your country; I must know where you propose to conduct me." He was on this occasion very communicative, and requested that I should march towards the mouth of the Bashee by a route which he would point out, and that we should move at midnight. To this request I readily acceded, having observed during the day's march all the cattle to be driven in that direction. At twelve I marched [12 May], keeping a very sharp look-out on Hintza, whose manner I observed to be excited, and continued marching till eight in the morning, when it became necessary to halt and cook.

At breakfast the chief appeared particularly uneasy and evidently annoyed at the vigilance with which I watched him. He observed peevishly, "What have the cattle done that you want them? or why must I see my subjects deprived of them?" I said, "These are odd questions to ask, Hintza. You well know the outrages committed in the Colony by your people; it is in redress of these wrongs I march, and at your own request."

At ten o'clock I again marched. Hintza suddenly became in high spirits, and observed sarcastically, "See how my subjects treat me: they drive the cattle away in spite of me." "Hintza," I said, "I do not want your subjects' cattle; I am sent for the colonial cattle which have been stolen, and which I *will have.*" "Then," said the chief, "allow me to send forward Umtini, my principal

2 D

councillor, to tell my people I am here, that they must not drive away their cattle, and that the cattle of your own nation will alone be selected." This proposal I immediately agreed to, as it appeared to hold out some chance of success, although I could not divest myself of the opinion that Hintza was meditating some mischief. I particularly enjoined Umtini to return at night, and this he promised faithfully to do.

Umtini quitted the line of march at full speed, accompanied by one of Hintza's attendants, the chief exclaiming, in high spirits, " Now you need not go to the Bashee ; you will have more cattle than you can drive on the Xabecca "—a small river which we were rapidly approaching.

On my nearing the stream, it was found that the spoor or track of the cattle branched off in two directions—one to the left, up a high mountain ; the other to the right, up a very steep, abrupt, high, and wooded hill upon the banks of the Xabecca.* The river-bed below was rugged, precipitous, and covered with brushwood. Hintza said, " We must follow the track to our right ; the cattle which are gone to the left up the mountain are lost to us." This desire of his I resolved to follow, and crossed the Xabecca accordingly.

It had been remarked that this morning Hintza rode a remarkable fine and powerful horse, which he spared fatigue by leading him up any hill we came

---

* Alexander gives the river as Gnabacka. Schmidt's map (1876) gives it as Xnabeccana and Gnabecca.

across during the march. On the opposite side of
the Xabecca the ascent was steep, precipitous, and
woody. I was riding at the head of the column,
when I heard a rush of horses behind me, and called
out to the Corps of Guides, in whose particular
charge Hintza was. I then observed the chief and
all his followers riding up quickly to me and passing
me in the bushes on both sides. The Corps of
Guides called my attention to the circumstance,
and I exclaimed to Hintza, "Stop!" At this
moment the chief, having moved to one side of the
track which we were marching on, became entangled
among the bushes and was obliged to descend
again on to the path before us. I drew a pistol, at
which the chief smiled so ingenuously, I nearly felt
regret at my suspicions, and I allowed the chief to
ride on, preceded by some of the Corps of Guides,
his guards, who had pushed forward to intercept him
if he attempted to escape.

On reaching the top of this ascent, we found the
country perfectly open, and parallel with the rugged
and wooded bed of the Xabecca (calculated for the
resort, cover, and protection of the Kafir), a considerable tongue of land ran for about two miles
and terminated at the bend of the river, where was
a Kafir village. On reaching the top, my mind
was occupied with the march of the troops up this
steep ascent, and I was looking back to observe
their appearance, when the chief set off at full speed,
passing the Guides in front, towards the village in
the distance. Two of the Guides, active fellows,

Messrs. Southey and Shaw, set off, exclaiming, " Oh, Colonel, Colonel, look!" My first glance showed me the treachery, and both spurs were dashed into my horse's sides, a noble animal of best English blood. The chief was at least two hundred yards ahead of me, and for half a mile his horse was as fast as mine. It was a capital horse in good condition, given to him some months before by Colonel Somerset. After that distance I found I rapidly neared him, and when within a distance of forty yards I pulled out a pistol. It snapped. I tried a second, with equal ill success. At this moment Hintza's horse gained on me, and I found that in the pursuit I had rushed my horse with such violence I had nearly blown him, and that, if I must take the chief, it was necessary to nurse my horse a little. In about a quarter of a mile I again closed with him. I had no sword on, but I struck him with the butt end of a pistol, which flew out of my hand. He was jobbing at me furiously with his assagai. I rode upon his right to prevent him turning down into the bed of the river, which I supposed (as afterwards it proved) was full of Kafirs in waiting to receive him.

I was now rapidly approaching the Kafir huts, and the blood of my horse gave me great advantage over Hintza. I tried to seize his bridle-reins, but he parried my attempt with his assagai. I prayed him to stop, but he was in a state of frenzy. At this point of desperation, a whisper came into my ear, " Pull him off his horse!" I shall not, nor ever

could, forget the peculiarity of this whisper. No
time was to be lost. I immediately rode so close
to him that his assagai was comparatively harmless,
and, seizing him by the collar of his karosse (or
tiger-skin cloak), I found I could shake him in
his seat. I made a desperate effort by urging my
horse to pass his, and I hurled him to the ground.

My horse was naturally of a violent temper, and,
from the manner I had spurred him and rushed him
about, he became furious. Having now recovered
and running on his second wind, I could not pull him
up, and he ran away with me to the Kafir village.
I expected to feel a hundred assagais at me in a
moment, but all the Kafirs had gone down into the
river. I dropped the reins on one side, and with
both hands hauled his head round. I then spurred
him violently and drove him right upon a Kafir hut,
by which he nearly fell, and I got him round with
his head the right way, viz. back again, and did not
spare the spurs.

The Kafir's fall created delay sufficient for the
foremost of the Guides, Southey, to approach within
gunshot. Southey shot the Kafir Larunu, and as
Hintza was running into the bed of the river, called
to him to stop. At this moment I was within hailing
distance, and I desired Mr. Southey, " Fire, fire at
him." He did so from about two hundred yards
off. The chief fell, and I pulled up, thinking he
was knocked over. He was on his legs again in a
moment, and so close to the bush he succeeded in
gaining it. I made instant arrangements with the

troops to invest as much of the bush as I could, in the hope of intercepting him. In the mean time, however, with the utmost rapidity, Southey and my A.D.C., Lieut. Balfour, 72nd Regiment, pursued him into the bush, the former keeping up, the latter down the stream, when Southey was suddenly startled by an assagai striking the stone or cliff on which he was climbing. Turning quickly round, he perceived a Kafir, his head and uplifted assagai only visible, and so close, he had to recoil to bring up his gun. It was an act like lightning; either the Kafir would send the assagai first, or the shot must fall. Southey was first, and fired and shot the Kafir, whom to his astonishment he found to be the chief.

Southey immediately galloped towards me. There was a cry, " Hintza is taken," at which I was not a little delighted, and I sent the sergeant of my escort, Japps, to bring him to me in a rein or halter, but by no means to treat him roughly. In a few seconds Southey reported the melancholy truth. I say "melancholy " because I had much rather he had been taken, but I thanked Southey for his exertions, and there was no one act I could upbraid myself with as contributing to the chief's attempt to escape after the warning I had given him and the kindness and respect I had treated him with, and after having, merely to please him, marched, as he pretended, to his assistance.

I had the corpse brought up the hill carefully wrapped in the karosse, and laid near the Kafir village with every mark of decency. I had no tools, or I would have buried it. In the distance, with my telescope I saw the confederate Umtini, and observed by his gestures that he was exciting and calling together the Kafirs in all directions by means of messengers running from hill to hill. This is their ordinary method of communication, and it is nearly as rapid as our telegraph.

CHAPTER XXXVI.

MARCH ACROSS THE BASHEE TO THE UMTATA AND
BACK TO THE BASHEE—DEATH OF MAJOR WHITE
—DIFFICULT MARCH FROM THE BASHEE TO REJOIN
SIR B. D'URBAN ON THE KEI—ANNEXATION OF
THE TERRITORY CALLED THE "PROVINCE OF
QUEEN ADELAIDE," AND FOUNDING OF ITS CAPI-
TAL, "KING WILLIAM'S TOWN"—RETURN OF THE
GOVERNOR TO GRAHAMSTOWN.

I COLLECTED my troops, and saw many of my
officers look somewhat staggered as to what was to
come next, considering that they were such a handful
of troops in the heart of a country swarming with
people who were now our most avowed enemies.
Some of Hintza's followers were in my hands. These
I despatched to their countrymen, to tell them how
Hintza's treachery had cost him his life, and that I
should [not ?] make war upon them. I called the
officers to the front, and some of the influential non-
commissioned officers of the Hottentot companies,
and told them the Bashee was not far distant. I
should march upon it, and cross or otherwise as circumstances demanded, for I had been informed that
the bed was full of cattle, principally colonial. I was

now without a guide, for on this important point I
had naturally depended on Hintza. However, I
could distinguish the line of the bed of the Bashee,
to which it had been told me by Hintza that the
cattle would be driven, and the tracks of cattle all
converged in that direction.

Late in the afternoon the waters of the Bashee
were discernible and on its further bank a considerable number of cattle. The troops had been marching fourteen hours, but I resolved to push forward
with my cavalry, whom I ordered to lead their horses
down the precipitous banks of the river. I forded
the beautiful and widely flowing stream in an oblique
direction, and ascended the rugged and steep banks
of the opposite side by a cleft in the rocks, which
admitted of only one horseman at a time. After
gaining the heights, I immediately pushed forward,
and succeeded in capturing 3000 odd fine cattle, but
very few colonial ones among them, and had there
been an hour's more daylight, I should have taken
double the number. Night, however, came on,
and I bivouacked my party on the left bank of
the Bashee, ground well adapted for the security
of the captured cattle. This was the third day
since I left the Kei, and the troops had marched
84 miles.

Having observed at dusk that the cattle I could
not come up with were driven in the direction of the
Umtata, I resolved, as the moonlight was greatly in
my favour, to move at three o'clock in the morning
[13 May], leaving the jaded horses, weakly men,

and captured cattle, with as large a guard as I could afford, in the bivouac. I gave this command to Captain Ross, of the Cape Mounted Rifles, an old and experienced Peninsular officer, with orders to concentrate everything as soon as it was daylight. I told him that he might rely on it the Kafirs would attempt to retake the cattle.

A most gallant officer and dear friend, Major White, the Quartermaster-General to the Burgher force, had accompanied me, and had rendered me great assistance, having also been busily employed each day in adding to the topographical information so much required in this country. He proposed to remain in camp to make sketches, and asked me to give him a guard of one corporal and three men. I desired Captain Ross to give him six, to keep a sharp look-out on this party, and (as I anticipated what *did* occur) to reinforce it in case of need. I also particularly requested my friend White to go a very short way from the bivouac, and to keep a sharp look-out, for he might rely upon the enemy's showing the utmost activity to retake the cattle and destroy every man remaining behind.

Upon my return to camp, the first report was that Major White and all his party were cut off. On the first alarm by a shot, the old Peninsular officer Ross was broad awake, but his reinforcement only arrived in time to find the body of poor White lying pierced with wounds, and all his papers, double-barrelled gun, etc., borne off, and the party lying murdered near him. In him the Colony lost a man of superior ability and vast utility, a noble-minded public-spirited fellow, formerly a lieutenant in our service, and I a friend I was proud of.

During these disasters in camp, which my foresight had anticipated, I pushed forward, detaching Captain Bailie with sixty excellent men of the Hottentot battalion down the Bashee to a distance, then to bring up his right shoulder and rejoin me on the banks of the Kakke * River, equidistant between the Bashee and Umtata, where I proposed to halt and cook, if circumstances permitted me. I had no guide, and my movements were conducted by reference to a very defective map. I marched from the mountainous bank of the Bashee through a most beautiful and fertile country, strongly undulating and rich in pasturage, over which was visible the track of vast numbers of cattle. I pushed on with vigour until the bed of the Umtata was perfectly visible, but not a head of cattle was discernible. The whole country had been driven on the alarm and capture of the previous night. The enemy had assembled in vast numbers all around me, but I never could get near him, so wary and so vigilant was he. I succeeded, however, in taking one prisoner, and two Fingoes came in to me. From them I learned what I indeed saw—the cattle of the whole country had been driven, previously and by Hintza's orders, over the Umtata, those I had captured the night before being, as it were, the rear-guard.

* Mpako?

From the distance marched, the fatigue of the troops, and the powerful concentration of the immense population all around me, I naturally began to turn my attention to the security of the bivouac I had left behind and the captured cattle. I had previously directed Captain Bailie not to join me, if he found the country I had detached him into excessively difficult tô traverse. He was in that case to follow the bed of the Bashee a reasonable distance, and then return straight to the bivouac. My own observation of the country I had marched over confirmed me in thinking it would be impossible for him to join me. I therefore made no halt on account of any such expectation.

The enemy on my march back made some attempts on my rear. The officer, a Lieutenant Bailie, son of the man previously mentioned, a very sharp fellow, laid himself in ambush in the long grass and several times made the Kafirs pay dearly for their temerity.

On approaching my bivouac I saw all was secure, and did not anticipate the extent of the melancholy report I was to receive of the loss of my friend White, as before described. Captain Ross told me that he had been kept on the most vigilant alert all day; that every moment he expected a rush from the immense numbers of Kafirs all round him, and he was very glad to see me back.

Every moment the numbers increased around

me, and their daring to approach me indicated great confidence. I was perfectly satisfied that an attempt would be made at night to retake the cattle, and I made my defensive dispositions accordingly, giving the command of the picquet to an active officer on whom I could depend—Captain Lacy of the 72nd Regiment.

Scarcely was it perfectly dark when on came, in the most stealthy manner, a swarm of Kafirs. Their design was anticipated, however, by our vigilance, and the assailants were driven back with great loss. Captain Bailie had not yet returned with his sixty men, and I was very anxious he should do so, although I felt no great apprehensions for his safety, as I heard no firing in his direction, and I was well aware he would not give in without a desperate struggle. However, between eleven and twelve at night I heard him approaching—joyfully, I admit ; for he and his men had been marching from three o'clock in the morning, and taking into consideration the previous day's march, I then considered, and I now maintain, that these sixty men marched a greater distance than was ever traversed in the same number of hours by any infantry in the world. I was aware that unless they fell in with cattle they would have nothing to eat, and I had their dinners prepared ; the active fellows had eaten nothing from the previous night. Captain Bailie reported to me that he had had various rencontres with parties of the enemy ; that after dark he was closely invested, and several bold attempts were made to assagai his men in the very ranks.

Seeing the number of the enemy, their increasing hostility and daring, the difficulty of the road I had to retire by, being obliged to recross the Bashee by a path admitting of only one bullock at a time, it became necessary to make my arrangements with every skill and attention, lest the enemy should retake my capture, the abandonment of which would be contrary to the feelings of most of my party. Accordingly I made the soldiers cook at daylight, and went in among my doubtful troops— the new levies; for in my *soldiers* of the 72nd Regiment I had every confidence, as they deserved. I found my Hottentots, who are very sharp fellows, perfectly aware of the delicacy of our position, which, indeed, I did not attempt to conceal, as I wished to impress upon them that our safety and the getting away of the cattle depended on their silence and obedience and their never firing a shot without orders. They always called me "father." An old spokesman now said to me in Dutch, "We will do all our father desires, if he will stay near us, and not go galloping about to have his throat cut; for if we lose him we are all lost."

I sent Captain Ross over the river to establish himself on the opposite bank, and I placed parties in the river above and below the ford to keep the Kafirs from driving off the cattle, as they are very expert at this, and a few men could have effected it if once an opening had occurred.

So soon as the enemy saw me under arms and observed my retrograde movement, they disposed of themselves in the most dexterous manner, so as to attack me wherever able, and made frequent feints in one direction so as to attack in another. But so well were my orders obeyed, and so alert was every officer and soldier, fully aware that one error would occasion dire disaster, all these bold attempts were defeated : and I succeeded in crossing the river to the full extent of my most sanguine hopes. When I reached the open country about four miles from the river, the enemy had no cover or ground favourable for molesting me, and I pursued my march uninterrupted, but with great caution and in as compact a body as possible. Three thousand cattle cover a deal of ground, and but for the ability of the Hottentots as drovers I should never have succeeded in bringing them off.

In all my previous service I was never placed in a position requiring more cool determination and skill, and as one viewed the handful of my people compared with the thousands of brawny savages all round us, screeching their war-cry, calling to their cattle, and indicating by gesticulations the pleasure they would have in cutting our throats, the scene was animating to a degree. I continued my march and recrossed the Kei on the 17th May, and rejoined the main body under his Excellency Sir B. D'Urban, having completed a march of 218 miles in seven days and a half, over a rugged and mountainous country, intersected by deep rivers at

the bottom of precipitous ravines and rivulets difficult
to cross, having had to march for hours without any
road at all, bringing with me 3000 captured cattle
and 1000 Fingoes, who had flocked to me with
their families for protection, and added considerably to my difficulties; and all this effected without
the loss of an individual except those whose fatuity,
or rather indiscretion, had placed them—so contrary
to my caution and my anticipation of danger—within
the grasp and power of the undaunted and stealthy
savage.

On my reaching Sir Benjamin D'Urban, he gave
out—

"21 May, 1835.

"The Commander-in-Chief has again the gratification
of recording the military skill and indefatigable activity
of Colonel Smith, and the admirable discipline, zeal, and
determined spirit of the troops under his orders in the
recent expedition beyond the mouth of the Bashee. Upon
no former occasion—and there have been many during this
campaign where they have well earned praise for their
high qualities—have they displayed them in a more
eminent degree. They marched in seven days 218
miles ; overcame all opposition, notwithstanding that
this was obstinately attempted by several thousands
of armed and determined savages; crossed and recrossed
a large river of very difficult banks, and brought off from
the further side three thousand head of cattle which had
been plundered from the Colony. They have also achieved
a still more important service in the course of this bold
and rapid inroad : they have rescued from destruction and
safely brought in one thousand of the Fingo race, who
from their remote situation had been before unable to join

their countrymen now under British protection, and who would inevitably have been sacrificed to the fury of the savages so soon as they should have had leisure to think of them.

"For these services, effected too without loss from the ranks, the Commander-in-Chief returns his thanks to all the troops employed, officers and soldiers, and he especially offers them to Colonel Smith."

The Governor was much depressed at the unfortunate loss of the chief Hintza by his own treachery, not only from the natural feeling of humanity towards the individual, but because he fully anticipated the hold the canting party would take of it in England. Such men, stripping facts of all collateral circumstances, so changed the features of that incident as to twist it into the tortuous shape of their own cunning duplicity. For my own part, I was firmly based in my conscientious rectitude, of which Almighty God alone was Witness and Judge, and anything which man could say I disregarded. I admit, however, that at the moment I did not expect to be called a bloodthirsty murderer in every print in every quarter of our dominions, or to be shamefully abandoned by the Minister of the Colonies,* whose duty it was in such assaults honestly to have supported and sustained me against the misled voice of the public, and not to have sacrificed me at the shrine of cringing party spirit when I had so faithfully, so zealously, and so energetically saved for him the Colony of the Cape.

* Lord Glenelg.

2 F

He remained in office long enough to repent and acknowledge his error. My own rectitude of conscience prevented me ever caring an iota for these miscreants' assaults, and I was ultimately thanked by the minister ; although not till I had undergone the ordeal of inquiry by a court of investigation, levelled at *me*, but assembled on Mr. Southey, by whose hand the chief lost his life (August and Sept., 1836).

The Governor prepared to move into the colony, as soon as he had taken possession of the country on the right bank of the Kei, some years previously wrested from the Hottentots by the Kafirs, and as soon as he had founded the city of King William's Town [24 May] immediately on the left bank of the Buffalo, and established corresponding posts throughout the newly added " Province of Queen Adelaide."

The army marched from its position on the Kei, establishing posts on the line of road towards Grahamstown, and headquarters were established on the 22nd May, on the site of the new city, King William's Town, and remained there till the 11th June, when the Commander-in-Chief returned to Grahamstown.

During this period, with a small force of cavalry and infantry, I made some most rapid and extensive marches throughout the whole of the new province, the object being, in virtue of the proclamation, to compel the Kafirs to return behind the Kei in the spirit of that conquest by which they had some years previously crossed it. A more harassing duty for myself and troops cannot be imagined, although the troops had the best of the fatigue, for after each excursion I took fresh parties.

The day previously to headquarters returning to Grahamstown a General Order was published, of which the following is an extract :—

"The Commander-in-Chief publishes three reports made to him on the 1st, 3rd, and 7th inst. [June, 1835] by Colonel Smith *at length*, because they are full of valuable instruction for young officers (whose attention, therefore, is earnestly invited to them), setting forth in the clearest and most emphatic manner how such duties should be performed, as well with regard to arrangement of plan, as to activity and energy of execution; and, above all, they furnish a practical illustration of this great military principle, which should be foremost in the mind of every soldier, and which so strikingly characterizes this distinguished officer, 'Nil actum reputans, siquid superesset agendum.'"

After thanking the troops, the Order continues—

"It diminishes the regret of the Commander-in-Chief at quitting this personal command, that he leaves them in charge of Colonel Smith, an officer in whom they must all have the fullest confidence as well on account of those high military qualities which they have witnessed, and which have made him a main cause of the recent successes, as because they know from experience he is a soldier, and will always have a watchful care of all that can contribute to their health, comfort, and convenience.

"Colonel Smith, C.B., is appointed to the command of the District of the Province of Queen Adelaide and all the troops therein, until his Majesty's pleasure be known."

CHAPTER XXXVII.

HARRY SMITH LEFT IN COMMAND OF THE NEW
"PROVINCE OF QUEEN ADELAIDE" AT KING
WILLIAM'S TOWN—DEATH OF LIEUTENANT BAILIE
—HARRY SMITH JOINED BY HIS WIFE—FORAYS
ON THE KAFIRS—CONCLUSION OF PEACE.

UPON my taking the command, my first object
was to provide for the security of the various posts
established by his Excellency ; to facilitate communication by improving roads, fords, etc. ; then to
endeavour to compel the Kafirs, in conformity with
my instructions, to withdraw beyond the Kei and
sue for peace. I endeavoured by every means in
my power to assure them that peace was within
their reach, and that if hostilities were continued, it
would be due to them alone. I most assuredly
never allowed the troops one moment's repose from
the furtherance of the great object—a peaceful
possession of the province wrested from the
enemy.

Of the many patrols which I sent out, one consisted of sixty of the 1st Battalion of the Hottentots
under Lieutenants Bailie and Biddulph. I had
frequently employed Lieutenant Bailie on such

duties. His achievements were always to my
perfect satisfaction, and I had implicit confidence in
his judgment, discretion, and bravery. The evening
this patrol went out, I proceeded some distance
with it, impressing upon Lieut. Bailie the necessity
there was for vigilance. Above all he must never
divide his party, as utility and safety consisted in
union. With this injunction I left him, and for ever.
It will appear that this excellent officer had received
some information by which he hoped to effect great
service, and he divided his sixty men into two bodies,
thirty with himself, and thirty with Biddulph. They
were to meet at a given point of rendezvous well
known to both. Biddulph reached the rendezvous,
but Bailie's party never again appeared. They were
cut off to a man. Biddulph, having heard no firing,
after waiting for some time, believed Bailie to have
returned to my camp. I had so much confidence in
this officer's ability, that I was not in the slightest
apprehension for his safety, and as to sending out
parties in quest of him, I had no clue whatever, for
Biddulph could not even give an opinion where he
could have proceeded to. Afterwards, on the conclusion of peace, it was ascertained that with his
small party he protracted a most gallant and un-
flinching resistance for four days against many
hundreds of the savages, who had hemmed him in
in one of the deep woody ravines of the Tabendoda*
Mountains, a resistance which did not cease till his
ammunition was exhausted. It is most extraordinary

* Alexander says " the Intabakandoda range " (vol. ii. p. 248).

that, though I sent patrols in various directions, no one ever heard the report even of a musket.

Being thus established "Governor" of a Province, and my dear, faithful, adventurous, and campaigning wife being impatient under her unusual separation, we resolved with mutual gratification that she should start to join me—a distance of nearly 800 miles over a wild country of bad roads, difficult passes, and deep rivers. But what will not woman undertake when actuated by love and duty? Such distances are travelled in large covered or tilted waggons drawn by ten, twelve, fourteen, and even twenty horses according to the road. The roads may be of deep sand, hard, or over mountains; but they are invariably rough. One of the judges' circuit waggons was kindly placed at my wife's disposal, and she, her maid, dogs, and two faithful servants started. Reliefs of horses were collected on the road at the usual stages by authority, my wife paying for the same. She travelled at an average rate of 70 miles a day, receiving, wherever she stopped the night or for refreshment, every attention from the families of the Dutch Boers, most of whom were, or had been, under my command, and with whom I was very popular. She reached Grahamstown much fatigued from the jolting of so unwieldy a thing as a Cape waggon, but no other vehicle can bear the shock caused by the roughness of the mountain roads. On reaching Grahamstown she found it necessary to rest for a day or two, after which the troops of Volunteers spontaneously prayed

to be her escort to Fort Willshire, about halfway
between Grahamstown and King William's Town,
the furthest point to which I could venture to proceed
from my command. On the day we were to meet,
so punctual were we both that her waggon and my
escort appeared on two heights on either side of
Fort Willshire at the same instant, and we were
again united in gratitude to Almighty God.

The next day we proceeded to the seat of my
government, King William's Town, where my dear
campaigning wife was again under canvas, surrounded by all the circumstance of war.   There
was, however, little " pomp " in my posts, every man
who strayed a few yards from the cantonment being
murdered to a certainty. We only occupied the
ground we stood on, and chains of sentries were
round us each night, as hundreds of Kafirs were
watching every post night and day for the purposes
of murder and plunder, and most daring attempts
were frequently made to carry off cattle from the
very centre of our camp. My tents were near the
garden of an old missionary station which had been
burnt during the war; and in that garden two
Kafirs were shot while attempting to steal my cows.

Close to King William's Town, and somewhat
under cover of it, I had a large Fingo encamp-
ment. One night the Kafirs in great force made a
desperate attempt to destroy them and their camp
and carry off their cattle. But the Fingoes, even
before the picquet in readiness for the purpose could
reach them, not only defended themselves most

gallantly, but bravely beat the Kafirs, left them lying dead in their camp, and pursued them until daylight. I shall never forget the screeching, yelling, hooting, Tower of Babel noise made in the dead of night by so many hundred desperate savages fighting with every degree of animosity that bitter hatred and enmity inspire. But so well did the Fingoes conduct themselves, that no further attempt was ever made to molest them.

In all the many forays I made on these determined barbarians, I endeavoured to impress upon them, through the medium of their women, that submission and a desire on their part for peace would be readily listened to, and that they alone would be the culprits if the horrors of war continued. The many forays I ordered are best described in a General Order, of which the following is an extract:—

"7 August.

"With reference to the General Order of the 1st July, when the Commander-in-Chief had last the satisfaction of thanking the troops in the Province of Queen Adelaide, he now desires to record his approbation of their continued and gallant and excellent services as reported by Colonel Smith during the latter part of June and the whole of the month of July. These have been hardly and brilliantly achieved, with great loss to the enemy and the capture of 5000 head of cattle. And for these the Commander-in-Chief desires to express to the officers and soldiers his approbation and his thanks, which are especially due to Colonel Smith."

If ever these anecdotes meet the eye of the

public, let it bear in mind that although as an *united*
enemy nothing could be so contemptible as the poor
athletic barbarians, yet to inflict any punishment
upon them the most rapid and gigantic marches
were requisite, and every patrol must be conducted
on the most vigilant and scientific principles.   Most
enterprising men were watching every movement,
ready to take advantage of inactivity or error.   On
one occasion a most desperate attempt, boldly
planned and executed, was made on a redoubt near
the frontier, and only repulsed by the soldiers of
the 72nd Regiment hand to hand.   On the whole a
more harassing duty was rarely undertaken.

My Hottentot levies—the 1st and 2nd Provisional Battalions (not enlisted soldiers)—began to
be very tired of the war.   The excitement of cattle-
hunting no longer existed ; and in lieu of it, when I
sent them into the bush they encountered an enemy
fully as gallant as themselves.   After the loss of
Lieutenant Bailie's party, too, they became somewhat cowed ; and I never sent any of them out
without a proportion of our own redcoats.   From
the various communications I began to receive
through the women, it was evident that the Kafirs
also were heartily tired of war.   In order, therefore,
to accelerate peace, I determined to make from Fort
Cox (commanded by the gallant officer of that name)
a desperate and very extended attempt on the tribes
of the great chiefs Macomo and Tyalie, who were
in that neighbourhood.   I therefore reinforced
Major Cox with all the troops I could spare, and

sent him very detailed instructions, dwelling particularly on the attainment of my object, peace. Any overture was to be received cordially, but no cessation of hostilities was to be permitted without previous communication with me; which a few hours would effect. This enterprise was so ably conducted by my gallant comrade, and so energetically supported by officers and soldiers, that Macomo sued for peace; and I consented to a provisional cessation of hostilities whilst I communicated with the Governor at Grahamstown.

Sir Benjamin immediately sent out Captain Warden and Major Cox. Both officers were personally known to Macomo and liked by him; and he with his council and Tyalie met them beyond our posts [15 August].* The basis of the treaty was then communicated to the chiefs, who consented to almost everything, the articles were taken to Grahamstown by Captain Warden, and Major Cox, to my deep regret, sent back the reinforcements I had furnished him with. I was so convinced that the chiefs would not conclude a peace on these terms, that I marched back to Cox the troops (or rather fresh ones), and wrote to the Governor to request that, in the event of Macomo, as I anticipated, demurring to the terms, I might be sent to conclude the peace. The whole turned out as I expected. Macomo, seeing we were willing to make peace, at his second meeting with Cox and Warden [25

* For Warden's report of the conference, see Alexander, vol. ii. p. 335.

August] rose in his demands, and was most violent and even insulting in his conduct. Warden, in conformity to his orders, came to me 30 miles off; and at dusk I was in my saddle, and troops were marching in all directions on certain points around Macomo.

On my arrival at Fort Cox, I sent a summons to Macomo to meet me with his chiefs in front of my picquet, describing to him the position of my troops, and pointing out that the line of his retreat over the Kei, previously left open for him, was now intercepted. I added that if he was not with me in two hours after the receipt of my message, I would sweep him and all his host off the face of the earth. This bold menace had the desired effect, and he speedily met me.

I went out [6 September] with only Cox, Warden, and my A.D.C., to show I did not anticipate treachery, although I had some able support hard by. On meeting me, Macomo was in a state of terrible agitation, as was his brother Tyalie. The spot was near the place called the grave of their father, the great chief Gaika. I therefore, in their own mode of incantation, invoked Gaika to our council, for whom they had profound respect and veneration, and then most abruptly demanded a repetition of his dying injunction to his sons Macomo and Tyalie, which was to remain in peace and amity with the English and never make war upon them. I would not allow the chiefs to have an opinion, much less to give one, saying, "You made war in the most brutal and unjust manner upon our colony, without observing *your own* and *our* unvaried custom of declaring war, but burning, murdering, and spoiling all you approached. Beaten in war, you sue for peace, and peace is granted to you. On a second meeting called to ratify it, you rise in your demands. You are insolent and overbearing to two officers for whom you profess respect and esteem. Now I read the only terms and conditions on which I make peace with you. Unless you accept them after the several days you have had to deliberate on them— for they are the very same articles you previously accepted without any reserve—you shall return to your people. I give you half an hour to reach them, after which I will instantly attack you, and never cease until you are all destroyed. I am here to command, not to *listen*." (" Listen" is a most impressive expression in the Kafir language and habit. It means everything.)

This decided mode of dealing with these treacherous savages, with whom self-will alone is law, astonished them, and they all agreed to the former treaty. Tyalie, an ignorant fellow, began to talk, but I shut his mouth in a voice of thunder, and threatened to make peace with the others and exclude him, which settled his presumption. The whole body—chiefs and council—then formally ratified the treaty, and all accompanied me to Fort Cox, where I regaled them with all in my power. I told them they should soon see the difference in me between a friend and an enemy ; that as I had waged vigorous war on them, so would I teach them by every kindness to become men and shake off their barbarism.

The Governor came to Fort Willshire, halfway between Fort Cox and Grahamstown, to meet the chiefs [dates of meetings, 11 and 17 September]. The tribes had become, in consequence of the war, somewhat unruly, and I do believe that at the moment the chiefs, with every desire, had not the power to restrain many lawless and predatory acts of their followers, pending the final arrangement of the new order of things.

On the conclusion of the treaty of peace, a deputation was sent to Kreili and his mother, Nomsa. Kreili was now the great chief in place of his father Hintza. If a Kafir has any heart, this youth Kreili showed one on all after-occasions to me, for my kindness to him when he was in our camp with his father. I ever found him docile and reasonable, and ever had paramount authority with him.

CHAPTER XXXVIII.

HARRY SMITH'S ATTEMPTS AT CIVILIZING THE KAFIRS
—THE CHIEFS MADE BRITISH MAGISTRATES—A
CENSUS TAKEN—A POLICE FORCE ESTABLISHED—
A GREAT MEETING OF CHIEFS—WITCHCRAFT FOR-
BIDDEN—A CHIEF PUNISHED FOR DISOBEDIENCE
—A REBELLIOUS CHIEF AWED INTO SUBMISSION
—AGRICULTURE AND COMMERCE INTRODUCED—
NAKEDNESS DISCOUNTENANCED—BURIAL OF THE
DEAD ENCOURAGED—BUYING OF WIVES CHECKED
—HOPES OF A GENERAL CONVERSION TO
CHRISTIANITY.

DURING the assembly of the chiefs and their great
men at Fort Willshire, I had many and long con-
ferences with them. They had become British
subjects at their own request, and now each chief
was appointed a magistrate in his own tribe and
district, with orders to look up to me and report
to me as the Governor of the Province. To intro-
duce a new order of things diametrically opposed
to their former habits required much consideration;
and the success of the undertaking depended on the
gradual introduction of innovation and change. I
joyfully and enthusiastically entered upon the task

of rescuing from barbarism thousands of our fellow-creatures endowed by nature with excellent under-standing and powers of reasoning as regards the *present;* for there was only one man among them—Umhala, the chief of the T'slambie tribe—who had an idea of the *result* of measures, or futurity. I saw that innovations must be so introduced as to render them agreeable, not obnoxious, and that anything acquired by conciliatory and palatable means was an important point gained. I requested each chief to give me one of his most able councillors, and several messengers on whom he could depend, to accompany me to King William's Town, now the "Great Kraal" or seat of government, that we might freely communicate, or, in their expression, "that they might have my ear." This they all cheerfully assented to. The Governor returned to Grahams-town [25 Sept.], I to my "Great Kraal" with my new court, and the chiefs to their tribes.

By this arrangement much of the territory, indeed almost the whole, between the Kei and the Keis-kamma was restored to the previous occupants. But the labour and difficulty I had to prevent locations on the tracts of country reserved for military purposes and sites of towns is not to be described. Fre-quently I have been compelled to resort to very harsh measures; but I never would admit of any arrangement bordering on a compromise. I started on the principle of Yes and No, Right and Wrong. I was ever inflexible, and I ever strove most energetically to establish that faith in my word and uncompromising justice which aided me beyond anything to effect what I ultimately did. I closed the door to all appeal or reference to events which occurred prior to the conclusion of peace. In their own words, "the old kraal was shut," never to be reopened. It was fortunate for me that I adopted this policy, for no records of the Court of Chancery embraced more retrospect than my new subjects were disposed to. They were all by nature subtle and acute lawyers. The councillor given me by Macomo was an old man of great ability; Lords Bacon, Thurlow, and Eldon were not more acquainted with our laws than was this old fellow with the laws of his people. He had been Gaika's Prime Minister and Lord Chancellor, and was attached to the English. With this old fellow I spent six hours a day for several successive days, until I made myself thoroughly acquainted with their laws and rights of person. Although these closely resembled the law of Moses given in Leviticus, and, if correctly administered, were excellent, I soon discovered that might was right, that the damnable forgery of sorcery and witchcraft was the *primum mobile* of oppression and extortion, and that under the cloak of punishment for this offence there was committed oppression of so barbarous and tyrannical a kind as it was hardly to be conceived that beings endowed with reason could perpetrate on each other. The following sketch will give some idea of what commonly takes place.

In Kafirland the witch-doctors and the rain-makers are in the confidence of their respective chiefs. Whenever any individual renders himself obnoxious to the chief or any of his family or influential men, he is accused of bewitching either the chief, his wife, or child, or cattle, or any other thing, but no one is ever considered capable of this sort of sorcery but a man rich in goods, viz. cattle.

A witch-dance is then called, special care being taken to summon the individual upon whom it is intended to affix the crime. An old hag, perfectly naked, comes forth; the assembled people dance round her in a circle; she is, in their expression, to "smell out" the person who has bewitched the supposed sufferers. After a variety of gesticulations, this hag approaches the individual already named by the chief, and literally *smells* him, proclaiming him the culprit. If he is very rich, the chief and his *pagate*, or councillors, are satisfied with "eating him up" (the native expression for having all one's property confiscated under an accusation of witchcraft); if not so, or if he is very obnoxious, they have various punishments, such as putting him at once to death by a species of hanging, or rather strangulating by a leather thong, throwing the poor wretch on the ground upon his back, tethering his arms apart above his head, his legs apart and fully extended, then bringing large quantities of large black ants,* throwing them upon him, and leaving him exposed

---

* These ants are most venomous—creep into the eyes, ears, etc., and cause a pain which no creature was ever known to bear without lamentation; in all other punishments not even a sigh escapes them.— H. G. S.

until the pain and anguish of the stings put an end to his existence; burning the body all over with large flat stones (the poor wretch on whose account I punished Umhala so severely * had thirty large places burned on his person); taking the accused to the edge of a particular precipice and hurling him down; and several other methods. No individual, man, woman, or child, is safe. The witch-doctors are in the confidence of the chief, as much as the Inquisitors are in that of the Pope, and no more arbitrary oppression is exercised on earth than by these Kafir chiefs and witch-doctors.

I soon saw that the witch-doctors and rain-makers, *i.e.* fellows who professed and were believed to be capable of bringing down rain in time of drought, would be my formidable opponents in introducing a new order of things, as their supposed power, if I succeeded, must ultimately be annihilated.

Having thus made myself acquainted with the laws of the barbarous people whom I was to govern and lead on to become civilized beings and British subjects, I was in a position to begin proceedings. At my suggestion, the Governor appointed magistrates to each tribe, consisting principally of officers of the army. With Macomo and Tyalie and the widow Suta, and with the heir-apparent Sandilli, Gaika's young son, I had Captain Stretch; with Dushani's tribe, the widow Nonibe,† and her son,

---

* See p. 441.

† Alexander, vol. ii. p. 222: " Nonubé, the mother of the young Siwana of the T'Slambies, . . . is the great widow of Dushani."

I had Captain Southey; with Umhala and the T'slambie tribes, Captain Rawstorne.

The missionaries all came back to their respective missions, and with the magistrates, the missionaries, and other aid afforded by the kind attention paid by Sir Benjamin D'Urban to all my wants, I proceeded to take a nominal census of the whole male population arrived at puberty, with the number of their women, children, etc. At first the Kafirs were much opposed to this, but through the aid of my councillor Ganya, the common sense of which they have a great share, and my patient explanation of the utility of the measure, I succeeded. I found I had upwards of 100,000 barbarians to reclaim who had no knowledge of right or wrong beyond arbitary power, desire, and self-will. To attach the people to the new order of things was of vast importance; to lessen the power of the chiefs equally so; but this had to be gradual, for if I removed the hereditary restraint of the chiefs, I should open the gates to an anarchy which I might not be able to quell.

A fortunate circumstance occurred, which enabled me to make gigantic steps. The Kafirs have a barbarous festival, when all the maidens are compelled to attend to undergo a sort of " Rape of the Sabines." These maidens, during the festival, are appropriated by the chiefs to themselves and their followers, and then sent back to their families. Old Ganya, who came to tell me this, said, " Now you have an opportunity, by preventing this brutal custom, to restrain the lawlessness of the chiefs, and to win the hearts of their subjects." He added that there were many fathers of families in camp, who had come to appeal to me for protection. I immediately gave them an audience,* as I invariably did every one who desired to see me. I acquired great ascendancy by first ascertaining through the interpreter the grounds on which they had come, and when they were ushered into the presence, exclaiming, " Ah, you want so and so ! " The poor wretches were much astonished at this, believing that I had the power to divine their thoughts ; and I frequently saved myself from listening to a string of lies very plausibly linked together.

I also established with every magistrate a police of Kafirs, and I had a considerable number with me, to apprehend delinquents and culprits and summon the heads of the kraals. These police carried with them from the magistrate a long stick with a brass knob. This is a custom of their own. Fakoo has a cat's tail on his wands of office. At headquarters I had a very long stick with a *large knob*, which was always held by my Gold Stick when I was in council, or upon trials, cases of appeal, mandates, issuing proclamations, etc. And when I seized the stick, held it myself, and gave a decisive order, that was formal and irrevocable. For when once I had decided, no power could induce me to swerve from that decision.

* The author seems inadvertently to have omitted the rest of this particular story.

When the police were out, if they were treated with contumely, and the head of a kraal refused obedience or compliance, this stick was stuck in his cattle-kraal, and he was obliged to bring it himself to the authority whence it emanated ; while so long as it remained in the kraal, the proprietor was under *the ban of the Empire*, excommunicated, or out-lawed. The fear they had of this wand was literally magical. I never had to use military aid in support of my police but once, and then I did so, more as a display of the rapidity with which I could turn out troops and rush them to the spot than from any absolute necessity. Such was the respect for these policemen, that the neighbours of a delinquent would voluntarily turn out in their support, and I always rewarded such support by a present of cattle from my treasury (formed from fines levied for offences).

Having now begun to have some weight and in-fluence among the whole of the tribes, and having taught the people to look up to me rather than to their own chiefs, I had next to re-establish the power of the chiefs as derived from myself. I therefore, with the sanction of the Governor, resolved on a great meeting on the 7th January of all the chiefs, their relatives, councillors, rain-makers, and as many as chose to attend. I had previously pre-pared English clothes for Macomo, Tyalie, Umhala, and some others, with a medal, which was to be the emblem of their magisterial power. Some thousands assembled in a most orderly and obedient manner. I had taken very good care to strengthen my force at headquarters, for I made it an axiom never to place myself in such a situation with these volatile savages as not to be able to enforce obedience to my commands like lightning.

I gave them a sort of epitome of their own history, especially of the Kafir wars. I dwelt particularly on their cruelty and treachery in the late war, and reminded them that they had voluntarily proposed to become British subjects. I then administered the oath of allegiance to all the chiefs in the name of their respective peoples. Two councillors from Kreili (the new Hintza and Great Father) whom I had invited to the meeting, proposed that they should take the oath of allegiance too, which of course I could not accept, all the inhabitants beyond the Kei being independent. It is a curious fact that after this meeting had been held, and the messengers from Kreili had disseminated throughout the tribe the improved state of things under my rule, Kreili himself and many of his influential men were most anxious to become British subjects, and I received many deputations to that effect.

To return, however, to my meeting. I described the duties of the magistrates, British and native, and the necessity of the people's obedience, and declared that, while no one should be " eaten up " * or any way punished except for robbery, etc., I should oblige them to be obedient to the laws and the jurisdiction of their respective magistrates.†

* See p. 433.   † See Appendix V.

After this meeting, my system began to work with the greatest facility, and the rain-makers, who had most scrupulously kept aloof from me, began to pay me visits, particularly the chief of that department of deceit. I received these first visitors with great ease and ceremony of reception, made them all presents, and dismissed them without any discussion of their power and respectability. At the great meeting I had prohibited every branch of witchcraft, so that the rain-makers, being fully aware that the axe was laid to the root of their power, thought it as well to worship the rising sun and court me. Knowing that the presents would bring back the great rain-maker, and induce the little rain-makers to come to me, I was prepared, on the visit of the great one, to prove to him the fallacy and deceit by which he led the people to believe that he possessed a power which he knew he did not.

One day when the great rain-maker was in my camp, and many others, as well as an unusually large number of Kafirs, I assembled them all for the avowed purpose of hearing a disputation between the " Great Chief " or " Father," as they invariably called me, and the rain-makers. My first question to them was, " So you can make rain, can you ? " I never saw in men's countenances more caution. I said, " Speak out, speak freely to your Father." The great rain-maker said he could. I then showed him one by one all the articles on my writing-table, knives, scissors, etc., my clothes, my hat, boots, etc.,

etc., asking, "Can you make this?" "No." "Do you know how it is made?" "No." Having explained everything and how it was made through the medium of my invaluable interpreter, Mr. Shepstone, I then called for a tumbler of water. I showed all the people the water, and asked the rain-makers if what was in the glass was of the same quality as the water or rain they invoked. All agreed "Yes." Their anxiety was intense. I then threw down the water on the dry ground, which immediately absorbed it, and desired the rain-makers to put it again in the tumbler. They were aghast, and said, "We cannot." In a voice of thunder, I said, "Put the rain again in this glass, I say." I then turned to the spectators. "Now you see how these impostors have deceived you. Now listen to the '*Word.*'" (This is the phrase they use in giving orders and decisions on all points of law and in trials.) I took my wand of office, planted it violently before me, and said, "Any man of my children hereafter who believes in witchcraft, or that any but God the Great Spirit can make rain, I will 'eat him up.'" I then left the meeting and the rain-makers thunderstruck and confounded.

On principle, however, I never directly contradicted or prohibited their customs, or left them without hope or a friend; so in about two hours I sent for the great rain-maker and two or three others,—clever, acute fellows all, and I said, "Your Father has now proved to the people that you are impostors, but as you have been taught to fancy

that you possess a power you have not, I must
provide another and an honest livelihood for you,
and I shall expect you to assist me in administering
the new and true laws."   I then made each presents,
giving them so many bullocks apiece—a stock-in-
trade.   These fellows were many of them of great
use to me afterwards.   By the line of conduct I
had pursued, I had carried them with me instead of
rendering them my secret and bitter enemies.

In Umhala's tribe, I heard of an awful case of
his " eating up " a man for witchcraft, and afterwards cruelly burning him with red-hot stones.
The poor wretch, so soon as he could move, came to
me and showed me the cicatrized wounds all over
his body—how he had lived was a wonder. I
kept him closely concealed. I sent for Umhala
and his English magistrate and council to come to
me immediately.   This Umhala was a man of
superior intellect, and the only one who could judge
cause and effect, and future results.   He never
quailed in the slightest, as all others did, under my
most violent animadversions.   He gave me more
trouble to render obedient than all the other chiefs.
Still, he respected me, and I him; and he afterwards showed more real and permanent affection
for me than the others.

Upon his arrival, he did all in his power to find
out what I wanted him for, and he apprehended
the real cause.   So soon as he and all his people
were assembled in my courthouse, I went in *with
my wand behind*, borne by my great councillor

Ganya. Umhala then saw something was coming. I came to the point at once, as was my custom. " Umhala, did I not give the word—no more witchcraft ? " He boldly answered, " You did." " Then how dare you, Umhala, one of my magistrates sworn to be obedient to my law, infringe the Word ? " He stoutly denied it. I then brought in the poor afflicted sufferer, and roared out, " Umhala, devil, liar, villain, you dare to deceive me. Deny now what I accuse you of." He then confessed all, and began to palliate his conduct. To this I would not listen, but seized my wand to give the Word. " Hear you, Umhala! you have eaten a man up. Give back every head of his cattle, and ten head of your own for having eaten him up. And you forfeit ten head more to me, the Great Chief, for my government." He was perfectly unmoved, but I saw that he intended to do no such thing. I then deprived him of his medal of office, and said, " Now go and obey my orders," and I desired the English magistrate to report in two days that he had done so. He had 30 miles to return to his kraal.

According to my custom, I sent the " news " all over Kafirland immediately. I sent out a Court Circular daily. I had no secrets. This they much admired. There never were such newsmongers. Their greeting is " Indaba " ("the news"). The mode adopted to give the news was by so many messengers running out at night-time in different directions, waving their cloaks or karosses. The whole country is strongly undulating, and there are always a number of fellows on the look-out. My messenger called out the news. Others took it up, and so it passed from hill to hill by a sort of telegraph; and every day I could communicate information throughout the whole province in a few hours. This open procedure was of vast importance.

The hour arrived when the news of Umhala's obedience should be received by me. The report came that Umhala had not obeyed my order nor did Captain Rawstorne think he would. This letter was brought me by two Kafir messengers. I had held two troops of cavalry ready to march to reinforce the post of Fort Wellington at Umhala's kraal. I sounded the assembly, and in five minutes they were on the march. When I ordered Rawstorne to "eat up" the chief, a thing never done before in Kafirland, my old councillor Ganya asked me in consternation what orders I had given, and when I told him, he said, " Then war is again over the land." For in old times such an act as seizing any of the cattle of a chief was regarded as a formal declaration of war. I roared out, " Either obedience or war. *I will be Chief*, and Umhala shall see it, and every chief and man in Kafirland." I seized all Umhala's cattle, and I desired the magistrate cautiously to count every head, to give him a regular receipt, and send a copy to me. The cattle were to be guarded by Umhala's own people. I saw that now was my time to establish or lose my power throughout my government. For this Umhala was much looked up to throughout Kafirland, and regarded as the boldest warrior, having distinguished himself by many daring acts in the war.

The news was sent out, and I immediately summoned to my "Court" Macomo, Tyalie, Suta, and Gazela, a chief of whom I must speak hereafter. I knew that this would so intimidate all parties that there would be no danger of a war. Scarcely was Umhala's cattle seized than he sent in succession the most penitent messages, promising to obey my orders and never transgress again. I would not "listen," but desired Umhala to come to me, and meet the chiefs for whom I had sent. He boldly, though penitently, came, as did all the chiefs I had sent for.

I then had a council, told everything that had occurred, and asked if Umhala merited what I, the Great Chief, had done to him, being one of the magistrates who had sworn allegiance and obedience. There was a mutter of assent. I had previously instructed Ganya to watch my eye and to speak in mitigation of punishment. I said, "Now, Umhala, you see how insignificant you are, unless obedient, and how powerful I am. I will be obeyed, and I will 'eat up' every chief who dares disobey me or sanction witchcraft. Here is your medal of magistrate, which I place under my foot."

The crowd were perfectly petrified, and looked at old Ganya, who stood up and made a most eloquent speech. (Some of the Kafirs speak beautifully.)

He dwelt on their own desire to be British subjects
and my exertions for them ; and then turned most
judiciously to Macomo and Tyalie.   " Now, sons of
my old chief, whose councillor I was, the great
Gaika, speak to our Chief for Umhala ; and I hope
he will 'listen.'"   Macomo instantly stood up, and
spoke capitally and to the purpose.   Umhala sat
unmoved, until I said, "Now, Umhala, all depends
on you.   Can I 'listen' or not ? " He spoke
modestly, but powerfully. I made a merit of forgiving
him, put his medal again on his neck, ordered his
cattle to be restored the moment he had returned
the cattle of the burnt man and paid the fines ; and
I immediately sent off the news throughout the
province.   Umhala returned, received all his cattle,
and reported to me that he had got every head
back, and had paid his fines and restored the cattle
to the sufferer.

This decision and determination established most
effectively my absolute power.   I was fully prepared
for some underhand work on the part of the chiefs,
and it was speedily started through the instru-
mentality of Macomo ; but the *people* whom I protected were with me, and nothing occurred which I
was not informed of immediately.

Macomo had driven his cattle to graze over the
Keiskamma contrary to treaty and my orders, where-
upon I strongly desired that he would never do it
again. This offended the gentleman, a restless, turbulent, uncontrollable spirit, and he sent to all the other
chiefs to say that if they would join, he would strive

for independence. At all the courts this message
was received most contemptuously. Tyalie turned
the messenger from his kraal; Suta and young
Sandilli were indignant and would not " listen ";
Umhala listened, but his council opposed the
measure, and a subordinate chief of Umhala's, a
noble little fellow, Gazela, stood up and spoke out
like a man. "You, Umhala, and all know how I
fought during the war, and never was for giving in
until I saw we had no chance of success. Macomo
made peace. He has received more kindness than
all of us put together. He is now false, and wants
to make us break the word given to our Great
Chief," etc.

All this I knew in a few hours. I sent for
Macomo, received him as usual, and said, " I have a
fable to tell you." They are very fond of speaking
in parables themselves. I then recounted a tale,
viz. myself and himself. I never saw a creature in
such a state of agitation. "Now," I said, "if you
were the Great Chief, what would you do?" He
threw himself at my feet, bathed in tears. "Ah,
Macomo," I said, "if I were only to say the Word,
your people would no longer *know you.*" Oh, how
Ganya did abuse him! "Ah, cry," he said; "your
tears can't wash away your sins. You caused the
last war, disregarding the dying words of Gaika.
You are now treated with every kindness, yet
treachery and that same restlessness which has
plunged the Colony and Kafirland in blood, still
guide you." I said, " Rise, Macomo, and go. I will

not touch my stick and give the Word for *two hours*. I must cool. Englishmen are generous, but they must be just to all. I must consider for two hours how my actions may be guided, but for the good of all my children, *go*."

He never had such a lesson. I sent for him and forgave him, with a full assurance that on the next offence I would eat him up and banish him over the Kei. I sent off the news, and my authority was ever after perfectly undisputed.

I now began to turn my attention to teaching them cultivation and the use of money. In the former I had but little difficulty compared with what I anticipated, although previously their fields had been cultivated by their women in a miserable manner. I gave them Hottentots to teach them, and I had soon several chiefs with ploughs and good yokes of oxen. The chief Gazela, a man of great use to me, and with more idea of honesty than any one, had also a commercial turn. I proved to him that it was by the use of money that *we* became a great people, and could make everything and do everything, and I made him perfectly understand our banking system—which I could induce no other Kafir to attend to. Gazela sold me some bullocks for the Commissary. Afterwards he let out horses to people travelling at so much a day, and he induced others to sell me cattle; this I considered the greatest step towards civilization.

The missionaries had all returned to me, and were excellent good men, doing all in their power.

The chief Tyalie, in the English clothes I had given him, attended divine service every Sunday, and the missionaries had a considerable degree of moral influence; but as to spiritual instruction or conversion, few indeed were the converts. Macomo knew more theology than many Christians, but was still a perfect heathen. Had I remained long enough, as cultivation and sale progressed, I would have built churches, and by feasts and slaughtering cattle have induced all influential men to attend; I would have had schools, and, by educating the children, would have reared a generation of Christians, but to convert the aged barbarian was a hopeless task.

The world does not produce a more beautiful race of blacks than these Kafirs, both men and women; their figures and eyes are beautiful beyond conception, and they have the gait of princes. It was one of my great endeavours to make them regard appearing naked as a grievous sin, now that they were British subjects; and no one was ever permitted in my camp, much less in my presence, but dressed in his karosse. This karosse is the skin of a bullock, but beautifully dressed so as to be pliant and soft, and then ornamented by fur, beads, buttons, etc. The head-dresses of the chiefs' wives are really beautiful. No creatures on earth are more the votaries of fashion than these Kafirs. In Grahamstown I could procure no beads and buttons of the mode of the day, but great quantities exceedingly cheap, which the Kafirs would not buy because they were out of fashion. I therefore

bought up the whole. I had always about me some
of the rejected buttons and of the blue beads that
had been once their delight, and I found fault with
every button that was not of my shape and every
bead that was not of my colour. The discarded
buttons and the blue beads were soon established
as the *haut ton* of fashion.

My wife, who took equal interest in the reform
of these poor barbarians with myself, was always
surrounded by numbers of the chiefs' wives and
hangers-on, particularly the queens Suta and
Nonibe (the former was Gaika's widow, the latter
Dushani's, and both had sons in their minority). She
taught many of them needlework, and was for hours
daily explaining to them right and wrong, and
making them little presents, so that she became so
popular she could do anything with them.

The Kafirs have a horror of burying their dead,
or even touching them. They will carry out a
dying creature from their kraal, mother or father,
wife or brother, and leave him exposed to wild
beasts and vultures for days, if nature does not
sink in the mean time. I not only prohibited this,
but I had three or four Kafirs who died in my
camp regularly buried. (Many came to me to be
cured of diseases.) In each case I made my Kafir
messengers dig the grave, and I, with my interpreter, read the funeral service over the dead.
Then the news was sent over the land—the Great
Chief does it, and whenever any one came and told
me he had *buried* his deceased relative (I took care

2 G

to *prove* it, though), I gave him a bullock, and sent the news over the land.

The Levitical law as to uncleanness is fully in force among the Kafirs, and they practise circumcision, but not until the age of puberty. It is a great ceremony, after which the youths are able to marry, provided they have enough cattle to buy a wife from the father. (A plurality of wives is tolerated. Macomo had eleven, all very handsome women.) This buying of wives is the great source of all robbery and inroads into the Colony. I just began to prohibit it gradually by making the parents of the bride and bridegroom contribute to the establishment of the newly married pair, and myself giving a present.

I directed the magistrates to decide all cases of law themselves, but when they were in any doubt, to send me, for my approval, the parties and the opinion or decision proposed to be given. This strengthened their power and also mine, for whatever I once decided on, I never revoked, and admitted of no appeal or renewal of the subject.

Having thus gained an ascendancy over these people never attempted before, my mind was dwelling on the great and important subject of their conversion to Christianity, and many is the conference I had with the missionaries upon the subject. Of ultimately effecting a general conversion I never despaired, but I was convinced it could only be through the educating of the youth and at the same time introducing habits of industry and rational

amusement.   The Kafirs, like the Hottentots, are
great lovers of music and have remarkably good
ears.   I have been wonderfully amused at observing
the effect the playing of our bands had on many
who had never heard them before.   Some would
laugh immoderately, some cry, some stand riveted
to the spot, others in a sort of vibrating convulsion,
others would dance and sing, all were animated and
excited beyond measure.   When poor Hintza heard
the bagpipes of the 72nd, he closed his ears with his
hands and said, "This is to make people cry.* I
like the bugles and trumpets.   When I hear them
I feel like a man."   Thus with the aid of music I
should have made some advance towards Christian
conversion.

* So Alexander, vol. ii. pp. 134, 135 : " A Highland piper was ordered
to play for Hintza's amusement.   Hintza was asked what he thought
of the music.   He answered, that some of it reminded him of his
children at home and made him cry, and that he supposed that the
instrument had been invented by us out of regard for the General
[Sir B. D'Urban], to imitate his crying when he was a little boy, and
to remind him of the crying of his children."

CHAPTER XXXIX.

LORD GLENELG ORDERS THE ABANDONMENT OF THE PROVINCE OF QUEEN ADELAIDE, AND APPOINTS CAPTAIN STOCKENSTROM TO SUCCEED HARRY SMITH ON THE FRONTIER—GRIEF OF THE KAFIRS AT THE CHANGE—JOURNEY OF HARRY SMITH AND HIS WIFE TO CAPE TOWN—HE IS EXONERATED BY LORD GLENELG, AND RECEIVES TESTIMONIALS FOR HIS SERVICES TO THE COLONY —LEAVES CAPE TOWN JUNE, 1840, ON BEING APPOINTED ADJUTANT-GENERAL OF THE QUEEN'S ARMY IN INDIA.

In the midst, however, of all I had effected, and all my visions of what I could effect, the most crooked policy ever invented by the most wicked Machiavellians blasted all my hopes for the benefit of the 100,000 barbarians committed to my rule, and the bright prospect of peace and tranquillity for the Colony (for the frontier inhabitants began to be in a state of security which was security indeed).

The Minister for the Colonies, Lord Glenelg, an excellent, worthy, and able man, but led by a vile party, under the cloak of sanctity and philanthropy, directed the Province of Queen Adelaide to be restored to barbarism, the allegiance the Kafirs had sworn to to be shaken off, and the full plenitude of their barbarity re-established. It is grievous to reflect that any well-disposed individual like Lord Glenelg, believing he was doing good, and under the influence and guidance of others, should have thus blasted the bright prospects of such rapidly progressing civilization.

But so it was. I was removed from the administration of affairs and my command, and replaced by a man * violently obnoxious to Kafirs and colonists. Owing to the view Lord Glenelg had taken and the *ton* given, I was upbraided with every act of violence and oppression the curse of war can impose, and branded as the murderer of Hintza throughout the newspapers of the world. Every act of the murderous Kafirs during the war was regarded as a just retaliation for previous wrong; everything the colonists said or did or suffered, treated with contempt, and they themselves believed to be the cause of their own misfortunes. While our country's treasury and private contributions were open to the sufferers of the world from the temperate regions of Portugal to the snows of Poland, the ears of the public were deaf to the cries of the widows and orphans in the once happy and rapidly thriving province of Albany, although its settlers had been induced to come from England and there lay out their capital, were good subjects, loyal and true, and

---

* Captain Andries Stockenstrom, afterwards Sir A. Stockenstrom, Bart. Lord Glenelg's dispatch was dated 26th Dec. 1835.

regularly paid their taxes, and therefore had a right to expect protection from the Government. All rule and just and good government was banished under the influence of the philanthropic party, who, by perversion of facts, evidently desire to lead others (this Colony certainly) to the devil for God's sake.

Do not let it be supposed that a man with a conscience so clear as mine, with a head and heart so bent on exertion for the benefit of others, tamely submitted to the opprobrium so cruelly, so unjustly heaped upon him—I, who, while regarded by the world as a monster stained with innocent blood, who had waged war contrary to the tolerated rules and precedents of warfare (which is a scourge in its mildest and most modified shape), was at the moment regarded by those I was accused of oppressing as their " Father," " their Great Chief," in whom they implicitly confided and believed contrary to the strong prejudices of previous habit. No, I wrote a letter to the Minister explanatory of every procedure—I opened his eyes—and I received from him the atonement contained in the extracts following :—

Extract from a dispatch of Lord Glenelg to His Excellency Sir B. D'Urban, dated May 1st, 1837.

" IV.—I perform a duty highly agreeable to me in declaring that Col. Smith is entitled to the grateful acknowledgments of His Majesty's Government, not only for his Military Services, but for his zealous, humane, and enlightened administration of the Civil Government of the

Province placed under his charge, and of the adjacent
district. I am especially indebted to him for the very
valuable suggestions which he afforded to Lt. Governor
Stockenstrom, who, I have no doubt, will gladly avail
himself of advice founded on so much observation and
experience.

" (Signed) GLENELG."

*Extract from a dispatch of the Right Honourable Lord
Glenelg to his Excellency Major-General George F.
Napier, Governor of the Cape of Good Hope. Dated
13th November, 1837.*

" But I cannot close this communication without adverting to the high gratification with which I have read the
testimony contained in the voluminous papers before me
to the conduct of Col. Smith. That officer's name is
never mentioned but to his honour either by the Governor
or the Lt. Governor; and in the superintendence of the
Province of Adelaide under circumstances of the most
trying nature, he appears to have been distinguished alike
by the energy with which he maintained the public tranquillity, and the kindness of heart which won for him the
affectionate gratitude of all classes of the people.

" (Signed)   JOHN BELL,
" Secretary to Government."

But although this palliated his error towards me,
it in no manner re-established me in the eyes of the
world at large, and Lord Glenelg was bound, as a
man of honour, to have instigated Majesty to have
conferred upon me some mark of distinction, which
should have at once proclaimed my merit and the
injury His Lordship's misconception had done me.
The Colony and the Horse Guards, however, took a

far different [view] of my merits and services, which I must relate hereafter.

To return to my children. So soon as the Kafirs heard of this change, the general exclamation was, "Ah, it is ever thus with the English, always changing towards us. We were never before so happy; never so protected; never saw such an improvement amongst us; our chiefs will eat us up as before." The chiefs again feared their people. Lamentation and grief throughout the land were excessive. Hundreds of men and women were around my house and tent, lamenting and praying me not to abandon them, and, as far as their knowledge went, invoking the protection of the Great Spirit, to preserve me and my wife to govern and instruct them.

I will candidly admit, I grieved too, for although at the outset, as I took stock of my enthusiasm, I was often led into a belief that my hopes would prove illusive, the consummation of my most sanguine desires had now been effected; daily I saw improvement progressing, not only by rapid strides, but on such a broad and firm path as to ensure its permanency and induce the conviction that ten years would have brought the Gospel of Christ and all the blessings of civilization among the thousands of benighted barbarians around me.

It now became my duty, and one which I trust I executed with every zeal, to do all I could to render the change palatable to the Kafirs and to disabuse them of their bad opinion of my successor.

The odium with which they regarded him I believe I much mitigated. To himself I wrote so soon as he arrived at Grahamstown, laying before him the exact state of the frontier district, and recommending him to convoke a general meeting of all the chiefs and their councillors at King William's Town, to explain to them the new order of things. I said that I would call such a meeting for any day he would name, and I was of opinion that it would have a better effect were I present than otherwise.

My successor was a sensible man, and at once saw the advantage of the arrangement I proposed, felt my attention and readiness to assist him, and named a day. I convoked a meeting accordingly, and desired Kreili, the great chief, to send a deputation. I had been in the habit of communicating constantly with Kreili and the more distant chiefs, Fakoo, Vadana, etc., and sending them all the news, thereby establishing myself the *Great Chief*. I took the usual precaution to reinforce my post, for when I told old Ganya that I should leave on the day following the meeting, he exclaimed, "Then we shall have a row!" A meeting, similar to the one I had convoked on the 7th January, was accordingly held, and in a long explanation I delivered over the government to my successor. Nothing could be more orderly than the conduct of the people, and the expression of their regret. My successor then explained to them their new position. Tyalie, always a forward fellow, spoke to him in the most insolent manner; but I gave him such a dressing,

reminding him his bullocks were fat (meaning that
he was rich) under me, thus, if I only said the word,
I could "eat" him "up" in a moment.

I shall never forget that afternoon ; never were
my feelings or those of my wife more excited. Our
house and tents were surrounded by hundreds ;
every chief and every one of the chiefs' wives took
off some of their various ornaments and put them
upon me and her ; some wept aloud, others lay on
the ground groaning ; and the man whom I had
visited more than others with the weight of power,
Umhala, showed more real feeling then, and even to
this day often sends me messages of friendship and
regard ; while Gazela and a fine young chief by
name Seyolo, who had defended the rocks on the
heights of the Poorts of the Buffalo, declared life was
no longer worth having. The way the women shed
tears around my wife was piteous to behold. Barbarian emotion when over-excited is uncontrollable,
and nothing could exceed this demonstration.

The next morning I and my wife and staff departed from King William's Town, the seat of
my labour in war and peace, and although every
demonstration of feeling was suppressed, I now
admit my heart was full. I had laboured day and
night, God alone knows how I had laboured, and to
be so unkindly treated by the Minister of my
country was galling to a soldier whose good name
is his only hope in the world. 'Tis true, a rectitude
of conscience sustained me which nothing could
shake, but human nature is weak enough to desire

others should think well of you, while inwardly and
mentally you exclaim, " God is my Judge."   I was
attended by my successor and by the officers.   The
soldiers whom I had given such gigantic marches
turned out to cheer and bid me farewell, while
thousands of Kafirs followed me and my wife, yelling
as if in despair.

The parting with my old councillor Ganya and
some others, as well as my Kafir messengers at Fort
Willshire, cannot be described.   Ganya, poor old
fellow, came to me in a state of abject poverty,
although a man of great influence throughout Kafirland.   I enriched him most deservedly, for his
assistance to me was invaluable and his attachment
to me faithful, while the most educated and upright
man could never more zealously feel or desire the
welfare of his country and countrymen.

This barbarian was a most extraordinary
character.   He died a few months later, as he told
me he knew he should, having lost his Father, his
friend and benefactor.   My messengers were very
peculiar fellows, too ; they were all selected by the
chiefs themselves, men, therefore, of their own interest.   In a country where writing is not known, all
communications, treaties, rules, laws, etc., are given
viva voce and by message, and these fellows were
brought up from infancy in that department.   Their
power of memory is not to be believed.   I had one
man from Macomo, by name Mani, a handsome
fellow who had been shot through both thighs in the
war.   My interpreter would read a long list of orders,

etc., addressed to Macomo of eighteen to twenty
paragraphs. He would then say, " Mani, do you
understand all ? " He would occasionally ask for
some explanation ; then he would go to Macomo, 34
miles off. If the chief did not detain him, he would
be back with me after doing 68 miles in 28 hours,
apparently not in the least fatigued, and bring me
an answer or comment on each paragraph in the
order written down with a correctness not to be
credited. I declare I have been frequently thunderstruck.

There is a curious law in Kafirland which shows
how human nature in a state of barbarism provides
for its own wants. " The secret and confidential " of
our diplomatic and military correspondence is with
messengers provided for in this manner : it is death
for any one entrusted with a communication to
divulge its purport to any one but the chief of whose
tribe he is a member. Thus if Mani was entrusted
with a message from me to Macomo, it was as safe
in his company as possible. If Tyalie had met him
and demanded its purport, he would have died ere
he divulged it. All messengers would give me the
purport of their messages from one chief to the
other if I demanded, being the Great Chief. Thus,
while secrecy is provided for, the supreme authority
reserves to himself the power of discovering plots
and conspiracies. Poor Mani! I see him now at
my feet weeping. I do believe that poor barbarian
would have been cut to pieces limb by limb without
a groan if it would have served me, and many

others would have done the same. To this day
I remember with gratitude their attachment. It
was like that of the most faithful dog, with this
difference—reason told them we parted for ever.

Upon nearing Grahamstown, the whole of the inhabitants turned out to meet me, presented me with
an address, begged me to name a day agreeable to
me for a public dinner, and if there was any consolation to the feelings in the sympathy of those whom
I had so served in need, whose trade I had again so
brightly re-established, I had a full measure of it.

I accepted the dinner as an opportunity of
thanking the inhabitants for their assistance, obedience, and desire to meet my wishes, and telling them,
as they regarded me, to render that obedience and
respect to my successor which loyal subjects were
bound to render to any one their King had placed
to rule over them.

We accomplished our journey from Grahamstown to Cape Town, I riding, my wife again in a
waggon. On this occasion, I had bought a very
nice light one, and had it fitted up with swing seats,
etc., so that she travelled in comparative luxury.
All Grahamstown turned out to take leave of me,
and I could not fail to remark the difference between
my entrance into the beleaguered town and my
quitting it, flourishing in trade and prosperity.

At every town upon my road down dinners
were given me in the Town Hall, and every Boer,
or Dutch farmer, came to see me. I never had to
deal with fellows who were more docile, if you took

them in the right way, viz. by kindness, by interesting yourself in their welfare, and by an inflexible adherence to " Yes " and " No."

Our journey down was delightful, through a country full of large and small game, and many is the gallop I had after ostriches, which require a fleet and right good-bottomed horse to ride down.

As I approached Cape Town, my many friends came out in shoals to meet us, and I was received in the metropolis of the Cape by every public demonstration of affection—ever so gratifying to the soldier who has worked hard to serve his country—from the noble Governor, Sir Benjamin D'Urban, to the mendicant.

I may, without any degree of mock modesty, say I worked hard, and assert that from the period I left Cape Town, the 1st January, 1835, to 18th October, 1836 (22 months), no man ever rode more miles, made more night marches or such long ones, or wrote more letters than I did. My correspondence was immense from the number of posts, and having to carry on a war over a vast extent of thinly populated country, and in peace to defend a frontier of 140 miles.

Soon after my arrival at Cape Town, a despatch was received from Lord Glenelg, which was highly complimentary to me.*

A public meeting having been convened under the sanction of the Government, this communication was made to me :—

* Given above, p. 454.

"At a meeting of the inhabitants of Cape Town and its vicinity, held in the Commercial Room on the 18th September, 1837, the Honble Hamilton Ross in the chair, it was resolved—

"That as the zealous, humane, and enlightened administration of Colonel Smith, during the time he commanded on the frontier, merits the gratitude and thanks of the colonists at large, the following gentlemen, as a mark of their esteem, have concluded to invite him to a public dinner."

Of course I accepted the compliment, which afforded me a good opportunity publicly to record my procedure, my gratitude to many distinguished individuals and to the colony at large, my regret at the system established among the Kafirs having been abolished, and my everlasting feelings of respect and veneration for the Governor, Sir Benjamin D'Urban, whose instrument alone I was, and whose support and approbation of all I did or proposed enabled me to effect all I had done; and, lastly, though I was far from being a man addicted to view things darkly, my foreboding, based on a knowledge of every circumstance on the frontier and the conflicting interests of the colonists and Kafirs, that chaos would again be re-established.

Unfortunately, my prediction has been but too truly verified. Such was the disgust of hundreds of valuable members of the Dutch population and wealthy farmers, they emigrated in masses and seized the country of the Zoolus, and have been a thorn in the government of the Cape until lately, when matters have been adjusted and Port Natal added to the British possessions.

Had my system been persisted in, and the order of things so firmly planted and rapidly growing into maturity been allowed to continue, not a Boer would have migrated. I am proud to say I had as much influence over the Boers as over the Kafirs, and by a kind and persuasive manner in expostulation, had they meditated such a step, I could at once have deterred them.

The whole colony being desirous of substantially exhibiting their gratitude towards me, subscriptions were opened for the purpose of presenting me with plate in demonstration thereof. Although each subscription was limited to half a guinea, £500 was very speedily subscribed.

Upon the articles of plate is this inscription :

" Presented to Colonel Henry George Wakelyn Smith, C.B., by his numerous friends at the Cape of Good Hope, as a token of their admiration of his distinguished military and civil services in that colony and in Kaffraria, 1835–6. Palmam qui meruit ferat ! "

The two Hottentot battalions, officers and men, had previously set this example, and by their 800 men a magnificent candelabra was presented to me, like the other plate, manufactured by one of the first workmen in London.

This substantial mark of their consideration bore the inscription :

" Presented to Colonel Harry George Smith, C.B., as a testimonial of respect for his distinguished military services during the late Kafir War, and the consummate skill and benevolence subsequently displayed in the civil administration of the conquered province of Queen Adelaide, which so eminently contributed to the peace and security of the colony and the amelioration of the condition of the barbarian thus brought within the pale of civilization."

The plate presented by the zealous officers is inscribed :

" Presented by the officers of the Cape of Good Hope Provisional Infantry to Colonel Henry George Wakelyn Smith, in testimony of their high sense of the eminent services rendered to the colony by his skill, gallantry, and unwearied activity in the field against the Kafirs in the year 1835, and by his subsequent, able, humane, and zealous exertions for the promoting the civilization of the native tribes as the best means of establishing with them a secure and lasting peace."

Lord Hill being desirous to mark his approbation and that of my Sovereign for the services above recorded, was kind enough to appoint me to the responsible, important, and elevated post of Adjutant-General to H.M.'s Forces in India ; and in the very ship which brought the newspaper gazette of my appointment did I embark for my new destination, the ship waiting from Saturday until Thursday for me. [June, 1840.]

Little was the time thus afforded for me to prepare for embarcation, but a soldier must be ever ready, and my wife's cheerful exertion soon prepared everything, although our hearts were full at leaving so many valuable, dear, and faithful friends and a

2 H

country in which we had spent eleven years of happiness and some excitement, and ever received as much kindness and hospitality as the most sanguine could desire.

So short was the time that my friends in Cape Town who were desirous to pay me some mark of their respect could do no more than present me on the morning of my embarcation with the following address :—

"*To* COL. H. G. SMITH, C.B., etc.

" SIR,

"We, the undersigned inhabitants of Cape Town, do ourselves the pleasure of offering you our sincere congratulations on your recent appointment to serve in a country which can, better than this Colony, reward its brave and zealous defenders.   But, cordial as our wishes are for your welfare and advancement, we deeply regret that the very circumstances which open brighter prospects to you must terminate your residence amongst us, and deprive this Colony of the services of one, whose well-known and long-tried courage and abilities have been once more tested in the performance of most difficult and important duties within our own observation.

"The few years which have elapsed since the most brilliant of your services to this Colony were achieved have not dimmed our recollection of them, and on quitting our shores be assured you leave a name behind you which will never be forgotten by the present, and will be made known to, and remembered by, succeeding generations of the Cape Colonists.

"The suddenness of your departure prevents very many from joining in this expression of our feelings towards you ;

but to whatever quarter of the world your well-earned promotion may lead you, South Africa will learn with deep interest the history of your future career, and rejoice in the tidings of your prosperity.

"We have, etc."

To which I replied—

"Cape Castle, 4th June, 1840.

"GENTLEMEN,

"I thank you most cordially for your congratulations on the mark of distinction which Her Majesty has been pleased to confer upon me, by appointing me Adjutant-General to the Queen's troops in India.

"On my return from the frontiers, you received me with warm congratulations—the services of which you were thus pleased, in a manner so gratifying to me, to express your approbation were of recent occurrence—but the feelings expressed by you in the address with which you have this day honoured me, prove that the recollection and appreciation of a soldier's services may outlive the excitement produced at the moment by success, and I pray you to believe that the recollection of the feelings so warmly and kindly expressed will never cease to dwell in my memory, and will be matter of exultation to me in whatever clime or quarter of the globe it may be my lot to serve.

"During a residence of eleven years, I have met with invariable kindness from all classes in the Colony—I may say, from the community at large ; and although I cannot but feel that an honour of no ordinary class has been conferred upon me by Her Majesty, yet I say from my heart that I now quit your shores with deep regret.

"I have the honour to be, Gentlemen,

"Your most obedient, humble servant,

"H. G. SMITH, Colonel."

And the Governor of the Cape, Sir George Napier,* issued the following General Order :—

"Headquarters, Cape Town, 1st June, 1840.

"In consequence of the promotion of Colonel Smith to be Adjutant-General to the Army in India, the Commander-in-Chief takes this opportunity to express his high approbation of that officer's services during his residence in this Colony, and he feels confident the officers and soldiers of this command will be highly gratified by so distinguished a mark of Her Majesty's favour and approbation being bestowed on an officer of such long and gallant services in nearly every part of Her Majesty's Dominions.

"As one of his companions, and as an old Comrade in Arms, the Major-General offers Colonel Smith his warmest congratulations and best wishes for his health and happiness.

"The Orders of the Garrison of Cape Town, and of the guards and sentries, etc., as established by Colonel Smith, C.B., are to be considered as Standing Orders for this Garrison, and will be strictly observed accordingly."

However gratified we were by this distinguished mark of Her Majesty's approbation, we left the Cape of Good Hope as if we were leaving for ever our native land, and in that patriotic expression " My native land, good night" is comprised all the most feeling heart of man can participate in.

Ah, Cape of Good Hope, notwithstanding your terrific south-easters in the summer, your dreadful north-westers in the winter, your burning sun, your awful sands, I and my wife will ever remember you with an affection yielding alone to that of the " Land of our Sires !"

* He succeeded Sir B. D'Urban, 22 Jan. 1838.

CHAPTER XL.

VOYAGE FROM CAPE TOWN TO CALCUTTA—HARRY
SMITH'S DISAPPOINTMENT AT NOT RECEIVING
THE COMMAND IN THE AFGHAN WAR—HIS CRITI-
CISM OF THE OPERATIONS.*

ON the voyage we encountered terrific gales of
wind; one night a squall took us aback, carried away
our topmasts, and shivered our sails into shreds in a
moment. I never knew or could conceive before what
the force of wind was capable of. This excessive
violence lasted only twenty minutes, leaving us a log
on the water. The gale continued three days, and
on the 18th June, 1840,† we had staring us in the
face a watery grave. It was the anniversary of the
day on which I and two brothers escaped the
slaughter of the eventful field of Waterloo. The
same Divine Hand, however, protected us, and the
91st Psalm was again read in devotion and gratitude
to the Almighty and Eternal Lord God, "Who alone
spreadest out the heavens and rulest the raging of

---

* With Chapters XL. to XLIV. compare the extracts from letters
given in Appendix VI.

† On this very day twelve months, this ship, the *David Scott*, was
burned in harbour in the Mauritius, having previously buried her
captain at sea on the voyage from Calcutta.—H. G. S.

the sea ;" and we reached Madras Roads in safety, after a most boisterous but quick passage.

I embarked six horses, one of which died at sea, and all the rest were much bruised and injured.

At Madras we had many friends. The Governor, Lord Elphinstone, whom we had known as a boy, and to whom we were of use at the Cape on his way out, was then in the Nilgherries. So soon as he heard of our arrival, Government House and all its luxuries were placed at our disposal ; but we were already hospitably put up with one of my oldest and dearest friends, Dr. Murray, the Inspector-General, who had for many years held a similar appointment at the Cape, one of the most able professional men in the world, and as an officer in his department never surpassed. Poor fellow! in two years it was my melancholy duty to report his death at Kurnal, in the Upper Provinces of Bengal, where he fell a gallant victim to an epidemic disease. To his exertions to avert the progress of its fatal ravages, and the rapidity with which he travelled from Calcutta in the sickly part of the rainy season, may be attributed a loss irreparable to the service, to his family, and to his friends.

From Madras to Calcutta we had a beautiful passage, flying along the coast and passing the famous temple of Juggernauth with the rapidity with which its votaries believe they ascend to the Regions of Bliss. On reaching Calcutta we were surrounded by old friends of the army, and many civil servants and military officers of the Honourable Company's

Service whom we had known at the Cape, where they had repaired for the recovery of health. Lord Auckland received us with every kindness, and his Lordship's amiable, accomplished, and highly educated sisters showed us the most marked attention, kindness, and hospitality. As to the Commander-in-chief, Sir Jasper Nicolls, we became, after some time, as it were members of his family.*

Sir Jasper Nicolls is a man of very strong common sense, and very wary of giving his confidence, or, indeed, of developing any of his intentions. At first I thought he was a rough, hard-hearted man. I soon discovered, however, he was one of the best men of business I ever served, with a warm heart and a degree of honesty of purpose never exceeded. His dear good wife is now, alas! no more —she died at Rome on their return to their native land after years of travel, toil, and burning suns. Her ladyship and daughters and my wife possessed a union of hearts and feelings which gradually increased until, on the death of Lady Nicolls, one important link of that chain of union was snapped, but is now riveted in the most fervent affection for the daughters.

In the career of military life, no man can

---

* Colonel Harry Smith was appointed on 21st August, 1840, to the rank of Major-General (in the East Indies only). Writing to his friend Captain Payne, 72nd Highlanders, on 17th January, 1841, he says, "I get on very well here with the public functionaries of all descriptions, tho' they are odd fellows to deal with. But I have very much learned to restrain an impetuosity which never produces so favourable a result as moderation, for, if right, it frequently makes you wrong."

reasonably expect that so rugged a path can be traversed without some personal disaster, and so it was with me, previously one of fortune's spoiled children.   Lord Auckland, from report and a knowledge of my exertions and successes at the Cape, had imbibed a favourable opinion of me, and had the Burmese made war in 1842, as was expected, it was his Lordship's intention to appoint me to the command of the troops destined to repel invasion and re-establish our superiority.   I had also a faithful friend in the Lieutenant-Governor of the Upper Provinces, Mr. Thomas Campbell Robertson—a man of superior ability and acquirement, and more versed in the history and affairs of India than any man I ever sought information from except Mr. Thoby Prinsep.*   As I was likely to spend some years in India if appointed Adjutant-General, as I had some reason to expect, I had, when at the Cape, read thirty-three authors, made copious notes, and generally studied the history and geography of this immense Empire.   This acquired knowledge enabled me to converse with such practical and experienced men with great advantage to any information and knowledge I had previously obtained.

After the death of the celebrated Runjeet Singh, the state of our North-West Frontier, bordering on the seat of commotion, and ultimately bitter war, in Afghanistan, was far from settled, and it was

---

* Henry Thoby Prinsep, Member of Council at Calcutta, 1835–1843 ; Member of the Court of Directors of the East India Company, 1850–1858 ; Member of the Indian Council, 1858–1874. Died 1878.

contemplated that the Sikhs might interrupt our communication with our troops, so fearfully extended from any base of operations, and with the country of this doubtful ally intervening. Under these circumstances, I placed my ready services at the disposal of Lord Auckland and the Commander-in-Chief. Soon after this the insurrection at Cabool commenced. Poor Elphinstone and I had been friends for years,* and I had frequently impressed upon him the difficulty of his position, the probability of an attempt on the part of the restless and independent-spirited Afghan to shake off that yoke so injudiciously imposed upon him (especially as our rupees were no longer so lavishly, so indiscreetly scattered to acquire an ascendency which, if necessary to acquire at all, should have been acquired by the sword, and maintained by the sword, sheathed in inflexible and uncompromising justice, equity, dignity, and honour), and the necessity of his ever considering himself in the greatest danger when he felt the most secure ; but I must not set my foot on a field which to describe would require volumes. The war broke out. The energy of a Wellington or a Napoleon would have saved the destruction of that force ; it was perfectly practicable, as I then pointed out. The Lieutenant-Governor and I were in hourly communication ; I showed the military steps we ought to pursue, and he urged them on the Government, and offered to bear any responsibility

---

* Elphinstone had commanded the 33rd Regiment during the years of the occupation of France, 1815-1818.

with the Commander - in - Chief. Lord Auckland
was a sensible but timid man, and the Commander-in-Chief, ever most judiciously and correctly
averse to the occupation of Afghanistan, was reduced to defensive measures at the moment when
the most vigorous and initiative steps ought to have
been taken with the velocity of lightning. The
moment was lost. If time, that irrecoverable
engine in war, is neglected, disaster, as in this
instance, must ensue. Before the outbreak at
Cabool, when my dear friend Elphinstone, from the
dire misfortune of sickness, was compelled to request
his relief, the Lieutenant-Governor urged the
Government and Lord Auckland to send me up.
I offered my services on the condition that I had
the supreme and uncontrolled military authority
from the source to the mouth of the Indus and was
aided by a civil servant; and Mr. George Clerk,
the Political Agent for the Punjaub, a man of first-
rate abilities and activity, most popular among the
Sikhs, whose country and resources intervened
between our distant operations and their base,
offered nobly (for we were personally strangers) to
serve with and under me.

Sir Jasper Nicolls, why I do not to this moment
know, was opposed to my being employed, although
Lord Auckland wished it, and Major-General
Pollock was gazetted by the Government—"by the
express recommendation of the Commander-in-
Chief"—but only to the command of the Upper
Indus, not the Lower, where Major-General Nott

was senior officer. Consequently, when these two officers' forces united, they were like the Corps d'Armée of Napoleon in Spain, jealous of each other, the junior * was disobedient to the senior, and that *ensemble*, on which success in war hinges, was lost.

The only reason I could ever suppose influenced Sir Jasper Nicolls in his reluctance to employ me— for I know he had the highest opinion of my activity —is that he apprehended, if I once got the command, the wealthy Persia would have been attempted, and my progress alone interrupted by the Caspian Sea. His thought day and night was to get back the army from its advanced and dangerous position. Whereas had the troops been rushed to the scene of action, as they might have been (for on the commencement of the outbreak, the Khyberies were with us), and Brigadier Wyld's Brigade moved by forced marches to Jellalabad, other troops rapidly following in succession, and when Wyld arrived at Jellalabad, the whole of the weakly men, women, stores, etc., been securely placed in a small *Place d'armes* constructed for the purpose during Wyld's approach, while General Sale's and Wyld's forces combined precipitated themselves on Cabool, the force then would have been saved, the spirits of the troops would have been sustained by the knowledge of succour approaching, the enemy proportionately depressed. Thus a want of exertion and decision in rendering support caused a disaster

* *I.e.* Nott.

and a loss England never before sustained. It is needless here to enter into dates, number of marches, etc.; the thing I have described was a simple matter of activity and well within the scope of possibility. As soon as he arrived, Lord Ellenborough saw the necessity of withdrawing the troops from Afghanistan, but was precipitate in availing himself of the period so to do—which certainly was not at the moment when our military prowess, the prestige of our arms, and our national character for supremacy required to be re-established. A government proposed by the Afghans should have been set up by us ; then the sooner we abandoned a nominal conquest, the better for the true interests of British India. So astonished was I at the immediate withdrawal, that I wrote the Memorandum No. 1. In the meanwhile the Governor-General had left it optional to General Nott to retire by Guznee, but had issued several peremptory orders to Pollock to retire. When Nott, however, proposed his forward movement, Pollock was also directed to move. I then wrote the Memorandum No. 2, and as the campaign developed, No. 3.* The moment the Afghans were

---

* In Memorandum No. 1, dated " Simla, 7th August, 1842," the policy advocated is, " strike a decisive blow which will maintain our prestige in India, and then abandon Afghanistan, which ought never to have been entered."

In Memorandum No. 2, dated " Simla, 29th August," he states that his policy has been adopted. But the method involved " A division of force ; an advance into the heart of the enemy's country ; the siege of two cities with no positive means, one the venerated city of the Prophet, Guznee, the other Cabool, the capital ; a retreat ; the destruction of the base of these operations, Candahar." The plan, therefore, involved too many risks.

assailed and the invasion pursued, they quailed
immediately, and did not evince the courage and

In Memorandum No. 3, dated "Simla, 7th September," he says
that the evacuation of Candahar before Cabool and Guznee had been
reduced was contrary to all military science. "Nott's column is now a
single ship in the midst of the Atlantic Ocean surrounded by hostile
fleets." "The science of war dictates that as rapid a concentration
as can be effected of the forces of Nott and Pollock should be made to
Guznee—reduce it, hence to Cabool. Thus the union of force ensures
one of the primary objects in war—'one line of operations, one base,
and a union of resources.'" "A kind of drawn battle with fluctuating
advantages is worse to the general cause than if no attempt whatever
had been made to 'strike a blow.'" "Our force is on the verge of
winter in the prosecution of two sieges—having abandoned its base
previously to the reduction of either, and it has a fair probability of
being distressed for food and forage." "Our present base Jellalabad
is of the most difficult and almost inaccessible character—and a whole
country, the Punjaub, between it and our natural frontier." "If the
enemy knew how to apply his means, he would fall upon either Nott
or Pollock."

These Memoranda, marked "confidential," were sent to a number
of Indian officers of high rank, civil and military, and their answers
(preserved) show a general acceptance of Harry Smith's views.
Among them is the following letter from Henry Havelock and note
from Broadfoot to Havelock :—

"MY DEAR GENERAL,
       "I have the pleasure to return the Minutes which Broadfoot,
the most gallant and talented fellow that I met beyond the Indus, has
read, as you will see by the accompanying note.

"I too, though all unworthy to be mentioned in the same day, have
perused them, and agree with you in every point, excepting one or two
minor matters which those only who were in Afghanistan could be
correctly informed upon.

"I feel like a man worn out, which is perhaps not surprising after
having had my mind pretty much on the stretch for four years, but
will come and speak to you upon General Skelton's affairs to-morrow
morning, by God's help, and try to get a look at the charges.

"I thought Sir R. S[ale] would not go home. He is to blame, but
generally takes odd views of things and then is not easy to move. He
ought to make a personal fight for his pension.
                              "Ever yours very truly,
                                        "H. HAVELOCK."

"MY DEAR HAVELOCK,
       "The bearer will deliver to you General Smith's minutes.

perseverance in the cause of their country of the Swiss and Vendeans. If they had done so, the three divisions of Pollock and Nott and England, moving as they were upon the falsest of military principles, would have been sacrificed; but in all wars the folly of one party is exceeded by that of the other, and that which is the least culpable succeeds. This example of the want of union and energy on the part of the Afghans shows how easy it would have been to have crushed the insurrection by adopting vigorous measures at the moment.

But to revert to my own command. If the Governor-General had selected me and given me the authority I desired, viz. the whole line of the Indus, with the aid of Mr. Clerk (whose popularity with the Sikh Government and nation was so great that the resources of the Punjaub would have been at his command, and consequently at my disposal for the use of the army, which stood so much in need of them), I would have waged war upon a great scale upon the Afghan, razed his forts and fortresses from one end of his country to the other, established a government, remained in the country until order, rule, and authority were firmly established; then when the invincible character of our arms had been maintained, marched out of the country triumphantly,

I have read them with much interest, and am much tempted to give you some of the reflections they have given rise to, but if I began I should run into a dissertation. Give the General my best thanks, and believe me,

"[G. Broadfoot] [Signature cut off].
" Major Havelock, C.B."

and not have sneaked out of it, as we did, with our tail down, like a cur before a hound. That our national character for consistency, equity, and superiority has suffered by this melancholy attempt on Afghanistan is daily experienced throughout India. Would Scinde, Bundelkund, and Gwalior have dared to resist us but for the example afforded them in Cabool, that British troops could be not only beaten, but annihilated? The whole of the transactions of this period afford such a lesson to all Governors and Military Commanders, it is to be hoped posterity will never forget them. First principles in government and war can never be departed from: though success at the onset may attend irregularity, in the end disaster will assuredly prove that consistency, rule, and the true principles of strategy are indispensable to the achievement of conquest. To buy the good-will of the influential men of nations is folly and extravagance and the most temporary authority that can be attained. Conquest must be achieved by force of arms, by the display of irresistible power; then held by moderation, by a progressive system of amelioration of the condition of the people, by consistency and uncompromising justice. In this way the great movers of mankind, Fear and Self-interest, perpetuate subjection.

CHAPTER XLI.

SIR HUGH GOUGH SUCCEEDS SIR JASPER NICOLLS AS
COMMANDER-IN-CHIEF IN INDIA—AFFAIRS IN
GWALIOR—BATTLE OF MAHARAJPORE—HARRY
SMITH MADE K.C.B.

AT this period [1843] the time of command of
Sir Jasper Nicolls expired, and Sir Hugh Gough,
the hero of Barossa and of China, was appointed
Commander-in-Chief. Headquarters was at the
time in the Himalaya Mountains at Simla, and, Sir
Hugh having expressed a wish that I should meet
him, I and my dear wife started in the middle of
the rainy and unhealthy season on the 18th July for
Calcutta by dâk.* By this slow process you are
carried at the rate of three and a half miles an hour
in a sort of wooden box called a palanquin. You
railroad flyers would regard it as slow indeed for a
journey of 1300 miles. We reached Allahabad, and
from thence proceeded by steamboat and found my
new Commander-in-Chief. The parting with Sir J.
Nicolls was as painful as affectionate. With every
member of his highly educated and accomplished
family we were on the most intimate and friendly

* "Dâk: post, relays of palanquins or other carriages along a road"
(Anglo-Indian Dictionary).

terms, and he was kind enough by letter to say that he
ever regarded me as a "most upright, straightforward gentleman and soldier."   On parting, I could
not fail to express regret that he had not appointed
me to command in Afghanistan, the only time I
ever agitated the subject.   His answer was, "My
reasons then are fully in force now, but it was no
want of the highest opinion of your abilities."   I
shall ever entertain the highest respect for Sir Jasper
Nicolls as a most shrewd and sensible man, laborious
at papers, expressing himself by letter in as few
words as the Duke himself, and possessing a clear
and thorough knowledge of the affairs of India and
its army.   In his great error of command—I allude
to Afghanistan—there he was ever consistent, always
opposed to the occupation of that country, so distant
from our resources, so ruinous to our Treasury, but,
though right in principle, he should have yielded to
the force of circumstances at the moment, *restored
the fight*, and ultimately given back the country to its
lawful owners.

We were both received by Sir Hugh Gough and
family with every demonstration of a wish to culti-
vate that mutual friendship and good understanding
which education dictates and the good of our service
and the rules of the social compact demand.   We
were only in Calcutta from the 1st to the 12th
September, but twelve more laborious days we never
passed, what with an excess of correspondence, the
meeting with innumerable old friends, the formation
of new, the *fêtes* to the new Commander-in-Chief, a

great military dinner to Lord Ellenborough, etc.,
and, added to it all, the muggy heat and damp of
Calcutta. The twelve days accordingly appeared
to us almost months, from excitement and fatigue
mental and bodily.

His Excellency had no recreation from his
labours and indefatigable exertion, exposing himself
to sun, wind, and weather both by sea and land
in the most enthusiastic manner. Such was the
state of affairs in Scindiah's Dominions, it was
evident that British interference alone could establish any peaceful order of things. It was therefore
not only expedient, but necessary, to assemble an
army for the purpose of supporting diplomacy or of
acting in open war. Lord Ellenborough intimated
this to Sir Hugh, who, with his characteristic energy,
sought information on all points, and soon saw his
position, his resources, and the means at his disposal
to collect that army which should be irresistible if
compelled to take the field, or adequate to making
a demonstration which would no less surely bring
about the required result. To assemble an army in
India requires much arrangement and consideration.
There are various points at which the maintenance
of an armed force is indispensable ; the extent of
country in our occupation entails in all concentrations
particularly long and tedious marches : lastly, the
season of the year must be rigidly attended to, for
such is the fickleness of disease and its awful ravages,
that it would need an excess of folly to leave it
out of the account.

Affairs at Gwalior were still in a most disturbed state. The country was divided into parties. One of them, since the death of the Maharaja Scindiah [5 February, 1843], had adhered to the widow, a girl of only fourteen, but intriguing, designing, and in the hands of a cunning fellow, a sort of Prime Minister. This party was the strongest, and was inimical to the British Government. Hence it became necessary, in virtue of existing treaties, to re-establish by force of arms that amicable relationship which the tranquillity of India demanded, as well as to support the interests of the Maharaja, Scindiah's heir by another wife, a boy of ten years old. An army with a very efficient battery train was accordingly assembled at Agra under the immediate command of His Excellency, while a large division under Major-General Grey was concentrated at and in the vicinity of Cawnpore. While negotiations were in progress, the troops were to move on Gwalior to menace the hostile party, so that we might secure the object in view by negotiation rather than at once appeal to arms. The headquarters army marched from Agra direct on Dholpore upon the Chumbul, while the division under General Grey was to create a diversion and threaten Gwalior by a march to southward. According to the rules of strategy and correct principles of military combination, this division of the threatening or invading forces may with great reason be questioned, when we reflect that the army of Gwalior consisted of 22,000 veteran troops and for years had been

disciplined by European officers and well supplied
with artillery, and thus an overwhelming force might
have been precipitated on Grey and his army
destroyed, for he was perfectly isolated and depen-
dent on his own resources alone. This, however,
had not escaped the observation and due consideration of the Commander-in-Chief. As we calculate
on the power of an enemy, so may we estimate what,
according to his system of operations, he is likely to
attempt. On this occasion it was considered that if
the enemy made a descent on Grey, his division was
of sufficient force to defend itself, while our main
army would have rapidly moved on Gwalior and
conquered it without a struggle through the absence
of the chief part of its army, (for strategy is totally
unknown to a native army, which usually posts itself
on a well-chosen position and awaits an attack).

The leading incidents which led to the outbreak
of war have been so recently and so distinctly
recorded, I have only to observe that the policy
pursued by the Governor-General was of the most
correct character. He gave the State of Gwalior
full time for reflexion, and demanded only such an
arrangement as could alone restore the youthful
Maharaja to his birthright, and produce harmony
within the State and peace and tranquillity without.
It admits of considerable discussion whether or not
the Governor-General was justified in crossing the
Chumbul, and thereby invading the territory of a
kingdom he was treating with, when one of the great
preliminaries had been granted, viz. the surrender

of the Dada Khasgee Wala, the adviser and lover
of the young widow and the Prime Minister.
However, the army under the Commander-in-
Chief crossed the Chumbul by ford above Dholpore,
while Grey's Division entered the dominion of
Scindiah *viâ* Koonah and crossed the boundary,
the river Scinde, in the neighbourhood of Kohee,
avoiding, however, the Antree Pass, which would
have exposed his advance to considerable interruption. The army, after crossing the Chumbul, moved
into a position on the Koharee rivulet (the banks
of which are intersected by small ravines so as to
be impassable but by certain roads), and about eight
miles from the ford of the Chumbul. The position
was one rather chosen for the pomp and ceremony
of a visit from the widow, the Maharaja, and the
Court, which was expected in the then state of the
negotiations. This meeting was all arranged,* but
never came to consummation. The army were so
jealous of Grey's advance, they concluded, and
naturally from their own Mahratta character (being
the most fickle and deceitful people, and capable of
any treachery to advance their desires), that while
the Governor-General was encouraging this meeting,
which was to be attended by a considerable body of
the Mahratta army, Grey's division would move
into the rear and seize the capital and the fortress
of Gwalior. The suspicions of natives (naturally
jealous and ready to impute evil to all around them)
are not to be calmed, and the army prohibited this

* For 26 December, 1843.

meeting (if the babe widow and her party ever seriously meditated it) and moved forward in a hostile attitude, crossing the Ahsin rivulet, which runs parallel to the Koharee at a distance of eight or nine miles.

I was in the habit of taking long rides every morning to make myself well acquainted with the country. When out riding on the 28th December, I fell in with a patrol which the Quartermaster-General of the Army had been directed to take out for the purpose of reconnoitring the enemy, who, according to information, had crossed the Ahsin and posted himself between the villages of Maharajpore and Chounda. The former is advanced on the plain between the two rivulets, the latter is below the Ahsin, the banks of which are also intersected by innumerable small and impassable ravines. I accompanied Colonel Garden, the Q.M.G. On my return I gave in the memorandum as follows :—

"Camp Hingonah, 28th Dec. 1843.

"Note on the position of the enemy on the left bank of the Ahsin River :—

"From what I saw this morning, I calculate the force of the enemy to be 10,000 men, and he fired from ten guns of small calibre. His position appeared to be on the plain in dense masses of troops, his left resting on the broken ground of the Ahsin River, his guns drawn out in front, his right 'en air,' as if *more troops* were coming up to occupy the position selected. The sooner, therefore, it is practicable for our army to occupy the right bank of the Koharee and place itself in front of the enemy's line, the better, not only to prevent a further advance of the enemy, but to

enable a general action to be fought in two hours, when
desired. This, however, is a single view of our army, as it
does not take into consideration Major-General Grey's
Division. It therefore rests mainly to be considered whether
General Grey's troops should not be so brought into direct
communication with the main body as either to attack
simultaneously the enemy's left flank, or be so posted as to
act upon the line of the enemy when 'en déroute' of our
main body. To do this it is obvious that the exact position
of General Grey must be ascertained. If the information
of the strength of the enemy renders it expedient to await
direct communication with General Grey, some little delay
is involved. On the contrary, if a general action be at
once desirable, it may be fought by eleven o'clock to-morrow,
Friday the 29th inst. To effect this, the army should
march, crossing the Koharee disencumbered of the 'impedimenta' of war, before daylight the 29th inst. The
distance hence to the enemy's line is within eight miles.
To fight this action early in the morning is most desirable,
in order to enable the pursuit of the fugitives to be protracted, therefore effective, and to ensure the capture of
every gun.

"The morning was very hazy, and the smoke of the
camp combining with it made reconnaissance difficult."

The army marched before daylight on the 29th
Dec.* in three columns, all of which reached their
ground with the utmost precision. The enemy was
attacked [Battle of Maharajpore], every gun (54)
taken, and the defeat general; but never did men
stand to their guns with more determined pluck,

* "The Governor-General, with the ladies of his camp, rode on
elephants beside the advancing columns" (Trotter, *India under
Victoria*, vol. i. p. 100).

every gunner being bayoneted or cut down at his post. It was the same at Puniar [General Grey's victory of the same day.] The result of these battles is well known. I was mentioned in the dispatches of the Commander-in-Chief, Sir Hugh Gough, and was rewarded with a step in the Most Honourable Military Order of the Bath, from C.B. (I had worn that decoration since Waterloo, twenty-nine years before) to K.C.B., the Great Captain of the Age writing to me as follows :—

"Horse Guards, 29 April, 1844.

"SIR,

"I have the satisfaction to acquaint you that the Secretary of State has, upon my recommendation, submitted to the Queen your appointment to be a Knight Commander of the Most Honourable Military Order of the Bath, of which Her Majesty has been most graciously pleased to approve.

"I have the honor to be, Sir,

"Your most obedient humble servant,

"(Signed)   WELLINGTON."

"Major-General Sir H. G. Smith, K.C.B."

To which I replied—

"Headquarters, Army of India, Simla, 23rd June, 1844.

"MY LORD DUKE,

"I have this day had the honour to receive your Grace's letter, 'Horse Guards, 29th April,' acquainting me with an expression of satisfaction that Her Majesty had, upon your recommendation, been graciously pleased to appoint me a Knight Commander of the Most Honourable Military Order of the Bath. While my gratitude to my

Sovereign is unbounded, my heart dictates, it is to your
Grace I am indebted for every honorary distinction,
promotion, and appointment I have received during a
long and an eventful period of the history of the world.
Among the many thousands of the gallant soldiers who
so nobly fought and conquered under your Grace, I
may conscientiously hope none could desire more zealously
to do his duty, or was ever more actuated by personal
devotion or inspired with greater confidence throughout
the numerous struggles of war, than he who now renders
his grateful thanks for this mark of distinction so honourable to the soldier, and thus conferred by Her Majesty
through the recommendation of his Commander-in-Chief,
the Great Captain of the Age.

" I have, etc.,
"(Signed)   H. G. SMITH.

" Field Marshal His Grace the Duke of Wellington."

I have now served my country nearly forty years,
I have fought in every quarter of the globe, I have
driven four-in-hand in every quarter, I have never
had a sick certificate, and only once received leave
of absence, which I did for eight months to study
mathematics.   I have filled *every* staff situation of
a Regiment and of the General Staff.   I have commanded a Regiment in peace, and have had often a
great voice in war.   I entered the army perfectly
unknown to the world, in ten years by force of circumstances I was Lieutenant-Colonel, and I have
been present in as many battles and sieges as any
officer of my standing in the army.   I never fought
a duel, and only once made a man an apology,

although I am as hot a fellow as the world produces; and I may without vanity say, the friendship I have experienced equals the love I bear my comrade, officer or soldier.

My wife has accompanied me throughout the world; she has ever met with kind friends and never has had controversy or dispute with man or woman.

HARRY SMITH.

APPENDIX TO CHAPTER XLI.

ON THE BATTLE OF MAHARAJPORE.

In a letter to Sir James Kempt, dated "Gwalior, 15th January, 1844," Harry Smith sketches the events which led to the battle, and cites his memorandum of 28th December given above. He continues—

"The army did march as described in Sir H. Gough's dispatches in three columns, each arriving at its designated post in excellent time—which I freely admit was scarcely to be expected, having to disengage itself from a mass of laden elephants, camels, and bullocks and bullock carts, etc., resembling rather the multitudes of Xerxes than anything modern, and having to traverse ground on the banks of rivulets most peculiarly intersected by numerous and deep small ravines, the pigmy model of a chain of mountains, but even more impassable. On such ravines was posted the enemy's left flank; his right extended towards the village of Maharajpore, which he had filled with Infantry and ably supported by batteries enfilading its approach, his extreme right again thrown back upon the ravines of the Ahsin River, as described in the little pencil sketch enclosed, thus realizing the surmise in my report, 'his right "en air," as if other troops were coming up to complete the

occupation of the position.' If we could have caught
the enemy in the state he was when reconnoitred the
previous day, easy indeed would have been the victory.
These Mahrattas, nor indeed does any Indian Army, know
no more than to occupy a strong position and hold it as
long as able, sticking to their guns *like men*. Having
observed the enemy's position the day before, it was obvious
to me this morning that he had advanced very considerably,
and that he held the village of Maharajpore in force, which
I rode through the day previous. Upon a plain, and that
plain covered with the high stalks of Jumna corn, not a
mound of rising ground even to assist the view, reconnoitring is nearly nominal. However, so impressed was I from
what a nearer view the day before had given me and what
I then saw, that the enemy attached great importance to his
left flank, the line of his retreat if beaten, I ventured to advocate that flank as the most eligible point for a weighty attack.
However, things were differently conducted and as the heads
of columns appeared, the enemy instantly opened a well-
directed cannonade, particularly from the vicinity of the
village of Maharajpore, and Sir H. Gough ordered an
advance. His dispatch tells the tale, and the mode of resistance, the enemy's guns, etc. I need, therefore, only bear
testimony to the gallantry of the enemy's resistance, which
in my conscience I believe and assert would not have been
overcome but for our gallant old Peninsular comrades, the
39th and 40th Regiments, who carried everything before
them, bayoneting the gunners at their guns to a man. These
guns were most ably posted, each battery flanking and
supporting the other by as heavy a cross-fire of cannon as
I ever saw, and grape like hail. Our leaders of brigades in
the neighbourhood and in the village had various opportunities of displaying heroism, Valiant, Wright 39th and
my Assistant, Major Barr, remarkably so, and many gallant
fellows fell in this noble performance of their duty. The

enemy was driven back at every point with great loss, yielding to force, not retiring in haste. A more thorough devotedness to their cause no soldiers could evince, and the annals of their defeat, altho' an honour to us, can never be recorded as any disgrace to them. Turn we now to General Grey's division. For many days before the 29th our communication was totally interrupted, and the wisdom of the route and the disunited approach to Gwalior must be tested by the fortunate result, not by the established rules and principles of strategy. Grey's dispatch is not so well written as it might have been, I am led to understand, nor does he give full credit to the old Buffs for their gallant *double allowance* with which they contributed to the achievements of the day and the capture of the enemy's guns, every one of them. The old 50th had its share too, and the blockheads in the East, who 'haver' over their wine of India's being in a state to require no British troops, are wrong: for, liberally contributing the full meed of praise to the Seapoy Battalions, that praise is so rested on the British soldier's example, the want of that 'point d'appui' would entail a dire want indeed, that of victory! Now if we regard the victories recently obtained over the Mahratta force, 28,000 men whose discipline has gradually been improving under Christian officers since 1803 (the days of Lake and Wellington), well supplied with cannon and every implement of war, animated by a devotion to their cause not to be exceeded—in a military point of view they are achievements in the field which yield alone to Assaye and rank with Dieg, Laswarree, and Mehudpore, and in a political point of view, their importance is immense, struck in the very heart of India, within the hearing almost of the seat of government of our Upper Provinces, Agra. Remembering the disasters in Affghanistan, which still, as they ever will, hold their baneful influence over British India; reviewing the recent bloody murders, and present confusion and anarchy at Lahore; the still unsettled state of Bundelkund; the sickness in Scinde (that accursed Scinde), the grave of our army; the intrigues at the court of Nepaul, which have been rife and ˌready for mischief pending the late contest—then may my Lord Ellenborough and our country congratulate themselves upon the re-establishment of the 'Prestige of our Arms' as a sure foundation of our Indian Empire, the very base of which was tremulous, for it is well known that these Mahrattas have been *advocating hostility in every court of the East.* It is to be hoped, therefore, coupled with Lord E.'s moderation and the equity of his acts in thus re-establishing the youthful Maharaja on his throne, that our country and its Government will regard this as no war of foreign invasion, no war of conquest and unjust aggression, but one of absolute necessity to maintain the one Power paramount in India on the faith of old treaties of amity, and a demonstration to the present disturbed states of India, to the well-disposed, and to the World, that the British Lion will be ever triumphant; and that it will accordingly treat the soldiers who have achieved victories of such political magnitude with the liberality shown to *the heroes exiled* from Affghanistan, their discomfitures conjured into triumphs of valour, their miserable retreat through the Khyber Pass into deeds of glory inferior to none but the passage of San Bernardo by Napoleon. In this hope we may venture to trust a fair construction will be put on our acts, and that I may see my gallant comrades promoted as they deserve, and honoured in the manner recent services have been.

"I shall ever regard this battle as one of the most fortunate circumstances of my life, if the majority of its remainder is to be spent in India, by its having acquired me that experience in Indian warfare all require, and above all, to hold in just estimation your enemy, a creed I have ever

advocated, and to a certain extent, in every instance practised. In the late conflict *no one* gave our foe credit for
half his daring or ability; hence our attack was not
quite so scientifically powerful by a combination of the
different arms as it might have been, and the defects of
the unwieldy machine called the British Indian Army
rendered most glaring :—its appalling quantity of baggage,
its lack of organization and equipment of the soldiers,
its want of experience in Generals and in officers, the
extreme willingness but total inexpertness and inaptitude
of the soldier in the arts of war, in the conflict, on picquet,
on every duty which a protracted campaign alone can teach
effectually. In this country almost every war has been
terminated in one or two pitched battles fought so soon
as the one army comes in sight of the other, and accordingly all the science attaching to advance and retreat, the
posting of picquets, reconnaissance of the enemy, the daily
contemplating his movements, both when he is before you
and on the march, are lost, and war is reduced at once to
'there are people drawn up who will shoot at you, so fire
away at them.' You blindly and ineptly rush upon them,
drive them from the field with considerable loss, take
all their guns, and never see the vestige of them after.
Thus we must judiciously and with foresight organize ourselves for a campaign in the Punjaub—a very probable
event—for the armies of India are not now the rabble
they were in Clive's time, but organized and disciplined by
European officers of experience (many French), and the art
of war has progressed rapidly among our enemies, whose
troops are invariably far more numerous than those we
oppose to them ; thus by superior ability we could alone
calculate on their defeat. As it is, we calculate alone on
the bulldog courage of Her Majesty's soldiers, and our loss
becomes what we lately witnessed.

"To obviate these deficiencies, apparent even to the

most inexperienced eye, we must in the first place reduce our baggage, next give our Seapoys canteens and haversacks (a Regiment told me they were exhausted for want of water, the water-carriers having run away). We must then, every cold season, have divisions of the army assembled, and post the one half opposite the other, with outlying picquets, etc., and daily alarms, skirmishes, etc., then general actions with blank cartridges. Without this the British Indian Army will remain as it now is—a great unwieldy machine of ignorant officers and soldiers. The drill of the Seapoy is good enough, and that of his officer, and never will attain greater perfection, but unless the officers in their separate commands know how, as I call it, to feed the fight, to bring up or into action successively in their places their command, when the attack is ordered, I defy any general to defeat his enemy but by stupid bull-dog courage. It may be conceit in Harry Smith, but if 10,000 men were given him in one cold season, if by sham fights, etc., he did not make them practical soldiers, he would resign in disgust, for the material is excellent and willing, but now, like a dictionary, it contains all the words, but cannot write a letter.

"I have given you no account of the death of our gallant old comrade Churchill; he was game, and tho' not free from many errors he had virtues, and his loss cost Juana and me some honest tears.

"Young Somerset is a fine, gallant young fellow who received four wounds, three severe ones, but is doing well, thank God both for his sake and his father's. As I cannot write to all my many friends, if you think this letter would amuse any of my *old comrades*, soldiers such as I aim at making, Lord K.,* Sir J. Lambert, Sir T. Reynell (if better), Sir A. Barnard, pray send it. Lord F. Somerset I do not

* Lord Keane.

name, as I know you show him all my effusions which meet your own approbation.

"Juana was under a heavy cannonade with Lady G., Miss G., and a Mrs. Curtis on their elephants. Juana had this command of Amazons, and as she was experienced and they young, her command was anything but satisfactory.* This Gwalior is a very extraordinary place. I have had some long rides in every direction, and the *débris* of the army of Scindiah now disbanding are as handsome, well-clothed and appointed soldiers, as regular in their encampments, as Frenchmen, and inclined to fight in their gallant and vivacious style.

"Thus our credit in the victory is the more.

"Faithfully, dear friend,

"(Signed)   HARRY SMITH."

---

* Sir Charles Napier, writing to Harry Smith early in 1844, treats humorously of the presence of Lady Gough, Juana Smith, etc., under fire at this battle. "I congratulate you on your feats of arms. You had a tough job of it : these Asiatics hit hard, methinks. How came all the ladies to be in the fight? I suppose you all wanted to be gloriously rid of your wives? Well, there is something in that; but I wonder the women stand so atrocious an attempt. Poor things! I dare say they too had their hopes. They talk of our immoral conduct in Scinde! I am sure there never was any so bad as this. God forgive you all. Read your Bible, and wear your laurels."—W. Napier's *Life of Sir Charles Napier* (1857), vol. iii. p. 45.

CHAPTER XLII.

AFFAIRS IN THE PUNJAUB—SIR HENRY HARDINGE SUCCEEDS LORD ELLENBOROUGH AS GOVERNOR-GENERAL—OUTBREAK OF THE FIRST SIKH WAR —BATTLE OF MOODKEE.

Cawnpore, 7th September, 1846.

THE narrative by way of my history which ceased in 1843 must now be renewed, as it embraces the most important period of my eventful life, as far as public services go. In my capacity of Adjutant-General of Her Majesty's forces at Headquarters (which in the cold weather moved about on the plains, in the hot enjoyed the cool and bracing atmosphere of the Himalayas at Simla), I had every opportunity of watching the gradually gathering storm in the Punjaub, until it was suspended over our heads in November, 1845, ready to burst, though where, when, or how no one dared venture a decided opinion. Most certainly, however, no one contemplated a powerful invasion, or imagined that the Sikhs were in communication with the [princes ?] and influential men of British India so far as Delhi. At the period when this was written, the history of the rise of the Punjaub as a nation was well known to all, but ere these pages come to light it may be

2 K

forgotten or partially so. A slight compendium of this history is therefore annexed.

The kingdom called the Punjaub extends from the Hindoo Koosh (a branch of the Himalayas) on the north, is bounded by that range on the east, by the Indus to the west, by the Sutlej, to its confluence with the Indus, to the south. However, a considerable portion of the territory *south* of the Sutlej was under the rule of the Lahore Government, and this became the seat of the great war in 1845-6.

This tract of country was consolidated by the conquest of various independent principalities by the ability, enterprise, and foresight of the celebrated Runjeet Singh, who raised himself to pre-eminence and absolute power from the middle class of society. Hence the old Sikh families, the ancient Rajpoots, although subdued into obedience, were ever distrustful of him and he was ever obnoxious to them; hence the seeds of discord which so rapidly sprung up on the decease of Runjeet Singh, and which concluded in this war so fatal to the Sikh.

The whole Punjaub contains about a quarter of a million of Sikhs, the chief part to be found around Lahore and the beautiful city of Umritsir. A Sikh cultivator is seldom seen. The Sikhs, although professing a religion of Brahmanical tenets and established by their great priest and prophet Govind Gooroo, drink to excess, eat opium and bangh (a species of wild hemp possessing narcotic and intoxicating qualities of the most enervating description), and regard the abstemious Hindoo and the sensual

Mussulman with contempt. Hence the labour of the fields and every other labour fall upon the two latter races, and they have always been favourably disposed to the British.

Runjeet Singh's great policy was a firm adherence to the rulers of British India. He had observed in 1811 [1808 ?] the discipline of some of our Seapoys who formed an escort to Mr. Metcalfe (ultimately Lord Metcalfe) on an embassy to the Court of Lahore. This escort, when treacherously attacked by a fanatical sect not then subdued to Runjeet's authority, called Akalies, so boldly and ably defended itself, that, observing the effect of discipline, the acute Runjeet instantly set to work to organize his own army on a similar footing. He invited foreigners, especially Frenchmen, to enter his service, and was liberal to many of them in the extreme. Under such instruction, a most powerful army sprung up, composed of Cuirassiers, Light Infantry most highly equipped, numerous Artillery (in which Runjeet had great faith), and beautifully appointed and organized Infantry. Runjeet spared neither expense nor exertion, and such a spirit of superiority and strength was infused into this army that it believed itself invincible and the most powerful in the world. Runjeet died in June, 1839, leaving this powerful army, estimated by us as of the following strength :—

40,000 Cavalry, regular and irregular, among which a Brigade of Akalies in cuirasses and chain armour, " The Invincibles."

120,000 Regular Infantry.

Innumerable Irregulars—every inhabitant being a soldier.

400 pieces of cannon ready to take the field, (for Runjeet had spared neither pains nor expense to improve the breed of horses, and his efforts were attended with great success.)

From the death of Runjeet Singh in 1839 to 1845 a succession of revolutions and murders of Kings and Princes continued, first one party, then another, supporting a reputed son of Runjeet on the throne, who was as sure to be murdered in the sanguinary struggles of that Reign of Terror. A Hill family, elevated for their personal beauty rather than their talents (although some of them were far from wanting abilities), became conspicuous, and many fell with the puppets of their creation. This family received the soubriquet of Lords of the Hills, Jummoo being the fortified hold of the head of the family. Its most conspicuous members were Goolab Singh and Dhyan Singh. Dhyan and his son Heera Singh were both Prime Ministers, or Wuzeer, and both were murdered in 1844. Such was the power of the standing army, it acknowledged no other authority, set up Kings and deposed them at pleasure, and at the period of the commencement of the war, a boy (Dhuleep Singh), born of a Hill woman of great ability and reputed the son of old Runjeet, was the nominal King, Lal Singh was Wuzeer, and Tej Singh Commander-in-Chief of this rabble (though highly organized and numerous)

army. It must be obvious that such a state of
things could not last. The resources of the treasury
were rapidly consuming, and with them the only
power of the Queen Mother, the Rani or Regent,
which consisted in her presents and consequent
popularity. All the foreign officers had absconded
except one Frenchman, a man of neither note nor
talent, and a Spanish Engineer by name Hubon, a
low-bred man, but clever, acute, and persevering.

The British Government of India had acknowledged this Regency, and was desirous to retain
amicable relationship with the Punjaub, but in the
middle of the year 1845, so unruly and clamorous
for war was the Sikh army, all negotiations terminated, and a state of uncertainty ensued which made
it necessary for British India, without declaring
hostility, to place itself on a footing to resist it,
should so mad an enterprise ensue.

Meanwhile in 1844 Lord Ellenborough was
recalled, and succeeded as Governor-General by
Sir Henry Hardinge, a statesman and a soldier of
Wellington's, in either capacity celebrated for
judgment, ability, and foresight. Upon his very
arrival, he saw that a rupture with the Punjaub was
sooner or later inevitable, and he drew up an able
document on the prospects of British India in such
an event, which he submitted to the Directors.
Immediately afterwards he commenced moving
every possible soldier, and commanded the material
of war up to the North-West Frontier, while a large
flotilla of boats was built at Bombay for the purpose

of bridges, and sent up the Indus and thence into the Sutlej opposite Ferozepore, where they were sunk under the left bank of the river. By these arrangements, dictated by a perfect military knowledge and by that foresight which bears the stamp of prediction, Sir Henry Hardinge, in the autumn of 1845, had in readiness for coming events nine regiments of British Infantry, three regiments of British Cavalry, a most powerful train of Field Artillery (with upwards of 100 field-guns, 6 and 9-pounders, and a powerful battering train in progress), a large force of Regular and Irregular Cavalry, and forty regiments of Native Infantry. The isolated post and fortress of Ferozepore had been reinforced by twenty-four field guns, a regiment of British Infantry, and Cavalry and Native Infantry, until a force of upwards of 7000 men composed a Corps under Major-General Sir John Littler, for the double purpose of defending Ferozepore from insult and watching the ghauts, or fords, of the Sutlej. The assembling force was put into Brigades and Divisions, and equipped to take the field either on the initiative or defensive.

In December all negotiations and communications between the Regency and ourselves had ceased at the dictation of the Sikh army, which was clamorous for war with the British, and openly vaunted it would place the Rani and her son upon the Imperial Throne of Delhi, and a correspondence was actually established with that city and the line conducting to it, for the supply of provisions to the

Sikh army. This act of treachery on the part of
British subjects will show what would be the
stability of British rule in India on any other basis
than that of military power.

The means of obtaining information on the part
of our political officers, as results prove, was defective ; nor can any credit attach to Sir John Littler
as a watchful outpost officer, when the enemy
gradually crossed by boats (not a bridge) an army
of 70,000 men of all arms, with an immense train of
artillery and overwhelming force of cavalry, with
stores enormous, and positively established themselves under the Commanders Tej Singh and Lal
Singh, ere our authorities were aware of it, civil or
military, fortified a strong position near and embrac-
ing the village of Ferozeshuhur, and made a demonstration as of attack in front of Ferozepore. This
was in the middle of December. This development
and invasion called for, and was met by, the
most active and vigorous measures on the part of
the Governor-General and Council. Every available regiment was pushed forward without waiting
to assemble Divisions and Brigades, although all
were in order, and a very able organization was
effected, as far as the programme went. The troops
made double or forced marches, with the result that
the force of cavalry under Brigadier White, the 1st
Division under Major-General Sir Harry Smith,*

---

* On Sir Harry Smith's appointment to the command of the
1st Division, his duties as Adjutant-General devolved upon Lieut.-
Colonel Barr.

and one Brigade of the 2nd Division under Major-General Gilbert, reached Moodkee much fatigued and exhausted on the morning of the eventful 18th December. One of the most able and enterprising movements at this stage of the war was the evacuation of Loodiana, except its fort, by order of the Governor-General, and the march of the troops thence on Busseean, which reinforcement, joining the troops on their hasty march on Moodkee, ensured the victory about to be contended for.

On the 18th December a considerable force of the British army had reached Moodkee, much exhausted, as has been said, by the necessary length of marches and a want of water and the power of cooking. Brigades were assembled, but not Divisions. The troops had some of them barely reached their bivouac, when the advance of the Sikh army with clouds of cavalry demanded an immediate turn-out in preparation to resist an attack of fresh and infatuated troops, excited by personal hatred, natural vanity, and the stimulants of spirits, opium, and bangh. In place of awaiting the coming storm, our united forces being compact, each arm in support of the other, the whole on an open plain ready to receive the onslaught, our troops were hurried unnecessarily into the field, and the cavalry and artillery rushed into action. Our cavalry and artillery had driven back the Sikh cavalry most gallantly into a very jungly or bushy country, when the enemy's infantry brought them up and occasioned a very considerable and most unnecessary loss. The

infantry meanwhile advancing, the right Brigade of
the 1st Division upon the right of the army under
the command of Brigadier Wheeler, but under the
eye of Sir Harry Smith, was fiercely assailed by an
almost overwhelming force of Sikh infantry. These
it boldly repulsed, and, continuing to advance, took
six guns and caused the enemy an inconceivable
loss. The dust was so darkening, the enemy could
only be discovered by its density and the fire.

The first part of this action was on an open
country with occasional large dense and thorny
trees, into which the enemy climbed and caused the
50th Regiment great loss. This Brigade (H.M.'s
50th, and the 42nd and 48th Regiments Native
Infantry) was more engaged than any other part of
the army. Many officers and upwards of 150
soldiers of the 50th were wounded. Brigadier
Wheeler was wounded severely; Major-General
Sale, Q.M.G. of H.M.'s Forces, who had attached
himself to Sir Harry Smith, mortally. On this
occasion Sir Harry Smith greatly distinguished
himself on his celebrated black Arab " Jem Crow,"
by seizing one of the colours of H.M.'s 50th Regiment and planting them in the very teeth of a Sikh
column, and gloriously did the Regiment rush on
with bayonet, and fearful was the massacre which
ensued. The left Brigade of the 1st Division was
engaged to the left of the line under Brigadier
Bolton of H.M.'s 31st Regiment (who fell mortally
wounded), while the Brigades of the 2nd Division
under Major-General Gilbert and Major-General

Sir John McCaskill occupied the centre. Sir John was shot through the heart.

It is a curious circumstance in this battle that so obscured was all vision by the dust, that it afterwards appeared that the bulk of the Sikh forces passed in column along the front of the 1st Brigade of the 1st Division, and when repulsed by the 2nd Brigade 1st Division and [ ] Brigade 2nd Division, were driven again across the front of the 50th, the advance of which was pushed by Sir Harry Smith. After the troops were halted, the dust dispelled and the moon was up and shining brightly. The 1st Brigade 1st Division then formed an obtuse angle with the rest of the army. This brigade had gone right through the Sikh repulsed columns. The 1st Division this day took twelve of the seventeen guns captured from the enemy.

The Division lost at Moodkee—

Killed.	Wounded.	Missing.	Total.
79	339	19	437

Both Brigadiers were knocked down, and one died of his wounds.

After the action the troops returned to their camp, which they reached about half-past twelve.

CHAPTER XLIII.

BATTLE OF FEROZESHAH (OR FEROZESHUHUR) 21ST
DECEMBER, 1845, AND RESUMED BATTLE OF
22ND DECEMBER—THE ARMY MOVES INTO POSI-
TION AT SOBRAON.

EARLY in the morning of the 19th parties were
sent out to bring in the wounded, and our cavalry
outposts pushed forward to cover this, as also to
enable our artillery to bring in the captured guns,
amounting to seventeen. The enemy having made
a reconnaissance with a large body of cavalry, which
created an alarm in the camp, the troops were turned
out and took up a very faulty position in front of
Moodkee. In this village there is a very tenable
little fort, which was of great use to us. About one
o'clock, the enemy making no forward movement,
the troops were turned in to cook. During the
afternoon all was quiet.

On the 20th every arrangement was made for
the care of the sick, wounded, stores, etc., at
Moodkee, and the troops, well completed in ammunition, prepared to march on the memorable 21st
December. As yet no direct communication was
established with Sir John Littler, in command of the

7000 men at Ferozepore. These were still isolated
and subject to a weighty attack of the enemy, who
could attack with facility and still hold his position
around the village of Ferozeshuhur. This was
strongly fortified and bristling with cannon, and
there was plenty of water for both men and horses.
Hence our object was to effect a combination with
the Ferozepore force ere the enemy anticipated us,
unless his correct information of our movements led
him to attack either one or both of our columns
moving mutually to a point of concentration, for
Littler's force was ordered to move out and meet
our advance. (This was by no means a difficult or
dangerous movement, the distance from Moodkee to
Ferozepore not exceeding that from the Sikh army
at Ferozeshuhur.)

The troops marched from Moodkee in order of
battle (almost crossing the front of the enemy's
position), and moved in the direction of Ferozepore,
from whence Littler's column was also moving to
effect the junction, which took place about ten o'clock
in the morning. Sir H. Hardinge, as Governor-
General, had interdicted any attack upon the enemy's
lines until the junction was effected, a most fortunate
interdiction for British India.* So soon as the army
was collected, Sir H. Hardinge turned to Sir H.
Gough and said, " Now the army is at your disposal."

---

* It will be noted that Sir Harry Smith, in spite of all that followed,
supports Sir H. Hardinge's military judgment in the famous dispute
on this occasion between him and Sir H. Gough. A contrary view is
taken in Gough and Innes' *The Sikhs*, etc., p. 107.

Sir Hugh made immediate arrangements to attack, although much most valuable time was lost in those arrangements, nor were Generals of Division made the least aware of how or what or where they were to attack. The army was one unwieldy battalion under one Commanding Officer who had not been granted the power of ubiquity. My opinion may be called one after the result, but I formed it while the troops were arranging in order of battle. I now record it leisurely and most deliberately. Had I commanded, I should have moved in contiguous columns of brigades, my cavalry protecting my advance up to the enemy's position till within range of his guns, the troops so moving as to be able to anticipate any movement of the enemy to the discomfort of Ferozepore, and to enable me to throw the weight of the attack upon the right of the enemy, if, as I apprehended from all I had heard, he was as assailable upon his right as on any other given point. I say I would have thrown the weight of my attack upon his right, because he was most formidable in his entrenched position, and if that right was to be carried as I anticipated, my victorious troops could have acted on the line of his retreat, which, being comparatively left open, gave him an opportunity to avail himself of it, and not to fight with that desperation that even bad troops will show if they are hemmed in. So soon as my advancing columns had attained to barely within the range of the enemy's guns, I would have carefully reconnoitred him, and compared ocular demonstration with the accounts of the enemy's interior arrangements of defence afforded by spies, taking with me each General of Division as I passed the front of his troops. This reconnaissance would have enabled officers in command to see their way. The whole weight of my attack should have been on the enemy's right and right centre, which would have given me the advantage which the principles of war so justly and truly demand, "To be superior to your enemy on the point of attack." The enemy's position was his favoured one, semicircular, the centre near the village of Ferozeshuhur, where there were good wells, and also pond water for cattle. By a weighty attack on a given point, the half of the enemy's cannon in position would have been lost to him and innocuous to us. Whereas we attacked in what may almost be termed lines of circumvallation of the enemy's crescent, thus presenting ourselves as targets to every gun the enemy had. Our artillery was massed about the centre of the army ; six-pounders opposed to the enemy's guns in embrasures, and of a calibre or weight beyond the range of our six-pounders ; hence the mortality and wrongly imputed inefficiency of that arm, a noble arm when called forth in its legitimate field.

The 1st Division, mine, was separated, the 1st Brigade, under Brigadier Hicks, being to the right of the mass of artillery, the 2nd Brigade to the left of that arm, which covered from three-quarters to a mile of ground. The whole Division was regarded as the reserve to the centre of the army. Sir John

Littler's, the Ferozepore force, was on the left. In this order the army advanced to the attack. There was plenty of daylight; the imputation of attacking too late in the day is unfounded, as I will plainly show, although I was not then, nor am I now, an advocate for so precipitate an attack, made without any knowledge of the enemy's position beyond the lies and contradictory stories of spies. An attack on a rear-guard ought to be precipitated *coûte que coûte;* an attack on an army delayed until science can be applied with the greatest decision.

Having posted my right Brigade, I joined the left and correctly posted it, strictly in obedience to the orders I had received from the Commander-in-Chief in person. My Division thus posted, I rode forward with a desire of having a look at the enemy's position, and came up to Sir H. Hardinge, who was in doubt what some guns were upon our left, which had just been brought into action. I galloped forward to ascertain, and reported they were of Littler's force, that his attack appeared to me one of no weight from its formation, and that, if the enemy behaved as expected, it would fail. Sir H. Hardinge said, " Then bring up your Division." I explained I had only one Brigade; I could bring up that. He ordered it up, and I pretty quickly had it on the move to the front, to the left of Gilbert's, or the 2nd Division, and to the right of Littler's.

At this moment Gilbert's left was not only checked in its advance, but actually falling back, and I had some difficulty in establishing myself on the front line in consequence of the broken troops falling back upon me.   Scarcely was I firmly established, when Major Broadfoot, the Political Agent, rode up and said, "Be prepared, General.   Four Battalions of Avitabile's* are close upon you in advance; I have it from correct information—a man in my pay has just left them."   The smoke and dirt rendered everything at the moment invisible. I saw, however, that to resist this attack, which was evidently made to take advantage of our check, and penetrate our line between Littler's right and Gilbert's left, I must bring up the right of my Brigade.   I endeavoured to do so, and with H.M.'s 50th Regiment I partially succeeded, under a storm of musketry and cannon which I have rarely, if ever, seen exceeded.   My native troops staggered and some receded, while the gallant old 50th bore the whole brunt, opening a rapid fire. At this moment poor Major Arthur Somerset † was struck down, a most accomplished soldier for his experience, and of a promise to emulate his great ancestor the Duke, had Almighty God been pleased to spare him to his country.   I never saw a more cool, judicious, and gallant officer than my dear and lamented friend, Arthur Somerset.   If the tears of a veteran could decorate the hero's tomb, every vein

* General Avitabile, an Italian, had been employed by Runjeet Singh in training his troops.

† Son of Lord Fitzroy Somerset, afterwards Lord Raglan, and great-nephew of the Duke of Wellington, his mother (a daughter of Lord Mornington) being the Duke's niece.

upon it would be full. Poor youth! "Sic transit gloria mundi!"

The enemy was at this moment in his bearing noble and triumphant. So fast were officers and men falling, I saw there was nothing for it but a charge of bayonets to restore the waning fight. I, Colonel Petit, and Colonel Ryan put ourselves at the head of the 50th, and most gallantly did they charge into the enemy's trenches, where such a hand-to-hand conflict ensued as I had never before witnessed. The enemy was repulsed at this point, and his works and cannon carried, and he precipitately retreated. I pushed forward with the 50th in line until we reached the enemy's camp. All order was broken by the tents, but my orders and example were "Forward! Forward! Forward!" I saw a village occupied by the enemy full in my front, about 400 yards away. By this time I was joined by many stragglers of regiments from my right or Gilbert's Division, but no one from my left or Littler's. I was therefore apprehensive of my left flank, nor was I aware (from the obscurity created by the dust) whether the four Battalions of Avitabile's were repulsed, or indeed where they were. I resolved, therefore, to carry the village, which I soon did in gallant style with H.M.'s 50th and a detachment of the Honourable Company's 1st European Light Infantry under Captain Seaton and Lieutenant ——. The colours of H.M.'s 50th were gallantly borne forward by Brevet Captain Lovett and Lieutenant de Montmorency.

I was the first officer in the Head-quarters village of the Sikh army, Ferozeshuhur, and I planted one of the colours of H.M.'s 50th on the mud walls. A scene of awful slaughter here ensued, as the enemy would not lay down their arms. The village was full of richly caparisoned and magnificent horses, and there were camels around it innumerable.

After about half an hour the dust cleared away upon my left, and I saw that Avitabile's Battalions had been driven back by my charge, but Littler's Division had made no impression upon the enemy where he attacked. The victory appeared complete on my right; crowds of advancing, straggling officers and soldiers came up, and I resolved again to push forward. The evening was fast closing, but before dark I carried the enemy's camp half a mile beyond the village, and endeavoured to collect and form the stragglers upon H.M.'s 50th—amounting, I conceive, to near 3000 men. For the first hour, so excited were the men, I could make no formation, which I little regarded at the moment, expecting every instant to hear the victorious army upon my right. Not doing so, on the contrary, hearing the enemy in force close to my front and right (it was very dark), I saw at once I had pushed the victory far beyond [the ground held by our army], and that my position was critical in the extreme. I therefore made a vigorous and determined exertion to establish a formation, and I got the 24th Regiment Native Infantry—one of my own Division—in line upon my right under Major Bird, and about 150 of the 1st European Light Infantry under Captain Seaton, and proceeded to form the whole in a semicircle in front of the enemy's camp, my flank being well refused towards the village. Scarcely was this first formation effected, when the enemy made rather a sharp attack upon my right and drove back the formed troops. The darkness prevented the enemy continuing his success, and the noise and clamour of my troops in the endeavour to form indicated that I still held my ground. Thus I was compelled to reoccupy my right and contract the circle of formation. In this arduous duty I (and the Service still more so) was deeply indebted to Major Hull of the 16th Grenadiers, who, after he received a wound of which he died in a few hours, continued to do his duty, and aid me beyond my expression under a murderous fire of musketry, grape, round shot, and grisaille.

I at length got all the stragglers, consisting of some of H.M.'s 9th Regiment under Major Barwell,

The 19th Grenadiers Native Infantry

„ 24th Regiment   „   „
„ 28th   „   „   „
„ 73rd   „   „   „

and many others, upon the 50th, which was well in hand.

The moon arose, and the night was as bright as day. The enemy soon discovered the weakness and isolation of my force, and gradually closed in upon me, keeping up a most destructive fire. My

A.A.G. and Q.M.G. were both wounded, their horses killed—every officer and soldier dead-tired, so that many were killed fast asleep, both officers and men. I was fully aware of the importance of my post, in the very centre of and beyond the enemy's entrenched position, and although I could hear nothing of our army or see any bivouac fires, I resolved to maintain myself to the last. The loss, however, became every moment more heavy, and officers and soldiers were restless and sensible of their critically advanced position. The enemy got a gun to bear directly on my rear; my course was decided for me, and I at once saw indications of the impossibility of maintaining myself any longer.

It was now three o'clock in the morning. To withdraw without being compromised was a most perilous operation, for I was surrounded, while the enemy were shouting and cheering, beating up troops, and calling out to us in French and English, as well as Hindoostani, that we were in their power. I therefore feigned to attack, opened a fire and under the smoke quietly drew off, H.M.'s 50th leading. For the last arrangement, this was my reason—if I were opposed, the 50th would charge through such opposition; if pressed on my rear and the native troops rushed past me, I then had a rear-guard of H.M.'s troops which I could depend on. The enemy never discovered my retrograde movement until I was out of his power.

I then marched straight, leaving Ferozeshuhur to my left and continuing my route (guided by the

moon and the dead soldiers on the line by which
I advanced).   I soon fell in with a vedette, and,
concluding all was right and seeing a bivouac fire,
regarded it as the picquet of cavalry from which
he was posted.   Upon reaching the fire, I found it
belonged to the wounded men of H.M.'s 62nd·
Regiment and others, under some surgeons, who
knew nothing whatever of our army.   It was pre-
sumptuously urged upon me by several officers, who
ought to have thought before they spoke, to move
on Ferozepore.   My answer was decided enough.
" The Commander-in-Chief with his army is not far
from us, meditating an attack as soon as it is daylight, and find him I will if in h—ll, where I will join
him, rather than make one retrograde step till I
have ascertained some fact."   At the moment a
large flame mounted up, as if soldiers were lighting
a large fire.   I exclaimed, " There's my point, friend
or foe."

In about three-quarters of a mile I reached the
fire, the village of Misreewalla, where I found a
Brigade of Cavalry, some Irregular Horse, some
Horse Artillery, and two or three thousand stragglers
of every Regiment in the army.   I halted my people
and got hold of some spirits, which I issued to my
gallant 50th and all the Europeans.   Soon after I
reached Misreewalla I met Captain Lumley, A.A.G.
of the Army and at the head of the Department
(General Lumley being sick, and Major Grant
desperately wounded at Moodkee).   I was delighted
to see him, concluding he came direct from the

Commander-in-Chief. He said, "Sir Harry Smith, you are the very man I am looking for. As senior officer of the Adjutant-General's department, I order you to collect every soldier and march to Feroze-pore." I said, "Do you come direct from the Com-mander-in-Chief, with *such an order?* If you do, I can find him, for, by G——, I'll take no such order from any man on earth but from his own mouth. Where is he?" "I don't know, but these in my official [position] are the orders." "D—— the orders, if not the Commander-in-Chief's. I'll give my own orders, and take none of that retrograde sort from any Staff officer on earth. But why to Ferozepore? What's the matter?" "Oh, the army has been beaten, but we can buy the Sikh soldiers." "What!" says I, "have we taken no guns?" "Oh yes," he says, "fifty or sixty." "Thank you," I said; "I see my way, and want no orders." Turning round to my A.G., Captain Lugard, I said, "Now get hold of every officer and make him fall in his men."

At this moment Captain Christie, in command of an irregular Corps of Horse, a most excellent officer, came up and said he knew the direction the Commander-in-Chief was in and could point it out. I was delighted, and I marched off every man able to move to join Sir Hugh Gough, sending forward my wounded A.G. to report my whereabouts and what troops I had with me. The Commander-in-Chief was as delighted to hear of me and my troops as I was to find His Excellency. His orders were to move up in support of the attack which I well and

truly anticipated he meditated, when to my astonishment I saw the village of Ferozeshuhur full in my
front two miles distant, the very post I had carried
and occupied the night before, and from which, after
having held it until three o'clock that morning, I
was compelled to withdraw, or I should have
remained there nearly by myself.*

The attack was made on the part of the enemy's
camp he still held, namely, his right, which had
repulsed Littler's attack on the afternoon of the 21st.
It was now carried without a check. The 1st Brigade
of my Division, especially H.M.'s 31st Regiment,
greatly distinguished itself and suffered severely.

Scarcely was the victory of the 21st and 22nd
December over, when a fresh body of the enemy

---

* Sir Harry Smith's capture of the village of Ferozeshah and his
retention of it during the night were vaguely referred to in Sir H.
Gough's dispatch in these terms : "I now brought up Major-General
Sir Harry Smith's Division, and he captured and long retained
another point of the position." On this circumstance General Sir
James Kempt, in a letter to Sir Harry Smith dated "5th April, 1846,"
makes the following comment, which I give for what it may be
worth :—

"Sir H. Gough does not in his public Dispatches of the action
mention your carrying the village of Ferozeshah, or allude to the
difficulty in which you were placed, and my *first* impression was that
he had written the Dispatch before he received your Report. But as
Gilbert in his Report of the proceedings of his Division (which has
been published in India) says that after driving the enemy from their
position opposed to him, he was induced (from circumstances which
he mentions) to withdraw from the position they had so gallantly won
and to take up a position *under instructions* 400 yards in the rear,
where he bivouacked for the night—*this*, and Littler having also
withdrawn on your left, fully accounts for the unprotected state in
which you were left after carrying the village. But Sir H. Gough
could not mention you in the way which your service deserved in the
public Dispatch without telling the whole truth, and letting the public
know how miserably the thing was managed."

(which had been watching Ferozepore or threatening an attack if the garrison was withdrawn, and
had been deluded through Littler's very judiciously
leaving his camp standing) came vaunting upon the
left of our line and opened a fierce cannonade upon
us, literally within what had been their own camp
and entrenchments. The ammunition for our guns
was fully expended, and our troops were literally
exhausted, and we could not attack what would have
been an easy prey under other circumstances. The
whole of the enemy withdrew and recrossed the
Sutlej unmolested, for our troops were in no condition to pursue. Our numerous wounded required
to be collected, our stores to be brought up, our
troops to be refreshed.

From the march of the troops from Umbala and
Loodiana upon Busseean, our men had fought three
actions, the battles of Moodkee, Ferozeshuhur, and
that of the 22nd December, gained three victories,
and endured great fatigue of marching and privations, especially of what is so important to the native
troops, water.* In a day or two the whole were

---

* Colonel T. Bunbury writes of the battle of Ferozeshah : "Everybody was so famished with hunger that Sir H. Smith, hearing that
(one of our officers had secured a lamb), sent to beg of us a mutton
chop. But he was too late. The sheep had been slaughtered, cooked,
and devoured" (*Reminiscences of a Veteran*, iii. p. 289).

The same story is told in a letter of a private soldier, dated
"January 5th, 1846" (printed in the *Cambridge Chronicle*, 25th April,
1846): "The Governor-General, the Commander-in-Chief, the General
of Division, the A.D.C., and the whole of the staff—with this one
exception, they rode and we marched—fared the same as ourselves—
without food, without water." The same writer relates, "General
Smith has command of the 1st Division. He exposed himself very

fresh, and we moved forward on the line the enemy had withdrawn by. The 1st Division was on the right of the army, and subsequently Brigadier Cureton's Brigade of Cavalry (two troops of Horse Artillery, H.M.'s 16th Lancers, 3rd Light Cavalry, and a corps of Irregular Horse under a Captain Hill) were posted again to my right and under my command. My outposts were opposite the enemy. At Sobraon, which afterwards became so renowned, the enemy threw over a bridge and had a ford near it; they ably constructed *têtes du pont*, and showed an intention to cross. To do so was an act of madness which could not be contemplated by any reasoning faculties, although ultimately demonstrated.

It appeared to me that our army was not posted where it ought to be, and I strongly recommended to the Commander-in-Chief to move up the left bank of the Sutlej, so that his centre should be opposite Sobraon, and his left be kept in direct communication with Ferozepore by an intermediate corps under the command of Sir John Grey, which could also watch the reputed fords and ferries on that part of the river on his front,—the right of the army,

much, too much in fact, for when the whole of the men were lying down to escape the shower of shot, the gallant General remained on his horse in front of the line, exhorting the men to lie still as they could not get up and live, and when they charged the guns, he led them in truly gallant style. His escape was truly miraculous." "The gallant General Smith has just passed—he looks somewhat thinner, and no wonder, for he has a very busy time of it. I hope to God he will come off unscathed, and may he receive the reward of his services from his sovereign."

namely, my command, Cureton's Cavalry and my own Division, to be posted opposite the ford and ferry of Hurreekee. The Commander-in-Chief called for the distribution of the army as I proposed, which I gave in, accompanied by an explanatory letter to His Excellency. In forty-eight hours it was adopted, and the army moved into the celebrated position opposite Sobraon. Here the enemy constructed a bridge of boats and pushed over his whole army, most strongly fortifying and entrenching himself on the left side of the river, a movement unparalleled in the history of war from time immemorial. It may be asked, Why was he permitted? Answer, Because we could not help ourselves. The right or enemy's bank was high and favourable for him in every way, and the bridge was judiciously thrown over at a bend of the river; hence the natural formation presented a formidable *tête du pont*, which the enemy entrenched and filled with cannon of the heaviest calibre. We could not contend with him, our heavy guns not having arrived, and the left bank of the river being nearly perfectly flat. Thus he could cross, and did, unmolested, and duly pushed his outposts forward and ours back, until it was deemed necessary to counter-fortify our camp in his front, which was done by bringing some of the heavy guns from Ferozepore. My Division and command being well to the right, I had a line of outposts from the confluence of the Beas and the Sutlej to within a mile of the enemy's entrenchments at Sobraon.

CHAPTER XLIV.

SIR HARRY SMITH DETACHED FROM THE MAIN ARMY
—HE REDUCES THE FORTRESSES OF FUTTEYGHUR
AND DHURMCOTE—COMBINES WITH COLONEL
PHILLIPS AT JUGRAON, AND AFTER CHANGING
HIS ROUTE TO LOODIANA ENCOUNTERS THE
ENEMY AT BUDOWAL, AND LOSES SOME PART OF
HIS BAGGAGE—HE RELIEVES LOODIANA, AND,
BEING REINFORCED AND THE ENEMY HAVING RE-
TREATED, OCCUPIES HIS POSITION AT BUDOWAL.

ON the 16th January the Commander-in-Chief sent
for me, and told me the Governor-General was
desirous that the small fortress of Futteyghur and
the larger one of Dhurmcote, both slightly garrisoned
by the enemy, should be reduced, as under their
cover he was drawing supplies from the left bank
and crossing them over. His Excellency said, "A
Brigade will be sufficient to send, the 3rd Light
Cavalry and some Irregular Horse; but who will
you send?" I replied I had rather go myself. Sir
Hugh Gough was much pleased with my offering to
do so, for I subsequently ascertained it was the
Governor-General's desire I should be ordered. The
Commander-in-Chief said, "When will you march?

there is no hurry." I said, "Soon after this time to-morrow I shall be writing my report that I have reduced them both." He laughed and said, "Why, the distance to Dhurmcote is twenty-six miles from your right." I replied, "I know that; still, what I say shall be, provided that the officer and the Engineers supply me in time with the powder I want to blow in the gates in the case of necessity." I said to myself, "However, powder or no powder, I march."

When I reached camp, I found that, without my knowledge, the Commissariat had sent almost all the tent elephants and other transport into Ferozepore for provisions; some, however, arrived in the night. These provisions I laid hold of, and I collected every animal in camp for the use of the troops ordered to move, and I marched two hours before daylight. On my approach Futteyghur was abandoned, and I pushed on to Dhurmcote, which I reached by two o'clock in the afternoon, and found it occupied, but without any gun deserving the name of cannon. I invested it immediately with the 3rd Light Cavalry and Irregulars (the infantry not being yet up), and summoned the garrison to surrender. It received my flag of truce, and the leader or *killadar* came out and made a variety of stipulations, which I cut short by saying, "You may march out with your arms, ground them on the glacis, and I will endeavour to secure all hands six weeks' pay. Go back to the fort. I give you 20 minutes to consider, after which I shall make no

terms, but open my cannon upon you." I waited
25 minutes, and no communication being made,
although I rode close to the works myself and
beckoned to them, I ordered our 9-pounders and
a howitzer to open a few shots. The Sikh flag was
then hauled down, and a white one hoisted. I
allowed the garrison to march out and lay down
their arms as prisoners of war, and as the Infantry
arrived, I immediately occupied the fortress and
commenced improving its defences. I was thus
able to report, as I had promised, to my Commander-in-Chief.

I had orders to reconnoitre the country around
to ascertain its resources and the feeling of amity
or hostility of the neighbourhood. Near me the
villages were Mussulman and well disposed. Dhurmcote itself belonged to a Sirdar in the enemy's camp,
but the people, when the hand of power was manifested, were civil and brought me all the supplies I
required.

Having made so long a march on the 17th and
being desirous to put the fortress in a state of
defence, I had resolved to halt on the 18th, when I
received a communication to say that on the 19th
I should receive a reinforcement of two troops of
Horse Artillery (viz. 12 guns), H.M.'s 16th Lancers,
and the remainder of the corps of Irregular Horse
under Brigadier Cureton. Upon these reaching me,
I should have a Brigade of Cavalry, one of Infantry,
and 18 guns. With this force I was to move on
to Jugraon, thence open a communication with

Busseean, the line nine miles to the interior of Jugraon, on which our enormous battering train, stores, treasure, and ammunition, covering an extent of ten miles of road, was marching. I was informed that I might get hold of H.M.'s 53rd Regiment at Busseean, and if so, they were to obey my orders. Under any circumstances, I was to open a communication with Loodiana (distant from Jugraon, by the direct roads *via* the little fortress of Budowal, twenty-five or twenty-six miles), it being threatened by Runjoor Singh's army of 50 guns and 30,000 men, which had crossed at Philour by boats and was in position at Baranhara, seven miles from Loodiana. The force at Loodiana, under Lieutenant-Colonel Godby, 30th Regiment N.I., consisted of one Regiment, the 5th Native Cavalry, the 30th and 36th Sermoor and Nusseeree Battalions, and four guns Horse Artillery.

On the 19th I marched the Infantry to Koharee, halfway to Jugraon, which divided the distance, and I left orders at Dhurmcote for Colonel Cureton to move on the 20th to Jugraon, where he was to join me, which was effected accordingly. On reaching Jugraon, I received a report from Lieutenant-Colonel Phillips, commanding H.M.'s 53rd Regiment, to whom I had sent orders to Busseean to move on without delay to Jugraon. He begged a day's halt, representing that his transport was done. I had opened a communication with Colonel Godby commanding at Loodiana. I received the most pressing and urgent reasons for my joining him, and I was equally urged by the Governor-General and the Commander-in-Chief to move on to save Loodiana and drive back the invaders under Runjoor Singh and the Rajah of Ladwa. Hence the necessity to concentrate every soldier I could lay my hands on for the purpose. I therefore sent Lieutenant Smith of the Engineers over from Jugraon to Busseean, with a written order for Colonel Phillips to march immediately—provided it were possible. He marched, and the 16th Lancers and guns had reached me.

I here annex a narrative written at the Period.

"When I reached Jugraon on the 20th January, all accounts agreed that the enemy was still at Baranhara, thirty miles from me, between Loodiana and Philour, a fortress of his on the right bank of the Sutlej, under cover of which he had crossed and perfected his invasion; but that he had also occupied with a small garrison the fortress of Budowal, which had been abandoned by the troops of a chief in amity with us, and that he had near it some two or three hundred Horse. He was also known to possess a fortress called Gungrana, regarded as very strong, to my right (that is, its parallel) about ten miles from Budowal into our interior, where there was also Cavalry.

"I got hold of the 53rd Regiment on the evening of the 20th, the day I arrived at Jugraon. My force therefore stood thus: eighteen guns, one Regiment of English Cavalry (16th Lancers), one Regiment of Native Light Cavalry, one Regiment of Irregular Horse, two Regiments of British Infantry (H.M.'s 31st and 53rd), 250 convalescents, and two very weak Regiments of Native Infantry (the 24th and 47th). At Jugraon was a very tenable fortress occupied by the troops of a Rajah considered to be friendly, but in time of war and doubtful success friendship is precarious. I therefore occupied the fortress (or rather its citadel) by two Companies of my Native Infantry, and resolved as soon as the moon was up, viz. at half-past twelve, to march on Loodiana, leaving Budowal to my right, *i.e.* by the best, shortest, and direct road, and I ordered all baggage which consisted of *wheel-carriage* transport, to remain behind under the protection of the fort of Jugraon.

"Meanwhile, every two hours I dispatched instructions of these my intentions to the officer who commanded at Loodiana, whom I ordered to meet me with his force of four Horse Artillery guns, an excellent and strong Regiment of Native Cavalry, and four good and fresh Regiments of Native Infantry. All the while I believed the enemy's force to be at Baranhara, thirty miles from me, but only seven from Loodiana. My order of march was in writing, also my instructions for the baggage and detail of its guards, and I read them on the afternoon of the 20th to all the officers in command. I marched in the most regular order at the hour appointed, with the desire to leave Budowal to my right, and not move by the interior line, *i.e.* between Gungrana and Budowal, two fortresses in the occupation of the enemy, distant only four miles from *both* my flanks, so that my march would be subject to double interruption. The large force nearly equal to mine was to have approached me from Loodiana, within three miles of Budowal on its own side, on a strong hill and position I well knew of, Sonnact. The natives here were most hostile, and it is an axiom, and a very just one, in the conduct of war, 'distant combinations are not to be relied on.' Hence, although I calculated upon this combination, I did not rely upon it, but adopted my own measures for advance with caution and circumspection, relying alone on my own resources.

"When I had marched some sixteen or eighteen miles in the most perfect order of advance to within two miles of Budowal, as day dawned, I received a communication from Colonel Godby that the enemy had marched from Baranhara and was encamped around Budowal with his whole force, and from some villagers I ascertained that the enemy had received considerable reinforcements. I found myself thus close upon him, and he in force. I had one of two alternatives, viz. to move on, leaving Budowal to my right and most probably the moving Sikh army on my left—in other words, to force my passage ; or to leave Budowal to my left and make a *détour* towards Gungrana. To return to Jugraon I never contemplated, which would have exposed Colonel Godby as previously stated. The stake at issue was too great, hence I changed my order of march and proceeded with every precaution, leaving the

fort of Budowal on my *left*, and with my troops in
order of battle by wheeling into line to their left if
required. Several times during our night march we
had observed rockets firing, as if for signals, and at
broad daylight we discovered the enemy preparing
to interrupt my newly adopted line of march, though
his most ample preparation, as I afterwards discovered, had been made for my reception on the
more direct road by which I had originally intended
to move, and upwards of forty pieces of cannon
pointed there, so perfect was his information.

" So soon as the enemy had discovered that I had
changed my line of march for the relief of Loodiana,
he immediately attempted to interrupt my force by
moving parallel to my column through a line of
villages which afforded him cover and protection,
and by providing him with good roads facilitated
his march, while I was compelled to move in order
of battle over ploughed fields of deep sand. Hence
the head of the enemy's column, principally a large
body of cavalry, rapidly outflanked me a mile at
least, and his rear of guns and infantry equally so.
With great celerity he brought to bear on my
troops a considerable number of guns of very heavy
metal. The cavalry moved parallel with the enemy,
and protected from the fire of his guns by a low
ridge of sandhills. My eighteen guns I kept together close in rear of the cavalry, in order to open a
heavy fire on the enemy and to check his advance,
thereby attracting his attention, so soon as the fortunate moment which I saw approaching arrived.

"This fire, which I continued for some ten minutes, had a most auxiliary effect, creating slaughter and confusion in the enemy's ranks. The enemy's cannonade upon the column of Infantry had been previously to this furious. I had reinforced the baggage guard, and sent orders that it should close up and keep well on the reverse flank and as much ahead as possible. A few round shot ricocheting among the camels, many of the drivers abandoned their animals, and our own followers and the hostile villages in the neighbourhood plundered a part of the baggage : little of it fell into the hands of the enemy's soldiers.

"As the column moved on under this cannonade, which was especially furious upon the rear of the Infantry, the enemy, with a dexterity and quickness not to be exceeded, formed a line of seven battalions directly across my rear, with guns in the intervals of battalions, for the purpose of attacking *my* column with *his* line. This was a very able and well-executed move, which rendered my position critical and demanded nerve and decision to evade the coming storm. I would willingly have attacked this line, and I formed up a part of the 31st Regiment as a base, when so deep was the sand and so fatigued were my men, I was compelled to abandon the project. I therefore, under this fierce cannonade, changed front on the centre of the 31st Regiment and of the 53rd by what is a difficult move on parade even—a countermarch on the centre by wings. Then became conspicuous the majesty of discipline and bravery. This move was executed as accurately as at a review.

" My Native Regiments were very steady, but I now directed the Infantry to march on Loodiana in échelon of Battalions, ready to receive the word ' Halt, Front' (when they would thus confront the enemy's line if he advanced), and the Cavalry to move in échelon of squadrons, the two arms mutually supporting, the guns in rear of the Cavalry. The whole were moving most correctly and the movement was so steady that the enemy, notwithstanding his overwhelming force, did not attack, but stood amazed, as it were, fearing to quit his stronghold of Budowal, and aware that the junction of my force with that of Loodiana was about to be accomplished.

" I was astonished, I admit, at hearing nothing from Colonel Godby. I had reason to hope some of my two-hourly dispatches had reached him, and when at daylight I changed the direction of my march on account of the enemy having anticipated me, I sent Lieutenant Holmes with a party of Irregulars, cautioning him to look as sharp to his right on account of Gungrana as to his left. I soon after sent off Lieutenant Swetenham of the 16th Lancers, and a short time later Lieutenant Band Smith of the Engineers. All these officers reached their destination. From the repeated and urgent requests made by Colonel Godby that I should advance to his relief, from *his then knowledge* that the enemy had anticipated me, I had every reason (supposing he had secured no *positive information* of

my march from Jugraon or my orders) to expect
some co-operation or demonstration in my support,
as I moved towards him.   On the contrary, my
first messenger found his troops only turning out, he
having only just received my instructions, and his
force did not move off until the firing had commenced, about half-past seven or eight, at a distance
of between eight and nine miles—another illustration of the truth of the axiom, 'distant combinations
are not to be relied on.'   The natural expectation,
too, of Colonel Godby's move towards me cramped
my manœuvres, for had I swerved from the line on
which I expected his co-operation, his force would
have been compromised and in the power of the
enemy's weighty attack.   The reinforcement of four
guns, a strong and fresh Regiment of Cavalry, and
four Regiments of fresh Infantry is a powerful reinforcement to a large army ; to me it was nearly one-
half of the whole.   Decision, coolness, and determination effected the junction and relief of Loodiana,
while it cut off the enemy from his line of communication with Philour, under which fortress he had
crossed the Sutlej.

"A want of water in a position near the enemy
compelled me to encamp in front of Loodiana, but
I established my outposts close upon him, and
frequently made strong patrols up to his position,
intending, if he dared attempt to interrupt our line
of communication *viâ* Busseean (which I did not,
although I so closely watched him, anticipate, so
close was I upon him, and the fortress of Jugraon

before him), to move on, *coûte que coûte*, and attack
under any circumstances.   Indeed, my combined
force would well have enabled me to do so, had I
come up with him when on the march and out of his
entrenchments.

   " Meanwhile the Commander-in-Chief, with great
foresight and judgment, ordered the second Brigade
of my Division, under Brigadier Wheeler, a Regiment
of Native Cavalry, the Body Guard, 400 strong, and
four guns Horse Artillery, to move from Hurreekee
viâ Dhurmcote and Jugraon to join me, while a
second Brigade under Brigadier Taylor was ordered
in support to Dhurmcote, and the Shekawuttee
Brigade was moving on Jugraon.   Thus the enemy's
position at Budowal was menaced on three points.

   " He expected considerable reinforcements *viâ*
the Tulwun Ghaut, eight miles lower down the
Sutlej than Philour. He therefore, again with
judgment, abandoned his position of Budowal, in
which I was making vigorous preparations to attack
him, and fell back upon the reinforcement of 12
guns and 4000 of Regular Infantry of Avitabile's
Corps and a large addition of Cavalry.   This movement, however, must have been premeditated, for
the stores of ammunition and his fortifications around
the ford were not the work of a day. I immediately
occupied the enemy's position at Budowal, and
as rapidly as possible concentrated my force coming
from Dhurmcote and Busseean (viz. : Wheeler's
from the former, and the Shekawuttee from the
latter), while I dispensed with the service of Brigadier

Taylor's Brigade in reserve at Dhurmcote, feeling myself now sufficiently strong, and being aware of the importance of Infantry to the Commander-in-Chief, who to reinforce me had considerably reduced his own means in the immediate front of the main army of the Sikhs. This is the *précis* of the campaign leading to the Battle of Aliwal, and from this period taken up in my report of that glorious battle, herewith annexed." *

* Before sending the dispatch given in the next chapter, Sir Harry wrote in pencil from the field of battle the following short note to the Commander-in-Chief :—

" Bank of the Sutlej, 28th January.

"Hearing the enemy had received a reinforcement yesterday of twelve guns, and 4000 men last night, I moved my troops at daylight this morning to attack. I think I have taken every gun he had and driven him from the river. My guns are now battering him from the opposite bank. He came out to fight me. I expect fifty guns are on the field at least. My loss I hope not great. The Cavalry charged several times, both black and white, like soldiers, and infantry vied with each other in bravery. To the God of victory we are all indebted. God bless you, dear Sir Hugh. My staff all right. Mackeson and Cunningham, of the Political Department, bore heavily on some villages. The enemy required all I could do with such brave fellows to teach him to swim.

" H. G. SMITH,
" Major-General."

CHAPTER XLV.

THE BATTLES OF ALIWAL AND SOBRAON—END OF SIR HARRY SMITH'S AUTOBIOGRAPHY.

Major-General Sir Harry Smith, K.C.B., to the Adjutant-General of the Army.

"Camp, Field of the Battle of Aliwal, Jan. 30, 1846.

"SIR,

"My despatches to his Excellency the Commander-in-Chief of the 23rd * instant, will have put his Excellency in possession of the position of the force under my command, after having formed a junction with the troops at Loodiana, hemmed in by a formidable body of the Sikh army under Runjoor Singh and the Rajah of Ladwa. The enemy strongly entrenched himself around the little fort of Budhowal by breastworks and 'abattis,' which he precipitately abandoned on the night of the 22nd instant (retiring, as it were, upon the ford of Tulwun), having ordered all the boats which were opposite Philour to that Ghat. This movement he effected during the night, and, by making a considerable détour, placed himself at a distance of ten miles, and consequently out of my reach. I could, therefore, only push forward my cavalry as soon as I had ascertained he had marched during the night, and I occupied immediately his vacated position. It appeared

* Not received by the Secret Committee.

subsequently he had no intention of recrossing the Sutlej, but moved down to the Ghat of Tulwun (being cut off from that of Philour, by the position my force occupied after its relief of Loodiana), for the purpose of protecting the passage of a very considerable reinforcement of twelve guns and 4000 of the regular, or ' Aieen' troops, called Avitabile's battalion, entrenching himself strongly in a semicircle, his flanks resting on a river, his position covered with from forty to fifty guns (generally of large calibre), howitzers, and mortars. The reinforcement crossed during the night of the 27th instant, and encamped to the right of the main army.

"Meanwhile, his Excellency the Commander-in-Chief, with that foresight and judgment which mark the able general, had reinforced me by a considerable addition to my cavalry, some guns, and the 2nd brigade of my own Division, under Brigadier Wheeler, C.B. This reinforcement reached me on the 26th, and I had intended the next morning to move upon the enemy in his entrenchments, but the troops required one day's rest after the long marches Brigadier Wheeler had made.

" I have now the honour to lay before you the operations of my united forces on the morning of the eventful 28th January, for his Excellency's information. The body of troops under my command having been increased, it became necessary so to organize and brigade them as to render them manageable in action. The cavalry under the command of Brigadier Cureton, and horse artillery under Major Lawrenson, were put into two brigades ; the one under Brigadier MacDowell, C.B., and the other under Brigadier Stedman. The 1st Division as it stood, two brigades :—Her Majesty's 53rd and 30th Native Infantry, under Brigadier Wilson, of the latter corps;—the 36th Native Infantry, and Nusseree battalion, under Brigadier Godby ;—and the Shekawattee brigade under Major

Forster. The Sirmoor battalion I attached to Brigadier Wheeler's brigade of the 1st division ; the 42nd Native Infantry having been left at head-quarters.

"At daylight on the 28th, my order of advance was—the Cavalry in front, in contiguous columns of squadrons of regiments, two troops of horse artillery in the interval of brigades ; the infantry in contiguous columns of brigades at intervals of deploying distance ; artillery in the intervals, followed by two 8-inch howitzers on travelling carriages, brought into the field from the fort of Loodiana by the indefatigable exertions of Lieutenant-Colonel Lane, Horse Artillery ; Brigadier Godby's brigade, which I had marched out from Loodiana the previous evening, on the right ; the Shekawattee infantry on the left ; the 4th Irregular Cavalry considerably to the right, for the purpose of sweeping the banks of the wet nullah on my right, and preventing any of the enemy's horse attempting an inroad towards Loodiana, or any attempt upon the baggage assembled round the fort of Budhowal.

"In this order the troops moved forward towards the enemy, a distance of six miles, the advance conducted by Captain Waugh, 16th Lancers, the Deputy Assistant Quarter-Master of Cavalry, Major Bradford, of the 1st Cavalry, and Lieutenant Strachey of the Engineers, who had been jointly employed in the conduct of patroles up to the enemy's position, and for the purpose of reporting upon the facility and point of approach. Previously to the march of the troops it had been intimated to me by Major Mackeson, that the information by spies led to the belief the enemy would move somewhere at daylight, either on Jugraon, my position of Budhowal, or Loodiana. On a near approach to his outposts, this rumour was confirmed by a spy, who had just left the camp, saying the Sikh army was actually in march towards Jugraon. My advance was steady ; my troops well in hand ; and if he had anticipated me on the Jugraon road, I could have fallen upon his centre with advantage.

"From the tops of the houses of the village of Poorein, I had a distant view of the enemy. He was in motion and appeared directly opposite my front on a ridge, of which the village of Aliwal may be regarded as the centre. His left appeared still to occupy its ground in the circular entrenchment; his right was brought forward and occupied the ridge. I immediately deployed the cavalry into line, and moved on. As I neared the enemy, the ground became most favourable for the troops to manœuvre, being open and hard grass land. I ordered the cavalry to take ground to the right and left by brigades; thus displaying the heads of the infantry columns; and, as they reached the hard ground, I directed them to deploy into line. Brigadier Godby's brigade was in direct échellon to the rear of the right; the Shekawattee infantry in like manner to the rear of my left; the cavalry in direct échellon on, and well to the rear of, both flanks of the infantry; the artillery massed on the right and centre and left. After deployment, I observed the enemy's left to outflank me, I therefore broke into open column and took ground to my right. When I had gained sufficient ground, the troops wheeled into line. There was no dust, the sun shone brightly. These manœuvres were performed with the celerity and precision of the most correct field day. The glistening of the bayonets and swords of this order of battle was most imposing; and the line advanced. Scarcely had it moved 150 yards, when, at ten o'clock, the enemy opened a fierce cannonade from his whole line. At first his balls fell short, but quickly reached us. Thus upon him, and capable of better ascertaining his position, I was compelled to halt the line, though under fire, for a few moments, until I ascertained that, by bringing up my right and carrying the village of Aliwal, I could with great effect precipitate myself upon his left and centre. I therefore quickly brought up Brigadier Godby's brigade ; and, with it, and the 1st brigade under Brigadier Hicks, made a rapid and noble charge, carried the village, and two guns of large calibre. The line I ordered to advance,—Her Majesty's 31st Foot and the native regiments contending for the front ; and the battle became general. The enemy had a numerous body of cavalry on the heights to his left, and I ordered Brigadier Cureton to bring up the right brigade of cavalry, who, in the most gallant manner, dashed in among them and drove them back upon their infantry. Meanwhile a second gallant charge to my right was made by the light cavalry and the body-guard. The Sheka-wattee brigade was moved well to the right, in support of Brigadier Cureton, when I observed the enemy's encamp-ment and saw it was full of infantry : I immediately brought upon it Brigadier Godby's brigade, by changing front, and taking the enemy's infantry 'en reverse.' They drove them before them, and took some guns without a check.

"While these operations were going on upon the right, and the enemy's left flank was thus driven back, I occa-sionally observed the brigade under Brigadier Wheeler, an officer in whom I have the greatest confidence, charging and carrying guns and everything before it, again connect-ing his line, and moving on, in a manner which ably dis-played the coolness of the Brigadier and the gallantry of his irresistible brigade,—Her Majesty's 50th Foot, the 48th Native Infantry, and the Sirmoor battalion,—although the loss was, I regret to say, severe in the 50th. Upon the left, Brigadier Wilson, with Her Majesty's 53rd and the 30th Native Infantry equalled in celerity and regularity their comrades on the right ; and this brigade was opposed to the 'Aieen' troops, called Avitabile's, when the fight was fiercely raging.

"The enemy, well driven back on his left and centre,

endeavoured to hold his right to cover the passage of the river, and he strongly occupied the village of Bhoondree. I directed a squadron of the 16th Lancers, under Major Smyth and Captain Pearson, to charge a body to the right of a village, which they did in the most gallant and determined style, bearing everything before them, as a squadron under Captain Bere had previously done, going right through a square in the most intrepid manner with the deadly lance. This charge was accompanied by the 3rd Light Cavalry under Major Angelo, and as gallantly sustained. The largest gun upon the field, and seven others, were then captured, while the 53rd Regiment carried the village by the bayonet, and the 30th Native Infantry wheeled round to the rear in a most spirited manner. Lieut.-Col. Alexander's and Capt. Turton's troops of horse artillery, under Major Lawrenson, dashed among the flying infantry, committing great havoc, until about 800 or 1000 men rallied under the high bank of a nullah, and opened a heavy but ineffectual fire from below the bank. I immediately directed the 30th Native Infantry to charge them, which they were able to do upon their left flank, while in a line in rear of the village. This native corps nobly obeyed my orders and rushed among the Avitabile troops, driving them from under the bank and exposing them once more to a deadly fire of twelve guns within 300 yards. The destruction was very great, as may be supposed, from guns served as these were. Her Majesty's 53rd Regiment moved forward in support of the 30th Native Infantry, by the right of the village. The battle was won; our troops advancing with the most perfect order to the common focus—the passage of the river. The enemy, completely hemmed in, were flying from our fire, and precipitating themselves in disordered masses into the ford and boats, in the utmost confusion and consternation; our 8-inch howitzers soon began to play upon their boats, when the 'débris' of the Sikh army appeared upon the opposite and high bank of the river, flying in every direction, although a sort of line was attempted to countenance their retreat, until *all* our guns commenced a furious cannonade, when they quickly receded. Nine guns were on the river by the ford. It appears as if they had been unlimbered to cover the ford. These being loaded, were fired once upon our advance ; two others were sticking in the river, one of them we got out ; two were seen to sink in the quicksands ; two were dragged to the opposite bank and abandoned. These, and the one in the middle of the river, were gallantly spiked by Lieutenant Holmes, of the 11th Irregular Cavalry, and Gunner Scott, of the 1st troop 2nd brigade Horse Artillery, who rode into the stream, and crossed for the purpose, covered by our guns and light infantry.

"Thus ended the battle of Aliwal, one of the most glorious victories ever achieved in India, by the united efforts of Her Majesty's and the Honourable Company's troops. *Every gun* the enemy had fell into our hands, as I infer from his never opening one upon us from the opposite bank of the river, which is high and favourable for the purpose—fifty-two guns are now in the Ordnance Park ; two sank in the bed of the Sutlej ; and two were spiked on the opposite bank ; making a total of fifty-six pieces of cannon captured or destroyed.* Many jingalls which were attached to Avitabile's corps and which aided in the defence of the village of Bhoondree, have also been taken. The whole army of the enemy has been driven headlong over the difficult ford of a broad river ; his camp, baggage, stores of ammunition and of grain,— his all, in fact, wrested from him, by the repeated charges of cavalry and infantry, aided by the guns of Alexander,

---

* Eleven guns since ascertained to be sunk in the river, total sixty-seven ; thirty odd jingalls fell into our hands.

Turton, Lane, Mill, Boileau, and of the Shekawattee brigade, and by the 8-inch howitzers ;—our guns literally being constantly ahead of everything. The determined bravery of all was as conspicuous as noble. I am unwont to praise when praise is not merited ; and I here most unavowedly express my firm opinion and conviction, that no troops in any battle on record ever behaved more nobly ;—British and native, no distinction ; cavalry, all vying with H.M.'s 16th Lancers, and striving to head in the repeated charges. Our guns and gunners, officers and men, may be equalled, but cannot be excelled, by any artillery in the world. Throughout the day no hesitation —a bold and intrepid advance ;—and thus it is that our loss is comparatively small, though I deeply regret to say, severe. The enemy fought with much resolution ; they maintained frequent rencontres with our cavalry hand to hand. In one charge, upon infantry, of H.M.'s 16th Lancers, they threw away their muskets and came on with their swords and targets against the lance.

    •   •   •   •   •   •

"The fort of Goongrana has, subsequently to the battle, been evacuated, and I yesterday evening blew up the fort of Budhowal. I shall now blow up that of Noorpoor. A portion of the peasantry, viz. the Sikhs, appear less friendly to us, while the Mussulmans rejoice in being under our Government.

"I have, &c.,

"H. G. SMITH,

"*Major-General Commanding.*"

My loss during the 21st January was, of killed and wounded and sick taken, upwards of 200 men, but many of our wounded and exhausted Infantry were brought off in the Artillery carriages and by the noble exertions of H.M.'s 16th Lancers, who dismounted and put the sick and wounded upon their horses. My orders to the baggage guard (composed of 400 Irregular Horse, to which I afterwards added one squadron of Regular Native Cavalry) were only half obeyed, or our loss of baggage would have been next to nothing; but young soldiers are excited under a heavy cannonade and apprehend more of its deadly effect than I have ever seen the heaviest cannonade (not grape and canister) merit.

This short but most eventful campaign was one of great difficulty and embarrassment for the General (or myself). The enemy was concentrated, whilst my force was to accumulate contingent on a variety of combinations distant and doubtful.

The political importance of my position was extreme. All India was at gaze, and ready for anything. Our army—truth must out—most anxious, the enemy daringly and exultingly regarding himself invincible, as the *bold* and *most able* and energetic move of Runjoor Singh with his whole force throwing himself between my advance from Jugraon *via* Budowal to Loodiana most fully demonstrated. It is the most scientific move made during the war, whether made by accident or design, and had he known how to profit by the position he had so judiciously occupied, he would have obtained wonderful success. He should have attacked me with the vigour his French tutors would [have displayed, and] destroyed me, for his force compared to mine was *overwhelming;* then turned about upon the troops at Loodiana, beaten them, and sacked and burnt the city—when the gaze I speak of in India would have been one general blaze of revolt! Does the world which argues on my affair at Budowal suppose I was asleep, and had not in clear perspective a full view of the effect such success of the enemy would have had upon the general features and character of the war? It must be remembered that our battering train, an immense treasure, our ammunition, etc., etc., were not ten miles from me, occupying a line of road of ten miles in length.

The end was accomplished, viz. the battle of Aliwal and its results. In a few days after the victory I received from my Political Associate, Major Murchison, a very clever fellow, a long report, of which this is an extract: "I cannot help mentioning to you that the result of your decisive victory of the 28th has been the abandonment by the enemy of *all* his posts south of the Sutlej from Hurreekee upwards to Nunapoor Mackohoorvara, and the submission to our rule of a country yielding an annual revenue of upwards of twenty-five lacs of rupees. The post of the enemy at Sobraon is now the only one held by the Sikhs south of the Sutlej." And again, in a letter from Colonel Godby after he had crossed into the Jullundur with Brigadier Godby, "I have no doubt the battle of Aliwal will be esteemed in England as it deserves; it finished a most painful crisis both in India and in England, and its moral effect in Hindostan and the Punjaub was

2 N

greater than any other achievement of the war. In the Jullundur the natives speak of it as most unaccountable that the soldiers they thought invincible should be overthrown and driven into the river in two or three hours, and be seen scampering through the country before the people had heard of their defeat. The defeat was so cleanly and unquestionably done, that they ascribed it to supernatural intervention for the many atrocious crimes of the Sikhs, especially upon the oppressed followers of the true Prophet."

All men, especially Generals, reflect in times of peace and quiet upon their exertions, their enterprises, and the measures they adopted. Human life once extinct is in this world gone, and how gratifying it is under Divine Providence to feel that not a soldier under my command was wantonly, unnecessarily, or unscientifically sacrificed to his country! Had I adopted any other course at Budowal on the 21st of January than I pursued, had I not pushed the war entrusted to my conduct with vigour and effected a junction with the troops at Loodiana, they and the city would have fallen, and next our treasure, battering train, ammunition, etc., would have been captured or scattered and lost to the army; had I sustained a serious reverse, all India would have been in a blaze. I steered the course invariably pursued by my great master the Duke, never needlessly to risk your troops or fight a battle without an object. Hence the decisive victory of Aliwal and its wonderful results and important aid in repelling the Sikh army at Sobraon and seizing the capital of his vaunted glory.

Months have now passed since I conducted these operations,* and although reflection as a guide for the future prompts me to find fault with any movement or march, I cannot, but with the blessing of the Almighty, I say, " Results even cannot dictate to me—if you had done this or that, it would have been better."

Having disposed of my captured cannon † (I sent forty-seven to the fortress of Loodiana, and took five with me to Head-quarters, the most beautiful guns imaginable, which will, I believe, be placed in St. James's Park, London), provided for my sick and wounded, replenished my ammunition and stores, given over to Brigadier Wheeler the troops he was to command on the Upper Sutlej, and furnished him and the Political Agent, Major Murchison, with my views of their operations as a guide, I marched on the morning of the 3rd February on my route back to the Commander-in-Chief.

I had with me three troops Horse Artillery, two 8-inch howitzers, the 16th Lancers, the 3rd and 5th Light Cavalry, one corps of Irregular Horse, H.M.'s 31st, 50th, and 53rd Regiments, and 200

---

* He wrote these lines in September, 1846.

† No one but those who have encountered it, can be aware of the difficulty there is in disposing of the stores and captured guns of your enemy.   I had 52 to move, and most of their own draught animals had been killed in action or shot by the victors.   The country yields no resources in aid, thus I had to use the transport of my own 32 guns to send on to Loodiana 47 of the enemy's, and this delayed my return to Headquarters three days.—H. G. S.

convalescents, and of Native Infantry the 47th Regiment, and the Sermoor and Nusseeree Battalions. The rest of my Aliwal heroes remained with Wheeler.

I reached the right of the army on the 7th, and was received by the Commander-in-Chief with a burst of enthusiastic welcome * to be equalled only by that of the army at large. His Excellency addressed each Corps in terms as gratifying to them as to me, and I, Staff, Commanding Officers of Corps, Prince Waldemar,† etc., dined with the Commander-in-Chief, who again, in a speech when drinking our healths, bestowed upon us every encomium, and attached the utmost importance to the great cause—our signal victory. The Governor-General was at Ferozepore.

The ground I had been directed to occupy being

* A trooper in the 16th Lancers, named Eaton, writing on 2nd Feb., 1846, of the battle of Aliwal, says, "As soon as the Commander-in-Chief received the dispatches, which he did on horseback while reconnoitring, he leaped from his horse and gave three cheers, a salute of eighteen guns was fired, and the line gave three hearty cheers for us, their gallant comrades, as they called us." The same writer gives a very characteristic picture of Sir Harry Smith : "The General told us that when our regiment was in Lahore in 1837, the King thought us all gentlemen, but had he seen us on that day, he would have proclaimed us all devils, 'for you charged their ranks more like them than anything else.' As he left us we saw tears in the poor old man's eyes, and he said, 'God bless you, my brave boys ; I love you.'"—See *Cambridge Independent Press*, 4th April, 1846.

Of the above letter Professor Sedgwick wrote, "Excepting Harry Smith's dispatch, which nothing can reach, it is one of the most soul-stirring letters that has come from India."—*Life of Sedgwick*, ii. p. 102.

† Prince Waldemar of Prussia, travelling as Count Ravensburg, was present with his suite at the battles of Moodkee, Ferozeshah, Aliwal, and Sobraon.

filthy to excess, I begged to move my position, which I was permitted to do on the 8th. On this day the Governor-General arrived in camp. He sent for me, and received me with all the warmth of a long-standing friendship, and bestowed personally upon me all the praises he had so lavishly given me in his General Orders.

On the 9th, all Generals of Divisions, Brigadiers, and Heads of Departments were summoned in the afternoon to attend in the Commander-in-Chief's tent. I pretty clearly guessed the purport of such a summons. His Excellency explained to all that the enemy's most strongly fortified position was to be attacked at daylight, and he clearly detailed to each General and Commander his position and portion of the attack. In my own mind I very much disagreed with my gallant Commander-in-Chief as to the place of his attack being the most eligible one. I saw at once that the fundamental principle of "being superior to your enemy on the point of attack" was lost sight of, and the whole of our army, with the exception of my Division, which was reduced to 2400 bayonets, was held in reserve just out of the reach of the enemy's cannon. At daylight our heavy guns (which had been placed with the object of destroying or greatly impairing the enemy's defences) opened fire, and with apparent success where the fire was the most heavy, but to our astonishment, at the very moment of this success our fire slackened and soon ceased altogether, when it was ascertained that the ammunition

was expended, the officer in command of the
Artillery not having brought half the quota into the
field which was ordered by the Governor-General
and the Commander-in-Chief. Thus no time was
to be lost.

＊   ＊   ＊   ＊   ＊

At this point Sir Harry Smith's autobiography
breaks off. He laid down the pen, probably through
temporary illness, and never took it up again. In
place of any fuller account of the battle of Sobraon,
we have only the following passages relating to his
individual share in the victory. The first occurs in
a letter dated "Camp Lahore, 25th February, 1846,"
and addressed to his sister, Mrs. Sargant.

"Our last fight was an awful one. My reduced-in-
numbers Division—only 2400 bayonets—was, as in other
fights, placed in reserve, but pretty soon brought into
action, and as at Ferozeshuhur again I had the good luck
to turn the fortune of the day. In so doing I lost out of
my 2400 men, 635 killed and wounded [100 more than
out of 12,000 men at Aliwal]. My first attack on the
entrenchments was repulsed. I attacked when *I* did not
wish, and had to take ground close to the river on the
enemy's left, consequently our right. [Never catch a
butting animal by the horns, though, as a good soldier,
obey your superior's orders.] By dint of the hardest
fighting I ever saw (except Badajoz, New Orleans, and
Waterloo) I carried the entrenchments. By Jupiter! the
enemy were within a hair's-breadth of driving me back.
Their numbers exceeded mine. And such a hand-to-hand
conflict ensued, for 25 minutes I could barely hold my
own. Mixed together, swords and targets against bayonets,

and a fire on both sides. I never was in such a personal fight for half the time, but my bulldogs of the 31st and old 50th stood up like men, were well supported by the native regiments, and my position closed the fight which staggered everywhere. Then such a scene of shooting men fording a deep river, as no one I believe ever saw before. The bodies *made a bridge*, but the fire of our musquetry and cannon killed every one who rushed. The hand of Almighty God has been upon me, for I may say to you what all the army knows, I was foremost in the fight, and on a *noble* horse the whole time, which sprang over the enemy's works like a deer, neither he nor I nor my clothes being scratched. It is a *miracle* for which I am, I trust, even more grateful to my God than humble towards my comrades. You always so desired I should distinguish myself. I have now gratified you, although I so egotistically write it to my sister, and in every battle have I with my noble horses been exposed without a graze. The only thing was my stick shot out of my hand; my clothes are covered with blood in many cases. Poor Holdich * got a bad wound in the shoulder and arm. He is a gallant and cool boy as ever lived. He is at Ferozepore, too far off for me to go and see, or I should do so and write to his mother."

The words in square brackets are inserted from a letter to Mr. Justice Menzies of the Cape. The following additional touches are taken from a letter to Sir James Kempt, dated 24th February.

"I never was in such a hand-to-hand fight; my gallant 31st and 50th literally staggered under the war of cannon and musquetry. Behind such formidable entrenchments

---

* His aide-de-camp, now General Sir Edward A. Holdich, K.C.B.

I could not get in where I was ordered to attack, but had to turn my right close to the river, where, if left alone, I should have commenced. I carried the works by dint of English pluck, although the native corps stuck close to me, and when I got in, such hand-to-hand work I have never witnessed. For twenty-five minutes we were at it against four times my numbers, sometimes receding (never turning round, though), sometimes advancing. The old 31st * and 50th † laid on like devils. . . . This last was a brutal bulldog fight, although of vast political and definite results ; but my fight at Aliwal was a little sweeping second edition of Salamanca—a stand-up gentlemanlike battle, a mixing of all arms and laying-on, carrying everything before us by weight of attack and combination, all hands at work from one end of the field to the other."

Sir Harry Smith's services at Aliwal were thus acknowledged by Sir Henry Hardinge :

---

* A coloured print of the 31st Regiment at Sobraon was published afterwards by Ackermann. There is also a large engraving, "The triumphal reception of the Seikh guns " (at Calcutta), after W. Taylor, in which Sir Harry Smith is a prominent figure.

† The following extract from a letter from Lieut.-Col. Bellers, who believes himself to be the only officer now surviving who served in the 50th during the Sikh War (during the greater part of which he was Adjutant), shows that the admiration expressed by Sir Harry for the 50th regiment was fully reciprocated. "With us Sir Harry Smith was ever most popular, I may say, beloved : a strict disciplinarian, but never exacting more than was necessary. His figure on 'Aliwal' with his cloak on in front of our Division is well in my memory."

Mr. B. Genn of Ely, who served in India in the 15th Hussars in 1846 under Sir Harry, gives us the *soldiers'* view of him. "He was about the most popular man in the army. He always had something jocose to say. He would gammon us by complimenting us in comparison with some other regiment—then we should hear from the men of the other regiment that he had complimented them in the same manner. He would stroll round the tents, and there would be a cry, 'Sir Harry Smith's coming !' Then he would call out, 'Trumpeter, order a round of grog ; and not too much water : what I call "fixed bayonets " ! ' "

" To Major-General Sir Harry Smith, and to the brave troops he commanded, the Governor-General conveys the tribute of his admiration, and the grateful acknowledgments of the Government and the people of India. The service rendered was most important, and was accomplished by the ability of the commander and the valour of the troops."

The following tributes were paid by Sir Henry Hardinge and Sir Hugh Gough respectively to Sir Harry Smith's conduct at Sobraon :—

" The Governor-General has much satisfaction in again offering to Major-General Sir Harry Smith, K.C.B., commanding the 1st Division of Infantry, his best thanks for his gallant services on this occasion, by which he has added to his well-established reputation."

"In his attack on the enemy's left, Major-General Sir Harry Smith displayed the same valour and judgment which gave him the victory of Aliwal. A more arduous task has seldom, if ever, been assigned to a Division. Never has an attempt been more gloriously carried through."

CHAPTER XLVI.

(*Supplementary.*)

HONOURS AND REWARDS, AND KNITTING OF OLD FRIENDSHIPS.

THE news of the victory of Aliwal reached London on 23rd March.* It brought a sense of immense relief to the public mind, which had been as much disturbed as elated by the costly struggles of Moodkee and Ferozeshah. The relief was the greater inasmuch as exaggerated reports had already been received of Sir Harry Smith's rencontre with the Sikhs at Budhowal and the loss of part of his baggage. It was at once decided that the thanks of Parliament should be offered to the victorious General and his gallant army—and although a few days later came the news of the crowning victory of Sobraon, it was not allowed to affect the determination which had been arrived at. The victors of Aliwal were still to receive a special vote of their own.

None were so delighted at the news of Harry Smith's victory as the old Peninsular friends who

* The official dispatches not till March 26th.

had watched his career from the beginning, and while they loved the man, marked in him that military genius and gallantry which must bring him to the front if only fortune gave him his chance. At last the chance had come, and he had seized it according to their utmost hopes.

Captain Kincaid wrote on the 24th March to Mrs. Sargant—

"I congratulate you most heartily on the brilliant success of your gallant brother, who has nobly vindicated the opinion entertained of him by every one who has had the opportunity of judging of his rare professional qualities, for he is one of Nature's generals. History will no doubt do justice to his merits. The previous battles were won by the bulldog courage of the soldier, with the consequent unnecessary sacrifice of human life ; here is a great victory, gained over superior numbers with comparatively little loss—the judicious proceedings throughout stamping it as a general's, and not a soldier's, victory." *

* Kincaid, in his generous enthusiasm, wrote a letter signed "Veteran" to the *Times* of March 30th, to acquaint the public with his friend's past services and military character. Speaking of Peninsular days, he writes, "Those only who have served under a good and an indifferent staff officer can estimate the immense value of the former, and Smith was one of the very best, for his heart and soul were in his duty. His light wiry frame rendered him insensible to fatigue, and, no matter what battle or march might have occupied the day or night, or what elementary war might be raging, Smith was never to be found off his horse, until he saw every man in his brigade housed, if cover could possibly be had. His devotion to their comforts was repaid by their affection. . . . No one who knew Harry Smith (his familiar name) in those days could doubt for a moment that whenever he acquired the rank, and the opportunity offered, he would show himself a General worthy of his illustrious preceptor. . . . The battle of Aliwal speaks for itself, as the dispatch of Sir H. Smith would alone proclaim that he had been trained under Sir John Moore and finished under the master-mind of Wellington."

Sir James Kempt, the revered friend with whom Harry Smith had kept up a monthly correspondence from India, wrote in similar terms—

"You may well be proud, my dear Mrs. Sargant, of having such a brother as Harry Smith. . . . I have read many details of battles with real pleasure, but I felt something more than pleasure, I felt the highest gratification and delight in reading Harry's admirable dispatch. It is spoken of by every one whom I have seen in terms of the highest praise." *

The *Times* of 25th March, after speaking of Sir Harry's avoiding battle at Budhowal, continues—

" The judgment and caution of General Smith on this occasion may be advantageously contrasted with the headlong and indiscriminating valour which hurried our troops into the frightful conflicts of Moodkee and Ferozeshah.   In these actions it may literally be affirmed that Sir Hugh Gough had never seen the enemy until he was in the heat of action.   The Sikh position had not been reconnoitred ; the strength of the Sikh army was unknown.† . . . Sir H. Smith's action at Ulleewal is exposed to none of these animadversions."

* Sir James, writing to Sir Harry Smith himself on 5th April, said, " I well knew that you only wanted an opportunity to display the great military qualities which I knew you possessed in no common degree. . . . Most nobly did you perform your part and show how a battle ought to be fought when the troops are commanded by a skilful and brave General who feels himself 'at home' in the thickest of the fight, and who knows how to handle them, and how to make use of each arm at the proper time as an auxiliary to the other.   The Great Duke in his speech in the House of Lords makes *you* the Hero of the day. . . . On the day that thanks were voted to you in Parliament, I invited Barnard, Johnny Kincaid, Rowan, Alex. McDonald, and other of your old friends and comrades to dine with me, and we drank a bumper to your health and that of Lady Smith."

† Compare an extract from the journal of Sir C. Napier (*Life of*

The Aliwal dispatch in particular,* excited unbounded admiration. Sir Robert Peel said of it, "The hand that held the pen used it with the same success with which it wielded the sword." And Thackeray's praise of it in the *Book of Snobs* is a proof that it appealed to a master of literary craft no less powerfully than it appealed to a statesman :

"Let those civilians who sneer at the acquirements of the army read Sir Harry Smith's account of the Battle of Aliwal. A noble deed was never told in nobler language."

After referring to Sir Henry Hardinge's conduct at Ferozeshah, Thackeray continues—

"No, no ; the men who perform these deeds with such brilliant valour and describe them with such modest manliness, *such* are not Snobs. The country admires them, their Sovereign rewards them, and *Punch*, the universal railer, takes off his hat and says, 'Heaven save them.'" †

On the evening of April 2nd the thanks of both Houses were given unanimously by separate resolutions to the victors of Aliwal and Sobraon. In the House of Lords Sir Harry Smith received, to quote

---

Sir C. Napier, iii. p. 398): "[Hardinge's] army is for discipline the worst I have seen. . . . There were no picquets or patrols, not even when close to and in sight of the enemy ! I am told, however, that Harry Smith's Division was an honourable exception." And another from the same journal, dated "July 9" (p. 434): "Harry Smith is a good-hearted, brave fellow, and it gladdens me that he has been rewarded, for he was the only man that acted with any science and skill as a general officer."

* Written, as Sir Edward Holdich tells me, on the battlefield on the night of the battle, and hardly altered afterwards.

† W. M. Thackeray, *Book of Snobs:* "Military Snobs."

the *Times*, an "unreserved panegyric"[*] from his worshipped master in warfare, the Duke of Wellington. It cannot be doubted that the proudest moment of Harry Smith's life was that in which he read these words of one so sparing of praise. Some of them were in later days inscribed on his tomb.

"The distant points of the frontier were threatened; Loodiana was threatened—I believe it was even attacked, and the cantonments were burned; and then it was that Sir Harry Smith was sent with a detachment of troops towards Loodiana, taking possession of various points on his road—Durrumkote and other places, of which the enemy had taken possession by bodies of troops which had crossed the Sutlej. And I beg your Lordships to observe that, when Sir Harry Smith was sent, he had three objects in view: one to give security to the post at Loodiana, already reinforced by the arrival there of General Godby after the battle; the others to keep up his communications with the rear by the town of Busseean, a point of great strength and importance, with a view to the communication between Ferozepore and Loodiana, in the front line, and Ferozepore and Delhi in the rear, the point from which the heavy train and the means of carrying on the siege in the ultimate operations were to come. These must have passed between twenty and thirty miles of the enemy, while the main body of the army at Ferozepore was not less distant than fifty. These were the objects, to secure which Sir Harry Smith was detached from the army. He marched upon Loodiana, and communicated with the British commander there, who endeavoured to move out to

---

[*] Professor Sedgwick wrote similarly, "I do not believe the old Duke ever spoke so much praise in the course of his life before, and all he said was from the heart" (*Life of Sedgwick*, ii. p. 102).

his assistance. While he was engaged with the enemy on this march, which he made in order to perform a part of his instructions—namely, to maintain the communication with Loodiana, they came out from the entrenched camp and carried off his baggage. I desire to explain that, because it was the only check which the gallant officer met with throughout the whole of this operation, and in fact it is the only misfortune, trifling as it is, which has happened during the whole operations that have taken place in that part of the country. This loss of the baggage, such as it is, has been written up as a great misfortune ; but, in point of fact, it could not be otherwise. He was obliged to march within sight of the entrenched camp, from which the enemy had an opportunity of attacking him on his march. I beg your Lordships to observe that Sir Harry Smith had not only to secure his communication with Loodiana, but likewise to secure his junction with General Wheeler, who, alone, was not able to contend against the enemy. He performed all those objects, was joined by General Wheeler, and then moved on to attack the new position which the enemy had taken up near the river. And, my Lords, I will say upon this, I have read the account of many a battle, but I never read the account of one in which more ability, energy, and experience have been manifested than in this. I know of no one in which an officer ever showed himself more capable than this officer has in commanding troops in the field. He brought every description of troops to bear, with all arms in the position in which they were most capable of rendering service ; the nicest manœuvres were performed under the fire of the enemy with the utmost precision, and at the same time with an energy and gallantry on the part of the troops never surpassed on any occasion whatever in any part of the world. I must say of this officer, that I never have seen any account which manifests more plainly than his does, that he is an officer capable of rendering the most important services, and of ultimately being an honour to this country."

Lord Hotham, who had himself served under the Duke, said that Sir Harry Smith had had the advantage of seeing an extent of service which it had been the fortune of few to witness ; but besides, he had the natural advantages of a remarkably quick conception, unceasing activity, the most ardent zeal and devotion, and the most undaunted resolution.

In the House of Commons Sir Robert Peel moved the vote, with a recital of Sir Harry's many services to his country—

" Of the battle itself I will not speak ; the victory was complete, and it has been so admirably described by the illustrious commander, that I will not weaken the effect of his narrative.　And what, let me ask, have been the services of this gallant officer ?　These recent events have given new lustre to his glory ; but he was at the capture of Monte Video—at the attack upon Buenos Ayres ; he served during the Peninsular War, from the battle of Vimeira to that of Corunna.　He was then wounded in another action, but he was at the battles of Sabugal and Fuentes d'Onor and the sieges of Ciudad Rodrigo and Badajos, at the battles of Salamanca, Vittoria, Orthes, the Pyrenees, and Toulouse.　He was at Washington and at New Orleans, and finally he was at Waterloo.　What a series of noble services, and how rejoiced I am that there should be an opportunity, through this new and signal victory, of bringing before the gladdened eyes of a grateful country a long life of military exertion, and an unbroken series of military honours! After he had achieved that success for which we are about to give him our special thanks—after he had driven back the enemy across the Sutlej, he instantly returned to rejoin his commanding officer, Sir Hugh Gough. He arrived on the 8th, two days before the decisive victory gained by the forces under Sir Hugh Gough and Sir Henry Hardinge. But for his services in the victory of the 28th of January, I propose that there should be a distinct and separate vote—distinct and separate from that which I shall recommend for that not more glorious, though perhaps more important achievement accomplished at a later date by the whole British army."

Sir De Lacy Evans, an old friend,* took occasion to defend Sir Harry from the unfounded notion that he had suffered any sort of reverse at Budhowal.

On the 4th April Sir Robert Peel wrote to inform Sir Harry Smith that, on his recommendation, the Queen had bestowed on him a Baronetcy of the United Kingdom. To the title were appended, as a special distinction, the words " of Aliwal." † At the same time Sir Henry Hardinge and Sir Hugh Gough were raised to the peerage as Viscount Hardinge and Baron Gough. While, however, Viscount Hardinge was further granted an annual sum of £3000, and Lord Gough one of £2000, in each case for three lives, no such material reward was given to Sir Harry Smith.

---

* See p. 329.

† Sir Robert Peel, in a letter of 21st April, requesting Sir Harry's acceptance of a copy of his speeches of April 2nd, added, " Sir Robert Peel trusts that the special reference in the Gazette and the Patent for conferring a Baronetcy on Sir Henry Smith to the name of Aliwal (unusual in the case of a Baronetcy) will be acceptable to the feelings of Sir Henry Smith."

On April 6th Sir Harry was appointed a Major-General on the staff of the army in the East Indies, *vice* Sir R. H. Dick killed in action; and on the 7th Prince Albert and the Duke of Wellington wrote separately to acquaint him that the Queen had approved of his appointment to be a Knight Grand Cross of the Bath.

On April 2nd the General Court of the East India Company echoed the thanks already passed by the Board of Directors; and on April 6th the Court of Common Council of the City of London voted to Sir Harry Smith, along with Sir Henry Hardinge and Sir Hugh Gough, their thanks and congratulations and the freedom of the city. The Council of the Borough of Liverpool passed resolutions of thanks on the same day.

Let us now turn to the recipient of these honours.

On 20th May Sir Harry Smith wrote to Sir Robert Peel to express his gratitude to Her Majesty for the baronetcy conferred upon him and to the House of Commons and Sir Robert himself for the honour paid him in that assembly. He could not forbear adding—

"I have been fortunate indeed to be reared in the military school of our great Duke. To meet His Grace's unqualified approbation in the face of the world is an honour, I must admit, I have ever contended for, but never hoped to have thus realized."

A week later he sent his thanks to the Duke

himself, and also assured him "how grateful I and Juana, my Spanish wife, are, for the messages sent us."

On 16th June he wrote from Simla to his old Peninsular friend, Major George Simmons *—

"I have received," he says, "since the battle of Aliwal, more than 150 letters of heartfelt gratification. . . . From every old General I have served with left to us, from every old comrade of the Light and 4th Divisions, have I received every expression of their approbation, their happiness in my having realized their often-expressed anticipations. Your old friend Juana's good sense, which you so kindly give her credit for, keeps pace with her delight in all the congratulations of our friends. Then, George, comes the encomium of the Duke. Dear old Master, if I have done that which meets *your* approbation, then is the cup of glory full indeed, for it is to your example I have desired to apply any share of ability bestowed upon me. I have had, too, from him the kindest messages, and to his old friend Juanita, as he still calls her. . . . I have had a letter from Joe, who tells me your happiness was such that your nerves so thrilled through your desperate old wounds as to make you quite ill. . . . I begin to long to get once more to my native land; mine has been an awful banishment. I do so long to seize by the hand all those old friends who have so adhered to me notwith-standing my absence, and who thus so kindly feel my success and honours *their own.* . . . Our old dear and mutual friends, Sirs Kempt, Barnard, and Lord F. Somerset, have written in most enthusiastic terms."

* See p. 33. The letter has been printed by Col. Verner in *A British Rifleman* (George Simmons' diaries).

To another old friend, Mr. Justice Menzies * of the Cape, he writes on 26th June. After recounting the story of the campaign, he tells of his coming movements—

"I and Juana start *dak* in the month of July for Cawnpore, my division. She will leave the hills before cold, contrary to sense, but in strict usage, with her unvaried attachment."

After the significant statement, "I am out of debt," he signs himself—

"one who, if affection can make him so, is worthy of your faithful friendship, hot-headed Harry Smith."

The following letters explain themselves :—

"To Lieutenant-General Sir Andrew Barnard, G.C.B., K.C.H.,
  "Colonel 1st Battalion Rifle Brigade.

       "Cawnpore, India, 29th July, 1846.
 "SIR,

  "The honorary distinctions recently conferred upon me by our gracious Queen enable me to take supporters to my family arms. I have the honour, therefore, to acquaint you, and to request you to be so good as to make it known to my gallant comrades, the Rifle Brigade, both 1st and 2nd Battalions—having served with each Battalion from the storm and capture of Monte Video [through] the whole of the Peninsular War, and the crowning Battle of Waterloo—I have adopted a soldier of the Rifle Brigade, a 'Rifleman:' and out of respect to that immortal Light Division, of which the Rifle Brigade and 52nd Light Infantry formed for so many eventful

* See p. 331.

years the 2nd Brigade, in which I was the Major of
Brigade at the many affairs and battles this Brigade
was so distinguished in, the Coa, Pombal, Foz d'Aruz,
Sabugal, Fuentes d'Onoro, siege, storm, and capture of
Ciudad Rodrigo and of Badajos, Salamanca, San Millan,
Vittoria, the heights of Vera, Irun, crossing the Bidassoa,
Nivelle, Nive, many affairs near Bayonne, Tarbes, Orthes,
and Toulouse, involving many days' sharp fighting with
each named battle, and as no officer in the army has
posted so many outlying picquets of this Brigade as I
have, and as I am indebted to it and the great school
of the immortal Wellington for whatever knowledge of
my profession I may have acquired, by which my most
fortunate career has so prospered, I beg the support to
my arms of a soldier of the 52nd Light Infantry and a
Rifleman in token of my veneration for their Corps and
as a connecting link of former times with my present
fortune.   I have, etc.

" H. G. SMITH,

" Major-General."

"To Major-General Sir Edward Gibbs, K.C.B.,
    " Colonel 52nd Light Infantry.

" Cawnpore, India, 29th July, 1846.

  " SIR,

        "The honorary distinctions recently conferred upon
me by our gracious Queen, enable me to take supporters
to my family arms. I have, therefore, the honour to
acquaint you and to request you would make it known to
my gallant comrades, the 52nd Light Infantry, that in full
remembrance of the period I was Major of Brigade to
the 2nd Brigade of the immortal Light Division, of which
the 52nd formed so prominent and distinguished a part,
involving the glorious contests of the Peninsular War ;
I have adopted a soldier of the 52nd Light Infantry and

a 'Rifleman'—my own regiment. The many affairs and battles the brigade so nobly fought in (no man better knows than yourself) include the Coa, Pombal, Foz d'Aruz, Sabugal, Fuentes d'Onoro; siege, storm, and capture of Ciudad Rodrigo; siege, storm, and capture of Badajos, where you lost an eye, as my brigadier; Salamanca, San Munos, San Millan, Vittoria, the heights of Vera, that most irresistible attack, although on a fortified mountain; Irun, the crossing of the Bidassoa, Nivelle, Nive, the many affairs near Bayonne, Tarbes, Orthes, and Toulouse, with the numerous skirmishes each of these actions entailed upon light troops. To this Brigade and to the great school of the illustrious Duke of Wellington am I indebted for that knowledge of my profession which has led to my personal aggrandisement, and which has lately acquired me the approbation of the Queen, the Duke of Wellington, and an expression of thanks from my grateful country. I pray you, therefore, Sir Edward Gibbs, and the 52nd Light Infantry, to give me that credit for the feeling of a grateful comrade I desire to demonstrate, and that you and this renowned corps may regard me as not unworthy to take a soldier out of your ranks to support me, in conjunction with their brother-in-arms, a Rifleman, and as the means in declining life of remembering the gallant Regiment who taught me to fight for my country. I have, etc.,

> "H. G. SMITH,
> "Major-General."

In the autumn at Simla Sir Harry Smith was invested with the Grand Cross of the Bath by the Governor-General, Lord Hardinge. In the speech he made on this occasion, he exhorted young soldiers to draw encouragement from his career—

"In 1805, now 41 years ago, I entered the army, one of a family of six sons and five daughters. I had two brothers in the hottest part of the battle of Waterloo, and as your Lordship kindly asserted, I may, with humility, affirm, I have fought my way through the four quarters of the globe to my present elevated position, unaided by the power of aristocracy or the influence of wealth. I cite this as an example to my younger comrades that in our free and unrivalled constitution, the paths of ambition are open to all."

On 18th January, 1847, he was appointed Colonel of the 47th Foot, but was transferred on 16th April to the command of the 2nd Battalion of his old Regiment, the Rifle Brigade, vacant by the death of Sir D. L. Gilmour.

In the letter written to Major Simmons on 16th June Sir Harry Smith had said, "I wonder if Charley Beckwith ever bestows a thought on me whom he once loved as a brother." In the course of the autumn came a charming letter from that noble man,* and henceforth the flame of friendship burnt brightly till both gallant souls had passed away.

---

* Charles Beckwith, so often mentioned in the first volume, lost a leg at Waterloo. During his time of suffering he underwent a religious conversion. "I was carried away by the love of glory, but a good God said to me, 'Stop, rascal!' and He cut off my leg; and now I think I shall be the happier for it." Through casually opening a book in the Duke of Wellington's library, he became interested in the Vaudois or Waldensian Protestants, and from 1827 onwards spent a great part of his life among them as a father or apostle. He died in 1862 (see *Dictionary of National Biography*).

"La Tour, Turin, 26th September, 1846.

"My Dear Harry,

"The noise of the guns at Aliwal and Sobraon having died away in the echoes of the Himalaya, and the éclat and movement of those brilliant days having melted into the calmer atmosphere of ordinary life, I have good hopes that the handwriting of one who has never faltered for one moment in the deep feeling of respect and affection which he will cherish to his dying day for all his old companions in arms, will not be unwelcome.

"From the hour in which I saw your name associated with the army of the Sutlej, you may imagine how carefully I followed all your movements, how I rejoiced in your success, how anxious I felt in the usual intervals of doubt and trial.

"I laughed heartily when you lost your baggage, I knew full well the hearty damns that you sent after Sikhs, coolies, syces, and the whole rabble rout ; saw your keen face as you galloped on the sand, and admired the cool close order of your movements in the teeth of an enemy who held-in his very breath in anxious doubt and dread whether he should dare to touch you ; saw the noble array of your clear decided movement of Aliwal, and went along with you pell-mell as you drove your enemy headlong into the waters of the Sutlej ; triumphed in the crowning efforts of a long soldier's life, formed in the school of true science, common sense, and right-hearted action, and felt a secret pride that I had been formed in the same school and was able to estimate such men as Hardinge and Harry Smith. But what did Juana do in all this row? Was she on horseback abaxo de los cañonaços? Give my kind love to her and kiss her for me.

"Many years have now gone by, and our outward frames are but the shadows of what they were, but my

mind continues of the same sort. Character never loses
its indelible stamp. Thin and black, my hair is not yet
gray, and you would yet be able to recognize the Charley
Beckwith of the Light Division. . . . The last enemy has
done his worst on very many of our Peninsular companions.
Sir Andrew and some Riflemen still remain to dine
together sometimes in Albemarle Street. Charley Rowan
is letter A, No. 1. Old Duffy regulates the Club, Johnny
Bell cultivates dahlias at Staines, Will Napier misgoverns
the Guernseymen, Johnny Kincaid regulates the secrets of
a prison-house, Jonathan Leach writes histories; thus each
labours in his vocation, and has still a conceit left him in
his misery. The chronicle of the out-pensioners of Chelsea
is more spirit-stirring in its former than in its latter day. . . .
Adieu, Harry, and believe me that you may always depend
on the affection of

> "Your old friend,
> "CHARLES BECKWITH." *

Harry Smith was raised on 27th February, 1847,
to the full rank of Major-General, dating from
9th November, 1846. He received a further
gratification in an address from his native town,
Whittlesey, which had been prepared by the Rev.
G. Burgess, his old schoolmaster, then in his 82nd
year. His reply evinced that warm attachment
to his birthplace and native land which had been
shown in so many of his private letters during his
long exile. At length he was to see them again.

---

* Sir Harry passed Gen. Beckwith's letter on to Col. W. Havelock,
the "Young Varmint" of the Light Division (destined to die a soldier's
death at Ramnuggur two years later), and received a characteristic
letter of acknowledgment of the "treat" it had given to "yours
affectionately, Old Will."

Already in November, 1846, he had told his sister that he had taken his passage in a steamer which was to leave Calcutta in the middle of March, and that he would not " go mooning about the continent," but "come straight home." He sailed as he had said, and reached Southampton after eighteen years' absence from his native land on 29th April, 1847.

CHAPTER XLVII.

(*Supplementary.*)

IN ENGLAND ONCE MORE—A SERIES OF OVATIONS—
LONDON, ELY, WHITTLESEY, CAMBRIDGE—AP-
POINTED GOVERNOR OF THE CAPE OF GOOD HOPE.

SIR HARRY SMITH was received at Southampton by
the General commanding the South-Western District
and a guard of honour. Salutes were fired, and
bells set ringing, and he landed in the presence of
thousands of spectators. The corporation presented
an address, and had prepared a civic banquet. Next
day he travelled to London in a special train, which
was put at his disposal by the South-Western Rail-
way Company.

On the 6th May he dined with Her Majesty at
Marlborough House; on the 7th he received a
deputation from the inhabitants of his native town
of Whittlesey, who were desirous of making him
a presentation. It consisted chiefly of old schoolfellows.

A series of invitations poured in from Her
Majesty the Queen, the Duchess of Kent, the
Dukes of Wellington, Montrose, and Beaufort, the

Earl of Ripon, the Lord Mayor, Sir Robert Peel,
Sir J. Cam Hobhouse, Sir De Lacy Evans, etc.*
On the 18th May his old friend and commander,
Sir Andrew Barnard, presided at a dinner in his
honour given by the Senior United Service Club.
On the 20th the freedom of the City of London was
presented to Sir Harry at Guildhall.   He returned
thanks for the honour in stirring sentences such as
came naturally to him.

"It has been my fate to call upon the British soldier to
follow to victory, and never have I known him to fail.
The fear of defeat never entered the bosom of any one
man whom I have seen with the blood of John Bull in his
veins" (great cheering). "So long as England is true to herself and loyal to her Sovereign, she will stand, as she now
stands, the paramount power of the world" (immense
applause).

In the evening of the same day Sir Harry was
the guest of a memorable company, his old Peninsular comrades, the survivors of the Light Division.
They included Sir Hew Ross, Sir Andrew Barnard,
the Duke of Richmond, John Kincaid, Sir John
Bell, Jonathan Leach, and Major Smith (Sir Harry's
"Brother Tom").   Next day the *Times* wrote as
follows :—

"A hundred soldiers dined yesterday together in this
city, and all the gatherings of all the capitals of Europe

* Lord Malmesbury wrote in his diary for May 8th, "Dined with
the Eglintons. General Sir Harry Smith was the great lion of the
evening. He is a little old man, very clever-looking. She is a Spanish
woman, and has been very handsome" (see *Memoirs of an Ex-
minister*).

for half a century to come will not produce so memorable a reunion. If the muster roll of the Old Guard could be called and answered, a rival parade might perhaps be formed, but from no other body whose services modern history records could another such company be raised. The survivors of the most renowned division of the most famous army of England's most famous war were yesterday once more collected to welcome an ancient comrade whose victories in more productive but not more honourable fields have gloriously terminated a career commenced amongst those who bear this grateful testimony to the fruits of a spirit and character which their own society and conduct so largely contributed to form.

" On all sides is Sir Harry Smith receiving the due congratulations of his countrymen and the well-earned meed of his courage. For once, at least, the metropolitan season is supplied with a reasonable object of admiration and amusement, but we are much mistaken in Sir Henry's disposition, if this, of all the festivities which greet his arrival, will not convey at once the greatest gratification and the highest compliment. The same recollections which led the newly created baronet to pass by the ordinary attractions of blazonry and to turn to the days and comrades of his youth, to Ciudad Rodrigo and the Pyrenees, to the 52nd and the 95th, for those figures which should support his shield and tell of the deeds by which it was won, will teach him also to value the tribute which he yesterday received above any more gorgeous or imposing testimony. His cordial countrymen, his gratified friends—appreciation of his service and admiration of his conduct, he may meet elsewhere ; but at the festival in Willis' Rooms last night only, and there perhaps for the last time, could he meet his fellows and companions in that noble school in which he learnt his soldiership and to which he owes his fame. Well does it tell for England's justice that such merits are at length acknowledged, and that Sir Henry Smith comes back to find that his ancient comrades and his ancient deeds are no longer left without the decorations which have been lavished on more recent services.[*]

"It cannot be the least part of his satisfaction at this entertainment, to think that, but for him, a gathering so memorable would never have occurred. This was no anniversary of a recurring solemnity, no periodical festivity or customary reunion. It did not take place last year, and it will not take place next. The last rendezvous perhaps was in the plains of Vittoria, or under the walls of Toulouse, the next will probably never occur. Already is the circle of survivors closing rapidly in under a slower but more resistless enemy than even they ever faced before; the actors, like the deeds, must soon become subjects of history and examples for imitation, and it is but too likely that yesterday was sounded the last assembly of the old Light Division."

On the 30th June, Sir Harry with Lady Smith left London for Whittlesey, his native place, and by desire of the people of Ely stopped there on the way. The story is best told in the words of warmhearted Adam Sedgwick.[†]

"I was called away [from Cambridge] by the Dean of Ely to meet my old friend, Sir Harry Smith. I could not resist the temptation. So next morning (the 30th) I went to the station, and there I met the hero and his family party, and joined them in a saloon fitted up by the directors for their special reception. The entry into Ely was triumphant.[‡] Thousands were assembled, with flags,

* The Peninsular Medal had just been granted.
† For his early friendship with Harry Smith, see p. 5, 'n.
‡ On the opposite page is given a facsimile of the handbill issued for the occasion.

SIR HARRY SMITH'S

VISIT ᴛᴏ ELY

Programme of Procession.

Standard Bearer.

TRUMPETER MOUNTED.

Chief-Constable mounted.

Three Police Officers mounted,

Standard Bearer.

GENTLEMEN ON HORSEBACK FOUR A-BREAST.

BAND of the Scots Fusileer Guards.

Drums and Fifes of the Scots Fusileer Guards.

Chairman of Breakfast--& Rev. E. B. Sparke, & Rev. A. Peyton.

Standard Bearer.

SIR HARRY SMITH,

AND ATTENDANTS.

LADY SMITH, and Attendants.

PRIVATE CARRIAGES.

Standard Bearer.

Three Policemen mounted.

Persons who join the PROCESSION are particularly requested to attend to the Directions of the Persons appointed to marshall it, and who will wear a distinguishing Badge.

☞ *The Procession must be formed punctually at a quarter before Eleven.*

ELY June 29, 1847   CLEMENTS, PRINTER, ELY

branches of laurel, and joyful anxious faces. The Dean
had provided me a horse, so I joined the cavalcade. After
going through triumphal arches, and I know not what,
preceded by a regimental band of music — Sir Harry
mounted on the Arabian charger he rode at the battle of
Aliwal, and greeted by lusty shouts from thousands—we
all turned in to a magnificent lunch.* We then went on
to Whittlesey, a similar triumphant entry. I should think
not less than 10,000 men to greet the arrival of the hero at
his native town. He was much affected, and I saw tears
roll down his weather-beaten, but fine face, as he passed
the house where his father and mother once lived." †

At the station an address was read by Mr.
Thomas Bowker, to which Sir Harry replied that
he felt proud to set his foot once more in his native
place, and he was delighted to see the Whittlesey
Cavalry ‡ there before him, as he could not forget that
in that loyal troop he commenced his military career.

A ball was given in the evening, at which Sir
Harry joined in the set dances, but refused to dance
the polka. Next day he was entertained at a dinner
attended by three hundred persons, including Lords
Fitzwilliam, Aboyne, and Hardwicke, Professor
Sedgwick, and other leading men of the county, and
an épergne of the value of £300 was presented to

---

* Dean Peacock, who presided, referred to the character he had
received of Sir Harry from Sir John Herschel, as one not only valiant
in the field, but able to conciliate a foe and turn the enemies of the
British Empire into its friends.

† *Life of Sedgwick* (Clark and Hughes), vol. ii. p. 124. The *Illustrated London News* of 10th July, 1847, has an illustration representing
Sir Harry passing the house of his birth.

‡ Then commanded by his "third Waterloo brother," Captain
Charles Smith, with whom Sir Harry stayed during his visit.

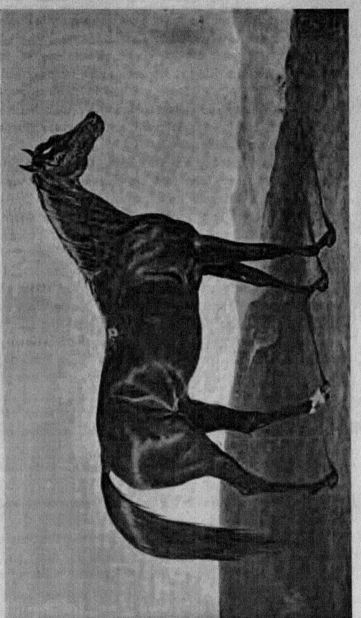

"ALIWAL," SIR HARRY SMITH'S CHARGER.

(*From a Picture painted by A. Cooper, R.A., in 1847.*)

[*Opposite p. 276.*]

hero down in time ; for the Queen's wishes are, as you know, a soldier's law.   I returned to Cambridge on Saturday. On Sunday . . . after evening chapel, I was rejoiced to find Sir H. Smith waiting at my rooms ; he took my bed, and I took Dick's. . . .   I spent a delightful quiet evening with my hearty and gallant friend.   We took a turn in the walks, but he was in plain clothes, and was not known by the multitude.

"Next day (Monday the 5th) began the great hurly-burly. On Monday John told me that more than one hundred people came to lunch at my rooms, no doubt partly drawn there in the hope of meeting Harry Smith, who (after the Duke of Wellington) was the most popular of all the visitors.   I could not be there myself except at very short intervals, as I was officially in constant attendance on the Prince. . . .   There was a grand cheer on Monday morning when Sir H. Smith had his degree. . . . The Vice-Chancellor that day had a dinner—the Queen attended—to a party of about sixty.   I presided in Trinity College Hall over a party of more than three hundred ; and a right merry party it was.   Sir Harry Smith was at my right hand as the Vice-master's guest, and among the distinguished foreigners were Le Verrier and Struvé.   If we had not as much dignity as the Vice-Chancellor, we had more numbers and more fun. . . .

"On Tuesday * we had the Installation Ode performed in full chorus, and of all the cheers I ever heard, the cheers after *God save the Queen* in full chorus, accompanied and joined by a thousand voices, were the most enthusiastic.

"When the Duke of Wellington was leaving the Senate House, a loud peal of cheers was raised for him ; and, immediately after, Harry was caught sight of. ' Cheers for

* The Whittlesey troop of Yeomanry Cavalry, under the command of Captain Charles Smith, formed the guard of honour at the Installation.

Sir Harry Smith' were called for ; and the Duke, turning back, laid hold of Sir Harry and turned him round, saying, 'There you have him.' Indeed, he is more like the Duke's son, so much is he attached to him." *

On Thursday "the corporation brought an address to Sir Harry Smith, to which he read them an answer. Soon afterwards he went away."

Professor Sedgwick tells the romantic story of Lady Smith's early life, and ends, "And now she is a pleasant, comfortable-looking dame with mild manners and soft, sweet voice." †

But the intoxicating hour of honours and ovations was quickly to give place to another period of hard service to Queen and country. During a visit to the Rev. T. Holdich at Maidwell Hall, Northants, Sir Harry received the news that he had been appointed to succeed Sir Henry Pottinger as Governor of the Cape of Good Hope and High Commissioner, and in September he was to leave England again. Another Kafir war was in progress, and Sir Harry's nomination gave the greatest satisfaction to the country. Before his departure his old friends at Glasgow presented him with a piece of plate of the value of £400 and upwards.

---

* A letter from the Rev. Canon Charles Evans tells us of an incident which took place *within* the Senate House. " I was present in the Senate House and stationed close to the platform on which Sir Harry was conversing with the Duke of Wellington, as we were waiting for the arrival of the Queen and Prince Albert, from whom I was to have the honour of receiving the Senior Chancellor's Medal. The undergraduates were loudly cheering the Duke, when laying his hand on Sir Harry's shoulder, he said, ' No, no, this is the man you ought to cheer ; here is the hero of the day.' Sir Harry Smith burst into tears and said, ' I little thought I should live to hear such kind words as these from my old chief.' I distinctly heard every word."

† *Life of Sedgwick,* ii. pp. 125-127 and 573.

On the 16th September, in reply to an address presented at Portsmouth on the eve of his departure, Sir Harry said—

"I trust, if it should be my good fortune to render any additional service to my Queen and country, I may be able to do it through other instruments than that called war. . . . If I can avert war, I will. If I can extend the blessings of civilization and Christianity in a distant land, where, without any affectation of humility, I can say that some years ago I sowed its seeds, it will be a gratification to me beyond expression to do so."

In the evening of the preceding day the 43rd, 52nd, and 60th Regiments had entertained Sir Harry at the George (the inn which had so many associations with his arrivals in and departures from England in early life).

In replying to the toast of his health, Sir Harry referred to the dinner given him on his arrival in London by the survivors of the old Light Division; to his own participation in every action recorded on the colours of the 52nd before him; and to the special praise given by the Duke of Wellington to the Light Division:

"When I have set the Light Division to do anything which was difficult and dangerous, requiring enterprise, the next day I found that division, with scarcely any loss, ready again to fight."

Sir Harry drew the moral, "He is the best officer who does the most with the least loss of life." On the relation of officers to men, he continued—

"Believe me, the tone of courage is taken from the officers; whatever the conduct of officers is, such will be the soldiers. And, gentlemen, if you knew the feeling of the British soldier in the field, . . . then would your devoted service be for the comforts and happiness of your men. Do not let it be supposed, gentlemen, because I talk of the comforts and happiness of the men, that I am one of those officers who I regret to say exist in the present day, who have a kind of twaddle in talking about 'the poor soldier.' In the country I am going to, I regret to hear it said 'the poor soldier' sleeps here and sleeps there, 'the poor soldier' wants this and wants that. It is the duty of every officer to provide to his utmost for the comfort of his men, and when comforts are not to be had, 'bad luck to the shilling.' And, my gallant officers, believe me, our soldiers are equally gallant men, and where the comforts are not to be had, they don't call themselves 'poor soldiers'; they call themselves the glorious soldiers in the service of Her Majesty."

In a later speech, replying to the toast of "Lady Smith," Sir Harry returned thanks for the honour to his wife—a wife who had participated in the hardships of almost every one of the gallant actions recorded on their colours; who had been three times besieged in her native city, and after being finally rescued, had followed him through the four quarters of the globe; a wife who had been not only honoured by all his comrades, but respected by those of her own sex.

On the 24th September Sir Harry embarked on the *Vernon* amid a great demonstration, by which he seemed much moved.

CHAPTER XLVIII.

(*Supplementary.*)

SOUTH AFRICA IN 1847—SIR HARRY'S RECEPTION AT
CAPE TOWN AND ON THE FRONTIER—END OF THE
KAFIR WAR—EXTENSION OF THE BOUNDARIES OF
THE COLONY AND ESTABLISHMENT OF THE PRO-
VINCE OF "BRITISH KAFFRARIA"—VISIT TO THE
COUNTRY BEYOND THE ORANGE AND TO NATAL
—PROCLAMATION OF THE "ORANGE RIVER SOVE-
REIGNTY"—TRIUMPHANT RETURN TO CAPE TOWN
—DISAFFECTION AMONG THE BOERS IN THE
SOVEREIGNTY—EXPEDITION THITHER AND BATTLE
OF BOOMPLAATS—RETURN TO CAPE TOWN.

MUCH had happened in South Africa since the period
1835-6 of which Sir Harry's autobiography has
given us so full an account, and it was his fortune as
Governor to encounter difficulties traceable to the
policy of Lord Glenelg of which he had himself seen
the short-sighted fatuity at the time when it was
adopted.

By Sir Benjamin D'Urban's treaty with the
Kafir chiefs of September, 1835, the country between
the Fish River and the Keiskamma was to be

occupied by those settlers who had suffered most
severely in the war, while in that between the Keiskamma and the Kei (to be called the " Province
of Queen Adelaide") a number of loyal Kafirs were
to be established under military protection. All
this was upset by Lord Glenelg's dispatch of 26th
December, 1835. No settlers were to be permitted
beyond the Fish River, and the Kafirs were to be
reinstated in the districts from which they had consented in their treaty with Sir Benjamin D'Urban
to retire ; while the compensation which was to
have been paid to sufferers from the war was sharply
refused. Well may Cloete write, " A communication
more cruel, unjust, and insulting to the feelings
both of Sir Benjamin D'Urban and of the colonists
could hardly have been penned by a declared enemy
of the country and its Governor." The immediate
consequence was the emigration from the Colony of
numbers of Dutch farmers (described by Sir B.
D'Urban as "a brave, patient, industrious, orderly,
and religious people "). In another dispatch of
Lord Glenelg's dated 1st May, 1837, Sir Benjamin
D'Urban, perhaps the best Governor the Colony
ever had, was recalled. He was succeeded by Sir
George Napier. The policy entrusted to the new
Governor was that of entering into alliances with
the Kafir chiefs. But experience soon taught him
that this was futile, and the only possible course was
that which had been pursued by his predecessor and
Harry Smith. " My own experience and what I saw
with my own eyes," he declared to a Parliamentary

Committee in 1851, "have confirmed me that I was wrong and Sir Benjamin D'Urban perfectly right; that if he meant to keep Kafirland under British rule, the only way of doing so was by having a line of forts and maintaining troops in them."

The Boers or emigrant farmers of Dutch descent who in 1835 and subsequent years, to the number of 10,000, left the Cape Colony as men shamefully abandoned by the British Government, settled themselves, some north of the Orange River, some across the Vaal, some in Natal.

To prevent those in Natal from joining any other European power, the British Government in 1842 took possession of Durban, and in 1843 of the whole of Natal. In 1845 Natal was annexed to the Cape Colony under a Lieutenant-Governor, Mr. West. But in consequence of dissatisfaction in regard to a settlement of lands, a new emigration of Dutch farmers began, and was in operation when Sir Harry Smith reached South Africa.

Meanwhile in 1845 Sir Peregrine Maitland, then Governor of the Cape, had established Major Warden and a small British garrison at Bloemfontein with authority over the emigrant Boers settled across the Orange between the Modder and Riet rivers, the Boers who were settled north of the Modder being left undisturbed. These had set up for themselves in 1837 a simple form of government at Winburg.

The treaty system failed to protect the settlers in

the eastern part of the Cape Colony from Kafir aggressions, and in 1846 Sandilli, the successor of Gaika, openly defied the British authorities; and a war broke out which was hardly ended when Sir Henry Pottinger, after holding office for less than a year, resigned the government of the Cape into the hands of Sir Harry Smith.

The *Vernon* entered Table Bay on 1st December, 1847. The first news signalled from shore was that five officers had been cut off by the tribe of Galekas under Boku, on which Sir Harry remarked, "Doing something they ought not, I'll be bound!"[*] A few hours later he and Lady Smith landed. "Amidst the most hearty cheering, mingled with the roaring of cannon, the Governor passed through the streets, at every moment recognizing and saluting old acquaintances. Immediately after his arrival at Government House he took the oaths of office. That night the town was brilliantly illuminated, and the windows in a solitary house that was unlit were completely wrecked by the populace."[†] That the new Governor and Lady Smith were received by the Colony as old friends was again shown when, at a public banquet, Judge Menzies proposed the toast, not of "His Excellency and his Lady," but of "Harry Smith and his Wife."[‡]

Sir Harry lost no time in grappling with public

---

[*] Told me by General Sir Edward Holdich, who sailed with Sir Harry as his aide-de-camp.

[†] Theal's *History of South Africa*, iv. p. 308.

[‡] Mrs. Ward, *Five Years in Kaffirland.*

business, and started by sea on the 11th December for the frontier. At Port Elizabeth he saw the chief Macomo, and, having upbraided him for his treachery, ordered him to kneel, when he set his foot on the chief's neck, saying, "This is to teach you that I am come hither to teach Kafirland that I am chief and master here, and this is the way I shall treat the enemies of the Queen of England." After-events may make us doubt the wisdom of this public humiliation of the chief. After having an interview at Sidbury with Sir Henry Pottinger, Sir Harry reached Grahamstown on the 17th. Mrs. Ward, who was there, writes in her diary—

"The shops were closed, every one made holiday, triumphal arches were erected surmounted by inscriptions proclaiming welcome to the new Governor and old friend. The very *bonhommie* with which Sir Harry had met his old acquaintances—even an old Hottentot sergeant with whom he shook hands on the road—procured for him a ready popularity ere he entered Grahamstown."

And at night—

"The frontier to-night was delirious with joy. Its own hero, its best friend next to Sir Benjamin the Good, has arrived. The town is illuminated, and beacon-lights telegraph from the hill-tops. . . . We watched the rockets ascending and the lights flashing from one end of Grahamstown to the other; the very Fingo kraals sent forth shouts, and torches flitted from hut to hut. But long before the lights were extinguished, Sir Harry Smith was up and at work. Three o'clock on the morning of the 18th found him at his desk, which he scarcely left till five in the evening."

But even on the day of his arrival in Grahams-town he had made history. He had released the captive chief Sandilli (an act of generosity afterwards ill-requited), and sent him the baton of office of a British magistrate; and, more than this, he had issued a proclamation creating a new boundary for the Colony, which was now to include the district of Victoria (to the east of Albany and Somerset), the district of Albert (north-east of Cradock), and a vast territory stretching from the old northern boundary of the Colony to the Orange River. The chief town of Victoria he named "Alice," doubtless after his beloved sister, Mrs. Sargant.

On the 19th, by the submission of Pato, it appeared that the Kafir War was at an end. The Governor at once set out for King William's Town, which he reached on the 23rd, and was again received enthusiastically. The troops—the Rifle Brigade and the 7th Dragoon Guards—were drawn up on the parade, and were praised in stirring terms for their services in the recent war. On another part of the square an assembly of two thousand Kafirs waited, sitting in a great hollow circle. Into this circle Sir Harry rode with his staff, and read a proclamation, which was practically a dramatic reversal of that abandonment by Lord Glenelg of the "Province of Queen Adelaide" which he had felt so bitterly in 1836. He declared the whole country between the Keiskamma and the Kei, running northwards to the junction of the Klipplaats and Zwart Kei rivers, to be under the sovereignty of the Queen, not, however, as part of Cape Colony, but as a district dependency of the Crown to be named " British Kaffraria," and kept in reserve for the Kafir people, over whom the Governor, as High Commissioner, was to be " Inkosi Inkulu," or Great Chief. Colonel Mackinnon was appointed to a post such as Harry Smith had held in 1835-36— that of Commandant and Chief Commissioner of British Kaffraria, with his headquarters at King William's Town.* Having read the proclamation, he gave an illustration of those dramatic methods of treating the Kafirs on which he had always relied, but which stirred some ridicule in England during the time of his Governorship. " He called for a sergeant's baton, which he termed the staff of war, and a wand with a brass head, which he termed the staff of peace. Calling the chiefs forward, he desired them to touch whichever they pleased, when each of course touched the staff of peace. After an address of some length upon their prospects if they behaved themselves, and threats of what would happen if they did not, he required them to kiss his foot in token of submission." [He was, of course, still on horseback.] " This they did also without hesitation. The ceremony concluded by

---

* After the abandonment of the Province of Queen Adelaide, King William's Town had been deserted. Mrs. Ward, early in 1847 (p. 147), speaks of " the ruins of what had once promised to be a flourishing town." " The walls of Sir Harry Smith's abode are still standing." Sir Harry now ordered Colonel Mackinnon to cause it to be laid out in squares and streets on both sides the Buffalo. He also established in British Kaffraria a chain of forts, and four military villages called Juanasburg, Woburn, Auckland, and Ely.

the High Commissioner shaking hands with all the chiefs, calling them his children, and presenting them with a herd of oxen to feast upon." *

On 7th January,† 1848, the Chiefs were called to a second meeting to hear the arrangements which had been made for the government of the new province. Sir Harry addressed them, after which they took oath to obey the High Commissioner as the Queen's representative, and to renounce witch-craft, violation of women, murder, robbery, and the buying of wives, to listen to the missionaries, and on every anniversary of that day to bring to King William's Town a fat ox in acknowledgment of holding their lands from the Queen. "Sir Harry then addressed them again, telling them what would happen if they were not faithful. 'Look at that waggon,' said he, pointing to one at a distance which had been prepared for an explosion, 'and hear me give the word Fire!' The train was lit, and the waggon was sent skyward in a thousand pieces. 'That is what I will do to you,' he continued, 'if you do not behave yourselves.' Taking a sheet of paper in his hand, 'Do you see this?' said he. Tearing it and throwing the pieces to the wind, 'There go the treaties!' he exclaimed. 'Do you hear? No more treaties.'" ‡

---

* Theal, iv. p. 311.

† The choice of this date shows Sir Harry's pleasure in restoring all his old arrangements. It was the date of the great meeting of chiefs in 1836 (see pp. 437, 438, and Appendix V.), and it was then arranged that on every 7th January there should be a similar meeting.

‡ Theal, iv. p. 315.

Things being thus settled at King William's
Town, Sir Harry proceeded to the country between
the Orange River and the Vaal.* Here Major
Warden at Bloemfontein had authority over the
emigrant Boers between the Modder and the Riet
rivers; the Boers north of the Modder were left to
themselves, and large tracts bordering on the
Orange River were assigned as reserves to the
chiefs Moshesh and Adam Kok, who could also
exact quit-rents from the farmers outside the
reserves.

"Sir Harry Smith came to South Africa with a
fully matured plan for the settlement of affairs north
of the Orange. He would take no land from black
people that they needed for their maintenance, but
there were no longer to be black states covering
vast areas of ground either unoccupied or in possession of white men. Such ground he would form
into a new colony, and he would exercise a general
control over the chiefs themselves in the interests
of peace and civilization. A system antagonistic to
that of the Napier treaties was to be introduced.
Those treaties attempted to subject civilized men to
barbarians. He would place an enlightened and
benevolent government over all. But to enable him
to do so, the consent of Adam Kok and Moshesh
must be obtained to new agreements, for he could

* On his way he stayed from January 12th to 14th at Shiloh, and
then selected a site for a town at the junction of the Klipplaats and
Ox Kraal Rivers to which he gave the name of his native place,
Whittlesea.

not take the high-handed course of setting the treaties aside." *

Accordingly, on 24th January he had an interview with Adam Kok. At first the chief gave himself great airs, and Sir Harry, losing his temper, threatened to have him tied up to a beam in the room in which they were sitting unless he acted reasonably. Eventually an agreement was signed by which Adam Kok, in return for a small annual income, ceded his claim to jurisdiction over all the land outside the Griqua reserve. At Bloemfontein the Governor received addresses from a number of Boer settlers. "Among them were some who had served under him in the Kafir war of 1835. At a public meeting speeches were made in which old times were recalled, and enthusiastic language was used concerning the future of South Africa, now that a true friend of the country was at the head of affairs. At this meeting the Governor observed an aged grey-headed man standing in the crowd. He instantly rose, handed his chair to the old man, and pressed him to be seated, a kindly act that was long remembered by the simple farmers, and which formed the subject of one of the transparencies when Cape Town was illuminated on his return." †

From Bloemfontein Sir Harry proceeded to Winburg, where on 27th January he had a conference with Moshesh, in which the latter, like Adam Kok, accepted his proposals. At Winburg twenty-seven farmers, heads of families, and twenty-two

* Theal, iv. p. 421.   † Ibid., iv. p. 422.

others presented an address, in which they requested
the Governor to extend British jurisdiction over
the country. He probably took this as representing the general feeling, but he could not wait for
further information. He had heard that a number
of the Boers in Natal were "trekking" out of that
colony. He therefore sent an express to their
leader, Pretorius, asking him to pause, and at daybreak on the 28th January (the second anniversary
of Aliwal) he was hastening towards Natal.

In a graphic dispatch written from Pietermaritz-
burg on 10th February, he describes his meeting
with the "trekking" farmers.

"On my arrival at the foot of the Drachenberg Mountains, I was almost paralyzed to witness the whole of the
population, with few exceptions, 'treking'! Rains on this
side of the mountains are tropical, and now prevail—the
country is intersected by considerable streams, frequently
impassable—and these families were exposed to a state
of misery which I never before saw equalled, except in
Massena's invasion of Portugal, when the whole of the
population of that part of the seat of war abandoned their
homes and fled. The scene here was truly heart-rending.
I assembled all the men near me through the means of a
Mr. Pretorius, a shrewd, sensible man, who had recently
been into the colony to lay the subject of dissatisfaction of
his countrymen before the Governor [Sir Henry Pottinger],
where he was unfortunately refused an audience, and
returned after so long a journey, expressing himself as the
feelings of a proud and injured man would naturally
prompt. At this meeting I was received as if among my
own family. I heard the various causes of complaint.
Some I regard as well founded, others as imaginary; but

all expressive of a want of confidence and liberality as to land on the part of Government. I exerted my influence among them to induce them to remain for the moment where they were, which they consented to do. The scene exhibited by about three or four hundred fathers of large families assembled and shedding tears when representing their position was more, I admit, than I could observe unmoved. . . . To prove, if it be necessary, the faith which I place in their loyalty, I may mention that on one occasion when the little waggon in which I travel, and which they call 'Government House,' was nearly upset when crossing one of the tributary streams of the great Tugela, thirty or forty men on the bank stripped and sprang into the water, exclaiming, 'Government House shall not fall—it shall not fall!' and their efforts saved my only home from being carried down the current."

Sir Harry proceeded to argue that the very existence of the Colony of Natal depended on its preserving its white population, and stated that he had therefore issued a proclamation to meet the grievances· of the farmers in regard to land, and had given Mr. Pretorius a place on the Land Commission. "If the measures which I have adopted conduce to the restoration of happiness to many thousands, tend to the preservation of a Christian community by the erection of churches, schools, etc., and are productive of general good, the glory of war will be eclipsed by the blessings of [establishing] harmony, peace, and content."

On 3rd February, from the emigrant camp Sir Harry Smith issued a proclamation declaring the whole territory between the Orange and Vaal rivers to be subject to the Queen. The country was to be divided into magistracies; taxes were to be raised for the support of a small staff and for erecting schools, churches, etc.; and the farmers were to serve the Queen when required. So arose the Orange River Sovereignty, destined to be known under altered conditions in turn as the Orange Free State and the Orange River Colony.

Meanwhile Pretorius, with the Governor's consent, had left the camp in order to ascertain the real feelings of the emigrant farmers beyond the Drakensberg. He seems to have thought that Sir Harry had promised him that if the general opinion of the settlers was unfavourable, the proclamation would not be issued. Sir Harry maintained that his agreement with Pretorius only referred to the Boers north of the Vaal, and in consequence of the agreement the territory they occupied was excluded from the terms of the proclamation.

Mr. Theal states that "in issuing this proclamation Sir Harry Smith was full of confidence in his personal influence with the emigrants. When Major Warden, the British resident, expressed an opinion that if the Queen's authority was proclaimed north of the Orange River, additional troops would be requisite, his Excellency replied, 'My dear fellow, bear in mind that the Boers are my children, and I will have none other here for my soldiers; your detachment will march for the colony immediately.' And in this confidence a garrison of only 50 or 60 Cape Mounted Riflemen were left to defend a territory more than 50,000 square miles in extent." *

The creation of the Orange River Sovereignty was reluctantly agreed to by the Home Government,† and the measures taken by Sir Harry to induce settlers in Natal to remain there, and others to come there, were to a great extent successful.

---

* Theal, iv. p. 427.

† The question was submitted to a Committee of Privy Council, whose report was approved on 13th July, 1850. They gave it as their opinion that to abandon a sovereignty virtually assumed by Sir P. Maitland in 1845 and proclaimed by Sir H. Smith in 1848 would be productive of more evil than good. But they add sentences which read strangely in these changed times. "We cannot pass from this part of the subject without submitting for your Majesty's consideration our opinion that very serious dangers are inseparable from the recent, and still more from any future, extension of your Majesty's dominions in Southern Africa. That policy has enlarged, and, if pursued further, may indefinitely enlarge, the demands on the revenue and the military force of this kingdom with a view to objects of no perceptible national importance, and to the hindrance of other objects in which the welfare of the nation at large is deeply involved. . . . Unless some decisive method can be taken to prevent further advances in the same direction, it will be impossible to assign any limit to the growth of these unprofitable acquisitions, or to the extent and number of the burdensome obligations inseparable from them. In humbly advising that the Orange River Sovereignty should be added to the dominions of your Majesty's crown, we think ourselves therefore bound to qualify that recommendation by the further advice that all officers, who represent, or who may hereafter represent, your Majesty in Southern Africa, should be interdicted, in terms as explicit as can be employed, and under sanctions as grave as can be devised, from making any addition, whether permanent or provisional, of any territory however small to the existing dominions of your Majesty in the African Continent, and from doing any act, or using any language, conveying, or which could reasonably be construed to convey, any promise or pledge of that nature. And we are further of opinion that the proposed interdict should be published in the most formal manner in your Majesty's name ; that so, in the contingency of any future disregard of it by your Majesty's officers, your Majesty may be able to overrule any such act, or to disappoint any such promise of theirs, without risking the imputation of any breach of the public faith."

But his belief that the settlers in the northern part of the new Sovereignty and over the Vaal would readily accept British supremacy when offered them by one whom they had known and trusted in the past—this belief proved fallacious. The sense of wrong created by the Glenelg policy could not be so easily assuaged.

By the 1st March Sir Harry Smith was back at Cape Town, " welcomed as a successful pacificator and benefactor with pæans of praise from all classes of the inhabitants. His meteoric progress over the length and breadth of the country—all at once dispelling the idea of the unwieldiness of the settlement and its dependencies—and the generous character of the mission he had so triumphantly concluded were regarded as the most signally happy events South Africa had ever witnessed. His Excellency's praise was on every lip, and his virtues were to be symbolized to future generations by an equestrian statue." *

But no sooner had he returned than he heard that among the farmers of the Winburg district (constituting the northern part of the new Orange River Sovereignty) there was a movement against the British authority which had been imposed upon them. To counteract it, Sir Harry issued on 29th March a manifesto of a rather unconventional kind. He bade the farmers remember all the benefits he had lately conferred on them [freedom from nominal subjection to native chiefs,

* J. Noble, *South Africa* (1877), p. 126.

etc.], and contrast the misery from which he had
endeavoured to raise them with the happiness of
their friends and cousins living under the Colonial
government. If they compelled him to wield the
fatal sword, after all he had attempted to do for
them, the crime be on their own heads. He concluded with a prayer to the Almighty in which
he suggested that the farmers might unite with
himself.

Such a manifesto is not to be judged cynically.
The religious passages were sincere and characteristic of their author, and calculated to appeal
especially to the people to whom they were
addressed. But the distrust of England was too
deep for such an appeal to have more than a partial
success. The disaffected party in the Winburg
district determined to make a struggle for independence, and invited Pretorius to come over the
Vaal to lead them. Pretorius arrived at Winburg
on the 12th July. At his approach, Mr. Biddulph,
the British magistrate, rode off to Bloemfontein
and informed Major Warden, who sent a report to
the Governor on the 13th.

On the 17th Pretorius reached Bloemfontein,
and Major Warden, being unable to offer resistance,
capitulated, and was furnished by Pretorius with
waggons to take him, his troops, and the refugees
who had sought his protection, to Colesberg. Pretorius with his force marched to a camp on the
Orange River in the same neighbourhood.

Major Warden's report of the 13th July reached

Sir Harry Smith at Cape Town on the 22nd.* On the same day he issued a reward of £1000 for the apprehension of Pretorius and made arrangements for collecting a force to put down the rebellion.

On the 29th July he left Cape Town for the Sovereignty, accompanied by his Private Secretary, Major Garvock, Dr. Hall, Principal Medical Officer, Mr. Southey, Secretary to the High Commissioner, and Lieutenant Holdich, A.D.C. (now General Sir Edward Alan Holdich, K.C.B.). The party travelled with three waggons.

I extract the following entries from Sir Edward's diary, which he has kindly lent me :—

5th August.—Reached Beaufort. Heard from Cape Town that Major Warden had left Bloemfontein.

9th.—Reached Colesberg, having been 11½ days from Cape Town, travelling 102½ hours at the rate of 6 miles an hour, making the distance about 615 miles. A hundred Cape Mounted Rifles and one gun had arrived from Grahamstown, with 30 of the 91st Regiment, and were encamped at Botha's Drift. Boers occupying the opposite bank.

15th.—Detachment of 91st and C.M.R. which arrived yesterday encamped at Botha's Drift. High Commissioner rode to Major Warden's camp at Botha's Drift to meet the rebel leaders, [Gert] Kruger and Paul Bester, who had been invited to a conference, but they did not come. About 60 Boers on opposite bank. No regular laager or appearance of defence. Mr. Rex (a settler in the Orange Settlement) crossed the river, and was civilly received by Pretorius and other leaders.

* "The Governor—likened to a thunderbolt in presence of an enemy—acted with characteristic promptitude."—Noble, p. 132.

16th.—A letter received from the Rebel camp, petitioning His Excellency to withdraw the troops. Boers would never acknowledge British Government, but would trek to their friends across the Vaal. No reply sent to petition.

17th.—His Excellency and staff left Colesberg and pitched camp at Botha's Drift. When on the way report arrived from Major Warden that the rebel Boers had left the opposite bank the preceding night, no vestige of them remaining. A Boer came across and confirmed the report that they had all trekked (about 100 men with Pretorius). They had 62 waggons in the laager. Various reports as to the cause of the sudden flight. One was that Pretorius had heard of an army marching against them from Natal *viâ* the Drakensberg. Detachment of 45th Regiment and C.M.R. reached Colesberg, and marched following day to Botha's Drift.

20th.—The force encamped together on Botha's Drift except 91st Regiment [which marched in on the 25th]. Preparations made for crossing the river.

26th.—Headquarters and staff crossed. In six days the whole force (about 1200), with 117 waggons and supplies for thirty days, followers, etc., had crossed a rapid river 240 yards wide, and that by means of a caoutchouc pontoon (then just invented and here put to a practical trial) and one small boat worked by a hawser. The pontoon had to be taken out of the water every night and refilled in the morning, and the line to be passed across and made fast to the bank each morning. Camp pitched on the north-east bank of the river, either flank resting on the river.

27th.—Commenced march on Winburg in following order :—Cape Mounted Rifles, two guns R.A., one Company Rifle Brigade, one gun, remainder of R.B., 45th and 91st, waggons (117), rearguard, composed of 20 C.M.R., servants, burghers, followers, etc. At 2 pitched camp to right of Philippolis. Camp formed in line. Cavalry on the right, infantry on the left, guns and headquarters camp in centre.

28th.—Camp at Fuller's Kloof. No tidings of the rebels. 250 Griquas under Adam Kok joined the camp.

29th.—Halt for breakfast at Touw Fontein. Rebels reported to have been in the neighbourhood the evening before. At 10 a.m. inspanned, fell in, and marched on Boomplaats in the same order as before. Route lay over an open plain. After an hour's march saw a herdsman at a distance. He reported that he had seen fires the evening before along the Krom Elbe* river, beyond a few low hills in the direct route, also about 20 Boers riding about that morning, but he believed more to be in the neighbourhood.

On approaching this low range of hills, through which the road led, we observed large herds of game, apparently uncertain which way to run. At length the herd crossed close in front of the column, as if avoiding the hill. A report (as above) having been received of Boers having been seen in the neighbourhood of the hills, Lieut. Warren, C.M.R., with three or four troopers, was sent to reconnoitre. On galloping up one of the hills for this purpose, he suddenly found himself close upon some 40 or 50 Boers, mounted and armed with "roers," who immediately retreated round one of the hills, apparently joining a large body; this was assumed from the dust that arose. The White Company (or Europeans) of the C.M.R. under Lieut. Salis were ordered to cover the front of the column in skirmishing order, and to feel round the hills, but not to fire a shot unless fired upon. General † and staff rode to

---

* Called in Sir Harry Smith's dispatch "Kroom Alem Boh," by Theal "Kromme-Elleboog."

† "Up to this moment he was confident that no European in South Africa would point a weapon against his person. In this confidence he had dressed himself that morning in blue jacket, white cord trousers, and drab felt hat, the same clothing which he had worn when

the front with tried troops. All waggons were moved up
well in rear of the infantry. The column had not advanced
many paces, when some one from the front cried out,
"There they are!" and on looking in the direction intimated, the hills were observed to be suddenly lined with
Boers in their duffle jackets and white hats, who soon
opened a brisk and regular fire, which at first did not
cause much more harm than to throw the leading party
rather into confusion. The order was given for the troops
to go "threes about" and make way for the guns. The
Boers fired so low that not much mischief was done.
The guns being brought to bear upon the enemy, the
infantry were deployed into line, and the waggons, under
charge of Mr. Green of the Commissariat, were withdrawn
further to the rear and formed up in circle (laagered), and
escort for their defence was composed of the servants
and drivers accompanying them.

The order of attack was Rifle Brigade to skirmish
over the hills to the right ; 45th to bear on the centre,
and follow up any opening made by the artillery ; 91st
Regiment to escort the guns, and the Cape Mounted Rifles
to sweep round to the left, where the Boers were advancing from their right, in good skirmishing order, into the
plains, with the evident intention of getting round to our
rear and in at the waggons. The 45th suffered a good
deal in the centre, and the Rifle Brigade on the right,
being too eager and not taking sufficient advantage of cover,
lost a good many, Captain Murray being mortally wounded
at the head of his company. The 91st were ordered in
support of the 45th and the General's escort (a party of
Rifle Brigade) to form the escort for the guns.

In about twenty minutes the first range of hills was

he met Mr. Pretorius in the emigrant camp on the Tugela seven
months before. He was exceedingly anxious to avoid a collision."
—Theal, iv. p. 437.

cleared, and pushing on with all arms we observed the
Boers reformed at a farm-house below, where they made
a good defence from behind walls, and especially from
an old kraal and the bed of the " Krom Elbe " river.
From the kraal Colonel Buller was shot, a bullet taking
a piece out of his thigh and killing his horse. The guns
were advanced over a stony hill, which in ordinary times
would have been deemed impracticable, and by their
steady fire, under Lieut. Dyneley, soon drove the rebels
out of their (natural) defence-works and they spread
across an open plain that intervened in great disorder.
(No cavalry available to pursue.) Their road lay across
a neck between two hills, where they again made a
stand, as if to cover their retreat, but were checked by
a demonstration of the C.M. Rifles and the Griquas and
other followers, who on observing the retreat had turned
up on the right in a very valiant manner !

The Infantry in the mean time under Major Beckwith (R.B.) had reformed, and marched in column across
the plain as steadily as if their ranks had never been
broken or thinned. A few shots from the R.A. soon
dispersed the group at the neck, who before retreating
had set fire to the grass. On reaching the neck, it was
observed that the rebels had dispersed over the plain
as fast as they could with tired horses. Halted at the
neck, to collect stragglers, and make provision for the
wounded and for bringing up the waggons. No water
to be had within three miles. Only about 40 of the
Cape Corps could be got together.*

Mr. Rex, with a party of Griquas, sent to bring up
the baggage, the wounded remaining at Boomplaats under
the superintendence of Dr. Hall, P.M.O.

* A picture of the sharp skirmish of Boomplaats (from a drawing
by the late Lieut.-Col. Evelyn) appeared in the *Graphic*, 17th Feb.,
1900, with some comments by Major-General C. E. Webber.

Advanced on Calvert Fontein, having been told by some friendly Burghers, who had followed rather close on the trek of the Boers, that they were collecting in great numbers round Calvert Fontein. Found that they were only collecting and carrying off the wounded, or something of this kind. There appeared to be no intention of waiting for any more of our fire. Reached Calvert Fontein at 4.30 p.m. (a great rush for water). Halted for the night. No trace of a human being. A picket of cavalry sent forward to reconnoitre and follow up the rebels till dark. On return reported having seen a large body of Boers at some distance, in great disorder, apparently " off saddled."

On roll being called, found the return of casualties to be—

Commander-in-Chief, Sir H. Smith, struck on shin (very slight), and horse wounded;* Colonel Buller, wounded in thigh (severely), and horse killed; 7 officers wounded (Captain Murray, mortally); Rifle Brigade, 8 killed and 39 wounded.

On strict inquiry among the men of the force, ascertained that 49 *bodies* of rebels were seen lying on the field.†

Waggons came up at 5.30 p.m. On arrival at the bivouac, a Dutch letter was received by the Commander-in-Chief, stating that the Boer laager was about 12 miles off, west of the direct route to Bethany, at the farm-house of one Jan Cloete.

30*th.*—Leaving the camp standing in charge of convalescents and officers' servants (Col. Buller in command), we marched at 3 a.m., cavalry in advance, guns (with port-

---

* " It was remarkable how his Excellency came out unhurt, for from the beginning to the end he was in the thickest of the fire."—Noble, p. 135.

† It appeared afterwards that only nine Boers were killed.

fires burning) following. A company of Rifles headed the column and were directed to sweep any suspicious places. Met with no impediment. On reaching Cloete's farm at 6 a.m. found no trace of any laager. Column arrived at Bethany at 10 a.m. There is a large missionary chapel and a few native huts around it. A good house belonging to the missionaries, who had deserted it. Sir H. Smith and staff took possession of house and yard. Breakfasted upon biscuits and brandy, aided by a little tea made in an old pot. A Boer came in from his house half an hour distant and professed to be "loyal," and said he had not been in the fight, though his son had. The son and another young man concealed in the house were brought into camp by Mr. Southey. They received a lecture and were sent off with the understanding that they were to bring in their "roers" next day, which they did.

Two prisoners were brought up from the rear, taken on the field with arms, one a Dutchman named Dreyer, the other an Englishman, who proved to be a deserter from the 45th Regt. Both were remanded for trial by court martial on arrival at Bloemfontein.

2nd Sept.—Arrived at Bloemfontein at 9 a.m. Troops formed up into three sides of a square (Commander-in-Chief and staff, etc., in centre). Proclamation read and sovereignty proclaimed under a salute of 21 guns. General Court Martial ordered and assembled under Colonel Buller, R.B., for the trial of the two prisoners taken in the field.

Bloemfontein, a small village, consisting of some half-dozen houses and some huts, prettily situated on the banks of a stream having its source in a bubbling fountain, and under a hill. A small fort (or stockade) had been built, which was commanded from every side. The rebels had taken possession of the various houses and at the Resident's house had even commenced ploughing.

Encamped on the opposite side of the stream to the town, very good ground and well sheltered by a hill.

Sept. 3rd.—Troops paraded at 10 a.m. in front of the camp for Divine Service. Service read by Sir Harry Smith.* Preparations afterwards made for the march on Winburg ; a small force to be left to garrison Bloemfontein under Col. Buller (disabled by his wound).

Sept. 4th.—Camp struck before daylight and troops paraded, when the two rebels (who had been found " guilty " by the General Court Martial of " being in rebellion and bearing arms against Her Majesty's subjects " and sentenced to death accordingly) were paraded in front of the troops assembled, in the very spot where, a short time before, the rebel leader Pretorius had demanded the submission of the British resident, and the sentence carried out—the rebels being shot in presence of the troops.†

6th.—Reached the Vet River at one. On the march joined by a party of friendly Boers, who greeted us with a salute from their " roers " and loud shouts, which caused no little excitement in the rear of the column. These Boers had formed a laager on the Vet River under a Field Cornet named Wessels, and had maintained their position against Pretorius and the rebels. [Gert] Kruger, one of the leading rebels, surrendered himself, and, professing penitence, after taking the oath of loyalty, was pardoned. Moroco, king of the Barolongs, also came in, with a small train.

* In connexion with this, I may quote a story told to my sister, Miss Moore Smith of Durban, by the late Sir Theophilus Shepstone. " Sir Harry always read part of the service on Sunday morning at Grahamstown [? in 1835], and was so particular that all should come that he imposed a fine of half a crown on every absentee. He read extremely well, and was very proud of it. One Sunday a dog came into the room when service was going on, and began to create a disturbance. Sir Harry stood it for a little time, then in the middle of a prayer said suddenly, ' Take that d——d dog away,' after which he continued his prayer in the same tone as before."

† The execution of Dreyer as a rebel was long bitterly resented by the Boers.

Sept. 7th.—At 5.30 a.m. crossed the Vet River. Reached Winburg at 10.30. Here the troops were formed up in hollow square, the Proclamation read, and the sovereignty proclaimed under a salute of 21 guns. Encamped on the far side of a stream on the slope of a hill. Village consisted of three or four houses and huts.

Sept. 8th.—Halt. King Moshesh and Sikonyela arrived in camp. Moshesh a clear-headed fellow and very sharp. He wore a general's old blue coat and gold lace trousers, with a forage cap.

Sept. 9th.—Troops paraded, and a Review took place for the benefit of Moshesh, who was much amused with the movements, and particularly astonished at the Artillery, these being the first regular troops that had been so far into the interior.

Sept. 10th, Sunday.—Halt. Divine Service.

Sept. 11th.—Review of Moshesh's army. Mounted men armed with old ' roers." Infantry with native weapons (assagais, etc.). About 700 paraded and performed a war dance. A fine body of men for savages and undisciplined as they were. Preparations made for leaving Winburg and returning to the Colony, Mr. Southey, secretary to the High Commissioner, remaining to collect fines, with an escort of C.M. Rifles.

Sept. 12th.—Leaving the troops to follow by ordinary marches, the Governor and Staff left Winburg in mule-waggons.

13th.—Reached Bloemfontein at noon.

15th.—Troops arrived from Winburg. Three guns R.A., two companies 45th, and a company C.M.R. detailed to garrison the "Queen's Fort" [now to be built]; the remainder to march back to their respective localities under Col. Buller.

18th.—Arrived at Smithfield on the Caledon River.

Great gathering of Dutch and English farmers. Sir H. Smith laid the foundation-stone of a Dutch church [which was never built, the village being afterwards removed—E. A. H.].

26th.—Crossed the Orange River. Arrived at Ruffles Vlet, a beautiful site for a town.*

On the 28th Sir Harry received an ovation at Graaf Reinet, and on 6th Oct. reached King William's Town. It had now grown into a pretty town, and it gratified him to see between 200 and 300 Kafirs hard at work in building houses and aiding in the cultivation of the gardens. Next day he held a meeting of chiefs, including Sandilli, Macomo, Umhala, and Pato. The superior chief, Kreili (the son of Hintza), overtook Sir Harry after he had left King William's Town, and showed every sign of affection, calling him "father" and "Inkosi Inkulu" ("Great Chief"). The whole meeting was considered of very good omen for the success of the system established in British Kaffraria.

After visiting Grahamstown, the Governor proceeded to Port Elizabeth. In reply to an address praying for the formation of the Eastern Province of the Cape Colony into a separate government, he asked "What is Germany with her 33,000,000 struggling after but union? These German states have sunk through their disunion, while Great Britain is

---

* Here, or near here, on 12th May, 1849, the town of Aliwal North was founded by Mr. Chase, the Civil Commissioner.—Wilmot and Chase, p. 417.

acknowledged to owe her strength and her greatness to the union of her people. Nor at the present time must we have separation here. When I was asked whether I would have a Lieutenant-Governor, I replied, 'Certainly not.' The office fulfilled no other part than that of giving rise to very unprofitable correspondence." * On the 21st October the Governor returned to Cape Town, and, as elsewhere, was received with enthusiasm and an address of congratulation. It stated that the vigour and rapidity with which the rebellion had been repressed, and the moderation shown afterwards, were characteristic of Sir Harry's genius as a soldier and of the generous sympathies of his nature, and concluded with a prayer that he might long preside over the Colony, and exercise that "justice and mercy" which had marked his career.

* Under Sir Henry Pottinger's rule the Eastern Province had had an able Lieutenant-Governor in Sir Henry Young, and there was a strong feeling during Sir Harry's governorship that the interests of the Eastern Province could not be ensured by a government at Cape Town. Sir Harry himself finally gave in to this view, and on 14th June, 1851, recommended "a separate and distinct government for the Eastern Province."

CHAPTER XLIX.

(*Supplementary.*)

THE QUESTION OF THE ESTABLISHMENT OF A REPRE-
SENTATIVE ASSEMBLY IN THE CAPE COLONY—THE
CONVICT QUESTION—KAFIR WAR—RECALL OF SIR
HARRY SMITH—HIS DEPARTURE FROM THE CAPE.

As early as 1841 the inhabitants of Cape Town had
petitioned that their present system of government
by a Governor and a Legislative Council consisting
of officials and persons nominated by the Governor
should give place to a constitution resembling that
of the mother-country, to consist, that is to say, of
a Governor and an Executive Council, both appointed
by the Crown, and a Legislative Assembly composed
of representatives freely elected by the people.
Lord Stanley, in reply, expressed a general concurrence with the prayer of the petitioners, but
desired further information. To this request no
answer had been received, when on the appointment
of Sir Henry Pottinger to the government of the
Cape, Lord Grey instructed him (2nd Nov. 1846)
that Her Majesty's Government entertained the
strongest prepossessions in favour of a representative

2 R

system, and desired the Governor's assistance and advice. "Some difficulties," he added, "may be wisely encountered, and some apparent risks well incurred, in reliance on the resources which every civilized society, and especially every society of British birth and origin, will always discover within themselves for obviating the dangers incident to measures resting on any broad and solid principle of truth and justice."

Sir Henry Pottinger, during his year of office, was too much occupied with the Kafir War to carry out the instructions given him in regard to the establishment of representative government, but the instructions he had received were repeated on the appointment of Sir Harry Smith. He lost no time in acting on them, and on the 29th July, 1848, the very day on which he started to put down the rising beyond the Orange, he transmitted to Lord Grey the opinions of a number of colonial authorities on the questions at issue, and stated that they all, and he with them, agreed on the main point that a representative form of government was desirable. Lord Grey then put the matter in the hands of a Committee of the Board of Trade and Plantations, who drew up the main lines of a constitution, which received Her Majesty's approval. On 31st January, 1850, Lord Grey transmitted this Report to Sir Harry. It laid down that all subordinate arrangements should be made by Ordinance in the Colony, and Sir Harry was instructed to collect information and make all other arrangements for this purpose.

Meanwhile the Colony had been thrown into a state of hysterical agitation by an unfortunate arrangement made by Lord Grey to send thither some convicts from Bermuda in H.M.S. *Neptune*. These convicts were Irish peasants who had been driven into crime during the time of the famine, and Lord Grey seems to have thought that on this account less objection would be taken to receiving them. But the name "convict" was enough. The colonists of the Cape believed that this was only a beginning and that their country was to be made a convict settlement and flooded with criminals. An Anti-convict Association was formed, and the Governor was petitioned to dismiss the *Neptune* as soon as she arrived to some other station.

Sir Harry Smith, who from the beginning shared the colonists' objection to Lord Grey's proposal, wrote to that minister on 24th May, 1849, begging him to revoke his decision, in accordance with the petitions which he had been forwarding to him since 1st January. On the 29th May he reported a combination of the people headed by the Anti-convict Association "to hold in abhorrence any person who may aid the exiles in landing, and may have any communication with them whatever," and to stop the supply of stores to Government. Government officials all over the country were resigning, but he was still making preparations to land the exiles and provide for their support on shore.* On July 24th

---

* In May and June, 1849, Sir Harry was seriously ill from a carbuncle on his neck. On 20th June he gave a ball at Government

he reported that all but one of the unofficial members of the Legislative Council had resigned, and that on the 17th he had promised by proclamation that the convicts should not be landed but detained on shipboard till Her Majesty's pleasure were known, while declaring he had no legal power to send them to any other destination.*

No reply had been received from Lord Grey to the many appeals which had been made to him, when on 19th September the *Neptune* arrived. A fresh storm of public passion arose, and for the first time since his accession to office the Governor assembled the Executive Council. They approved of all his measures, and agreed that it would not be legal for him to dismiss the vessel. He offered a pledge, however, that he would resign his office rather than assist in carrying out any measure for landing the convicts. This declaration allayed the feelings of more moderate men, but the extremists extended their operations, and included the navy and the whole body of executive and judicial agents

House, which many refused to attend owing to the agitation against the Government. Sir Harry, with soldierly punctiliousness, appeared among his guests for half an hour, but his appearance was so ghastly, and made the more so by his dark green Rifle uniform, that it was said " one might have imagined that he had just stepped out of his coffin."

* Mr. W. A. Newman (*Memoir of J. Montagu*) quotes a reply made by Sir Harry to the Anti-Convict Association on 18th June : " This is the anniversary of the Battle of Waterloo. For four and forty years have I served my sovereign—I say it with pride—and I would rather that God Almighty should strike me dead than disobey the orders of Her Majesty's Government and thereby commit an act of open rebellion."

of the Government under an interdict so long as the
Neptune should remain in Simon's Bay.

Sir Harry, while curbing the military from any
act of retaliation against the insults heaped on
them,* was not to be daunted from the line he had
taken up, and with his usual energy devised arrangements for supplying Government servants with meat
and bread. He was thus able to maintain his
position until 13th February, 1850, when, in answer
to a dispatch of 30th September, he received one
from Lord Grey dated 5th December, which authorized him to send the unfortunate convicts to Van
Diemen's Land.

To return to the question of the new constitution. On the receipt of Lord Grey's dispatch of
31st January, 1850, the Governor found himself at
a deadlock owing to the resignation of the five
unofficial members of the Legislative Council in
the preceding July. The convict agitation had
spread such a spirit of dissatisfaction in the Colony
that the Governor thought that a Legislative
Council filled up by men who were merely his
nominees, would not command public confidence.
He therefore arranged that the Municipalities and
District Road Boards should furnish him with the

---

* Chase writes (Wilmot and Chase, p. 458), " Sir Harry, perfect
soldier as he was, had an instinctive horror of shedding blood, which
was never more strongly developed than when he curbed the military
from retaliating the insults offered to Her Majesty and to themselves
by the mobs of the western metropolis during the anti-convict *émeute.*"
We may remember that he had shown the same spirit during the
Radical disturbances at Glasgow (see pp. 326–328, 335).

names of gentlemen whom they would desire to be appointed, and from these he would fill up the vacancies. He did not, however, commit himself to nominating the five highest on the list. As a matter of fact, he chose the four highest, although he believed their election had been largely procured by electoral devices emanating from Cape Town, and with them the gentleman who was eleventh, chosen as having the special confidence of the Eastern Province. No sooner was the Council thus constituted and assembled than the four gentlemen above mentioned resigned their seats (20th September), as a protest against the Governor's departure from the electoral results and against the fact that the Legislative Council was called on to vote the estimates and transact ordinary business instead. of merely preparing the way for a Representative Assembly. These gentlemen were treated in the Colony as popular heroes, and two of them, Sir A. Stockenstrom and Mr. Fairbairn, were deputed to proceed to England to carry on an agitation against the Governor. Their position was, however, an untenable one, and received no support from Her Majesty's Government.*

* In connexion, however, with the delays encountered in receiving the new constitution, Lord Grey was much reviled both in the Colony and in England. Sir W. Napier (*Life of C. Napier*, iv. p. 327) quotes the following epigram :—

> " This point was long disputed at the Cape,
> What was the devil's colour and his shape.
> The Hottentots, of course, declared him white,
> The Englishmen pronounced him black as night ;
> But now they split the difference and say
> Beyond all question that Old Nick is Grey."

The Governor in his difficulty had taken a step which was not well received. He had constituted the remaining seven members of the Council a Commission to draft the ordinances of the proposed constitution, and on 19th Feb. 1851 suggested to Lord Grey that, there being no chance of forming a Legislative Council which would have the confidence of the Colony, the draft ordinances should be ratified in England. This suggestion was accepted. However, in obedience to Lord Grey's further instructions, he set himself in September to fill up the Council, and found four gentlemen willing to accept the vacant seats. On 10th October the Council met again. On 16th December the draft ordinances which had received Her Majesty's approval in England were read for the first time, and the second reading was fixed for February, 1852. In spite of the great eagerness of the Colony to receive representative government, it was then proposed that the further consideration of the question should be deferred till the Kafir War was over, and this view had the support of all the four unofficial members and of two out of the five official members of the Legislative Council. When, however, it was represented to the Governor, he promptly replied from his camp at King William's Town, in words full of political courage and sagacious confidence—

"I desire the Legislative Council to proceed to the discussion of these ordinances as a Government measure, leaving each clause an open question. I apprehend far greater embarrassments to the Government by delay than by procedure. I am ordered by Her Majesty's Government to proceed, and my own opinion concurs in the expediency of that order. I see no cause whatever for apprehension as to any public disturbance. Under any circumstances, however, I do not view a war upon the borders as affording cause for deferring the grant of a representative government."

Thanks, then, to Sir Harry's firmness the business proceeded, although it was not till the time of his successor that the long-desired boon of Representative Government was actually received by the colonists.

Till the end of 1850, in spite of the Anti-convict agitation and the political unrest caused by the desire for a Representative Assembly, Sir Harry's administration had been apparently a highly successful one. He had felt himself able to send home the 1st Battalion Rifle Brigade in May, 1850, and so meet the demands for economy pressed on him by the Home Government. The Orange River Sovereignty had been at peace, and in British Kaffraria, under the rule of an able officer, Colonel Mackinnon, the Kafirs seemed, as in 1836, to be making rapid progress towards becoming orderly and civilized British subjects. But this happy prospect was now suddenly over-clouded.

However contented the Kafirs at large might be with the new system, the chiefs suffered a loss of wealth by being no longer able to "eat up" whomsoever they liked, and with the loss of wealth

a loss of dignity. They felt that their followers
were encouraged to appeal for justice to the British
Commissioner and that the feudal power of the
chief was being quietly undermined. Accordingly
the Gaika chiefs of British Kaffraria, Sandilli and his
half-brother Macomo, became intriguing agitators,
and found in the terrible drought and distress of
1850 an opportunity ready to hand for disturbing
the peace.

In September of that year, Colonel Mackinnon,
instead of his usual satisfactory reports, wrote that
the white colonists were alarmed, as a new prophet,
Umlanjeni, thought to be a creature of Sandilli's,
was preaching war against the white, while the
Kafirs had been on their side alarmed by a report
that the Governor wished to seize all the chiefs.
In consequence of this information, Sir Harry on the
15th October left Cape Town for the frontier.

Having arrived at King William's Town on the
20th, he called a meeting of Kafir chiefs for the 26th.
At this meeting great demonstrations of loyalty were
made, and the Governor was greeted with a shout
of " Inkosi Inkulu! " (" Great Chief!"); but Sandilli
was absent. On the 29th Sir Harry threatened him
that unless he came and renewed his allegiance, he
would "throw him away" and confiscate his property—and when this threat produced no effect,
formally deposed him and appointed Mr. Brownlee,
the Civil Commissioner, chief of the Gaikas in his
place.* The act showed perhaps an over-sanguine

---

* On the 20th December, Sutu, Sandilli's mother, was made chief.

estimate of the readiness of the Kafir mind to recognize British authority as paramount to that of their feudal chiefs; but at the moment it was approved by Colonel Mackinnon and other men specially acquainted with the Kafir disposition, as it was later by the Home Government.

At another meeting held on 5th November, the chiefs of the Gaïkas and other tribes acknowledged one and all that Sandilli by his contumacy had deserved his fate, and the Governor wrote to Lord Grey, " The crisis has passed, and, I believe, most happily." He at once started on his return journey, and after receiving various congratulatory addresses on his way, reached Cape Town on the 24th November.

But news of fresh turbulent acts followed him, and (to quote the words of Mr. Chase *) " Sir Harry Smith was to be pitied by all who loved him—and who that knew him did not ?—when he had to write in bitter disappointment to the Secretary of State on the 5th December, 'The quiet I had reported in Kafirland, which I had so much and so just ground to anticipate, is not realized, and I start this evening.'" He left with the 73rd Regiment on the *Hermes* for the frontier, destined not to quit it again for sixteen months, and then as a man superseded in his office.

Having landed at the Buffalo mouth on 9th December, he reached King William's Town the same night, and next day by proclamation called

* Wilmot and Chase, *Annals of the Cape Colony* (1869), p. 437.

on all loyal citizens to enrol themselves as volunteers. The Kafirs were arming, and the farmers with their flocks and herds had fled in panic from the frontier. After a meeting with the chiefs (14th), which was again considered satisfactory, Sir Harry moved his troops to positions round the Amatola Mountains to prevent any combined movement between Kreili and the Gaikas. He proceeded himself to Fort Cox. Here on the 19th he held another meeting, at which, except Anta and Sandilli (who had now been outlawed), all the chiefs were present with their councillors and 3000 of their people. When Sir Harry vigorously denounced Sandilli's conduct they apparently acquiesced, but asked the Governor why he had brought the troops?

From Fort Cox Sir Harry sent Colonel Mackinnon on 24th December with a patrol up the gorge of the Keiskamma in the direction in which Sandilli was supposed to be hiding, it being thought that when the troops approached he would either surrender or flee the country. Mackinnon was, however, attacked in a defile, and twelve of his men were killed. And so broke out a new Kafir War, a " fitting legacy," says Chase, " of the retrocessive policy of 1836," and, we may add, unfortunately not the last disastrous war to which those words could be applied.

Next day (Christmas Day) three of the four military villages which had been established in British Kaffraria not quite three years before, Woburn, Auckland, and Juanasburg, were treacherously attacked by Kafirs, many of whom had just shared the Christmas dinner of their victims, and the settlers murdered. The Gaikas sprang to arms; every chief but Pato joined in the rising; and of a body of 400 Kafir police 365 rushed to their tribes with their arms and ammunition.

Meanwhile the Commander-in-Chief was shut up in Fort Cox in the Amatola basin, with hordes of wild Kafirs filling the bush and heights on every side, and the prospect before him of speedy starvation if he remained, or death from a bullet or an assagai if he issued forth. Colonel Somerset from Fort Hare made two unsuccessful attempts at relief. In the second, on 29th December, after fighting for four hours, he was forced to retire. After this he wrote to Sir Harry, begging him not to move with infantry, or they would be cut to pieces, but to sally out with 250 men of the Cape Mounted Rifles.

"This Sir Harry, in the daring, dashing way so characteristic of him, gallantly did, wearing the forage cap and uniform of one of the Cape Rifles, and by this timely incognito he rode twelve hazardous miles through the desultory fire of the Kafirs on the way to King William's Town. At the Debe Nek, about halfway, a strong attempt was made to intercept the Corps, but Sir Harry Smith and his escort vigorously spurred through their opponents, and after a smart ride reached the town, having eluded six bodies of Kafirs, who little suspected how great a prize was then in their power." *

* W. A. Newman's *Memoir of J. Montagu*, 1855.

On the day of his arrival in King William's Town, 31st December, Sir Harry issued a Government notice of the most vigorous kind. " He hopes colonists will rise *en masse* to destroy and exterminate these most barbarous and treacherous savages, who for the moment are formidable. Every post in British Kaffraria is necessarily maintained." *

Meanwhile, on the news reaching Cape Town that the Governor was shut up in Fort Cox, the Colonial Secretary, Mr. Montagu, himself a Waterloo man, showed the greatest energy in raising troops and despatching them to the frontier. He sent in all 3000 men, chiefly Hottentots. On the arrival of the first levies (1600 men), Sir Harry wrote to him, "Your exertions are incredible, and they will enable me to take the field."

Accordingly, at the end of January he ordered Mackinnon to throw supplies into Forts White and Cox. This was accomplished, but he could do little at the moment beyond maintaining the military posts, and meanwhile difficulties were accumulating upon him. The Dutch farmers did not come forward as they had done in 1835, to assist in repelling an invasion from the colony;

* A good deal might have been excused in a document issued under such circumstances, but the word " exterminate" was not a happy one, and was frequently seized on afterwards by opponents of Sir Harry in England. How little it represented the writer's real feeling is shown by a sentence in a letter to his wife of 24th May, 1851 : "I hope yet to see all the ringleaders hung, while I would willingly *forgive* the poor wretches who have been led astray by the wickedness of others."

Kreili, the Great Chief beyond the Kei, was wavering; and, worse than all, by the beginning of February Sir Harry learnt that the Hottentots of the Kat River Settlement, people nominally Christians, though of late suspected of disaffection, had one and all revolted and joined the Kafirs, their hereditary enemies.

On the 3rd February, in once more appealing to the inhabitants of the colony to rally in their own defence, he said, " I regard this almost general disaffection of the coloured classes within the Colony as of far greater moment than the outbreak of the Kafirs."

At this time the British troops at Sir Harry's disposal amounted only to 1700,* of whom 900 were employed in holding a dozen posts. Accordingly he had only 800 "available to control 4000 Hottentot auxiliaries of doubtful loyalty, and to meet the hordes of well-armed athletic and intrepid barbarians in the field." †   Both Colonel (now Major-General) Somerset and Colonel Mackinnon had obtained successes ; the rebel chief Hermanus had been killed in attacking Fort Beaufort on 7th January; yet the enemy was still powerful and in the occupation of a mountainous country next to impenetrable.

Sir Harry was compelled to act on two bases, the one from King William's Town to the mouth of the Buffalo, so communicating by the port of

---

* Consisting of the 6th, 73rd, 91st, and 45th Regiments.
† Dispatch to Lord Grey, 17th March, 1852.

East London with the Western Province and with the sea ; the other from Fort Hare *viâ* Fort Beaufort and Grahamstown to Port Elizabeth, Fort Hare being connected with King William's Town by the garrisons of Fort White and Fort Cox. The troops operating on the first line in British Kaffraria were under the command of Colonel Mackinnon, and had their headquarters at King William's Town under the eye of the Commander-in-Chief. In April, after the arrival of the new levies, they amounted to 4700 men, of whom 1000 were occupying a line of seven posts. The troops on the second line were under the command of Major-General Somerset, whose headquarters were at Fort Hare. They amounted to 2900, of whom 900 were garrisoning six posts. The general plan of the campaign was to confine the war to neutral territory, to detain the Kafirs in Kaffraria, and eventually to drive them out of their fastnesses in the Amatola Mountains. The Kafir revolt would in this way, Sir Harry writes, have been crushed at once, but for the hopes raised by the defection of the Hottentots. That defection had indeed gone far. Although Somerset on the 23rd February had crushed the Kat River rebellion by the capture of the rebels' stronghold, Fort Armstrong, only a fortnight later 335 men of the Cape Mounted Rifles, including the very men who had so gallantly escorted the Governor from Fort Cox, deserted from King William's Town in a body. This was another crushing blow. "My horror cannot be described," Sir Harry wrote on the 17th

March. "I assure your Lordship that no event of my military career ever caused me so much pain as the defection of so large a portion of a corps to which I am as much attached as I am to that wearing the green jacket of my own regiment." This detachment of the Rifles had been drawn principally from the Hottentots of the Kat River Settlement and had been much excited by rumours of the punishment which was to be meted out to the Kat River rebels.

Having felt it necessary to disarm nearly all the Riflemen who had not deserted, Sir Harry now found himself practically without any mounted force at all, and wrote to ask for 400 young Englishmen to be sent out as recruits, with the promise of receiving ten acres of land after ten years' service. This request, however, was not granted. In order to anticipate any attempt at rescuing the Kat River prisoners at Fort Hare, Sir Harry moved out himself on March 19th, and by a masterly movement defeated the enemy at the Keiskamma, spent the 20th at Fort Hare, obtained another success on the Tab' Indoda Range on the 21st, and returning by Fort White with 1000 captured cattle, reached King William's Town on the 25th.

A Cape newspaper, politically opposed to him, wrote of Sir Harry's conduct in these few days—

"It is not a little gratifying to find the mingled fire and prudence of the veteran commander as conspicuous now as in former days. We see the value of such a leader more distinctly in comparing him with other officers of good standing and abilities."

And it quotes from the *Frontier Times*—

"Sir Harry Smith showed his usual energy, riding backwards and forwards to where the different parties were engaged and cheering them on. A new spirit has been infused among the troops and levies, and all speak of the bravery and activity of his Excellency." *

Fresh signs of disaffection in the Cape Corps made it necessary to disarm still more men, and the Kafirs were so much emboldened that but for the loyalty of the one chief Pato, who held the country between King William's Town and the sea, the Governor's position would have been barely defensible. He continued to send out patrols, which were invariably successful. Mackinnon scoured the Poorts of the Buffalo in the middle of April and at the end of the month penetrated the Amatolas; and Captain Tylden, in command of the position of Whittlesea, which was twelve times assaulted, saved the Colony for the time from the enemy. But larger operations were out of the question. "Had the Kat River Rebellion and the defection of the Cape Corps not presented themselves, Sandilli's reign would have been a transient one. I have been obliged to steer a most cautious course, one contrary to my natural desire in predatory warfare, but imperatively imposed on me by the dictates of prudence and discretion, my force being composed

---

* *Cape Town Mail*, April 5th and 8th, 1851.

generally of a race excitable in the extreme."   S
Sir Harry wrote on the 5th April.   Ten days late
he again complains of the little assistance give
him by the farmers.   " A few spirited farmers hav
performed good service, but where are the men wh
so gallantly fought with me in 1835—Van Wyk:
Greylings, Nels, Rademeyers, Ryneveldts, etc.
Once more, my advice to the frontier inhabitant
is to rush to the front."

Early in May Sir Harry received reinforcement:
from home, consisting of drafts for the regiment
already under his command (11 officers and 29(
men) and the 74th Regiment.   This he sent t(
Fort Hare to Major-General Somerset, orderinᵍ
him at the same time to be prepared to concentrat(
for a move into the great Kafir stronghold, th(
Amatolas.   Two more regiments were still to come
and Sir Harry believed that the force he would thei
have would be ample.   In acknowledging the re
inforcements, he wrote on 6th May, " I had mos
zealously clung to the desire of civilizing thes(
savages.   As regards the Gaikas generally, m)
attempt has been an awful failure, while I con
gratulate myself on having maintained at peace th(
T'Slambie tribes, comprising the half nearly of th(
population of British Kaffraria.   I am deepl)
indebted to the chief Pato."

On the 10th May he was gratified by receivinᵍ
the following letter from the Duke of Wellington :—

"London, 8th March, 1851.

"MY DEAR GENERAL,

"We heard on the day before yesterday of the renewal of your troubles at the Cape.

"The 74th Regiment and all the drafts from Depôts that can be sent for the Regiments at the Cape will be sent off as soon as possible.

"I have told the Government that I think that another Regiment ought to be sent.

"I enclose the copy of a memorandum which I sent yesterday to Lord Grey.*

"Not knowing the latest or the exact state of the insurrection, I cannot say in what stations it would be necessary for you to carry on your operations, or whether with more than one Corps.

"If with only one so much the better, but it will increase the security, confidence, and tranquillity of the

---

*   "Horse Guards, 7th March, 1851.

"It appears to me that this insurrection of the Caffres is general and quite unjustifiable, sudden, and treacherous.

"In my opinion Sir Henry Smith ought to have the means in Regular Troops and Light Equipments of ordnance to form two bodies of troops, each capable of acting independently in the field, each of which should give countenance and support to the detachments of Boers, Hottentots, and loyal Caffres, by which the rebel and insurgent Caffres should be attacked and driven out of the country.

"The occupation of the numerous posts in the country marked Adelaide in the map was very proper and necessary when the frontier was the Buffalo River, but it would be much better to carry it to the Key and there fix it permanently, and to form a place d'armes or fortified Barrack for Troops somewhere about King William's Town, between that and Fort Wellington, or possibly a little to the westward near the sources of the river.

"In such place d'armes there might be the means of giving cover to more than the small body which might be required for the permanent garrison."

Colony if you should be able to keep an efficient Corps in reserve in a second line.

>   " Wishing you every success,
>   " Believe me, ever yours most sincerely,
>   " (Signed)   WELLINGTON.

" Lieut.-General Sir Harry Smith, Bt., G.C.B."

It must have been satisfactory to Sir Harry to feel that in establishing his two lines of defence he had anticipated the advice of his great master.

While Somerset made a successful patrol against the combined Kafirs and Hottentots of the sources of the Kat River, and Mackinnon another in the Amatolas, there were still no signs of the submission of the enemy. Meanwhile news came of trouble with Moshesh in the Orange River Sovereignty, and the prospect of a new war there, and this was followed by a revolt of the Hottentots of the missionary station of Theopolis, 25 miles from Grahamstown. The period of six months for which the Hottentot levies in the army had been enlisted was now expiring, and there was no disposition among them to enlist again, and in this way the force would be reduced to 1800 men. Nothing could be done till further reinforcements arrived from England. "The almost general rebellion among the eastern Hottentots," wrote Sir Harry on the 17th June, "paralyzes my movements in British Kaffraria and compels me to hold a force ready for the protection of Grahamstown." Owing to the cutting off of the mails, his letters to his wife at Cape Town were now written almost entirely in Spanish.

The following letter to his sister Mrs. Sargant shows the feeling excited in him by Sir William Molesworth's attack on him in the House of Commons on April 10th, in which he was accused of burdening the empire by the annexation of 105,000 square miles of new territory and provoking his local troubles by high-handed and despotic government.

> "King William's Town, 18th June, 1851.
> "*Waterloo.*

"MY DEAREST ALICE,

"I wish I was half the active fellow now I was then, for I have need of it, seeing I am Her Majesty's 'Despotic Bashaw' from Cape Point to Delagoa Bay to the east, and to the great newly discovered lake to the north-west—without a legislature, and in the midst of a war with cruel and treacherous and ungrateful savages and renegade and revolted Hottentots. These Hottentots have been treated as the most favoured people, enjoying all the rights, civil and religious, of the inhabitants at large of the Colony—fed as a population when starving,—yet have these ungrateful wretches in great numbers (not all) revolted and joined their hereditary and oppressive enemy the Kafir, who drove them from the Kye over the Fish River, and who have destroyed them as a nation.

"I have had so much to do and some little anxiety of mind, although I sleep like a dormouse, that I have not written lately to one so dear to me, but Juana has. The war-making Kafirs are cowed by the continued exertions among them of my numerous and vigorous patrols, but they are in that state of doggedness they will neither come in nor fight. By every communication I have open to me, I offer peace to *the people*, but the chiefs must await my decision, their conduct has been so treacherous, cunning,

and deceitful. I have succeeded in maintaining in peace
and tranquillity nearly one-half of the population of British
Kaffraria, those fortunately next to the sea, while the
Gaika Kafirs, natives of the mountains adjoining the
Hottentot great location of the Kat Province, are all at
war. This shows my system cannot be oppressive, or I
should have had no friendly Kafirs, whereas the latter
escort my waggons with supplies, slaughter cattle, carry
my mails, assist me in every way in their power, which
affords better argument in refutation of the Radical and
garbled untruths, though founded on facts, of Sir W
Molesworth. I will give you an example [of one] among
other accusations of my despotism. The Kafir Hermanus
who by birth is a negro slave, was ever heretofore with his
people an enemy to the Kafir, because it was his interest
to be friendly to us. After the war of 1835–6, Sir B
D'Urban gave him a grant of a beautiful tract of country
within the Colony upon the ever-supplying-water, the
Blinkwater, stream. His title was disputed by some o
the colonists, and it was complained that *he* paid no quit-
rent as they all did. It was just, and only just, that if he
was protected by the government, he should contribute
equally with others, his quota for its maintenance. I
therefore, as a part of a general system, exacted a quit-
rent, a mere trifle, which was the best possible title and
deed of occupation, yet does this throating Sir W. M
bring forward this as an act of despotism. It is really
ludicrous.

"But for this inexplicable Hottentot revolution, I
would have put down the Kafirs in six weeks. These
Hottentots are the most favoured race on earth, yet have
a set of Radical London Society missionaries been preaching to them like evil spirits that they were an oppressed
and ill-used race, until, encouraged by violent meetings
all over the Colony upon the convict question, they have

met with arms in their hands, arms given to them by us, for the purpose of joining the Kafirs to drive the English over the Zwartkop River beyond Uitenhage.

"I have endeavoured to administer this government so as to allow the all-powerful sun to shine forth its glory upon all its inhabitants, whether black or white, equally, and I have no other object than the welfare of the people generally. I have said, 'Lay before me your wants; they shall be considered and your wishes met if practicable.' This was appreciated until the d—— convict question arose. The emancipated blacks in Cape Town, the Hottentots in the Kat River, held anti-convict meetings got up by white Radicals, who have thus induced the coloured classes upon this frontier and in many other parts of the Colony to believe that separate interests exist for white and black.

"The Kafir has been fostered by the most benevolent acts of kindness by me as a Governor. My study has been to ameliorate their condition from brutes to Christians, from savages to civilized men. They progressed in three years beyond all belief until some white-faced devils (the sable king often wears a white face) got in among them, persuaded the chiefs my object was their extermination, and while the *people* clung with avidity to my protection from the former tyranny they groaned under, the chiefs asserted their feudal authority, and such is man in a wild state of nature, he cleaves to the hereditary rule of oppressors of his forefathers—with tears in his eyes. I have seen many weep when they came to say to me farewell; 'Our country will be lost.' Let Sir W. M. and his myrmidons deny this; he cannot, but he can assert that just measures are foul, despotic, and arbitrary acts.

"Juana is in better spirits now since the reinforcements have arrived, I hope. Since I have received the dear

Duke's kind letter, Juana regards me as supported by o
friends and present master.* The latter gentleman and
understand each other. I will be *censured* by no man, bu
I will endeavour to obey where I can. He affronted m
by finding fault with an 'abortive attempt to reform th
Legislative Council,' which made my blood boil, althoug
my remonstrance was as mild as milk. I think the recer
attempt he and his colleagues have made to form
government has been fully as *abortive* as mine, and the
have discovered the impossibility of making legislators o
men who will not undertake office. Since the outbrea
all his communications have been most complimentary.

"Your brother

"HARRY.

"P.S.—I have been urged by many friends to sen
home some one to support the cause of my government.
won't. It is a weak line of conduct to appeal to friendshi
when conduct is in intention free from imputation of evi
Let Miss Coutts peruse this if she can. You had bette
copy it in your legible hand, for the enormous quantity
write has as much impaired my autograph as hard road
the fore-legs of a trotting horse, if England still produce
one. That she does asses, I know."

One of Sir Harry's nephews, writing home o
the 21st, says—

"My uncle's health, thank God, considering all things
is far from bad, but he is obliged to be very careful, and
cannot stand exposure to damp or cold. The Hottentot
are mostly in the colony in small bands, plundering the
poor defenceless farmers ; constant outrages are committed
by these rascals. . . . Sir Harry confidently expects tha

* Lord Grey.

two or three regiments will be speedily sent out, and sincerely do I hope they may, for to end the war with his present force is impossible."

On the last four days of June a combined movement to clear the Amatolas which had long been preparing was at last accomplished, the 1st Division under the command of Somerset co-operating with the 2nd under Michel (Colonel Mackinnon being ill), assisted by Tylden with 300 men from Whittlesea. The operations were conducted by four columns converging to a centre. They were completely successful, but Sir Harry saw no signs that they had hastened the end of the war, and warned the inhabitants of the colony that the beaten Kafirs were likely to go about in small marauding parties as " wolves "—an anticipation too sadly realized by the rush which was now made into the Colony, and the terrible depredations which accompanied it.

The trial of the Kat River rebels resulted in 47 of them being sentenced to death—a sentence which Sir Harry commuted to penal servitude for life ; so bringing on himself in some quarters the charge of excessive leniency. Chase, who considers the commutation a " grave mistake," excuses it on the ground that Sir Harry " pitied the poor creatures, knowing that they had been deluded into the belief that they are taught by the precept of the Bible to fight for independence with the sword of Gideon." *
It is better to accept the explanation given by Sir Harry himself in his dispatch of the 7th April, 1852.

* Wilmot and Chase, p. 458.

"Surrounded as I and Major-General Somerset were by these people drawn from the eastern and western districts, one false step or untimely exercise of power and martial law would have plunged the whole into the chaos of revolution. Her Majesty's troops must have abandoned their advanced positions and fallen back on Grahamstown, and the T'Slambie tribes would have risen as well as every curly-headed black from Cape Town to Natal." *

During July and August bands of the enemy filled the country between Fort Beaufort and the Fish River, penetrating later into Lower Albany itself, and burning and marauding wherever they appeared. It was natural that the colonists should appeal to the Commander-in-Chief to assist them. Feeling, however, that if he fell back from King William's Town, his retreat would be the signal for tribes on the east, hitherto passive, to join the Gaikas, he expressed his wish to continue operations in the Amatolas, and ordered Somerset to establish posts of burghers, if they would turn out, at every eligible point. Somerset replied that the burghers could not now withstand the attacks, and he had established a camp at Haddon on the Koonap; and a month later Sir Harry sent Colonel Eyre with the 73rd Regiment from King William's Town to Bathurst to protect Grahamstown and Lower Albany.

And so the war went on, the Commander ever sending out fresh patrols to harass the foe in his

---

* Cp. pp. 791 *bot.*, 792. The *Cape Town Mail* (some indication of colonial feeling) protested both on the 25th January and on 5th April against the military execution of rebels.

fastnesses,—on the 8th August he says that the 73rd regiment has now marched 2838 miles since the outbreak of hostilities,—maintaining every single post, yet still, for want of an adequate force, unable to effect any decisive action. Meanwhile there were fresh defections among the Hottentots in the Cape Corps, and news came from Warden in the Orange River Sovereignty that many of the Boers there would not assist him against Moshesh, and their fellow-countrymen over the Vaal were disposed to back them in their hostility to the British Government. He was bidden to act only on the defensive till troops could be sent to him.

In August the 2nd (Queen's) Regiment arrived from England, and soon after part of the 12th Regt. from the Mauritius. But there were a mass of hostile Kafirs and Hottentots in the Colony estimated at more than 6000, one body being in the Fish River Bush 30 miles to the north-east of Grahamstown, the other under Macomo in the Waterkloof 50 miles to the north-west, and in a patrol made by Colonel Mackinnon in the Fish River Bush on the 8th September, Captain Oldham and 25 men were killed and 41 wounded, and the bush was re-occupied by the Kafirs immediately. Meanwhile Somerset had failed in expelling Macomo, and Kreili and Fakoo seemed on the brink of openly throwing in their lot with Sandilli.

Under these circumstances, although now reinforced by the 60th Rifles and the 12th Lancers, Sir Harry asks on the 15th October for 400 English recruits for the Cape Corps and two additional regiments of infantry. Meanwhile there were fresh operations of the most arduous kind in the Waterkloof, and Somerset at the end of October succeeded in dislodging Macomo from his fastness. In consequence of that success, Sir Harry was able to write on the 1st November that he was now able to undertake tasks of a more extensive character, and proposed, after sweeping the Amatolas and driving the enemy from the Fish River Bush, if he concentrated there, to march across the Kei with three columns to invade Kreili, whose country was the great refuge of the beaten Gaikas, after which it might be necessary to send a force over the Orange River against Moshesh.

On November 12th, having received a despatch from Lord Grey suggesting that, failing the support of the Boers in the Orange River Sovereignty, the territory should be relinquished, Sir Harry forwarded it to his Assistant-Commissioners, Major Hogg and Mr. Owen, with a strong expression of his own views of such a proposal.

"If Her Majesty's sovereignty over this territory were now rescinded, the step would be regarded by every man of colour in South Africa as an unprecedented and unlooked-for victory to his race, and be the signal of revolt or continued resistance to British authority from Cape Town to the territory of Panda, and thence to the Great Lake. No measure during my administration of this Government has caused me so much consideration as that relating to the affairs of the Sovereignty. Property there, even during the late disturbances, has increased in value, and although the funds are not now flourishing, I am confident that locally they will speedily improve to a great extent. I am equally confident that if any change were made in the present state of things in the theoretical hope of gaining over a discontented party by yielding to their demands, such a precedence would evince weakness on our part, fraught with every evil, and perpetuate the belief that persevering resistance to Her Majesty's authority would ultimately ensure success. It would, at the same time, be not only disastrous to the parties now dissatisfied, but would sacrifice to the vengeance of the disaffected those who have remained loyal and faithful."

In this Sir Harry saw more clearly than most of his contemporaries. When, contrary to the strong opinion of the Colony,* the Sovereignty was abandoned in 1854, and a Republic hostile to England was allowed to take its place, only one man, the present Lord Norton, opposed the change in the House of Commons, and he on very narrow grounds, and Sir Harry Smith's successor in the Governorship of the Cape wrote in blind satisfaction, "The foolish Sovereignty farce is at length over, and we have done with it."†

* The *Cape Town Mail* of 9th Dec. 1851 wrote prophetically, "This abandonment of a really flourishing and promising British colony would be an Imperial calamity ; but the full extent of the mischief would not be understood until it became necessary, as in a few years it certainly would be found, to reconquer the territory so dishonourably and foolishly deserted ;" and Chase in 1869 speaks of the "abandonment of that splendid country, the Orange River Sovereignty, through a gross ignorance and a disgraceful misstatement of its capabilities, and permitting in its place the formation of the Free State Republic—one of the most imprudent acts ever committed, involving the Colony in entanglements, troubles, and cost, the end and consequence of which cannot be predicted."

† *Correspondence of Gen. Sir G. Cathcart*, p. 358.

In November, in the course of Somerset's continued operations to clear the Waterkloof, Lieut.-Col. Fordyce of the 74th and four other officers fell by an ambuscade, an incident the more unfortunate as the English public, unable to realize the enormous difficulties of the situation, was already much excited by the slow progress made in the war. Those difficulties were enumerated by Sir Harry Smith on 18th Dec. in reply to a querulous dispatch of Lord Grey. He reminded him that he had had to carry on a desultory war over an extent of country twice the size of Great Britain and Ireland, overrun by a most enterprising horde of savages, and to maintain twelve forts. Had one retrograde step been made, the *whole* population of British Kaffraria would have been in a blaze. What soldiers could do, his had done.

"So long as the insurgents held together and acted in large bodies, they were defeated on forty-five different occasions between the 24th Dec. and 21st Oct. . . . I have maintained throughout my positions and forts—no convoy has been cut off, and no rencontre, however sanguinary, has been unattended with success." Now that the reinforcements have arrived, they "will rescue the Colony from its misery . . . and relieve the Governor of the Cape from difficulties, obstacles, opposition, and rebellion, such as it has been the fortune of few men to encounter."

The worst was already past. In the middle of January Sir Harry reports that the operations beyond the Kei have met with signal success, that 30,000 head of cattle have been captured, 7000 Fingoes rescued from thraldom, and that a meeting of all the Gaika chiefs and their councillors has deputed emissaries to sue for peace, and that he has insisted on an unconditional surrender. At the same time he has seven columns of troops ready to move, if his terms are not agreed to.

Accordingly, when he received on 5th February a rather sarcastic dispatch from Lord Grey written on the 15th December, he was in a good position to reply to it. Lord Grey wrote—

"It is some relief . . . to find that you are so highly satisfied with the conduct of the officers and men under your orders, and that you regard the operations under Major-General Somerset on the 14th and 16th October as having been attended with important success. I confess that from that officer's own report, . . . that is not the light in which I should have regarded these affairs. The very serious amount of our losses, and the fact that at the conclusion of the operations of the last day to which your intelligence reaches, it was the rear, and not the van, of the British force which was engaged with the enemy, and that the latter must therefore have been the assailants, would appear to me scarcely to justify the tone of satisfaction with which you relate these occurrences."

In reply to this piece of civilian criticism, Sir Harry writes—

"Those, my Lord, who have witnessed military operations, and are best acquainted with their varying character, success attending them in one part of the field, while in others partial bodies may be held in check, will not consider the affair of a rearguard as the criterion by which to judge of their general result. Neither in ancient nor in modern war has a rencontre of the kind been so regarded. And the peculiarity of the present contest must be borne in mind; it must be remembered that this Kafir warfare is of the most completely guerrilla and desultory nature, in which neither front, flank, nor rear is acknowledged, and where the disciplined few have to contend with the undisciplined but most daring and intrepid many, in the midst of the holds and fastnesses of the latter. . . . The country in which the operations were carried on is far more difficult to ascend and penetrate than even the Amatolas; hence the gallant and enterprising exertions of the troops became the more conspicuous, and called forth that expression of my satisfaction dictated by experience in war, which enables a Commander to estimate justly the success he has obtained, and to commend as it deserves the conduct of his officers and soldiers.

"In my dispatch of the 19th November I have reported the ultimate success of Major-General Somerset's operations. Although the loss of Lieut.-Col. Fordyce and of the other officers who unfortunately fell by an ambuscade of not more . . . than 20 rebels, was deeply to be regretted, the success which I anticipated and have reported, but which your Lordship does not regard in the same light, founding your opinion on the affair of a rearguard, enabled me immediately to so organize the troops as effectually to watch and guard the frontier line to prevent inroads, and at the same time to invade the territory of the paramount chief, Kreili. The uninterrupted successes of the troops beyond the Kei . . . established their superiority far and near. Meanwhile I was enabled to collect a depôt of provisions for 1000 infantry and 500 horse at Bloemfontein, in case necessity should arise for a movement in that direction. . . . Thus, my Lord, viewing matters as a whole, you will, I think, consider me borne out by general results in having expressed my satisfaction at the conduct of the officers and troops, whose exertions and success I foresaw would lead to the result which has been attained, a general entreaty for peace by the enemy beyond the Kei, as well as by the rebels of British Kaffraria."

Peace was in prospect, but it was not yet attained, and after a week's suspension of hostilities, seven columns were again operating in the Amatolas. Little or no resistance was met with. A fresh operation in the Waterkloof was now determined on. Accompanying the troops himself, Sir Harry established his headquarters on 5th March at Fort Beaufort, and on the 9th at Blinkwater Post. On the 11th Eyre, after enormous difficulties in a precipitous country, captured "Macomo's Den"— a success of such magical effect that resistance seemed to vanish after it.

On the 17th March Sir Harry pronounced that the difficult and till then well-maintained positions of the enemy, the Waterkloof, Blinkwater, and Fuller's Hoek, were completely cleared, and he was at once moving with Michel's and Eyre's columns with fifteen days' provisions to dislodge Tyalie and penetrate into the heart of the Amatolas, while Somerset pursued the retreating enemy, and the Tambookies were assailed from Whittlesea. "Every part of the rebel enemy's country will then be assailed."

But in the same dispatch in which he announced that the enemy was being at last driven to bay, he had to acknowledge the receipt of Lord Grey's

2 T

dispatch of 14th January, informing him that for a want of "energy and judgment" in conducting the war he was recalled, and that General the Hon. George Cathcart would shortly arrive in South Africa to supersede him.   It is needless to picture the bitter mortification of the veteran Commander, who, after gallantly facing unexampled difficulties, saw the sweets of victory snatched from his grasp and the military qualities which had brought him fame condemned by a civilian of half his years. Lord Grey's dispatch—universally condemned in England and in the Colony *—and Harry Smith's vindication may be read in full in Appendix V. to this volume, their length precluding them from finding a place here.

It was a consolation to the recalled General to learn that the Duke of Wellington, speaking in the House of Lords on 5th February, had entirely repudiated Lord Grey's censure.

"I wish to express my sense of the services of General Sir Harry Smith, now in the command of the troops in the Colony of the Cape of Good Hope. Sir Harry Smith is an officer who, from the high reputation which he has already attained in the service, does not require any commendation from me. But having filled a high command in several important military operations carried on under his direction, and having been recalled by Her Majesty's Government, it is but just to him to say that I,

* Lord John Russell stated that the dispatch had never been seen by the Queen, and Lord Ellenborough, in a kind letter dated " Feb. 7," says, "What I am told is that Lord Grey recalled you, not without asking the Duke's opinion, but against it, after he had asked it."

who am his commanding officer, though at a great distance, entirely approve of all his operations—of all the orders he has given to the troops, and of all the arrangements he made for their success. I approve entirely of the conduct of the troops in all their operations. I am fully sensible of the difficulties under which they laboured, and of the gallantry with which they overcame all those difficulties, and of the great success which attended their exertions. (Cheers.) My firm belief is that everything has been done by the commanding General, by the forces, and by his officers, in order to carry into execution the instructions of Her Majesty's Government. . . . I am proud to say that I have observed no serious error in the conduct of these late operations. . . . The only fault I find with Sir Harry Smith is" [that after storming a native fastness he did not destroy it by opening roads into it for the movement of regular troops with the utmost rapidity].

The Duke, however, acknowledged that to do what he suggested was not the work of a moment.*

But the bitterness of his recall did not cool the energy with which Sir Harry maintained the war against the flagging enemy. The Amatolas were

---

* Sir George Napier, himself an ex-Governor of the Cape, wrote in April, 1852 :—" Had the Duke of Wellington ever seen the ' Cape bush,' he would not have said what he did about making roads through it ; the thing is quite out of the question. . . . You may rely upon it that Sir Harry Smith would never have delayed one day in making roads had it been feasible . . . As for Harry Smith, I am glad to see Lord Grey is abused by everybody for the harsh unjust manner of his recall. In my opinion the great mistake Smith made was in ever giving in to Lord Grey's folly of withdrawing a single soldier ; and when the war did break out, he should have at once acknowledged his error, and boldly demanded reinforcements to the extent of 5000 troops at once. I still hope he may be able to finish the war before his successor arrives, for till lately he had not force to do more than he did."— *Life of Sir W. Napier*, ii. pp. 310-312.

scoured again, and the satisfactory report brought in by Colonel Michel : "The Gaika tribes generally have migrated from these strongholds. Two companies may traverse with safety where heretofore a large column was required. I deem the war in this quarter virtually concluded." With such news the Governor returned to King William's Town on 26th March. On 7th April he wrote his last dispatch as Governor and Commander-in-Chief. He was able to say—

"I transfer the civil government without a single particle of business in arrear, and with a treasury without a debt, while all the civil officers have worked under me with energy and zeal. The war impending over the Orange River territory has been averted, while had its prosecution become imperative, I had collected an ample depôt of commissariat supplies at Bloemfontein. Amicable relationship has been established with the Transvaal emigrant Boers.* The turbulent Boers within the Sovereignty, when convicted of overt acts of disloyalty, have had heavy pecuniary fines inflicted on them, many of which to the amount of £1075 have already been promptly paid, which I have caused to be placed in the imperial chest and to its credit. Property rises considerably in

* By the Sand River Convention signed on 17th January, 1852, by the Assistant-Commissioners Major Hogg and Mr. Owen, and subsequently ratified by General Cathcart, the Transvaal emigrant farmers had their independence recognized, and being thus reconciled to us were detached from the Boers within the Orange River Sovereignty, who now had no one to look to but the British Government. The Convention was no doubt politic on the assumption that the Sovereignty was to be resolutely kept. When the Sovereignty was abandoned, it took a different character. But for this Sir Harry Smith was not responsible.

value, and the revenue of the Sovereignty exceeds its expenditure.

"The flourishing condition of Natal is deeply indebted to the able and judicious government of Mr. Pine, who, in a letter to me of the 20th March, thus expresses himself: 'The only service I have really rendered your Excellency was the sending the contingent into the Sovereignty; and the greater part of any merit there may be attached to that service belongs fairly to you. It is an easy thing for a subordinate officer to do his duty when he feels that he has a chief above him, who, provided he acts honestly and straightforwardly will support him whether he succeeds or fails. Such a chief I have had in your Excellency.'

"I relinquish the command of the troops . . . at a period when, according to the reports I have received, . . . the mass of the Gaikas have been expelled from the Amatolas—when the Kafirs, Cis- as well as Trans-Keian, have repeatedly sued for peace, and when the war is virtually terminated." *

On the same day Sir Harry issued the following farewell to his troops, dated " Headquarters, King William's Town ":—

"His Excellency Lieut.-General the Hon. George Cathcart having been appointed by the Queen to relieve me, I this day relinquish the command.

"Brother officers and soldiers! Nothing is more painful than to bid farewell to old and faithful friends. I have served my Queen and country many years; and attached as I have ever been to gallant soldiers, none were

---

* The supersession of the Governor at this crisis was no doubt a main cause of the war's being protracted, though in a less severe form, for some months longer. See Mr. Brownlee's report dated " Fort Cox, 4th March, 1852."

ever more endeared to me than those serving in the arduous campaign of 1851-2 in South Africa. The unceasing labours, the night-marches, the burning sun, the torrents of rain have been encountered with a cheerfulness as conspicuous as the intrepidity with which you have met the enemy in so many enterprising fights and skirmishes in his own mountain fastnesses and strongholds, and from which you have ever driven him victoriously.

"I leave you, my comrades, in the fervent hope of laying before your Queen, your country, and His Grace the Duke of Wellington these services as they deserve, which reflect so much honour upon you.

"Farewell, my comrades! your honour and interests will be ever more dear to me than my own.

"H. G. SMITH."

In a reply (also dated "7th April") to an address from the inhabitants of King William's Town, in which they assured him, "We could have well wished that Her Majesty's Government had thought fit to have left the final settlement of this war in the hands of your Excellency," Sir Harry chivalrously put in a plea for those who had inflicted upon him so bitter a humiliation. "You on the spot must have observed how slow the progress of the war occasionally appeared. It may therefore be readily conceived how much Her Majesty's Government must have been disappointed, who could alone judge of events by reports, and had not the various circumstances before them which were apparent to you."

General Cathcart reached King William's Town late on the 9th April, having taken the oaths as Governor at Cape Town on 31st March. Sir

Harry received him on the 10th with the same generosity with which in 1836 he had received Capt. Stockenstrom under similar circumstances, and, as General Cathcart writes,* devoted the whole of the day "to the purpose of giving me every insight into the affairs of the colony generally, and more particularly of the eastern frontier."

Next morning at 3, Sir Harry left King William's Town with his staff. In the darkness of night the inhabitants and troops turned out voluntarily, cheered him enthusiastically, and in considerable numbers escorted him to Fort Murray. Here, though it was still dark, he was met by a body of Kafirs under Pato, who greeted him with shouts of "Inkosi Inkulu!" and, refusing all other escort, he committed himself to their hands. He was much affected, we are told, at parting with his officers, and his voice was scarcely audible when he uttered his last words, "Gentlemen, take care of the soldiers. God bless you!" He then continued his journey with the friendly Kafirs, who were joined on the way by other parties of Kafirs, horse and foot. It was a strange and romantic spectacle.†

A few days later, on board the *Styx* he reached Cape Town. He was received by an immense concourse, cheering enthusiastically, and carried to his carriage under a triumphal arch. Though extremely unwell, he bore himself with his usual

---

* *Correspondence of General Sir George Cathcart* (1856), p. 36.
† *Cape Town Mail*, 20th April, 1852. Sir Harry's departure from King William's Town in 1836 was strangely similar. See pp. 458, 459.

energy, and from his carriage rose and briefly thanked the multitude, adding emphatically, " I have done my duty to the Cape of Good Hope." A public dinner was offered him, but in his situation he felt it right to decline it, upon which the conveners opened a subscription for a " more lasting tribute of respect and esteem." It took the form of a gift of plate.

During his three days' stay at Cape Town, addresses were presented to him by the inhabitants, by the tradesmen and mechanics, and by the inhabitants of Rondebosch, where he had resided both as Colonel Smith and as Governor. In his reply to the first, he said—

" In the service of this colony I have spent some of the best years of my life, and, excepting those during which I have been Governor, some of the happiest. At such a moment as this, nothing can be remembered by me, and I am equally certain nothing can be remembered by the citizens of Cape Town and the colonists at large, excepting what would serve to keep alive old kindness and good feeling, and to bury all past differences and temporary estrangements in oblivion."

To the tradesmen and mechanics, he said, " I am myself a working man. Whatever reputation I may have at any time possessed, I gained simply and solely by being a working man who put his heart into his work."

To the inhabitants of Rondebosch, after referring to the difficulties he had had to contend with and the failure of his efforts for the good of the Kafirs, he added, "Let us all hope that the distinguished officer who has succeeded me in the government will be able to settle permanently the elements which are already subsiding into peace, and let us all be ready to aid him, heart and hand, in his arduous undertaking." Those words were the expression of a noble nature incapable of jealousy.

On Saturday, 17th April, at 2 o'clock, Sir Harry and Lady Smith embarked on H.M.S. *Gladiator*. The multitude of people that turned out to bid them good-bye exceeded anything ever seen in the Colony before ; triumphal arches had been erected, the horses were taken out of the carriage, and cheer after cheer arose, to which Sir Harry, in spite of illness, responded with almost juvenile animation, while Lady Smith sat by his side in tears.*

Cape Town honoured itself in honouring the veteran who, whatever his faults of judgment, had served the Colony single-heartedly to the utmost of his strength, who by his military genius and promptitude in action had conferred upon it in the past enormous benefits, and whose warmth of heart and loyalty of character had endeared him to all who had known him.

As a Governor he had not been indeed beyond criticism. In his relations with Hintza in 1835 he had shown an excessive confidence in the protestations of a savage, and he had seen that confidence abused. The same fault committed in the closing months of 1850 had preceded events still more

* See *Cape Town Mail*, April 17th and 20th, 1852.

deplorable.   In questions of imperial policy his views were large and far-sighted.   In regard to his civil government, one may say that he had to face a series of situations which might well have puzzled the most practised statesman.   Standing alone with an unpopular Colonial Secretary and a Legislative Council utterly discredited, he had the task of smoothing the way for the introduction of representative government, unaided by the support of the people at large, who on their part, when a grievance presented itself, being without any constitutional means of enforcing their views, were driven to make a sort of civil war on their own executive.   Sir Harry was himself a believer in the advantages of popular government, but he was also a soldier who felt himself bound to render implicit obedience to his superior officer.   If in this situation he temporarily lost popularity and encountered obloquy and misrepresentation of the grossest kind, it can only be set to his credit.   As to his management of the Kafir War, for which he was recalled, one may safely leave his reputation in the hands of the Duke of Wellington.

The general judgment of the Colony upon him is perhaps expressed by Chase, who calls him " the eagle-eyed and ubiquitous, a better general than statesman," and adds—

" All men sympathized with the Governor on his recall. With some share of bluster (in the best acceptation of that term), he was in private life most warm-hearted, generous, and amiable, unforgetful of services done to him when plain Colonel Smith. Those who had the honour of being admitted to his confidence, and therefore best knew him, can bear testimony to his ardent desire to benefit the Colony and to his personal regard for its inhabitants. It is true, when under excitement, he employed somewhat strong expletives, which, like sheet lightning, are terrifying yet harmless ; but the writer can add from personal and intimate knowledge that, notwithstanding this blemish, he was, perhaps strange to say, a devout and religious man." *

Besides Whittlesea and Aliwal North, two towns in South Africa keep alive the memory of Sir Harry Smith's administration — Harrismith, over the Orange River, founded early in 1849, and Lady-smith, in Natal, founded in 1851. I may add that Sir Harry's autobiography now sees the light, only on account of the reawakening of interest in him and in his wife during those long weeks of the beginning of 1900 in which the fate of Ladysmith held the whole British race in suspense.

* Wilmot and Chase, pp. 417, 459. With regard to Mr. Chase's last assertion, it is perhaps worth remarking that Sir Harry Smith reflected the spirit of the Romantic School in his religious feelings as well as in much else.

The weakness which Mr. Chase previously mentions is thus referred to in the *Natal Witness* (Jan. 1889): " It was a common habit with Sir Harry Smith to threaten to jump down people's throats, —boots, spurs, and all ; and he once on a field of battle sent a message, seasoned with some fearful expletives, to a colonel that if he kept his regiment so much to the front, he'd have him knee-haltered. But the fine old General drew a line at swearing and never allowed of personal abuse."

CHAPTER L.

(*Supplementary.*)

AGAIN IN ENGLAND—LAST YEARS, 1852–1860.

BEFORE Sir Harry Smith reached England, Lord John Russell's Government had fallen, one main cause of its fall being a general and perhaps excessive dissatisfaction with Lord Grey's administration of the colonies. It was widely felt that Sir Harry had been made the scapegoat of the Whig Government, and there was every disposition to give him a warm welcome.

The *Gladiator* reached Portsmouth on the afternoon of Sunday, 1st June, and at seven that evening Sir Harry and Lady Smith disembarked and proceeded to the George. Next day he was visited by a great number of persons, both official and private, and at four the Corporation hastily came together to vote him an address. In sharp contrast to the terms of Lord Grey's dispatch, it expressed admiration for his " capacity and fitness for command" shown amid almost unparalleled difficulties. Sir Harry was brought to the Council Chamber to receive it. In his reply he tersely described the situation in which he had been placed. " I became a Governor without a Legislative Council, a Commander-in-Chief without a British army." Meanwhile the Mayor had been requisitioned to call a public meeting of the inhabitants. It was held to suit Sir Harry's convenience at a quarter to ten next morning, " military time." At this meeting, which was enthusiastically sympathetic, Sir Harry recalled an incident of his youth.

"Many years ago I embarked on my first campaign from your shores, unknown to the world, nay, I may say, *unknown to myself*, for no youth is aware of the latent qualities which may hereafter be brought forth. At the storming of Monte Video, an event which is not known to many of you, because it occurred before many of you were born, I was Adjutant of three Companies, and was fast asleep when they fell in. A brother officer came and shook me by the shoulder and awoke me, saying, ' The troops are falling in ; come, wake up.' I arose and exclaimed, ' Lord, in Thee have I trusted ; let me never be confounded,' and with many others came out unscathed from a dreadful storm. These words have guided me during my life."

In each of the two speeches Sir Harry showed the most magnanimous spirit towards the Government which had recalled him.*

The feeling displayed at Portsmouth was typical of that which prevailed throughout the country, and as he acted at Portsmouth so he acted throughout. He wrote in 1857, " All England upon my arrival again received me with open arms. I was requested

* *Portsmouth Times*, 5th June, 1852.

to stand as a member for Cambridge, for West-
minster, for Edinburgh, for Glasgow. I declined
to interfere with politics or to embarrass Her
Majesty's Government, which I say my position
enabled me to do, had not my desire been ever to
serve it faithfully and fearlessly." Perhaps his
determination not to pose as a man with a grievance was manifested most strikingly when, after
his arrival in London, while declining an invitation
of the United Service Club, he accepted one even
from Lord Grey. A writer in *Colburn's Magazine*
for November, 1860, is very indignant at this, and
calls it "the most lowering act" of Sir Harry's life.
But Sir Harry was only maintaining the generous
position he had taken up—that Lord Grey, even if
he had acted wrongly, had acted from a sense of
duty.*

But with whatever mixture of feelings Sir Harry
visited Lord Grey, he received another invitation,
we may be sure, with the most unadulterated
pleasure. On the 18th June he was the guest of
his beloved master and faithful defender, the Duke
of Wellington, at the Waterloo Banquet at Apsley

---

* Lord Grey fully appreciated Sir Harry's chivalry. He writes,
"On a question of this kind we were not at liberty to consult our
private feelings. This was fully understood by Sir Harry Smith
himself, of whose most handsome and honourable conduct I cannot
too strongly express my sense. He has shown no resentment against
us for what we did, but has fairly given us credit for having been
guided only by considerations of public duty. I feel individually very
deeply indebted to him for the kindness with which he has acted
towards me since his return."—*The Colonial Policy of Lord John
Russell's Administration* (1853), vol. ii. p. 247. Men will decide
according to their dispositions whether such conduct was "lowering"
to Sir Harry or not. It was at least part and parcel of his nature.

House—the last Waterloo Banquet ever held. Around the Duke's table, with Prince Albert and the Duke of Cambridge, sat between thirty and forty generals who had played their part in the struggle of giants thirty-seven years before. They included Lord Anglesey, Lord Hardinge, and Sir De Lacy Evans. At this gathering of glorious soldiers and old comrades, Sir Harry Smith's health was proposed by the Great Duke himself and drunk with the greatest enthusiasm.

Early in August Sir Harry and Lady Smith settled themselves at Belmont House near Havant, where they were near neighbours of another famous Peninsular and Indian soldier, Sir Charles Napier. A month later they crossed to Guernsey to visit their old friends Sir John and Lady Catherine Bell. Sir John as Lieutenant-Governor held a review of the Guernsey Militia in his friend's honour, and induced Sir Harry to address them. He spoke on a favourite topic—the power of an armed peasantry to resist an invader.

" In the mountains of the Tyrol, under Hofer, the militia peasantry of the country repelled the attacks of the well-trained battalions of Napoleon. In Algeria for nearly thirty years have the peasantry defended their country, which even now is not conquered, although 450,000 French soldiers have been sent there. In the Caucasian Mountains the peasantry have resisted for thirty years the efforts of 800,000 Russian soldiers to subjugate them, and the Russians have made to this hour no progress. In South Africa I have experienced what the determined efforts of an armed peasantry can do, for after having beaten the

Kafirs in one place, they immediately appeared in another. I state this to you to show what a brave and loyal people as you are, are capable of doing." *

After returning from Guernsey, Sir Harry visited Sir Charles Napier, and here met, for the first time for many years, his old friend and comrade of the Light Division, the historian, Sir William Napier. It was while the three brilliant soldiers were thus together that they heard, with an emotion easy to imagine, that their great chieftain, the Duke, had passed away (14th Sept.).† At the Duke's funeral on the 18th November Sir Harry rode as Standard-bearer, attended by Col. Garvock.

On 21st January, 1853, Sir Harry was appointed to the command of the Western District, and to be Lieutenant-Governor of Plymouth. His feelings on again obtaining employment were no doubt those expressed in General Beckwith's letter to him on the occasion: "We should all die in our boots, with our spurs on, if possible; at any rate, the grand affair is to keep the game alive to the last." Accordingly, he and his wife took up their abode at Government House, Devonport, where they remained till the autumn of 1854. It was a busy time when troops were constantly departing for the Crimea, and a great deal of hospitality was dispensed at Government House.

Mr. W. F. Collier of Woodtown, Horrabridge,

---

* *Portsmouth Times*, 11th Sept. 1852.
† *Life of Sir W. Napier*, vol. ii. p. 327.

sends me the following reminiscences of Sir Harry at this time :—

"He was an active General, to be seen everywhere. When inspecting or reviewing infantry, he usually rode his little Arab, Aliwal, and always, when the troops were in line, he would suddenly put his horse into a gallop and ride at the line as if he were going to charge through them (the men were, of course, well up to this trick and stood perfectly steady) ; the little Arab always suddenly halted within about a foot of the line. I have seen him perform this show for the benefit of the public often.

"He went to the public balls in his tight Rifle uniform of the time—a tight 'invisible-green' jacket, with tight trousers to match. It was very trying to the figure, and *his* then was rather spare and dilapidated, rather of the Don Quixote order.

"Lady Smith was a dear old lady, very kind, and very popular."

Sir Harry had distinguished himself from the beginning of his career by his zeal for the common soldier, and in his last years no old soldier appealed to him in vain. Through the kindness of Colonel L. G. Fawkes, R.A., I am enabled to give the following charming letter addressed by Sir Harry at this time to Sergeant T. Himbury, an old soldier of the 95th :—

"Government House, Devonport, May 20th, 1853.

"OLD COMRADE HIMBURY,

"I well recollect you. Upon the receipt of your letter of the 16th inst., I recommend your memorial to 'The Lords and other Commissioners of Chelsea Hospital' to have your pension increased to two shillings a day. There are few men now remaining in the British Army who have seen *so much* service and been in so many actions as yourself; and the fact alone, of your having been wounded when one of the Forlorn Hope at the important storm of San Sebastian, where we, the Light, Third, and Fourth Divisions sent our gallant volunteers, is enough. The Lords Commissioners are very kind to such gallant old soldiers as yourself, and, if they can increase your pension, I am sure they will. Let this certificate accompany your memorial, and let me hear that another, though not a forlorn, hope has succeeded. My wife well remembers your picking her up when her horse fell upon her, and again thanks you.

> "Your old friend and comrade,
>
> "H. G. SMITH, Major-General,
>
> "Colonel 2nd Battn. Rifle Brigade."

Sir Harry's interest was not confined to the rank and file, and early in June, finding on the appearance of the *Gazette* that various officers whom he had recommended for promotion for their services in South Africa had had their claims overlooked, he wrote some vigorous letters to Lord Hardinge, the new Commander-in-Chief, and in some cases obtained what he desired. In one of these letters (12th June) he adds, "I had a great sham fight yesterday on Roborough Downs, horsed four guns myself, and taught the troops a *forward* fight."

Early in 1854, we see the shadow of the Crimean War coming over the land. It was a new experience for Harry Smith to be at home when there was fighting to be done. But now Charles

Beckwith wrote to him from Turin, "I suppose, old boy, that our share in coming events will be reading the *Gazette* at breakfast, shutting the garden-gate, and turning the siege of Dendermond into a blockade." That was what it had now come to.

In March, 1854, Sir Harry had permission to appoint as his aide-de-camp Lieut.-Colonel Holdich of the 80th Foot, who had held the same position during the Sutlej campaign and in South Africa, and had since greatly distinguished himself in Burmah. Although Colonel Holdich resigned this position in 1856 in order to proceed with his regiment to South Africa (Major Hugh Smith replacing him), he remained closely bound to Sir Harry and Lady Smith to the end of their lives.

On the 20th June Sir Harry became Lieutenant-General (in South Africa he had had the local rank of Lieutenant-General, but no more), and on the 29th September he was transferred from Devonport to Manchester, being appointed to the command of the Northern and Midland Military Districts. Soon after he and his wife took up their residence at Rusholme House, which was their home till 1857, when they removed to Somerville, Victoria Park.

One of Sir Harry's first duties, after taking up his command at Manchester, was to proceed to Hull to supervise the military arrangements for the reception of the Queen, who was to pay a visit there on her way from Scotland. After being present at Her Majesty's arrival on the evening of 13th October, he dined by command with the royal party at the Station Hotel. Next morning he was on the *Fairy* when the Queen made a tour of the docks, but immediately afterwards left Hull on another mission of great interest. At the request of Lord Hardinge, now Commander-in-Chief, he proceeded on the 15th October to Paris to represent the British Army at the funeral of Marshal St. Arnaud, who had died in the Crimea. He was accompanied by his own aide-de-camp, Lieut.-Colonel Holdich, Colonel Brook Taylor, A.G. of the Manchester District, and Lord Arthur Hay, aide-de-camp to Lord Hardinge (representing the Commander-in-Chief). On the 16th Lord Cowley, the British Ambassador, entertained the military deputation at breakfast, and then conveyed them to the Invalides, the place of interment. Sir Harry was subsequently admitted to an audience of the Emperor at St. Cloud, of which he has left the following note :—

"After a very long conversation, the Emperor said, 'You will see the Queen, and I pray you to assure Her Majesty how sensible I, the French Army and Nation are of the mark of respect paid to us by sending to attend the melancholy funeral of Marshal St. Arnaud, an officer of your rank and reputation with a Deputation of British Officers. The amicable relationship which existed between the Marshal and Lord Raglan renders his loss still more to be deplored.'"

Sir Harry was back in London on the 21st.
Christmas, 1854, brought Sir Harry a double

sorrow. His "third Waterloo brother," Charles, died at Whittlesey on Christmas Eve, and four days earlier his old friend Sir James Kempt passed away at the age of ninety. On 17th January, 1855, Sir Andrew Barnard followed. On Sir Andrew's death, Sir Harry, who had been since 1847 Colonel of the 2nd Battalion Rifle Brigade, was appointed to the command of the 1st Battalion. In one of his strangely beautiful letters written on 27th January, Charles Beckwith grieves over the sufferings of the men in the Crimea, gives his friend some of his thoughts on the great mystery of death, and then refers in particular to the recent deaths of their old friends.

"What a good old fellow Sir James was! I did not feel Sir Andrew's loss so much, as they told me that his intellect had failed. I had a good letter the other day from Lord Seaton. All these men I regard as the patriarchs of all that is solid in England. These men and their fellows, the men of Alma, Balaklava, Inkerman, of the *Birkenhead*, and the Arctic Regions, I hold to be the foundation-stones of England. In them is incarnate the sense of duty and obedience as a fixed habit, not a sentiment or conviction, as the people say, but a true witness of the Omnipotent who wills it thus. . . . Adieu. Love to Juana. We must expect to be rather ricketty at the best, but we may toddle on. It is highly desirable that we may all go together as nearly as may be. Bring Bright to a garrison Court Martial, take care of your old bones, remember me kindly to any old fellow that may write to you, and believe me,

"Your affectionate friend,

"CHARLES BECKWITH."

It might atone for many faults in Harry Smith that he loved and was loved by Charles Beckwith.

The following letter to H.R.H. the Duke of Cambridge and the Duke's reply are self-explanatory :—

"Manchester, March 9, 1855.

"DEAR SIR,

"I cannot avoid expressing to Your Royal Highness my *delight* on reading the opinion so nobly given by you, when in the Chair, as to the Patriotic Fund, of the *value, worth,* and *zeal* of our Regimental Officers. In a service of fifty years I have ever found them the same, and ever looked up to and beloved by their soldiers. Your Royal Highness's expressions in the Chair are calculated to do vast good in these twaddling and criminating times, and to uphold that class of men, alone qualified to command British soldiers, who feel themselves that gentlemen best command them.

"H. G. SMITH,

"Lieut.-General.

"To H.R.H. the Duke of Cambridge, etc."

"St. James's Palace, March 10th, 1855.

"MY DEAR SIR HARRY,

"Many thanks for your most kind letter just received. I really am delighted to find that all my friends *approve* of my speech the other day. I felt it was a duty I owed to the Officers of the Army to state what I did in their favour, they having been most unjustly assailed from all quarters, and not a soul to take their part, which I felt was too bad. Never are there a set of men who have worked harder, and their trials have been great. You know my devotion for the service. I could

not allow such imputations to go by unanswered. The
Departments have been very bad, though I admit their
great difficulties, but the Army, as far as troops are
concerned, cannot be improved.

> " I remain, my dear Sir Harry,
>
> " Yours most sincerely,
>
> " GEORGE."

In May Sir Harry received with great pleasure
from Prince Adalbert of Prussia the beautifully
illustrated volume on the First Sikh War written
by the lately deceased Prince Waldemar, who had
fought in those battles as a volunteer, and had
gained the esteem and affection of his comrades.

On the 25th July Sir Harry wrote to Major
George Simmons—

> " I have not been myself since the 18th June last. I
> went to Preston to inspect some militia and a Depôt
> Battalion of the line, and I was wet for six hours. George,
> on *one* 18th June, I did not much mind a wetting. Age
> is a bore. Ah, poor dear Lord Raglan! He died, I fear,
> *of a broken heart.* I desire you write ' Dear Harry S——,'
> and not ' Dear General,' you old humbug. Juana sends
> you and yours her love, as does your old comrade,
>
> " HARRY SMITH."

As General in command of the Midland District,
Sir Harry was present at Birmingham on 22nd
November, when Prince Albert laid the foundation
stone of the " Midland Institute." On rising to
reply for the " Army and Navy," he called forth
vociferous cheering by the words, " I pray my

country not precipitately to make peace.   Let peace
be based upon the surest foundations."

A letter of Lady Smith's dated " 31st March,
1857," reminds us of the regulation ordering all
officers to leave the upper lip unshaven, of which
the effect is seen in portraits of Sir Harry after
this date.   "Your uncle is, thank God, quite well.
His moustaches are growing very nicely, and I
do think they become his dear old face."   A week
later he wrote to his nephew, Mr. George Moore
Smith, of Whittlesey, his native place, to express
his delight at "the pluck" he had shown during
some riots, when the rioters had cheered him for
going in among them.

On 5th May the Manchester " Art Treasures "
Exhibition was opened by Prince Albert, who wrote
the same night to the Queen: "After luncheon
[at Abney Hall] we donned our uniform, and drove
with an escort, etc., etc., to Manchester, some six
miles, and through the town—Sir Harry Smith
upon his Arab 'charging the multitude.'" *   On
29th June the Queen and various members of the
Royal Family, including Prince Frederick William
of Prussia, newly betrothed to the Princess Royal,
visited the Exhibition.   It was Sir Harry Smith's
duty to make all the military arrangements, and
he rode on the right of Her Majesty's carriage in
the procession.   When the Queen was about to
knight the Mayor, she turned to Sir Harry for his
sword, telling the Mayor at the same time that

* Martin's *Life of the Prince Consort*, vol. iv. p. 37.

it had been "in four general actions." On receiving it back he respectfully bowed, and, stooping over it, pressed the hilt to his lips. Her Majesty afterwards expressed a wish for the sword, saying, "Do you value it very much, Sir Harry?" and, needless to say, it was at once presented to her. Sir Harry had worn it from 1835.[*]

Sir Harry and Lady Smith having invited General and Mrs. Beckwith to come over from Paris and stay with them during the time of the Exhibition, the General replied, "You must understand that if I should come to England, I shall certainly present my wife to Juana. As to the Exhibition, it will be a thing to be seen and *felt*, but your house will be little better than a hotel for a part of the time, and I think much more of your blessed faces than of all other possible sights. I had rather see John Bell's 'old divine countenance' than that of Raphael himself."

That summer of 1857—the summer of the Indian Mutiny—filled the letters of Harry Smith and Charles Beckwith with gloomy forebodings. It is interesting to see the reminiscence of the old Light Division contained in the last words of Beckwith's letter of the 18th September: "Do you think 'Young Varmint'[†] can get to Lucknow? I

---

[*] Sir Harry felt a strong personal devotion to the Queen, and would speak of her as "the most gracious lady in the whole world."

[†] Henry Havelock's elder brother, Will, as before stated, was called in the Peninsula "Young Varmint," for "his keenness and daring in the saddle and in every manly sport." See account of W. H. by H. H. in Buist's *Annals of India for* 1848.

have some doubts. God protect him and bless him."

General Beckwith did not achieve the visit to Manchester in 1857, but wrote on 15th January, 1858, that he would like to come in the following July. He says—

"I am glad to hear from you, because you really know something of what is going on in the world, and, above all, something of the men who take an active part in directing its affairs. I have nothing but my own theories and the newspapers to direct me, two fallacious guides. It is impossible not to shed a tear on H. Havelock's grave. I wish he could have once more embraced his wife and daughters. There is another thing, Harry, that hangs on my mind, and that is Punjaub Lawrence. As far as I can see, nothing was foreseen and nothing was prevented from Calcutta. Everything — wisdom, counsel, action, foresight—came from Lahore. 'There was a little city and few men within it, and there came a great king against it, and besieged it, and built great bulwarks against it. Now, there was found in it a poor wise man, and he by his wisdom delivered the city; yet no man remembered that same poor man.' . . . My wife, the most simple-minded creature living, sends her duty to Juana, and I send my love. Is John Bell on the staff of your district? My kind regards to him. I think with reverence and affection of his 'old divine face.'"

In May Sir Harry Smith, Lord Burghersh and the Garter King at Arms were commissioned to go to Lisbon in attendance on the Marquis of Bath, who was to invest Don Pedro V., on the occasion of his marriage, with the Order of the Garter. The young queen, Princess Stephanie of Hohenzollern, visited the English Court on her way to Portugal, and Sir Harry and Lady Smith were bidden to a dinner-party at Buckingham Palace on 7th May, and to a State Ball on the 10th, given in connexion with her visit.

Lord Bath and his suite reached Lisbon on the 17th, a day before the Queen. They were present at various festivities held in honour of the royal wedding, and after the investiture at Belem Palace on the 27th were the guests of the King at a State Dinner. Sir Harry received from the King at this time the Order of St. Bento d'Aviz. It must have been very interesting to the Peninsular veteran thus to revisit under such different circumstances the place where he and George Simmons had bathed together forty-eight years before when convalescent from their wounds received at the Coa.*

Alas! the first letter he received from Charles Beckwith after his return told him, in sentences worthy of Thackeray, that Simmons, with his simple hero-worship of them both, had passed away.

"Todas son muertas! and amongst the rest old George Simmons, who went out of the world in a few moments with a smile on his countenance. The first thing George would ask was, 'Where's the regiment? My word, the General and Sir Harry will soon be here.'"

* See p. 33 *n.* It is characteristic of Sir Harry's kindness of nature that he now brought home from Lisbon some little presents for the children of his aide-de-camp, Major Payne.

He adds—

" I shall be ready to move on Manchester on the 14th July with my young wife. I hope to find you during an interregnum of giving dinners and dining out, as I want to comfort my head and heart during my stay in England, and have no reverence for cotton lords. Your blessed faces and those of the old stock that I may be lucky enough to meet, will mend up and comfort my soul which has passed through a dreary desert for the last thirty years. I had much rather see old Sousa e Silva * than Milner Gibson. In fact, it is not safe for me to get into a colloquy with this sort of chap, as I should certainly rap out something disagreeable. . . . Love to Juana. Corramba, how I shall enjoy myself at Manchester ! "

In July the anticipated visit duly took place.

On the 9th October, at Newcastle, Sir Harry inspected for the last time his own Regiment, the 1st Battalion Rifle Brigade. When he had inspected them and put them through some rapid manœuvres, he formed the men into square, and addressed them in words full of his lifelong affection for the corps. That was the only Regiment or Battalion, he said, in which he had taken his place in the ranks, and their services, their " everything, in fact," would never be forgotten. He then desired the men to let him get out of the square, observing that he well knew he never could get into it if they wished to prevent him.†

Early in 1859 Sir Harry had a bad fall and cut

* See p. 184 *n.*   † Cope, p. 451.

his knee. He went to London unwisely, inflammation came on, and he nearly lost his leg. Beckwith writes to him—

"MY DEAR OLD FELLOW,

"What a spoony of a Manchester doctor to let you set off! Why didn't you turn back? However, when you've got your nose in a given direction, you *never* turn back. . . . You see how a man may be 'severely wounded' being at ease and in his own house, after riding through showers of lead and iron unscathed. I am certain that you will have greatly profited by this occasional martyrdom, and that you are now much fitter to 'fall in' in the ranks of the celestial army."

For eight weeks the patient was confined to his room, and almost constantly to his bed. He reports his return to Manchester on 12th April and adds—

"In a few days I hope to mount Alice's * pony. I have suffered very much occasionally, but my pluck never forsook me. My greatest distress was to see my dear old faithful wife suffer so—her anxiety was intense."

Sir Harry's five-years' command of the Northern District was to expire on the 30th September. He hated the idea of being out of harness, and wrote in May to the Duke of Cambridge, begging that he might be reappointed, but the Duke replied that, though his feelings were strongly in favour of continuing Sir Harry in the command he so

* Miss Alice E. Smith (daughter of Major Thomas Smith), now Mrs. Lambert, was a great deal with her uncle and aunt from 1852 onwards.

worthily filled, he could not, in justice to other officers, make an exception in his case. Accordingly Sir Harry saw his time at Manchester drawing to an end.

There, as in all his previous employments, he had gained the love and esteem of all who came in contact with him, by his high spirit, his generosity, and his kindness of heart, while they smiled at his soldierly inflexibility in little things. A lady who visited him at this time tells me how severe he would be on bad riders, or men who used a spoon to their pudding or left a wine-glass unfinished; how proud he was of his little beautifully-formed foot, and how when in bad health he would scrupulously dress for dinner, perhaps to imitate the Duke of Wellington, whom he made his pattern in all things; how he would ride a very strong and spirited horse, although it exhausted him; how he would take men into his employment from pure charity, because they needed assistance; how in society he would devote himself still to the prettiest woman present; how rigidly punctual he was in his house; how charming with children and young people; how he would go through whatever he felt to be his duty at any cost.

Sir Harry's departure from Manchester was therefore a time of severance from many friends. The Council of the City, in a formal resolution, requested the Mayor to assure him of their regret at his removal, and their thanks for the great courtesy and kindness with which he had discharged his duties. In his reply to the Mayor, Sir Harry wrote—

"After the approbation of his Sovereign, the greatest compliment which can be conferred on the soldier is to live in the affections of his countrymen. Thus to learn that the Council of the wealthy and populous City of Manchester appreciates any services it has been my duty to perform is, I assure you, most gratifying to my feelings. During the five happy years I have commanded the Northern District and resided in Manchester, I have received the greatest kindness and hospitality both in the City and in the neighbourhood, and joyfully do I record that during that period no single instance of any collision between the citizens and the soldiers throughout these extensive districts was ever brought before me. . . . The kindly feelings evinced by you, Sir, in your letter of transmission, are most forcibly impressed upon my mind, the more so as you include Lady Smith, the faithful partner of my joys, sorrows, and military career for so many years in every quarter of the globe."

Lord De Tabley wrote—

"I do assure you that, amongst the many neighbours who have had an opportunity of forming your acquaintance and cultivating your friendship during the period of your command here, there is no one who regrets the termination of the command more sincerely than I and my family. Most exceedingly also will the Regiment, which you have so kindly, more than once, inspected, miss the cheering and encouraging glance and word of the General they were always so glad and proud to see. As you say, time passes, but I trust that friendship and kindly feeling will remain."

Similarly, Lord Derby, "the Rupert of debate," wrote from Knowsley—

"Your retirement will, I am sure, be a subject of very general regret. I hope that Lady Derby and I may have the pleasure of again seeing you and Lady Smith at this place. I beg of you to place me at the feet of the Doña Juana, and to believe me, my dear Sir Harry,

"Yours sincerely,

"DERBY."

To Major C. W. Meadows Payne, his second aide-de-camp, whom he had first met in South Africa in the thirties, Sir Harry wrote a warmly affectionate letter of farewell.

"Manchester, 30th Sept. 1859.

"MY DEAR OLD AND VALUED FRIEND PAYNE,

"This day closes for the present our Military Career—but no change in our circumstances can effect any change in that Fraternal Love which has endeared us to each other for so many years. During the last five years, while my A.D.C., you have been of the greatest possible service to me in both your official and private capacity, my interests have been yours, and the frank confidence I have ever reposed in you has been observed with every regard for my honour.

"It may happen, even at my advanced age, I may be again employed—if so, I hope you would again join your General who so valued your services.

"Meanwhile, Payne, may every blessing attend you and yours, and may every Veteran General have such a Friend as yourself to confide in.

"Your old friend,

"H. G. SMITH.

"Major Payne, A.D.C."

There was one other loved friend from whom Sir Harry had now to part. His little Arab " Aliwal " had been ridden by him at Maharajpore and at all the battles of the Sutlej Campaign ; it had come home with him to England in 1847, accompanied him to the Cape, returned with him in 1852, and had since served him faithfully in his commands at Devonport and Manchester. A lady, the daughter of Sir Harry's aide-de-camp, Major Payne, writes—

" My sister and I have a vivid recollection of the lovely horse, and how, when we used to meet Sir Harry when we were out walking and he was riding, he would call out, 'Stand still, children,' and then come galloping up at full speed, and Aliwal would stop at our very feet ; [*] and my mother used to tell us that on the anniversary of the Battle of Aliwal, when there was always a full-dress dinner at the General's house, some one would propose Aliwal's health, and Sir Harry would order him to be sent for. The groom would lead the beautiful creature all round the dinner-table, glittering with plate, lights, uniforms, and brilliant dresses, and he would be quite quiet, only giving a snort now and then, though, when his health had been drunk and the groom had led him out, you could hear him on the gravel outside, prancing and capering. The horse was now old, and Sir Harry, in his new house in London, would not be able to keep him ; and though Sir Robert Gerard (now Lord Gerard) kindly offered him a home, Sir Harry feared that his old age would perhaps be an unhappy one, and he resolved to shoot him. My father and the faithful groom were with Sir Harry when he did so, and I believe they all shed tears."

[*] Cp. p. 657.

That night Sir Harry's place was vacant at dinner, and he was seen no more till the following morning. The following epitaph on his horse in Sir Harry's handwriting is still preserved:—

"Near this Stone is buried Sir Harry Smith's celebrated Arab charger of the Purest Blood,

'ALIWAL.'

Sir Harry rode him in the battles of Maharajpore, Moodkee, Ferozeshahur, Aliwal, and Sobraon. He was the only horse of the General Staff that was not killed or wounded. He came from Arabia to Calcutta, thence to Lahore; he has marched nearly all over India; came by ship to England, thence to the Cape of Good Hope and back to England. He was twenty-two years old; never was sick during the eighteen years in Sir Harry's possession. As a charger, he was incomparable, gallant, and docile; as a friend, he was affectionate and faithful."

On leaving Manchester Sir Harry and Lady Smith visited Sir John Bell at 55, Cadogan Place, London, and took a house for themselves a few doors off (No. 15), which they entered at the end of November.

The letters of General Charles Beckwith show him to have been vexing himself for years with the question, "How is England to defend herself against invasion?" Although Harry Smith's letters to him are not in my hands, I do not doubt that he had also deeply pondered the same momentous problem. Neither of the friends forgot the famous letter which Wellington, in their eyes the wisest of all Englishmen, had addressed in 1847 to Sir John Burgoyne, and in which, after saying that he had studied our Southern Coast piece by piece and did not doubt that a foreign army could be landed at many points, he added—

"I know no mode of resistance excepting by an army in the field capable of meeting and contending with its formidable enemy, aided by all the means of fortification which experience in war can suggest.

"I shall be deemed foolhardy in engaging for the defence of the empire with an army composed of . . . a force of militia. I may be so, I confess it. I should infinitely prefer an army of regular troops. But I *know* that I shall not have these. I may have others.

"I am bordering upon seventy-seven years of age passed in honour. I hope that the Almighty may protect me from being the witness of the tragedy which I cannot persuade my contemporaries to take measures to avert." *

These solemn words of warning were present to the minds of Beckwith and Harry Smith when, in 1859, they saw the public mind seriously alarmed by the fear of invasion, and an army of citizen soldiers springing up in its defence. They would have been untrue to their master if they had not gladly hailed the Volunteer Movement, and seized the opportunity of aiding their country to put its defences in order. Harry Smith, as we have seen, had told the Guernseymen of the immense value of a citizen army. On 17th May, 1859, he wrote at Manchester the following memorandum :—

"1. I am one who thinks that the most formidable enemies are the armed population of a country—take Switzerland, America, Spain, etc., and I have never seen more formidable opposition than by armed savages even.

"2. I would therefore *gradually* enroll every man in

* Sir H. E. Maxwell's *Life of Wellington*, vol. ii. pp. 361-364.

England who has a vote, and teach them to *shoot.* That is all we require at present ; plenty of time to talk of a little drill and embodiment.   And as we may become threatened by war, I would enroll all gamekeepers and their helpers as Light Infantry, or rather *Riflemen.*   I would enroll all the navvies, give them arms, but call them 'Pioneers.'   I would enroll all the Railroad men, not to take them from the rail, but teach them to *shoot.*

"3. I would never talk of war, but thus show such a set of Bulldog teeth as no sensible enemy would like the grip of.   All this in aid of the Regular Army, the Militia, etc.

"4. I would erect such works at Plymouth as I have long ago pointed out : no *great* fortifications ; *outworks* of strength, on points which would render it unassailable. So at all our ports, etc.

"5. Why, when *the* Napoleon threatened us with invasion, Mr. Pitt had 800,000 men with arms in their hands ; 200,000 more enrolled.   Every waggon, boat, etc., was numbered, and alarm-posts established everywhere throughout England.   By heavens, if any enemy, or *enemies*, thought of invading us, England would ' chevaux-de-frises ' like a porcupine's back, with lots of men everywhere.   These are our resources if our Navy let them land.   And we should have *swarms* of little steamers with Armstrong's guns on our coasts.

"6. I should like some 'Places d'armes' on the Reigate Hills range—small, but capable to resist all but a siege.   These points being occupied add to the defensive, and are capital Points of Rendezvous.

"7. If the war * is protracted and our neutrality shaken, we must go back to the old constitutional plan of Ballot for the Militia.

"8. All I have here written about would be easy,

* *I.c.* the war then being waged in Italy.

feasible, and requisite if a large French Camp was forming in Boulogne, Cherbourg & Co., but, as yet, John
Bull's steam is hardly up.　Government measures of
defence upon the basis of *strict neutrality* would be
acceptable to the People, and, by Government being
energetic, the People would think there is more necessity
than they see, and would rally round it in defence of
Queen, Country, 'pro aris et focis.'　And if they did not
get their steam up, give them a touch of 'The blessings
of Tortona'＊ and various other interesting anecdotes of
war and contributions, etc., etc.

"H. G. S."

Sir Harry's interest in the question was still
shown after his removal to London.　The *Times*
of 19th December having discussed in a leader
whether the country would be wise in following
Lord Palmerston's advice and spending £10,000,000
on fortifications, or in trusting its defence merely
to its fleet, army, and volunteers, Sir Harry again
put his views on paper in a letter to the editor
(which, however, seems not to have been published).
I give a few extracts :—

" 3. What you state as to Fortifications is truly correct.
They must ever be regarded as auxiliaries, and no mode
of defence would be more objectionable than 'large
fortifications,' absorbing, as you observe, the men required
in the field.

" 4. 'Should we not take our stand upon the ocean and
the coast rather than assume that an enemy will make
good his advance into the country?'　On this allow me
to observe that, in war, one of its first principles is to

＊ Tortona was laid waste in 1155 and 1163 by Frederick Barbarossa.

ensure a 'reserve.' This, if we were defeated at sea (which I by no means anticipate), your *small* fortifications around your arsenals, docks, etc., and upon a few points on the most vulnerable side of the capital, would secure.

"7. A movable Column or Columns of Riflemen and Armstrong's guns might not arrive at the point in time. Defences must be permanent and leave nothing to chance.

"8. The assertion that 'No force would ever attempt a landing on a hostile shore in the face of 2000 Riflemen supported by good artillery,' is very correct, but it must be observed that this small force would cover but an atom of the coast, and the enemy would land on either flank, leaving a force in front of the 'atom of defence.'

"11. Arm the People, who have demonstrated their readiness. Place such an armament under a system of organization which would ensure obedience. That authority to emanate and be exercised direct from the Crown, and to descend by a continuous chain of responsibility from the Crown to the private. Thus would England be so armed as to prevent the melancholy exhibition of a Panic, as injurious to her trade throughout the world as it is degrading to her position as a State. Nothing so well ensures the friendship of nations as irresistible power.

"12. I conclude by asserting that the Navy, some small fortifications, the Army and Militia, and the 'Rifle Volunteers' (in other words, 'the Armed People of invincible England') will ensure her defence as effectually as they will re-establish her 'prestige' throughout Europe and the world."

At Glasgow, when the survivors of the "Sharpshooters" of 1819 met to consider the question of re-embodying the old force, they wrote to their

old commander, and received a letter from him full
of reminiscences of his Glasgow days, and full of
encouragement to them to do what they were
proposing—

"London, Feb. 7, 1860.

"My war cry for England has ever been, *Arm the
people!* . . . Some of my gallant and experienced
comrades who write upon the subject of the defence of
England take as extreme and one-sided a view as some
of our leading journals do on the other—the one declaring the inutility of Volunteers, the other that they
are omnipotent. I ask either of these extremities—If
you saw a large French army in battle array, which
must occupy a large tract of country, with artillery,
cavalry, and *their* sharpshooters, how do you propose
to check their advance? I cannot conjecture the reply
of either. But this I will assert and maintain, with my
last breath—It is alone to be done by a combination of
regular troops, as a barrier and a reserve, with swarms
of riflemen everywhere as powerful — most powerful—
auxiliaries. We must bear in mind that the distance
from our coast to London is barely three days' march,
hence the object of the enemy is to advance by a *coup
de main* to seize London. Could I say loose troops
would stop them? No. But a combination would ensure
their defeat, and then let loose the sons of Britain, with
this command—'*Forward* and shoot; you shall all be
supported at the requisite points.' Should any enemy
have the audacity to attempt our shores, could he avoid
our ever invincible Navy, I as a General of some experience in war, would be proud to command a combined
force as I have described, and 'Let deeds show.' . . .

"One word more. *Tease* not our youths as Volunteers
with the minutiæ of drill—a few things are alone necessary.

To march in quick time, to march in column, form line, gain ground to the right and left, to advance again in line, to extend and occupy bridges or walls ; a rallying square may be practised. Soldiers require these alone in the field. Then, to be *good shots.* Pluck enough they have, and, with prompt obedience, England's regular army, so nobly supported and its numbers so increased, can, may, and *will* defy the ——.

"Let our watchword be,

"' Arm the People.'

" Ever faithfully yours,

"H. G. SMITH.

" To Peter Mackenzie, Esq., *Gazette* Office, Glasgow." *

When others were timorous of the Volunteer Movement as a danger to public order, Harry Smith saw in it the possible salvation of the country which he had served valiantly with the sword and could serve now only by words.

His spirit was still high, and it chafed him to live in London without horses and on a diminished income. He had never had the art of saving money, and he now writes (7th March) to Major Payne—

"You would laugh to see me poring over twopences. Hang me if I know how people in England live. I hate London, and I love you, Tom.

"Your friend,

" HARRY SMITH."

He says in the same letter that he had taken a cold at the funeral of his old friend Sir William Napier, but when he writes again on 12th June he gives a better report of himself.

* *Glasgow Gazette,* 11th Feb. 1860.

"Everybody tells me I look well. I am thin, but as active as ever. I want horses and that stirring exercise. I *say nothing*, Tom, but I do feel the loss, for the last fifty years having ever had a right good stud. But you can't eat your cake and have it. London full of *the world*, a most heartless reunion ; it is for the *girls* a regular Constantinople. Tom, do write often. I don't care what the subject of your letter may be, so that it is not melancholy. Say it rains or don't rain ; yesterday 'twas fine, to-day pouring with rain again."

Two months later the old man has had a warning that his sands are nearly run. He asks his "dear old Tom Payne" to copy a paper which he has drawn up.

"You won't d—— me, won't you? I have not been well lately with violent palpitation of the heart, and I should not like to slip my wind without an attempt to secure for Juana the pension of my rank which must be an especial [one ?]. I have consulted Yorke and Bell, who agree in my course ; but, Tom, I am no nearer dropping off the hooks for doing this.

"Yours,
"HARRY SMITH.

"I write *on my back* to-day, but *much better*. Say nothing of all this."

The following letter, addressed to Major Payne by Colonel Shadwell (Q.M.G. at Manchester), though of the nature of a false alarm, shows the coming of the end, and how it struck home to those who loved him.

" Manchester, 15th Sept. 1860.

"MY DEAR TOM,

"You will probably have heard from London direct of our dear old friend Sir Harry's alarming state. From Alice's account this morning, he was yesterday morning *in extremis,* and ere this has most likely breathed his last.

"It has come like a thunderbolt on us, as only five days ago Lady Smith wrote to us in such good spirits about the dear old man.

"We saw him, I am now thankful to say, when in town for a few days the middle of last month.

"I presume, from the intense agony he has endured, that he has succumbed to an attack of angina pectoris.

"What a friend we have lost! so true, so constant, so generous, so kind, and then to think of dear Lady Smith! I shudder to think of what her state will be when she comes to realize it.

"My wife is quite upset by it, and so am I.

"Always, my dear Payne,

"Yours very truly,

"LAWRENCE SHADWELL."

On the 12th October, at 1, Eaton Place West, which had been his home for the last six months, the end came. Sir Harry had reached the age of 73 on the 28th June preceding.

A year before, in sending his nephew George Moore Smith a subscription towards the restoration of St. Mary's, Whittlesey, he had written, " I enclose a cheque for *our* subscription to the repairs of the Dear Old Church, which I do most willingly, and should do more willingly if *our* bones could

repose with our fathers." But though the church
where his father and mother lay was closed for
interments, he could still be taken to Whittlesey,
and there in a corner of the new cemetery he was
laid to rest on the 19th. All business in the little
town was suspended for the day, and some thousands
of the inhabitants of the town and district lined
the route of the procession. The Rifle Corps of
Ely, Wisbeach, March, Ramsey, and Whittlesey
were represented at their own request, and with
arms reversed preceded the hearse from the station
to St. Mary's Church, and thence to the cemetery.
The coffin was borne by eight old soldiers who
had all served under Sir Harry, and had all won
medals; the pall-bearers were six Whittlesey gentlemen, most of them his schoolfellows. Among the
mourners were his surviving "Waterloo brother,"
Major Thomas Smith, his nephew Lieut.-Colonel
Hugh Smith, Colonel Garvock, his Military Secretary at the Cape, and Colonel Shadwell, whose
letter has been printed above. Three volleys were
fired over the grave by the volunteers of Whittlesey,
March, and Wisbeach.

A sum of £700 was subscribed to found a
memorial to Sir Harry Smith's memory, and was
spent on the restoration of that part of St. Mary's
Church, Whittlesey—the chapel at the end of the
south aisle—in which, when it was used as a
schoolroom, he had received his early education.*
It is now known as "Sir Harry's Chapel." On the

* See p. 1 *n.*

south wall was erected a monument of white marble surmounted by a bust of Sir Harry, executed by Mr. G. G. Adams, A.R.A.* It bears the inscription :—

"This monument was erected and this chapel restored in 1862 by public subscription to the memory of Lieutenant-General Sir Harry G. W. Smith, Baronet of Aliwal, Knight Grand Cross of the Most Honourable Order of the Bath, Colonel of the 1st Battalion, Rifle Brigade. He entered the 95th Regiment in 1805, served in South America, Spain, Portugal, France, North America, the Netherlands, India, and at the Cape of Good Hope, of which he was Governor and Commander-in-Chief from 1847 to 1852, and on the Home Staff to 1859, when he completed a most gallant and eventful career of fifty-four years' constant employment. He was born at Whittlesey, 28th June, 1788,† and died in London 12th October, 1860. Within these walls he received his earliest education, and in the cemetery of his native place his tomb bears ample record of the high estimation in which his military talents were held by his friend and chief, the great Duke of Wellington.

"Coruna, Busaco, Fuentes d'Onoro, Ciudad Rodrigo, Badajoz, Salamanca, Vittoria, Pyrenees, Nivelle, Nive, Orthez, Toulouse, Waterloo, Maharajpore, Ferozeshuhur, Aliwal, Sobraon, South Africa.‡

"O Lord, in Thee have I trusted ; let me never be confounded."§

---

* Called by Lady Smith, "not *quite*, yet like my own Henrique!"
† The date should be 1787.

‡ The first twelve names represent the 12 clasps attached to Sir Harry's Peninsular medal ; for Waterloo, Maharajpore, and South Africa (1853) he had separate medals ; the remaining three names are those of his clasps for the Sutlej Campaign. He wore, besides, the Grand Cross of the Bath and the Portuguese Order of St. Bento d'Aviz.

§ See p. 653.

On Sir Harry's tomb in the cemetery, Lady Smith caused to be inscribed the last sentences of the extract from the Duke of Wellington's speech of 2nd April, 1846, given above (pp. 558–560), though in a slightly different version.

After her husband's death, Lady Smith resided for some years at 19, Robertson Terrace, Hastings, and later at 79, Cadogan Place, S.W. Passionately cherishing her husband's memory, she was the beloved friend of all members of his family, and the goodness of heart and active sympathy which she showed to some who were heavy-laden will never be forgotten by their descendants. The editor of this book recalls from his boyhood the proud and animated tones in which she would speak of "Your uncle Harry"—pronouncing the name with the full Continental *a* and a strongly trilled *r*. Her noble heart ceased to beat on the 10th October, 1872, and she was laid with her hero in his last resting-place at Whittlesey.

Of the other close friends and companions of Sir Harry Smith, Charles Beckwith died in July, 1862, among the Piedmontese whom he had served so truly ; Sir John Bell in 1876, having lived to the age of ninety-four.* Sir Harry's sister, Mrs. Sargant (of whom it has been humorously said that she was " the only person in the world of whom he was afraid "), died in 1869; his youngest sister,

---

* In his last years the gallant old General would say that " he did not care any longer to go to the club and meet *a lot of old fogies whom he didn't know.*"

Miss Anna Maria Smith, in 1875; his brother, Colonel Thomas Smith, C.B.—the last survivor of the family of eleven—in 1877. Colonel Smith's widow still lives at the age of ninety-three, fresh in body and mind, though it is ninety-three years since her husband sailed to the Peninsula under Sir John Moore.*

Few words are necessary in bringing this book to a close. If it has been a long one, the Editor can only plead that Harry Smith put more into his seventy odd years than would make the lives of half a dozen other men.

The autobiography shows us the strong family affections of his boyhood, his abiding reverence for his father, who had made him a *man* and a bold horseman, his love of brave soldiers like Colborne and Barnard and Pakenham, his supreme worship of his great master and example, Wellington. Such were the influences under which he was trained for the service of his Sovereign and of his country. In the hour of responsibility it was seen that he possessed in rare harmony qualities on which that training had not been thrown away—"an ardent spirit, which inflamed a whole army with kindred ardour, combined with a power of self-control which kept the mind clear and calm in the most difficult emergencies — the union of fiery passion with temperate reason."† A born leader, he never lost the confidence of the officers and men who were under his command—he had it as clearly amid the

---

* She died Jan. 10, 1902.   † *Cape Town Mail*, 5th April, 1851.

anxieties and disappointments of the Kafir War of 1851-2 as after his marvellous campaign of Aliwal. His soldiers literally loved him, both for his bonhomie and for his lifelong zeal for their welfare.*

Sir Harry Smith was above all things a great soldier. In his civil administration of the Cape, undertaken at a time of enormous difficulty, his success was less brilliant than elsewhere, but even here he justified Havelock's opinion of him: "There is no species of business which Harry Smith's mental tact will not enable him to grasp." History will approve of the firm stand he made against mob-rule in the time of the Anti-convict agitation, and, seeing events in true perspective, will forget little errors of judgment (magnified at the moment by party-feeling) when set side by side with his zeal for the good of the Colony and his far-sighted perception of England's true policy in South Africa.

Such practical mistakes as Harry Smith made, both within the Colony and in his dealings with Kafir chiefs, were due to a generous, chivalrous disposition, which was ready to put the best construction on other people's conduct and to attribute to them a goodness of heart resembling his own.

---

* I visited last year at Ely, Mr. B. Genn, late of the 15th Hussars, who had served under him in India in 1846, and who had fired over his grave. As soon as I had opened the door, a fine engraving of Sir Harry greeted me. It had been bought at a sale. The old veteran spoke of his commander always as the "dear old man." When I asked him if he thought him a good General, he fired up quickly, "Why, think of the battle of Aliwal! Not a mistake anywhere."

With an open foe, in warfare, he was caution
itself, but he was too little of a Macchiavelli to read
treachery in the smile of a seeming friend. A
generous open nature was similarly responsible for
such flaws in his character as his hastiness and
warmth of language under provocation,* as his extravagance in money matters (strangely contrasting
with the severity in many respects of his own life),
and a little vanity in regard to his own achievements,
a vanity perhaps not more real than other men's,
but occasionally less carefully concealed.   If he
sometimes seemed to his subordinates an exacting
master, we may remember that during his whole
career as a soldier he had never spared himself.

If any one were disposed to take an unfavourable view of this or that trait in Harry Smith's
character, I hope the picture given of him in these
pages would be a sufficient corrective. Praised by
Wellington for his generalship as hardly any man
else was praised, acknowledged by Havelock as the
man who had made him a soldier, he had through
life the warm respect and love of a score or two of
brave and worthy men, such as D'Urban, and John
Bell, and Kempt, and Barnard, and Kincaid, and
George Simmons, and Charles Beckwith. They
recognized his rare military genius : they respected

---

* The following characteristic story has been sent me by Major
J. F. Anderson, of Coxwell Lodge, Faringdon : " Sir Harry was very
quick-tempered, and on one occasion (during the Kafir War of 1835 ?),
when my father remonstrated with him as to an order he gave, he said,
'Learn to obey, sir,' and ordered him into his tent under arrest. In
the evening he sent to ask my father to dine with him ! "

him because, in his own words, he had always been "a working man who put his heart into his work:" they loved him for what Lord Raglan called "the chivalrous and gallant spirit" which had been his guide in his military career; because he was fearless of danger, indomitable in energy, over-flowing in kindness, magnanimous and placable towards those who seemed his foes, loving his friends, even to his old age, with the ardour of a boy. Little wonder that one of the noblest and largest-hearted of women also pardoned his faults and adored him as only few men have been adored.

Historians may perhaps find some matter of instruction in the autobiography now presented to them. But is it too much to hope that it may have a still happier fortune, and that young Englishmen and Englishwomen yet unborn may be kindled to a noble emulation by the brave and glowing hearts of Harry and Juana Smith?

APPENDIX I.

" E'er since reflection beam'd her light upon me
You, sir, have been my study ; I have plac'd
Before mine eyes, in every light of life,
The father and the king.   What weight of duty
Lay on a son from such a parent sprung,
What virtuous toil to shine with his renown,
Has been my thought by day, my dream by night :
But first and ever nearest to my heart
Was this prime duty, so to frame my conduct
Tow'rd such a father, as, were I a father,
My soul would wish to meet with from a son.
And may reproach transmit my name abhorr'd
To latest time, if ever thought was mine
Unjust to filial reverence, filial love."

MALLET.

1806. *Nov.* [*Oct.* ?] *9th.*—Sailed from Falmouth under convoy
of His Majesty's ship *Ardent* (Capt. Donnelly), *Unicorn* frigate,
Daphne, 20-guns ship, *Pheasant* and *Charwell*, Sloops-of-war,
with a fleet of about 25 transports, a store-ship for the Cape of
Good Hope, and a merchant ship for the East Indies.   The force
consists of a Company of Artillery, under Capt. Dixon ; three
Companies of the 2nd Battalion Rifle Regiment, under Major
T. C. Gardner ; 17th Light Dragoons, Col. Loyd ; 40th Regiment
of Foot, Col. Browne ; and 87th, Col. Sir Edward Butler ; the
whole under Brigadier-General Sir Samuel Auchmuty.   Brigadier-
General the Hon. William Lumley, Brigadier of the Horse ;
Lieut.-Col. Bradford, Deputy Adjutant-General ; Lieut.-Col. Bourke,
Deputy Quartermaster-General ; Captain Blake, Assistant Adju-
tant-General ; Lt. Tylden, Brigade-Major to Sir Samuel ; Captain
Roach, Brigade-Major to General Lumley ; Mr. Baddock,

Deputy Paymaster-General; Mr. Bissett, Deputy Commissary of Accompts; Mr. Redman, Deputy Inspector of Hospitals. A fine breeze until the 12th, when we were becalmed in the Bay of Biscay. Lovely weather.

13th.—A breeze sprung up which increased into a gale. Blew dreadfully hard. Sea ran mountains high. Continued until the 16th, when it gradually died away; a heavy sea still running, with the heavy rolling of the ship, sprang the main piece of our rudder. We made a signal of distress, which was instantly answered by the Commodore, who made a signal to the *Charwell* to come alongside us, which she did, and hailed us. She immediately sent a boat on board with her carpenter. Soon after the *Unicorn* came up with us. She also sent a boat on board, with a lieutenant, midshipman, and carpenter, with everything requisite to repair our rudder, which was soon done. A steady breeze until the 18th, when it again blew hard. The *Daphne* and a Transport with 150 men of the 40th Regiment parted convoy in the night. Still continued to blow until the 23rd, when we were becalmed. Lovely weather. Captain of the ship took an observation for the first time since at sea. Latitude 47° 35' North.

24th.—Breeze sprung up. Lat. 39° 37'. Breeze freshened. Continued until the 30th. Commodore lost a man overboard. Lovely weather. In the evening observed two large whales close to the ship. They followed us some time and greatly amused us. Lat. 32° 9'.

Nov. 1st.—At daybreak discovered land, to our great delight. It proved to be the Canary Isles. In sight of them the whole of the day. The ground appeared mountainous and barren, with an aspect bleak to a degree. Beautiful weather, with a fine breeze which soon carried us into the Trade winds. The flying-fish begin to be innumerable.

Nov. 4th.—Lat. 23°. A shark passed close under our stern.

Nov. 5th.—Lat. 21° 40'. Fine fresh breeze. The *Harriet* Transport, with the Artillery on board, made a signal of distress, which proved to be from the death of her captain. Flying-fish so numerous, they resemble large flocks of larks. Some of them were by accurate observation seen to fly from 100 to 200 yards and upwards.

Nov. 6th.—Lat. 18° 31'. Fine fresh breeze. In the evening an unfortunate flying-fish flew on board us, being close pursued by an enemy, which measured 8 inches from head to tail, and 9½ from the extreme of each wing. Tail forked like a mackerel. Cooked him for breakfast the next morning. Every one tasted him.

Nov. 7th.—Lat. 16° 53'. Thermometer 80° in the shade. Weather very warm. Signal from Commodore for Commanding Officers of Corps. A fine turtle close to the ship. We wished for him on board. To our astonishment, although a considerable distance from land, we were in shoal water the whole of the day, supposed to be a sand-bank, the water by times being quite discoloured. Commodore, not meaning to put into any port, made a signal for the troops and seamen to be put on short allowance of water, two quarts per man, all ranks.

Nov. 8th.—Lat. 15° 19'. Therm. 84°. Scorching hot. Speared some fish at the bow of the ship.

Nov. 9th.—Lat. 15° 12'. Therm. 82°. Fine weather, but no breeze. Caught two venata with bait. They resemble a mackerel as much as possible, except that they are about twice as large. Cooked them. Coarse, hard and bad eating. A flying-fish flew on board and fell into a tub of water.

Nov. 10th.—Lat. 14° 34'; long. 23°. Therm. 83°. *Pheasant*, Sloop-of-war, made sail in search of land, which must be the Cape de Verd Isles. Suppose she made it, as she joined convoy in the evening.

Nov. 11th.—Lat. 12° 57'. Therm. 82°. Venata are innumerable. It is very amusing to see them leap out of the water in pursuit of the poor flying-fish.

Nov. 12th.—Lat. 10° 49'. Therm. 82°.

Nov. 13th.—At 10 a.m. every appearance of a storm. The clouds put on a terrible aspect. Fortunately it was not violent, going off with torrents of rain. Five minutes before 5 p.m. a waterspout was observed to the westward, which emptied itself in torrents over the bow of the *Pheasant* without intermission, until 5 minutes past 5.

Nov. 14th.—Dark cloudy weather. No observations.

Nov. 15th.—Lat. 7° 53'. Therm. 83°. A boat of the *Charwell's* swamped as they were about to hoist it up. All hands overboard, but saved. Went on board the Commodore with returns to the General.

Nov. 16th.—Lat. 6° 38'. Therm. 86°. Sultry close weather,

with storms of thunder and lightning. Stark calm, with tremendous showers, the rain coming down in torrents, not drops.

Nov. 17th.—Lat. 6° 17'. Therm. 82°. Weather less sultry, with heavy showers. A large flight of birds resembling ducks ahead, so close together in the water they resemble a floating island. Loaded rifles and fired at them, but to no purpose.

Nov. 18th.—Lat. 6° 1'. Therm. 84°. No breeze. Tremendous thunderstorm, with torrents of rain.

Nov. 19th.—No observation, being cloudy dirty weather. A signal for masters of transports to go on board Commodore. A brig sent home for inattention and not obeying signals. The troops on board her were distributed on board different ships. Wrote letters home in hopes of being able to send them by her, but a breeze springing up prevented our lowering a boat, to my great disappointment.

Nov. 20th.—Lat. 4° 44'. Therm. 82°. Nice breeze but rather ahead. At 6 p.m. the *Pheasant* passed us under all sail. On coming alongside the Commodore she hoisted his ensign, which was immediately returned by him. It is always done when a ship parts convoy. Suppose she is sent forward to Buenos Ayres.

Nov. 21st.—Lat. 3° 45'; long. 26° 38' West. Therm. 82°. Fine breeze.

Nov. 22nd.—Lat. 3° 14'. Therm. 81°. Squally. Wind changing often and suddenly.

Nov. 23rd.—Lat. 2° 30'. Therm. 80°. Weather cool, considering how near we are to the sun.

Nov. 24th.—Lat. 1° 49'. Therm. 82°. Fine breeze but rather ahead. Evening squally. A strange sail to windward. Proved to be an American.

Nov. 25th.—Dark and cloudy. No observation. Plenty of wind.

Nov. 26th.—Lat. 15' South; long. 32° West. One of the sailors caught an immense large albacore with a spear. Took three men to haul him in. He had a curious prickly fin upon his back, which he could completely hide in a crevice so as not to be perceived, and when hurt would set it up. Sea completely covered with flying-fish. A signal made for our ship to take in tow the *Three Sisters*, a small brig, she being to leeward. Ran down to her and obeyed the signal.

Nov. 27th.—Lat. 1° 29'; long. 32°. Speared another large

albacore, which measured 4 feet long and 2 feet 9 inches in circumference.

Nov. 28*th.*—Lat. 3°. Therm. 82°. Signal made by Commodore signifying land in sight, bearing south-south-west, upon which he altered his course one point more to the westward. Supposed to be the island Ferando Noronha.

Nov. 29*th.*—Lat. 4° 12'. Therm. 84°.

Nov. 30*th.*—Lat. 5° 27'; long. 34° 15'. Therm. 81°. Took in tow the *Osborne,* a large ship with Dragoons on board.

Dec. 1*st.*—Lat. 6° 39'. Therm. 82°. At 6 o'clock a.m. a signal made by Commodore signifying land in sight, supposed to be Cape Augustin.

Dec. 2*nd.*—Lat. 8° 20'. Therm. 82°. Have observed for these two or three days the flying-fish have almost entirely disappeared.

Dec. 3*rd.*—Lat. 10° 3'. Therm. 81°. The two merchant ships, the *Lincoln* and *Loyalist,* the former bound to the East Indies, the latter store-ship for the Cape of Good Hope, parted convoy. On altering their course every ship hoisted her ensign, which was returned by them by way of farewell. Had a pretty effect.

Dec. 4*th.*—Lat. 12° 42'. Therm. 81°. Lovely breeze. A signal for masters of transports to caulk and prepare their boats for landing.

Dec. 5*th.*—Lat. 15° 24'. Therm. 80°. A schooner in sight to the westward bearing down for us. Overhauled by the *Charwell,* and proved to be a Portuguese bound for San Salvador.

Dec. 6*th.*—Fresh breeze. No observation.

Dec. 7*th.*—Lat. 19° 26'. Therm. 82°. Observed a shark which followed the ship a long time, accompanied with three pilot fish. Threw a bait to him, upon which one of his pilot fish swam to it and tasted, and reported accordingly to its master. Observed the breeze to die away by day and blow by night.

Dec. 8*th.*—Lat. 20° 8'. Therm. 86°. Dreadfully hot.

Dec. 9*th.*—Lat. 20° 48'; long. 39° 34'.

Dec. 10*th.*—Lat. 22° 5'; long. 40° 29'.—A signal from Commodore signifying land in sight, supposed at first to be Rio Janeiro, afterwards proved to be Cape Frio, about 40 miles distant from it. Therm. 85°. A tremendous thunderstorm, louder than anything I ever heard.

> " Loud thunder from the distant poles ensue,
> Then flashing fires the transient light renew."

Dec. 12th.—Beating all day off Cape Frio, endeavouring to get into port. Wind ahead. At 9 p.m. wind came round. Weathered Cape Frio.

Dec. 13th.—Made the bay. On the first appearance of the land it put me in mind of the following lines in Thomson's *Hymn on the Seasons :—*

> " Should fate command me to the farthest verge
> Of the green earth, to distant barbarous climes,
> Rivers unknown to song ; where first the sun
> Gilds Indian mountains, or his setting beams
> Flame on th' Atlantic Isles, 'tis nought to me,
> Since God is ever present, ever felt,
> In the void waste as in the city full,
> And where *He* vital spreads, *there* must be joy."

Appearance of the land before the entrance of the harbour, mountainous and woody. At 7 p.m. came to an anchor at the mouth of the harbour. The darkness of the night prevented our going in. The hills surrounding illuminated with the most vivid lightning I ever saw, equally beautiful as awful.

Dec. 14th.—At 12 weighed anchor. The entrance of the harbour is very grand. On the left hand is an immense rock called the Sugar-loaf, which it correctly resembles. At the foot of it is a strong battery. On the right hand is a pretty little fort, apparently very strong, having three tiers of heavy guns. At a small distance from the mouth of the harbour is a little island with a fort upon it, which gives the bay a pretty and rather romantic appearance. As soon as the Commodore came to an anchor, he fired a salute of 19 guns, which was immediately returned by the different batteries, the echo of which in the surrounding hills was beyond description grand.

General, Staff, and Commodore went on shore to call upon the Viceroy. When in the boat the *Ardent* fired a salute of 15 guns to them. The General obtained permission for the officers and a proportion of men to go on shore.

Dec. 15th.—Went on shore, and was highly delighted with the town of Rio Janeiro. It is very large but irregularly built, situated on a spacious and commodious bay. You land nearly opposite the Viceroy's palace, which stands on the south side of a large and regular square. You see nothing scarcely but poor slaves carrying immense loads, and friars in their cocked hats going to and from the monasteries. Their carriages resemble in some manner our single-horse chaises, but badly made and drawn by two mules. On the near one rides the charioteer, in a huge cocked hat; the off one is in the shafts. They go astonishingly quick. Saw but few horses, those small and bad. The mules are most beautiful animals, and the inhabitants tell you are much more serviceable then the horses. They are as clean about the legs as our race-horses, and full of spirit. Fowls and ducks plentiful, but rather dear. The oxen and sheep are small and bad. Pigs in abundance. Fruits of all sorts. Pines are larger than ours, but not so fine flavoured; you get them for 6d. apiece. Oranges, lemons, limes, sweet and sour, bananas, yams, etc., etc. They make no butter or cheese. They get it from England or America. The grandees, when they appear abroad, are carried in a kind of palanquin, which is borne on two negroes' shoulders. Most of these are blue, and adorned with fringes in general of the same colour. They have a velvet pillow, and above the head a kind of tester with curtains. He may either lie down or sit up. (See Guthrie.)

I must think, from what we have seen of the inhabitants, Guthrie speaks too harshly of them. They paid us every attention—nay, so much so that they were troublesome; and were honest in their dealings. The canoes afforded us great amusement. They are rowed by two or three negroes, according to the size of them— not with oars, but a thing resembling a spade. They appear, as they go along, to be digging the water.

I went into one of their monasteries, the chapel of which was very grand. There was also a capital library. The monks were extremely polite, and showed us everything particular. Their service is in Latin. There are four monasteries, and two nunneries filled with poor wretches of girls, who are not allowed to speak to their own fathers. I dined in what they call a cooking-house. The host showed us into a miserable back room looking into the kitchen, where was a black fellow cooking. My stomach was not yet turned. No glass in the window (but that is the case with all the houses, except those of the grandees), and the light shining through the pantiles over our heads. We had for dinner first some macaroni soup, half oil, and scraped cheese to eat with it; afterwards some mutton chops swimming in grease, pork chops in a similar way, a pair of fowls we could scarcely pull to pieces, not an atom of flesh on their bones. There was also a piece of thin beef rolled up with the stuffing in it and roast —a famous dish for a hungry mastiff dog. These being removed, we then had a cold plum-pudding, which was very good. We drank at dinner bad American bottled ale, afterwards some decent port wine. When we called for our bill, we were all amazingly astonished. It came to 4880—*whats*, we could not tell. We afterwards found it was about six dollars. They give you always their bills in that way in some imaginary coin about half a farthing value.

Dec. 16th.—Did not go on shore. At 6 p.m. a Portuguese brig came into harbour, laden with poor wretches of slaves just taken from the Guinea coast—the most horrid sight imaginable.

Dec. 17th.—Went to see a grand review of the Portuguese troops. They performed pretty well. There was a regular regiment of militia, and a volunteer, with some dragoons and artillery, amounting in all to about 2000 men. After it was over, all the English officers were presented to the Viceroy. Nothing more worth setting down. All of us quite tired of the place, and anxious to get away.

Dec. 23rd.—Sailed for Buenos Ayres. Nice breeze.

Dec. 24th.—Lat. 24° 47'. Out of sight of land. Therm. 80°.

Dec. 25th.—Lat. 25° 32'. Therm. 76.° Blows hard, with a heavy sea.

Dec. 26th.—Lat. 26° 51'. Heavy swell and no breeze. An immense shoal of porpoises swimming towards the north. In hopes of a fair wind, as they always swim against the wind.

Dec. 27th.—Lat. 27° 48'. Stark calm. At 4 a.m. a strong breeze sprung up, but quite ahead.

Dec. 28th.—Lat. 27° 52'.

Dec. 29th.—Lat. 27° 29'; long. 47° 9'. Went on board the Commodore. A large shoal of porpoises by their swimming portending a fair wind, which soon sprung up.

Dec. 30th.—Lat. 30° 21'.

Dec. 31st.—Lat. 32° 11'. Anxious to get along, but the wind against us.

1807. *Jan. 1st.*—Lat. 32° 20'; long. 51° 15.'

Jan. 2nd.—Lat. 32° 30'. Wind against us.

[Remainder apparently written afterwards.]

Landed four miles north of Monte Video 16th Jan., had a sharp skirmish with the enemy.

19th.—A regular battle. Licked them confoundedly.

20th.—A very severe action. The enemy's loss very great.

3rd Feb.—Stormed the fortress of Monte Video. A severe conflict. Indeed, our loss, as well as that of the enemy, was very great.

16th Jan., 1807.*—Sharp skirmishing with enemy.

17th.—Ditto.

18th.—Ditto.

19th.—A regular and victorious battle in the open field.

20th.—They made a sortie ; were repulsed with great loss.

From the 20th Jan. to 3rd Feb. constant skirmishes. On the morning of the 3rd Feb. stormed the fortress of Monte Video with severe loss on both sides ; but carried it.

7th April, 1807 [7 *June* ?].—Colonel Pack made a sortie from Colonia with 1000 men to meet Colonel Elio, whose force consisted of 1500. Entirely routed him, and took six pieces of cannon.

3rd June [5 *July* ?].—Attacked Buenos Ayres by assault. Was made prisoner, and confined three days and three nights.

Embarked for England, and arrived at Falmouth 5th Nov.

1808.—Embarked at Harwich for Sweden latter end of May [April ?]. Sailed soon afterwards. Was two months in Gottenburg harbour, when we sailed for England, and refitted at Portsmouth for Portugal. Landed about 30 miles north of Lisbon latter end of July [August ?]. Marched through the south of Portugal into Spain. Had a very hot action with the French between Villa Franca and Calcavellos 3rd Jan., 1809. The loss was nearly equal on both sides. Take it all together, the most severe conflict I ever saw.

Embarked at Corunna in January, and reached England soon after.

Ready to embark again.

* In this and the following items, the story given above is repeated.

APPENDIX II.

Letter I. Endorsed—"*7th May, 1813. From Eleanor on Stona's marriage.—H. G. S.*"

Whittlesea, May 7th, 1813.

My Dear Henry,

From the ardent desire which you have long expressed concerning Stona's marriage, it will, I am convinced, give you pleasure to hear that the nuptials are at last solemnized. The ceremony took place on Tuesday, which was the fourth of May. Mr. Coleman was father, and of course led the bride to church. Stona, Kate, Charles, and Anna Maria followed, and my Uncle Ground's John in a handsome livery, and Stona's own servant (who is a particular smart-looking young man) dressed in a drab coat, and a gold band on his hat—all new for the occasion—attended to receive the bridesmaids' parasols at the church door, and remained there in waiting during the ceremony. When concluded, the party returned to breakfast at my Uncle Ground's, where were assembled to meet them a group of relations consisting of about two and twenty. Each of us was presented with a white favour, the ringers and servants also. There were forty favours given away. The bride and bridegroom, accompanied by Catherine, set off at twelve for Cambridge, and from thence they proceeded to London. I assure you they cut a dash. The postboy of course had a favour on his hat, and James, Stona's man, attended them on horseback as far as Ramsey. Unfortunately it was a Newmarket meeting, and Cambridge was so full that they could not get beds, were therefore obliged to proceed another stage that evening. About five the next day they arrived in the

Metropolis, and when they had dined, they dressed for Covent Garden Theatre. Stona repeatedly expressed a great wish that it was possible to meet you in town. Neither the bride nor bridesmaid would, I can venture to say, have had any objection to that. Never poor fellow I think was in a greater agitation than Stona during the ceremony and two days before. When he was being married he trembled in such a manner that Anna Maria expected no other than he would drop the ring—and he was himself much afraid lest he should have fainted at the altar. . . .

I must not omit to tell you what a very pretty place Stona's house is, and so handsomely furnished that I declare it is enough to make me long to be married. . . .

We are now always changing our Curates; next week Mr. Cook is going to leave us, and that handsome gentlemanlike man, whom I mentioned to you in my last, Mr. Powis, is to take his place. The young ladies, they say, will become very religious, and many of them attend prayers.

I have, since writing the above, received a letter from you for which I thank you a thousand times. Believe me, I am not offended at the remark you made respecting my age, and the next time I hear from you, I expect the letter addressed to " Mrs. Eleanor Smith." You will, my dear Henry, be six and twenty in June.

My Mother, I am happy to say, is better than when I last wrote, though still rather delicate. My Father goes into quarters on Sunday. Wisbeach, as usual, is to be head-quarters.

Mrs. W——, I fear, has not added much to her happiness by marrying W——, for he is excessively idle, an *epicure*, a free *drinker*, and a *notorious debauchee*. With such a man, can any woman be truly happy? . . .

I hope you will lose no opportunity of writing, for, as I have frequently observed, it is the greatest pleasure I can have in your absence. Would to God we could have you among us. I never wished for you more than I do now. My Mother is quite delighted that you wish to see us.

As you do not say anything about Tom, I conclude he is well. Pray give my love to him, and tell him that Mary Smith * is a pretty little black girl, and generally allowed to be more interesting than ever her sister was.

* Afterwards married to Charles Smith.

All your friends, my dear Henry, join in affectionate remembrance to you and Tom; and sincerely wishing you health and happiness, believe me to remain, dearest Henry, your truly affectionate sister,

ELEANOR.

Addressed—

Brigade-Major Smith,
2nd Light Brigade,
Pd. 3/   Light Division,
Portugal.

Letter II. Endorsed—" 19th *August,* 1813. *The last letter my dear Mother ever wrote to me. She died on the* 12th *December,* 1813, *Sunday.—H. G. Smith.*"

Whitt^r, Augst 19, 1813.

MY BELOVED CHILD^N,

What words shall I find sufficiently expressive to congratulate you upon y^r great escape from the great perils and dangers you have been exposed to, where so many of y^r brave countrymen have fallen? But to God alone must the praise be given, who has preserved you both, I hope to be an ornament to y^r country and a blessing to y^r friends, and may God Almighty of his infinite mercy still hold his protecting Arm over you both, and may we never lose sight of him, and have always his goodness in our sight as never to neglect our duty for his great mercies towards us at this time and all others.

This, my dear Harry, is an anxious time, and, tho' we have not a Lett^r from you, by the *Gazette* we know that you are safe.

As for Tom, I think he never intends to write to eith^r of us again, but I am proud to hear of him from you as being so brave a fell^w, and hope to have Lett^{rs} by the next dispatches. We can make every allowance for not hearing from you at this time, as indeed you must be so much ingaged, but pray write whenever you can, and indeed it is one of my greatest comforts.

I have been very ill, so much so that I never expected seeing eith^r of you again, but with the blessing of God I am a very great deal bett^r, and with the kindness of y^r Fath^r and the attention of y^r Sis^{rs} I look forw^d with the hopes of seeing my beloved boys once more under their parental roof. . . .

We have been extremely healthy for a length of time that y Fath' and Bro' make great complaints some time for want of something to do.

Poor R⁴ Binfield is no more. He payd the great debt of nature about three weeks ago, after being a very great sufferer. When he was taken to be buried, his Corpse was preceeded by six Girls dressed in white with white turbans, and baskets of flowers in their hands, whʰ they throwed into the grave as soon as the Corpse was let down. The Pall was supported by six of the schoⁿ in white Hat-bands, and the whole Schᶦ follwᵈ in the same way. It altogether was a pretty sight, but rath' too romantic, but you know the woman. . . .

Yʳ Sisʳ Sargant is not in very good health, and is gone to Cromer. It is upon the Norfolk coast, and is a very fashion-able Bathing-place. The rest of the Family, I am happy to say, are well. As for yʳ dear Fath', I think if you could see him you wouᵈ think he had grown fat. We all Unite in Love to you and Tom, with best wishes for yʳ healths and prosperity. Pray write soon, and may God Almighty preserve you both is the fervent prayer of yʳ affecᵉ Moth',

E. SMITH.

Eleanor desires me to say she is much oblidged to you for yʳ Lettʳ and will write soon, and Betsy also says that unless Tom will write to her she never will write again.

Addressed—

    Brigade-Major Smith, Light Brigade,
       2nd Light Division, Portugal.

  Post paid to Falmouth.

Letter III. Endorsed—"15ᵗʰ *Oct.* 1813. *From my Father, say-ing my Mother was pleased with my Letter after a fight in Spain.—H. G. S."*

Whittlesea, Octʳ 15ᵗʰ, 1813.

My Dᴿ HARRY,

    Your Mother receiv'd your letter the other day and myself one about a fortnight back, both of which gave us great satisfaction, particularly as you were both in good health and safe. We were in hopes as the French were so much beaten by our brave fellows, and Soult having had so good a specimen of the superior Abilities of Marshal Wellington (superior they are indeed, for he is certainly the first General in the world), that he wou'd have been glad to have got hived, and not have exposed himself again to the second part of the same tune.

I was very sorry to hear of your Horse's accident, as it must be a great loss, but it was an accident and cou'd not have been prevented. My Horse I bought for you to send into Portugal has turned out very unfortunate. He has had a bad Cough on him for near a year, which continued getting worse, and I was fearful of its terminating in Glanders. Had he been quite well he was worth two hundred. However, I was under the necessity of sending Long Will to Bridge Fair, and selling him for what he wou'd fetch, which was fifteen pounds, leaving me a loser of at least £100, for I was at great expence with him.

I was happy to find Cap^n Stewart's horse turn'd out so well, but you clapt your seal over the amount and we cou'd not read it. Send me the amount when you write again. As to news I have none, for Eleanor gives you that in all her letters.

I must say I feel hurt at Tho' not writing at all. . . . I am very proud to hear so high a character of him as an adjutant. Major Percival came from Portsmouth with Bob Hotchkin to London, and seeing an offic' in the coach in 95th uniform, he asked him if he knew Capt. Smith, and he asked him which, Henry or Tom. They had a great deal of conversation, and he said he believ'd Tom to be one of the best adjutants in the service. A poor unfortunate Cripple he was. Bob was with Gen. Murray at that noble business. He came Home extremely ill indeed of Dysentery.

I am sorry to tell you poor Mr. Moore * I think is wearing up fast. He has been severely afflicted with Rheumatism. He is better of Pain, but left so weak and low that he can scarcely ride on horseback. . . .

If any one is coming home that you can trust, I wish you wou'd send me some flower seeds, but I am in great hopes you will bring them yourself.

The Allies seem to be licking the French in Germany well, and I hope will drive them into Peace.

* Vicar of St. Mary and St. Andrew, Whittlesey, and cousin to Harry Smith's mother.

We one and all unite in Love and affection to self and Tom, praying God to protect you both is the prayer of your affect. Father,

J^{no} SMITH.

Addressed—

Brigade-Major Smith, 95th Reg^t Rifle Corps,

Light Division, Light Brigade.

Serving under

Marshal Wellington,

Spain.

Letter IV. Endorsed—"14th Dec^r, 1813. *My dear Father's Letter announcing my poor Mother's Death.—H. G. S.*"

Whittlesea, Decr 14th, 1813.

We have received, my Dr Harry, your letter dated Sante Pe, Novr 14th, and it was read by myself, your *Dr Mother*, Brothers, and Sisters with infinite pleasure in finding you were both unhurt, and with gratitude to the Almighty for the preservation of you both in this and in every other danger you have so often been expos'd to.

But, my *Dr Boys*, what pain, what affliction is it to me to tell you it is the last letter your poor dear Mother will ever hear or read more from you.

You have been apprised of her ill health by your Sister Elean^r, and we did not wish to distress your feelings by repeatedly telling you the ill state of her health, for we were in hopes she might have got well again. But alas! her D^r soul quited this earthly abode on Sunday morning, Decr 12th, in hopes of a joyful resurrection, which her pious, virtuous, good life entitled her to hope for in her blessed Lord and Redeemer. Oh Harry! she prayed constantly for the return and welfare of you both; she suffer'd much in anxiety; she dearly, very dearly lov'd you and adored you, and in her last prayers never lost sight of her dear Boys abroad. She died in her perfect senses even to the last moment. I hope she did not suffer very much in the separation of soul and body. . . . Your poor distrest father, Brothers and sisters all unite in the strongest love and affection for you both. God Bless you.

J^{no} SMITH.

2 Z

Send a proper direction. Pray write to me on the Receipt of this.

Remember, my D' Boys, that this letter is equally addrest to you both by your very much afflicted Parent.

Addressed—

> Brig'-Major Smith,
>> Light Brigade,
>>> Light Division,
>> Commanded by Col. Colborne,
>>> Serving under Marq. Wellington,
>>>> France.

Letter V. Endorsed—"*19th Feb'y*, 1814, *after my poor mother's death, from my sister Eleanor.—H. G. S.*"

Whittlesea, Feb'y 19th, 1814.

MY DEAREST HENRY,

I received your melancholy and affectionate letter on the seventeenth, and only waited to answer it until we could purchase a pair of Wild Ducks to send with it to Mr. Angelo, who has very politely offered at any time to forward our letters abroad. Heaven has indeed, my dear Brother, thought proper to lay upon us a most heavy affliction; every day proves to us the severity of our loss and the inestimable value of her who is gone. You have indeed, my poor Henry, lost your best friend. Never parent more truly loved a child than she did you. Never shall I forget her the last time she read a letter from you. When I went in, she raised her languid face from the pillow, and holding up the letter to me, said with a heavenly smile, "I am quite purely [i.e. *well*] to-day, my love, for I have had such a delightful cordial "—meaning your letter. I have witnessed two deaths and heard of many, but never such a one as our angel mother's. For two months before her death, she was not able to walk upstairs, but was carried up and down every day, and laid upon a sopha in the dining-room. On the 10th of December,* she was so much worse, that we requested her not to leave her bed, but she earnestly begged to be brought downstairs, and as soon as she had recovered a little from the fatigue of being dressed and removed, she told us that

---

* Query, 11th? See preceding letter.

she felt her end approaching, and summoning my grandmama, my aunts, and all her children around her, she took a long and affectionate farewell of every one separately with as much calmness and composure as if she was only going a short journey. With my father she requested to be left alone, and continued talking with him for a considerable time. She lamented greatly that she could not see her other three boys, and wept when she left you her blessing. All the day she spent in dozing, praying, and speaking peace and comfort to her afflicted husband and children. Frequently she held up her hands to look at her poor black nails, and would often request my father and brother to feel her pulse, and begged they would tell her if it did not get lower every time. She mentioned every particular respecting the disposal of her clothes, and gave orders about being laid out and for her funeral, and turning to my father, meekly said, "If not too much expense, I should like a vault." Oh, Henry, what a day was that! To describe our feelings is impossible, but from your own on receiving the intelligence of her death, you may form some idea of ours who witnessed it. It was some consolation to us that she did not die below. She loved to be carried upstairs. My father lay by her side all night, and from her calm and comfortable slumbers was in hopes she would awaken rather better. But when she awoke, she complained of being in a little pain, which did not continue long. In about an hour after, with her hands clasped in prayer, she breathed her last. Who, who beheld such a scene as this could refrain from exclaiming, "May I die the death of the righteous, and may my last end be like hers!" The highest respect we can pay to her ever-lamented memory is to aim, my dear Henry, at her perfection, that by a virtuous life here, we may be re-united to her in Heaven. My poor Father is better than he was, but still continues to feel his loss greatly, as do we all. But the conviction of the eternal happiness of her for whom our tears flow blunts the edge of our affliction. Our loss is most assuredly her gain. It is for ourselves that we lament, and selfish indeed should we be to wish for her return. Elizabeth is my father's housekeeper, and Anna Maria and her, by their attention to him, endeavour to assuage the bitterness of his regret. Charles, by his own wish and the request of his dear departed mother, is under the tuition of my Uncle Davie, who performs to the uttermost—nay, I must say, exceeds the extent of his promise, a convincing proof of his regard for her to whom he made it. Charles neither boards nor sleeps in our house. At least, he does not breakfast or dine with us, but he always comes in at eleven for some refreshment, drinks tea, and sups with us constantly every evening, and on Sunday we have his company all day. He is a very amiable, promising youth, and I cannot speak too highly of my aunt and uncle's kindness to him, nor of his gratitude to them. Sam, by his own choice, is to be a surgeon and apothecary, and by his good talents and attention has gained the approbation of his father and brother. He is a very respectable English scholar, and might have been a good Latin one if Mr. Binfield had taught him properly, but by experience it is proved that, though Mr. B. may understand that language himself, he is incapable of teaching it to others. An opportunity has, however, presented itself for Sam learning Latin in perfection, if he will be but diligent. Mr. Pratt, our new curate, is allowed to be a classical scholar of considerable eminence, and he has promised to instruct Sam. . . . Since my father was in practice, he never had so little business as he has had for these last two years. It is the general remark, that such a healthy time or so long a continuance was never remembered. I was concerned to see your friend Captain Eeles' name in the list of wounded at the late Engagement in Holland. I sincerely hope that the war is nearly at an end, and that we may again meet, though the late melancholy change in our family will render it both a happy and painful meeting. But you must be confident that you have still many friends left, who dearly love you, and believe me, no one better than myself. . . . All your friends, my dear Henry, join in affectionate remembrance to yourself and Tom, and believe me to remain if possible more than ever

Your truly affectionate Sister,
ELEANOR MOORE SMITH.

Letter VI. Endorsed—" 13th *July*, 1815. *From my Father after Waterloo, thanking God he had three sons unhurt.—H. G. S.*"

Whittlesea, July 13, 1815.

MY DR HARRY,

Never did I receive two Letters with such pleasure as your two last since the fight at Waterloo. For three of you to have been engag'd and to come off unhurt, must have been not the fate of chance, but Providence seem'd to have watch'd over you all and protected you. How grateful we all ought to be to the Almighty. I assure you my Prayers have ever been offered up to the Throne of Grace, praying for the Protection of you all, and a safe return to England. This has been one of the most glorious, and most decisive, Battles that has been fought this War. What a shocking sight to see the *Gazette*, it contain'd full four Columns and a half of kill'd and wounded, and amongst them so many Names I had so often heard spoke of. Poor Major Bringhurst is among the kill'd, an only Son, and his poor father almost broken-hearted.

Poor Mr. Moore is at my house, broken-hearted, and a most distrest object in Health. . . .

Poor Sudbury is dead, he has been a poor creature for many Weeks. . . .

Your Mare was put to Cervantes, a Horse of L⁴ Fitzwilliam's; she is very well, and lying in my Wash ground with my Mare and foal, I think the handsomest I ever saw. I am sorry to hear Charles' Mare is like to have bad feet; if so, the sooner she is disposed of, the better. Tell Tom and Charles I expected to have heard from them long ago.

Give my Love to your Wife and tell her how much I felt for her, before I heard of your fate, well knowing that she must have been dreadfully alarm'd.

Your blood Mare is worth, Buckle tells me, a great deal of Money. Her Dam is dead, and they have sent to him for her to Newmarket to breed from.

Your sisters have told all the News, therefore I conclude with my Love to your Wife and Brothers join'd with all at home.

I am your affect. father,

J. SMITH.

Write soon.

Addressed—

Major Smith,

95ᵗʰ Regᵗ of Rifles,

Serving under the

Duke of Wellington,

France.

Letter VII. Endorsed—" 31" *Dec*, 1816. *My Father's Letter announcing the death of my good Grandmother, 83 years old.—H. G. Smith, Col."*

Whittlesea, Dec' 31", 1816.

My DR HARRY,

After a very short tho' not painful illness, your poor old Grandmother paid the last debt of nature in the 83rd y^r of her Age. During the whole of the time she lay on her death-bed she retained her senses, and died calm and reposed, a Blessing which God grant we may all do in the same manner as she did, a Pattern of true Piety and Benevolence. The changes in our family have within these last seven y^{rs} been great, and *one of them* painful and very distressing to me, having lost that Companion whose Conduct endeared her to every one who at all knew her, and, that being the case, how much more so must I have felt her Loss! But these are trials we must all expect to meet with, and let none of us in our *gay moments* forget how soon the case may be our own. . . .

I find the House is to be sold, but times are so bad here now that no one has got any money to purchase, however desirable they may be. I hope if Charles and his Lady shou'd marry, they may become the Purchasers. . . .

Since the Death of poor old Jack, I have lost my Uria Mare, which I was obliged to have shot. I afterwards bought a fine big Horse five y^{rs} old, one I expected wou'd have proved valuable. After keeping him about ten Weeks he made his exit as rotten as a Hare, so you see I am one of those unfortunate Beings in the Horse way. I must now be satisfied with my little Mare and my good old Gig Horse ; when you are tired of your bay Mare, forget not she is a particular favourite of mine. . . .

Remember me most kindly to all my friends, particularly Col. Achmuty, Bell, and my old friend St. John.

Tell Charles we have not written to him as you wou'd be able to tell him every particular. I hope his Mare turns out well and that he is able to hunt her. How are all your Horses ? I hope you have had good hunting ; it has been very wet here, and very heavy riding.　I suppose the same with you.

Give my Love to Juana, and tell her the whole of her Brothers and Sisters do also.

I remain,

My Dʳ Harry,

Your affect. father,

Addressed—　　　　　　　　　　　　　　　　　JNᵘ SMITH.

Lieut.-Col. Smith,

Rifle Brigade,

Town Major,

Post pᵈ.　　　　　　　　　　　　　　　　Cambray,

France.

Letter VIII.　Endorsed—" 18ᵗʰ *March*, 1822.　*Eleanor as to the Genealogy of my Mother's family.—H. G. S."*

Whittlesey, March 18ᵗʰ, 1822.

MY DEAR HARRY,

. . . You have desired me to collect for you all the information I can of the Moore family, but that is very little. My good grandfather Moore always used to say that he was descended from that great though unfortunate man Sir Thomas Moore, who was beheaded in the reign of Henry the eighth. Alice always says that she is sure we are descendants, the arms are undoubtedly the same. When my poor Mother was very young, my aunt Stona told her that she was descended from no mean family, and to prove it unfurled a genealogical table which reached half over the room, but my Mother was then so young that she never could recollect much about it. She used to say that she remembered seeing a number of Gabriel Moores. This table I am sorry to say was destroyed during the riots in London. At that time my aunt Stona lived in London and lost a great many valuable things.　Our great great grandfather was the first

of the Moores who lived in Whittlesey, and he was an Attorney
and came out of Buckinghamshire.

. . . I must now say farewell, and with kindest love to
yourself and Juana, believe me, dear Harry, to remain your truly
affectionate sister,

ELEANOR MOORE SMITH.

Addressed—

Lieut.-Colonel Smith,
Rifle Brigade,
Glasgow,
Scotland.

[See Appendix VIII., p. 794.]

Letter IX. Endorsed—"2*nd* *Sep*ʳ, *reporting the death of my poor
and venerable Father, 2*nd* *Sep.* 1843, ¼ before five o'clock in the
Morning; rec*d* at Cawnpore 31*st* Oct*r*, 1843.—H. G. S."*

Whittlesea, Sepʳ 2, 1843.

MY DEAREST HARRY,

. . . Our beloved father breathed his last this
morning at ¼ before 5 o'clock. . . .

About three weeks ago Charles perceived an evident
alteration in his appearance. He became ill in health that week,
and on Wednesday, Augˢᵗ 16ᵗʰ, he took to his bed. His poor mind
was in a most distressed state and his terrors extreme. Unable to
bear the suspense, Anna Maria and myself set off for Whittlesea,
Saturday, Augˢᵗ 19ᵗʰ. Eleanor had come to Charles's from
Northampton a few days before, and on the Monday morning as
we got to W. on the Sunday Tom arrived. We found our poor
father very ill, but certainly not like immediate dissolution, tho'
his state was very precarious. We tried to rouse him to recollection and to soothe him, and oh, blessed be the Almighty for the
mercy, we so far succeeded as to be convinced that we restored
him to happiness and peace. Tho' not able to retain recollection
of us for many minutes together, he was ever conscious that his
children were about him; he blessed us, recognized us, asked us
to pray for him, to repeat the Lord's Prayer, and one day he told
us he had *hope*, that God was a God of mercy. He never uttered

indeed two connected sentences, and he rambled incessantly, but the character of his ramblings was altered—bits of hymns, parts of the Psalms, exclamations to the Deity took the place of cries of terror, etc. He was *happy*—our voices reached him and soothed him, and he would reward us with a word or a look of love. He would lie in bed and amuse himself with fancied dressings of himself, talk of driving, etc., entreat to get out of bed, and would sit a few minutes in his chair. On this day week we got him out of bed, when his happiness was beautiful, but oh, the heartrending appearance he made ! He was *literally* a skeleton ; he had not an ounce of flesh on his whole body, he was a breathing death. He knew us all, smiled on each (the four daughters and Charles), dressed himself in imagination for a walk and a drive, tied his handkerchief on his neck, and when he had fidgetted away the blanket in which he was wrapt, and I put a light chair cushion in his lap, saying, " It is cold, we must pull up the apron of the gig," he smiled and said, " What fun it is ! " After a little while he asked to go home ; we laid him in bed and thought he was dying. It was, however, but exhaustion, and he rallied again, but he was never more so rational as this.

Oh, Harry, all my desire now was to gain something for you. I tried him, asked him if he recollected you, spoke the name " Harry " in a marked manner, and oh, Harry, you will thank me for this—at length he said, " Harry, yes, God bless him." I had touched the string. Some time after he addressed a set speech (made of broken sentences) to Col. Smith, in which he said he " thanked "—" noble deeds "—" to be praised "—and much more that could not be gathered ; but this was enough, his darling son was not forgotten. He spoke much of William, always saying, " William, I am coming," and once he said, " Stop, Stona—I'll go with you." He took decided notice of Anna Maria, but he held all our hands as we sat by him, and would stroke them and take them to his cheek, and even to his lips and kiss them. When he awoke in tears and we spoke to him, it vanished and he became calm ; and even when we prayed by his side, if we told him not to interrupt us, he would become quiet, seem to catch some sentences, become soothed and fall asleep. The last three days he became very ill and the pains of death racked him greatly, and it was *very* sad to see his sufferings. He was dying all yesterday and all the night, and oh, what an awful night we passed by his bedside ! He appeared to suffer a good deal from convulsive affection of the muscles, but the strength of his constitution was really wonderful. It was a hard struggle indeed for the victory. After many hours' most laboured breathing, he became gradually lower and lower, and at length with one sigh, one struggle, one effort, he breathed his last at $\frac{1}{4}$ before 5 o'clock this morning, Sept. 2nd, having reached the great age of 87. We mean to lay him beside our beloved mother on Wednesday afternoon. . . .

I must close my letter, praying God to bless and comfort you, and grant that hereafter we may all meet in Heaven and there form one happy family again. . . . Kind love to you both from all.

     Believe me your fond sister and friend,

                       J. A. SARGANT.

APPENDIX III.

D.Q.M. General's Office,
Cape Castle, [2 June ?] 1834.

Your Excellency having been pleased to submit for my
perusal various documents relative to a scale of diet fixed by a
Board of Officers, of which the Hon. Colonel Wade, now Commandant of the Garrison of Cape Town, was President, directing
me to return them with any remarks which my experience of five
years as Commandant of that garrison may enable me to afford,
I beg to observe.

    *   *   *   *   *   *

There are several officers under whom I have served whose
example I have ever endeavoured to imitate. The most conspicuous of them are Sir Sydney Beckwith, Sir A. Barnard, and Sir
J. Colborne. The leading principle by which these officers of
distinction were actuated was that of kindness to their soldiers,
and an endeavour to maintain discipline by seeking out the meritorious to reward and commend rather than the guilty to punish.

For the attainment of discipline and good order two modes
are to be adopted, encouragement and punishment. Towards
well-disposed men, the first is always preferable; the latter, however, must be appealed to, but I have ever found great severity in
punishment less calculated to maintain discipline than a mild

* I possess this document only in the form of rough drafts. The
document as here printed is therefore to some extent a compilation.
It is clear that the Board of Officers were proposing a more stringent
treatment of prisoners than that which Harry Smith had adopted and
which they maintained was more lenient than was permitted by the
Royal Warrant.

administration of the great power Military Law vests in the hands of those in command.

In the study of my profession, to no branch of it have I paid greater attention than to the prevention of crime and to the reform of the ill-conducted, and the results of some years' experience enable me to affirm that it ought to be the duty of all officers, in the first place, to endeavour by wise and salutary regulations to render every one under their command happy. Cheerfulness is the mainspring of discipline, and the desire to reward merit while crime is held in execration, ought ever to be the delight of the officer. And although for acts of disobedience and insubordination, or neglect of duty, I would, *as I have done in this garrison,* inflict corporal punishment to the utmost of my power, not only to punish the offender, but to strike terror into the hearts of the spectators in the ranks, for more moderate crimes, to see a fellow-creature, a comrade, dragging on a miserable existence from week to week, nay, month to month, in a solitary cell, or expected to be capable of daily labour and occasionally to attend drills *on bread, rice, and water,* his bed a watchcoat, *affording no public example,* is a species of protracted cruelty I am as yet not prepared to inflict.

Confinement or the loss of liberty for a long period is in my mind, under the most modified circumstances, a punishment severe indeed. During the period I was Commandant, I made it a point to visit the prisoners (whenever there were any) every Sunday, and the surgeon of the week did the same during the week. I had written me a report to that effect. My object was to see that they were in every respect as clean as the meritorious soldier at duty, to ascertain that their rations had been according to the scale hung up with my signature in their cells, duly furnished them, and of a good quality, and by conversation with them and pointing out the impropriety of their conduct to ascertain their character. Many sentenced for a long period I have taught to read and write; in the case of others, what little knowledge they possessed I have improved by lending them books, etc., and in the proportion of ninety-nine in a hundred has my kindness been attended by the most beneficial results. Some whose conduct in prison was particularly good, and whose previous character was not heinous, I have remitted several weeks' confinement, ordering them to report to me every Sunday, "My conduct has been good." In no individual instance, to the best of my recollection, has this leniency been abused, and I will mention that in no garrison in His Majesty's dominions was heinous crime less frequent than in the garrison of Cape Town whilst under my command.

No man is so degraded as not to be susceptible of kindness, and no man so much requires a friend as he who has none even in himself. Many is the vicious character I have reformed as captain of a company by conduct of this sort, re-establishing a man in his own good opinion and in that of his comrades. The want of a *point d'appui* in distress has been the ruin of many an individual, both civil and military, and in my estimation the *morale* amongst the soldiers tends far more to attain discipline and happiness than the severe administration of rigid justice. There are many of my brother officers, I am aware, who differ very materially with me in this opinion, but, as practise makes [perfect], I maintain that my system is the best, which, when combined with a vigour of action in all military points, excites emulation in both officers and soldiers and induces them to look up to their commander as their friend.

*   *   *   *   *   *

The Royal Warrant now provides the sum of sixpence per diem for the maintenance of prisoners without any reference to "bread and water," to ensure them being furnished with wholesome and sufficient food. I cannot, therefore, for a moment conceive that reflection would put a construction upon my prison-regulations as positively contrary to the Royal Warrant.

Not only by inclination and predilection am I in all military acts guided by the practice in the Light Division of the Duke's army, but [in this case] by Lord Hill's circular letter bearing date 24th June, 1830.

My reasons, therefore, for submitting the scale of provisions I drew up to the approval of Sir Lowry were—

(1) The practice in the Duke of Wellington's army.

(2) The practice of the Light Division, ever construing all orders and regulations to the benefit of the soldier.

(3) The Royal Warrant.

Although I very much differ in opinion from the Board as to the scale they have fixed, I approve very highly of a distinction being made between the diet of prisoners sentenced for long and short periods.

H. G. SMITH.

APPENDIX IV.

Grahamstown, 30th Jan. 1835.

The Kafirs, from the manner in which I occupied all the passes in their rear, had been beautifully harassed, and now fly from the sight of *one* of our people as rapidly as they flew towards him until I stirred them up a little in their own country. So you recommend shrapnel, grape, howitzers, shells! Well done! We will take your advice: for old Johnstone* says true, you are the best general he knows. I am sadly off for officers and assistants in my office. Selkirk Stewart would be to me worth all the clerks in my office, and old Johnstone all the officers I have in the field, Cox excepted. The quantity I have to write and to do is really incredible, and you know how quick I can get through my work. The people here are astonished. But I have eased my labours very much by establishing boards of gentlemen of the place and officers, one of clergymen for the destitute families, one to receive the claims of all persons whose property has been seized for military purposes, one to inquire into the burgher force, a clothing board for the burghers, a labour heretofore beyond even me. All these boards submit their proceedings to me. I approve or disapprove, and act as supreme. Even thus, much of my time is occupied; but it has reduced my labours much.

* Col. W. Johnstone was then living at Cape Town See p. 58.

Bivouac between Fish and Keiskamma rivers,
close to Mount Somerset, 13th Feb.

Viva Enrique !

MI QUERIDISSIMA MUGER,*

I have been in the field since Saturday last, sleeping in the bush, *never better*. Was on horseback yesterday 28 hours, attacked the Kafirs in five points like fun, gave them a good licking with a trifling loss on our parts; seventy-three killed, counted on the field, lots of wounded. Took 2500 head of cattle, goats, sheep, etc.; gave them some of your shrapnel shells, but want a few of my old Riflemen, although all my fellows are willing enough and full of fight. Do not be afraid of Enrique. He takes good care of himself, and never moves without 30 Cape Rifles as an escort.

A shocking accident occurred the night before last. The 72nd and other troops lay in position waiting for daylight to attack; though every precaution was taken and there was no fault, some one cried out, " The Kafirs !" and the men jumped up and fired on each other before the officers could speak. Three men were killed, and more desperately wounded. This rather hindered my operations, because it alarmed the enemy. However, thank God, I have done as much as I expected.

You cannot think how well I am. Nothing fatigues me, and although my force is only 1200 men and 800 horses with four guns, yet my operations are over an extent of 4000 square miles of country. We were marching from 7 o'clock the 11th till 8 o'clock the 12th. No one tired. This morning we want nothing but some grog, which I momentarily expect. God bless you, old woman, and do not be afraid. Our God will take care of us both. *Adios, alma mia.*

ENRIQUE.

Grahamstown, 26th and 27th Feb. 1835.

My Fish River trip was a very lucky one, and has had a great effect on all the Kafirs. It is reported and believed that they are all flying into Hintza's country. He is a very powerful chief who has been wavering in his policy towards us. He is, I believe, at the bottom friendly, although he wishes to keep as

* " My dearest wife ! "

much of the stolen cattle as he possibly can. It is decided that the 75th Regt. remain on the usual frontier line, and that the 72nd all go into Kafirland. The former are as much mortified as the latter are delighted. To-day I go to Hermanus Kraal, next day near to Fort Willshire to select a camp for our invading force to assemble on. We are to select the most effective men of the Burgher force, and send the remainder to the second line. The Chief is now all for invasion. Paddy Balfour will be my A.D.C.

I should like you to see me with my escort, a trumpeter, a sergeant, two corporals, and six fine fellows of the Cape Corps, five led horses, Guides (a corps all well mounted), etc., and generally five or six smart young fellows of volunteers; but I would give all the pomp and glory of war for one quiet evening with *mi vida* at Charlie's Hope,* though I am now writing by a nice little wood fire, as comfortable as can be when away from my beautiful wife. You are in no danger, *alma mia*, of being supplanted here. This is the most dull, stupid, and horrid place on earth, celebrated for the most ugly of the *fair sex.*

I have just been to inspect three detachments of Burghers. I will give you a detail. One consists of 62 fighting men and horses, 50 non-combatants, 28 waggons. Another of 118 fighting men and horses, 80 non-combatants, 36 waggons. Only conceive what an army, and every individual wants something, either shoes, shirts, bridle, saddle. It is perfectly ridiculous, but yet when the poor fellows thus dragged from their homes are in the field, they are good-humoured and willing and shoot well enough. Oh! my old woman, glory is a fine thing, domestic quiet is better. It was well enough when I was at the head, but now second fiddle is slow. I am lazy and forget when things do not fly like lightning.

All our own country is free from Kafirs, much more so than in times of actual peace; still every post the postmaster comes to me for escorts. To-day I blew him up and called him an ass. The panic with which the people were seized here will not wear off for years. Had twenty Kafirs shown themselves in the neighbourhood of Grahamstown a day or two before my arrival, all would have either run away or shot one another.

* His house at Rondebosch, near Cape Town.

What amuses me much just now, is that those who funked the most formerly are the most valiant now that the danger is dispelled.

In two months I will, with God's blessing, be with my dear old wife to talk over my labours, which Heaven knows have been heavy enough. I have gained credit for two things—one, licking the Kafirs ; another, blowing up the lazy idle rascals who will neither work, fight, nor do anything but draw rations.

So you are a schoolmistress? Mind teach the young ones to sew and work. It will do them more good than to read and write.

Love to all, and the sum total of all my love, affection, regard, esteem, everything that is dear, to you, *alma mia.*

ENRIQUE.

5 o'clock, 27 Feb.

When once I am in the field, I will work in my own way. *Master* is always floundering in the midst of information, whilst I like to take a look at the ground, march, and take possession. Thank God, I have been heretofore very lucky indeed. Do you recollect poor Thompson saying, when the ants were swarming in the house, " Oh, sir, it is great luck, great promotion for you somewhere "? It is very ridiculous, but I often think of it.

I long to march, although I well see I shall have all the trouble of war and marches without the all-stirring spirit of War. Ah, Venus and Mars! Enough of the latter. I begin to think a quiet life of Darby and Joan very agreeable. The fact is, it is better fun to be *together* as heretofore : only this is such a *naked* country. At Genadendal there was one pair of breeks between three boys, but here neither boys nor girls nor women have breeks or sarks either.

I have been writing all day, still it is with much delight I keep on writing to you, *alma mia* . . .

God bless my dearest virtuous wife.

ENRIQUE.

Grahamstown, 6th March, 1835.

Thank God, my dearest old woman, you are well. . . . To-morrow the troops commence their march upon the base of our future operations between Fort Willshire and the Block Drift or the line of the Chumie, which runs into the Keiskamma near the Fort. I went up there last Saturday and had a beautiful ride of three days, doing everything I had to do and returning a day and a half sooner than I was expected. It is really wonderful how I bear work. I spread my karosse and lie down with my saddle-bags under my head, and after thanking my God and blessing my dear old woman, am asleep *in a moment.* The bivouac we are going to is really one of the most beautiful things I ever saw, and, thanks to the late rains, the grass everywhere is up to the horses' fetlocks. To-morrow I start with my escort—my corps of Guides, my led horses, my interpreters, my secretaries. How you would laugh to see such a motley group!

So I am to take care they do not shoot at me from the Bush? That story about old Jem * and me was founded on very little truth. In the middle of my Fish River fight, just as Jem was cooking some coffee and I was writing, when we were surrounded by soldiers, three shots were fired *at the whole.* I certainly jumped up and rattled the impudent rascals " out of that " pretty quick ; but, old girl, I am too much of a Rifleman to be caught napping without every precaution of war. But they do put such trash in the papers occasionally, it is quite amusing.

Camp near Fort Willshire, 12th March.

I wish you could see me, because then, you know, I could see you. It is very delightful to unbend and not act always the great man, although I assure you we laugh in camp sometimes famously. I almost kill Hallifax at some of my roar-outs to the soldiers. Yesterday morning, just before daylight in Fort Will-shire, I desired his bugler to blow the "rouse," which you well remember. He said he did not know it. " D—— you, sir, blow something." So he blew up a *quadrille,* and I began to dance. I thought Hallifax would have laughed till he died. What a burlesque upon our school of war !

Grahamstown, 16th March, 1835.

When I came flying down from Fort Willshire the other day it was, as you may suppose, for the purpose of inducing my master to get under weigh and not to mind a Kafir and a half, which

---

* Major William Cox.

Col. Somerset's *arrangements* with nearly 3000 men were going to catch. Master and I very nearly fell out. In his string of operations in last week's paper, signed by Kitty Dutton, my attack on the enemy's position was left out. After some little jaw, he said he thought it too bold a thing to attempt with the force under my command, so I bristled up and said, " Rely upon it, whenever I hear of a Kafir, so soon will I be at him with whatever force I can collect. This is the way to treat so contemptible an enemy, although too much caution cannot be adopted to prevent a surprise, or too much activity used in following up any advantage obtained. This, sir, is my maxim, and one which shall guide me throughout the campaign." "Oh, it is a very proper feeling, but *discretion* is also to be observed."

I have at last spurred him into a move, and I hope we shall get on and bring things to a close, for I am really tired of this slow work. I want to be at Charlie's Hope again.

17th March.

The 72nd Regiment marched yesterday for the camp at Fort Willshire, and the whole of the troops will be in motion, I hope, to-morrow to concentrate. Sir Benjamin has given out a General Order appointing me to command the 1st Division.

1st Division : 100 of the Cape Corps, 40 Corps of Guides, two 6-pounders, 300 Swellendam Burghers, the whole of the 72nd Regiment, the 1st Provisional Battalion of Hottentots, 430 strong. Officered by H. Peddie.

2nd Division, 2 guns, 750 Burghers, 200 Cape Corps, Lieut.-Col. Somerset.

3rd Division : 250 Burghers, 50 Cape Corps, two 3-pounders, 2nd Provisional Battalion, 374 strong (an excellent body of men), Major Cox.

4th Division : 500 Burghers, Field Commandant Van Wyk.

The troops will thus advance—

Left.	Left-Centre.	Centre.	Right.
Van Wyk.	Major Cox.	Me myself and Sir Slow as far as he goes.	Col. Somerset.

Lieut.-Col. England is to command the ordinary Frontier Posts and Grahamstown and has 1800 men, just 100 more than

I had when I took the command here, re-established villages and posts which had been so shamefully abandoned, and invaded Kafirland with 450 men, so that I think the 2nd line may be considered safe and no necessity for any panic. But really it is astonishing to see how they funk.

His Excellency has just sent for me, good old man, to say he is not pleased with his General Order of yesterday appointing me to the command of the Division. He says it cramps my power, so he has put in orders that I am to be second in command, continuing my duties as Chief of the Staff, by which means I can order everybody about like himself. It also gives old Peddie a command, which I am very glad of.

18th March.

In this stupid little room in which I am writing, I think rather too much of an old faithful woman at Charlie's Hope, but as I hope soon to lick Tyalie, I hope soon to be with her. But my hair has grown grey. I think, if it progresses as heretofore, I shall have a white top altogether. Not quite so bad as that either! But it is grey. Oh, I should like at this moment to ride into the dear little square! I can hear your voice when I left you on the 1st January, as plainly as possible. Do you recollect the glove in the hackney coach in London?* And so it will be again, *alma mia !*

20th March, 8 o'clock.

Don't be jealous, but my landlady has just sent me a present of half a dozen of champagne and two stone bottles of curaçoa, rather a treat to me the latter. The former I will astonish somebody or other with in the bivouac. Fine campaigning this, is it not?

I have just packed my leave-behind box and remaining papers, got a canteen of brandy for Paddy Balfour and myself, and ten pounds of tobacco for my escort, filled the two bags *you* made with tea and sugar, put up my knife, fork, and spoon, and thirteen plates into a leather letter-bag. The tea-kettle is tied to my saddle-bags. We make *carbonada* on a forked stick, oh, so good it is! quite different to what it is when done in a frying-pan : you then stick the one end of the stick in the ground, whilst the hot

---

* See p. 212

meat hisses in your face as you recline on your karosse *à la Turque.* Very fine. But the old round table at Charlie's Hope would do as well!

I really am capitally equipped, and if you were like me, *young,* I should like to have you with me. God knows but it will be cold before we get back. This Grahamstown itself is the coldest place in Africa. The moment you are five miles from it, the climate is much milder. Not a tree near it, scarcely a bush, and such bleak cold-looking hills you cannot conceive, as cold as the Pyrenees—where you rather roughed it than otherwise in the old paved tent. Do you remember when old Billy Mein, 52nd, used to come and drink with me grog made of very bad rum? We were not so nice then as to have brandy.

I have desired you have a Grahamstown journal sent you, and I beg you not to believe more than one-half of the alarming lies that will be published in it. This place ought to be called "Necessity," for it is the mother of invention.

Adios, alma mia di mi corazon. You have a good long letter this time.

ENRIQUE.

Camp near Willshire, 25th March.

Up at four; sing out to cook for coffee; "Minni" (sergeant of the escort), "feed horses"; "Japps, rouse up the escort"; "Up saddle, camp." Marched as soon as light into a nice bivouac. I have a most beautiful bush, and a still better one for His Excellency, and one between us both for Kittie. Capital breakfast; cows give lots of milk. Secretaries all at work building me a hut. Twenty men on fatigue building one for His Excellency, who has not yet arrived.

Nine o'clock. "Escort, up saddle"; "Japps, order Pompey for me and Minni's horse for Captain Jervis. We are going to look for a new line of road." Return to camp at one, having chalked out my road and sent a hundred men with Jervis to repair it. Report of five Kafirs prowling about the camp. Their spoor discovered back over the Keiskamma. Learn that His Excellency is not to leave Grahamstown for a day or two. Much mortified; I have built him a noble hut. Have a most capital hut myself, just completed, and wish *una vieja muger que se llama Juana* was within it.

Just received a report that some cattle are seen on the other side of the river. "Japps! a horse and my escort." "Ah, ah, sir!" Up saddle and off.

Just come back. I fancy I see some, and send out a patrol of 50 men under Field-Commandant Lindé, Swellendam Burghers. The finest old fellow upwards of 70 I ever saw, except my poor old Padre. Just such a game old fellow as *he* is. Order dinner. Bruintjes (you must be acquainted with him); Painter and Minni you know; all these are occasionally called in my delicate voice. Our conversation is now beginning. "Well, Bruintjes, what's for dinner?" "Some skin beef I can for soup mak." ("Don't make such a jaw, men; I can't hear what my cook says.") "Some pampoose too, sar, what master bring from Kafirland. Leetle onion, sar; a leg mutton for rost, sar; some bock what left yesterday, sar, what the Boers send master for hash; dat plenty, sar." "Yes, by G—d, plenty, Bruintjes. Well, good fellow, mind, coffee ready directly after dinner, then you shall have your grog. Keep me waiting, no grog. Japps, what the devil are those loose horses doing here about my hut?" Japps, in a voice something between thunder and the croak of a frog, roars out, "Heigh, you d—d Boers! You take way your horse from Coronel." The prospect of a good dinner makes me think I am dirty. "Painter, lay out my dressing things, lots of water, and a clean shirt." A glorious splash, the water as cool as possible, the day not being so hot as yesterday. I think in a day or so it may rain. All the better for our grass. The cow-boy, "Black Jim." "Well, Jim, what do you want?" "Kraal to be made for master's cows." "Very well, Jim; but make a kraal for the calves too." "Yah, Mynheer." "Or no grog." "Yah, Mynheer." "Now, be off."

"Field-Commandant Dreyer wishes to speak with you, sir," says the orderly sergeant. "Well, Dreyer, why the devil won't you come in? What a ceremonious humbug!" "Coronel was busy write." "Oh, you be d—d, and come in sit. Well, vaar is the Kafir?" "I canno say, meinheer. Coronel must loup into Kafirland." "How can I, Dreyer? I must wait for the Governor." "Well, where is the Governor? He must come; my mans is tired for 'nix mak.'" * "Can't help it, Dreyer."

---

* *I.e.* tired of doing nothing.

"Well, Sandford, what do you want? Paddie Balfour, and be whipped to you, don't make such a noise. Japps, send this order to Commandants Lindé and Dreyer." "Yas, sar."

Sandford. "Colonel, I want an escort for empty waggons to Grahamstown." "How many?" "Twenty-two." "By Heavens, we shall eat up all our stores, lying idling here: I will order an escort. Let them make haste back, and lots of rice and spirits, mind." "We are getting very short of beef too, sir." "Damnation, I hear nothing but bad news. Orderly, tell Greyling and Nel" (two capital Boers) "to come to me *immediately.* I will get meat, Sandford. Any more bad news?" "No, sir, plenty of stores as yet." "Well, Ford, did you bleed them?" "No, the camp is very healthy, and the wounded at Fort Willshire are all doing well." "Send for Adair. Order an escort for Sandford's waggons. Ford, come and dine with me, and be off now, I am busy. Well, Greyling and Nel, where are the bullocks and sheep?" "I know no tings, sar." "The devil you don't. Be off both of you immediately beyond Fort Beaufort. Bring me 40,000 sheep." "Nay, Mynheer." "Well, go and bring me as many bullocks and sheep as I shall give you an order for, when I and the commissary have made our calculations. Here, Andrews" (the Dutch secretary), "make out passports and authorities for all persons to aid and assist Greyling and Nel to go to Beaufort for sheep. Well, sir, what do you want?" (A great fat stupid-looking Boer standing at the hut door.) "Mynheer, mi vrouw——" "Andrews, what the devil does he want?" "To go home, sir, or to have his gun mended." "No, sir" (in a very low voice); "I want to go to my vrouw, but by G—d I can't." "No more shall you. Go to your camp, and be ready to shoot Kafirs. Here, bugler, sound the grog-horn." Then such a hurrah! "Almost dinner-time, Painter?" "No, sir, only five." "You are wrong." "No, sir, I am right." "You, sir, why do you contradict me? It is six by my appetite. Well, Hallifax, what is going on in Fort Willshire?" "Fort Harry, sir, will be finished in a day or two." (A little post he has established as a look-out, and named after me.*) "Wounded doing well." "Are you going to stay and dine?" "With great pleasure." 'So uthey" (captain of Guides), "let this way-post be sent to Captain Jervis,

---

* See p. 737.

who knows where to place it at the turn-off of the new road."
" Well, Bagot, what is it ? "   (He commands a battalion of Hottentots.)   " Shall I post any additional sentries to-night ? "   " *Why !* "
" Five Kafirs were about the camp."   " I care not a —— if 5000
were around' my camp.   I will post my own picquets, ah ! and
sentries too—or vedettes, as I call them ; ah ! and take good
care of our camp too.   Five Kafirs shan't take us, be assured."

Well, old woman, this is a little specimen of one of my days
in camp ; so that you may readily conceive what a holiday a ride
is.   But all this is good fun enough, compared to the quill-driving
in Grahamstown.

✱   ✱   ✱   ✱   ✱   ✱

What shall I do to-morrow ?   Think of old Juana.   Yes,
because I do nothing else, I believe ; although all the fellows
wonder what the devil I am made of.   I am here, there, and
everywhere.   No party do I ever send out but in two seconds I
am amongst them ; when they, look grave I sing (*beautifully*,
as you know), and the Boers laugh at my gaiety beyond everything.   A young, big, fat Dutchman has just come to my tent
door, saying that he has no blanket, and that it is very wet.
What is he to do ?   " Go to the devil, and warm yourself, you
spoony.   Make a fire, sir, and sing over it.   I have given you
grog.   Why, I never had a blanket campaigning for ten years.
You want pluck, sir.   Be off."   This is the way I go on almost
day and night.

Night scene.   " Hallo, sentry."   " Sir."   " What the devil
are the dogs making such a noise about ? "   " Don't know, sir ;
they always make a noise."   " Are the horses right ? "   " Yes,
sir."   " What horse is that, biting himself so ? "   " That horse is
master's old horse, what carries the canteen."   Then sleep.   In
an hour, " What horses are those I hear moving ? "   " Some
escort with letters for Coronel."   Out with a lucifer : light
candles.   Sometimes the letters are worthy a candle, oftener cock-
and-bull stories.   Lie down and sleep again.   " Sentry, near
daylight ? "   " No, sir, moon."   " I wish the dogs were at the
devil."   " Make too plenty noise, sir."   Sleep.   Soon after, awake,
look at my watch.   " Hallo, bugler, blow the rouse ; Japps,
feed ; Bruintjes, coffee.   Painter ! "   " Coming, sir ! "   " Where
are the straps to my trousers ? "   " Under your 'ead, sir."   " Why,
what an ass you are !   Leave them in my boots.   You, Jim,

where's the milk?"   "Here, Mynheer."   "Balfour, where are you?"   "Coming, sir."   "Why, the shadow in your tent makes you look like the knave of clubs." . . .

Adios, hija.   Tu fiel, fiel,

ENRIQUE.

Camp on the Debe Flats,
8 o'clock on the night of the 1st April, Tom Fool's Day.

We are now pretty well collected, and Master is quite ready for anything.   He is really a perfect soldier in the field, and to hear him laugh when I blow up the fellows in Dutch (that is, *my* Dutch)!   But his delight is to dine and breakfast with me, particularly the latter.   Our breakfast to-day was really perfection.

I have some excellent guides to all the passes in the ridge of hills which we are going to stir up to look for cattle.   This Kafir war is nothing else than that.   Read of Walter Scott's Borderers, and you will learn what Kafir warfare is:

> "He would ride
> A foray on the Scottish side."

It is just that.   You gallop in, and half by force, half by stratagem, pounce upon them wherever you can find them; frighten their wives, burn their homes, lift their cattle, and return home quite *triumphant.*

4th April.

Last night at eight o'clock, on our return from a march of twenty-two hours, I received your dear letter.   Yesterday I roared myself into one of my Vittoria lost voices,[*] and to-day I am whispering and swearing exclusively for my own amusement, for no one hears me.   Old Doyle says I am still in advance in the talking way, and could afford a year's silence at least.   Murray is sitting with me; he is my great friend.   Your description of your robbery and the "cuchillo "[†] is highly amusing.   I ought to publish it in this army, and show what a Spanish woman dare, for, by heavens! here I have some arrant cowards.   The Boers of the old Commandos talk of the glories of former times, when the Kafirs had only assagais.   But now that they have a few guns, which they use very badly, Mynheer funks.   There are, however, some very fine fellows amongst them.

---

[*] See p. 100.   [†] "Knife."

Quite delighted to hear of the " Green Jacket " getting on the windows. We want very much some " Green Jackets " * here, for this warfare has all—nay ! more than all—the fatigue of any other without the real excitement of war. Oh ! the noise of the devils of captured cattle. Above a thousand head of cows and calves are now roaring in our ears.

Headquarters, Camp on the Debe, 5th April, 1835.

Our Hottentots are the most willing fellows possible. I call them my children, and all their little complaints, wants, and grievances they lay before me, which I listen to most patiently, for I exact a deal of work from them. . . . I will send off a warning order to the troops to march to-morrow at daylight. I always like to give the fellows all the warning I can. *Arrangements*, as His old Excellency calls them, are leather and prunella ; for though he writes them beautifully, and in the most military and technical terms, there is not a soul in this camp who understands what he means; so that the pith of the matter is contained in the words, " March at daylight to-morrow, Monday, the 6th instant, commissariat and other waggons following column." There it is, and all hands understand that it takes just two hours for our commissariat train to arrive, from the moving off of the first waggon to the arrival of the last, when the road is good. You, therefore, General Juana, conceive what it must be when there is any serious obstacle to pass. It is really quite ridiculous to see the proportion of soldiers to the waggons ; for when stretched out on the road, each with eight bullocks, it looks as if each soldier had one waggon at least.' You, General Juana, accustomed only to regular armies (except a few guerrillas or so), would laugh to see our motley group, with every costume of a mean kind which can be imagined,—the Boer with his old white slouch hat, his long gun, his miserable saddle and bridle ; the Hottentots with a little low-crowned hat, black jacket and trousers; the 72nd's men with crackers,† their pipe-clayed belts left behind, and a little ordinary pouch substituted for the large one, wearing a forage cap with a large red leather peak, which makes every man look exactly as if he had sore eyes ; old Dutton strutting about the camp in the paraphernalia of a Kafir chieftain's wife.

* *I.e.* soldiers of the Rifle Brigade.
† *I.e.* brown, buckskin trousers (Munro, *Records of Service*, i. 205).

Camp on the Buffalo, daylight or nearly so,
Friday, 10th April, 1835.

The Third Division, under Jem Cox, and the Fourth Division are going to remain here to hunt the rebel chiefs, while the First and Second and Headquarters go on to Hintza to bring back the captured cattle. I hope twelve days may see us back here again.

Bivouac on the Gunga Rivulet, six miles from the
Gonoube River, 4 p.m., 11th April, 1835.

I am writing on my knees, the table not having arrived in the waggon just yet, in a most beautiful bivouac on the banks of a woody streamlet with beautiful water, and grass up to the knees. We have marched twenty miles from the Buffalo upon the main road into Kafirland over very open country without seeing anything but some Kafir cranes, two khorans, and three partridges. Lots of kraals, but all have been deserted for some time.

I am half afraid Master is only to go to the Gonoube to-morrow—six miles—and halt the next day. Such slow work is quite dreadful. Last night I had a regular fight with him. He funked dividing the army—nay, actually gave it up for all I could say or do. I was perfectly mortified. However, in the middle of the night he changed his mind, and I had it all my own way. He is far too scientific for this guerrilla warfare, always full of combinations and reserves, and rears, and fronts, and cautions and dangers, and false movements, and doubts and fears. The greatest fault one can be guilty of is dash. Yet it is *the thing*, and there is nothing to fear.

I wish you were with me just now. The tent is all pitched, my table up, the rushes laid down, all my clothes put inside (as it looks as if a heavy dew were going to fall), a large heap of beautiful dry wood laid ready to light at daylight. The soup has been on at least two hours. Our dinner, I hope, will be good, for *me* most certainly, for all I care about is soup with rice, and I eat such a lot, about five times as much as when with my dear old woman. We get also a lot of beautiful pumpkins from the Kafirs' gardens, which help the soup, and we boil it with our rice. To-day, had there been time, we should have had a hare, which one of the men brought me yesterday ; which I ordered to be stewed with rice and a piece of ham (Viva España !). But then we ought to have had *un poco de aceyte y una cabeza de ajos.** . . . I wonder how I write Spanish. Do you understand it or not? I get on just as fast with it as English, anyhow; and if you do not understand, 'tis you who have forgot your own language, and not I how to write it.

.　　　　　　　6 o'clock, evening. 12th.

No ladies or any cattle brought in to-day, but I think we are running the whole population to earth on the Kei. There are great marks or spoors of innumerable cattle having been driven towards it. This should be our *boundary*. It is as bare of wood as the fens in my country, or even your country, scarcely covert for a hare, much less for the wily Kafir, whom I look upon just as a wild beast and try to hunt him as such. I little thought that the pains I took to make a huntsman of myself would here-after befit me for a general of renown in Kafir warfare. But so it is. "Right ahead" and a "forward cast" will soon ensure you "Woo-hoop," or as you call it "Oo-oop." (Don't "queeze" me, it is very "estraordinary," you always do so.)

I hope that you may hear from me every week. I do my best to ensure it, and as yet I trust you have not been disappointed. If you are, be assured it cannot be helped. The distance is so enormous, and the odd devils we have to send as escorts with the mails do not, like regular soldiers, enable one to say that it will arrive on such an hour on such a day. The Hottentots are to be trusted, poor fellows; but the Boers are too fond of sleep-ing. Although I get on famously with them, I have no *particular* opinion of their pluck, and always have about me my twelve men with double-barrelled guns, my escort, with old Japps, whose very holloa! would frighten a Kafir if his shot did not. Twelve more plucky fellows I never saw, and they watch me like hawks. If I move, they are after me and all round me, and every night mount sentry over me. If I whisper, Japps hears me. My bugler is no great hand as a musician, but the gamest fellow I ever saw (I am my own trumpeter, *n'est-ce pas, ma femme?*); but all our fighting is now over. It is quite an affair of Smith-field Market now, or will be in a few days.

* " A little oil and a clove of garlic."

Daylight on the 13th April.

We were all ready to march, when Master sent for me, and because Somerset's division is not up yet, has ordered a halt. I remonstrated, but it was of no use. He became touchy, talked of principal combination, military errors, etc. So I dropped the matter, as I always find it best to do at the moment, and renew it hereafter. Upon the whole, we are doing very well, but I fear he does not think so. He has been disappointed in not fighting a general action ; which is a thing as likely to occur as that, *if* such were the case, the Kafirs would beat us.

They are in terrible dismay. Last night (for always two or three of them creep near us), the wind being favourable and the night very still, my Kafir guide sitting by the fire distinctly heard one call to another, " Ah, ah, the troops are come, and we shall be all killed." In my tent I heard their howl. I will indulge in another wash, although it cannot wash away the stain of this day's delay.

A nice cool morning, and I hope the day may be so too, for we have no shade. Not that I care about it ; my hands are as black as my face, and that is the colour of dear little Moira's nozzle, and my head about as gray as her nose. A big Dutchman just put me in half a rage. He came for a bullock skin. I gave him the order on the commissary, and the brute said he did not know where or who the commissary was. Now surely it was right to blow up such a fellow? I have improved in my Dutch wonderfully, almost as much as your dear Spanish figure has progressed towards the Dutch.

This lost day is a bore. I shall be tired of it *all* soon. Indeed, the little excitement there was in the warfare has subsided, now that we have no enemy and I cannot make my little patrols. I have no ambition to be a Smithfield Market drover. We will make Hintza's Kafirs drive our cattle back, and guard it too. As I have before told you, it is wonderful how these devils can make the cattle go, when they are ever so tired. I feel delay more than ever, but a light heart (which thank God I possess) keeps me the most lively fellow in the camp. All the fellows in camp rejoice in me, thank God, and the soldiers would go to the devil for me. I feed them well. Two of the wounded fellows passed me yesterday, those with assagai wounds who had been with Murray. "Well, my boys, how are you?" "Oh, quite well, sir." "Ah, it is me who gets you into such scrapes." "We will soon be ready to fight under your honour again with all our hearts and souls."

Halting-day, 13th April (continued).

We are just going to take a ride—Master, me, and escort—upon the road to the Kei, with some of our guides. And then such questions as he will ask these fellows, who are as ignorant of what he wants to come at as possible—the name of this hill, and the other, the source of this river, and that t'yaron, sometimes with impatience. But the dear old gentleman sets down all this to the credit of science and information, and thinks my guerrilla ideas are far too wild. To-day he said, " In your view of the case there is no combination. All is trusted to a blind succession of chances." So I bristled up and said, "General, war in itself is a succession of chances, like all other games. But science must be its basis, and the great science of war is to adapt its principles to the enemy you have to contend with and the nature of the country. If you do not, you give *him* so many chances of the game." This rather posed him. " Oh, certainly, I do not deny that. On the contrary, I agree with it." I did not like to push him any further, for the great danger I have to avoid is that of assuming towards him a dictatorial manner; and God knows my manner is *brusque* enough, soften it down as I will. I am obliged sometimes to speak out ; but I do so with every endeavour to avoid hurting his feelings.

14th April, 4 o'clock in the afternoon.

Just arrived from a march. We have taken a Fingo, a Kafir of an inferior order, who has given us very important information. He states that Hintza has all the Colonial cattle collected and ready to restore to us, and that he is within two days' march of us at his residence near the missionary station of Butterworth. I ought to have told you where we are : which is, as the crow flies, within six miles of the Kei, but twelve miles by the waggon road. The bed of the river is very evident, and the country now most beautiful again, intersected with ravines on a minor scale like those of the Pyrenees, beautifully studded with gardens, and with pumpkins innumerable.

15 April, 4 o'clock in the morning.

Just received a beautiful letter from Master, which put me in great alarm—full of very military reasons why our march to-day should be delayed, and begging me to come to him that we might discuss it. So off I started from my barrack-sheets and karosse, and after a little preamble I found him much more easily turned into my path than I expected. So we start to-day at seven. The enemy is so disheartened now, that I think if you were here with your female attendants and that large knife, with a red cloak on, the sable foe would fly before you.

" Now, Paddy Balfour, you ugly beast with your moustaches, pour out the coffee, and be d——d to you."

> " Battle over, sleep in clover ;
>   Who so happy as we in camp ? "

I am in great spirits this morning at having overcome the delay. " Up saddle."

6 o'clock, 15th April.

This day has turned out much more auspicious than my utmost desire anticipated. I told you in the morning I was in high spirits, because Master consented to march down to the Kei. So I took care to be long before my time on horseback at his tent, with the advanced guard and my escort. He said with his usual politeness, " Pray, do not wait for me, Smith. Go on." The hint was quite enough. It was all I wanted, and off I set in as fast a shuffle as I could keep the cavalry horses in, down to the river (about 11 miles). We could observe the tops of the hills (almost mountains) on the other side covered with Kafirs. The more there were, the more I pushed on. On my arrival at the ford, I was challenged from the opposite side by " Hallo, English, do you know what river this is? This is Hintza's country. What do you want here?" I halted my troops, and made my Kafir desire one of them to lay down his arms and to come down to the river to speak to me. They were dreadfully frightened, but at last one laid down his assagai and by degrees in about an hour approached my Kafir. I told him to say that we were come to make Hintza give an answer to our former demand; that we would enter their country for the present as friends. All depended upon themselves and Hintza whether or not we were afterwards enemies.

During our conference we were joined by His Excellency, who highly approved of what I was doing. I went close to our side of the river—my Kafir sitting in the middle, Hintza's Kafir on the opposite side—and had a long jaw,* which ended in our entering Hintza's country for the moment as friends, and sending off for him. But no Kafir was to come near us with an assagai. The Kafir was a clever fellow, and wanted me to name a place to meet Hintza. I told him Hintza should have been on the river to meet the Governor, and we should march on until Hintza came. His Excellency was satisfied, so I said, " Now, sir, let us cross immediately." He was full of two or three little doubts, fears, military precautions, when I could stand it no longer, and roared out, " Mount ! " " Now, General," I said, " I will cross, and you will see every fellow fly before me. Then pray send the whole army on."

It was as I said. The fellow with whom I had the parley came up to me on my ascent from the river and told me he would desire the people to keep out of my way and would lead me wherever I might like to go. He is a most civil, athletic savage, 6 feet 3 inches high. He is now sitting with me, having eaten half a sheep, and his manner is really very fine. He liked my gingered tea exceedingly, but could not bear brandy. We have just had a visit from three of Hintza's councillors. He himself is in the upper country. We have told them what I have before stated, and they are to send off for their king immediately. They promised fairly, and seemed terribly frightened when we threatened them with Fakoo in their rear.

I can talk Kafir wonderfully—*Asapā*, " come here " ; *A Bāmbā*, "good-bye"; *Ekwee*, "yes". Now that is a great deal to learn in one day, besides crossing a river and getting over a flock of *sheep* rather than *soldiers*, pleasing a master, writing nonsense to an " auld wife," and orders for the camp, blowing up fifty people at least, shaking hands with some fifty Kafirs, and giving them tobacco, and a breakfast to two of them, who were highly delighted. The graceful air and gentlemanlike manner in which they thank you is really astonishing. No French marquis of the *ancien régime* could exceed their bow and expression of countenance. The

* Alexander has a picture of this scene, with others of the war, drawn by Major Michell, Surveyor-General.

knowledge they have, too, of passing events is totally surprising. They are perfect politicians, and talk to me of the general policy of our countries.

4 o'clock, 16 April.
On the road to Butterworth, Hintza's residence.
Gona Camp, 7 miles over the Kei.

Hallifax, who literally loves me, has made a fort, which he and Bingham—the impudent rascals!—call Fort Harry, just above Fort Willshire; and last night they sent me a copy of a drawing they have made of it, and which I send to you. It is a very useful little work, I assure you, and must be admired by you because its name is Harry.

FORT – HARRY.

Hallifax et Bingham fecit

Old Pato has just arrived with the waggons and one of his chiefs, come, he said, to learn *the news.* He has sent a message to his cousin Hintza. Old Pato says Hintza is a *great chief.* We must wait patiently with him, and give him time. He is a *great chief.* So I told him, great or small, if he or a messenger from him were not in to-morrow, I would be at his people immediately. At this old Pato and his captain laughed fit to kill themselves. They are two monkey-faced rascals, but they are dressed like Dutchmen, and really very well-behaved fellows. *Adios por el momento.*

3 B

17th April, 4 o'clock in the afternoon.

After rather an uninteresting march, the country being very monotonous, here we are in the most beautiful and highly cultivated valley, close to Hintza's residence and immediately in front of the missionary institution of Butterworth, formerly occupied by Mr. Ayliff, but now abandoned. We breakfasted in a nice little ravine with good water and visits innumerable from the Fingoes, whose cattle are grazing all around us, giving the air of harmony, peace, and confidence. These Fingoes are a race of men formerly dispersed by Dingaan's tribe. They took refuge in Kafirland, and are but ill treated and little looked upon by the Kafirs. They are exceedingly inclined to befriend us, and if Mr. Hintza is not what I know he will be, we will arm all these Fingoes and use them as an instrument of vengeance against their oppressors. They are a fine athletic set of fellows.

Master is very communicative to me, and, I am vain enough to think, takes my advice, but it is difficult to advise. My mind is not enough awake to the subject. When the responsibility is mine, my versatile disposition turns the subject in a thousand ways, and at daylight a bright ray of intellect has heretofore been kind enough to say, " Enrique, do so-and-so." It is really astonishing when I reflect upon my late career; everything has occurred to me as if by inspiration. All my little successes have flashed across my mind in an instant, and have been to the utmost of my power as instantly put into execution.

Midday, Saturday 18th.

One of Hintza's principal councillors, who came to us the first day, has just come in with a long tail, and claims an audience. He is a little shrewd-looking old fellow with a tiger-skin karosse, and brings as a present and token of good faith and amity a bullock.

We have given him a saddle and bridle, and oh, the delight of the fellow! Thirty-five are sitting round me, having thrown off their karosses, as naked as they were born, one, a great orator, holding forth to the honour of the British nation—I dare say a great humbug; however, we can humbug too. I have just given all of the councillor's tail a piece of tobacco, and his orator a tinder-box; also to two a knife apiece, and oh, such kissing of hands! He says Hintza will be here to-night or to-morrow.

7 o'clock.—Oh, it has just begun to lighten tremendously, and the thunder rolls ten thousand cannon. Such vivid lightning I scarcely ever saw, like a blue light at sea, and lasting almost as long. Heavens, what a storm! I must shut up my desk. Good God, how it blows and rains and lightens! The candle is almost flapped out with the walls of the tent; I will finish this page though, if possible, rain or no rain. Viva Mr. Hintza's country! You are a changeable fellow, hot and cold, wet and dry, light and dark in a moment. Blow, rain, thunder, lighten, but pray let me write to my poor old wife, for I can't go to my bed yet, the rain so spatters through my tent.

> Evening of the 19th, Sunday.

About 2000 Fingo captains have come in to say they must return into the colony with their wives and families, which will be granted them, so that I shall have a pretty increase of my cares. These are, as I have before told you, real game fellows, and, supported by my best of Hottentots, will drive more cattle out of the kloofs on the bed of the Kei in one day than we could in a week. It will be a measure of great policy, too, to bring with us a settlement of people so well disposed towards us and place them upon our new frontier. They appear to be of a much more docile nature than the wild Kafir, whose head is mischief and heart deceit.

I therefore hope to see them and their families comfortably located on a good ground and their huts built before winter, and hereafter they must be taught to build cottages. I feel convinced that nothing would tend to the civilization of these poor people more than domestic comfort in a nice cottage in place of lying all together like dogs in a kennel. . . . Good-night, my soul, my love, my wife.

ENRIQUE.

> 9 o'clock at night, 19th April.

I have just received a deputation of *royal blood*. The look-out officer reported to me that about one hundred Kafirs were coming towards the camp in a friendly manner and without assagais, so off I started with my orderlies to meet them, making sure they were from Hintza. On my approach I halted them, and desired one to come out, when out came a tiger-karosse man. He said he was the captain, Kuba, come to pay his respects to the Governor, and asked the *news*, which is their mode of wishing to know whether we are friends or foes. I told him that four of his people might come with him, and I would then conduct him to the Governor. The Governor told them the news was with Hintza. This was all they could get from him, but he was very civil.

We encamp in a very curious way—not as in the Peninsula, the General some distance from the camp. We are all in a square, the troops outside, the General and staff and all the commissariat and oxen and waggons within. Sentries outside of the whole.

I have just returned from poor old Master, who now is *very kind* to me, and treats me with the most marked attention. He said, "Well, have you sent the sketch of yourself to Mrs. Smith?" "Oh yes." "Do you know what Michell says?" "No, sir." "Why, that if he could get you to stand still for one minute, he could make a perfect likeness of you." "By God, sir, I have not time to stand still." "I believe you," said the old boy; "you have not stood still;" and he shook my hand.

20th April.

I have just ordered Bruintjes to bring me a camp-kettle lid full of embers, and now am quite warm. Such a cold day as this would put me in a fever about you, were you here, lest you should get cold, lest you should not have all you want. For years now (that horrid thing, Time!) you have been accustomed to luxury. When I was first *troubled* with you, you were a little, wiry, violent, ill-tempered, loving, always faithful, little devil, and kept your word to a degree which at your age and for your sex was as remarkable as meritorious. How often have I admired you for it! Had it not been for your own good sense and faith to me, I should not have had my dearest love as a young woman, nor an old Boba to whom to pour out the feelings of an affectionate heart. But please Almighty God, I shall have this old woman with me, until we both dwindle to our mother earth. And when the awful time comes, grant we go together at the same moment!

It is time we changed our camp. This delightful valley, so beautiful in its crops of Indian and Kafir corn, the hills around, so luxuriantly clothed with grass, are all now eaten off or trod down by the innumerable bullocks, horses, and animals we have with us, and bear the countenance of what you have so often seen —war and devastation. When we march to a fresh bivouac, all is again green and gay.

> "Battle over, sleep in clover;
>   Who so happy as we in camp?"

Answer, "Enrique with his Juana at Charlie's Hope." Oh, I must tell you of the compliment the Kafirs paid me the other day by calling me a *beauty!* They yesterday, after looking at my feet in my brown boots, asked the interpreter where I put my toes, and then like great baboons they laughed at their own wit, so that we all turned to and laughed also.

The soldiers were very much amused yesterday with me, when cross-questioning one of the Hottentot deserters. I asked his name, which was—what do you think?—Henri Smith! By Jupiter, how the fellows laughed! However, I had my jaw too by saying, "All Smiths are sharp, active-looking fellows, and so is our deserter rascal."

I am glad to see those rogues leave the Kafirs. Nothing disheartens the brutes so much as the supposition that you know what they are doing. They will, on account of it—we are given to understand—change their plans even. It is just so with a wild beast (you were a sportswoman once, you know, dearest). Head a wolf, fox, hare, any *bête de chasse*, and it will change its whole plan of escape immediately. So it is with the Kafir.

10 o'clock, 20th April.

Somerset's division, or rather the *débris* of it, has just arrived in twos and threes, forty times worse than the army of Burgos was in the pig-shooting days which you witnessed. This is the way in which it has marched these three days. To-morrow His Excellency inspects this division (what a name for it!), and I will answer for it we will still muster a few horses fit to do something.

23rd April, daylight.

My fifty Fingoes just coming in like Trojans. I have ordered each 3 pounds of meat. Upon my word, I never saw

anything so fine as my fifty Fingoes, all with their assagais and
their shields, and singing as they marched along, all aroused
as if the blood of their forefathers was flowing through their
veins, when their nation was independent and important
amongst the other savages. They then gave me a war-whoop,
and jumped, and then sang again most melodiously in a
deep sonorous voice, with a most harmonious bass. Nothing
villainous in their countenances, but full of heroism and fine
feeling.

9 *at night.*—Oh, such a Johnny Raw as old John Bell sent up
to us to-day, young——! The General did not know what the
devil to do with him, and sent for me. I soon appointed him a
Volunteer to the 1st Provisional Battalion, and as he had neither
tea, sugar, coffee, nor brandy, he was a pleasant fellow to join a
half-starved officers' mess. I set him up with 2 lbs. tea, 4 lbs.
sugar, 4 lbs. coffee, and a canteen of brandy, with this good
advice: "Be broad awake, sir, and learn to speak quick." I
was very near telling him to get his hair cut. Tell dear old John
to send us no more such trash.

> Bivouac on the T'solo, a small stream running into the T'somo,
> which runs into the Kei, 30th April, 1835.

Viva Enrique!

Mi Queridissima Muger,

Since the 24th, I have not been able to talk with you,
and in these six days your old man has worked wonders. *Hintza
dined with me yesterday, and is my son.*

On the morning of the 24th instant, His Excellency having
waited nine days for a communication from Hintza and none
arriving, proclaimed hostilities to a chief named Kuba (Lynx-eyes),
and fired a gun in great ceremony. Knowing pretty well that
nothing but the most vigorous and indefatigable exertions would
bring this fickle chief to terms, I had a little bit of an army
of both divisions told off for me, with which I immediately
commenced operations, the results of which are detailed in
the accompanying two letters. With them I send my dear old
woman a copy of the General Order on the subject.

On the afternoon of yesterday, on my return, His Excellency,
who was most highly delighted at my success, informed me that
on the 27th and the 28th, he had received communications from

Hintza, but he had refused to treat with any one but himself.
"Right, sir," says I, "by G—d." He continued, "This afternoon you will see him himself, or I am the most deceived of
men." (However, I held in readiness a detachment of fresh
troops to march against Boku at two o'clock in the morning on a
fresh venture.)

About four our picquets reported a body of horsemen coming
in. We sent out Beresford to meet it, and in rode the *Great
Chief*, a very good-looking fellow, and his face, though black, the
very image of poor dear George IV. He seemed perfectly satisfied of his safety among us, and acted majesty with great dignity,
though nearly naked like the rest. He said to the Governor that
he was ready to proceed to business.

His Excellency, therefore, read sentence by sentence a long
story of grievances, which our interpreter *spoke*. Hintza paid
great attention, occasionally made a remark, and when it came to
the terms on which we would make peace, he sighed two or three
times; then gave a toss of his head and said he would consider
of them.

I asked him to dine with me. He and one of his councillors
came, and you would have laughed to have seen us all. He fed
himself very well, ate enormously, drank only water, but lots of
coffee, with pounds of sugar in each cup. After dinner he began
politics. I soon saw he was for coming to terms. He said he
looked upon me as his *Father*. I therefore soon cleared my tent
of all but myself, the Interpreter, Hintza, and one of his councillors.
In deep whispers he proceeded to talk over the present state of
affairs, pointed out the insubordination of many of the chiefs
under him, and, to make a long story short, we swore eternal amity
and friendship and privately concluded peace on *our* terms. The
whole was to be publicly ratified in the morning.

I stuck to my *son*, turned out all the troops, and assembled
all the officers. The Governor appeared at their head, I and
Hintza and his councillors opposite. I having pledged myself to
be his patron and answer to the Governor for his fidelity (which
highly pleased him), he then ratified all the conditions of our
treaty and shook hands with the Governor and with me.

I then said, "Now let it be proclaimed far and near that the
Great Chief Hintza has concluded a peace with the Great King
of England, and let the cannon fire."

Three guns were loaded and fired in succession accordingly. Hintza was delighted. All our prisoners had been released. We had a capital breakfast together, and soon after gave him his presents. I never saw a creature so delighted. He swears by me. The main points of our treaty are these (there are several minor ones) —that he shall within five days give up 25,000 head of cattle and 500 horses, and that this day twelvemonth he shall pay 25,000 more and 500 more horses. He is to place two hostages in our hands for the fulfilment of his treaty, but as to hostages, he says, " Why, I will remain with you myself." He is to order the rebel chiefs to submit, and to consider our enemies his. I am quite amused with the fellow. Now, old woman, I give myself more credit for my negotiations than anything else, and God knows I have been the humble instrument for concluding this arduous and laborious war most satisfactorily. I have followed the enemy everywhere, driven him out of every den, captured 25,000 head of cattle in all, and concluded an honourable peace. The poor Excellency is most delighted. The labour I have encountered from the morning of the 24th to the afternoon of the 30th has astonished everybody, nay, even myself. It is nearly equal to my ride up from Cape Town.

Hintza's son is just come in, a very fine young man about nineteen or twenty. I am to have the honour of his company at dinner, with that of his papa, my son. . . . Oh, to-day my heart was full to overflowing ! I had taken prisoner the brother of a chief called Chopo. I told him yesterday that he or his brother must pay 500 bullocks for his ransom. Then he said, " My liberty is a hopeless case "; and he sighed and looked so melancholy, I quite pitied him. He was a very handsome, nice youth. After peace was proclaimed, I sent for him and liberated him, and I declare he made such demonstrations of real gratitude, that the poor savage saw a tear steal down my cheek. I could not help it. Poor fellow, how delighted I was to have it in my power to confer the great boon of liberty on a poor fellow-creature ! —almost a reward for my labour, I declare.

To-morrow we begin to turn our heads towards home, but we must wait for the cattle. Hintza has sent in all directions for it, and it is to be here in five days from to-morrow's sun.

How you would laugh to see me walking about the camp with Hintza leaning on my arm !

Four o'clock, 30th April.

What do you think has been my occupation for this last half-hour? One very much in my way. Stringing a large necklace of glass beads for young Hintza. I have just hung it round his neck in three rows.

1st May.

Just four months to-day since I left you, dearest. What a time it does appear! Good heavens! four years at least.

There never were such game fellows as these Hottentots. The other night in the Kei, after a terrific march, when we got up to the enemy, I halloed them on like a pack of hounds, and, upon my word, they flew past me through the bush like buffaloes, making everything crack before them.

Only fancy, my dear old woman, what must have been my five days' late campaign. I never shaved from the 24th to the evening of the 29th, nor did I ever comb my hair. My toothbrush my only luxury. I changed my pantaloons because in a cattle hunt the mimosa bushes literally tore them off. The difficulty of obtaining information where anything is going on occupies every moment one has off horseback. One of the days I was out, Paddy Balfour—meaning well, God knows—sent my led horses with the infantry, and at night I had the gratification to find myself 25 miles from them. We had lots of cattle, but killing and eating two hours after dark is rather a bore. Luckily, one of the men gave me a bit of tongue—no salt nor biscuit, but I was delighted with it. Next morning, on joining the infantry, having had no cup of coffee, I was so hungry, by heavens! I could have bit a piece out of my wife's shoulder, when one of the escort hauled out of a dirty haversack a bone of a goat, which he had already had a gnaw at. So I turned to at that, and gnawed it as greedily as little Moira seizes everything out of one's hand. However, after joining my horses, I had a real good breakfast, and we then marched 25 miles over mountains steeper than the Pyrenees, and the weather down in the Amava was exceedingly hot. However, we have overcome all difficulties.

8 o'clock in the evening, 1st May.

I have written a very long letter to dear old John Bell. I wish I could let him be behind the scenes in one of my councils with the chief. Such rascals as they are, trying to overreach you. My delight is for a long time to keep playing with them, as though thoughtlessly about to concede their request, then suddenly to turn round when they least expect it, show them what they are aiming at, and then say, " No, decidedly not. A man never changes 'the word.' It is written—the cannons have fired." This figurative and metaphorical mode of speech they are very fond of. I carry on all our negotiations in this way, until it comes to the point. Then I disrobe the question and put it in plain matter-of-fact language. Altogether it is good fun for the moment, but I can see that as these rascals are bereft of their fears they will become troublesome and try every shift in their power.

We expect Thomson up daily. Master and he will have a long ride or two—I think to decide on eligible spots for a line of posts along the Kei. It is decided we take possession of all this country; but as yet we have not touched upon it to Hintza, to whom it matters but little, as we take possession of no territory belonging to him personally, but of a large portion of his brother Boku's. There does not appear to be any particular love between the two.

2nd May, 5 o'clock.

Just going to send His Majesty his coffee. I sent him one cup yesterday morning, and asked if he would have any more He said, " Oh yes ; I have a large belly."

Later.—On the march to-day met Boku coming in with 20 cattle—all the Colonial cattle he has, the villain.

We had a great scene in camp to-night. There are about 150 followers of these chiefs in camp, and some of them have been murdering the poor wretches of Fingoes, who have placed themselves under our protection. So His Excellency got very naturally irate and blew them up considerably. After to-day's march I recommended that all their assagais should be given up. By way of intimidation Hintza said his people would throw them. So I said I was delighted. I went in amongst them and ordered them to lay down their assagais. They began to untie them and really get ready to throw. So I laughed like the devil, and in a voice like thunder ordered the picquet of thirty men standing with their left flanks towards them about fifty yards off to wheel up to its left, which brought their front immediately opposite the group of Kafirs, at the same time ordering my corps of Guides to file round their rear.   The cowards were electrified, and immediately roared out, " Oh, we will give them up ! we will give them up ! " and in two minutes they were collected.   I then went in amongst them with tobacco, and oh, such fun as I had throwing it in amongst them and making them scramble for it !

Hintza, who is really gentlemanlike in his manner, his brother Boku, another brother, and Kreili—Hintza's son—dined with me.   And I made them laugh too, although at first they pretended to be rather sulky at their men's arms being taken away.   I allowed the chiefs to retain theirs.

Cox reports that Tyalie, etc., are in a state of the most miserable alarm.   He cannot get near any of them.   They are flying about in small parties, literally afraid for their lives.

3rd May, 10 at night.

My son Hintza and I have been at loggerheads very much this afternoon.   I let him alone all day, although I could see he was doing nothing nor intending to do anything.   At 4 o'clock I summoned him, Boku, and their great councillor Umtini to a talk, and demanded that the two messengers should go to Tyalie and Macomo.   They struggled in every possible way.   I stormed with the Articles of Treaty in my hand, marched down an additional picquet, doubled the sentries, and then said, " Hintza, my son, I am pledged to the Governor for your faith, and my head is likely to be cut off for your infidelity, so that if you do not fulfil every tittle of the Articles of Peace, we will carry you, Hintza, Boku, Vadana, and your son Kreili, with us into the Colony and keep you until the good faith we have expected from you be extracted by force."

You never saw fellows more astonished.   I then made Hintza and his great councillor Umtini come and dine with me.   Hintza and he at first were awfully dull, but ate a good dinner.   I had six sentries around my tent.   After dinner I cleared it of all but the Interpreter, and then said, " Now we will have a talk, and I will again ' give you the word.' "   The sentries were told off, and when I said, " Are you there ? " every man was to roar out, " Yes, sir."

We parted friends, he in a funk, his followers all disarmed. I marched him down to his tent with ten sentries. Ninety men of the 72nd Regiment are round him, and every minute I make them sing out " All right ! All right ! " from sentry to sentry. En la moda Española, "Sentre alerte ? Alerte soy."

Poor devils ! If Hintza had been educated and had lived among well-disposed Christians, he would have been a very fine fellow. I like him and Umtini, but I hate all the rest except young Kreili, his son, who is a very nice modest youth.

4th May.   Monday morning, daylight.

Did I tell you that last night Hintza said he had rather at once pay the 50,000 head than half in a year ? To this I agreed. I have therefore promised Hintza that if in five suns more he brings us the whole of our demand, I will return him 5000 bullocks and 100 horses. Probably this may act upon him, for he will certainly keep them for himself.

6 o'clock, 4th May.

My Royal Son has grown particularly modest or *cold*, for he asked me to give him a pair of pantaloons. I gave him two. His delight when you give him anything is quite " estraordinary."

Oh ! to-day the uncle of Maquay came in to see me. He says (literally) his heart is full to me for my kindness when I might have taken his life. All his wives thank me, and he will never cease to love me. When he went away, he held my hand, kissed it, and bid me good-bye, wishing me all the cattle in the world ! A fine manly-looking fellow. When he was quite out of sight, I sent for him back and made him several presents. His gratitude almost overflowed. I let him go first to see if he came in the hope of getting something, but no, it was pure gratitude. One can scarcely consider such a being a savage. If so, he had better remain in his present state.

Poor devils ! these little opportunities of kindness make me very happy for the moment. It is hardly fair so to frighten them, but without it nothing can possibly be done with them.

I was perfectly satisfied with the message sent to-day to Tyalie and Macomo. I summoned Hintza and all the royal personages into my presence and desired them to send their message to the rebels. Hintza told Boku to speak. He did so very slowly and impressively to the purport I wished.

5th May, an hour before daylight.

They trumped up a tale in the camp last night that the Kafirs were going to make an attempt that night to rescue their chiefs, by help of a body without. I laughed at it most heartily, but as Master placed much credit in it as a likely thing to occur (very likely!), why, to please him I took the necessary precautions, as he terms it. Amongst others, I desired Captain Murray of the 72nd, should the attempt be made, to go in very quietly to Hintza's and Boku's tent and put them to death, but not to do so until there was a probability of a rescue ; so their escape was pretty well provided for, I think.

All is quiet, however, as I ventured to anticipate, contrary to the opinion of all other persons, or nearly so, in camp ; but they none of them have been quite so often on outlying picquet as *you* have been, or accustomed to the little constant services of danger on which I have been for a number of years. (What a conceited old rascal you are, Mr. Enrique!)

This is the 5th sun ; now for the faith of my son. I expect some of the 25,000 head, but not all, because I know he has not had time to fetch it since the Peace, so far off had he driven it.

Oh, how all that delay at Grahamstown has altered everything ! It might have been all over a month ago, the farmers in their homes, the families who had suffered from the invasion in possession of cattle and roofing their houses or rebuilding them ; land apportioned to those who wished for it in the new boundary ; every Kafir tribe dreading the name of an Englishman from the rapidity as well as force with which he strikes ; thousands of pounds saved to our country ; and last, but by no means least, I at home with my dearest faithful wife.

2 *o'clock.*—I have just given out the order of march for the 1st and 2nd Divisions for to-morrow, the 6th ; the latter to cross the Kei, and continue its march back to the Colony with the captured cattle, Fingoes, etc., and all the impedimenta ; the first division to move into the camp just on this side of the

Kei, where we halted and bivouacked the first day after we crossed.

My tent just filled with Dutchmen come to bid me good-bye. They all march to-morrow, thank Heaven. I do pity them ; but if ever Job had had to deal with them, I feel satisfied he would not have acquired his character for patience. I am liked by them, however, and, notwithstanding the many rowings I have given them, am glad to part friends with all that are good for anything.

Afternoon.—The poor Boers keep coming in to bid me good-bye, and with all their hearts. God knows, it is with all my heart I say good-bye. I would never attempt to learn Dutch now. Such is my horror of the language, a bevy of beautiful maidens could not tempt me into a Dutch parley.

9 *at night.*—The Clarksbury party have at last arrived—lots of parsons ; and we march to-morrow towards the Kei.

Boku was to have brought 600 head of cattle in to-day for the murder of Purcell and Armstrong. His messengers came after dark, bringing in nineteen head. So I sent Paddy Balfour to kick them out of camp, and the Interpreter to Boku to say I had done so.

Later.—I have just given Kili, or Kreili, a necklace for his mother. The youth was quite delighted. You cannot conceive a more handsome half-black fellow. He has such a gentlemanlike figure. At first I thought he wanted intellect, but to-day I find it is nothing but modesty. We were talking of the Kei and the rivers which fall into it, when he became quite eloquent, and described the great river, its source, and tributary streams far better than his father or the prime minister. My Royal guests were in great spirits indeed. Hintza talked much about his fifteen queens. They have increased five lately. At first he acknowledged to only ten. He says he loves them much. He never ceases to think of them, when I do not bring out the long paper. He is always horrified at the long paper. I told him to-night we were going to cross the Kei to-morrow. He said, "Very well ; I am doing all I can about the cattle, but I, like others, must have time. I cannot perform impossibilities. The cattle are so far off, they could not be here within the five suns."

Morning of the 6th.

The day has turned out so wet, I have been obliged to countermand the march of the two Divisions. The roads here are so steep and so slippery in descending and ascending to and from the Kei, they are totally impassable to the waggons. Therefore discretion says "halt," and patience says "the devil."

If you were to see how Paddy Balfour works for me now, how he tries to have all my things about me right and comfortable! And in the field he is a very useful and a proper plucky fellow, and *now* knows something about his business, as do a very few more of them—ignorant enough at first, but all, all, most ready and willing to learn. They fly to obey, nay, even anticipate my wishes. Thank God! I never wish to serve with a nicer set of fellows.

How it does rain! Well, a fine day to-morrow. How it used to rain in the Pyrenees, *ti acordas, mi pobrecita?* * Oh, how I pitied you some days, although I never said so! But the most varmint thing you ever did was to get on your horse that cold day and ride to Mont de Marsan to return the poor kind woman her bridal basin.† No person on earth but you would have done that.

I do not think I told you that in one of his notes to me Master expressed a wish that I would move Cox's 3rd Division from the immediate vicinity of the enemy, that is, from the Amatola to Brownlee's missionary station on the Buffalo, at the point where the high-road crosses into Kafirland. I said, "What is the object, sir?" "Oh," he says, "then the army will be concentrated." "Sir," I said, "the sole object I have aimed at and studied is to send the troops in every direction in detachments strong enough to protect themselves, because such is the practice of the enemy. I have never yet sent out any detachment that they did not do something, either take some cattle or a horse or shoot a Kafir or two." So he said, "Very well, let the 3rd Division remain where it is." However, to please him, I have sent 300 of Van Wyk's 4th Division there, because it does not matter whether they are there or in any other place, they are so sick of the war, although they have done much and good service and are real game and plucky fellows. So by agreeing in trifles, as I told you, I succeed in getting the essentials as I like.

* "Do you remember, poor child?"   † See p. 168.

Ah! all this is very fine, but I am naturally so lazy a fellow I long to be back again. I do not mind the fox-hunting part of it, but the dry official writing is awful.

Hija, I have just thought of a very nice amusement for you, and one which would be very probably hereafter useful to me. Copy in a book everything descriptive of what we have done, my scenes with my followers, my descriptions of the war, Kafir chiefs, policy, etc., in short, everything but my *touterias.** The rest I will some day publish in the life and adventures of Harry and Jenny Smith.

7th May.

This wet weather does put me in mind of the Pyrenees—that cold camp we had on the very top of them, when our tent was floored with large cold stones, the only time I ever smoked a little, when you made me a little paper segar, and tea, too, to drink with it.

It is so cold, too; however, cold or no cold, in future, if I campaign again in a friend's country, my Juana must be of the party; I cannot again be separated. But in this savage warfare, it would have been folly, nay, the height of cruelty, to have brought you.

Half-past 12.—Hang the rain! it has begun again as hard as ever.

Oh, how I see you now, I think, at Government House in your fancy dress, your dearest shape so divulged, *aquella gracia Española*, the remembrance of our youthful days and what you have gone through for me, brought back by the costume; all the room admiring you and your dress, and in that room one heart in which the universal admiration is concentrated, because he knows that love of a woman is his own, and knows what others do not—the qualities of her mind, the generosity of her heart, the superiority of her character, void of all littleness, the strength of mind of a noble-hearted man, the soft feelings and affection of the most delicate of her sex !—

> " Yet are Spain's maids no race of Amazons,
>   But framed for all the witching arts of love."

I see you sitting thus dressed at dinner. How I watch you

* " Nonsense."

sometimes when I see you animated, your dear full bosom heaving, your eyes flashing fire, whilst with a heart of innocence and joy you are recounting some of our old campaigning stories, and the listeners wonder that a creature so delicately framed could have endured such awful fatigue and for one unworthy of her! Oh, God bless her!

5 *o'clock.*—My master has just sent me a confidential communication which in the strictest confidence I impart to my own soul for *her*, *her* sacred ear alone. It is a copy of his ultimate treaty of peace with Hintza when the latter has fulfilled the engagements of his former treaty; a copy, that is to say, of his proclamation declaring the territory conquered up to the Kei to belong to his Britannic Majesty, including the territory beyond the T'somo. That is, the new boundary-line of this colony is to extend to the sea, up the Kei, following the course of the T'somo to the Stormberg. It will include a most magnificent track of country, I assure you.

The whole is framed upon various conversations which I have had with him.

I have just sent for Umtini, and have desired him to tell Hintza that as two days have passed beyond the time named in the Treaty and he has done next to nothing to fulfil it, he, his son, Boku and Vadana with their retinue, are our prisoners-of-war, and that we now demand the 50,000 cattle and the 1000 horses before he is liberated. Umtini began a parley, but as usual I took hold of the Treaty of Peace, thumped it and gave him "the word," then assumed the civil and asked him what he wanted. He said, a sheep, some biscuit, and some tobacco. We shook hands, and so we parted.

9 o'clock at night.

Just done dinner. We had Major White there, the Assistant Quartermaster-General, a very excellent fellow, very fond of me and argument. I never argue except with old Johnstone, but White, Murray, and Beresford had plenty to say, laying down the law about everything. These kind of conversations make one laugh sometimes, but oh! how I do hate man's society; the same monotonous ideas day after day. Give me strong exercise all day and lots of women to talk with at dinner, and then to my own home with *my own*. But times alter, and so do I. Give me my own fireside, my own wife, my dogs, my horses, my domestic happiness, and let me alone.

Just finished a very long and laborious report for His Excellency, with comments upon his ideas of the new frontier line its defence, and the force to be kept in the field for the purpose of driving the hostile tribes, even though they make peace with us, across the Kei. Near us they cannot stay. I differ very little in a general point of view from my Master, but he is for not occupying a post nearer than thirty miles to the Kei, I am for occupying a more advanced one, within ten or eleven miles of it, and patrolling frequently up to it. There is a degree of weakness which I am averse to avow in proclaiming an extensive territory as ours, and not placing a soldier upon it within thirty miles of the boundary. These posts will be all fortified so as to prevent any aggression on the part of the enemy, and a moderate time after the proclamation I would shoot every Kafir not authorized to remain in our territory.

Head Quarters, east of the Kei, 8th May, 1835.

Now, my dearest old companion, comes the tug of war !

As I expected, but dare not previously say so, I am to be kept upon the frontier, Heaven knows how long ! My Head Quarters are to be on the Buffalo, where there was a nice house, a missionary station. It has been burned, but as the walls stand it may soon be made habitable. Come to the welcoming arms of your faithful husband !

9th May.

On the Kei, ready to cross to-morrow, when a great ceremony will be performed, in proclaiming our conquered territory. The new boundary is to be the Kei. This is better than the T'somo, as the T'somo runs far too much in Hintza's country.

How I long to get to the Buffalo, to see where and how I shall build our house ! Williams of the Engineers is ordered up with Sappers, etc., and that is to be his first occupation. We are going to found a town there, to be called William's Town ; but this is a secret.

I fear this cunning rogue, Hintza, will give us some trouble ere we get the cattle. He is a shuffling scoundrel. I am making him go with me to-day on a bit of a tour. He says he can get the cattle if I can help.

God bless you, dearest woman; the pleasure I think on, dream on, is in some degree banished by a knowledge of the fatigue which you must undergo. God bless you! But when we meet we will forget all, and then, in light marching order, once more we will go together, together everywhere. As the old man campaigns so well, why should not the old woman?

ENRIQUE.

Fort Smith, 18th May, 1835.
On the right bank of the Kei, about seven miles from it.

Viva Enrique!

This is the 9th day, and I have not sent a word to my dear old wife. The hand of the Almighty God has been again upon me. Since I last wrote to you from the other bank of the Kei, I have made one of the most extraordinary marches ever made by troops, but I enclose a copy of my despatch.

One day (Mr. Hintza's, the scoundrel) was an awful one, I assure you. What with hunting him, and taking the cattle at night, I was rather done, I admit; but I had some mutton chops and coffee, and in an hour was fit again for a night's march. At three o'clock did I again set off on a venture. Though it was not successful as to bullocks, it had a fine political effect, that in three days from the bed of the Kei, a British force was in sight of the bed of the Umtata, etc.

Oh! if I could but describe the countenance of Hintza when I seized him by the throat and he was in the act of falling. A devil could not have breathed more liquid flame. I shall never forget it. I have his bracelets for you, and, what is more, the assagai he sent flying after me, as also his bundle. The pains I took to conciliate and treat kindly that savage! A pack of fox-hounds would have followed me all over the world with a half of it, but such blackguards as these fellows are, cannot be described. They are the most determined and practised liars in the universe.

We do not march till the day after to-morrow, for all I can say and do. But being now within the Colony, it is quite ridiculous how much at home we feel. I had a long letter from Cox to-day. He has had an interview with Tyalie and Macomo, who are anxious for peace. I know not what they will think of our having taken possession of their country.

Poor man ! what a loss Major White is to us all ! He lived with me, poor fellow, and we were mutually much attached. I have told him a thousand times what would occur. I even on one occasion forbad his going with me, only he promised so faithfully to stay with the column. He is universally regretted.

19th May.

This day at 12 o'clock we liberated Kreili, Vadana, his uncle, Sotoo, a councillor, and Nomsa, a councillor, and Piet Chingele, a half-Hottentot villain—Kreili having agreed to fulfil his father's treaty of peace.

We march to-morrow, leaving Warden with eighty Kat River Legion, one officer and twenty men, Cape Mounted Rifles, eighty of the 72nd Regiment, and one howitzer.

This is the advanced post of my command, and forty-eight miles from my Head Quarters, the Buffalo or William's Town.

20th May.

Marched from the Kei, and arrived and bivouacked on the Gonoube Hill, above the river of that name, at three o'clock, and immediately chalked out a redoubt to contain fifty men ; Lester, 72nd Regiment, to command.

21st May.

All the troops at work at daylight finishing the redoubt, which is named Fort Wellington.

May 23rd, Buffalo River, and our winter quarters, which is to be called King William's Town.

The house, as I think I have before stated, has been burnt, but the walls and the chimneys are standing. We will soon, therefore, put a roof on to it, and it will be a snug little box enough. There is a capital garden full of fruit trees, young and flourishing : peaches, apricots, plums, apples, pears, some vines ; very rich land, and ground enough to grow quantities of Indian and Kafir corn.

The site for the town is beautiful. The main road will run through it, and the river also. It will be perfectly magnificent.

The poor old Governor is so kind to-day. At dinner I asked Thomson where we could get rafters for the house. "Oh, we must cut them where we can." "No," says Master, "let the dimensions be immediately taken and I will send off express to Grahamstown for them." I felt this more than anything, because I often talk to him about you, and he saw I was pleased. He is a wonderfully good-hearted man, and wants nothing but a little more nerve.

I will soon have up more soldiers. We are generally to have here about 1200 men. I only hope so many will not be assembled as to induce Government to send out a Major-General to supersede me.

King William's Town, 26th May, 1835.

The old Master is all kindness to me. When he speaks of the new province, he always calls it "Your province." I shall also have the command of the whole of the frontier from Algoa Bay to the Kei, or I would not stay.

8 o'clock at night, 27th May.

Had a most beautiful ride to-day, and took 17 head of cattle. Two milch cows, worthy a place in my dairy, have been placed there, and two, less valuable, have been discarded. I have named three places—one "Kempt's Valley," another "Barnard's Vale" and "Ford," a third "Hotham Hill." I follow the bed of the Buffalo upwards to my estate. The road, which *will* be good, but is now a path, took us up to my estate and Murray Castle, where formerly I took 5000 head of cattle and on this occasion the present few. We crossed the river three times, all good fords but one, the stream most clear and beautiful, and each succeeding valley more calculated than the former for a village or a farm or anything. It is certainly a most beautiful country, this Province of Queen Adelaide.

King William's Town, 7th June, 1835.

My own Queridissima Muger,

I returned to Head Quarters last night after a foray of eleven days, during which I have again, thank God, rendered my country very essential service and the enemy considerable loss. . . .

I mention all this to you to show how rejoiced I must have been on my return, after such hard labour, to receive your *queri-dissima carta*, telling me you were on the road, since the 4th June, Thursday.

11th of June, 8 o'clock at night.

His Excellency started very early this morning for Grahams-town. I have sent off Paddy Balfour to meet you, and my trusty ensign Low, with 20 of my most faithful Hottentots to accompany you, and never to quit your waggon. Paddy will also turn out 20 cavalry.

15th June.

I have had 30 men at work all day, and all the Artillery, poor fellows. The delight with which they do anything for me is quite amusing and gratifying, but I rather think all their labours are to please *you*, for I heard them talking of your nice house at Cape Town, and then to come and live *here* in a tent! The Scotchmen said it was " an awfu' change," and they all rubbed, and swept, and laughed, and I jawed, and gave them a glass to drink your health.

22nd June, midday.

Last night I would not write, hoping that by trying not to think quite so much of you I should not dream, and kick about so, and this morning I had so much to do I could not, but nothing would do. Oh, such nights as I pass! I really believe the sentry thinks I am mad, such questions I ask him. To-day it is raining like the deuce, so I am conjuring up flowing rivers again and 5000 impediments. How in the name of wonder did you get on when I was away from you? You had nothing to do. I to-day have plenty, but I can settle to nothing, and I am so irritable, I am quite ashamed of myself. I feel satisfied Balfour has reached you. This is a consolation to me, for I know he will exert himself, and take the greatest care of you, and he has been with me now long enough to learn how to over-come difficulties. God grant I may hear from Balfour to-day, and that to-morrow I may meet you at Fort Willshire.

24th June.

Surely this day we shall meet. Oh, such a night as I have had! I could neither sleep, nor toss about, nor dream, nor anything, but lie and listen, hoping every moment to hear the footsteps of horses crossing the ford, bringing me letters from you and Balfour, saying when—oh, when !—I was to be at Fort Will-shire. Oh, such a merit as I make of it, when people ask me if they may go to fetch their wives ! " D—— it, sir, I cannot go for my own," although, poor fellows, I do so long to say, " Yes, you shall have leave." But it must not be. There is plenty here for every one to do yet, and for more too if we had them. I imagine your itinerary : the 18th, Uitenhage; 19th, Quagga Flats; 20th, Grahamstown ; 21st, halt; 22nd, Hermanus Kraal ; 23rd, Willshire ; 24th——. Oh, dare I hope it, my own dearest, that this night I shall receive thee ?

APPENDIX V.

HAVING closely applied myself to become thoroughly acquainted
with your wants, I have now lived long enough amongst you, my
children, to observe them.

Field Commandants, Field Cornets, and Heads of Kraals—
the Laws of our Country are rules established by the authority of
its King, or Governor, and his Councillors, to direct the conduct
and secure the rights of its inhabitants. You have all lately been
received, at your own request and humble desire, and in the
mercy of his Excellency the Governor, as British subjects, consequently are now governed by the British law, which, widely
differing from your own, will require on my part some explanation, in order to point out to you the necessary procedure in
cases where the interpretation of the Law, and its coercive power,
is required. Having been placed over you by his Excellency the
Governor as your Ruler since the day peace was concluded, and
as he holds me strictly responsible to him to see justice duly
administered to all—that the Laws are neither outraged, nor
individuals oppressed or ill-used—so have I, since that period, as
you all well know, watched over your rights and interests, for
your benefit, so to govern you that gradually you might become
so accustomed to our manner of proceeding, as to enable you to
observe the impartiality with which the Law is enforced, falling
equally heavy upon those who are its aggressors, rich or poor,
black or white, and equally protecting all. I have therefore
called together this large assembly, personally to explain to
you, to the best of my ability, the mode you are to adopt as

Magistrates, when crime is brought under your observation, in conjunction with the British Resident.

Whoever it was among you who first suggested the idea of your becoming British subjects, deserves to be marked by you as a man who has rendered you the most eminent service. Did not your great father, Gaika, on his death-bed, assemble his sons around him and with his dying breath tell them to hold fast the word of peace with the English? This you did not do: what ensued? You were almost utterly destroyed, soon would have been annihilated, and driven from your native country; your women and children were starving, almost the prey of wild beasts, and the widows of 4000 of your warriors lament their husbands slain during the war; the greater part of your cattle starved or taken; your plunder, so treacherously seized from the Colony, lost to you from the robberies of others; you were in a lamentable, nay, a deplorable plight; you sought and asked for mercy—it was granted you. You also begged to be received as British subjects; this has been granted you, and you are *now* the subjects of the most powerful nation, whose laws, manners, customs, and institutions are the wonder of the world. This was your state when I took you "out of the bush," since which three moons have barely passed over your heads; land has been given you, your gardens are flourishing; your clergymen are returned to you, hoping to forget your sins in observing your penitence; a trade is established for you; your persons and property are protected by the equity of the British law—no man can now be "eat up," unless found guilty of crime, and condemned by your judges; and in place of being the beaten, the degraded, humbled, mortified people you were in the bush, you are taken by the hand, and called "brother" by the greatest nation under the protection of Almighty God. You tell me that you are naked and ignorant, that I must teach you to clothe yourselves, to know good from evil, that you are willing to learn, and that you wish to be real Englishmen. Mark me, then. Years ago the English were as naked as you, and ignorant as you, as cruel as you were in the late war; but the bright day which has opened upon you, dawned upon them; they first learnt to believe in the omnipotent power of Almighty God, who judges every man according to his actions; worshipped, honoured, and obeyed Him; they loved their neighbours as themselves, and respecting their property, ceased to be thieves; they believed all that the ministers of God told them; they sent their children to be taught to read and write; they learnt the use of money, and carried on an honest trade with each other, selling their skins, etc., and buying clothes as you see us all now dressed. Some were labourers in the field, some tended the herds and flocks, some made implements of husbandry, built houses, made arms, and every other thing you see your brother-Englishmen possess; while others made laws to govern the whole, under the King, whom we all love. Thus civilization gradually advanced, while we became acquainted with the works of art; knowledge increased, we threw off the yoke of despotism and barbarism, cast away our vicious habits, and put to death or banished by the Law every one who by sin, crime, and wickedness was a pest and an enemy to society at large. Do you suppose that we have all these things by lying sleeping all day long under a bush? No; but by habits of daily industry, working as you see me do, and all the people around me, each day becoming wiser than the other: and by avoiding the evils of yesterday, striving to improve ourselves to-day. Such now may be your case, provided you cease to do the following things :—

I. First, to " eat up " one another. This is theft.

II. To murder or kill any one.

III. To believe in witchcraft. This is all folly and ignorance of the worst description. Did not Eno's " rain-maker " desire you to go to war, and encourage you by telling you that you would beat the English, the greatest nation in the world, whose power exceeds yours as much as the waters of the Keiskamma do the pools of the Penla rivulet? How dare the villain tell you such lies? Was he not the first man shot when the troops moved on Eno's kraal, after I came amongst you, and was then as much your bitter enemy as I am now your true friend?

IV. Perjury, or giving false witness against any one.

V. Setting houses on fire, and destroying property.

VI. Rape. And above all (having this day taken the oath of allegiance)—

VII. Treason, or lifting up your hand against the King, the Governor, his officers, magistrates, soldiers, and subjects.

The British Law punishes these crimes with death; by avoiding them we have become the great, powerful, and enlightened and happy nation you see, going about the world teaching others to imitate us, and we are now instructing you. Do you wish to be real Englishmen, or to be naked, and almost wild men? Speak, I say, that I may know your hearts.

✱   ✱   ✱   ✱   ✱   ✱

You have spoken well; your brothers will assist you. This day has his Excellency the Governor clothed your Chief Magistrates and Field Cornets according to their rank, to show you how England expects her subjects to appear. From this time henceforth no more presents of clothes will be given you; by trade (as we do) you must clothe yourselves, and look no more to me for presents but for some important and good service rendered to the State. Such I will reward, because his Excellency the Governor loves to reward merit. Since you have been under my protection the oldest men tell me there has been less crime than they ever knew: but this, though it pleases me, does not satisfy me. There shall be no stealing, one from the other; above all, from the King—or, as you would term it, the Great Kraal—the Governor or his people. Beware, I say, of theft, and as I protect you, so will I punish you, until the Law, by the rigour with which I will wield it, shall root out this evil from amongst you. Our clergymen will teach you what God expects from you, what you must do to expect God's mercy and love in the next world : thus you will all learn to love God. You may send your children to school, or you are wicked and base parents ; and by your good example and speaking the truth, teach them what they may become with the advantages of an education, which you have not, and could not receive. Above all, do not despair or despond, or say, " We are poor people ; we know nothing." Rouse yourselves : remember what I have told you, that the English were once as you now are, and that you may become what they are at present.

In the great change of laws by which you are now governed, one of the most important is that of not tolerating your being " eaten up." Now, this protects the weak ; the strong from time immemorial possessed amongst you this power, which custom made a right of the Chief, though it was a curse to you : do not therefore suppose that the English Law while it protects one part injures the other. No, such is not the case ; your Chiefs who from custom possessed this power by which their kraals were filled with cattle, and by which they were enabled to reward those who performed good service, must, your merciful and provident

Governor says, receive an equivalent; besides, being now your magistrates, much of their time and attention will be taken up for your advantage. You must therefore contribute to their support and dignity.

A regulation is now framing that each kraal pay so many cattle or calves in the hundred annually to each other [each chief?] on the day the ox is paid to the King of England for the land which you possess, and which he had conquered from you. No time will be lost in carrying this arrangement into effect. Thus you see, Macomo, Tyalie, Umhala, and the others of your kindred who from birth possess rights and privileges, you will be hereafter amply provided for.

To the heads of kraals and villages do I now address myself.

You are responsible for the good conduct of the people of your village; if you exert yourselves and do your duty, crime will be checked and ultimately stopped. No man ought to be absent without your knowledge. No man can return with cattle or horses without your knowing it, and whenever a crime shall have been committed by a kraal, I will make the whole responsible to me, if they do not produce the offenders and the stolen property. You shall leave off this wicked practice of stealing from one another in the way you do; the English Law will make honest men of you—you shall not steal.

You must see that your people are active and industrious, that they work in the garden; it is the duty of men to work in the fields, not of women; they ought to make and mend your clothes and their own, and to keep the children clean, wash your clothes, cook your food, and take care of the milk. You well know from observation what work the English do, and what their women; this you must imitate, and not sleep half your time and pass the rest in drowsy inactivity; these things you must do, and you will soon reap the fruits of your labour.

Magistrates and all assembled! As you wish to be real Englishmen, you must observe their manners and customs in everything; and as you are rapidly ceasing to believe in witchcraft, and at the death of any of your friends and relatives (an affliction to which we are all liable) beginning to omit the witch-dance and the burning your huts and clothes, so do I now call upon you to bury your dead, as you see we do, and not drag out the corpse ere the vital spark is extinct, and cast it forth for food for wild beasts and birds of prey—the thought, even, makes a Christian and a civilized man shudder.   To the first man who has the misfortune to lose one of his relatives, if he decently inter him, will I give an ox. How can you bear to see those whom in life you loved and cherished—your aged father, who taught you your manly exercises and provided you with food ; your mother, who nursed you as a child, who attended you in your sickness, who for years watched over you, contributing to your wants or wishes ; your brother, sister, nearest relation and dearest friends, dragged from amongst you ere dead, and thrown out to the dog ?   We English not only make coffins to bury our dead, but raise upon the spot where our dearest friends' earthly remains are deposited, monuments to perpetuate their virtues ; and when wicked men whose lives have been forfeited to the offended laws of our country for any of the crimes which I have enumerated to you are buried (for we even bury them also), such spot is marked with the ignominy it deserves ; and our youth, as they pass the tomb of the good man, have an example of the respect due to virtue set before them ; or are taught to abhor the crime which merited an ignominious death by the wretched mound which marks the sinner's grave.   Thus as you loved your relatives in life, so you are bound to cherish their memory, and deposit their mortal remains in their parent earth.   Englishmen not only do this, but the clergyman prays over the grave, and these matters of moment connected with the immortality of your souls the missionaries will teach you when you attend Divine worship. But *your dead you must bury*, as I point out, if you wish to be real Christians and Englishmen.

At this great meeting let me impress upon you, that all previous animosities among yourselves be forgotten, and while the great English nation now regard you as British subjects and brothers, love your neighbours as yourself, fear God, honour your King, and the Governor, his representative.

APPENDIX VI.

EXTRACTS FROM SIR HARRY SMITH'S LETTERS FROM INDIA, TO
HIS SISTER, MRS SARGANT.

Loodhiana, 12th Feb. 1842.

You must excuse, dear Alice, my referring you to Sir James's
letter for information as to the tragedy of Cabool, but my labours
now are great. He sent me such a character to give Lord Ellenborough. I had also a very handsome letter from dear Lord
Fitzroy Somerset, saying his son was with Lord E., and he would
thank me "to instil into him some of that chivalrous and gallant
spirit which has been your guide in your military career."

Juana unites with me in love to you all, dearest sister, and if
I am actively employed you shall not have cause to accuse me of
a want of energy, pluck, or decision, with a jealousy of time, that
thing of all others in war for which all great generals have been
remarkable. "Time is everything in War," says Wellington, and
daily experience verifies it.

HARRY.

I suppose you started, like a half-broken horse, when I told
you I was driving four-in-hand. You will start again, I hope,
when I say after having had the use of it since I have been in
India, having driven it from point to point seven hundred and
two miles of good roads and bad, I have sold it for £700.
It is gone as a present to Shere Singh, King of the Punjaub at
Lahore, the son and successor of old Runjeet. There's a bit of
luck for you !

Simla, 3rd June, 1842.

My dearest Alice,

On the 24th May I received your letters of 31st March and 6th April. And while you wrote them full of that excitement and ardour for the fame of your country and the ambitious honour of your brother, he was quietly pruning rose-water trees, training jessamine, lopping forest trees, and improving his *ways*, like Cincinnatus, with this exception, I fear—that in his case, there is no chance of being drawn from his retreat into activity and the service of his country.

It rejoices me to see the vigour with which the people of England always meet disaster and rush to its reparation with heart, hand, and pocket.

I am of the War Party. Money will overcome every difficulty, expended with economy and supported by energy and activity.

My Lord E. is *now* of a pacific turn, and, as I told you last month, our troops are ordered to withdraw.

Simla, July 1, 1842.

This L[ord] you have sent us as a Moghul, by the powers, he is an arbitrary boy, and veers about like a weather-cock. Maybe a wonderful scholar, but, rest assured, unless he materially changes, ——. "The wind bloweth where it listeth," but terrestrial rulers must be guided by locomotive principles slower than steam-coaches.

Poor dear old Father! my heart aches when I think what age reduces us to. I inherit many of his noble ideas as to courage, I hope. His has been a wonderful career of strength both of mind and body. We unite in love to all. God bless you, dear Alice.

HARRY.

Simla, 7th Sept. 1842.

The great Lord arrived yesterday. The Staff and Commander-in-Chief were ordered to his Lordship's own house to receive him. I was the only person introduced. He came up in a most ready manner, shook hands, and said, "I am delighted to make your acquaintance, General Smith. I have heard a great deal about you indeed." I was very near laughing and saying, "I hope no *harm*," but as Great Moghul he is our king. He is a wild fellow, depend on it. His A.D.C.'s are all great friends of mine. I hear his Lordship prides himself on his *military ability.* It is more than my note and its continuation* are inclined to do. Oh, the grievous procedure since November last!

Simla, 15th Oct. 1842.

You will rejoice to learn that Lord E. has taken a great fancy to me and treats me quite as an old friend. Upon the receipt of any news of importance he will run down to my house to tell me or write a note. I have had frequent long conversations with his Lordship. He has a perfect knowledge of the affairs and state of India and the mode to preserve it, and, although he jumps to very rapid conclusions, they are usually just and accurate, therefore cease to be classed as errors.

I have done two or three military things for him with which he was highly satisfied, and in the military shows and spectacles he proposes for our camp at Ferozepore upon the return of the army at the Indus and the reception of the monarch of Lahore, Shere Singh, his Lordship tells me I must be prepared to assist him.

. . . Once more adieu, dear sister. How I long once more to visit my native land! What a period of banishment has mine been! Out of thirty-seven years' service, I have only been six in Great Britain, five of that in Scotland.

Ferozepore, 15th December, 1842.

MY DEAR ALICE,

It is not often I complain of a want of time, but I may venture this mail to do so, such humbug, as well as serious matters, am I engaged in. Our Moghul is non-compos, as sure as eggs are the produce of fowls, with all his pomp and trash, to meet an army of imaginary victors.

Loodhiana, 17th Jan. 1843.

Our Moghul is mad, undoubtedly—a species of military madness, of pomp, ceremony, renown, and it is incredible to what an extent of frenzied excitement he has worked himself up. Among

---

* See p. 476, *sup.*

other acts of extraordinary folly, so at enmity with the cause of
Christ and so calculated to sow discord between Hindoos and
Mussulmans, is his dragging these old portals about called the Gates
of Somnauth, a temple which *once* existed, but is now a Moslem
ruin. He conjured up in his imagination that Hindoos would
flock in myriads from every quarter of pagan India to sacrifice at
the holy shrine of these memorable portals, whereas not a votary
of Brahma ever, even out of curiosity, came to look at them, their
history being obsolete among an ignorant people. Mussulmans
are indignant at this attempt to degrade them in the eyes of those
whom their swords subdued, and the holy Cross of Christ stands
appalled, while all Christians shudder at this sacrilegious attempt
to perpetuate the barbarities of Paganism by contributing towards
its maintenance. The attempt has, however, been as futile as
monstrous. Our course is not one to sow discord amongst
those we have conquered.

Our united love to poor old Father and you all.

HARRY.

Simla, June, 1843.

MY DEAREST ALICE,

The state of poor dear Father from your description is
melancholy indeed. "Yet is their strength then but labour and
sorrow." Poor old man! an iron though never over-robust frame
has enabled you to endure much, to struggle against difficulties,
to contend with excitement, and to bear great bodily exertion.
God's will be done! All things must end, and our only prayer
ought now to be, however painful the blow we must anticipate,
"Lord, now lettest Thou Thy servant depart in peace." And we
must add, "Almighty and most merciful Father, grant that he may
receive Thy salvation." "Beats the strong heart, the less the lips
avow." Heaven bless him!

Our m—d Moghul has started from Agra to Calcutta by order,
we hear, of the Court of Directors. He therefore may be regarded
as *en route* to Downing Street to encore his "song of triumph."
He is a fickle fellow, but has told me twenty times, "The moment
I am not fully supported from home, I go." He was always very
kind to me.

3 D

Allahabad, 9th Aug. 1843.

A wish was expressed by Sir J. Nicolls, as also by Sir H. Gough, that I should proceed to meet the latter in Calcutta. In three days after the receipt of this wish, I and Juana started dâk, as it is called; that is, in a wooden box, a palanquin, somewhat like a giant sailor's trunk, borne on the shoulders of four men by a pole projecting fore and aft, with four other men to relieve them, eight to each palanquin. The eight men are again relieved at about ten-mile stages. The pace is not rail-road; it averages three and a half miles per hour.

The heat we endured until we reached Delhi cannot be described. After that we got through the greater part of our *day's* work by night; from hence we shall steam it, and complete a journey of 1300 odd miles.

Calcutta, 10th Sept. 1843.

I like my new master much, and with his Irish heart he appears readily to warm to me. He is very much delighted at my exertion to join, but I am cruelly worked just now, writing from four o'clock every morning till dark, then dinners, parties, balls, etc., so that even my aptitude to labour must fail if our Staff did not relieve me.

18th Jan. 1844, Gwalior.

My dearest Alice,

As I know my welfare is one of your leading stars, I tell you I am all well, and likely to be decorated with the Star of Gwalior !

Our Chief is a gallant fellow, but no genius as a tactician on strategic principles, but he licked the foe and took every gun (56), right well served and every gunner bayoneted at his gun; while the Division under General Grey on the same day beat the enemy opposed to him, several miles distant from us, and took every gun he had (25).

The devils before us had the most pluck, though, by far.

You had a brother and two nephews in the field. Hugh's * regiment was the most distinguished with General Grey. Indeed, theirs was the brunt of the battle, and the youth behaved nobly,

* Hugh Smith, son of Harry Smith's "Waterloo brother," Thomas.

all his comrades say. Harry's * corps was but little engaged, yet I
saw the boy looking as cool as his usual placidity renders him.
I had a most narrow escape. A cannon-shot contused my right
leg and carried away my stirrup and leather, passing under the
horse's chest. The force of the ball against the stirrup nearly
threw the horse on his side. I thought my leg was smashed, so
benumbed was it, but it was not cut. I never got off, nor until I
could move my toes upon a return of sensation was I aware that
my leg was whole and my stirrup was gone; the very leg I was
wounded in years ago. Thank God, though still black, it is all
right now. My horse, a noble Arab,† which I rode all day (my
other horses, of course, being out of the way), had two slight
wounds besides his miraculous escape from various round shot.

Among a set in India, it is the *façon de parler* that India could
be kept with Seapoys alone. He who says this is a fool.
They could not keep it, though transferred to them by England's
best blood. There is on earth nothing equal to the "British
soldier."

Now for your gratification. Poor dear Juana, who was on an
elephant under the fire of cannon, is to be "Lady." Poor dear
old wife, she has been very far from well for some time. The
Commander-in-Chief, who is a very warm-hearted fellow, says he
insures me the K.C.B., which will please you more than me. . . .
We are also to have a brass star for every officer and soldier made
out of the captured cannon, and as Juana is again a heroine, I
want a gold star to be made at the jeweller's who makes mine, according to the sketch enclosed, which she would wear as a brooch,
the enamel part representing the ribbon.

May God bless you all is the fervent prayer of all us stars of
Gwalior!

Faithfully your brother,
HARRY.

As you have fancy in such things, make me out some sort of
arms for approval; but I like my present crest of all things, as it
resembles a game-cock; and remember I am Sir *Harry* Smith—
none of your Henries.—H. G. S.

---

* Harry Smith, son of the "third Waterloo brother," Charles.
† See pp. 673, 674.

Camp Umbala, 18 March, 1844.

MY DEAREST ALICE,

You must forgive me this post, but what with marching, my report going home, etc., I have a mass of papers and business on my table, which must be cleared to-day. For I never have *one* thing any *one* day that I do not finish; and my table every evening is as clear as an Indian sky. God bless you all !

HARRY.

Simla, 1 July, 1844.

DEAREST ALICE,

As to the shield, I prefer the one I returned. But we must have a better elephant. His hind legs are all wrong.

Now for the motto, which, believe me, I have not lightly chosen, and which I intend pertinaciously to adhere to—" Inter milites miles." As a boy, as I was a jawing fellow, I always had a great sway among my comrades: and progressively the truth neutralized the vanity of the assertion that I had ever been looked up to in my profession. Thus, " Inter milites miles "—" A soldier among soldiers." And, thank Heaven, I have served with soldiers.

Pray be sure I do not adopt or assume anything bordering on the preposterous or beyond the limit of decided right. Are you sure this Vandyked sort of a coronet is right for the lion to dance on ? I wish that lion was a Rifle soldier; but I suppose that cannot be. I must fight for supporters. Then I would have a Rifleman and a 52nd soldier, the component parts of my gallant old Brigade in the Light Division. If the Rifleman could be put on duty, Brother Tom would correct his uniform and position. Your brother,

H. G. SMITH.

Rest assured all of you, no *honour* is half equal to the love I bear you all in heart. I am the same

HARRY.

Simla, 1st July, 1844.

Lord Ellenborough's government has been one stamped with indelible proof of striking ability, exertion, zeal, and assiduity, but founded on no just and firm principles of future durability, establishing and altering things at the moment without reflecting whether for ultimate benefit to posterity. Such innovations in established government require a gradual introduction, and must not be prematurely forced if they are to be a wholesome fruit and for the welfare of such a vast and heterogeneous nation. He saw clearly many existing errors, many practices which required reform or were capable of amendment; but jumped to such rapid conclusions that in the most instances the remedy increased rather than alleviated the evil.

India is an ancient and peculiar country, replete with prejudices and bigoted to custom. The introduction of any change requires to be gradual to effect a benefit. Such benefit his precipitancy usually defeated. The complicated systems of modern governments obviously found their origin in those simple forms of patriarchal rule not as yet in the East obliterated. Laws must be adapted to the people; their nature must be gentle and calm, and not marked by any outward appearance of strong feeling. He was elated in success beyond all bounds of moderation, in reverse depressed below all conception, in difficulties wavering and undecided; thus evincing a want of that moral courage without which, in situations of great responsibility, the most consummate ability and zeal are useless, and a straightforward, bold, and plodding fellow of very inferior talent makes the better governor. In the military execution of a large portion of his duty his zeal for the nominal welfare of the soldier has been unbounded; but it must not be regarded as illiberal or uncharitable if I remark that this appears to be founded on a personal vanity which has acquired for him the appropriate soubriquet of a Brummagem Napoleon. With great affectation of liberality, accompanied certainly by several such acts, he has shown a miserly parsimony a great governor should avoid,—just, probably, in principle or founded on rule; but such a principle (however anomalous the assertion) must bend to circumstance in all states, whether in the civil or military branch. Hence my lord drove the Seapoy army into mutiny by an indiscreet exercise of what I admit was a right, but one which the Seapoy did not understand under very trying and peculiar circumstances, and in the midst of this mutiny moral courage was wanting. By conceding the pecuniary point, mutiny in that army of mutineers had been reduced to implicit and unqualified obedience. The matter was unadvisedly smoothed over, and the *strong* goes to the wall. Militarily, too, my lord had another awful fault : one which, had he continued long enough as Governor-General, would have sapped the true base of discipline that every soldier must look up to the authority placed immediately over him, and all to their Com-mander-in-Chief. Whereas he would correspond with officers commanding regiments, even with individuals ; would frame orders which were indeed within his legitimate province, but which etiquette, or, what is a better reason, common sense, demands should be previously submitted to the Commander-in-Chief, for an opinion as to how they would work ; would appoint officers to civil departments without any reference to their military character for rectitude, or whether they could advantageously be spared from their regiments. Thus it was evident that the fundamental principles of good government were not respected, and, while these interior errors existed, external ones of great magnitude were in operation ; but these require more time to dwell on than I can bestow. As a whole, Lord Ellenborough's administration will be extolled by the home government. He can speak, and will well defend himself. He has some great acts to boast of (whatever their intrinsic merit) which will so eclipse the appa-rently little ones I have recorded (which still are the component parts of one great whole, like wheels in a watch) that he will be deemed a noble martyr and become ere long President of the Board of Control. India will be the gainer by his removal and by the man (if I mistake not) who succeeds him, my old friend Sir Henry Hardinge. By way of summary of my lord's character. An excess of vanity, and contempt for the opinions of others or their feelings, but, as with many a man, not naturally a bad heart where self-interest and aggrandisement are not the controlling powers. In early life he had not been taught to withdraw his thoughts from self-will and to fix them upon the dictates of con-science, to watch narrowly the rapid movements and changes which take place in all men's ideas, to form distinct notions of the intellectual faculties of others and the result and operations of his own acts. Had such been the case, it is more likely he would have acquired just habits of thinking and been more accustomed to analyze his own feelings and trains of thought. If a man of his great capability and powers of reasoning be placed in early life in minor situations of responsibility, and thus be afforded opportunities of observing the diligence and aptitude for industry of those around, and subsequently succeed to supreme authority, he has acquired an *indispensable quality*—that of giving every one his meed of credit, until he has displayed inefficiency or incompetency.   In the profession of my lord's father * every man is innocent until found guilty, but with *our* " Law " every man was guilty who ventured an opinion in variance with his own. Lord Ellenborough has been very kind to me, and as I ever feel for any man under a visitation, so I do for him, and I have written to him.

Simla, 12th Sep. 1844.

My dearest Alice,

What do you think I have been at work at for the last month ? Some memoirs of my life and Juana's and my adventures—all from memory. I have got into *Jamaica*, and have written nearly 400 pages of closely-put-together foolscap. Will you like to decipher and correct it ? It will be done in a fortnight—that is, the rough ; for as yet I have never read over one sheet I have written, but rushed ahead as water finds its level. There are a variety of stories and events in it.

The new Governor-General is winning golden opinions by his deportment and the regularity with which he transacts business. He says in his letter to me the labour is incessant, much of it trifles which ought to be settled in the departments they belong to. He has hit off one of the great evils of this government pretty quick evidently.   The rumour here is very general that, Sir Hugh Gough not having taken the hint to make way for Sir Henry Hardinge, it will be renewed in a less evasive communication. If he be made a peer and they give him the pension as in the case of Lord Keane (my dear old friend who is fast decaying), I am of opinion Sir Hugh Gough would willingly return to his native land, covered with honours, wallowing in wealth, possessing a good heart, a gallant hand, and *no* ——.

It is wonderful how fortune adheres to some men, and supplies all the deficiencies of nature.

You addressed a letter to me the other day " Sir Henry." My name is and shall be Harry.

* Edward Law, Lord Ellenborough, Lord Chief Justice of England.

Simla, 15th October, 1844.

Well, I have finished the anecdotes of a very long military career from my entrance into the army in 1805 to the end of the campaign of Gwalior. It is a voluminous tale, containing upwards of six hundred pages of foolscap, written all over without margin in my beautiful autograph as closely as this paper, but I fear ten times as illegible. I have never read a page of it since my scrawling it over at full gallop, and wish you well through it. If I am to send it, great circumspection must be used as to names and descriptions of men and events, or they might do others an injury (which Heaven forfend) and myself too. Whether it may not be advisable not to print it all until I am on the shelf in our retreat or in my grave for the benefit of my widow remains for you and Sir James Kempt to decide on inspection.

I very much regret to say the new Moghul has begun his career as Governor-General in a very little, calculating way, as a banker's clerk might be expected to do; and all accounts from Calcutta agree in saying that he funks responsibility beyond conception, throwing himself into the hands of understrappers. This won't do for India. It must be governed by energy and decision. "Sic volo" like my lord Ellenborough. It would appear that if these two men's minds could be manufactured into one, the corn being preserved and the chaff scattered to the winds, then a Governor-General would be manufactured appropriate for the *rôle*. The Company servants, civil and military, are an *exclusive* race of beings and of all things must be controlled. There is now a sort of reaction from great control to concession and a seeking the opinion of others. I hope he is only studying his lesson.

I am sorry indeed to hear poor Nancy* has been unwell. God bless her, she was a wild, light-hearted thing once, like my wife.

Umbala, 14th Jan. 1845.

My book is in the hills. Harry Lorrequer would make a good story of it. You may ask him if you like, and let me know what he says of it. I ought to expect half the proceeds. It is a book that would take wonderfully. Suppress actual names.

* His youngest sister, Miss Anna Maria Smith.

All my old comrades would speedily know the hero and heroine of the romance. I hope to return to my dear old wife by the middle of March.

HARRY.

Simla, 15th March, 1845.

Your description of railroads astonishes the eyes of a Whittlesea man. It is a very curious circumstance that one of the Romans' great roads ran down to Eastrey near Charles' farm, that is, between our two old fields, from which I have fetched up old Jack from grass many a time, and Charles' large farm (the Decoy is the name, I think). These railroads will have an effect on the world, whether for good or evil, and will change its population to one community, either saints or devils or a bastard mixture of both.

Simla, 1st May, 1845 (the Merry Month).

I have not a word of news to give you. Affairs in the Punjaub are like the waves of the sea, agitated more or less, but not by the wind, but the blast of the mutinous trumpets of the rabble army. I hope we may have a slap at it, because I rely upon Sir Henry Hardinge desiring to give me a command, which I firmly believe Sir Hugh Gough would not oppose, for I never got on smoother with any of my generals, and he is as warm-hearted a fellow as ever breathed, and does right and acquits himself manfully to the extent of the powers the Lord has bestowed upon him.

.I am glad to observe the English feeling which strikes at so condemnable a system as that of opening letters. I would rather fight to put down a Revolution arising from private correspondents than cock a pop-gun to maintain so nefarious a breach of all public and private confidence. We are in danger enough from the Mesmerites telling us in a deep sleep what is going on in the next room (a three-feet wall intervening), without having recourse to the other side of a thin sheet of paper.

Juana's health is capital, thank God, but I am never half so well in the hills as on the plains. Nothing can be more beautiful than our situation, but I love the winter gallops on the plains as flat as the Bedford level.

Simla, 24th Aug. 1845.

By the last mail's papers, as well as by your letter, I see that dear Sir James Kempt was at the Waterloo Dinner, and I have this day written to congratulate him.

The way in which the Duke, dear old and modern hero, drank his health was truly flattering to Sir James and most gratifying to all his many and faithful friends. But I really wish some of the glories of the *Peninsula* were occasionally commemorated by such fêtes. Many of the battles are superior to Waterloo in the annals of the art of war; but not being succeeded by such momentous political results to all Europe (ah! to the world), they are suffered to dwindle into oblivion. Nor is there a medal on the breast of any cicatrized hero to hand down to posterity the glories and victories of the previous age. History to the educated will do it, but a few petty baubles in possession of the many families of Great Britain would ocularly demonstrate " My grandfather, sire, uncle, or brother achieved this in battle," and thus the courage and patriotism of the sire would descend on the son.*

Every ass in India is covered with medals, though the sum of his fighting does not equal one of *our* days. The battle of Salamanca was the most scientific the Duke fought, Vittoria in result the greatest, Talavera in slaughter equalled Waterloo,—yet these names and many others are only seen upon the colours of regiments. My old corps, having no colours, has no record of its deeds.

As to writing to Mrs. Holdich, Lord alive, it gives one no trouble, especially when cheered by the happy feeling of doing right. I suppose a million or so of letters go through my hands per annum; one or two more or less is like a drop of water in the ocean or a hogshead in Whittlesea mere.

Headquarters, Simla, 1st Sept. 1845.

Oh that I was in England, partridge-shooting!

MY DEAREST ALICE,

—Ah, what a bore! A note from the Commander-in-Chief to prepare a very heavy report, which will take me some hours, when I was anticipating a comfortable talk with my dear sister. With all my writing, however, half an hour makes little

* The Peninsular medal was granted in 1847.

difference, although on the most conspicuous part of my writing-desk is pasted in large characters the tenth verse of the ninth chapter of Ecclesiastes.*

When shall I enjoy that liberty so pleasing, when emancipated from all the shackles and labours, bars, bonds, and tempers, which business lays on us, and which we have to contend with? Alas! memory takes us by the hand and leads us back to our early haunts, habits, and friends—the flower garden of other years— and points out all the blossoms we may never more behold, although in imagination as beautiful as ever. Still hope encourages us in such sweet sensations and sustains us in the belief there may be some years of quiet and recreation in store for us, surrounded by those we love, and eased of the labours of public life. Many of my old comrades say, " How could you, Harry, get on without something to do?" I laugh, for I am ever busy. I love books and gardens. I am as interested in the growth of a pet plant as in the results of my more arduous labours; and the charm of the word "home" often inspires me to exertion.

Now, dearest Alice, to my report. My head must be full of cannon, musquets, sabres, rations, tents, transport for baggage, sick, lame and lazy, shirts, shoes, pipeclay, tobacco, soap, etc., etc.

HARRY.

Left bank of the Sutlej, 28th Dec. 1845.

MY DEAREST ALICE,

Your old brother Harry has only a few minutes to say to you and his dear friend Sir James Kempt he has at length in India had an opportunity of distinguishing himself as much as you both could wish, in the three most sanguinary conflicts with the Sikhs, and he with his own hand, the first man in, planted the colour of H.M.'s 50th Regiment on the walls of the head-quarter village from which the great battle was named, Feroze-shuhur. A bloody fight it has been, as you will see by the papers. I was with the old 50th hand to hand in their trenches when four battalions of Avitabile's (so called from having been drilled by that officer) bore down in furious onslaught upon my Division which I now command—two Brigades, H.M.'s 31st and two Native Regiments in one, the 50th and two Native Regiments in

---

* " Whatsoever thy hand findeth to do, do it with thy might."

the other. In the affair of the 18th my Division took twelve guns and a howitzer; in the great battle, three fine standards; and on the 22nd my Division made a furious charge and completed the victory. I was placed on the night of the 21st in a most critical and perilous position in the very middle of the whole Sikh (though beaten) army, completely surrounded by thousands, and at three o'clock succeeded in drawing off my troops, and received the thanks of Sir H. H.: "Smith, it was your boldness and audacity that *saved* to us the victory." Poor old General Sale asked leave on the 18th to serve with me. I gave him a Battalion, at the head of which he received his mortal wound. Our loss has been as great in proportion as in our most bloody fights in the Peninsula. All my Staff were wounded, A.A.G. and A.Q.M.G. in two places. My A.D.C., Eliza Holdich's son, wounded in the hand, one horse killed, one wounded. Myself and my horses escaped, with the blessing of Almighty Providence, without a scratch. I was in the saddle from half-past two on the morning of the 21st to four o'clock in the afternoon of the 23rd. My dear, dear gallant young friend Somerset received his mortal wound close to me, and fell in my A.D.C.'s arms. Tell Sir James I will send him next mail copy of my report; this, I cannot. I have no clerks as when A.G. Dear Juana is at Meerut, thank God, well out of the way. Your old humbug of a brother's name *up* in the army, I do assure you, especially with Sir Henry Hardinge and Sir Hugh Gough. Sir H. H. treats and takes and asks my opinion for as much as it is worth, as my dear, dear friend Sir James would. Heaven bless you, I know this will gratify you and Sir James. So I send this on a thick scrawl of paper. I have not time to read it over.

HARRY.

Camp on the Field of Battle, Aloowal, 1st Feb. 1846.

MY DEAREST ALICE,

I have only one moment to say I have gained, in a separate command of 2700 cavalry, 32 guns, and 9000 infantry, one of the most glorious battles ever fought in India, driving the enemy over the Sutledge double my numbers, posted in an intrenched camp with 75 guns, 52 of which are at my tent door, the others lost in the passage of the river. or spiked in its bed.

Not a gun did they get over. And oh, the fearful sight the river presents ! the bodies having swollen float of men, horses, camels, bullocks, etc. Thousands must have perished, many threw away their arms and fled headlong into the broad river and difficult ford. They had about fifty large boats, which added to the confusion. Some of them were sunk, my thirty-two pieces of cannon pounding them all. Never was victory more complete and never was one fought under more happy circumstances, literally with the pomp of a field-day ; and right well did all behave. I brought well into action each arm as auxiliary to the other, but see my dispatch, which will be published as soon as you get this. I have not a moment to write. Send this to dear Sir James Kempt, and tell him my being thus distinguished I owe entirely to his friendship and good opinion of me. Send this to him, for I have not a moment to write.

Your brother,

HARRY.

To W. M. Ford, Esq., Staff Surgeon, Chatham.

Headquarters, Simla, 4th May, 1846.

The enemy we have had to contend with lately are proper varmint fellows, and had they been commanded by Massena's, Ney's, Soult's, Augereau's victors, they would have made us look sharp to have victor'd them. I never saw men shot out of trees before. At Moodkee the bold rascals got into trees, shot our fellows in the rear, at first without our knowing where the shot came from, but when we discovered the *where*, it was the most extraordinary thing I ever saw to see half a dozen fellows out of each tree come rolling down like cock pheasants or capercailzie. When repulsed from their guns and position, they would sometimes throw down their musquets and come on sword and target (they all carry excellent swords) like antient Greeks.

APPENDIX VII.

A. *Copy of a Despatch from Earl Grey to Governor Sir H. G. Smith, Bart., G.C.B.*

Downing Street, January 14, 1852.

Sir,

I have received and laid before the Queen your despatches of the 5th and 19th of November, reporting the results of the operations of the war since the date of your despatches by the previous mail.

2. I learn from these despatches that another month of this distressing warfare has passed away, and though the force at your disposal had been increased to a very considerable amount no advantage of any real importance has been gained over the enemy, while the loss of Her Majesty's troops has been exceedingly heavy, that very distinguished officer, Lieutenant-Colonel Fordyce, being included among those who have fallen.

3. I have said, that no real advantage has been gained, because, while you state that positions of extraordinary strength have been stormed, and it is clear that the most determined courage has been shown by Her Majesty's troops, these successes (if they can be called so) have been entirely barren of useful results; and it appears from the reports of Major-General Somerset, and particularly from his despatch dated the 9th of November, that the ground thus hardly won could not be retained, and that the position which was carried at the price of such heavy loss to the 74th Regiment on the 6th of November, was only held until the Major-General "withdrew the troops in the afternoon," when it would seem that there was no obstacle to its being re-occupied by the enemy, and that in fact it was so.

4. For several months your despatches have been of a similar character. You have described to me operations which I have constantly been assured had been attended with success, and had inflicted heavy loss upon the enemy, while there could be no doubt that the troops had fought with their accustomed gallantry ; but at the same time I was quite unable to discover that any ground had really been gained, while it was obvious that the enemy, far from being discouraged by their supposed defeats, were from month to month increasing in boldness and determination ; and the lists of casualties but too clearly proved that the loss they had inflicted was at least as certain, and bore no small proportion to that which they were believed to have sustained.

5. It was impossible that I should continue to receive intelligence of this description by many successive mails without being led to entertain very serious doubts whether the war had been conducted with the energy and the judgment which were necessary to bring it to an early and successful issue; but distressing as was the anxiety which these doubts occasioned, I have not hitherto allowed them to induce me to deprive you of that support which I know it is of the utmost importance to the public service that those in high military commands should be able to rely on not having lightly withdrawn from them by the advisers of the Crown, when, in situations of difficulty and danger, success does not at once attend their exertions.

6. But the information I have now received has converted what was before only a very serious doubt, into conviction ; and it is my painful duty to inform you that having consulted my colleagues on the subject, they have concurred with me in coming to the conclusion, that upon a careful review of the events of the war and those which preceded its breaking out, there is evidence, which it is impossible longer to resist, that you have failed in showing that foresight, energy, and judgment which your very difficult position required, and that therefore we should not be justified in shrinking from tendering to the Queen our humble advice that the Government of the Cape of Good Hope and the conduct of the war should be placed in other hands. It has accordingly been my duty to submit to Her Majesty my advice that Major-General Cathcart should be appointed to relieve you, of which Her Majesty has been pleased to approve, and that officer will very shortly proceed to the Cape for that purpose.

7. I need hardly assure you that I cannot make this communication without great pain and sincere reluctance, and that nothing but a sense of imperative duty would have led my colleagues and myself to take the course we have felt ourselves compelled to adopt.

We do full justice to the ardent zeal for Her Majesty's service which you have uniformly displayed, we have not forgot how greatly you have distinguished yourself on former occasions, and what a high military reputation you have deservedly obtained; but we have been compelled to believe that, perhaps from the failure of your health, and your being no longer able to exercise as close a personal superintendence as formerly over the conduct of affairs, you have failed in giving either to your military operations or to your political measures bearing upon the war, that character of vigour and judgment which are necessary to inspire confidence in the inhabitants and troops, and to command success. I must remind you that the first error which was committed, and to which I believe the failure of a policy otherwise sound, and the calamity of the war, are mainly attributable, was the premature reduction of the British force under your command. I must take upon myself a share of the blame for this mistake, inasmuch as I had probably too often and too strongly pressed upon you the importance of reducing the number of troops as soon as this could be safely done. Still your discretion was unfettered, you were left to decide for yourself when the troops should be sent home, since this was a point on which a judgment could only be formed on the spot; and the error, therefore, was your own of supposing that a large proportion of the force which you found in the colony could without danger so soon be dispensed with.

8. I must also remind you, that up to the eve of the actual breaking out of hostilities you continued to send me the strongest assurances that there existed no real danger, and that the apprehensions expressed by the frontier farmers were unfounded. Even when the war began, you were so little aware of its true character that you made no application to me for additional force; and neither in your public nor your private letters did you give me the slightest intimation that such aid was required; and the reinforcements, which were immediately despatched, as well as those which have been subsequently sent, have all, with

the exception of the last, anticipated your demands for them. It is not for me to express any opinion on the detail of your military operations; but it must strike even an unprofessional observer, that by the employment of means which you considered adequate for the purpose no serious impression appears to have been made on the enemy. It follows that you have either been entirely mistaken in your judgment, and have consequently led Her Majesty's Government into error as to the character of the war, and the amount of force required; or else that you have failed in using with effect the force at your disposal.

9. With regard to the political measures bearing upon the result of the war, I must refer you to the despatch which I have been compelled to address to you by the present mail on the neglect of the precautions obviously required, in order to obstruct the supply of ammunition to the enemy. The fault in this respect must no doubt be in part attributed to the Colonial Secretary, whom you had left in charge of the Government at Cape Town; but if you had intimated to me that Mr. Montagu could not alone adequately discharge the arduous duties which devolved upon him in your absence, I should not have failed immediately to have afforded you further assistance, by the appointment of a Civil Lieutenant-Governor, to reside at Cape Town during the war,—a step I propose adopting, now that the necessity for it has thus been disclosed to me.

10. I must also observe, that you have, I believe, truly represented to me, that if you had had the Kafirs only to contend with, the war would long since have been brought to a close; and that what has made them such formidable enemies has been the assistance they have derived from the rebel Hottentots, too many of whom had been trained as soldiers in the ranks of the British army. But if this is, as I believe, a correct view of the subject, I must regard it as a most fatal error that the first instances of treason amongst this class of the inhabitants of the Cape were not dealt with more promptly and more severely. I cannot resist the belief that, had this been done, the contagion of disaffection would have been stayed, as the prompt punishment of the real traitors would have calmed the fears naturally excited amongst the white inhabitants by seeing their impunity, and would thus have prevented the colonists of European descent from being led to entertain and display that indiscriminate

jealousy of their coloured fellow-subjects, which has been, as there is too much reason to fear, the means of driving into disaffection many of the latter who were not originally inclined to it.

11. Lastly, I must regard it as a grievous error that you have allowed the administration of the Orange River Territory to remain too long in the hands of an officer in your own opinion unequal to the task, and that by this and other mistakes in your management of the Dutch inhabitants of the frontier districts, you have failed to conciliate that important class by whose cordial co-operation there can be no doubt that you would have been enabled to bring the war to a much earlier termination than there is now a prospect of; while, on the contrary, by the distracted condition of the Sovereignty, your difficulties in Kaffraria have been very seriously increased. The manner in which, by judicious management, Mr. Pine has succeeded in Natal in securing the confidence and attachment of the Dutch farmers, as described in your despatch No. 193, clearly proves that, if properly treated, they may be rendered loyal and useful subjects of the Crown.

12. It has been with much reluctance that I have entered into this review of the errors which you seem to me to have committed, but I have thought it due to your position and to your high reputation to show that Her Majesty's servants have not determined to advise the Queen to supersede you in the midst of the war without sufficient cause for doing so; and for this reason, painful as it has been to me to write to you in such a tone of censure, I have been compelled to point out the errors into which you have been betrayed. It is, however, some satisfaction to me to be able to add, that I have no doubt it has been your judgment only which has been in fault, and that, to the best of your ability, you have endeavoured to acquit yourself of duties of no ordinary difficulty; nor do I doubt that in more regular warfare against a civilized enemy, and if your military operations had been less complicated by political difficulties, you would have achieved the same success by which you had formerly been so much distinguished.

I am, &c.

(Signed)   GREY.

Lieut.-General Sir H. G. Smith, Bart.

B. *Memoranda to serve as Data in meeting the accusations brought forward in Earl Grey's Despatch of the 14th January, 1852.*[*]

Camp Blinkwater, 12th March, 1852.

1. I am not aware that the not bringing a war to a speedy conclusion with inadequate means is a proof of incompetency in a General, nor even when his means and those opposed to him are nearly balanced. It rather argues the strength and prowess of the enemy. History affords many instances of long and protracted wars, conducted by men of consummate ability, who constantly had occasion to report the result of glorious and sanguinary victories which, however immediately successful, did not do more than merely *lead* to the conclusion of the contest. I have had to contend with, I may say, an invisible enemy, hardly ever to be met with in an assailable position. In other wars to which I allude officers of rank may have fallen, but their fall, however greatly to be deplored, was not considered of importance in connection with the conduct of the campaign. The loss of Lieut.-Colonel Fordyce I much regret. He showed himself with his telescope outside the bush and was picked off by some skilful Hottentot—a chance which might happen to any soldier. The other officers who rushed to aid him fell under similar circumstances. I am at a loss to understand how casualties of this description can attach culpability to the General. If every General Officer were removed from his command because his career was not a continued current of success, not one would retain it. In the instance immediately in question I assert that the troops were eminently successful, their success enabling me to carry operations into a distant part of the country, the important result of which best speaks for itself.

2. Earl Grey attaches blame to me for not having given the necessary "vigour and judgment" to my military operations, or to the "political measures bearing upon the war." A reference to my detailed instructions to the officers in command of the constant patrols will, I think, sufficiently show that the movements of the troops have been carefully watched over and well directed.

---

[*] I am not aware what use, if any, Sir Harry made of these "memoranda."

I am not aware that it is the duty of a Governor and Commander-in-Chief to *head* patrols. On one critical occasion, when a vigorous personal example was required, when it was necessary to show that I was regardless of the sudden and extensive desertion in the Cape Corps, I hesitated not for a moment to take the field in person, in direct command of a large patrol; and by some rapid and completely successful movements not only restored full confidence throughout the army, but in all probability arrested the further spread of disaffection. But although this energetic and decided step upon my part was at the moment called for, and although in former days as Colonel Smith I led patrols under the late Sir Benjamin D'Urban and gained some reputation as a bush fighter, my position as Governor and Commander-in-Chief and the interests of Her Majesty's service directed me to place myself at some central point, from which the general movements of the troops could be best controlled and the duties of the Civil Government equally administered. Neither of them were ever delayed a single day. For this purpose no position could be so advantageous as King William's Town—the base of general operations, the very focus of all movements.

3. Earl Grey states that I have failed in using with effect the force at my disposal. I have some experience in war, and I assert that no body of Her Majesty's troops was ever more energetically applied under more appalling circumstances of difficulty; and none were ever more successful. And although the troops have been so unceasingly and energetically employed, they have suffered no privation, so well have I cared for their provision; while at the same time so rigid has been the economy I have observed and enforced, that many thousands of pounds have been saved to my country. The comments of Earl Grey on my not having done as much with the force placed under my command as might have been done, would be very natural if such were in point of fact the case. But it appears to me His Lordship has not drawn this inference from my voluminous and explanatory despatches, nor borne in mind the dates of arrival of reinforcements; but has reached this conclusion through the medium of irritable disappointment, the flippant statements of indirect correspondence, and the garbled statements of the opposition newspapers. I will therefore analyse the mode in which these reinforcements reached me and their respective dates of arrival.

It is perfectly correct that I never asked for troops until the war was far advanced and had assumed a much more formidable appearance than was originally anticipated. I then recommended that two Regiments of Infantry should be sent out in addition to those already arrived or on their passage. These had been already ordered, the 43rd Light Infantry being one, the 1st Battalion Rifle Brigade the other. I always reasoned that, as Lord Grey had so repeatedly and peremptorily directed a reduction of the force at the Cape, he would see the necessity, if he desired to retain British Kaffraria, of at once sending reinforcements. My reasoning was correct. I also relied upon a general turn out of the frontier population, and neither I nor any other man anticipated a Hottentot Rebellion.

On the 25th April, 1851, drafts for Regiments, amounting to 300 men, reached the Cape in the *Singapore*, Peninsular and Oriental Company's steamer. I landed them at the mouth of Buffalo. On the 12th of May, the 74th Regiment reached the Cape, after a passage of 58 days in H.M. Steamer *Vulcan*. I landed it at Algoa Bay, so as to move on the interior line of defence. On the 8th August the 2nd Queen's arrived, a period of 86 days having elapsed since they were ordered for embarkation, a delay which caused me great disappointment. I landed them at the mouth of the Buffalo, having been compelled to detach Lieut. Colonel Eyre and the majority of the 73rd to within the Colony for the defence of Lower Albany and Graham's Town, a service which he most effectually performed.

On the 29th July I received authority to send to the Mauritius for the Reserve Battalion 12th Regiment. Commodore Wyvill, with his usual energy, placed H.M. S.S. *Hermes*, under that most energetic officer, Captain Fishbourne, at my disposal. She sailed from Simon's Bay on the 24th July, touched at the mouth of the Buffalo, received my orders to proceed to the Mauritius, and on the 27th August, with the greatest expedition, landed as I directed the whole Regiment at Algoa Bay, so as again to reinforce the interior line of defence.

On the 29th August, 200 drafts for Regiments arrived from England.

On the 19 Sept. the 60th arrived, after a very tedious passage of 66 days in H.M. steamers *Retribution* and *Sidon ;* and were landed at the Buffalo. At the same time a detachment of the 12th

Lancers arrived after a passage of 76 days in the *Berkshire* Transport. The head quarters and remainder of the 12th Lancers did not arrive until the 4th Oct., after a very slow passage of 91 days. The horses for the Regiment were in readiness at King William's Town. The whole of the troops were in the field on the arrival of the 60th, which Corps also marched in three or four days, that is, as soon as they were able after their long voyage. I am not aware that any delay occurred in the application of these reinforcements, which were, on the contrary, employed in the most energetic manner; and, as results prove, with military judgment. Yet before their services could be well felt, Earl Grey relieved me from my command, because Lieut.-Colonel Fordyce, a very gallant officer, placed himself, to look through his telescope, within shot of a paltry ambuscade of Hottentots.

After I had invaded Kreili's country, the 43rd Light Infantry arrived. They were sent immediately into the field as an escort of provisions to Forts White and Cox by way of initiation; and on their return were at once moved on the Kei in reserve and support.

It was intimated to me that the 1st Battalion Rifle Brigade would, as one of the Regiments I had asked for, be immediately sent out. So great, however, had been the delay, that I wrote to Earl Grey saying that our successes against the enemy were such, that if this Corps had not left England I did not then require it. A few days before I was relieved it reached the Cape after a passage of *eighty-four days.* I ordered it to Algoa Bay, thence to the Blinkwater, to preserve that country, which I had just cleared, from any reoccupation by the enemy. This was the only service I had for it; and as it had not arrived two months previously as I had expected, I deeply regretted its having left England. In the then state of affairs it was not required. I appeal to every General Officer in H.M. Army if more could have been done, and I turn to my own local experience, and cast aside the theory of abstract and disappointed expectations.

4. With respect to my "political measures bearing upon the war," my conviction is that my central position at King William's Town—the best in a *military* point of view—enabled me effectually, by personal care and supervision, to preserve the neutrality of the formidable T'Slambie tribes, who, had I been absent, would assuredly have joined in the revolt. No man was

ever surrounded by greater embarrassments; but in the midst of them I preserved my position.

5. Earl Grey alludes to the state of my health. It is assuredly not so good as it was twenty years ago; a half-century of unremitting service in every quarter of the globe must naturally have made some inroads, but no measure of government, civil or military, has ever, from this or any other cause, remained neglected for one moment.

6. Adverting to Earl Grey's remark as to the premature reduction of the force, in which he confesses to participate in the blame (if there be any), I must observe that he most emphatically urged the measure upon me, desiring my reasons for delay in the event of my not carrying it into effect. I could more honestly, at the moment, reduce the force than give reasons for not doing so. I am now censured for having *met the views of Her Majesty's Government.*

7. Previously to the outbreak, I undoubtedly sent continued assurances to Earl Grey that no real danger existed. I believed what was brought before me by the officers directly associated with the Kafirs. I could myself see nothing on the part of the people indicative of a hostile feeling. If I have been deceived, Europe in the present age affords various and similar examples. Upon the first outbreak of the war, I was certainly ignorant of its real character. No one apprehended the rebellion of the treacherous Hottentots. And had the burgher population turned out, as I had every reason and right to expect, it would have never taken place, and the Kafir rebellion would have been quelled at the outset. Opinions after results are easily and may be decidedly given.

8. As to the supply of firearms and ammunition, and the want of energy imputed to myself and to the Secretary to Government in suppressing their introduction, a reference to my despatches will show that all that was possible was effected.

9. Earl Grey proceeds to regard as a most fatal error my having failed to deal more promptly with treason on the part of the Hottentots. My position at the time referred to was one, I believe, of as great difficulty as man was ever placed in. The *whole* Hottentot population at that period had been taught they were an " oppressed and an ill-used race," and that the precepts of Holy Writ tolerated their seeking redress by arms. Some thousands

of them were in my camp, with a few hundreds only of British
soldiers; while General Somerset was surrounded by Hottentots.
When evidence was forthcoming, I proceeded to military trial.
But I must advisedly assert that had I, at that period, executed
the condemned, the torch of revolt would have blazed throughout
the Colony. I am regardless of an opinion to the contrary
advanced by any man. I assert as an undoubted fact that by my
course of proceeding I weathered a storm which would otherwise
have burst over me with irresistible fury; that the exercise of
sound discretion in this instance saved the Colony; and that a
contrary course would have ruined it. To strengthen this assertion, I desire to remark that a few weeks only have elapsed since
the legislature of this Colony was deterred from passing an
ordinance for the prevention of "squatting" on Government
lands, a very general impression prevailing that the Hottentot
population would arise to resist it. In the course of enquiry
facts will show the difficulty of my position, and bear me out in
my line of proceeding; in the correctness of which I rejoice, and
shall do so to the latest period of my existence, reflecting that
sound judgment saved the colony. The white inhabitants were
very naturally excited by the treachery of their Hottentot
servants, and jump to the conclusion that hanging a few would
have been a sovereign panacea. I know as much of the
Hottentot character as most men; and the contrary, I say, would
have been the effect.

10. Earl Grey regards it as a grievous error that I have not
removed Major Warden. I honestly admit that that officer might
have done better; I had, however, no one to replace him; and
he acted zealously and to the best of his abilities. He is very
popular with every well-disposed and loyal Dutchman. His
Lordship proceeds to remark that by this and other mistakes (a
somewhat comprehensive application of censure) I have failed to
conciliate the Dutch inhabitants. I need not scruple to say that
for many years I was most popular with them. Perhaps my too
anxious desire to serve both those within the Colony and beyond
the Orange River has been an error. Their not having turned
out, as they pretended they were desirous to do, is attributable to
no proceeding of mine; and if honesty of purpose and kindness
of manner fail to conciliate, I am as irresponsible for the effect
as incapable of seeking the good will of any one by other means.

Earl Grey observes that Mr. Pine has succeeded in conciliating many of the Dutch inhabitants of Natal. The Lieut.-Governor acted upon my precedent and by my advice; and has repeatedly declared his perfect concurrence in the policy which I originated, which has led to the present contented condition of the Natal Boers.

11. In his concluding paragraph, Earl Grey states that he has entered into a review of the errors which it seems to him I have committed, regarding it due to my position and to my high reputation to show that Her Majesty's servants have not determined to advise the Queen to supersede me in the midst of these errors without sufficient cause. I have served my Sovereign and my Country, as few soldiers have had the good fortune to have the opportunity of doing, for nearly fifty years. During that long service I have never, until now, received the slightest censure. The difficulties which have surrounded me at the Cape of Good Hope have been unparalleled. Earl Grey might have awaited the result of operations which I apprized him were in progress and which have been attended with eminent success. However much it may appear to his Lordship that I have failed in using vigour and judgment, facts will speak for themselves; and exonerate a General from the stigma of deserving the greatest indignity with which he can be visited—removal from the command of a victorious army devoted to their Queen and Country and serving in the highest spirits and with every confidence in their veteran Commander.

True copy of recorded Memoranda.

JOHN GARVOCK, Lieut.-Col.
Late Priv. Sec.

APPENDIX VIII.

Sir Harry Smith's Paternal and Maternal Ancestry.

(1) John Smith, = Martha,
of Warboys, Hunts.   dau. of John Wakelyn, gent.,
Whittlesey.

Wakelyn Smith, = Susanna,
of Whittlesey,   ob. 6 March, 1804,
drowned 14 July, 1759.   dau. of — Smith.

John Smith, = Eleanor,
n. 1756, ob. 1843.   n. 1760, ob. 1813,
dau. of Rev. George Moore.

Henry George Wakelyn,
n. 1787.

(2) Thomas Moore, = Jane.
of Boreton, near Buckingham,
Head bailiff in 1546, 1551, 1565,
ob. 1589.

Raphael Moore, = Ann Dix.
of Bucks, ob. 1603.

Thomas Moore, = Oswald,
of Bucks, ob. 1641.   dau. of John Clerke,
citizen of Oxford.

Thomas Moore, – Ruth,
of Ely, ob. 1662.   dau. of Edw. Woodman.

Thomas Moore, = Mary,
of Haddenham and aft. of   ob. 1729, æt. 56,
Whittlesey, an attorney,   dau. of Cadwallader Coker,
ob. 1728, an. æt. 75.   of Bucks.

Thomas Charles Cadwallader Moore, = Eleanor,
of Whittlesey,   ob. 1735, æt. 31,
ob. 1764, æt. 71.   dau. of W. Wiseman,
of Eastry Hall.

(Rev.) George Moore, = Alice,
n. 1731, m. 1758, ob. 1763.   ob. 1816, dau. of T. Ground, Whittlesey,
m. 2ndly, in 1775, John Stona (ob. 1789).

John Smith = Eleanor Moore.

Henry George Wakelyn.

CPSIA information can be obtained at www.ICGtesting.com
Printed in the USA
BVOW03s1526101115

426583BV00013B/76/P